The Life and Loves of a Countryman

Joey Swinbank-Slack

Copyright © 2024
All Rights Reserved

Published in 2008 by Joey Swinbank-Slack Matamata
Copyright © Joey Swinbank-Slack

All rights reserved. No part of this publication may be reproduced or transmitted in any form or by any means, electronic or mechanical, including photocopying, recording, or any information storage and retrieval system, without permission in writing from the publisher.

Cover design by Joey Swinbank-Slack
Pictured are Bridget, Monique and June

To an angel—my mother.

Acknowledgments

Thanks to Yvonne and Zara for helping me with the computer work!

This is the story of my life and loves.

For my love of three young women, my love of shooting, horse racing, fishing and travel.

The periods in this book are from my birth under the shadow of Cross Fell in 1927 'til my departure from England in 1977 as a tax exile.

My first true love of the heart was Bridget, from the tender age of childhood into my late youth.

My second love was June, when in my early manhood, to whom I proposed marriage.

My third and lasting love was Monique, a schoolgirl and a beauty of France. There were other lovely girls I courted, but the three mentioned loves were true loves of the heart.

My love of fine cigars, of which I smoked many thousands, starting at the age of nine years, and not forgetting that elixir of Scotland.

My horse racing activities were mostly in the north, meeting many personalities of trainers and jockeys mentioned in this book.

My trips on the Continent, on one of which I was arrested and jailed by Franco's police.

And of becoming great friends with one of Franco's secret/political spies, being entertained by him, and of Spain's top military brass, and of my blood brother, one of Hitler's tank commanders.

I think you, the reader, will enjoy the various stories as my life unfolds as much as I have enjoyed living them.

Joey Swinbank-Slack

1

I first saw the light of day on 2nd June 1927, on a little farm at the foot of Crossfell, the highest mountain in the Pennine Chain. The little house was Kirkland Hall. My father ran this farm of 134 acres, about 120 swale dale ewes with their followers and a few Cumberland short-horn cows with their calves, and then helped his father, who farmed at Skirwith Hall. Both places were rented from our 2nd cousins, Le Fleming's of Rydal Hall, Windermere. Well, I was my mother's third and last child. Adam was the firstborn, and Cathie the second.

Then we would walk back home, all downhill, stop to pat and speak to Rose, the cart horse, which to me was a special meeting, to speak with Rose. Then, behold, when I was 12-14 years old, I was myself working with Rose rolling the cornfields with an iron horse roller, crushing all the lumps of soil flat and the small stones pressed into the soil so that it made the cutting of the corn at harvest time more easy for the binder. Then Rose and I sowed acre upon acre of turnips, and if it was hot weather, I used to take my shoes off and walk behind in the stitches or rows in my bare feet. This was a grand time, the peewits swooping and crying, laying their eggs, the skylarks singing their hearts out. Those days one could hear all of this, all of nature singing, the only noise was of the horses' gentle plod-plod-plod or of her, Rose, breaking wind! I loved this period because I never liked noise, and the smell of horses, in and out of the stable, is like a loveable perfume.

To show some aspect of my grandfather's hardness, one Christmas when I was three years old, my family was invited to Christmas dinner at Skirwith Hall to dine with my grandparents. I have vivid memories of it to this day. We lunched in the morning room instead of the dining room proper, the meal went well until a small Christmas cake arrived at the end of lunch, with a little toy red Robin perched on the top of it. Of course, I wanted the little toy bird; I can still see it now, almost in my 86th year. I did not make too much fuss about it—Mother always vouched this for me—well, all of a sudden, Grandfather pounded to my chair. I was on cushions to make me a bit higher, he grabbed me by the scruff of my neck and landed me out in the hallway and literally thrashed me to within an inch of my life. Thereafter I could not get my breath back for ages, wracked with huge sobs for a very long time. My mother was too frightened of Grandfather to do anything, but she told me in later life she had never seen or heard of such a small child of three receive such a thrashing. However, I had my revenge, or shall we say the last word with this horrid nasty man. When I was perhaps six years old, my grandfather died and was taken to the church in Skirwith on a flat 4-wheeled farm wagon pulled by four horses. I saw that coffin laying there, with branches of yew round about it in the entrance to the garden at Skirwith Hall, and in my small way, I said to myself, "You're going away, you nasty old man, a good job!" and away he went.

However, when I was four years old, we moved to the village of Skirwith into a house called 'South View' and my father put a man into Kirkland Hall as his father was demanding more and more of his time at Skirwith Hall. South View was in the middle of the village overlooking the village green and the pub, the Sun Inn, at the bottom near the beck. It was at this house that I became ill with measles. I got almost better, then had a relapse, and my life hung in the balance. The village and district nurse was a lovable lady called Nurse Snowball (this was her real name). When I eventually did recover from measles, Nurse Snowball gave me a little sugar pig with a lovely pink nose and tail, telling me when I was allowed outside, I had to be sure and go and visit her in her house in Church Street, which was about 200 yards away. At my tender age, it seemed miles away, almost in another country, however, she gave me directions and a description of her house, which had a silver plate on the door. I found Nurse and she made me some hot cocoa, she was a very kind woman.

Shortly after my recovery began, she moved on to other places. After this illness, the doctor informed Mother that I had been left with a weak heart.

My friend at this time was a boy called Frank Strong, whose father was a second horseman for Grandfather, and Frank's mother was a bit peculiar. We used to play in the back, tickling trout or lifting stones and finding 'bullheads', small fish with a big head. One day Frank had taken his sandals off, rather than get them wet, and could not find them again. So, eventually, we went home to his house and told his mother, Lizzie, he had lost his sandals. Well, his mother blamed me and dragged me 50 yards to my mothers' house, slapping my face and boxing my ears. She was a common slut of a woman, now I cast my mind back, Mother told her off, but all mother got was abuse. My father wanted the husband sacked, but my grandfather would not. However, within the year, Lizzie Strong was taken to the lunatic asylum, Garlands at Scotby, Carlisle, where I believe she remained for the rest of her life.

At the same time, there was a small farm where Mr & Mrs Howson lived, and outside on the opposite side of the entrance to Mr Howson's garage (he had a black Rover car) was a heap of soft sand. One day he, Howson, was driving his car out of the garage, I was on the sand heap, his car almost touched the sand, so I threw a handful of sand at his car (and in my tiny hand, all of four years of age, it must have been an egg cup full). Howson jumped out of the car and slapped me around the head, something awful, until I more or less saw stars and, to make matters worse, wet myself, I couldn't help it. It seemed I was doomed to have my head and ears knocked off. I blame these slappings for my severe tinnitus later on in life.

It was when I was about six years old when Grandfather died that Father moved into Skirwith Hall and farm of 1050 acres that had been farmed by the family for almost 400 years. Skirwith Hall was a lovely old long fronted house built of pink sandstone quarried on the farm, as were the farm buildings. Its walls at the front and ends were covered in ivy, which had to be clipped and trimmed each year. The ivy was a haven for nesting sparrows, and at the lower reaches, blackbirds, the odd crack in the stonework near two of the bedroom windows, nests for Blue Tits, the chatter of these birds in the morning was a lovely thing to listen to, especially the one big fir tree in the garden, where a song thrush perched at the very top in full view used to give his beautiful music to the sky at large. I never tired of listening to his beautiful melody. In the apple trees, which were very large, never having been trimmed, there was always a wood pigeon, giving his soft *coo, coo, cuckoo cuck*, stopping abruptly on the latter note, across the beck in some oak trees, another pigeon would reply. There in the stack yard at the end of the saw bench was a very spreading, lovely, deep-coloured copper beech tree where each year, a wood pigeon made its' nest and reared its young. As I tell later on of my love for shooting, I never shot any wood pigeons or ducks next to the house. It was, I used to think, a sanctuary for them. This was at first Mother's wish, which I even then understood, though the sparrows on the building roofs and in the huge Dutch barn got a few lessons from my air gun.

The Dutch barn was at that time the biggest in the north of England, with three huge bays where the harvest of oats, wheat and barley was stored. This middle bay was then reserved for the resident threshing machine and the resident steam engine, the former had a forged iron plate on it with Grandfathers' name on giving the address at that time as Carlisle, not Penrith. With the steam engine going back and forward up the middle bay, over many years, belching smoke and steam, the acid of this gradually rusted and ate holes in this section of the barn. The side sections were almost like new. I think it was in the 1960s Father had the middle section all removed, when the steam engine was done away with and more and more cereal was grown, I have seen all three sections full, with stacks outside and the threshing machine outside, sheeted up. There was also running right through the middle of the lower lands, from the village to the end of the farm, the Briggle beck, as children we used to tickle trout and lift the stones to catch bullheads, a small fish 3-4 inches long with a large head, the local name for this fish. The beck was full of brown trout, from end to end, and also a haven for wild ducks, the mallard, they used to nest in hundreds, also a lot of water hens when the latter were nesting, we would take the eggs, breaking one first to make sure they were not too far hatched if they were, we would leave them alone, but these eggs were as good as the plover eggs to eat, we used to have plenty of the latter too. At one side of the stack yard stood a lovely dovecote. This building was an artist's delight. It would, I think, be amongst the oldest, if not the oldest, in England. It was said by a few "experts" to be around six hundred years old. Built of rough sandstone and mortar, with sandstone slabs for slate, which were held on by sheep bones, the inverted /\ shaped top open at each end, rested on the four-sided sloping roof the wooden beams, all of oak, in the '/\' and the interior were all held together by wooden pegs—not a nail. All four interior walls were latticed from the floor to the very top with pigeon holes, all of the sandstone slabs, I somehow never counted them, but I should think each side would be a least 200 nesting places or holes. These are what the Lords of the Manor bred and ate in bygone years—I regret I never had this building listed. It was so ancient and lovely because when I sold the estate in 1977, which was resold again two years later, the latter owner, without a thought or a word, demolished it. A crying shame, I was very angry and upset when I heard the news, it was, in my eyes, pure vandalism, a part of old and ancient England gone, to make way for, I believe, a cow shed.

The farm itself was approximately 1050 acres, of which land next to the house was in the region of 600 odd acres. Three outlying fields, one and a half miles distance, two near Ousby and one on the road to Kirkland one mile away. The three latter fields were always good for a few hares and snipe. With the enclosure act somewhere in the eighteen hundreds, the farm was allotted 265 acres of low inland fell land. I used to shepherd this ground with Spot and my pony Star as this 265 acres lay above the village of Ousby, three miles away. I used to cut through various old tracks for shortcuts, making it perhaps two miles. This was good sheep grazing and latterly was used for a small number of cattle in a dry period. This ground was enclosed by a stone wall nine-tenths of all the way around. It was a work of art. All the stones had to be sledged to the site by horses, carts would have been no good, the ground being too steep and rough. Some of the stones in various parts were of limestone, and in these, one could see the clear impressions of sea shells, proving that this area many millions of years ago had been under the sea. The limestone had not been carried from afar. These were quarried on site, other stones in parts of the walls were of iron which were an extremely heavy lot to deal with, as there had been the excavation of iron ore in this area many years ago. Quite often after the winter snows (sheep were never left up here when the snows started to fall), the stones would move, causing parts of the wall to fall, making a gap, where when sheep were put back in, they soon found these gaps and would escape to the open fell the ground. Father used to send half a dozen men, I used to go with them when I was 14 years old, to mend these gaps, mostly they would only be 2-3 yards long and were soon mended, but I remember the iron stone, the big ones, I could not lift some of them, they were so heavy and the limestones were very sharp, they would cut ones hands, but more than three-quarters of the wall was built of ordinary rock stones.

This allotment, as we used to call it, was also always good for two covey of grouse, which Father and I shot each year. A pair of peregrine falcons nesting on a cliff face only 400 yards away. I used to watch them stoop to kill many times, most elegant in their flight, he told me when he was a boy, he shot these grouse with a single barrel, 32 bores of which were in the gun cupboard. I had tried to get cartridges for it, but to no avail, it was obsolete. This then was Skirwith Hall, my domain for many years. I was pleased because, from the sporting point of view, I had everything, grouse, pheasant, partridge, wild duck, rabbits by the truckload, pigeon and trout. I was in my element.

Half a mile below the allotment is a sheltered valley beside the Ardale beck (very good for trout). There was a flat space of ground about 30 yards across (circular). In the middle was an old blackish piece three yards across. It was recognised that it was an old camping place for the Roman soldiers, from this site ran a Roman road cutting right across Skirwith Hall allotment, the markings of this road are there to this day disappearing over the horizon, possibly to meet up with Hadrian's Wall in the far north. Near the top end of the allotment facing the open fell, just under a scree of rocks, was an open mine shaft going straight into the hillside. The opening had fallen in quite a lot, leaving a small hole that I used to crawl into with Spot, exploring for foxes. They used to visit this cave-like place because their strong scent was always hanging in the air. Inside was quite large and cold, one could stand quite easily, the mine only went in for about six yards. There, the roof had fallen in, but between the fallen rocks of the roof, enough space for a fox to go further inside. There were rabbit bones and old grouse carcasses, remains of the fox's meals. Spot was always excited by these foxy smells, but he was too large in the body to squeeze further through. Beside this old mine shaft was discovered a stone axe head, dating from the Stone Age. I believe this is now in Tully House Museum, Carlisle. Beyond and to the right top side high stone wall, about 500 yards away, one can still see the old iron mine workings, with quite a lot of iron ore lying there in the open, far above all of this lies the majestic flat-topped "dome" of Cross Fell. The highest peak in the Pennines at just under 3000 feet, the face of the "dome" crag-like, strewn with boulders and inhabited by a colony of ravens, these were always wheeling overhead, giving their deep cronk call. As well as home to numerous foxes having their lairs deep inside, amongst the boulders, the plateau of Cross Fell is so flat that with a little arrangement, it would be very easy to land light aeroplanes there. Cross Fell is also the home of the Helm wind, a peculiar wind in that one can walk through it and out the other side, so to speak, this phenomena has been the research of various professors and experts for many years, and none have come up with anything concrete yet.

So the second phase of my childhood started. In 1933-34 at Skirwith Hall, here we had what seemed to us the world to run about in. I was at school in the village with the small children's teacher, Miss Taylor, who biked five miles each day from Eden Hall. She was a good teacher, kind but firm, and she had me reading and writing in no time, not like the teachers of today whose pupils leave school and are unable to do either. Miss Birch, the Head Mistress, was also a very good teacher and very, very firm. We were always a bit scared of her, but later in life, she became a very good friend of Mothers' and myself. On the farm, one of the workers was Bob Carrick. He had been with my grandfather for quite a while, he had four children, Alan, Jack, Bill and Lena. We, Adam, my brother and Cathy, used to play a lot with them, and we used to go to their house in Newtown to eat Mrs Carrick's homemade buns and gingerbreads, Mrs Carrick's' house was always in a mess, and herself also, but she was kindness itself, her stockings were like concertinas, tied below the knee in their own knot, her fireplace was always chock full of ashes from a week of the fire, there was no running water in the house, hot water was a boiler beside and heated by the open fire, the lavatory was outside, an earth one, 15 yards away, to be emptied with a shovel, this cottage did not belong to Skirwith Hall, but belonged to the Abbey estate of Cyril Parker; however, we just loved being at Mrs Carrick's, because we could do what we liked, and the lady of the house, could not care less.

Father used to grow quite a lot of oats, a small acreage of wheat, and a lot of turnips and Swedes for the fattening of lambs and beef cattle. When the turnips were sown and were small plants, it was my job, at the age of eight or nine, to scare the crows off by banging a thick short stick on a piece of tin, make as much noise as possible, otherwise, the crows could clear a few acres in half an hour. At one stage, there was one field, Skaws Gill, of forty acres in Swedes, well I, with my tin and stick, could hardly keep the crows off such a big field. If I was at one end, the crows would be at the other, they got used to the small boy banging away. In due course, when I was nine, Father gave me a .410 shotgun to use against the crows. He came with me a few times to see if I handled the gun alright. I had been, in any case, many times with Father shooting and knew all the aspects of the shooting drill safety, etc. The gun was made in Belgium, 32inch barrels and chambered for 3inch cartridges of which Father always bought the American Remington Kleenbore in 3inch green ribbed cases, as he had found, and myself also found, that the .410 cartridges of Eley make were useless and would not stop a rat. The Remington cartridges were so good, plus the 32-inch barrels of the .410. I could kill pheasant (when Father was not around) at 40 yards, wild duck left and right at 40 yards, high pigeon, no trouble, and rabbits quite often at 50 yards. All of this game was either on the wing or running, in the case of the rabbits. Father was most pleased by my quickness in learning to shoot so well (I had another surprise for Father later on) that he and I would, in the summer holidays or at weekends, do a lot of ferreting to try and stop the rabbits eating the crops. Twice or three times a year, a professional rabbit catcher would come and trap the rabbits. There were thousands of them before Myxomatosis came along.

When I was nine years old, most of us at school would try our hand at smoking cigarettes. I could never just get away with it, they made me feel either sick or about to be sick, so I tried a pipe, of course, I put cigarette tobacco in—that was no better. I thought, one day, why not try one of Father's panatelas? When he was away one day, Father had a good supply of cigars and panatelas plus Egyptian cigarettes in the Smoke room, cum office. He got a regular supply from

The Life and Loves of a Countryman

Rothmans of Pall Mall; this was when Rothmans was Rothmans, not as it is today, a conglomerate of firms all different but all the same.

One day Father and Mother were away, so I thought, now is my chance. I took one panatela from one of the barrels—they came in barrels of 50—and were beautiful to look at and had a nice perfume when smoking. I took it outside into the old dovecote and lit it carefully like Father did, and I was off, gently puffing away, not trying to inhale, like most of my village friends would try to, and end up coughing like mad. I was quite content to sit there with Spot and I was rather surprised and pleased to find I did not feel dizzy or ill. After I had finished it, it took a long time, I know—I thought no more cigarettes for me—only cigars. Each week I would take one from the Smoke room; this went on until I was almost twelve. When Father must have been suspicious, he caught me in the dovecote and gave me a good dressing down. I was frightened indeed, then after the telling off. He asked me if I had liked his panatelas. I told him I did, in a trembling voice, he said, next time you want one, you must come to me and ask for one. I could not believe my ears or my good luck at being let off so lightly. I let a week go by before I plucked up the courage to ask him, however, I did, he took me into the smoke room and held the barrel out for me to take one. He did not hand me one himself—I took one, then he helped himself—now he said, let us smoke together. We sat down there and then and smoked and talked about ferreting and the dogs. I think Father, maybe, did not believe me that I enjoyed them and that I may be sick and that would put me off. He was rather surprised to see that I could smoke a cigar quite professionally and finish it as well. After that, we would often smoke together. I was at school in Carlisle and I used to buy my own small cigars. They were called Copes Courts. I think they were in packets of five and flattish, not round. I preferred them to Manikin's; I had no trouble buying them from the tobacconist at all.

2

It was also about eleven years old. I thought I would like a pony. Father would not buy me one because, for one thing, he did not like them and for another, money was not plentiful. I had saved up 3 pounds and 10/-shillings now and one weekend, I went on my bike to Penrith to see my friend, Hugh Longrigg, who went to the same school as I did and whose father was secretary of Kidd's Auction Mart, Hugh was my best friend at this time, I had seen in the local paper, the C.W. Herald, of a Shetland pony for sale at a farm beside Penrith, Hugh and I went to see this pony, belonging to Mr Brownrigg of Scaws farm, he was a nice kind man and he let me see the pony named Patsy, she was a little beast, Mr Brownrigg said get on and have a ride, he produced a bridle and I jumped up on Patsy, I soon fell off, I had only been used to the big broad backs of the cart horses. Anyway, I asked Mr Brownrigg how much he wanted for the pony, and he said 5 pounds. I said right, very well, and shook hands. I hurried home very excited to tell mother, not father, of my purchase, as I had only 3 pounds 10 shillings. I asked Mother if she could loan me the 30/- shillings needed and Mother did. It was all she had, not a penny more, so I hurried to the local haulier, Joe Brown, who lived in the vil- lage. He had one small lorry and I asked if he could go to Penrith right away to pick Patsy up. He said okay, so I went and gave Mr Brownrigg the 5 pounds and I was the proud owner of a lovely pony. Joe Brown duly delivered Patsy at Skirwith Hall, I asked Joe how much I owed him for the trip and he said 7/6. I asked if he could wait a day or two, he smiled and said, of course, he would. I thought I would ask Father, whom I always addressed as Dad, but he was not too pleased with the pony. "Dad, can you please lend me 7/6 for the delivery of Patsy to Mr Brown?" Dad refused and now I was in a quandary. Mother had no more money, however, her brother, Uncle Willie, was helping out on the farm with some shepherding and staying with us. So mother asked him, and it came to pass, Uncle Willie paid for the carriage of Patsy.

At no time in my young life did father buy me a pony—I had others, or a motor car or a gun. I had to buy my own. He was a very good father to all of us, but to get him to buy anything like a pony was too much for him. I had no money for a saddle for Patsy, so I rode bareback. Two years were to pass before I got a saddle. Mother got me one from Lancaster's in Penrith. I tried it out, it was a nice saddle, but I could not manage it. I preferred bareback, so Mother took it back to Mr Lancaster. I used to go ferreting, watching the cornfields and turnips from Crows with Patsy and Spot. I used to shoot running rabbits from Patsy's back at a gallop. She soon got used to the gun. I was shooting six days a week now. If I was not boarding at school, then it was weekends. Afterwards, I was a day boy and then I shot every evening in summertime till dark. I think, looking back, this was the best time in my whole life, not as a late teenager, but from the ages of nine to fourteen years, they were perfect. When I outgrew Patsy in due course, Mr Jack Proctor, the manager and head auctioneer at Kidd's Auction, lent me a very nice pony. She was 13.2hh.

Tommy Kitchen was one of the rabbit trappers. He was a grand sort of chap and we all loved him. He used to sleep in the men's quarters during his visits of trapping times, he used to bring his melodeon with him, and I used to sit in the kitchen at night with the other men and maids and listen enraptured. At this time, when I was eleven or twelve, I was busy breeding ferrets in a hen house. I was going to make a fortune at it, as I was breeding these nice little creatures, Father and I would set off towards the end of the farm, where there was a long L-shaped wood of Scots Pine, this was one large rabbit warren and we would take six or seven ferrets, our sandwiches and plenty of cartridges, Father with a 12 bore, me with the Belgium .410 the one he had to give 4 pounds 10/- for and 32inch barrels. I have the gun with me today, although the shot pattern is now useless and worn out. We at first used to walk to Black Wood as it was named, but it was a mile away, and the ferrets were heavy. Together with guns and cartridges, eventually, we would take one of the tractors with a small trailer behind. This was much better. I would put the first ferret in the hole, father and I would stand to one side, he and I maybe 12-15 yards apart, more or less knowing which direction the rabbits would run, and shoot all day. Many times we would kill 200-300 rabbits in one day. The best bag was 534 in one day between us. My first introduction to this sort of thing was when I was nine years old. When I was twelve, I could outshoot my father and he was an expert. Quite often, I would shoot and kill rabbits only five yards from father, all of this in the middle of the pine trees. He never said a word if the kill was too near him. He had confidence in my ability to shoot straight. I used to even shoot running rabbits only feet in front of my dogs and never pricked a dog yet. Well, with the ferreting place, Black Wood, as I said, was one big warren, rabbits could come out thirty yards away, ferrets as well, so we had to keep a sharp eye on things, and if the first ferret either got tired or lay up with a rabbit it had killed in the burrow, we would put another one down further on. We would rarely use the sixth or seventh ferret but would go through four most times, and if a ferret did lay up, which was also quite often, I would put a small box down the whole mouth with a little hay inside, the hole I would choose for this was the one the ferret went down first, block the box of hay in with a spade, and as many other nearby holes, and go home hoping the ferret would find the hay and go to sleep inside the box, sometimes they did, really early in the morning I would be there with my dogs hoping the ferret would be in the hay.

Sometimes they were, but very often, there would be a small round hole, which the ferret had dug and escaped, but they never went too far. I would set Spot to work to find them and he would soon point at a hole, ears cocked, and then I knew the ferret would be there, or another sign was rabbits bolting from holes for no reason, which meant something was pushing them out. After their night's slumber, when they dig themselves out, they love to start working again on their own. They start by bolting rabbits through habit. I used to watch what the dogs were doing, going from hole to hole. They used to do this on tiptoe. I suppose by instinct, at the hunt, Spot could hear all of the noises underground before I ever could, and when he pointed to a hole, he was always right. We seldom kept them and shot rabbits in the summertime to eat, for the price was too low, 3d each and many would be shot too hard for the town housewife. Though in winter, I used to make my cartridge and pocket money by ferreting, but into nets. A clean kill by pulling the rabbit's neck and the flesh was not bruised, in fact, white like a chicken. This is what the rabbit dealer liked and gave a fair price to them.

By now, in 1938, Gyp had a litter of puppies on the third of March. She had five, but one of them was dead. She had one more the next day. The father of these puppies was a dog from a neighbouring farmer from the village, Mr John Jackson, whose son Robert was my brothers' best friend. This dog's name was Rip. He was the cattle dog for Jackson's. He was a mongrel and had a dash of Alsatian in him. He was a good fighter too. Well, I wanted to keep a puppy from Gyp, so Father let me. I kept a male. He was black with tan points and white dots on his forehead and a white tip on his tail. I named him Spot. He turned out the be the best friend and all-around dog I have ever had in my life. I trained him to ride on the backs of the farm horses. He would sit on the crossbar of my bike with his front feet on the handlebars. The crossbar must have been very uncomfortable for him. He would do anything I wanted of him. At one time, I had a super ferret called Puggy. She was a white female, small, she would come when called by her name and also she was extremely docile. I got her used to Spot, and vice versa, and eventually, I had Spot picking her up in his mouth from the rabbit burrows and either putting her down at another hole or bringing her to me. Puggy was the only ferret I had that never bit Spot, and she never lay up in a rabbit hole if she took longer than usual. I used to call her name down the hole. Sure enough, she was there in no time, sometimes licking the blood from her lips from a kill, or her claws, full of rabbit fur, trying to get one to turn to bolt it. Spot would have killed for me. One day I told him in his and my language, he was the only dog I used to train and speak a doggy cum human tongue to get my sister. In an instant, Spot flew at Cathie's throat. This surprised me immensely. From that moment, I knew for Spot that I was his only master and friend.

In 1939-1940, I had 36 ferrets. I had started to breed them, as the year before, good young ferrets could fetch up to one pound each, so I thought I would get in on this lark. I had most of them in a hen house, partitioned off, but the partitions were only two feet high, and when the ferrets were big enough, they had the know-how to scale the partitions and therefore have the run of the whole hut. I had to put my trousers inside my stockings, otherwise they were up inside my trousers like a flash. They knew me as the bread and butter man, I supposed. Most of the ferrets, with much handling, were soon docile and gentle, but there was always the odd one or maybe two who would love to bite no matter what. Anyway, in a short time, I took 20 ferrets to Daltons Auction Mart in Botchergate, Carlisle. Daltons sold everything from safety pins to tractors, hens, ducks etc., on each Saturday, all sold to the highest bidder. Uncle Willie, my mother's brother, went with me to keep me right, so to speak. My ferrets were a picture and handled well. One had to handle them in front of the audience of buyers so that they could see they were quiet and did not bite. Ferret after a ferret was put up, bids started and stopped. The most I had that day was five shillings, the lowest price was 2/6, and the commission for Daltons was always high. I cannot remember exactly, but I did not breed many ferrets after this episode.

3

It was about this period, when I was about twelve years old, that I met my first girlfriend. Bridget was her name. Her parents were Captain Cyril and Mrs Parker, who had moved into the Abbey at Skirwith on the death of Captain Parker's father. The father and Mrs Parker, his mother, built the Church of St John in the village of Skirwith and, I believe, also the village school. When their eldest son, Tom, brother of Cyril, was killed in the Great War, Mrs Parker commissioned the builders to add a Lady Chapel to the Church—a beautiful Lady Chapel it is. Also, the Church is a very beautiful one and is well known as the Cathedral of the Fellsides. Well, it seemed as if this last building project was finished, it left Mr and Mrs Parker (sen) very strapped for cash, and they never recovered, always living like many other landowners, way above their income. The family had a few farms, two at Skirwith of approximately 300 acres, three, I think, at Culgaith, one of them, Stain Gills, would be approx 400 acres, the other small, and I think two were at Stapleton, north of Carlisle, wettish land, but rents those days were low. They had to be, as farm income was at a low ebb. The war improved farmer income, but that is another thing.

When old Mr Parker died, he was in debt and never paid his bills (his son Cyril was the same). His bill at Rothmans for cigars and cigarettes was over 500 pounds on his death. In those days, that was quite a sum, and of course, death duties faced his son Cyril, the father of my first love.

How I met Bridget was when her parents moved into the Abbey, they thought to give a big party for the children of the village, poor or rich. We were all asked about this party which was held in the village hall. There would be about 25 children in all. We would play the usual children's games, have a good meal prepared by caterers in Penrith, Birkett's I think, pull many crackers etc. Bridget was opposite me at the table, and we pulled the crackers together. I won and got the joke piece of paper which I thought was very funny and then gave it to Bridget to read. She laughed, so we pulled more and more, swapping the joke papers, and then we played together for the rest of the party. Thus began my first true love. It lasted until we were in our late teens, then Bridget moved down to Bedford as a land girl with a family named Archer, of Beadlow Manor, near Bedford, but before this, she and I had some wonderful times together. We would go riding and ferreting. She was an outdoor girl.

On Tuesdays, a market day at Penrith, everyone went to Penrith on market day. Not only was it auction day for livestock, but there were the travelling stalls set up in Dockray and the local produce in the market hall beside the George Hotel. It was also a drinking day for the farmers, in fact, for all and sundry. Well, on Tuesdays, the Regent Cinema always had a matinee at about 2 pm. Bridget and I used to go to these matinees most Tuesdays. Her parents knew this, but it let them get on with their drinking, knowing she was only at the pictures. We used to take a back seat upstairs, the cinema was never crowded, and this is where Bridget taught me how to kiss. I had a love for her even when she eventually married the son of a Captain Archer and I know for certain Bridget never stopped loving me until the day she died from Multiple Sclerosis, aged, I think, forty-four years. Bridget's father, at this time in our tender years, did not like me at all. I was very small, and not only that, he thought as a tenant farmer, I was not good enough, or my family, though what he did not know my pedigree was much grander than his, tracing back to John of Ghaunt, the grandson of William the Conqueror, 1134 and beyond, hence the de Lancaster in my name, from the ancient Dukes of Lancaster. However, later on, his opinion of me changed to one of genuine affection, but Mrs Parker was always fond of me from the beginning and used to ask Cathy and I to tea at the Abbey. Bridget would be, at this period, 8 inches taller than me. However, when I left school, I caught her up and passed her in height. Her father, she told me, called my father "that little squirt" – behind, of course, my father's back. (My father was only 5' 6', taken after his mother, who was very small—but our male line before this were all over 6 feet and 15-18 stone in weight). Bridget brought her husband up to Penrith in due course. She was now Mrs Gerald Archer—of Beadlow Manor, Bedford—a farmer. They came into the George Hotel bar. It was a Tuesday market day. I had a surprise. He was the very caricature of a country bumpkin—a round, red turnip face to match! The only thing missing was a straw sticking out of his mouth! Bridget had made a poor choice. I did not take to him at all, and neither did her father—who eventually had to go to Archer's place and rescue her. He was beating her up.

4

When I was thirteen, my mother thought it was time that I was confirmed. On my return from school, I was packed off twice a week in the evenings to the Vicar, Father Kewley, very high church. As I have said elsewhere in this book, he was a fine gentleman of the First Order, of graceful manners. He was portly and had sight only in one eye. None of us knew of this until he told Dad one day when he was on his weekly visit to Skirwith Hall, a needle (I can not remember whether a darning or knitting needle) had gone through the side of his eye, doing damage behind, to all outwards looks, his eye was no different to the other.

Father Kewley duly instructed me in the religious side of life, preparing me for my Confirmation later on by the Bishop of Carlisle. Lessons took place in his study, across a little courtyard separate from the house. The walls were lined with many hundreds of books of all sorts. He alone had hundreds of paperback Penguin books. He loved novels or books of all sorts. Two of his other great loves were the cinema and ice cream. When there was a diocesan conference at Carlisle, he did his best to go to two films that day and eat as much ice cream as he could. He had a small saloon car. I suspect bought by Miss Childs, one of the Kewley fillies and a chauffeur who lived in the village. During my religious lessons, the vicar's big fierce dog D'if was always with him by now, though D'if was an old dog, content to lie on his carpet next to his master. The trouble was D'if would fart, most of the time filling the room with a smell like rotten eggs. If D'if would let off a loud one, the vicar would look at me over the top of his spectacles with a smile and say, "Sorry about that, but you know he is getting rather old now", which of course, was true, he asked if I minded, I said no, I understood. This pleased him, for he and the dog were devoted to each other. Near the end of my learning with Father Kewley, he told me the facts of life, sort of anyway. He asked me if, during the night, had I had any wet dreams. I did not know what he meant, so he explained about erotic dreams and my sperm coming, had I had any sperm come? I said no. I thought that was when one was twenty-one years old. I knew nothing at all of these things. He saw I was as innocent as the snow in this aspect. Before I was confirmed, he told me I had been his best pupil ever and was most pleased with me and gave me a silver and ebony cross with Christ on it and a book, Taglioni's Son. I still have them today.

In the school behaviour book, he and Miss Birch tore the pages from it, concerning my having sworn at Miss Birch when I was eight or nine years old. I had a clean record! A few years later, Father Kewley left to go to another living in Shouldham in Norfolk; he went, I think because hardly a soul went to church at Skirwith. Cyril Parker, now a patron of the living, hated the vicar for some reason. When a younger man, he had at a garden party taken off his jacket to fight the vicar but was stopped by his father. It was slowly getting him down preaching to four or five people each Sunday. The fact was, he was too good for Skirwith village. The people never appreciated what a good man they had until he left. He and I corresponded until he died—at Shouldham in Norfolk.

The opening of the war did not alter things very much for me. I thought at school if the French were with us, we would win very quickly. How wrong I was. The neighbouring farmer, John Jackson of Red House, had bought his son Robert a TB broodmare. She was a beauty by Highborn II, she had two or three foals and Robert had a ¾ blood horse of about 15 h.h and I wanted to borrow her for a while, or as long as the war lasted. Mr Jackson wanted all his grazing for his cows and too many riding horses did not improve anyone's image. She, it was a mare, was really too big for me. I could not reach the stirrups from the ground unless I got on a big stone first or at a gate. I said yes, I would have her. Her name was Laura and she could mark time at a canter, but once off the bit, she had a mouth-like iron, which I was to learn of at a later date. Before this, I had never ridden in a saddle, only bareback. Bridget and I did many miles on Laura but only at a trot or walk. Bridget liked to be in the saddle and me behind, and on instructions, I had to place my hands on her breasts. These were very pleasant times. She had beautiful breasts too.

In July 1941, coming home on my bike from the train at Langwathby, I was looking forward to a bit of rabbiting in the evening with Spot. He was always there to meet me at home, lying waiting for me on top of the hill outside the garden facing New Town over the beck. Spot never missed, and sometimes he would be at the railway station, three miles away, waiting. Well, this evening, the 4th of July, as I arrived over the shortcut across the field from the road, there was Spot in his usual place. I dismounted my bike, and all of a sudden, I felt like lead. One foot would hardly go past the other. Spot jumped up, greeting me with his usual enthusiasm. I just could not respond. It was all I could do to get up that last hill. I could not have anything to eat, so Mother put me straight to bed. It was Friday and I stayed in bed till Saturday, feeling very ill. My sister Cathy, who by this time had joined the WAAF, had a boyfriend, Flt Ltn Basil Tatham, flying Hurricanes. He was a very handsome man, Basil, and beautifully mannered. Well, it came to pass on Saturday, 5th July, Basil and two of his pals were on exercise over the area in their Hurricanes, and so they thought they would let Mother know he was there. He had been to the house quite a few times with his pals, where they would have home-killed lamb, and strawberries, and cream from the farm, cream so thick, one had to pull it out of the jug with a spoon, well Basil flew so low over the house he nearly knocked the chimneys off. He flew back and forward, time and again. Mother came to my bedroom and told me to come and wave at Basil's plane and his friends, Mother was waving a white tablecloth from the window, but I had no energy to get out of bed. It was then that Mother thought there was more to my listlessness. The next day, I did not go to church or to school. That was the day five of my turkey eggs hatched out under a broody hen, five out of five eggs. I could not go and see them. Mother saw that one of the men fed them. The next day, I was still ill, so the doctor was sent. Dr Sacks came as usual at express speed in his rover, had a look and said he would be back first thing the next day, so he was and took a blood sample. On the 11th, Dr Sacks came at the same time as the ambulance and I was carried downstairs by a kindly big man. I wasn't very heavy, for in my diary, I see I was five stones, 7½ lbs and 4 feet 9 inches in height—and I was off to the isolation hospital in Penrith. I had succumbed to Para-typhoid, the doctor thought it may have been from an ice cream eaten at Carlisle, because quite a lot of days, I would spend all my luncheon money of 1/6 on ice cream, I with a pal or two, would have one ice cream in Wool- worth's, one in another shop and another in the milk bar in Bank Street if we had money over from these ice creams, we would ask for a milkshake, and Hazel behind the milk counter would make us the biggest she could, they were super, and so was Hazel. This typhoid germ, though, was never pinpointed. There was only one other person in the hospital with the same complaint as myself and that was a girl of about eleven years old, I think from Lazonby.

The Ministry of Health came to inspect and disinfect all of the drains at Skirwith Hall—Father was not pleased. Of course, when one has Paratyphoid, the nurses give you nothing to eat at all. As it was explained to me, one's intestines become like wet blotting paper, food, if taken, would break through the walls of the intestines and of course, you would die. I was in Hospital for 31 days, and for 21 days, I did not have anything to eat, only liquid drinks and not in great quantities. This is the illness, I believe, that killed Prince Albert, Queen Victoria's husband. Was I hungry? I dreamt of all the dishes mother would make for me, pigeon, rabbit stew, plenty of eggs... I loved them all. The head nurse was Miss Egglestone from Culgaith, whose brother worked at Langwathby Railway Station, where I took the train to school. She was a lovely young woman and kindness itself. Mother visited me four times but could only speak to me through a small window from another room in my ward; my bed was not far from the window. Fortunately, I was always terribly sad when Mother left. It must have been hard for her to come as her mother did not drive. She visited me on Tuesdays and on market days. Father would park in the Crown Hotel garage; he never took Mother by car to the hospital. Mother had to walk, and it was a hard walk from the middle of Penrith right to Beacon Edge, where the Cottage Hospital was. All uphill and steep, a good half mile of slogging. I was not allowed out of bed until about three days before I came home. When I did get out of bed, I was given a bath with Dettol in it by Nurse Egglestone. I was very shy of this, however with not walking for more than three weeks, flat on my back, I was as weak as a kitten. My feet would not bend if I tried too hard to bend them and walk correctly. They hurt terribly, so for three days, Nurse Egglestone used to help me, one arm around my waist, to walk again. On 11th August, I was home again to my mother, dogs and guns. Two days later, I was out shooting and shot three rabbits, then out fishing on 17th August, I got four nice trout from the beck that ran the entire length of the farm, not a big beck, but excellent for trout, most of them from half a pound to three quarters, odd ones at a pound, it was Eldorado when I landed a one-pounder. Bridget used to come and see me quite often, as I was more or less persona non grata at the Abbey.

Three weeks after I came out of the hospital from typhoid, I had an accident on Laura, ran right into a tree and was knocked out for thirty-six hours; I awoke to find Dr Sacks tickling my cheek in the Cottage Hospital. It began with the loading of oats out of stooks from the high side of the farm. Fields were named High Woods, though there were no woods, my brother Adam was on one of the tractors, leading the corn into the Dutch barn. This was the biggest of its kind at that time in the north of England. I was on Laura, opening and shutting the odd gate as he went through various fields. This was so the stock in the field he was crossing did not stray due to open gates. I remember having to get off Laura for one gate as the latch was too far down for me to reach from the saddle, to get on I remember getting back into the saddle by first climbing a few bars of the gate that is where my memory stops. Adam seeing I had not arrived at the next gate, 300 yards further on, got off his tractor to open it himself. He saw Laura running without a rider. There was only one tree in the near middle of this field, a massive old oak with low spreading branches, that is where he found me, lying on my back with my head on Spot's body, like a pillow, my collar stud in a biggish dent beside me. Spot must have known something drastic had happened and he was there to try and help and comfort me. He was a great dog. Adam soon raised the men at the farm doing the stacking of the corn. Lifted the gate off its hinges, the one I had climbed on to get up on Laura, took me to the farm, about 500 yards away and got Mother, so they told me later. Then they put me in the back seat of the car. This was a standard 20 specially built for Commander Torbock of Crossrig Hall. It was higher than the usual car of that era, with mahogany picnic tables, and one could stretch one's legs full length in the back. She was a powerful car and could start from a standstill in top gear. In fact, Father hardly ever did change gear once on the run. My head was in Mother's lap, Adam drove me to Penrith at maximum speed. He was a superb driver, his hand on the horn going through the middle of Penrith. He must have done 60 mph through the town itself with no traffic lights, then straight to the doctor's surgery. Dr Sacks was on his rounds, so the other partner, old Dr Eddington, came out to the car. He took one look at me and shook his head. I was, of course, out cold and cold and clammy to the touch. Dr Eddington then advised Adam to take me to the Cottage Hospital, the one I had come out of only three weeks ago and put to bed. I don't know what the treatment was, except it seemed to keep me warm. Four days later, I was x-rayed by Dr Melville Eddington Jnr, Dr Sacks' partner. He was a hard case, Dr Mel, as he was known by all and sundry.

He enjoyed putting the needle in one arm from a distance, like throwing darts, in fact, some of the partnership's clients, if Dr Mel was on duty, would quietly go away and come another day. I myself have been on the end of Dr Mel's long arm. I was always very nervous when he was alone on duty, he was reputed to be the best salmon poacher in the district. He was indeed a man's man.

It turned out my X-rays showed five broken ribs and bruising. Dr Sacks strapped me up and I was back home at the end of eight days but put to bed. I remember my bed had a big hollow in it, for the full length, almost like lying in half of a cut-down pipeline, this aggravated my ribs, and I was unable to sleep, so Mother moved me to her room into the big double bed for a week, I had to stay in bed for six days, Bridget came every day to see me.

I went to see Vicar, who had been most concerned for me. Vicar then was Father Kewley, not a Catholic, but the High Church of England. He was a complete gentleman. He had three women around him—one was Miss Childs, his lady housekeeper, a very genteel lady she was, Miss Barton, his cook and Miss Birch, the headmistress of the village school who also played the organ at church. They were known throughout the Diocese as "the Kewley Fillies". He wanted for nothing, Father Kewley. His fillies waited on him hand and foot. My father was Vicars Warden, and each Thursday, Father Kewley would come for afternoon tea walking the mile from the village. Afternoon tea in those days was a feast, and after tea, the cigars would come out together with the whisky decanter. Many times the Vicar would return home not quite the worse for wear but definitely very happy. In fact, one Thursday in winter, after imbibing just that bit too much, Joe Varty, Father's pig man at that time and who lived in the servant's quarters, had to walk him home to the Vicarage with the aid of a storm lantern, we called them in those days, stable lamps.

Joe Varty was a general farm worker who had been with

Father for 30-40 years. When father persuaded the agent for Le Fleming's that he would have to increase his turnover to go along more modern lines, he would like a first-class piggery built. The agent had to borrow the money in the first place, as landowners had for years overspent on themselves. Well, a very modern piggery was built, and also, if pigs went bust, it was easily converted to a cattle shed. I think it was built in 1936-37. Joe was made head pig man and Jack Carrick, Mrs Carrick's son, not long after left school, his assistant. Jack used to take epileptic fits. I think there were 50-odd breeding sows, and they did well for Father. At this time, Mother had a housemaid named Ginny Little. She was a grand sort and could stand up to men if they taunted her too much. She was sex mad, one night with Mother's consent, she wanted to try a joke on Joe, that she would get into his bed and pretend she wanted Joe to make love to her. This particular evening at about 8 pm, Joe went out to relieve himself before mounting the stairs to his room, Ginny saw her chance and slipped up his staircase from the great kitchen and into his bed. We were hiding in the small kitchen next to the great one and when Joe went upstairs to bed, we quietly, with Mother, crept to the doorway leading to his room, which was just overhead. This was before electricity got to the world. It was either candles or paraffin lamps. Joe, once in his room, unable to discern Ginny in his bed due to the shadowy scene of light, got undressed and into bed. Ginny was doing her job well. She got on top of him, nearly scaring poor Joe to death. Joe was out of bed in a shot, saying to Ginny, "Nay lass, it's not right. The mistress would not be pleased". Ginny tried her best to see what Joe had to offer, but as the agent Mr Porter, once talking with Father of general things, Joe's name cropped up. Major Porter said he believed Joe was a "cock virgin", never known to have slept with a woman, and he, Joe, was no poofter either. He was an extremely nice man and a very faithful one too. I think one day in 1942, Joe was not feeling very well at all. Father thought the symptoms rather like pneumonia, so he put a light mustard dressing on Joe's chest and covered it with thick brown paper, this, of course, next to the skin and Adam drove him to Penrith to his brother Tom's place, where he would have more care than that of the maids at Skirwith Hall. Dr Sacks was also Joe's doctor and later on, Dr Sacks spoke with father and told him that the mustard dressing plus the brown paper had saved Joe's life, even though he was slightly blistered by the mustard, this was the type of remedy used for pneumonia in the calves, only more mustard was used. Joe made a good recovery and returned to the farm to work with his pigs. Father installed a steam potato boiler in the piggery, in a 14ft x 14ft square room at one end of the piggery opposite the meal room. The boiler was fired by coal or coke and held 3 or 4 cwt of potatoes. It did not take long for the potatoes to cook. We, children, used to go and eat a good many of them when nice and hot. The boiler had not been installed for very long.

One day, Father, not far from the piggery, heard loud shouts and more frantic shouts coming from inside. He ran in and found Joe with a strong piece of stick in both hands, holding down, as hard as he could, the arm of the safety valve whereas no excess steam could escape. The dial of the safety valve had gone right across the red strip and was on the danger line. The boiler was on the point of exploding and ready to take Joe with it. Father took it in at a glance, knocked Joe aside, where he fell to the floor. Of course, the steam escaped in a rocket-like blast, nearly lifting the roof. It was a near one for Joe, whom her father said was as white as a ghost. Father had to explain to him the workings of the boiler, safety valve etc. Joe was a simple soul, one of nature's gentlemen, he could not drive a tractor, but his large piggery, 50 yards long and 30 feet wide, was spotless. Another episode with the boiler concerned Joe's assistant Jack Carrick (an epileptic). Again one day, Father heard loud shouts from Joe in the piggery, so Father rushed and there was Jack with his head and half his shoulders stuck underneath the boiler fire with hot cinders and ashes falling onto his head. He had had a fit and when Jack had a fit, he would let out such an unearthly scream cum shout that he had frightened Joe so much that he was unable to help him. In his fit, Jack had quite unknowingly crawled under the boiler fire. Father pulled him out, loosened his collar stud and waited till he came round, poor Jack, he could never remember anything of his fits, but this time he had a few souvenirs, three or four mostly cinder burns, small but a bit painful. Jack's brother, Alan, worked on the farm for a short while. He was easily upset if there was a row after one such fallout left. I think he was with us for about six months. He joined the Merchant Navy and went through hell on the Murmansk run. He said the Russians would not let them off the ship there. Alan said the British seamen used to throw the Russian workers, mostly women, cigarettes onto the dockside and there would be an unholy scramble for them. Alan said the Russians were like animals. He had ships go down in front and behind him, he came through the war in one piece, but I think his nerves must have suffered.

At nine years old, I was sent to Grosvenor College, Carlisle as a weekly boarder. Brother Adam was there at the same time, also Robert Jackson and one more boy, four of us. I was the youngest by far. My parents perhaps thought it best for me to get away from dogs, guns, ferrets and ponies for a while. I might learn better though I was doing quite well at the village school. By now, under Miss Birch, I was a neat and good writer and could read very well. I read many books, and I loved them as a present from people, arithmetic, okay, etc., but there hung over me the black cloud of telling Miss Birch to bugger off and my stubbornness to apologise. So Carlisle it was, Grosvenor College had a grand name, and in my opinion and now at eighty-five years old—that was all.

In no time at all, I was the only boarder, Adam being now a day boy, Robert Jackson left to go to Appleby Grammar school, the other boy left, and then I was on my own with the Headmaster and his wife, Mr & Mrs F.L. Harrison. Of course,

I started off in the infants class. I thought how stupid to be with these little ones. I knew far more than they did most of the time. They would be chanting nursery rhymes like "Up the rocky mountains, down the rocky glen", in this atmosphere. It was not long before I decided that I was not going to bother learning anything and shut my mind down. For one thing, whatever I tried in my writing style, which was very good, never satisfied my teacher, Miss Grant. As a result, my writing got worse and worse. In all things, I went backwards. The dreary part of things was in the evenings, when all alone in the sitting room come dining room, with Mr and Mrs Harrison. He was old and feeble, she was stout and robust, kind in their way, but had had no children of their own. One maid came to cook, Ethel. She was nice and made a very good steamed sponge pudding. When evenings came and after supper, Mr and Mrs Harrison sat up to a big open fire and I sat at the other side of the room, with the big dining table between me and the fire. In winter, it was cold with no heating. Never once was I invited to sit by that fire, instead, if I got a bit fidgety, Mr Harrison would give me columns and columns of figures to add up. I'm not sure, but they may have been called cubes. This is about the only thing I learned at school, how to add figures quickly, whereas now, my younger son can only add figures with a calculator. There was also an assistant master in the senior room by the name of Scott, a young chap; I suppose in his late 20s, he fancied himself a bit as a dandy. He liked cigarettes and one day, as we were being marched to our gym beside Carlisle railway marshalling yards, he got a cigarette out, so I asked him if he smoked Woodbines that seemed to be too much for him and in a flash. I never saw it coming—he smacked me over my face and ear, I should think, with the whole of his weight behind it, for a second or two. I was completely at sea—stunned—what had happened! I was almost on the ground on the pavement. This is another smack on my ear(s) that I blame for tinnitus. Scott never said a word, neither did I, but I knew if I had had my .410 I would have shot him dead on the spot. Scott must have realised he had gone too far because, at the gym, he was trying to toady up to me all the time. I took no notice of him then or at any other time after this episode. He knew he had made a mistake. If he ordered me to do anything, I just ignored it and he knew about it.

At about this time, there was a boy at school by the name of Wills from Scotby near Carlisle. He used to, by the encouragement of Masters and Headmistresses, report any pranks or little misdemeanours to the head. There was one day, I was sent to the Headmaster. It was he who administered punishment six times and for each time—six of the best. Due to this boy Wills! I had on me a tin of itching powder, so together with four or five other boys, I gave each some of the powder. We would make an excuse and pass by Wills and drop the powder down his shirt neck, he was scratching himself before I started on him, but after the final dose, he was in a bad way, he complained heartily to the headmistress, who when her temper was aroused, was a very formidable woman, I was blamed straight away and was sent down for another six of the best, on my way back from the head, to my seat, I pulled Wills ears so hard he yelled, well this time there was no doubt who the culprit was, so down I went for another six of the best, but this time I had had enough, I refused to bend over, the old head was beside himself with fury, no one had had the audacity to refuse punishment before.

In the end, he called on two senior boys, big ones too!! He had them hold me down, which was quite easy for them to do. I was only 4.9 feet and 5 inches and ½ stones, but the head was a bit exhausted by his wrath, so the last six of the day for me were not so bad. I don't know if it was a record, but I had 36 strokes of a very whippy cane that day. I did not tell my parents—Father would not have been amused by my antics. When school finished for the day, I had to catch the LMS train to Langwathby at 4:20 pm. Wills had to catch his bus, I had to pass by his bus station, so I thought to myself. I would give this underhand teachers today a thick ear, but I was thwarted in this, as Wills realised I was going to "get him" and requested help—from the Headmaster himself, who escorted Wills the quarter mile to the bus station, with me shadowing some ways behind. The head was apparently not amused, as in the post the next morning, Saturday, there came to mothers hand a letter from the Headmaster, desiring me not to attend his school anymore. I had to tell Mother what I had done etc. Wills, so Mother straight away took me down to Carlisle to see the head and his wife. I had to apologise, which I did and promise to be a good boy, which I think I kept. I had not to keep this promise very long, as I left school within the next year.

5

When I would be eleven or twelve, my father's uncle would come into my life. Uncle Charlie was my great Uncle. He being the half-brother of my father's father (my grandfather). My great-grandfather was named Isaac. According to Father, he was 18 stones but as solid as a rock, also according to my father, Isaac could carry two sacks of beans, one under each arm, each sack containing sixteen stones, making thirty-twoa stones in all with each sack, he had three wives and 18 children, four of whom died in infancy, he had a very fine aristocratic face and a beard shaped like the tail of the blackcock, he was Charlie's father.

Uncle Charlie was almost the twin of that great film star, Sir Aubrey Smith—a man's man who lived a man's life, he was 6ft 4inches, a big angular face, with a big aristocratic nose and always a twinkle in his eyes, a great sportsman, and a crack shot, he and his brother Tom had gone to Canada to the Klondike, to dig for gold, they made a fortune in the process, but Charlie blew most of his on wine, women and song, and his brother Tom, was shot in a saloon bar in Edmonton, seemed he was not quick enough on the draw. I well remember Charlie standing many times in front of a roaring fire in the morning room at Skirwith Hall and recounting his adventures in those tough lands in Canada's wild north. The ground was too hard to bury the dead until summer and even then, a bonfire had to be kept lit for days on end before the ground was diggable.

Huts of stone with a turf roof were what he and many others lived in at the diggings. I remember him telling me about the notorious bandit Soapy Smith. Charlie was at a place called Skagway, a gold mining place, in those days, a rough and tumble place full of miners, women and booze. The local sheriff was a man named Frank Read, he the sheriff had heard that Soapy Smith and his gang were on the way to Skagway, likely to see what the pickings would be, i.e., robbing the miners, which, as a lot of gold was being dug could be pretty good indeed, Frank Read waited at Skagway end of the bridge over a stream entering the village, Charlie, a few feet away from the sheriff, Soapy Smith arrived at the other end of the bridge, which was not too long. Frank Read told Soapy to back off, whereas Soapy started to draw, but Frank Read drew and shot almost simultaneously with Soapy. Soapy dropped dead, but Frank Read was also fatally hit as Soapy hit the ground. Frank Read, his last words were, "I've got the son of a bitch at last," then Frank dropped dead also. Charlie was a witness to all of this and was, as I have said, told to me word for word many times by him when I was eleven years old. Afterhis brother was shot, Charlie tried hard to find the killer, but those days, and in the vastness of Canada, and the mode of travel, he did not succeed. When the Boer War broke out, Charlie decided he would like more adventure, so he enlisted and went out there. In one of the skirmishes, his horse was shot dead from under him, and this, on his birthday, when the war was over, he came home to England. He arrived at Penrith Station, word had gone around the district that he was on his way back, he was a most popular man, so Penrith's Brass Band was organised, and Charlie was met off the train with the band playing "For He's A Jolly Good Fellow" on the platform. The band then played him all the way down to the Gloucester Arms Hostelry, which was a favourite haunt of Charlie's' and many of his friends in those days, the band, after some lubrication, continued to play outside. No wonder the Yellow Earl liked Charlie. He was a man's man like himself and was a gentle giant unless some fool got in mind to annoy him, then like the Earl, he would be quickly dispersed off by a hefty fist. He had hardly any money, having lived life as it came. However, the Earl of Lonsdale, the Yellow Earl, and he were great friends. One day the two of them were in conversation, and the Yellow Earl asked his friend how things were with him. Charlie told him things were a bit difficult wherewith, without more ado, Lord Lonsdale asked him if he, Charlie, would care to rent a farm of his that was becoming vacant very shortly near Askam, Penrith. Charlie said he was most interested and thanked his friend but added he would be unable to pay the full rent for a year or two, he at first needed to buy stock and this would take all his remaining capital. The Earl told him not to worry; he could have the farm for a nominal sum of a few pounds per annum until he was back on his feet, so to speak. Charlie took the farm and, for a few years, paid little or no rent and, on many occasions, dined with Lord and Lady Lonsdale and guests, which included most of the Royalty and nobles of Europe at Lowther Castle. Later on, when I was in my late teens and early 20s, Lady Lowther (the wife of Anthony, Viscount Lowther, the heir to the Earldom who unfortunately died before reaching the title) told me about Uncle Charlie dining at Lowther Castle. She said, "Your great uncle used to tell such stories at the table that he had the guests spellbound, and at the same time, they would be so risqué that we ladies would be embarrassed and do nothing but blush." But of course, the Yellow Earl was indeed a man unto himself, with an income of three hundred thousand pounds a year (in today's terms, perhaps a hundred million pounds), all spent on pleasure and on the welfare of his estate workers and mine workers. He, the Earl loved to box, and he liked a man who could box and stand up to him. In this, Charlie excelled as a boy at school, he had knocked out his Headmaster and then his school days were over, just as he wished. The same build as his Lordship, Charlie gave as good as he got from his friend. They used to box regularly when the Earl was in residence. The latter never liked a man easy to knock down, so in Charlie, hehad the ideal partner; they were great friends for life. Lord Lonsdale was the only man to put John L. Sullivan on his back and broke his hand doing it.

At Skirwith Hall, 6 or 8 men ate their midday meal and some their evening meal, supper, in the big kitchen, 3 or 4 slept in the quarters over this kitchen, a nice big airy room with three beds in. The meals were huge, great barons of beef, pigs were killed regularly for the bacon and hams, these sides of bacon called flitches, hung from the ceilings of the big kitchen and the small kitchen adjoining, 75 to 80 sheep were killed each year, some were lambs, some two or three years wethers, for consumption in the house, The men and maids would dine at the long kitchen table, on forms each side, the head man for midday would sit at the head on his chair and do the carving for the rest of the company, this was the Shepherd, Fern Crowther.

The head horseman was Isaac Strong, the husband of Lizzie, who slapped my face and head so hard when I was small in the village. Isaac was a kind man, strong as a bull. On most nights, I would watch them in the kitchen washing themselves. If any of the men had a boil on his neck, this was the time of day for treatment. Almost all of the men were great chewers of tobacco. Black twist came like a small rope. They would cut an inch off the black rope, pop it into their mouths and chew. This was also a good cure for boils, so if any of the men wanted treatment after washing, he would ask one of his workmates to squirt it for him. This entailed a good mouthful of tobacco juice being spat onto the offending boil, usually on the neck and rubbed in. It seemed to do the trick. After this, Isaac would grab me and give me what he called a dry shave. He would have 2 or 3 days of stubble on his chin, which he would rub his face against mine quite hard, making me squeal, then he would put me on top of the kitchen mantlepiece, which was about 6.6ft high and very narrow. I was always frightened I would fall off, but I never did, then he would lift me down with a big loud laugh.

One day when Father and Mother left for the market at Penrith on Tuesday. I was in the main courtyard and found the kitchen door locked; I found this strange, so I hopped up onto a big stone slab outside one of the windows. The slab was almost like a mounting block, and I found Isaac on top of the big kitchen table, on top of one of the maids, her with bare legs waving about, making quite passionate love to her, quite a surprise for me, I gave it much thought, but never mentioned it to either of my parents. That was part of the life of the maids and the men when the boss and his wife would be away. They would start to play and had little else those days. A kitchen maid would get 2/6 a week, with the rooms maid at 5 shillings per week, all found, with perhaps one weekend off ina month. They had to ask permission if they wanted a weekend or Saturday off and had to be in by 10:30 pm. Failure to be in at this hour led to a reprimand by Mother, three offences and they were sacked, otherwise if left to their own devices. It was thought and probably right that they would get themselves pregnant, a few did, and of course, then, in the 1930-40s, it was a mighty big slur on a girl's character to have a bastard child. Not many people wanted to hire them if the news got around. My mother had one young woman as a kitchen maid, whose name was Mary Bouch, she was a grand worker and a nice person, but she was one of the girls who just could not say no to a man. I think she had, by the time she came to Skirwith Hall, about seven children, all illegitimate and mostly by different fathers. She admitted this, she became pregnant at Skirwith Hall and her mother asked her why she did it so often to get pregnant, her reply was, "I can't help it, it just happens." Most of Mary's children were brought up by a woman in the village of Ousby, her name I cannot remember. She used to foster them up to a certain age. What happened to Mary, I do not know, but I often wondered.

There was another maid name, Elsie Webster, she was young, quite smart, and was courting Joe Varty, the pig man's nephew. He was also a smart-looking young man. By this period of time, the maids could go out most weekends but had to be in by still the same hour of 10:30 pm. Elsie never came in until after midnight many times, no matter how her mother demonstrated with her. Also, she and the others were supposed to leave the house by the rear courtyard and down the drive at the rear of the premises. Elsie took the shortcut across the front lawn, but after a while, this was detected, as she wore a good path in the grass by keeping to the same one time after time, this was not tolerated, and she had to toe the line. Elsie was also a complete headache for Mother. I do not know why Mother put up with her so long, she had complete butter finger and proceeded to break all or, as it seemed, most of the crockery in the house. She just dropped everything. One day I was in the big kitchen, Elsie was washing the dishes after lunch at the big stone sink, which was 5ft long by 2.5ft wide. All at once, there was a tremendous crash, and there lay on the stone-flagged floor, 8 large dinner dishes. She had dropped the lot at once, this was almost the last straw for my mother, and on her next outing off, she went to see Nathan Arnison of Arnison & Co, the family solicitor, to see if she could deduct the cost of all these breakages from Elsie's wages, this to teach her a lesson. Mr Arnison said no, she could not, as it was not lawful. The rate Elsie was breaking stuff, which would have meant no wages at all for years. Shortly after this, Mother decided enough was enough and parted with Elsie.

6

Bridget and I were still sweethearts, and by now, she would be fourteen years old. She had copied me and gone into ferrets. She had two, a bitch and a dog. She did her own ferreting on her father's estate, Skirwith Abbey, for her pocket money and had to as her father was crippled by death duties and his own fathers' debts gave him practically no pocket money. She, Bridget, used to sell her rabbits, as sometimes I did mine, to Jack Goodfellow, who lived in the village, so it was very handy for us both. We still used to go to the picture matinee at Penrith on a Tuesday and kiss all through the thing. One day, Bridget said why can't we meet at night? No one will know. Her father kept a tight eye on her. I asked how can we manage it; we schemed it up. She would slip out of the Abbey at 2 am one morning, on such a night, and throw a pebble to my window. I myself would have a rope from one of the horse-drawn carts and, at the pebble on the window, tie the rope onto my bed's leg, which was against the wall near the window, with no fear of the bed sliding on the floor and making a noise. The day arrived and I smuggled a good rope from the farm, hid it under the bed and just after 2 am, there it was—the pebble, quickly I tied the rope around the bed leg, and I was down in a flash to meet my sweetheart, my dog Spot, who used to sleep under the big travelling saw bench in the sawdust, met us, he had not barked as he knew Bridget well. We spent two hours in the barn, heavy petting. Then it was time for Bridget to go home and myself up the rope and into bed. Bridget had half a mile to go, mostly across our drive and her father's park. To me, it had been a wonderful night. We were in love. Bridget told one of the housemaids at the Abbey what we had done.

Of course, it was not long before I had my leg pulled by the village joiner, Edwin Kitchen. His joiners shop was the centre for gossip of all types, but one thing neither of our parents found out. So short of pocket money was Bridget she managed to persuade her parents to let her come to Skirwith Hall in the spring and plant potatoes for 10 shillings a day, which she did. She and I would work side by side with what we called a brat around our necks. This 'brat' was a sack that was cut to put over one's head and shoulders and cut off in front to make a big pouch in which potatoes were put, maybe two stones at a time and walk up the stitches or rows, and drop the potatoes in at 18inch or 2ft intervals, full sacks of potatoes would be placed at intervals to replenish our brats. Bridget loved this kind of thing and it got her out of the atmosphere of her parents, who did nothing but quarrel and drank like fish. I believe I have said before, Bridget never went back to school after her 12th or maybe 13th birthday, she had been at Rhodene, but her father was unable to keep up paying the fees, so that was all the schooling she got, and allshe witnessed was the ritual of her patents on market day and Fridays swilling drink down. Her sister Pam, who was, I think, 3 or 4 years older, got fed up with the family squabbles and way of life and joined the ATS. We saw her only on home leave, which was seldom. At least Bridget was paid for her work in the potato field, but I never was. Father always promised to pay, but that was that.

    I was also a good hand at hoeing turnips, and for the first year of which I was learning, and of course, at first, it is slow work, I hoed a section of a field by myself, for this Father promised me 4d a hundred yards. Anyhow, in my second year of hoeing, I was able to keep up with the men. We would then be 8 or 9 of us all together, one behind the other, going at a fair speed, but also able to talk together without shouting. Such were the conversations; time really flew, a forty-acre field, all done by hand before one knew it was finished. There was one very hot sunny day. Men and I were hoeing turnips (Swedes). I was about fifteen years. It was dusty as the hoes flew among the small plants and thirsty with the sun beating down on one's neck. There were 2 or 3 men chewing tobacco and having a good spit now and then. Thirst did not seem to bother them.

John Dixon, now headman after Ferns' retirement, was next to me and chewing beautifully, so I asked him, "John, give me a chow. I'm as thirsty as the devil." John pulls out his black twist and cuts off and inch for me. I popped it into my mouth and chewed contentedly like the rest. This was my first introduction to chewing tobacco, so on we hoed. After perhaps eight minutes, I had good saliva going and spat some out and swallowed some… to my regret, another five minutes, I had swallowed too much and became quite dizzy, but now we were at the end of the stitch, and at this end, a nice firm stone wall, I could not go on and spat the tobacco out and lay down behind the stone wall to recover my senses, things were going around, the men laughed and carried on, I recovered slowly, and was not sick, but did not feel well. Did some more hoeing, but slowly only. My heart was not in it! I went home with the men, so Father would not suspect anything, but I went to bed without my dinner and was not well the next day. I had a temperature and fever and stayed in bed. It had been such a boiling hot day. My parents thought the sun had given me slight sunstroke, perhaps it had, but I blame the black twist mostly. Also, when I was 15, I hoed most of a fifteen-acre field myself—perhaps ¾ of it, it was Little Milles, by the Langwathby Skirwith road. Father promised me payment of 6d per 100 yards, so I set to work with a will and took my lunch and tea and Spot with me. The weather was good, and I enjoyed myself. The plants were easy to part, as the soil in Mille's was a good reddish soft brown, but nearing the end or finish of my ¾ of the field, the plants were getting too big for the home, then it became a hands and knees job with a sack cut in two and used as knee pads, this was a slow slog, on hand and knees, because by the time I had finished, the plants were a foot high and very thickly sown. This sowing of seeds thickly was before many years later known as precision sowing; this was the sowing of each individual seed on its own, a few inches apart, saving a lot of waste. However, I was pleased with myself, even though I had missed Bridget on market days in the pictures.

She gave me a big wave from the car as she went with her parents on Tuesdays when I asked Father for the payment. Yes, he said, next week will do, and so it went on. I am still awaiting payment sixty-five years later on, though I know now I shall never get it. Father died two years ago.

I thought to myself, well, this means I shall have to shoot a few of Father's pheasants to catch up on my pocket money, as well as more rabbits. I shot quite a few pheasants with the .410 and the Remington Kleenbore Express cartridges. Of course, I dare not for the life of me let Father know. I would then have been in a lot of trouble. Mother was in the know, though. To sell the pheasants was quite easy, there came around once a week a small lorry from Lazonby, calling at farms to see if they had any hens or rabbits, eggs, etc. for sale. It was driven by a tremendously kind chap (I'm afraid his name escapes me, though it may have been Fred). I explained to him that for the next few weeks, I would meet him at the back of the farm with a few pheasants and not breathe a word to anyone. Fred knew what I meant, and it would be no problem, so due course, for about four weeks, I would take the pheasants from the hiding place I had and pass them on to Fred for instant cash, 6 or 8 a week I sold, together with a heap of rabbits.

To also make up my cash flow, due to the nonpayment of hoeing, I started to trap rabbits at the Black Wood end of the farm, a mile away. I would put as many traps as I could (this was in the gin trap era) on my bike and cut off to Black Wood, where it was one big rabbit warren and set my traps, about thirty of them. Spot used to watch intensely and tiptoe around the holes. He did this tiptoeing as once before he had not known what traps were and stepped on one I had set and got his foot caught. It had not only hurt him but had surprised him. After that incident, he was most careful, then off home, we would go. I liked to walk whenever I had the chance and not be encumbered by a bike or such, then I could use the .410 quickly, as I nearly always carried it with me. The next morning, Spot and I would set off on foot with the .410 to inspect the traps; I would follow the beck quite often and shoot a few wild ducks. These ducks we ate at home as they were so good, I shot a good few left and right with the .410, birds easily at 40 yards, yet a few years ago, I read in Shooting Times magazine a well-known writer on shooting articles wrote that the .410 was no use at all except at perhaps 20 yards. He may be right in one aspect, i.e., the English Eley cartridges were no good at more than 20 yards. Then onto the traps, I was quite skilful in settingthem. I had watched the professional rabbit catcher very closely and knew my job. The results were plenty of rabbits to sell. I used to line five couples along Spot's back, of course, legged and gutted, myself with a stout stick over my shoulder with as many more and start for home. Spot also knew his job, he would walk beside me in a slinking walk so that the rabbits would not move and fall off if a couple started to slide off his back. He would stop and look up at me. I knew his expression, so I would put the rabbits right for him and off we would go again. On odd times I would be in thought and not notice Spot had stopped, then I would notice he was not beside me and look back. There he would be, maybe 30 yards behind, not moving, with a couple of rabbits almost off his back. His pained expression was, "You had taken no notice of me" he was a great all-rounder—Spot.

When the owner, Michael Le Fleming of Rydal Hall, (they were a very old family, their forebears having come over with William the Conqueror, there being a General in the family and a title, which along the way became extinct. I am not sure how long the Le Fleming's owned Skirwith Hall, but it must have been for a good few hundred years, Lady Le Fleming having lived there herself) and his brother Dick came on their annual shoot with various friends, one of whom was Admiral Sir Bromely Wilson, who used to tease my mother with his ditty of, "Here is the missus of the house, with a mouse in her blouse," Mother used to blush at this. Another extremely kind man at the shoot was Major Mounsey, later Colonel, Commander of Carlisle Castle. After one shoot, in wartime, there was a Captain Flood, whom it was said (I took it all in) wore corsets to help keep his wasp waist. The captain was a nice chap but could not hit a 'barn door flying,' I carried his cartridge bag on one shoot. I knew he could not hit anything. I do believe, though, towards the end of the day, he shot a rabbit at 10 yards. I would take Spot on these shoots, some guns brought their own dogs and most of these would be sick in their master's cars because there was always a lot of cleaning up for the beaters to clean, i.e., the farm men. Well, Spot was head and shoulders over all of the gundogs that came to Skirwith Hall, impeccably obedient and a superb retriever. He would seek birds and find them long after the other dogs had given up. Due to this, a few of the guests would pump me about my shooting game. I knew if I told them the truth, it would be reported to the Le Fleming's and then to Father, so I always replied that for the game, I was not allowed. I only frightened pigeons and crows of the crops and rabbits also, with my .410. As soon as they realised that I only shot with a .410, they believed me. They would have changed their minds if they could have seen me in action with my 'little gun.' These were the times when farmers grew many acres of Swedes. At Skirwith Hall, Father would grow 70-75 acres to fatten many hundreds of lambs up for the market. The Swedes were good game holders of partridge and pheasant, but especially the former. 150 brace of grey partridge would be shot on this day by the 6-8 guns, and most partridges would be shot in the Swedes. One field of 40 acres, named Scaws Gill, would keep the guns happy for almost half a day. The game was always walked up; on wet days, the Swedes would soak through all but the best waterproofs. Also, it was hard going for the beaters who had to carry the cartridges as well as the game, but Kale was the worst to walk through on wet days because it would be as high as one's neck. One passage through and one would be soaked. The farm men, acting as beaters, hated the guns to shoot hares, of which there were plenty and very heavy ones. When a hare got up, one could almost hear every beater saying to himself, 'Miss the bloody thing for hell's sake,' but the only one to miss them was poor old Captain Flood; maybe his corsets were too tight.

I carried the cartridge bag of Michael Le Fleming once after lunch and was almost overwhelmed by the whiskey fumes from him, but of course, most of the guns had the same perfume after lunch, a few even before the shooting started. The shooting lunch was quite a long affair, held in the dining room, sumptuous meals all seen to personally by Mother, with whisky and cigars galore provided by Father. After the day was over, Michael would say to Father, "Well, Guy, it's yours now. Help yourself!" meaning the shooting.

My father used to tell us that in his Father's Day, at one of the Le Flemings shoots, his foreman at that time, by the name of Robert Dalton, received a good charge of shot in one side of his face. Dr Stephenson of Temple Sowerby was sent for, who proceeded to extract as many pellets as possible. At the end of the day, when by this time Dalton had been patched up, so to speak, he was called into the Smoke room. Mr Ritchard Hughes Le Fleming was there and also the gun responsible for Daltons' agony. The latter apologised the most profusely and gave Dalton a gold guinea. Dalton was taken aback, accepted the guinea and thanked the guest and told him, "For your kindness and the guinea, sir, I would stand up and you can have another shot at me." This was repeated by him in the Sun Inn that night with great glee. They were hardy chaps in those days, these times, such an episode would entail hospitalisation, no work for weeks, sick pay, the police, solicitors, lawyers and the courts! Robert Dalton's period, his acceptance and his reply. I think I should apply to more things in life these days than to resort to solicitors, etc., the sharks of mankind.

Trout fishing was a great hobby of mine. The briggle beck ran right through the middle of the lower lands of Skirwith Hall for a very good mile, and there would be another two miles of good trout stream at Kirkland and High Close. The latter trout were not as big as the briggle trout, the latter, some of which would be a good ¾lbs, a few at 1lb. The beck was full of brownies and had plenty of dubs in it. Dub is a nice-sized pool created by the beck turning and making a corner. It was very difficult to fly fish because of the beck's' elder trees, but many low branches were cut away by Father and myself to make casting a line, whether for fly or worm made, easy. We also had many shot rabbits hanging up through the summer months from the trees overhanging the beck; these would be maggoted and made good food for the trout because what we caught were very plump ones.

My best season of all was that I landed 355, but of these, I would throw 50 back again as too small. Of course, the beck was at its best after a heavy rainfall making it just nicely coloured. My best bag had been in these conditions when it just rained and rained nonstop. One of these days, I was fishing with maggot, and the fish just kept on biting and biting. I had not many hooks with me, maybe half a dozen, loosing some in the tree roots and odd ones with a biggish trout. By the time I had reached the end of the Skirwith Hall stretch, I was loaded with 75 trout and no hooks left. At the end of the beck, however, there was a nursery garden called Beck Mill Nursery, run by Mr Alf Britton, who was quite famous for his lectures and lantern slides around the north of England. I thought, *well, the fish are still hungry,* so I popped over the fence, went to see Alf and asked if he had any fishing hooks. He hunted around and came up with three or four worm hooks. Well, I had no worms, however, I knew I could soon get a few worms under the stones or a log. This I did and started to fish homeward bound. By now, it was becoming dusk, I had not had a morsel to eat all day except breakfast and now it was dusk. However, I was not at all hungry and time had gone by without my realising it. I had Spot and fish were biting. Nothing else mattered. I reeled in another 20 trout and came into the home at 9 pm, by now Mother was getting worried and was on the point of asking the men who boarded in to go and look for me, however, she was used to me staying out late, with my mind always on the hunting side of things, by now I was tired and hungry. What with the weight of the fish, etc., I was ready for some warmth and food, so I gave Spot his uveka and milk (in modern times, I suppose this is doggy cornflakes and milk). Mother fried me three of the biggest trout. They were delicious, trout fresh from the stream or river took a lot of beating, and to bed with my hot water bottle, I was soon asleep.

I would be fourteen years old and had overgrown my Shetland pony, Patsy. Our neighbour, Mr John Jackson of Red House farm, had, a few years before, bought his son Robert a racehorse broodmare. She was also a good-looking one by Highborn the Second. Robert had put her to the local Hunter Premium stallion, Merely-a-Minor. He was a beautiful horse, a bay full of quality all around. He had also done quite well on the track, he was standing at Newton Reigny, Penrith, at the farm of Jimmy Rowlandson, but of course, the stallion travelled all of Cumberland and quite a lot of Westmoreland with his stallion man, all on foot, staying at various places for the night and also meeting other mares at these places.

Robert Jackson, five years older than I was fortunate to have a father who loved a good horse and let his son indulge in hunting with the Cumberland farmers with the best money he could buy. Always extremely well turned out, horse and boy, Robert had a yearling filly to sell by Merely a Minor out of his mare Miss Fitz. I went to see the filly and liked her right away. As a foal, she had got herself badly staked in her chest and had to have 50-60 stitches in, but the stitching had been very well done. She was scared, but only lightly. I asked Robert how much he wanted and he said 35 pounds. I had this amount, so we did a deal there and then. The next day, I went with Robert again, he put a halter on the filly and I led her home. She was well-behaved, as Robert always handled his foals well. He even taught them to jump rails or bales of hay when they were foals and already had named and registered the filly at Weatherby's Helm Star. The helm bit comes from the Helm Wind, which blows from Cross Fell. This can be a right hurricane at times. I paid Robert two days later in 1 pound and 10/- notes, and he very kindly gave me 3 pounds back for a lucky penny. I was most pleased with this. I was now the owner of a full-blooded racehorse, though, through her injury, we knew Star, as we now called her, would not grow to the usual height of a thoroughbred. She stopped growing when she reached 14.2, and now I had no proper riding clothes. Robert told me he had some breeches from Harry Hall that he had outgrown. Would I like to try them on? He also had a pair of riding boots, also too small for him. I tried the breeches; they were just right, very elegant with buckskin on the inside legs, and the boots just right, very supple and of the finest quality. I paid Robert for both 30/-. I was now set up and most pleased. I wanted a nice riding jacket, which I acquired a little later on at the Durafit shop in Penrith; Mr Wilson measured me for it and made a very good job of the jacket, with double slits in the back.

I started to break Star in right away, as she was rising two (classed as a yearling), putting her reverse into one of the stable stalls and mouthing her with the Clydesdale bit with keys, it was far too big, but I had nothing else, and that with the big horse breaking gear, all too big, I did this for two weeks, never having broken a horse in at all, just watching Fathers' horsemen do the job, then I lunged her for a couple of weeks, left and right, then I drove her with two reins from behind, doing figures of eight and driving her round buildings, stacks, all end of things. By now, she had done everything asked of her. She was quick to learn, had a nice sensitive mouth and was ready to mount. I mounted her in the stable at first when she was tied in, which she did not seem to mind. I thought, right now, into the field with you. I led her into the first field on the driveway and mounted her. She walked away on demand and trotted on demand. I did this for fifteen minutes and thought that it was good enough for the first time, she had done everything asked and I was thrilled. Father looked on at a distance.

I must have been fifteen years old when Ma decided I needed some extra education. Dad didn't believe in all this at all, wanting me to work on the farm. However, Ma persisted and went to see Father Kewley to see if he would give me tuition. He was be delighted and he told Ma. The price was discussed and finished with two mornings a week at 5 shillings and hour, six hours a week total. Ma paid for me herself from money left to her by her father, my Scottish grandfather. Monday and Thursday mornings were set aside by Father Kewley for my lessons. If was still there, farting away as usual, but now very old and full of rheumatism. The Vicar very soon had me taped, so to speak, as to what I knew from learning at Grosvenor College. He taught me new ways of maths, etc, but the marvellous thing was that his teaching was so readily understood. He had the gift of explaining what seemed to me so hard a problem so simply and easily. His knowledge just flowed from him into me. He was to teach me for two years; I will say this now in my old age if this man had taught me from the age of ten—I would never have started working on the farm. I could have gone to great heights. We were really now firm friends; there are now in the church very few of his calibre, if any. The Vicar who followed, J.C. Wilson, was a clever and nice man but a gossip, going from house to house, each occupant knowing all the intimate goings on of the other. All his visitors in the clerical line were poofs, without exception and so it remains to this day. The clergy as a whole are a bunch of homos and myself now. I have no respect for them, from the highest to the lowest.

Star became the best pony anyone could have had. She could take a bullock or cow out of the herd and stick to it like a leech, better than a dog could. If I was driving ewes and lambs when the lambs were being tailed and castrated, and if a lamb was too tired to go on, stop, I would lean down from the saddle, pick the lamb up, put it over her withers and walk on, Spot and she got on well, she let him jump onto her back without any trouble, I would lunge her at a slow canter, many times with Spot up. Star enjoyed all of this, she would put up with a few couples of rabbits slung over her withers and so far up her neck. I used to shepherd the sheep on the far-off piece of land above Ousby called the allotment of 265 acres with Star and Spot, see they were alright, non-maggoted or put the strays out. There was also grouse on this piece of highland four miles from home. Star was an excellent jumper and also very fast. The first time I went to a gymkhana was at Gamblesby, a village fair. There was a race of one mile round for ponies of 14.2hh. I thought I would enter Star for this race, which she won easily. I think the first prize was 3 pounds. This made my day. Bridget's father was one of the judges. I went in for best pony etc but won no more that day.

The next entry for Star was at Cliburn, where she was on a handicap of so many yards behind the others for a start. Why this, I don't know, as this was nothing to do with her first win. The organisers at Cliburn were preparing for a few races that particular day. I did not know then, but I knew later on this type of thing was called 'flapping' or 'flapping races' at the opening of the Cliburn races. It was a terribly rainy day, pouring down. By the time Star was due to race, I had borrowed my brother's good riding mack and rode the race in this. Star and I did no good, and the light-coloured Mack was a different colour at the finish. My brother was not pleased. Robert Jackson had run Laura, the one I had broken my ribs on. She also was nowhere. We had walked the horses seven miles there and seven miles back in pouring rain. It was fun. Robert's father then would not allow him to run any more of his horses in flapping races because, by Jockey Club rules then, it was illegal as far as they were concerned. Any horse running in them, and I believe persons to run under rules, i.e. N.H, involved in flapping, were declared persona non grata. To me, I did not think I would ever be involved with racing or race horses. For one thing, money-wise, I could not see it happen.

The men, who had got the Cliburn races up, then thought

they would create a flapping committee too and did so create the Eden Valley Racing Association. At one time, there was racing on most Saturdays at various villages, together with some sort of sports with ponies and hounds trailing. The next year I prepared Star as best I could for the first race of that season at Temple Sowerby. This was on a big flat field with the river Eden on one side and a naturally elevated grandstand on the other. I had brought Star in from the grass six weeks before, thinking that was enough time to prepare her. Jimmy Curwen, the blacksmith, shod her, but the shoes were not light ones. I had her in one of the stalls in the main stable. I was unable to persuade Father to give me a loose box. She exercised once a day for an hour. I knew nothing about training but had read a bit about it only. The big day came, and off I set to walk Star to Temple Sowerby, four miles away. The new Vicar of Skirwith, Father Wilson and his boyfriend, Jim Peel, were keen to go and have a bet on her if there were any bookies. He, the Vicar, took his camera and set off in his very battered Ford 8, passing me on the way. I got to the field of operations in good time, wearing my second-hand riding breeches and boots from Robert Jackson and my new hacking jacket looking quite smart. There were plenty of bookies in attendance, giving the place a very real race atmosphere. The local brass band was playing and Star seemed to be in the mood. There was also in attendance one of the most colourful of characters in Cumberland (though Temple Sowerby was just over the border in Westmoreland), his name was George Willie Chappelhow, George Willie, also known as One-Eyed Willie, had only one eye, but he saw more than most men with two, one never knew whether one could trust Willie. He was as shrewd a man and as slippery as a box of monkeys, a most likeable man, he could charm a hen off its nest, and Willie liked to have a bet as long as he knew the chances of winning were great. Well, George Willie had imported a pony, a black one, it was said to be from Manchester, a very elegant pony, a filly named Rushholme. She was looking at every part of the racehorse, also imported specially to ride her was one of these sidelined jockeys. A sideliner is one of those chappies the professional racehorse trainer has discarded, one that has possibly not been too honest with his master.

Willie, his sons and cronies, came over very casually, as if not concerned, to give Star the 'once over' and ask me innocent little things like how long she had been off the grass. I told them six weeks. Star really looked as if she had just come off the grass. She was still a big girl all over. They studied her heavy shoes and returned to their 'camp' well satisfied that they had a sure thing in their 'Rushholme'. I heard, on moving about on Star, Willies' son Arnie, 'that yan' (one) of Joey's can't win for over big of its belly and girth heavy shoes on'— (Cumberland dialect), but to make sure of his horse winning, One-Eyed Willie, who had many friends in the Eden Valley Racing Club especially the handicapper and most of the committee, spoke to them and they put my horse Star, on the scratch mark. They gave Rushholme 50 yards in front of me, in fact, I was the only one on scratch. The bookies were getting nervous about One-Eyed Willie's betting. He had been along the line of them, perhaps 15 or 20, together with his sons and had struck simultaneously. The bookies knocked Rush- holme down to odds. After Willie had his plunge, he came round once again to see Star, his one eye gleaming and seemed well satisfied with himself, seeing he had got my horse handicapped behind all the others. Star was 10/1 at the bookies. I hardly did any betting those days but had 2 pounds on 10/1, the Vicar and Jim had 10/- each and there was no place betting. We were called on at the appropriate time over the loudspeaker system to line up for the race, which was one mile two times around the track, which was roped off on the inside. The starter gun, a 12-bore, went off. Star was off like a rocket in a second or two. I was onto Rushholme, who was about two yards off the inside rope. I thought I'd got your measure now. I put Star to pass on the inside. The jockey on Rushholme, the Manchunian, glanced over to my side, saw me coming to pass, and pulled right over to cut me off. I had the rope on my left leg (left-hand track) and rubbing boots with the chappie from Manchester, watching his dirty trick made me instantly boil. I swore a few hot and filthy oaths athim to move over. My anger and the tone of my voice must have taken him by surprise because he did move over and was very sharp too. Then I was past him at the brief fracas had given Star a breather. We passed easily everything else in the race and won by 30 lengths pulling up. The Vicar had taken a photo of the finish, no other horse in sight. I was most pleased to have won, and to have won so easily and to have given One-Eyed Willie and his cronies of the committee a slap down. The bookies were jumping for joy that they had come out on top, especially against their old foe Willie. In one of the races later on that day, about six or more of them, unable to take the bend next to the river, finished up in the middle of it, two riders taking a very sudden cold bath fully clothed. I beat Rushholme every time we met that year. The next season George Willie bought another horse named Tony; he was 16 h.h an ex-racehorse, he must have damaged his knee at some time, as he had a lump on one side the size of a goose egg, but Tony could gallop. Arnie, Willie's son, always rode him; I don't think Willie trusted anyone else after his big loss when I beat his Rushholme at Temple Sowerby. I never raced against Tony, as I always put Star in the 14.2 h.h races, except one time at Culgaith, I entered her in an open race against him and she won. I had put one of the boys from the village upon her, Raymond Trevaskis, who was only about six stones. This time, the handicap was by weight, and Star, who was a pony up against the full-sized horses, received a lightweight. She still had to carry some lead, so I had prepared a lead cloth out of clover seed bags, tightly woven stuff, made it into pockets for the lead. It looked the part, or mostly. In this race was a local farmer, Reg Bateman, who had a horse named Snowball, a grey, also an ex-racehorse. I cannot remember if it was a gelding or mare, but the horse looked the part and had won quite a few flapping races quite easily.

Reg was also a man who liked to bet and also a big friend of One-Eyed Willie. Both had had a good dig that day on Snowball, well the horses were called in, and the 12 bores went off. Star with Ray on, he was only thirteen years old, was off a bit slower, again it was a mile-long race, but much like the one I had described before. This was three times round, left-handed. *Snowball soon passed all in front of him, Reg riding his own horse. He was not a heavy man, Star some way back by 15 lengths,* I thought to myself. *Ray is not doing so well, however, he was sitting pretty still and riding correctly.* In the final lap, Ray had moved Star into second place, two lengths behind Snowball, then he put Star on the ropes to pass on the inside, by now she was opposite Snowball's shoulder and pressing when Reg all at once saw his bet going under, put his whip in his left hand and started to flail it in the air as much as possible. Star, with no room to move over, refused to go past the flailing left hand of Reg. If she had gone forward, she would have been hit over the head, so Reg won and no questions were asked by the committee, who was in on the 'good thing'. Once again, Star almost upset their best-laid plans. Ray had ridden a very good race and had remained quite cool. I had taught him how to ride. In fact, I taught him on Star, so she knew him well. Ray, at that age, would smoke twenty cigarettes a day and, later on in life, go on for sixty a day.

One other little episode at these flapping races concerning Snowball was at Whinfell Park, just outside Penrith on the Appleby road. Reg, One-Eyed Willie and their cronies, the committee men, had a big plunge on Snowball. I got to know that they had doped it, what substance I don't know, but the horse was absolutely on its toes, almost unmanageable. Arnie, George Willie's son, was riding. He was much lighter than Ray and fearless was Arnie. It was impossible to get any money from Snowball. It was odds on with a vengeance. Reg, Willie and pals had seen to that. The horses were called in for the right-hand track this time, twice round. Snowball, by this time, was really on a high, and as the old 12 bores went off, at that very same split second, so did Snowball—in the opposite direction, of course, he took no part in the race. Arnie had a devil of a hard job not only to stop the horse but also to control it. It ran right off the track across this very large field, where Arnie managed to stop it against a hedge while helpers ran to his aid. Once again, Willie and his pals came unstuck, but the same night he would be planning his next offensive. The same day as Snowball went potty, I raced Star, riding myself, in the mile for 14.2 h.h. against a horse named Flicka. This one was owned by Frank Allison from Brough, a garage owner and a charming man. His son Cliff was riding, who was, later on, to gain fame as a racing car driver, he was good, but his career was cut short by a very bad crash and Cliff was badly injured, if I remember rightly, he used to ride his horses bareback in these flapping races. Flicka was good; I had beaten her a few times before and vice versa. This day we lined up, Flicka 50 yards ahead of myself, on scratch. We lined up and were off. Star was always very quick off the mark (except for once). I was up to Flicka very quickly passed and made the pace hot. This was my own undoing. I had not given Star one breather, with the result in the last half furlong, she had shot her bolt and Flicka beat me by two lengths. I never made that mistake again.

7

I had made friends with an enchanting little lady through the local gymkhana and flapping racing. She was Netta Baron, her father was a dentist in town. Netta had a nice pony at that time, which she raced in the 14.2 h., who has the class against Star, sometimes finishing second to me, named Spoilt Child.

Well, I asked her out and we courted for about a year and very often at weekends. We would meet at Eden Hall, she on her pony, myself on Star. It was almost the halfway mark for both of us. We would put the ponies in Arthur Lancaster's' boxes at the Home Farm and go out and have tea at the hotel. Then we would go for long walks beside the River Eden, young love, it's a wonderful thing. One day or one evening to be exact, I wished to go and see Netta, no cars available, so I asked Jim, the Vicar's boyfriend if he had a bike and, if so, if I could borrow it. He said he had and I could, so off I set for Penrith, 8 miles but far from easy. It was the toughest and hardest of bikes. It was so hard I had to get off up the hills and push as if something was wrong and I should think with the gearing. I duly arrived at Penrith, took Netta to the pictures and then went back to her home. I wasn't looking forward to that 8 mile journey home with the monster. It took me quite a while to get back.

The affair between Netta and I cooled off somehow. In later years, she married a young man by the name of Oliphant, a nice young man. My wife and I met him and Netta at a party given by John Bell, the baker in Lazonby and she looked well. She had had a baby, and I think the same year, Netta was found dead in her bath, poor Netta, she was a very tender and loving girl, my mother liked her a lot and she was a good judge of character.

I had by now left school, and as I was small and not too strong, so Father thought, I passed my time shooting and fishing with great abandon with my two faithful, Spot and Star, ferreting around the various crops which Father encouraged.

All rabbits were shot as they bolted with the .410 pigeons I shot in the hundreds in wintertime, keeping them off the turnips. There was one winter in the '40's that was so hard and long with snow, always a foot deep even on the open fields, the pigeons at a shot would rise then land again on the same place. They were so hungry, in fact, I saw the cruelty in my shooting, as the birds were, then I stopped shooting at them and let them eat.

One morning however, Father came to my bedroom. I was still fourteen years old he said to me, "Get up, I want you to start to plough today. Haterslyis off ill."

He was one of the tractor men, so I got rather excited. I could drive a tractor quite easily, but had never ploughed, however, Father started the tractor for me with no starter buttons, tractors then only had the starting handle, and I could barely swing them. My wrists were no thicker than a sparrow's leg. The tractor was Fordson, the small ones (before Fordson Majors came out). This particular tractor had a high top gear, which, when on the road, I thought was great fun at 20mph.

We hitched the plough onto the drawbar. Hydraulics had not been invented then. This was a trailer plough made by Ransom Simms & Jefferies, a two-furrowed one. One could alter the depth by twisting a long lever from the driver's seat. This was quite easy if kept well-greased. The plough and tractor were greased up, as it was usual, with all machinery before work. This was the ritual. Off we went to an 18-acre field that had grown turnips; the next crop was to be oats, under sown with grass seed mixture. I think Father chose this type of field for my debut in ploughing because if my furrows were not straight, it did not matter a lot. Not like ploughing a lea (or grassland), Father showed me how to 'set out' the first furrow and how to come back into it to 'throw it out' then back in again, to step out exactly each end and the middle for the next set out, further over the field, possibly 40 yards across, so the whole thing would be equal at the finish of that plot. At the hearing (that is a space from where to lift one's plough shares out of the ground at the end of the field, or end of each run furrow and be able to turn around without stopping and into the ground again). We made, with the tips of one of the ploughs shares, a skim mark 5 or 6 yards from the wall (most of the fields were walled in) right around the field. At this mark I would pull the chord that tripped the lever or catch, and the shares would lift out of the ground, making a neat finish. Then when the field was ploughed, there remained the hearing, the 5-6 yards to finish off. That entailed either starting by the wall side as close as one could or to start at the edge of the ploughing and plough towards the wall, going round and round the field until the 5-6 yards were turned over. The final furrow of all is to be made as shallow as possible in the case of turnips ground, as next year it would be grass after the binder had finished. The shallow furrow, when harrowed, would then be almost levelled off, leaving the field smooth.

Father stayed with me for half an hour so that I had the hang of things. When he had gone, I had Spot sit on the wide footplate or beside the gear lever on top of the axle. Sometimes he was not too comfortable, so I would put a thick sack on top of the big round mudguards and he would lie there. If the sack started to slip with him on, he would soon get a better position, he travelled many miles and fields like this. I quite enjoyed ploughing and, after a few weeks, became quite good at it. Father had no hesitations about putting me to ploughing lea (grassland). The only thing at the start of my new career was to start the tractor, so having my 10 am sandwich and at tea time, I would sit beside one of the big wheels or behind a wall and leave the tractor running. Eventually, I could swing the starting handle round and round as hard as possible to get her going, then all of a sudden the handle would be torn out of one's hand, spinning backwards at 100mph. No good putting one's thumb around this one!

On spring days, ploughing was quite a pleasant job. The gulls and rooks would be almost landing on the plough to get the worms and grubs, the rooks used to cram their little pouches under their beaks, full to over-flowing, then fly off to the rookery across the beck from Skirwith Hall amongst the oak trees and back again to load up, odd crows as we called them, had the odd coloured feather in them and I would recognise them and take notice of how long it took them to fill their pouches and fly off to feed their young and be back again, say a distance of ½ to – ¾ of a mile, it was only a few minutes, I never carried a watch, in fact, I did not own one, my sister gave me one year later, which when I got wet one day, I put my trousers on top of the Aga cooker to dry, I forgot my watch was in them, Well hours later of course, the Aga had melted the plastic glass face, some had run into the works and that was that. I bought another one when I was twenty-nine in Munster, Germany, which I still have and it still keeps perfect time. Those are the only two watches I have owned in my life. Without a watch, I could tell the time of day to within fifteen minutes through habit. The feel of the day, and I suppose latterly for myself, watching the sun, it was the 'feel' of the day I went by mostly, perhaps like those birds that migrate or when mating time comes around, they 'feel' it's time to move or to find a mate.

I would come across many nests of the plover (the peewit), as we called them locally, some full with four eggs, some just started with one or two eggs. Of course, the nests were just a small scooped hollows in the soil, nicely done though, no grass or feather lining like many other birds, these nests when I ploughed up to them, I would get off the tractor, make a little nest, hollow maybe 3ft onto the new ploughed land, remove the eggs from the original nest and put them in the one I had just made and carried on. The plover whose nest I would move, watching and making plenty of noise, would run about maybe 20 yards away or fly very low overhead, screeching her cries of woe or anger. However, when I would move on, she would be back at the new nest within two minutes. They never deserted their nests, as possibly a partridge or pheasant may do. The only thing ploughing with the tractor, one only heard the noise of the engine, no birds singing or the like. One thing though about the tractor, if I wanted to have a cigar and had no matches, I would dip a straw or piece of paper into the petrol tank, then take a wooden-handled screwdriver, touch the engine casing with the metal end, hold the tip of the screwdriver within 10th of an inch from a sparkplug, this caused the spark to jump to the piece of straw or paper doused in petrol and hey presto, I had a good flame and a good smoke. These tractors had a small petrol tank holding 1½ - 2 gallons. This was only to start the tractor with when cold, run for five or ten minutes, then switch over to the main tank of paraffin, T.V.O. I had seen the tractor men doing this, otherwise, I would not have known. I did not smoke good Havana's on the tractor; I had now, for day-to-day smoking, been introduced to Burma Cheroots by Uncle Alex. He had smoked these in India, these were made and imported from Rangoon by a firm named Scott and the first I smoked were small Scott's No.2. Black in colour and very mild, these ones were a bit on the tight side to draw, but very good, then I got onto Scotts No.1. which were as thick as a large Havana, extremely mild and would last for two hours. I think I paid 9d each and got them from Bertha, the tobacconist in the straits in Penrith, these Burma's had an extremely light and delicate perfumed smoke, different from all other cheroots or cigars. One could smell them a mile away.

After a year of non-stop tractor work, I found my ankles in the mornings, getting out of bed, would not bend, they would loosen up later in the day, my brother had had the same problem, starting, I suppose, too young, from the continued vibration of these old types of tractors, the footplates on each side attached to big enclosed mudguards, these had a fair amount of vibration and for one growing up, young bones, that sort of thing, it was not good. Eventually, I stopped doing so much of the tractor work and Father put me as an assistant shepherd, when not shepherding, I, in springtime, after the lambing, would take Rose, the horse I had known as a baby, out to roll the newly sown cornfields or to sow the turnips. To roll the cornfields, I had a metal roller 8ft wide with a flat platform on top of it with a ledge side and back about 3 inches high. This was to put the large stones that were too big to crush into ground, some were too big, or sometimes there would be one we called a set-fast which was a boulder under the soil with so much jutting out of the ground, these were liable to break the binder at harvest time, so these ones I would mark with a slender post hammered into the ground beside the offender. Horses still did a lot of work on the farm even though there was a modern tractor, but slowly they were faded out. Father got another Fordson, still, three or four horses were kept for rolling the cornfields and sowing turnips and for feeding turnips to the various fields that held ewes and lambs. This work with horses was slow, but looking back, by far the best, one could study the sky, the hedgerows, and trees and listen to and watch the birds singing, especially the skylark of which we had hundreds, it was a joyful period of life, the hayfields were cut by the mowing machine pulled by two horses, with the driver sitting on top of and between the wheels, cutter bar on the right, coming upon partridges or curlew nests, as there were plenty in the hay fields, were easily seen by the driver as the horses were not too fast.

The eggs would be removed, the grass cut, eggs replaced and marked by a long hazel stick so that the next hay-making machine would know of a nest and take precautions and go around them. Unfortunately, at this stage, many birds deserted their nests because of being lifted too many times. The other consolation being if there were very young birds, only a few days old, one could rescue these without having them cut up. However, as tractors took over this work of mowing, they became faster and faster, drivers unable to see in time, or couldn't care less, dozens of nests and young were run over or had the mower cut them up.

When there was a fell gathering, that is, all the shepherds from adjoin- ing villages for many miles would all start to gather on a certain day, either for clipping of the wool, tupping time or compulsory dipping. This is when all shepherds would make a full sweep of the fells. They would take the gathered sheep to the various shedding places for their various owners. This was a hard day's work, but at the same time, exciting. The dogs seemed to love these days too, knowing they would, during the course of the day, meet many others of their kind, either making friends or an enemy and have a fight. It did not matter. They enjoyed themselves even though they had probably run anywhere from 10-15 miles that day. At night when the sheep were at the homestead, the dogs would have worn their pads raw then they would lie down to lick them the morning after. They would be a bit stiff to start with but willing to do it all again for their masters, fine intelligent dogs them all, sheepdogs, collies and scotch beardies.

Those days we had not the use of a land rover to be taken on to the top of the fells, Joe and I, then later on, Len and I had to walk from Skirwith Hall up to Skelling farm, 2 miles away to collect Beeby, who would be waiting for us with his two dogs, one was a large black and tan named Roy, one could hear Beeby shouting at this dog of his for miles. Beeby, who had a voice that could travel, he himself was the brother of Mrs John West, the tenant farmer of Skelling, a raw-boned man of leather beaten face, very kind and would chat for hours, when talking, he would spit a lot, very expertly too. The strange thing about Beeby's life at Skelling farm was that he slept in the hay barn or in a hallway off the hay barn on the floor but covered with plenty of hay, he had to bring the meals from the house on a plate himself, across the yard and his sister, the farmers' wife, cosy inside with fires and nice beds, I never questioned him on this side of things. Mrs West, his sister, seemed to be a kindly woman, though terribly disfigured by a huge red birthmark covering a good half of her face and all of her nose. In later life, this birthmark turned much worse and, in fact, became grotesque, with large warts covering her nose.

She had a beautiful daughter and a nice son, who grew into a very nice young man. Beeby, I believe, died one hard winter in amongst the hay. However, to get back to meeting Beeby at Skelling, we would all three proceed to Ousby across an old track which was right of way, to call on Bobby Little at Town Head Farm.

Bobby was a non-stop pipe smoker, and would spit in great juicy streams of tobacco for yards. His dogs used to keep their distance because he used them for target practice; I think he did this quite unconsciously, though. Bobby had a cat in his farmyard, which was like a tiger in its rage and any strange dog that came into the yard, as it happened that morning, it would run at the nearest dog with its eyes blazing, hair straight on end, spitting and howling like a demon, it would jump on top of the dog, its' claws doing overtime in scratching, in seconds that dog would howl and run for its life as if all the demons in hell were after it, the cat would then in a flash be onto the next dog and the next repeating the process, our dogs would all be put to flight out of the yard and wait for us at a respectful distance. I often wondered what Spot would have done to that cat. The two never met, and never in my life have I seen a cat so wild with pure fury. It was incredible, for she never bothered Bobby's own dogs. After waiting for perhaps fifteen minutes for Bobby to pack his sandwiches, we had to wait because he had just finished milking his 12 or 14 cows, then off we set. On our backs with bottled tea, this would be for our 10 am break, lunch and tea, and weighed quite a bit. Our gathering ground was to go to the other side of Cross Fell, down to Bullman Hills below the peak and gather all sheep up to the shedder and holding pens, all built of local stones and rocks, just below Skreeds Hut, an old mining hut from the lead mines a long time ago. Skreeds Hut was stone built and very good indeed, snug and warm with a good fireplace, table and cupboards. Various shepherds would bring wood and coal to burn. It was a good shelter in bad weather until the ramblers burnt the table, cupboards and the door and tore slates from the roof. I believe now the ramblers or green peace lot have repaired it, more or less claiming it for themselves. This is where I saw a good many grouse and promised myself a day or two shootings because the shooting rights were the property of the Lord of the Manor, who owned Skirwith Hall, our cousins, the Le Flemings.

It took until midday to round up the sheep of many owners as well as so many strays from afar, then came the shedding. The main flock would be held in the large enclosure and led down a walled in corridor or channel so only one sheep could go through (not two side by side). It was a case of following the leader. There would be about three men doing the shedding. The first man would shed one lot of sheep with its specific mark of tar or paint on its' fleece or perhaps a coloured horn. The latter mark making shedding easy, more so than tar or paint. The second man, another mark, the third another mark, when these three lots of sheep had been shredded off into their various pens. I have omitted to say that each man doing the shedding stood by a small wicket (gate) only about 2ft 6in high and 2ft wide. This was opened and shut, as the case maybe, when his sheep came, he opened it and his sheep would walk through to his pen. The ones he did not want to be walked on to the next shedding man and so on. The various shepherds would then set off to their homes with their respective flocks. There would still be many more sheep left to shed, though, the process would be repeated until the last flock, and usually, these would be the strays from afar.

Odd times one or two sheep would be from Middleton-in-Teesdale, or other places possibly only 5-6 miles away because bear in mind this is the Pennine Chain, all open country for many miles. It was always the same farmer who took the strays away at each gathering. It was very late at night that first fell gathering. I was very tired when we eventually got the sheep home, or almost home, because we left the sheep that night in a field a mile away from home to pick them up the next morning. All day on foot from 4 am until 8-9 pm at night, dogs and all of us were ready for bed. The strays were sorted out by the various farmers because even though shredded, there were always 3 or 4 of other people in each and everyone's flock. These would be taken to the Melmerby sheep meeting ten days later which was held on the village green in front of the Shepherds Inn, pens would be made of hurdles and the strays would be, if 12 or so from one farm, driven on foot, if only one or two from various farms, by land rover or trailer or in the boot of cars. Everyone would crowd into the Shepherds Inn except the village policeman – put 2 shillings in the kitty and drink his fill. When the kitty was empty, another 2 shillings would be put in. The committee chairman, Mr Frank Wales from Lown-thwaite, was a teetotaller, drank only maybe two, at the most, glasses of lemonade. He was an extremely kind and charming man and there would be perhaps 3-4 more fans of lemonade, which made it great for us beer drinkers, even though I was too young, I stuck to the beer.

It has been told to me and by my father at that why perhaps Frank Wales was teetotal—his father, in the days of pony and traps, was a fair drinker on market days (like many others of those days) calling at all the pubs on the way home. One such market day, old Mr Wales, from market one Tuesday in summer, arrived home the worse for wear. He had a row with his wife, he went into the house, grabbed his 12 bores, his wife ran across the yard and was just rounding a corner of a building when her husband fired, he missed but only just, blasting a fair chunk of sandstone out of the building's corner, the marks are there to this day at Lownthwaite, this was possibly why Frank was teetotal. Frank of the stray sheep committee had two sons, one named Frank, who was also teetotal and one named Thomas, who was a drinker who became Master of Fox Hounds of the Cumberland & Cumb Farmers Pack. He was master for very many years, well-known and well-liked, as were all other members of the Wales family.

Back to the stray sheep shop, at 2 pm, the sheep were started on. In my day, the sorting out of these would be Bill

Teasdale of Gale Hall. He had the Shepherds Guide, a book of all the different markings of sheep from the Eastern Fellside, on hand in case of difficulty. Shepherds came to this meeting from far and wide. Each collected his own and went his way. Sometimes 2 or 3, maybe only one, would have such poor markings that no owner could be pinpointed, usually, these would be kept in a small paddock well fenced, then advertised in the local paper. If not claimed, they were sold and the money was to be put into a reserve for new hurdles or such. On one occasion, I think it was dug into to give a presentation to Mr Wales of a very nice clock on his retirement from the chairmanship of this committee. I well remember some of these fell gathers when it was so wild and stormy and misty, one could scarcely see, one particular day of such, there was a new tenant farmer at Bank Hall, Kirkland (the village I was born in) his name was Joe Morton, having taken on the farm from his near relative Tom Morton, who had been killed by a savage kick in the back by a Clydesdale horse, Joe was new to this part of the fells and this gathering was his first at his new farm, it was a day when it was wild and wet, we started gathering Kirkland Fell which lies directly above the village and in front of Cross Fell. Halfway through the day, the fell mist came down thick. I was nearby at that moment with another farmer who had farmed just across from my birthplace, Jake Ridley from Ranbeck, Jake had the reputation of being very bad-tempered, but he was always friendly towards me. This day we could see very little, then rain started to fall heavily. We sheltered behind a huge rock and passed an hour or so smoking his, Jakes, cigarettes. He was a very wild bad-tempered man. I had seen him, once only, threaten to bash the brains out of a salesman who had left one of his farm gates open, wielding his long shepherd's stick. He almost carried out his threat. He was in a tremendous fury. However, here I was, just as the mist came down to blot everything out, only a hundred yards away from him, we both got together behind an enormous rock for shelter, it was good, from the storm, being behind the rock was like going into a nice cosy room. We talked and talked, dogs at our feet. Jake was a big cigarette smoker. I did not have any cheroots or the like with me, so he insisted I join him with his pack of cigarettes, we smoked the lot, almost a full packet of Capstan, at the same time, we wondered how Joe, the newcomer was faring, Jake and I decided to call it a day, as time was getting on and the weather no better, the mist still thick, we knew where we were and the way down to the inland fields so off we set. At the fell bottom, we walked out of the mist and home, arranging to do the job tomorrow. Tomorrow came when we learnt Joe, the newcomer, had kept on walking in the mist, walking 5 miles across the fells, then coming down, to come out at Melmerbly, missing the village in between of Ousby.

There is no doubt about it when the mist comes down too thick, try and see it out, and if unable to, due to loss of daytime, always head downwards, I have done this quite a few times, but usually, the mist will lift to a certain extent. These were grand days, shepherding, wandering over the fields and fells with the dogs at a leisurely pace, mile after mile on foot. From the fells on clear days, one could see for miles, even to the Solway coast, the sleepy fellside villages chimneys smoking and some- times hear Skirwith church bells ringing out. This church was named the Cathedral of the Fellsides. The ravens swooping low and unafraid, the pair of peregrines, I would often watch, stooping at a colossal speed onto a young grouse or rabbit, the lower fells were alive with rabbits, this was before myxomatosis, the old grouse would cackle and strange as it may seem, quite often a covey of partridges on one of the front slopes of Kirkland fell just above Kirkdale beck.

A few snipe on the boggy lots of pond and keeping an eye on all of these was Reynard, himself and his family. I often saw foxes on my shepherding fell days, once coming over a ridge with a rocky face from above, I came upon a litter of them about 8 weeks old, 6 of them. I caught them at play on the grass below for an instant, then, in a flash, they were in the rocks and inside their den, my dogs were not fox orientated and did not know what to do about tackling them, the den was well chosen because the rocks the vixen had chosen, were very large and would have needed a few strong men to lift them, I left them in peace to play another day, they were a lovely little bunch of fun. Looking back on my shepherding days, I was only a worker for my father, but they were the best days of my life. I had not a worry in the world. I had the best mother and father any young man could have had, no worries like the tax man or bank manager to contend with, no money troubles, and life was good. On a sunny day in summer, I would sit down in the bracken, or a nice hillock, lord of all I surveyed, take a nice big Burma cheroot, contemplate all in front of me, and smoke the smoke of sheer peace and bliss. Alas, one is young only for a very short time, it was true, one of Ma's little sayings, 'The days of thy youth, are the days of thy glory.'

The first shepherd I was assistant to was Joe Wilson, a thick-set, round-faced, jovial chap with a smile like a full moon and with a bent nose. This organ had been broken at the sport he loved, Cumberland and Westmoreland style wrestling, in a fall at some time, his opponent, accidentally of course, on the fall had hit Joe on the nose with his head squashing this tender organ and these were big men of 16-18 stones. Joe's happy nature and huge smile made up for the slight disfigurement. Joe's brother, John Barker Wilson, lived in Mungriesdale, a big solid man of 18 stones, who latterly kept the rather famous Mill Inn from there. It was he who, at one time in his young days, was for quite a few years the champion of Cumberland and Westmoreland style of wrestling in Great Britain. He was so good that Lord Lonsdale (the famous Yellow Earl) took him to London for an exhibition in the, I think, White City Stadium. He also, like Joe, had—a very kind jovial face and nature. Joe was such if anyone of his dogs did the wrong thing in its work of shedding sheep or sorting etc, Joe's temper would rise, this was not very often, he would raise his shepherd stick high in the air to give the dog a good thump, the dog cringing at his feet in fear of the stick landing on its' back, but with the stick in mid-air, ready to come down, his anger vanished as it always did, I don't think he ever hit a dog in his life. He was too kind, not like one of his predecessors, Albert Fawcett. He was the shepherd before Joe, he was tall, all bone and muscle and his muscles and veins in his arms stood out like thick ropes. All of the shepherds in the East fell side were frightened of him because of his temper, which was ignited at the slight- est thing. A group of shepherds got together for the annual agricultural show at Alston one year, specifically to give Albert a thrashing. They thought 5 or 6 would be enough to handle him. Albert always went to Alston shows as they knew, so when Albert appeared in his Sunday best suit with his shepherd's stick, itself like a small tree, they made their move. Albert saw what was happening, he threw off his jacket with a great flourish and advanced to the attack. He looked so ferocious when he was in a temper, his face like a demon incarcerated, that they all fled. No one at any time dared face him, when aroused, his fury was enormous. The extent of his vile temper was such that if one of his dogs did wrong, he would wind a rope or a few lengths of binder twine doubled or trebled around the dog's neck and hang the poor hopeless dog from the nearest tree till it was dead.

His wife, Hilda, was a large, homely, kind-natured woman whom we all liked very much. She remained a family friend all of her life. She at writing this, is still alive and in her late '90s living with her daughter at Langwathby Hall. She must have gone through many agonising years with Albert because, for one thing, every six months, he would face the sack wherever he went, Father sacked him twice. The second time round, he only took Albert back because of Mrs Fawcett, Hilda pleaded for him, I think she was at her wit's end as they had nowhere to go; too many sheep farmers knew him. He was extremely strong, I saw it for myself, one day he was sent to bring one Swaledale tup with horse and cart from a field near the bottom of the farm. Being one animal, it could not be brought home with the dogs, it was only possible to 'drive' sheep in numbers of 4-5 and upwards. The horse cart had very wide sides on called 'shilvings' for loading corn sheaves on to. Albert caught the tup, a full-grown four-year-old, in a corner of the field. There were a dozen others, so that made it easy, he tied the tup's legs, got a good hold of it and lifted it into the cart, clean over the wide high side as if it were a lamb. That tup would have weighed 16-18 stones; normally, it would take two strong men to do this, the height of the shilvings being 5ft from the ground.

Moving every six months meant another house for Hilda to scrub clean from top to bottom, and she was herself super clean. Things had to be just right for her and on top of this, with six small children to cope with, many times she would come and see her mother and have a cry over her ill fortunes. I think the second time at Skirwith Hall, she used to come and bake sometimes, she was an excellent baker too. When Albert retired years later with Hilda, she had stuck by him in a retirement bungalow at Langwathby. He had become a very quiet and amicable man, his temper seemed to have left him, he passed his time helping his son-in-law farming at Langwathby Hall. I had many a chat with him and noticed the great change in him for the better. His retirement did not last many years as he died comparatively young, only in his late 60s.

Getting back to Joe Wilson, he and I, in winter times, had to feed 600 lambs fat on turnips. These turnips (Swedes) were cut from the rows in the turnip fields. Father grew 75 acres a year by hand, picked up by gripes (shorthand forks) and loaded into, at first, horse carts, then in later years, tractor and trailer, then he would put them in small heaps about 15 cart loads, spaced in line up the field with about 25 yards distance between each heap. The next line of heaps would be 30 yards across from the first line and so on. The lambs being barred off the first line of heaped turnips by sheep netting the full width of the field. Before winter set in, every heap was covered by a thick layer of straw which were held down by plenty of earth.

Rows and rows of deep wooden troughs, all made from timber on the estate, would then be lined up at the first heap close to the wire. On the trough and sheep side of the fence, we would place a turnip cutter which cut the turnips into long one-inch square strips, they would go down a chute into a basket called, in Cumberland, a 'swill'. These swills would hold about 2 or 3 stones of the weight of cut Swedes. At first, these turnip cutting machines were turned by hand, this was hard work, so Joe and I took turns to turn the handle and cut. Joe turned the machine more than I because he was as strong as a bull, but before the lambs had the turnips, they would be fed half a pound of whole oats each, fed into the troughs from a sack; they used to go mad for this once they had found a taste for them. Cutting by hand took many hours, so the next year, father had an engine put in each of the two turnip cutters, as quite often we would be cutting for two different lots of sheep. With the engine in, it was quite easy to work and took a quarter of the time. This was much more pleasant. In very wet weather, with so many hundreds of lambs continually around the troughs, which of course was bare soil, urinating day after day. Filling the troughs with turnips entailed many journeys on foot back and forth, cutter to troughs and visa versa, it became a bog of mud. Sometimes our gumboots would be pulled off our feet with the depths and suction of the mud, the lambs once at the troughs and eating never moved, until they were full, then they would go onto drier soil and lie down.

Once the first heap of turnips was finished, we would move the troughs one by one, Joe at one end and me at the other end, up to the next lot of turnips 25 yards away, and so on for each lot and across the field, in this way, almost the entire field was well and truly fertilized. At intervals, the lambs were taken to the sheep pens at the farm and inspected by Father to see which ones were fat, those that were, were sent off to the Penrith market on Monday mornings to be graded by men from the Ministry of Agriculture, and one or two expert farmers, who would have the confidence of the M.A.F.

Lambing time was hard work if the weather was bad, the Helm Wind and driving snow, almost like bullets hitting one's face, on one of these periods, a very dirty night of sleet and snow with the Helm behind it, a lot of ewes had decided to give birth, in the morning there were 75 lambs dead. What a turmoil the lambing field was in. Most of the ewes would have twins, and quite a few had triplets. I skinned about fifty of the dead lambs so as to put the skins, like coats, over the live lambs, if a ewe had live twins, one was taken off and a skin put over it and given to a ewe who had lost her lamb. The skin put on the live lamb would of course, come from her own dead lamb; she would recognise the smell of her own and almost always 'adopt' the youngster in a coat. To make sure these ewes would take 'new' lambs, there were perhaps 40 small lambing huts placed around the walls of the lambing field for this purpose, and any sick ewe or ewes with weakfish lambs, they would be put into these huts 5ft x 5ft, bedded with sawdust, fed and watered. If the ewe turned out to be difficult and would not let the lamb suckle and kept dunching the lamb, then a collar would be put on her and she was then tied short to the side of the hut. She could get her head up and down to eat or lie down but unable to dunce the lamb. The lamb would then be hand pushed under the ewe to suckle and the ewe held to stop her fidgeting about. After two or three times of this, the ewe would take the lamb and let it suckle. Then they would be let into a specially built temporary grasspen of about one acre to enable us to keep an eye on her and others like her. Occasionally there would be such a ewe who would never adopt a lamb, no matter how hard we persevered. These odd ones used to show a great deal of bad temper and if not tied up in the hut, would certainly kill the lamb we would be trying to get her to adopt. In these foiled circumstances, which were rare thank goodness, we would just let her go and run with the ewes that had proved barren and sell her fat in the autumn.

We once had a ewe that had lost her lamb while lambing. By lost, I mean we were unable to find it. Joe, Father and I looked all over but with no luck. Perhaps a dog or fox had gone with it, the ewe was beside herself with grief, bleating non-stop, running up and down the lambing field, quite demented, sniffing at all the other newborn lambs belonging to other ewes, trying to take one herself, she was upsetting the other new mothers, we caught her and put her in one of the little huts until we had finished our rounds. We had to check the rest of the ewes to lamb and the ones that had already lambed, which were fed once a day with one pound of oats and minerals per head and inspected twice a day. Later in the day, a ewe had triplets, good strong lambs. I put one of them in a sack and went over to the demented ewe, took the lamb out of the sack in front of the hut, the ewe inside saw what I was doing through a space in the front bars and went mad with joy trying to get at the lamb, I opened the door, but before I could put the lamb down inside, she had dived past me and out, she did not run away, she was almost knocking me down to get at the lamb, I put the lamb inside the hut and she ran in and made all the soft mothering sounds that she could possibly make, it was incredible! The lamb had no skin or smell of her own lost lamb, but here she was, taking a stranger with all the emotion she could. This was enough to make a strong man cry. She was so good I did not shut her in. I left the door open.

8

It was now 1944, Father had grown 25 acres of potatoes and needed plenty of help to pick them. He approached the M.A.F for 15 or 20 Italian prisoners of war, who were in the P.O.W camp Merrythought,

   8 miles from Penrith on the main road to Carlisle. The Italians arrived to pick up the potatoes; they were a happy lot of young men but did not like work. There were exceptions, but this was rare, they started on the potatoes but were terribly slow. Children of 8 years old would have been better and, at the slightest drizzle of rain, would stop work and quote the Geneva Convention. They were supplied with coffee and snacks from the farm but brought most of the food with them from camp. Father and my brother Adam would give them plenty of cigarettes as an incentive, which they took eagerly. They were always very well-mannered chaps. However, picking potatoes on showery days proved a complete waste of time.

   The first drop of rain, they would down tools for the day, so farther refused to have them anymore, he got the Land Girls in from Lazonby Land Army Hostel and had the potatoes finished in a few days, just as well because it poured with rain for weeks just after the girls had fin- ished, they were very efficient these Land Girls. Later my brother, who was now more or less running the farm, hired a Land Girl and billeted her with one of the married men called Jeremiah Head and his wife. Jeremiah had been hired three years before from, of all place names, a village called Lickpot. Two Italians were hired from the Camp on a day-to-day basis for general work on the farm. They were delivered early in the morning by army and dropped off at various farms. These two were named Louis and Lunghini Menardo. Louie's surname I cannot remember, but he was aged about twenty-two, good-looking and very strong, he had a nice character and was a good worker too. On thrashing days, which was once a week, the sacks would be filled in the barn in 12 stone sacks. Some to transfer to one of the corn lofts and some to another. One of these lofts had to go up a flight of 20 stone steps outside and against the building to a landing, then into the corn loft itself. The sacks were loaded in the barn onto a tractor trailer and taken to the bottom of these steps and the men would then have the sacks slid onto their backs by a man on the trailer and up the steps, steep ones at that. Well, Louie would grab a sack on the trailer, pull it to the side, put it over his shoulder and run up the steps to everyone's amazement, he relished in being the fastest and it seemed strongest than the other men, but he was younger by far, Father liked all of this, he would praise Louie and give him an extra packet of cigarettes, the other men took it all in good part and were never jealous of this act of Louie's. I could take the sacks up, but it was hard work, as I was slender, now tall, but only weighed 9 ½ stones.

The other, Lunghini, was from Milan, he could only struggle up the steps with sacks, so he was put on the trailer to hand the sacks to the men doing the carrying, he also was a good-mannered young chap, maybe twenty-five years old, Louie was a country boy bred and Lunghini, a townie.

That was the difference, Lunghini and I used to often work together, either cutting thistles with long-shafted sickles or loading turnips from the long storage clamps for the lambing ewes and to the various fields that held ewes and their lambs to keep the milk at them. This was a daily job and he would teach me a few words like, 'donne mi un baccho, bella Signorina', 'Io vi amo' and tell me stories of his exploits in the brothels in Milan, of which he seemed very fond of. He liked the sunshine but did not like cold weather or rain, one day when working with Lunghini, we stopped for a tea break at 3 pm, I unwrapped my sandwiches from a newspaper and saw the headlines, Germany had occupied all Hungary and Lunghini taught me the Italian version which was 'Germania occupa touta L'ungaria'. I never forgot these little bits of Italian.

In the end, they were not allowed to work. I believe it was because Italy changed sides in the war, before he left, Lunghini gave me his identity disc, No. 16188(6), which I still have, with a few coins with holes in that he had threaded out for a neck chain. Both had tears in their eyes, so had Mother, who had grown fond of them as we all had. When they said farewell, our own men, too, were sorry to see them go, we had a good bunch of men, some of whom had been with grandfather and who either retired in old age or died in harness.

I went to visit Merrythought before they finally left, riding Star and leaving Spot behind. He might have been run over by a car. It was a long ride of about 15 miles there going by Lazonby. Coming back through Penrith, it was 16 miles, making 31 miles total, cantering most of the way on the verge, Star could stick to 6 inches of verge, never wavering. We were given a tremendous reception by all of the Italians. Star seemed to fascinate them. I wrote to Lunghini a few years later but had no reply. The Italians vacated Merrythought and before long, it was occupied by Germans.

Father was keen to have a German worker, as his father had had Germans working for him in the First World War and liked them very much; Germans liked agricultural work, it seemed. So Father applied for a German to live in, as a few other farmers also did. The truck arrived and dropped off a young, fresh-faced youth, nineteen years old. He did not speak English but seemed to understand it. His name was Heinz, and he was a bit arrogant, did not communicate much and did his work and that was that. Myself being about only two years younger, wanted to make friends with him, but it seemed he did not want to do so.

One evening, it was summertime after work finished at 6 pm, I thought to go and shoot a few rabbits, this before myxomatosis, there were thousands of rabbits, at the same time I thought, I'll ask Heinz to go with me, so I handed him my favourite .410. I handed the gun to Heinz first before I said come on Heinz, let's go and shoot some rabbits, at the same time giving him about 20 cartridges, I saw him rather surprised, he hesitated, smiled and said, "Are you sure?"

I said, "Why not?"

"Oh, thanks," he said, so off we went. Spot worked the rough grass reeds in various corners and we bagged quite a few rabbits, some of which we took home to eat, it was then I noticed Heinz was speaking very good English to me, we did the same thing for many nights and he became more and more friendly. He also lived in the men's quarters in the house, eating with Joe Varty and one other young man who later joined the Merchant Navy. Heinz enjoyed the food, he told me he was an ardent Nazi, believed completely in Hitler and had been a Hitler Youth. That is why before, he would not speak any English and did not believe in, what he called all the propaganda put out by the BBC and newspapers. It was all lies, he said, but and he was most serious—'when you gave me the gun and a lot of cartridges, me a hard Nazi, I could not believe it. I could have turned on you and shot all of your family'.

I told him I never thought of that, no he said, I am now beginning to think I have maybe been wrong to have been a Nazi, but still think Hitler is a wonderful man. Since that day, Heinz became more and more into the bosom of the family; he spoke perfect English learned when he was a prisoner in America, wounded and taken there to a hospital for a few months or so.

At Skirwith Hall, he never overstepped his mark to take a bath; the single men used the kitchen sink like the maids used to. It was 5ft long and 3 wide and 6 inches deep. He did not care to bath there, so Mother offered him the use of the bathroom. Mother was taking pity on him, so young and no family, a long way from home. No he said, thank you very much, I am a prisoner and it is not my place to put on your family, I will do like I did when I was a soldier, I will wash in the back, which was 50 yards away, so this he did with relish, even in full winter Heinz would strip nude, scrub himself hard as he could. This, of course, behind a few trees so that he was out of view, I used to sit on the bank and talk to him, he liked to be clean because he said he had been on the Russian Front.

On the way through Russia, the people welcomed them with open arms and many soldiers, in the cold of winter, would bed down with a family in their little houses, no more than mud huts, in a corner of the main room, there would be great brick or stone heater cum cooker, where the family would all huddle on top of it. At a few stages in the German Army push, sleeping this way many times, he told me the Russians were full of lice with the result, he had gotten lice too, he said he and the rest of the soldiers would strip and search for the lice and they were so big they would hold them to a match and the lice used to explode and go pop. He also said the Russians were extremely kind and generous and would give freely of any goods they had, but that they were at the same time very poor. They had these lice because they never changed their clothes, wearing the same things year after year. When at a village water pump or stream, the German soldiers would strip to the waist to wash, the old women would put their long pinneys over their faces and run away, shouting something in their tongues. They did not like to see men exposing so much bare skin, even though the soldiers had their trousers on.

Also, the Russian people welcomed the German army in with open arms, they were tired of Stalin's purges, this changed when behind the army came the SS, Heinz did not say anything of this at the time, but later he told me quite genuinely, the front line soldiers were just doing the job of fighting and made friends with the population, he realised later as well what the SS and Gestapo had done. He was in a tank regiment under Guderian and was one of the first lines of tanks to arrive almost into the suburbs of Moscow. He said it was almost impossible to stop the Russians. They just came, in wave after wave, to be mown down. Others would come on and take the rifles of the fallen. He said there were just pile upon pile of dead women soldiers also, which he told me were hard to discern as they looked like men, the Russian prisoners had to be frisked to see which men were and which were women. He told of the atrocities the Russians did to them, many Germans captured being crucified and nailed to barn doors by their testicles, but of course, what he did not know at the time was the SS and Gestapo coming in behind the main fighting army, had started it all in a most savage way. The Russians, on the retreat of the German army, seeing what had been done to the populace by the Gestapo and SS, took bloody revenge. Heinz understood all of this when he realised the German propaganda was mostly lies. He turned overnight almost and became very pro-British.

One day before we went to start shooting rabbits, he took out his knife, cut the side of his hand, and said to me to give him my hand. I asked why, and he replied that we were going to be blood brothers for life. I held out my hand. Okay, that's a good idea. For we were firm friends in that short time, he cut my hand and we rubbed the cuts together, blood to blood, then we hugged each other. We were now blood brothers, this man, who had been a hard Nazi soldier, turned out to be the only true and best friend I had in my life. One day I asked Heinz if ever he had done the goose step. He did not know what I meant, I explained and he was vastly amused at this marching style of the Germans to be called so, he went to the far end of the courtyard 40 odd yards and stood rigidly, like a ramrod, face set and stern and started the goose step, I was amazed, Heinz was like an automaton, a robot, absolutely rigid the only part of him seeming to move were his legs, themselves as straight as a die and almost up to his chin in rigid and perfect precision. I was witnessing something here at this moment that not many people ever would when 10 yards from me, he put his left hand to his mouth and started to play the oomph, paa paa, and trumpet sound combined. He saw I was most sur- prised and at the same time pleased he had shown me, he said can you play the music like me, I put my hand up to my mouth and started to play, just like he had, perfectly, now it was his turn to be surprised, we had many a duet together in the pubs in Germany in later years, at the Karnivals, we were indeed two brothers.

Heinz worked for father for a few months, then Adam wanted him to be hen man, looking after 60-fold units of hens, whose eggs went to Fair- bains Hatchery at Carlisle (my brother had 60 units looked after by another worker). These had to be moved every day and put in as straight a line as possible, with Heinz the line was as if a string had been put along to keep them straight, no it was German thoroughness, he told me it was a very easy job, he would finish his morning's work of carting water, washing all the water buckets out first with a scrubbing brush, the water was carted from field troughs by a horse with a very low set cart, in drums, when this finished he would hunt a few rabbits with one of Spots sons named Caesar, this one was out of a whippet and he could catch rabbits this dog.

On a nice sunny day, he would sunbathe, he used to (to build up his strength) suck three raw eggs every day. It's a wonder he could face eggs after you read another story I have to tell of his exploits, he also got me onto sucking eggs, and they are very tasty things. In the evenings after we had done our shooting, we would drink milk, he would drink pint after pint, he loved the stuff.

When Heinz was in America, he had a rather an amazing story to tell me. When he was in camp there were two, as he put it, two little black girls who worked in the kitchens, one was called Margaret, she was 17 years old and quite nice, she liked Heinz a lot and he used to make love to her on the kitchen table on a regular basis, he used to tell me many times of his little black girl.

One day he walked out of camp and got a lift to the town, only four or five kilometres away, went for a beer in a bar where he got into conversation with a red-headed young woman, they talked for a while and she invited Heinz to her house, 20 kilometres away in another town, off he went with her, she had a very smart house, a large saloon car, seemed to have plenty of money and lived alone. She asked Heinz to stay with her for a while into, six weeks. During that time, the young woman wanted sex, sex, and more sex, all day and all night, she fed him on eggs and more eggs to keep his strength up until, after six weeks he could take no more eggs and no more sex, he'd had more than his fill. One day when she was out having her hair done, he walked out into the town, walked up to the nearest policeman to give himself up and told him, "I am an escaped German prisoner and I'm giving myself up." the policeman looked him over (for Heinz was in civil clothes given to him by the redhead) and told him to push off. Heinz, at that time, had a foreign accent, but so did most of the Americans, he tried again, the policeman again told him to push off, this time in an angry tone, or he would lock him up. Heinz thought these Americans were a crazy lot and started walking to the camp.

He soon hitched a lift and reported into the head of his section, this chap said, "Welcome back, we were almost about to report you missing' and was pleased to see him back. I was almost on my hands and knees, he said, it was a wonder Heinz could face sucking eggs at Skirwith Hall after this episode, but perhaps it was to keep fit for Ginger.

There was another German working on a farm about 2 miles away named Ernst Neuman, very tall and strong, with a broken nose from boxing, he had been the champion of his regiment. He had met Heinz in the camp at Merrythought, Ernst saw how Heinz was living and all the comforts of family life, treated like one of the family, so he told Heinz of his troubled way of life. He was treated like a dog, had to sleep on straw in the cow byre, his meals were given to him in the byre; he had nowhere to wash except the animal water trough. Heinz got a little bit mad at this, he went to see this farmer, Mr E Watson of Broats Farm, Skirwith, told him he had better give Ernst a room and proper meals, a proper place to wash and quickly, or else, he was warned, Mr Watson duly obliged, he knew Heinz's look and I know whatever the consequences, Heinz would have sorted him out. Ernst and he used to run (in summer) five miles every evening after work to keep fit for their boxing, running in a triangle from Skirwith Hall to Kirkland, 1 ½ miles—Kirkland—Blencarn 1 ½ miles, Blencarn—Skirwith Hall 2 miles, arriving at base sweating like two young bulls, they were gluttons for work and sport, doing both with a good will, no wonder the German soldiers at the front was a very hard man to beat.

Now I had my licence to drive, I used to drive Heinz and Ernst to Merrythought to report and get their pocket money, somewhere about 10 shillings a month, the exact sum I'm not sure of and a huge lump of fruit cake. Heinz liked to box also, he had done well in his regiment, so Ernst and he decided on 2 weekly bouts in one of the lofts at Skirwith Hall. What they needed were boxing gloves, through the camp grapevine, they found out there were 2 pairs they could have at a camp near Longtown on the other side of Carlisle. One Sunday I drove them over to pick the gloves up, that week we had 2 nights arranged for boxing in the loft, Heinz put Ernsts' gloves on and I put and tied Heinz's gloves, Joe Varty, the pig man who shared a room with Heinz, was timekeeper, three rounds, each round was of two minutes, at the end of each round Joe had to bang on a tin bucket as the gong, one bang on the bucket and they started, Heinz was 4 inches shorter than Ernst, blows were landing, Heinz got hit with a few sharp ones, Joe started to shout at Ernst not so hard, poor chap, one of natures gentlemen had not seen a boxing match in his life, he thought Heinz was going to be killed or badly hurt, he for- got to look at this watch for the 2 minutes stop, with trying to get Ernst not to hit so hard. The two boxers realised their timekeeper was not so good at his job so they stopped, Joe, most concerned that Heinz had not suffered permanent damage, calmed down. He gave me the job and the watch, do for two more rounds I timed them while Joe watched and shouted for Heinz to be careful, with tears almost flowing down his cheeks, he stopped watching them box after the first week, it was too much for him.

One day Heinz wished to write a letter in English to a former English man he knew when in camp at Burton on Trent, a Mr John Willshie (I am not exactly sure of the spelling of this surname). He asked Jeremiah, one of the other farm men, the one who came from the village of Lick-pot, how to spell a certain word he was stuck with, Jeremiah told him after scratching his head, "A dun't now, ah' niver bin 't skeal."

Poor Jeremiah could neither read nor write, what he had said should read, "I don't know, I have never been to school." *This rather tickled Heinz,* he thought, *in this modern era everybody should be able to read and write.* After this, he always showed much kindness towards Jeremiah and even offered to try and teach him to read, but Jeremiah wasn't interested. He said he was too old at 45 and he was married with a nice homely wife who looked after him like a broody hen looks after her chicks, this was quite true of Jeremiah's wife.

There were always a few village dances here and there at the weekends and one Saturday night in the Drill Hall at Penrith. I thought it a good idea for Heinz and I to see what they were like, as Heinz had only his prisoner suit with patches, he said it was not possible, so I asked Dad if he would lend him one of his old suits, which he did, with a shirt and tie, plus shoes, the shoes were just a shade too big, but they did the job. The next Saturday night we went to the Drill Hall, first though we had two pints of beer each at the Crown Hotel, Eamont Bridge where the owners, Mr and Mrs Timeswood, knew me, they had three daughters who then helped in the bar and dining room, on our arrival the eldest daughter June, asked who my friend was, Heinz and I had prepared for this, he was to be Harry Watson, don't know where we conjured this name from, from Liverpool, his English was good, and if he thought he was not sure, break into the Cumberland dialect and slang of which he was also very good at.

It worked and no one was any the wiser, he was fair-haired

and fresh complexion, as we were. We went to the Drill Hall, it was my first visit to this place, it also had a reputation for fights there, and there was nearly always a policeman on duty in the porchway. Heinz enjoyed himself immensely; he was an excellent dancer as well as an excellent player of the trumpet, trombone, piano and zither and was quite good with the violin. This first night, there was a fight between a young Polish man and two or three local boys. Heinz was keen to have a go-to break it up but realised his cover might have been blown, so we stood back until all quietened down and got on with the dancing.

Of course, Heinz going out was strictly forbidden, and in civilian clothes more so, we had a fright one Saturday afternoon when he was free from farm work. We were stopped. I was driving the Blue Lady, as we now named the V8, on one of the side streets in Penrith by a police- man who waved me down, he asked where we had come from, I told him, "Where are you going?"

I replied back home, "Alright."

He said, "Let us go. He perhaps was looking for someone else but that made me a bit nervous, but we did not go home, we had just arrived and we wanted a few beers and to visit Joe Varty's brother, who lived in town. He always had a bottle of whisky which was my new drink. Tom Varty and his wife were in on our secret of Harry Watson. One thing I was always nervous of the policeman that day, and also at other times, was the petrol, petrol was rather scarce and as Heinz and I did quite a bit of motoring to make it spin out, for every four gallons of petrol, I would add one gallon of tractor vaporising oil (paraffin) which made quite a bit of smoke come out of the exhaust.

Sometimes if we were too short of petrol, I would mix it in half, but this was rather too much because, behind us, we almost had a smoke screen, so I stuck more to the four-to-one. That is why I was always apprehensive about going through the main streets of towns and tried to stick to the side streets.

Petrol at the time was also of poor quality, but to obtain more petrol coupons, I had bought a 600cc motorbike, a very old model, from a neighbouring farmer, John Sanderson of Burrell Hill. John could not be bothered to farm, so he rented all his land off, the motorbike I never used, it was too hard to start anyway, but I applied to the authorities for petrol to enable me to shepherd the fells and the far allotment of 265 acres, I duly received a nice supply, but I wrote back to say that I covered 5000 acres of rough fell and mentioning Cross Fell of 3000 feet, by the return of post I had as many petrol coupons that would keep Heinz and *I are happy for a long time if one does not ask, one does not receive,* I thought.

The vicar, Father Wilson, was well supplied with fat hens by Heinz, unknown to Adam or any of us, Heinz told me this in Germany many years later and the vicar never breathed a word either. One day while working with his sixty field units in a field at the lower end of the farm, there he saw a man with a gun leave his car on the verge of the road and go into the woods. Heinz thought he should not be there at all. He stopped work and ran over to apprehend this stranger. With his sheath knife ready he grabbed the man, put his arm in a half nelson and told him this was Skir- with Hall land, what was he doing? The man told Heinz he had been given permission to shoot pigeons, the man named all the members of my family and in the end Heinz let him go, after first extracting the chaps' name which he gave. Heinz said he was so frightened he did not stop to shoot but drove away. It turned out Dad had given him permission to shoot a few pigeons on this particular plantation. He was from the next village, Langwathby, his name, I think was Alderson. Here was a German guarding the land of an Englishman at knifepoint.

The months passed quickly while Heinz was with us, he enjoyed his work and did with great gusto. He was well liked by all of the other staff. He wrestled with Joe Wilson the Cumberland and Westmoreland style and still boxed with Ernst, we shot a lot of rabbits together, he rode Star, pub crawled and danced. He had a girlfriend at Culgaith named Ginger, she was a bit rough, I thought, but Heinz said she was alright to keep him healthy and she also kept Ernst healthy. Went to church on Sunday if he had time off, but one thing upset him.

He thought he would treat himself to a beer at the Sun Inn in the village, the landlord, Fred Hodgson, ordered him out in great style and if he could have walked properly, he would have thrown him out or at least tried.

Fred was a First World War soldier, a Canadian by birth who had married a close relative of the pub's previous tenant, the latter having no one to take over, mentioned it by letter to Fred and his wife Florrie, who lived at what is now Thunder Bay, Canada. Fred had been shot through both legs pretty badly and could only waddle, swore at everyone like a trooper, except the vicar who used to go and play scrabble with him. Also, he had a son in the army, so no German, no matter how nice, was going to drink at Fred's pub.

The war was drawing to a close now; I kept every cutting with the news of the three fronts from the Daily Mail and had piles of them. Heinz and his comrades at Merrythought told me to my face, we are just waiting for Mr Churchill to give the word and we are ready to go and fight the Russians. They fully expected this from a man. They were keen to start and were disappointed when they were not called for. I think it's a pity they were not. There would not have been the trouble which the Western world has gone through in the period after the war. England went to war so that Poland could be free, to no avail. They were still enslaved.

In the course of Heinz's stay with us, Dad employed another German, Rudolph Peterman, from near Oberammergau and where his parents had a restaurant. He was on a daily basis being dropped off by the army truck, he had a bit of the intellect in him, not very well-liked by the other prisoners, they told me he was an informer, perhaps he was, but he worked well very good manners and he was an excellent artist with a crayon, one day he was in the garden clearing the leaves and generally making things tidy, Ma was playing the piano in the drawing room, the french windows were open on to the lawn, Ma was quite a good pianist, Rudolph stood and listened when Ma had finished the piece she was playing, he came forward, hat in hand, congratulated Ma on her playing and asked if he may play a little, he sat down and played. Ma was quite amazed and pleased, he had asked, for he was a superb and very serious pianist, he played music from the great composers with the greatest of ease. The music just flowed through his fingers. After that first episode, each day he was at work, Ma had him play for her for about and hour each day. He one day asked if he could make a sketch of the front of the façade of Skirwith Hall, he was given the go-ahead, he took a chair and sat on the middle of the lawn for two days, he finished two sketches, both in pencil, each from a slightly different angle of the house. Then showed them to us, they were extremely good, in fact excellent. Rudolph signed them and presented them to Ma and Dad. Ma had them framed and hung. I have one of them still.

Now it was time for Heinz and his comrades to go to their homes in Germany. Heinz to his parents and girlfriend Gisela, who used to write to him, full of hope to get married, her father had an electrical appliances factory, I think. Heinz was excited as he had decided to be an electrician on his return, he told me it should be a good trade as most of the houses had been blown down and needed electricity for lighting and cooking etc... He was certainly looking ahead.

I drove Heinz back to Merrythought for the last time, he had said his farewells to his friends in the village and my family, Ma and Dad, gave him 10 pounds to help him on his arrival in Germany. There were tears in all our eyes and his also, it was a sad parting. We missed him. It was not long, however, before a letter arrived, telling us of his arrival, about his family and his girl Gisela and thanking us all so much for his stay with us. I will say this, though, he came to us a German and left as an Englishman, my friend, Henry Watson from Liverpool.

Ernst did not go back at the same time as Heinz, perhaps three months later, he missed his friend firstly because he had no others nearby, sec- ond his farmer and wife were unfriendly towards him, so he used to come each night to see me, we sat in the kitchen and he still drank his 3-4 pints of milk, Ma used to automatically put a huge jug in the table for him, we just talked, he would stay an hour maybe two and then go back to his farm sad. I was sorry for him and his rather sad existence. He was not a clever man, just a simple everyday chap.

Now Heinz had gone, I carried on my life as usual, shepherding with Joe. By now, Bridget and I had cooled off, we were still great buddies and liked to be together, but my own love had somehow cooled down. I never had a lot of true friends; somehow, at one stage or another, I would be let down by them.

After the war, everywhere started to open up for us young ones. Before, travel of any distance had been limited, we now popped over to Ire- land either to buy a suit because coupons for clothes were still on, or buy silk stockings for girlfriends. We could go racing (horse) to Yorkshire and all over Scotland, farmers balls and hunt balls. Each week we would be in our dinner jackets, many times two a week, getting back at 3-4 in the morning after seeing some girl home or calling at friends for the 'one for the road' and lingering till dawn, then we would get into our working clothes and straight to work with no sleep, Dad would not have been amused if we had taken to bed for a few hours, it was our fault we had come back too late.

We had a good little band of us, me now I was 20, there was Eric Loth- ian (bank clerk), Robert Jackson (neighbouring farmer), Mac the vet (real name Maurice McSporan Macmillan) whose homeland was Camp- belltown in the Mull of Kintyre, a loveable and fun-loving chap, Ian Findlay also a vet (later on he married Robert Jackson's sister) and Bobby Dickson (whose father had the County Motors Garage in

Carlisle),

Bobby was a playboy and spent money like water—too much.

We all used to go to these balls and dinner dances, one such was the Farmer Ball at Dumfries, we stayed the night in the County Hotel, on one such night, Tom Mitchell, who stood as an independent candidate for Penrith, and borders were with us and after the ball climbed to the top of the monument cum fountain outside the hotel, almost getting himself arrested and soaked to the skin, he later in life was President of West Cumberland Rugby Team. The next day if we stayed the night, we would repair to Robbie Burns pub, The Globe, up a tiny side street, Dumfries is the town of Burns. Robbie's bar, a very small low room, is where we put a few drams back. He has scratched a verse from one of his poems, "Coming through the Rye," with a diamond on a window pane.

9

It was at a Farmers Ball that Adam met a girl who had really taken his eye and arranged to meet her the next day in the hotel bar. She was a Dumfries girl, what Adam was worried about was if she had good legs because he was unable to see them the night before with her evening dress so long, the girl turned up, her name was Pat McGeorge.

There was only Adam and I now at home with Ma and Dad. He, being five years older than I, had his own band of friends. I caught up with them later on, in the meantime, there was an estate to sell at Eden Hall of 400- 500 acres, a family called Hindley from Burnley bought it for 60,000 pounds. They were cotton millers from Burnley in Lancs. Their eldest son was Airlie, he also for his surname added to his mothers', making him Holden-Hindley. They were a very nice family. The Hindley's wanted a good farm manager, Adam knew just the man. The trouble was he was then working as a stud manager at Tara Stud in Ireland for Clifford Nicholson, the Lincolnshire potato king. Tara was a beautiful place standing some of the best T.B. stallions available, I had been there myself, his name was Tommy Iceton. Adam went over to Ireland; spoke to Tommy, telling him about the Hindleys' job. They had given Adam more or less carte blanche to get Tommy wages, car, house, etc. Mrs Iceton was feeling homesick for the north of England. This was also Tommy's homeland, so without more ado, he took the job as farm manager and was there until he retired, his son taking over from him at Tara and I believe when Clifford Nicholson died a bachelor, he left this young Iceton very well off indeed, in fact, I think the whole stud.

Adam sold Airlie 60 of his fold unit hens and all, why I don't know because they were money spinners; however, they were moved on a convoy of tractors, two units to a tractor. Adam was left with his other 60 units plus 300 birds on the free range in the middle of the farm.

The estate of the Hindley's was already well laid out as a sporting estate with its small woodlands here and there together with a 20-acre pond, the new owners made an excellent pheasant shoot, gamekeepers the lot, entertained on a fair scale at Eden Hall and their large home in Burnley, Read Hall. Adam was invited to every single function, shooting parties each Saturday with a guest list of the best and richest, including King Peter of Yugoslavia. I knew the Hindley's well, meeting them many times at the George Hotels' annual New Year's Eve Ball, hunt balls, farmer's balls, etc, and not once was I invited to even a meal with them. They would invite Adam to shoot in front of my own person. They knew I was a more than good shot. This carried on until my brother's death on October 8th 1952, when at Adams' funeral, in the hall at Skirwith Hall, Mrs Hind- ley, Airlie and a few more were gathered there, she—Mrs Hindley said to me in front of Ma 'Joey, I think you and Airlie have now to be friends' as if we had been enemies, of which we were not, I replied 'one just can- not be made to have friends Mrs Hindley like that in a few minutes', she was taken aback, I left it at that and they realised they had ignored me far too long. I did call on Airlie once on a Saturday night, he gave me a box of Lonsdale cigars which were extremely good, maybe I should have made friends, but I also had my pride. I was nobody's lap dog.

My brother Adam had by now got the dairy side of the farm going at full steam, in actual fact, the monthly milk cheque was a lifesaver for the farmers, sheep and beef were, at that period, not too profitable. I used to help in the cow byres washing and drying cow's udders and washing and disinfecting the milking equipment for which I was paid 10 shillings a week, my sole income at that time, except for rabbit catching. At hay time and harvest, I helped to milk the cows and then back to the fields, the milk lorry of the Express Dairy from Appleby came into the courtyard and collected the milk churns from a large stone built-up slab, then outside the kitchen window, for 5 shillings per week, Beattie, the driver did this otherwise the milk churns were supposed to be on a stand by the roadside, company orders.

Beattie was not a very nice chap. He had run over and killed Johnie the postman on his bike and also Bobby Hope, who was an engineer and mechanic and was killed on his motorbike on one of the small narrow country roads that abound in Skirwith/Kirkland Blencarn areas, the roads were only 8-10ft wide in some places. The Express Dairy certainly lived up to its name, the milk lorry drove too fast, always, one day I was in the courtyard and Beattie came in at full blast, as usual, he pulled up to the slab at the kitchen window, loaded the churns and he pulled away (Spot was lying on the cement not far from the slab). As he turned away, his front wheels went away round Spot, but as the back wheels cut the corner inwardly, they went right over his hindquarters. I saw just too late to shout him away, his eyes and mine met the same second the wheels crunched him under and I could see the great pain he was in, I carried him into the stable, laid him under the manager on a good bed of hay as he looked at me with his lovely soft grey-brown eyes with an expression that is still in my heart. An expression of tremendous love, and I wept and wept as I knew and he knew that we were parting company. My great and true friend throughout my childhood and my youth, always waiting for me at any time of the day and night, he did everything I had ever asked of him, he would sit on the hill overlooking the beck and the shortcut I used to take from the school train at night and watch and wait for me, greeting me with faithful adoration. Mother said she knew when I would be coming home as he was always in place half an hour before I was due.

I nursed him for perhaps two hours, his tongue very white, I stroked him and spoke to him and tears flowed off my cheeks, he would lift his head and look at me with love, my heart was broken, I could do nothing for my friend although he must have been in great pain, then he slipped away from me. I weep as I write this. I am in the stable nursing him now, seeing into the past with great clarity, our eyes still meeting. I buried Spot in the front garden where I could see his grave from my bedroom window; I put him in my one and only raincoat and planted a few daffodils there. I have had 5-6 dogs in my lifetime, one or two very good workers and good friends, but never one like Spot. He was everything a boy, youth or man could ever wish for in a dog, he was family. When I was ill as a child, as I often was, Mother would bring Spot to my bedroom where I would talk to him and pat him, he would lie all day, bedside my bed being reluctant to go out at night to his bed in the hay barn. Very quickly, I had lost two of my best friends, Spot dead and Heinz gone, returning to his homeland. It was a very sad year for me, I felt lonely for the first time, but I had a wonderful friend to share my troubles and sadness with at all times, then, and the rest of my life, was my Mother. She was always there to share my sadness and there to comfort me, she was an angel on earth, my mother. The most gentle of people at all times, she never once at any time slapped her children or even scalded them. She was so gentle, I think as children, we knew Mother should not be upset, as she was so kind.

Now I could drive on the roads, I wanted a car of my own, I had saved 170 pounds, there was a car advertised in the local paper belonging to Mr Charlie Bailey of Appleby, the car was an MG saloon, long and rak- ish, Charlie wanted 300 pounds for it, I asked if I could drive it for a few miles which I did, I drove it home for Dad to see and asked if he would go halves, as I had not enough to buy it outright, he refused so I took it back to Charlie and told him father would not go halves, he asked if I worked for dad, I said I did, he then said if I was you I wouldn't work for the old bugger any more, he was not put out I had taken the car back, but he was amazed that the biggest farmer in the area could not put 150 pounds down for a car for his son. Dad already owed me over 100 pounds for hoeing turnips a few years ago. He still owed me this money plus another 100 pounds for when I worked for him for a year at 2 pounds per week when I was twenty-two years old, I let it stand on to get it in one lump—till the day he died. Ma took pity on me and a week later gave me a cheque for 150 pounds, but I did not buy the car or any other than I thought it would be better if I bought some swale dale ewes to breed from for a better income than 10 shillings a week, from this, I had to buy my own clothes and boots. A few weeks later, Len Bellas was shepherd Joe Wilson, who had married Len's mother, a widow, was offered a manager's job by his wife's son in laws farm near Wigton. Len was a very good shepherd and a very nice man but not blessed with the best of health.

Len and I cut off for Kirkly Stephen's annual ewe sale of swale dales so that I could then run them on the fells and not interfere with Dad's pastures. I bought 60 yearling gimmers, ready for tupping that year at 3 pounds to 3 pounds 10 shillings each. Len kept his eyes like a hawk on the pens the ones I bought went into, as he said there was quite a bit of stealing sheep straight from the ring into new pens at these auctions, I arranged the transport home there and then, when they arrived at Skirwith Hall Len and I marked them with the Kirkland Hallmark with the tar, TA in the near ribs and a long bar on the offside flank and a fork bit in the near ear. The TA was the mark of a previous tenant, Thomas Atkinson of Kirkland Hall, where I was born. Dad did not bother to change it, after this Father gradually wore out his own swale dales with TA, these ewes having the Skirwith Hallmark of a gelders horn on the near side hip and pop on the offside shoulder, both ears ends clipped across.

Now I had my own flock, I was rather pleased but the first winter I had them was the most severe and prolonged, there were many farmers on the immediate fell sides who lost a great many of their breeding stock. Dad always insisted at the first sign of snow that we bring all the breeding black-faced ewes down from the allotments to the shelter of land near Skirwith Hall, the meadows and Lime Kiln field at Kirkland Hall and this we did on the occasion of this severe winter. But at the lambing time, my own ewes heavy in lamb themselves thin, the majority of sheep farmers on the Kirkby Stephen fell sides, did not feed hay or cereals to their young gimmer breeding stock, the result was when our ewes were eating their fill of hay and crushed oats and minerals, my young ewes just stood aside looking on as the others fed, the end result was my stock lambed, or a good many of them lambed down with little or no milk, mostly the latter and I lost eight ewes dead.

In July, I had, of course, the wool and about 20 gimmer lambs and 15 tup or male lambs running with their mothers. The rest would still be there for next season's mating.

Len kept a good eye on them for me as well, in fact, he was so sorry that I had had such a bad start with the breeding that he picked six of Dad's best gimmer lambs for me, putting my tar mark and earmark on them, he had to be careful for Dad had an eagle eye when it came to sheep.

In the next year or so, I did quite well with my sheep, having at one time until 1956, 120 ewes running on Kirkland fell. However, when it came to getting my wool cheque, I had to ask Dad for it because my wool, though weighed and graded separately, went with the rest of the big wool sheets in Dad's name. I think he still owes me for quite a few sheets of wool. I fattened my wethers off on cut turnips, Len and I in the autumn and winter, cutting turnips with the turnip cutting machine for 600 or more sheep, by now I was getting 1 pound in wages, though Dad had me down at full wages for the tax man's benefit.

One year, the last I had with my ewes and lambs, 1953, I paid my first visit to my blood brother Heinz in Germany. I had 80 wethers to sell at stores (sold for others to get fat), in my absence, Dad sold these at Lazonby mart for 2 pounds each on a rising market, five weeks later, they would have made 4 pounds 10 shillings each, I was annoyed at and dismayed at Dad because there was no reason to sell mine. Especially when I was not at home, it took a long time and many demands before I got my 160 pounds.

It was on New Year's Eve, 1948, at a dinner dance in the

George Hotel, that I met the second girl I was to really love in my life, her name was June Haigh, she was nineteen years of age, blonde, tall and elegant, it turned out she was a very good horsewoman, tennis player etc., a beautiful tomboy, in no time at all I was head over heels in love, we went to a good few balls that winter and dining out at the best places in the area, she had many young men trying to court her but at the moment, I held her eye.

June's parents, whom I got to know very well, were Willie and Doris. Willie had sand and gravel quarries near Darlington, North Yorks, he also had about twelve horses in training with various trainers, the principal one being Michael Everitt, the latter an elegant chappie, always with his rolled umbrella and immaculately dressed. Doris, a lovely petite woman with an engaging smile, bought her clothes at Marshals & Snelgrove, she was always very chic and where Willie went, Doris also went, for the present at any rate. Willie, like myself, always wore a bow tie and, like me, no clip-on things. He was a big drinker of whisky and a big gambler, he had a big fob pocket always with a big fistful of 5-pound notes in it.

My first date with this lovely girl, who was a dog lover and owned two Keeshounds, was on 5th January 1949, on New Year's Eve. We had danced together until 2 am, she then went home with her parents, I was unable to see her home myself as I was with my brother Adam in his car, he and I finished up at the vet's house, John Barr, at 5 am.

The next day, I saw in my diary, I was tired but got up at 7 am and fed the turnips to the sheep. About 200 left, all alone as the shepherd was on holiday (a day off). I took June to the County Hotel in Carlisle for dinner, where I was well known by the manager and his wife, Mr and Mrs Atkin- son, Maurice, Cherry, the head waiter, Dick, another waiter, Leo and Hector, Hector was only about 5ft tall, he was the wine and lounge waiter, his jacket pockets always chock full with change and Mr Cioli, the volatile Italian cook, they all became my friends until they died.

Mr Cioli was not to be tampered with in the kitchen. He would throw knives at his staff in the kitchen. They were scared of him if things went wrong. When he knew I was in the dining room, he would send one of the waiters to see what I would like to eat, usually dinner. Anything off the menu he would make for me. We got on well because he liked horse racing and he liked to gamble. I had many an hour talking and racing in his little office in the kitchen. The sporting life would be out, it was hard to listen to him because his English was very broken, but he was a charming man. When he retired, his son Leo took over and was head chef for a few years (no relation to Leo, the waiter).

The staff then were excellent, an excellent Hotel, well run and good food, we had a bottle of wine then went to see Oliver Twist at the cinema, on the way home we had a puncture, I was driving Dad's V8, the Blue Lady, named by Heinz, which dirtied my hands making it impossible to embrace June after that, however, that did not matter, we made a date to meet on 11th January when we wined and dined at the George in Penrith, then we went to the local cinema, the George, run by Leslie Walker and his wife Lucy, this was perhaps the best hotel for many miles for good food, spotlessly clean and very good staff, the head waitress was Dolly and very good at her job, the tables were always laid with pink embroi- dered linen and excellent cutlery, the best dinner dances in winter were always at the George and on Boxing Day and New Year's Eve, it was in- vitation only by the Walkers and the owner, Frank Street whose wife was sister to Leslie's wife, Lucy.

Then, one dined at the George, a full three-course dinner for 19 shillings and the remaining of it I used to give Dolly for the tip.

On the 12th of January, I took June to the Queen's Hotel at Tirril for dinner, then to the cinema again. I did not worry about the expense. I was in love, I would just have to catch more rabbits and knock a few of Dad's pheasants off for a boost of earning. On the 13th, I took June again to Carlisle and had lunch at the County Hotel, then went to see Spring in Park Lane, Herbert Wilcox's, with Anna Neagle and back to the County Hotel for afternoon tea and had dinner with June's parents at High Heskett. They had taken rooms in the local pub there for a while, I suspected something was not quite right about this, Willie was sliding downhill financially. On the 9th Sunday, I took June to once again the Queen's Hotel at Tirrill for dinner. I was overhead in love, on January 21st, we went to the County Hotel in Carlisle for dinner then went to see the film Bonny Prince Charlie and with the impetuosity of youth, my blood hotted up with love, I proposed to June, she was rather taken aback, she was nineteen years old and I was twenty-one, she said she did not know what to say, tell me in a few days I said, a week went by and I thought I'd better not hurry her with an answer when she did give it, it was I who was this time taken aback, she told me no, because I drank too much, which I suppose, at that time, I was quite a hand at knocking it back.

Her father Willie was a hard toper, at market day or racing day drinking bouts, he did not know when to stop and would often be a paralytic drunk. His driving licence was taken away from him three times, the third time for about fifteen years, which in the early 50s was pretty severe, his last offence was driving back to his home from Penrith, he had run straight into the rear end of a timber lorry near Eamont Bridge, laden with full trees sticking out for quite a long way behind, one of the trees went right through the passenger side of Willie's car and right out of the back window, missing Willie by a few inches, of course, if he had had a passenger, that person would have been decapitated. Willie, of course, dead drunk, was caught, fined and banned. I think that is what June must have been thinking, although, to this day, I have never had an accident of any sort in sixty years of driving all over Europe, touch wood.

I could out drink or keep well up with the old stagers like her father, One-Eyed Willie, Major Parker (Bridget's father) and a good few more, so I thought that it was a funny thing to say to me, it crushed my ego a bit, but I said nothing and we kept up our courting for a year, dinners, dances etc., I also did not slow down on my drinking, it was to me a nice past time after work, all day, to adjourn to the George in Penrith or the Crown at Eamont Bridge, these two hotels were the favourite watering places of the gentry and businessmen of the town. Also, characters like One-Eyed Willie, where 5-6 would get into a domino game of 1 pound a spot, this was beyond my pocket by miles. I was used to a penny a spot, though I stood my rounds of drinks with the others, man for man. June took at job at Lytham St Anne's near Blackpool, at a girl's school as PT instructor, she loved this sort of thing and all outdoor life, she came home for odd weekends by bus and left on Sunday nights by bus from Sandgate in Penrith. Eventually, she took a job in Singapore, for a while, some of her parent's friends had homes there, we wrote very often to each other and I still have all of her letters to me.

After June came home to her parents, who were by now living at Cliburn, in a little place named Rock Cottage, it was in the middle of the village, only 50 yards from the Golden Pheasant Pub, a place I never frequented until later in years, but I suppose it was handy for Willie. One weekend I was told June had been out for one weekend with another young chap, Jackie Egglestone, who was a local butcher by trade, I asked June if this were true and she said it was, I was dumbfounded, I had never thought of another girl, I left and was not in a good mood.

I continued to take June out for dinners and the odd dance, but things were just not quite the same. By now, June's parents had taken the hotel, High Force in Middleton-in-Teesdale, this place was famous for its rather beautiful waterfall. I went there on May 28th 1950, to see them and apologise for not being at June's 21st birthday on 24th May, as I was over in Dublin with Robert Jackson, our neighbour and good friend of Adam's and Eric Lothion, I spent a nice day with them and June also.

In August 1950, the owner of the Crown Hotel and I went to the Thrisk horse races. On the way back, I stopped the night at the Crown as Adam had run me in the day before and that night, I had no car. The owner, West Tinniswood, was a grand chap and a good drinker. He had three daughters, June, Ann and Mary, in that order, he welcomed a clique of us young chaps with open arms, I suppose, with a view to getting his daughters married off. They were all, each one in their own way, quite lovely. West and I would many a night drink until midnight before I left for home, he liked to drink at night, brandy and advocaat in equal portions, until he started to put too much weight on, then he switched to his other favourite drink of gin and martini, I would always stick to my whisky, West always had a tub of very good panatelas on the mantelpiece in his snug, where he and I and the clique retired to when the main bar closed, he always said to me, Joey, help yourself, which I did, smoking 3-4 a night for him on top of my other Havana's or Burma's, I was never without them.

Two weeks later I took another girl out to dinner, she was from Carlisle, a very pretty girl named Sheila Towil, Sheila's father was a great racing man, Ronnie was his name, a big friend of my mother's brother, Robert Tinning and of our neighbour at Skirwith, John Jackson, another mad keen racing man and liked to bet, and bet big, like Ronnie. Whenever I called to take Sheila out for dinner, Ronnie, also a great drinker, would sit me down and give me an enormous half-tumbler dose of scotch and if I brought Sheila home fairly soon, another big dose of half a tum- bler, for the way home, we would talk racing for ages. Ronnie had a friend in the whisky distilling world, in fact, this friend was the owner of the plant, his name was Graham Munro, a very big gambler.

I first met Graham about two years ago at Lanark races, I was with Uncle Bob (Tinning) and John Jackson, I rather think John's son may have been with us, Robert, in the car park at Lanark, my uncle and Ron- nie were having a biggish discussion with Graham about buying a case of whisky each, Graham said it was a bit difficult as all his output then went to America, however, the two were promised their whisky so I thought I would try my hand, I was I think nineteen or twenty years old—would it be possible for me to buy a case from him, he looked and said, of course, my boy, give me your address, I did and in due course, the whisky arrived it was Clan Munro and the charge was 3 pounds less than Graham had charged the other two.

In the car park, John Jackson tried his best to sweetheart a very lovely woman of about forty years old, who it seems was a friend of Graham's, he had had plenty of whiskies that day and it was showing, but he, John, was a charmer and had an infectious laugh. He was a ladies' man and women loved him, then he spotted me and tried his best for me to kiss this lovely piece, all in fun, we set off for home, saying goodbye to Graham and his friend, first stop Thorn Hill a hotel in the main street named the Buccleuch, John had a box of cigarettes with maybe a 100 in it, he was in his cups alright because he threw them all over the car inside, they were scattered from back to front then we piled out of the car, the hotel was a very good and popular watering place and for food of the racing fraternity, we always made a point of calling in. John had to be helped out though, after more rounds inside, then into the car, where he went to sleep.

I sold Father half the case of Clan Munro, he was himself a connoisseur of whisky. He said it was one of the best he had ever tasted, very smooth. It was a blend but a good one. I asked Graham for another case which duly arrived, again, I sold half to Dad.

For November and December, between work, I hunted with the Dumfriesshire hounds, with Sir John Buchanan-Jardine as M.F.H., a black and tan pack with much French blood in them; Sir John's passion was his hounds.

One night, I thought in December 1950, I asked Sheila if she would care to go to the show jumping ball at the Crown &

Mitre Carlisle, she said she would love to, on that particular night, my brother, Robert Jackson, Eric Lothian and I would meet at the Crown at Eamont Bridge, we duly met, then came upon the scene Bobby Dickson, a school friend of my brother's. The night wore on and I tried to move them but to no avail. I had not a car that night, I was in the hands of these other naughty boys. I phoned Sheila saying I would be late, explaining. By the time I got the others going, it was 11 pm, we got to Carlisle, the others went into the ball and I went to pick Sheila up. When I got there, she had changed out of her evening dress, her father told her to get it on again at the same time giving me a half tumbler of whisky, on top of a multitude of others I had had, off Sheila and I set, I had the car then, it was only half a mile to the Crown & Mitre, and we arrived just in time for the last dance, I was ashamed and apologised to Sheila, but I think, both of us knew that was that, and so it was.

Bridget wrote me from Bedford and told me she was quite happy, on February 23rd 1950, West Tinniswood's middle daughter Anne had her 21st birthday party held at her father's hotel The Crown, it was a superb do all round and lasted until 4 am, that was the day the Labour Party got in with a majority of 9, we were all disappointed but noted our candidate Scott, retained his seat over Robert's Liberal and Taylor's Labour. Anne, West's daughter, was courting at that time a young man learning to be a vet, he was at the vet's college in Edinburgh, who was to be quite famous in the north for his amateur jockeyship and also famed as a trainer, he was Tommy Robson, Anne and he married in later years.

Ma and I were on our way to pick up my sister Cathie from the ship RAKAIA, coming from New Zealand. She it seems, could not support her husband Jimmy Davies' goings on with other women. It seemed a pity because she had spent more than a year or two in New Zealand in a Nissan hut, waiting for, to be allocated a house which she eventually had. This was the man I refused to shake hands with when he left Eng- land with Cathie as his wife just after the war. The ship was delayed 24 hours because of gales so Ma and I booked into the Angel Hotel, Cardif, which was very good, it was somewhere to rest for Ma because the train journey was so long, a long time to wait. I think it was Birmingham and dirty. The trains then were shocking.

We were up at 5.30 am, took a taxi to the docks and a very kind dock superintendent when Ma explained her daughter was on board, let us pass and showed us on board. Cathie looked tired and thin, she had two children, Josephine aged four, of course, born here in Wales, and Michael, aged two, he was in his bunk and I bent down to say hello, he spat right full in my face. I thought, just wait, you little brat. Later in the railway carriage on the way home, he did it again, but I was prepared for retaliation. I spat right back and hit him full face, and pulled the hair on his temples hard upwards, making him squeal. He never did that dirty habit again and became a really nice boy.

Bridget was twenty-two years old on 24th April 1950; I sent her a card and phoned. I was sitting up now each night as one of my mares, Reva was due to foal, her udder was full and almost bursting but not showing wax or milk. Ma took turns for me after I had sat up all night for a full week and it was only after eight days of dripping milk she foaled a chestnut filly by Brio II, Reva was by Winter Halter, usually as soon as wax is formed on the teat end, they will foal within 24 hours but dripping milk for eight days was a bit abnormal, the foal had a leg halfway back, but I soon put that right, I watched a while, she was very motherly, then I went to bed, she had foaled at 12.20 am, it was her first foal.

In the morning, I went to see mother and foal, the foal was a very nice sort, rather stocky and strong, I saw when the foal went in to suck, Reva would squeal and kick out, the poor little thing had nothing to drink all night, usually a foal is sucking like a Trojan within twenty minutes of foaling, I got a couple of the farm men to help me hold her while I put the foal underneath to suck, for by now it was rather frightened to go underneath the mother, Reva was a hard case, in the end, we put a twitch on her, that quietened her down. I got the foal sucking well, let it have its fill, then left her to go to work because we were still lambing and were sorting out the fell ewes. We also had many tons of potatoes to sort for the market, they were better potatoes in those days, for one's health, perhaps once or twice sprayed, not like now, up to 18 times sprayed with pesticides, insecticides, defoliant, weed killers etc. No wonder that people are rotten with cancer because in all foodstuffs from fruit to cereal, the man in poisoning himself.

In June, I went to another 21st birthday party of a young man by the name of Ian Stobbs. His father, a bit of a snob, had the Greyhound pub at Shap. I called at the Crown Hotel on the way and took the three Tinniswood girls and Tommy Robson, too; Shap was only about 9-10 miles away. It is a cold and windswept, rainy place, a great deal of rough hill country mostly owned by Lord Lonsdale, however, we arrived at the Greyhound pub, and quite a few people were there, we gave Ian our presents. Mine was a silver fountain pen, Tommy Robson said to me, hey Joey, have you noticed people are buying their own drinks, I told him that's not possible, this is an invitation to a 21st party, I then asked Tommy and the three girls what they would drink and told them to watch me. Father Stobbs was behind the bar, I ordered. They were all spirits. I was served with a smile, then I took the drinks to my group and that was that, I thought to myself, if old man Stobbs is getting any money out of me tonight, he had better think again. It turned out to be an excellent party and toward the middle of the night people had noticed me not paying, so decided to follow suit. I don't think Father Stobbs would be too pleased. I thought it very mean of him to accept money continually if people offered he took it. We went home on a beautiful bright morning.

The next few weeks, I spent hoeing turnips. By now, Dad was paying me 2 pounds per week, I still had to catch rabbits which I did by lamping them at night with Jakob, our replacement for Heinz. Jakob Muller was from Romania and he was unable to return owing to the communist regime there, he was one of Adam's poultry men. Jakob carried the 12-volt car battery with a large car headlight that I had fixed up. We had Caesar, Spot's son, he was out of a whippet bitch I had bought a few years ago and Spot had mated with her (an accident), he was very good at this lamping at night was Caesar.

I carried the rabbits, sometimes I wish I had let Jakob have that job because we used to get so many, it was hard work. I split the rabbit money 50/50 with Jakob and sold all to Jack Pears of Culgaith, he was the local poultry dealer and a cut above the other dealers of that sort of thing, in fact, he was very gentlemanly, his wife also a cut above the rest would go around when he first started, in his little van to pick hens, ducks and turkeys up. They had one daughter, Jean, I think they had a son who was killed in the war. He was a collector of Stubbs paintings of gun dogs he used to show them to me sometimes, they were exquisite; Stubbs was a master of his art, alright. I came to know the Pears well and went to Jean's wedding to a vet. Each Saturday night, we would meet Mr and Mrs Pears at one of the hotels we visited, so between my day work and rabbits at night, I was rather busy. I was not courting any girl just then. June was at one of her jobs abroad and we wrote very often to each other. The weather in July became very wet, which made the Briggle Beck, the one that ran through Skirwith Hall land, very fishable. I was out for quite a few days, work permitting or evenings till late, by my diary catching 20-25 trout each outing, that was to eat, throwing the too-small ones back. Bridget came home for a while, I took her to dinner at the George Hotel and a few outings besides. I think it would be another two years later that, she married Gerald Archer, then her father had to more or less to rescue her from him. He was battering her about. On one occasion, she told me he threw her downstairs, hurting her back, I believe I have said elsewhere, when I met Archer once, I immediately thought he resembled a turnip. Bridget and I had no secrets from one another. It was after Archer threw her downstairs that Bridget started with pains in her shoulder, these pains lasted about 3-4 years, then slowly she became paralysed in one arm, then her legs, until she was chair bound for years.

On my excursions to Stockton horse sales, I used to stay at the Corpo- ration Hotel in Middlesbrough, just over the 'cause way'. I was rather intrigued by a very good-looking receptionist there, her eyes were soft and beautiful, her best point, but overall she was quite a lovely one, her name was Ester Gofton, she lived with her parents on a housing estate called Brambles Farm, I never seemed to get her for a date, either she was tied up at her work or I had to leave to go home, I used to visit her at her parent's two or three times and chat her up at the hotel. I took Ester out to the sales ring at the horse sales once for lunch, but the morning I called to pick her up, her mother, who at that time did not know me, answered the door and asked on seeing me if I was the new footballer. I replied no, I gave her my name and was invited in, Ester and I left for the sales and spent a nice day then I took her home, a little later I learnt the 'new footballer' was a chap called Ugollini, he was a goalkeeper for Middlesbrough club, not long after that Ester married him, I heard that he later left football and became a bookie in Edinbrough. Another girl I took out for a while was Nora Brown, she was petite, very pretty, had an enchanting husky voice and smoked cigarettes from a long holder. Her mother, I believe, was one of the ladies John Jackson used to pay court to, in more ways than one, in times now past. I had known Nora for quite a while, having danced with her at various balls, she always had the same escort, one day I phoned her to invite her to dinner and she accepted.

We went for dinner to the Crown Hotel at Wetheral near Carlisle, an excellent little place for good food, it became a foursome as I had invited my good friend Bill McGillivray and his wife Sylvia also, it was on the 29th March 1952, Oxford won the boat race and in the Penrith-Carlisle area it snowed all day. Nora was a very lovely girl, but we never fell in love, it was a good friendship, she worked as a doctor's receptionist in Carlisle for a Dr Miller whom she later married, they moved to Penrith, where I used to see her from time to time in the George Hotel, she had I think two sons of which she was immensely proud, I got to know her husband, a very nice man indeed. When I left England a few years later, I heard she had died from a form of cancer.

Come market day on Tuesday, at night, one or two of the vets and I went to a dance in the St Andrews Church rooms. These were held each Tuesday night for a certain period; Saturday nights was for the Drill Hall. I happened to dance with a girl whom one of the vets was courting, and she asked where I was from. I told her, straight away, she asked me to call her on the phone, which she gave me on the back of a cigarette packet, told me where she lived, with her mother, she did not believe in wasting time, she said we could get stripped off on the sofa, I could hardly believe my ears, the first time I had met her and she courting someone else, I had visions of making love on the sofa and her mother coming in, I thought not bloody likely, her name was Vera Monkhouse, she still I believe is single and lives in Penrith.

The village pub was quite a good, very old-fashioned pub with flagstones of sandstone on the floors, the beer was brought up from the cellar in jugs, straight from the barrel, no pumps and no bar as such. The darts cum domino cum bar room, with no bar, was the drinking room. If one was favoured, they could sit on the staircase or by the kitchen fire or in the little back room where the bottles were on a shelf, the cold tap for washing, and the stone steps leading to the cellar, which was open at the top, when the place was crowded at a hunt ball or such, there would be times when someone would take a step backwards and fall head over heels down these steps, by a good chance no one was hurt badly as to stop them drinking. After being cursed for being a 'son of a bitch', this was Fred's regular curse on all and sundry, the injured party was quickly back into his stride.

Fred and Florrie's two sons, twins Bill and Ted, would bring the jugs of beer up from the cellar, but by helping themselves also as customers by ¾ of the way through the night, the boys would be so far gone there was sometimes more beer on the floor than in the glasses. Neither of the boys could count right, giving either too much change or too little and they were fighting mad with each other, they would square up to each other and have a scrap in a full house, Fred or Florrie, however, would quickly stop it, until their backs were turned and they would flare up again. I myself have seen Bill, one of the twins, race out of the front door of the pub at full speed right across the main road, looking neither left or right, hard on his heels was his brother Ted, with either a bucket of urine or water from washing the floors, throw the lot over his brother then when that was done, it was visa versa, a veritable Laurel and Hardy scene, but one or the other could, if a car had been passing easily, been killed. The pub had no toilets then. Most of us used to go into the rear yard and pee against the kitchen wall, under the window or the barn or road outside of the house. It never smelled really bad, I suppose because of the never-ending rains of Cumberland.

Fred loved his rum, and Florrie did not like him drinking it. It cost money. He always had his pipe going no matter what, always it was Black Twist. Rum then was 2 shillings a quarter dram which was a much better measure than one got today in 1995. A measure today only fills one hollow tooth and what a cost! One of Fred's little tricks was on a dance night or an ordinary busy night if one offered Fred a drink, he would accept, take pay for it in front of Florrie, say good health and wait till Florrie was out of sight serving in the next room, quick as a flash Fred would press 4 shillings into my hand, taken out of the till which was a biscuit box open on the sideboard, and say 'when Florrie comes back, ask me to have another, she'll

The Life and Loves of a Countryman

think you are paying', I duly obliged, this was a regular thing of his, poor Florrie, thought I and others were in on it, were treating her husband, I have also seen Fred take a bottle of rum from the bar shelf, drink as fast as possible, then like a flash, hold it under the cold water tap, top it up to the bottles previous measure then back on the shelf with it.

Fred had a very good army pension from the Canadian government which, when paid in dollars, turned out to be the saviour of the Hodgson family, keeping them all nicely on booze until he died.

For us, a select few, in Fred or Florrie's eyes, she held the licence, closing hours did not exist. The customers who did not wish to stay behind were ushered out but not in a hurry. Then when this had been done, the select customers and friends were left, the front door was locked and the rear door also. I was there one night at about midnight on a Saturday. We were in the kitchen drinking and playing dominos when all of a sudden, a hush came over all, the village policeman from Melmerby and, Skirwith on his beat, was with us in the kitchen, cloak over his shoulder, looking most severe. No one could ever hear George come or go, for he was always on his push bike, silent as the night. Caught in the act, so to speak, but George Robinson, for it was he, was not only our law and order, he was a gentleman of the first order, he was a friend one in trouble could turn to, but he was not to be crossed either, in a gruff voice he told us all to clear out and gave Fred and Florrie a piece of his mind, he knew next Saturday night would be the same, but he came in like that to put a fright up everyone.

George once later on came up to me in the village. I had gone to use the phone box as my phone had a fault, he said, "Joey, your vehicle (land rover) licence ran out a month ago, best get it seen to." I told him I would.

Four-five weeks later, I again met him in the village, he said again, "Joey, I see that licence is still out of order," he said I had been warned and if he let me carry on without a licence people could be talking and maybe re- port him to head office for not doing his duty, I apologised and the next day renewed the land rover licence.

For me, our first village policeman was PC Inglis, his family hailed from Hawick in Scotland, he was a no-nonsense man, well-liked though because he was a fair man but would brook no nonsense. For example, with the bad boys who used to start fights etc. at the village dances, out came his truncheon, lay a few of them down and send to Penrith for the police van and off to the cells for the night, or he would just give them a good hiding, a boot up their backsides as hard as he could and send them home. Eventually, where he was in attendance, there was never any trouble at any of these functions; he was feared by this type of yobo. Not like when later in Harold Fells day in various vans, too much paperwork to do, the yobos got the upper hand until all village dances were done away with.

My brother had an old post office van for delivering his chickens, an eight or 10hp Morris, he lent it to me one Saturday night to go to Penrith for the Saturday night fever round of drinking. I started off for town at 5.30 pm and found I could hardly keep the thing on the road. If I turned a bit left, the van would want to go full left and like a flash, I could hardly keep a straight line, the same if I turned slightly right. I had met my pals, had a few drinks and I left town to return home by way of Eden Hall to call and have a last one at the Woodbines Hotel. I met a few people I knew and left there about 11 pm in the devil of a van, half a mile after the village of Eden Hall, in the direction of Langwathby, there is an acute S bend. I got into the S and with turning left, without warning, I was over the low hedge and into the field beside, the van on its side, I switched the engine off, I thought, *good grief, what is Adam going to say, there was nothing for it but to walk to Lanwathby to Hopes Garage to see Billy, the mechanic.*

I arrived and there was Billy talking to PC Inglis, *who now had his beat at Langwathby*, I thought, darn, Inglis will know I have been drinking, anyhow I explained to Billy and he got his car out of the garage and some rope and off we went to my van. PC Inglis stayed where he was, in the shadows, Billy soon had the van on its four wheels out of the field and towed me to the garage. There was little wrong with it. *Mudguard bent,* I think, anyway I left it at Billy's, who said he would run me home, PC Inglis appeared, saying, "I will go too," in we piled, got to Skirwith Hall, where I entertained both of them for an hour or more in the smoke room with extra large whisky's and PC Inglis laughing his head off, I gave him thirty doubled yolk eggs to take home for his wife, these were our police, grand chaps, hard but fair. Sometimes one of Skirwith Hall fell sheep would be found dead a few miles away on Hartside roadside, having wandered far from their heath. George Robinson, on his beat, would see the animals or some shepherd report on whom the animal belonged to by its markings. Twice this happened and it is the duty of the said owner to remove the dead animal or bury it because such a thing was not a nice sight for motorists passing by. George was such a man, he never called us to get rid or bury the carcasses, he buried them himself without more ado. When he would come to Skirwith Hall, he and Father would be in the morning room, a roaring fire (always a great fire in this room), a decanter of whisky and a good Havana each. As I have said before, George was more than just the law, he was a friend and gentleman. When he retired to Great Salkeld village near Penrith with his wife, I used to call on him quite often to say hello. He developed a leaky heart valve, he told me, but he would not have the operation, which then was a very major thing. Now, it is still a major operation but performed every day with great success. A few years of retirement and George died, missed by a great many on the fell sides.

I think it was after George retired that the next village policeman, always stationed at Melmerby, was a young chap by the name of Rule, and by Jove, he did Rule, by name and by nature, he frightened the life out of all the publicans on his beat, threatening them, storming into pubs on the closing hour and ordering the customers out, giving many no chance to finish their drinks, under threat of being taken to court.

At one pub run by an old woman, The Fox at Ousby, Mrs Graham, she would be about seventy-five years old, it was the same as Skirwith's Sun Inn with sandstone flags on the floor but a very snug kitchen and a better drinks room too. One night as Mrs Graham was just bolting the pub door, PC Rule ran his bike full pelt into it, almost knocking her down, at the best of times, she was a bit on the frail side, this went down not well with all and sundry. Everyone had had enough of PC Rule, he was covertly threatened and, I think, so scared he asked for a transfer, which he quickly got and was shifted down to Workington on the Cumberland Coast, coal miners and dockers, a hard lot, PC Rule started his iron law again, but within the month the lads at Workington had had enough of Mr Rule, they decided to teach him a lesson, a hard one at that, he was duly apprehended, thrown into the docks and had one of his legs broken for good measure, I should think that was a good lesson for the future PCs in that area, no one shed any tears for PC Rule.

Our next policeman was as good as George Robinson, his name was Sid Hetherington. Sid had a wife, son and daughter. He at one time had been a travelling thoroughbred stallion man, he liked the racing scene and he liked shooting, so I let him shoot wild duck on a very good syke (boggy piece of ground with a natural spring and plenty of watercress) and the beck at the end of Skirwith Hall. A grand flighting place with a bit of rough, if a pheasant or two got up, he would take those too. He also was one of nature's gentlemen; he and I would chat for hours about horses. He had been in Italy in the war and had visited a few of the famous studs there.

His hobby was making walking sticks and thumb sticks for hill climbing. He made Mother one which I still have. The crooks for the shepherd- ing sticks were made from the horns of the Swaledale tups. Boiled and moulded into all sorts of forms, from fish to dogs and thistles. I have one Sid made for me years ago with the scotch thistle and my name carved into the crook, his thumb sticks, like the shepherd's sticks, were all made from hazel trees, but the fork in the thumb ones were from deer antlers.

Sid's wife was not a strong person, ailing quite a lot, she could not bear the strong Helm Wind in Melmerby when it blew, so eventually, he asked for a transfer and got it on medical grounds because of his wife, a beat on the streets of Penrith where the climate was more mild, he then after a year or two retired, he used to still come and shoot my flight ponds and the beck near Beck Mill, with his black Labrador, his daughter after leaving school, went into the police force for a career, she was quite clever and in no time became Sergeant and a year or two later, Inspector. I expect at the time of writing this, she may be a Chief Constable, Sid's son, also and an academic is, I believe, a top accountant.

I called on Sid on one of my journeys to Cumberland from France with my son Joey Jnr. Sid's wife told us he was on his allotment and had had a heart attack the year before, we went to see him, he had just finished digging a piece of ground over and came to greet me. I thought, how tired he looked, but I did not tell him this, I told him all of the diggings was not good for chaps of his age. He laughed and said come on in for a drop of scotch and a chat, so we did, reminiscing about old times. He took me to his workshop where he made his walking sticks; he had a multitude of them and a good few Swaledale tup horns that his friends, the farmers on the fellside, kept for him. If a tup died, his horns would be kept or if the horns were growing into the side of a tup's face, then they would be cut off. Most of them were given to Sid. He was so well-liked he gave me to take back to France a very nice thumb stick that I still have. After that visit, Sid died the next year.

Our next policeman was Harold Fell, but now times had changed, the others had bicycles to go around their village beats, now Harold had a little police van, however, he lived up to what the others were (with the exception of you know who) and was a very good man. Harold was always extra tidy and smart, wore his uniform as if measured in Saville Row. He quickly became friends with the community and with us at Skirwith Hall, he could drink whisky like an old hand and had been in the navy in wartime, going around the world a few times. He had a few stories to tell.

10

One day Robert Jackson and I went together to Hexham races, it was as always, a Saturday and a Monday meeting, this particular Saturday, we both chatted two rather good-looking girls up. They were with their father and mother. Their names were Marilyn and Marjorie Moore from Warkworth in Durham County, or was it Northumber- land? The girls were about eighteen-nineteen years old, Marilyn was blonde and Marjorie was dark and Spanish looking. The end of the races came. By then, we had arranged to meet them down in Hexham town at the Hotel Beaumont. Robert and I had a whale of a time with the girls, their father, Alf, turned out to be a butcher in Warkworth and their mother, to me, was a bit of a gypsy type, very ordinary in her speech, however, the girls were quite pretty, for the moment that is.

What mattered, I flirted with Marilyn and Robert with Marjorie, we all arranged to meet at the races on Monday, again Hexham. Robert was hesitant, as always, with girls, Monday came and I went under my own steam as I wanted to get Marilyn on her own, we had an excellent day together at the races, I took her to dinner at the George Hotel, Choller-ford, a rendezvous for the racing fraternity then back to her home to Warkworth then I went home myself. Her parents were, as the French would say, 'tres ordinaire', especially the mother, she was inclined to be gypsyfied.

Marilyn and I made plans to meet up for the Newcastle races in a few days' time, which we did, meeting her sister and boyfriend, not Robert. After the races at a little hotel in Jesmonde Dene run by a Mr Donohue, Marjorie, I believe at the time, was a receptionist at this hotel and her boyfriend was staying there, semi-permanent. He was quite a charming chap, wearing a monocle, divorced and about 45 years old, and was in shipping, his name was Archie Catto, related to the Catto on the pound notes, at that time, Governor of the Bank of England, Archie and I be- came good friends and had quite a bit of fun together although I am not sure if he at that moment knew where he was going, not many of us re- ally do know.

Archie and I used to stay at the girl's parents' home in Warkworth and have quite fun at night when all was quiet with the girls, myself, I did not become involved too deeply, her mother was eventually to continually harp on at me ' when are you going to marry Marilyn', until my hackles signalled warning signs. They, the parents, thought I was a soft touch, always racing, always with big cigars, one thing with Marilyn, she had beautiful full and firm breasts which were a joy to handle and a delight to suckle, it's strange how a man in his courtship of woman reverts to the suckling of the female breasts, it is one part of the female anatomy a man first grasps at in the initial stages of each new courtship.

One day I took Marilyn to Silloth to see Mother, who had bought a house on the seafront there and was having a little holiday on her own. She had named the house Kirkdale, we called, but Ma was not in, I decided to walk along the seafront, knowing I would run into Ma and before long, there she was, I introduced Marilyn to Ma, and I could see Ma was not impressed, later that day when alone together for a few moments, she said to me 'this one not for you Joey, are you serious?' I smiled and said no. We courted for another six months, in my eyes, she was still a very pretty and elegant girl. The courtship was on her side, a very teasing hot affair, we would many times be on the point of making love and she would break away muttering hot, sweaty words like, 'we mustn't—its not right and wait', that was until one night driving towards Carlisle I pulled into a lay by just outside of Brampton and started love play, as usual things got hotter and hotter, she herself unable to stop, I plunged right in, Marilyn was soaking with her own juices. When it was all over, we carried on to where Marilyn was staying with some friends of her family, Ike Wilson and his wife near Hayton, Carlisle and dropped her off. An- other of Marilyn's little quirks was that she loved to light my Burma Cheroots for me no matter where we were and made a good job of it too. This was a comic friendship.

The weekend after, I had a letter from Marilyn saying she did not want to see me again, I read in between the lines and did nothing.

Ten days later, I went to Newcastle races and met up with Archie Catto. I told him about the letter from Marilyn, he told me he knew all about it and also told me it was written at the instigation of her mother, who thought when I received the letter, she would come running to her daughter with arms and heart open. That is what I had read in between the lines. I never saw them again until I was married a few years later. Archie, the nice man that he was, made the mistake of marrying Marjorie, later divorcing; I never met up with him again.

I have always been interested in racing and having a bet, reading all about it in Horse & Hound, of which I had stacks and stacks, until my sister burned them together with all of my war maps, clippings and writeups of the battles, quite a collection and worth a bit today, she thought my bedroom needed tidying up when I brought my bride back home.

Anyway, back to racing, I bought my first broodmare at York Repository; I was about sixteen years old and was on my way back by train from Warwickshire, staying the night at my Aunts in Leeds. I had seen an advertisement in the Horse & Hound of a stud—the Claverdon Stud, North Warwick, who was selling some brood mares. I thought in the paper the prices were right for me. At that time, bloodstock prices were low. I set off by train from Langwathby via Leeds to stay the night with my Aunt Kate and Uncle David. The next day I retrained for Birmingham from whence I would take a taxi to see this man of the brood mares, a Mr Brown of Claverdon Stud. I got off at Birmingham, got hold of a taxi driven by a very nice elderly driver, getting near our destination, the driver did not know where the stud was, he stopped in the village of Claverdon, at a picturesque cottage. I got out and knocked on the door, it was opened and a woman of about 35 asked what I wanted. I told her I was looking for Mr Brown of Claverdon Stud, she asked (strange to say) if I was doing business with him, I said yes, I may try to buy a broodmare, she then told me to take care in dealing with Brown, he was a dishonest man and no one liked him, I thought, just my luck to come all this way from Cumberland and be faced with someone dishonest, I was so near that I thought we might as well have a look.

I got back into the taxi, we had only another mile to go, the taxi entered the driveway to a lovely old house overlooking a lawn, the far side of the lawn in the front paddock grazed a few brood mares, maybe a dozen or more, I knocked and this huge man answered the door, he would be 6ft 6in and built to match. Mr Brown seemed a kindly man, he sat me down in the huge lounge on a huge sofa (settee). Seeing my age, he offered me a lemonade which I accepted, I saw no one else in the house and thought everything was very well-kept. We talked a short while, my taxi waiting outside, then he showed me the brood mares he had for sale.

They were aged and a bit thin, but some were well-bred. I remember one by Horus, he told me this one would be 300 pounds, too much for me, I chose one at 70 pounds, but I cannot recall how she was bred, we shook hands. He wanted a deposit, but I did not give any money, only saying I would pay when I had arranged to pick the mare up. I left in my taxi, the old gentleman had kindly switched his meter off while I had been with Mr Brown, perhaps a good ¾ of an hour. I set off back to the train at Birmingham, I cannot remember the cost of the taxi fare, but it was most reasonable and to boot driven by an English gentleman, we shook hands and I entered the station, it was quite empty and I had an hour or two to wait for the return trains to Leeds.

In the station, I strolled about and found some of the platforms out of bounds. As there was hardly anyone about, I took no notice; however, I was idly watching one of the platforms where something was causing some activity, I noticed by the side of a carriage a few officials—then King George VI, I was most surprised and delighted to see my king, he was alone and looked most sun tanned, I must have been no more than 25 yards away from him, it made my day.

Then it was back in the carriage on the way back to Leeds where Aunt Kate would be waiting for me, with, as usual, a large blazing fire in the living room. She always had enormous fires going and plenty of home-baked scones, buns and cakes, of which she was an expert like Ma. Ma and Aunt Kate loved each other like a couple of angels of, which they were completely happy in each others' company, both of them used to go for tea and cream buns to Mathias Robinson in the centre of Leeds and listen to the small orchestra there, they were at complete harmony with each other.

Now back to horses and my return train journey, I had Horse & Hound with me, the latest issue which, strange to say, I had not looked at much before, now I had time to do so, there were a few pages of horse sales from Newmarket of brood mares etc.

I started to read their sales, giving names, pedigree, prices and buyers of each lot sold and low and behold, here was a batch of brood mares' names that I had seen that morning at Mr Brown's Claverdon Stud, my eyes opened wider, the prices in the page in front of me were all in the region of 15-25 pounds, the Horus mare Brown wanted 300 pounds for was in the Horse & Hound for 15 pounds. The lady at the cottage from whom I had asked where Brown lived, her warning was ringing in my ears—be careful he is dishonest. I thought to myself, you dammed con, I had now made up my mind, even though we had shaken hands on the deal, to give back word, the first and only time in my life I have done that after shaking hands, but he was blatantly dishonest.

I got off the train in Leeds and went to the nearest phone box and rang Mr Brown. Told him I was not now taking the mare, he was most displeased indeed until I told him the reason, he never uttered another word. I caught a tram to Roundhay where I had some beautiful people waiting for me, it cost 2p and off I went. My sister Cathie was there too, coming to stay with Aunt Kate for a little holiday, Aunt Kate spoilt the lot of us and so did her husband.

Next day I had read in the Horse & Hound there was a mixed sale of hacks, hunters, brood mares etc at York Horse Repository, Auctioneer was Mr Botterill, forerunner of Botterills's sales of Ascot. I thought I would have a look over, so took the train from Leeds, Cathie decided she would also go. As far as I can remember, the station was not far from the horse repository, we arrived on foot from York Station to find sales had not started. There was plenty of hustle and bustle, grooms showing off the paces of their charges. I had a look around for the broodmares, finding only a handful, I chose one named Bodo, she was by BrioII and in foal to a stallion named 'George Here' a hunter premium one, I expect he had won a race or two, I liked the mare and seeing I was determined to be in bloodstock one way or another, I was going to bid for her.

The sale at the repository itself was an interesting affair, buyers would crowd the alleyway where the horse had to show their paces. Mr Botterill's rostrum at the head or top end of the alley. Horses would be brought in at the auctioneer's end and set off by sticks banging, a lot of verbal noise and trot or canter full blast to the other end of the alley (which I believe was paved with wooden blocks), here the crowd at the far end would watch the front action of the horse paraded then in a second they would part letting the horse coming at full tilt pass, the groom would then stop his horse, wheel round at speed and start on the return trip up the alley.

This was encouraged by a few whacks on the horse's rump from the gentlemen who watched to see his rear-end action and also the horse's reaction to a whack on the rump, it was the first horse sale I had been to and it was quite fascinating.

I had found the owner of the mare I was going to bid for,

a weaselly looking chap, very horsy, named Chris Pulleyne, he, it turned out, was a racehorse trainer from Yorks. I later looked him up in 'Horses in Train- ing' and found he was a very small trainer, he assured me Bodo was in foal and that George Here was a very smart-looking horse. In due time it was her time to go through or rather up the alleyway, being a broodmare, she was carrying (if she was pregnant) her first foal, she was not hurried, I bid 30 pounds, someone else bid 35 pounds and so on until at my bid of 60 pounds she was mine, my first blood broodmare.

One morning a few months later, I was passing through the field I kept Bodo in, and hey presto, there she was, as proud as punch showing off a lovely chestnut filly, I was highly delighted, the foal was straight in every way. I was now a breeder of bloodstock.

After the 6-8 days of birth, Bodo came into season, I phoned my friend Foster and took her over to the local stallion Merely-A-Minor, this was an exquisite-looking horse, full of St Simon blood, he had won some decent races and I think a Cumberland Plate, he was standing at Jimmy Rowlandson's church farm, a groom held Bodo, the foal locked securely in the lorry behind large rails, blinded with sacks, Merely-A-Minor, a bay horse came out of his box after teasing, stood immediately on his hind legs and walked this way to his mate of the moment, he always did this party piece. My pony Star was by him, Robert Jackson putting his mare Miss Fitz to him year in and year out, but Robert was a point-to-point enthusiast and made little of his stock, breaking them in at 4 or 5 years of age, then the hunting scene, he was a good hunter, hardly won any point-to-points because his training methods were no good. He would walk his horses for miles, himself getting out of the saddle and walking the last mile or two home on foot, putting in at the last week before a race a tremendous lot of work, with the result his horses finished last.

Merely-A-Minor's party trick of coming to his mare 20 yards or more on his hind legs was to lead to his death, but as an aged stallion, he came over backwards and broke his neck.

My first foal out of Bodo, now a yearling, I thought I would sell her, she was a nice sort, a good mover. I did not have the funds to try her in training, though I had by now about 14 pigs as another money maker, I still relied on rabbits and my wages, that is when I got it which were at now 1 pound per week. Cigars and cheroots and my courting were keeping my bank account low, in fact, I was now overdrawn at the Midland Bank, Manager, Mr Sharpe, father of John, the boy in love with my sister. However, I was not too worried about this.

I entered the yearling at the mixed sale of bloodstock at Stockton run by old Major Petch and his son, I borrowed Robert Jackson's horse trailer, hitched behind Dads land rover and set off. Ma went with me, we set off the day before because Ma wished to see some very good friends of the family in Middlesbrough which is possibly only 3 miles distance from the sales, to our friends in Linthorpe.

I duly boxed the yearling, groomed her up, fed and watered her, then waited for the next day. The sales day was nice and dry and the filly was about halfway into the catalogue, the time came, bidding started and stopped at 60 guineas. I told the auctioneer, young Petch, I was not sell- ing, he tried again as I walked the filly a few more times around, still no advance. I said no and young Mr Petch was now in a bit of a temper, I was telling him not to sell, in the same manner of when refusing to sell a cow or sheep, and he didn't like it, the result was the filly was passed out at 60 guineas, a smart man came up to me a short while after leaving the ring, he introduced himself as Capt Wilson, or Watson and asked me if I would sell at 60 guineas, I said no and that left but one thing, to load up and head for home, so endeth my first foray into selling bloodstock.

It was one of my quirks of nature. Whenever I was selling bloodstock in the future, I would invariably end up taking them home again, possibly rueing it the day after. I thought it over and the month after, decided to enter the yearling at

York Horse Repository, where I had bought her mother. I set off alone the day before, stabled her in a nice large box and stayed the night at the Station Hotel.

Next day the sales, and up and down this hell-fire alley with the yearling, walking sticks waving, verbal noise, making it hard to hear the bids, I don't know who was the more nervous, the filly or I. In the end, she was knocked down for 60 guineas to Mr TC West, Lane End, Gambling, Driffield, I set off for home. Four days later, I sold two of my lamb's fat @ 2/3 ¼ per pound and sold some fat cockerels to my brother for 7 pounds. They were pure R.I.R the same week I won 5 pounds 14/6 on the football pools, I managed to pay my overdraft off and be in a nice credit too.

My friend Bill MacGillvray from Scotby was a keen racing chap my own age and a head for summing up the odds in a flash, whereas I had to do a bit of thinking about it. Bill and I used to drive twice a week alone to the County Hotel Carlisle, to dine and drink wine for a celebration after a good bet on the horses and champagne. Quite often, I would stay with Bill and his wife, yes, he was married very young. He had already got a young girl pregnant, a daughter of Mickey Moscrop, the one who supplied the Le Fleming brothers and others with cartridges in the war years in exchange for being invited to the best of shoots. Bill told me he had almost got the girl's sister pregnant as well and she was only thirteen years old.

One day Bill and I had been up to Hamilton races, we went in his utility with him driving, had a good day betting, quite a few whisky's, Bill could never take a large quantity of drinks otherwise, he became yucky, on the way back we talked then I dozed off, I woke up, it seemed only minutes later finding the vehicle on its side facing the wrong way, I was on top of Bill and I quickly realised he had also gone to sleep, fortunately, no other vehicle was involved but just as I was climbing out skywards, a Jaguar pulled up to help us, it was our good bookie friend Willie Wight- man and his clerk. I nearly always had my bets with Willie, he was nearly always a point below the other bookies, but one could wheedle or squeeze at least a little more than he was offering, I had a credit account with him, Willie helped me down from the utility, he, his clerk, Bill and I all got to one side and heaved until we were on four wheels again, after fatherly words from Willie we were on our way again, but there came a hitch at 35mph, the utility developed a bad attack of the shakes, we both thought the chassis had got a twist in it so home we went at 30mph. Bill had the Ute checked the next day and it turned out it was one of the wheels that had a twist in it, not too bad after all.

His father, a grand chap to meet, always a twinkle in his eyes, was a first-class toper and a jovial man with it, his wife, also a lovely person, did not like him drinking so much in the house, he used to hide bottles galore in the hedge row or in the big potato heap that was used for the pigs. He and I would drink it straight out of the bottleneck. Bill's father, everyone called him Mac, had a jump jockey lodging with him by the name of Willie Tracy, an Irishman, who gave them tips, he rode at this particular period quite a few winners.

One night while dining at the County Hotel, Carlisle, Bill told me a horse he had a share in with his father, called Ormolu, it was running at Ayr, previously it had not been eating up and had not run well, so Bill got the vet to have a look at him, the vet soon discovered a very bad rear tooth, pulled it out and from there the horse ate everything and worked well. The trainer, whom I think was George Boyd, gave it a good trial from which Ormolu came through with flying colours. The big question for Bill was, could they trust Willie Tracy, who, so Bill told me, had been pulling horses when he shouldn't have. In any case, if he did decide to put Tracy up, the latter would not be told of the plans until he was in the paddock prior to the race. Bill told me he and his father were going to have a good bet, in fact, a killing, would I like to have a bet, but he, Bill, would put it on for me as he did not want any other bookie to smell a rat, I said yes, I would have 10 pounds on, I handed Bill a couple of those lovely old white fivers, with these notes you were a rich man. I was un- able to go racing with Bill as we were in the middle of lambing at home, this being the third week in March. In the event Bill did put Tracy up, after telling him in the paddock before mounting, that he Bill had put a fair sum on the books for him and so he had to win and was told to this effect, he won, I think at 7/1.

This was a nice windfall, so on the Saturday night following 29th March, Bill, his wife, myself and Nora, the one with the lovely husky voice, dined at the Crown Hotel, Wetheral (this was regular). This was another place where closing time did not exist for us, also, it was the day Oxford won the boat race and with us, it had snowed all day.

At a later meeting at Sedgefield, Tracy was booked to ride a horse named Colbert, this horse had won its previous race, Bill and the owner John, his last name I cannot remember, he was in the printing trade and lived at Corbridge, Northumberland, he was a nice man, not very worldly when it came to racing, trusting everyone implicitly, he spoke as if he had a permanent head cold. When Colbert had won his race previous to his next run at Sedgefield, John had got blind drunk finishing off at the Crown at Eamont Bridge, where he collapsed into a coma, nobody took much notice, but as time went on, maybe six hours later, in the very late hours, we got a bit worried, before he had vomited what looked like stale blood so our host, West Tinniswood phoned the local doctor, Frank Eddington, who came to see him, he told us John would be alright but to try and get plenty of water into him when the doctor had gone, we thought how were we going to get plenty of water down a comatose man.

One of the local vets was there, Mac (MacMillan), so we asked Mac to tube him (that is to put a tube down his throat and into his stomach), put a funnel at the top and pour water into him down through the tube, perhaps, fortunately, Mac had no equipment in his car as a tube used for cows and horses would maybe have been too big for Johns' throat and choked him. John started to come around bit by bit just after midnight, he had to stay the night at the hotel, he did not seem to have any after effects.

To get back to Colbert running at Sedgefield, John had a large bet, Bill was most unsure of W. Tracy, feeling sure in himself that Tracy was going to do the dirty and pull the horse. John's money had brought the price down to 3/1, the race itself a selling hurdle, Bill said it was a certain thing for Colbert to win, I myself had 5 pounds on the horse. The race started, Colbert going very easy mid-field, but at the finish, Tracy was nearly lying back in his stirrups pulling him in and he finished second, it was so flagrant, it was a wonder there was not an inquiry. After this episode, the MacGillvrays could not trust Tracy again, like a lot of other owners and trainers, he was asked to find other lodgings and, soon after this, went back to Ireland as he was getting very few rides, I never saw him again.

Bill's father, Mac, as he was known by, had bought a young three-year-old gelding from my neighbour, Robert Jackson, out of his mare Miss Fitz, I am unable to remember the sire of this horse, but he was named Cluaran. He was put into training with Hugh Barclay of Lockerbie, now the Barclays were a fair-sized clan, I knew them all very well, they comprised of Mother Barclay, a very serious and successful gambler, a great whisky drinker and a great character, one could hear her high pitched laugh from one end of the paddock to the other, especially when the whisky was flowing, she could out drink most men.

We get back then to where Cluaran was sent to them to train, it was not long before it was realised that Cluaran was a flyer, Mac, Bill's father was most excited. Now he could have a good bet, Cluaran ran and won his first race, a hurdle, in a canter, he was then poised for a race at Carlisle. The great day arrived, myself was there also, with Bill, Cluaran was paraded in the paddock, his price on the boards was at 5/1, but in a flash, before Mac had a penny on, he was evens, the Barclay clan in its entirety had got their money on, they were all there for a killing, I debated with Bill whether to have a bet or not and decided not to do so at evens, Mac was annoyed, he knew whom it was that brought the price down, he went into the paddock and told father Barclay off, the horse had to be pulled up and stopped from winning, now there was a flap on, I think the Barclay clan, all nearly had heart attacks, one of the brothers was riding the horse, Mac was in such a mood, old man Barclay had to do as he was told and stop the horse.

A quick family talk now took place, Mrs Barclay and boys, to save their big punt, more or less knew Cluaran would be stopped from winning the race, off they went in a rush to hedge their bets. This betting by the Barclay sons and running horses to suit their betting ways, I think, was the reason they got fewer and fewer horses to train. As the years went by, they had only a handful, but in their stable, there was one horse of when the coffers of the family were at a low ebb, this horse used to be wheeled out and very seldom beaten, carrying always top weight. A chaser, he was an absolute marvel, I believe also winning at Cheltenham, his name was Langton Crag and without doubt, he was the Arkel of the North.

Cluaran won one more race, then developed severe arthritis or maybe a muscular disease in his front pasterns, he was sent to the vet college in Glasgow to no avail, he did not run again, as I have said many times, nothing ever happens to a bad horse, but to a good one, everything happens, and always an ill thing.

My Uncle Bob Tinning—my favourite uncle, Mother's brother, it was he whom I used to go racing with very often, going up to his farm Aller-beck, where mother and eventually my brother Adam were born, set on the banks of the river Kirtle, where I used to fish for trout, good sized ones too, it was a lovely old place originally owned by Sir Edward Johnston Ferguson of Spring Kell. My grandfather bought it from him and raised his family of seven children there, and when he died, left each a good-sized sum. I stayed many times when I was a small boy at Allerbeck with Uncle Bob and his wife Aunt

Jean, I was always made welcome day or night. I would do the Scottish racing circuit with him, which was good fun, I would be introduced to many famous racing personalities over the years

One particular year Uncle Bob acquired from the Queen Mother, via Peter Cazalet's stable, a big liver chestnut horse named Lamento, he had shown great ability over hurdles, then had turned doggy and would not start in his races, just standing with his feet planted like a mule, there was even pock marks on his hind quarters where he had been shot at with a cartridge/s packed with either rice or wheat, this must have been done at Cazalets. I am sure if the Queen Mother had known this, she would not have been amused.

Uncle Bob put him with Barclays and won a race with him quite easily, I saw this race and thought, my word Uncle has a flyer here, but in his next two races, he refused to start, so he was brought home to Allerbeck to have another three or four months hunting with the Dumfriesshire pack, I used to hunt then on another of my uncle's horses, one named Laura's Lad, he was out of Laura, the more I had come off when I was thirteen and broke 5 ribs, this one was a go-getter taking his jumps like an old stager, but I noticed Lamento who was out regularly with my uncle up, the horse just loved this new way of hunting. Talking everything in his stride without question, he was a new and rejuvenated animal. More or less straight from the hunting field, he was entered in a three-mile hurdle race at Carlisle, not far for him to travel in cases he started thinking, I was there that day at Carlisle and I told Uncle Bob I was sure Lamento would win, he grunted a half laugh, I think he was nervous the horse would refuse again.

In the paddock, Lamento really looked the part, fit and fine, I wandered round to the bookies where he was 9/1, I thought by Jove that's nice and had myself 20 pounds to win. He remained at that price until almost the off, only dropping a point, I was standing alone, my friend Bill was not there that day, I watched closely through my glasses as they were called to the line. Then the tape went and they were off, Lamento with them, that is when I clapped myself on the back, I knew by his previous win and now he was running he was home and dried and sure enough, he won on a tight rein.

I asked Uncle Bob if he had won much on him, he had not had a bet, when I told him I had won 180 pounds he could not believe it. I think he was really jealous, things got a bit better when I had treated him to a few double whisky's, I did not rub it in saying I told you so, but left it at that.

Lamento, in his next race, once again refused to start, eventually, Uncle Bob, then hunted him for quite a few seasons, he proved to be extremely good and enjoying it, I should think it was the excitement of the hounds, horns and hunt. I went to the Lanark races with Uncle Bob and at one particular meeting, he was invited to dine with some of the stewards, he introduced me and asked if I could join him, I could, the food was excellent, so was the wine and as Uncle Bob liked cigars, I passed him one, a beautiful Ramon Allones, I offered my case to our friends either side, one took, the other had his pipe, not like today, it's impossible to have a smoke in any public place without people grumbling or scowling or being downright rude, before long there was an aroma of richness in the air then the port was served. The atmosphere was that of a gentle- man's club in London, I was most content and thanked my Uncle Bob for what turned out to be a most pleasant day.

On our return journey home, Uncle Bob said he had to call on the chef at the Annadale Hotel in Moffat, I did not ask why he wished to see the chef, we duly arrived in Moffat, a nice clean little Scots town, we pulled up at the hotel, and Uncle Bob went in the back entrance, I thought well I'll stretch my legs and invite Uncle to have a drink or two, into the kitchen I went where there was only Uncle Bob and the chef talking, in the middle of the kitchen was a long wooden table with about 40 cooked chickens on it, this would be about 6:30 pm, in the middle of the chickens was enormous ginger, fluffy cat slowly making his (or her) way through them, eating a bit here and a bit there, the chef took no notice whatsoever, it must have been an everyday occurrence for the cat which looked to be rolling fat. I thought to myself, what the eye doesn't see, the heart doesn't grieve. Eating in hotels 4-star or 1-star, guests never know what has been tampered with or happened to the food that is put in front of them, I told my uncle that I would never, ever eat in that hotel and never did.

Another case of hotel food I will mention and readers will notice I name the hotels, I do not cover them up using false names, these hotels are there today, but I expect, due to the passage of time, under new ownership or managers.

The hotel I now mention is the Edenhall Hotel near Penrith, at the time in question, the hotel was owned and run by Alex Beck, he himself was a good hotelier in his own way, but behind the scenes, the kitchens were a dirty mess. My wife and I were dining there with a neighbouring farmer and his wife, Bert and Christine Johnstone, Bert had a steak and complained to the waitress that it was tough, the waitress told the chef, who then came from the kitchen in a vile temper, waving his knife ask- ing what was wrong with the steak, Bert was so unnerved by the knife and the chefs' belligerent attitude he replied saying 'no it's a very good steak', the chef who was Spanish went back into his kitchen muttering under his breath, possibly disappointed he hadn't stuck his knife in Bert's ribs. One of the waitresses told me later (she was the granddaughter of Bobby Little, with whom I used to shepherd. The one with the cat that used to frighten the dogs to death out of his farmyard) that the same chef if anyone sent their steaks back to be done a bit more, used to throw them onto the kitchen floor, this is what happened to Bert's steak, stomp on and spit on them then send them back to the customer. It was the same if he disliked someone in the dining room, if he saw them early, he would, if they had soup—spit into it before sending it to the customer. One never knows does one what goes on behind the scenes. Alex Beck was warned many times by the local health people at Penrith to clean his kitchen up, he took no notice until their patience ran out, he got the final notice and date to commence the cleaning up just as he was leaving for Spain on holiday, but the local health would not be put off another time, he had to leave the cleaning up to an understudy, things were so bad it cost him at the end 5000 pounds.

In 1950 I had a two-year-old colt in training with Horace Barker of Redcar, he had Blue Meteor mentioned before, Horace was a charming little man, he would be no more than 5ft 3 or 4in, a good trainer. He used the sands at Redcar for his training, harrowing the sand very well before working the horses, my horse was out of Bodo by Emir D'Iran, who stood at Weststowstud named Price Ahmed. He was quite a nice sort but a bit gangly, he was at Horace's for a few months, I saw him gallop a few times and he seemed to go rather well. Just before he was due to run, Horace phoned up and told me the horse had slipped a curb, so I brought him home and turned him out with a slight blister, gelded him and later sold him for 150 pounds to Tot Kelso, who also ran and owned the Clifton Hill Hotel, Penrith. I think also at this time, Tot had his own licence to train on the flat, when he came to see the horse in question, Price Ahmed, I told Tot he had slipped a curb, but he did not know what I meant or where to look, poor Tot, he knew very little or nothing of a horse's conformation.

Tot had been banned by the Hound Trailing Association for 'lifting' one of his hounds halfway around the trail, substituting a new fresh hound and winning, he was soon found out and banned, then thought he would enter the world of horse racing, he was really quite a nice man with a very hard-working wife who started Clifton Hill from a house to a club, then a hotel. Tot did have a few successes on the turf, which seemed to perk him up. The only shadows were his being fined quite heavily by local stewards for one or two of his horses racing with ringworm.

Bill MacGillevray and myself went to the Dumfriesshire

Hounds hunt ball held at Lockerbie on 6th January 1950, my brother Adam and a few more of us were there and we stayed at Dinwoody Lodge Hotel, there was also staying at the hotel and attending the ball, a girl from Thornton Hall, Lanarkshire called Joan Chambers, Joan was 4ft 11in, red hair and she was a lovely petite, charming girl, I danced quite a few reels with her, then we all retired to Dinwoody Lodge for pre-bedtime drinks, after this, possibly around 3:30 am, Adam and I went to bed, Bill in his own room, he told me in the morning he had waited until all was quiet then went to Joan's room, she was awake, he told her he wanted to make love to her and in between getting the bedclothes to one side, Joan told him she could not as she had her periods, Bill, as usual, could not contain himself and ejaculated all over her tummy. I saw Joan in the morning and she was quite radiant, she and I had a few drinks then she opened her handbag and gave me a very nice tie, it was a maroon colour but one of the long type, myself only wore bow ones. I kept that tie for a very long time, but eventually, it got lost.

The same morning my brother, Robert Jackson, Eric Lothian and I were drinking in the Kings Arms, Lockerbie, after seeing the hunt meet- ing in the town square, we had retired to the bar, the owner, if I remember correctly, was Tom Gibson, he himself was a teetotaller and a nice young dapper fellow (whom in later years, once when I called, was a pathetic alcoholic) by now I was on my third panatela, warming up to some good Burma's a little later, when in rolled Bobby Dickson, he was one of my brother's school friends, his father had built up a rundown garage in Carlisle called The County Motors, this he turned into a thriving concern selling cars from the Standard Motor Company.

Bobby was a car enthusiast who raced cars at Le Mans and many other places, his mother and father doted on him too much. Anyway, Bobby arrived, declaring he was on his way to Edinburgh and wanting my brother to go with him. Adam had no time, he had his hens to see to. Bobby then asked if I would go with him, it was only for that day and night, back later the next day, I said I would, I had never stayed in Edinburgh before. We had more drinks and I then lit a nice big Scots No.1 Burma cheroot, I was getting them by now by post from George Murray Frame, a tobacconist in Ayr, 3p each, cheaper than Penrith.

We had a light lunch at the Kings Arms, I lit another cigar. This time, a Cuban and Bobby and I set off, he was driving a standard vanguard, brand new. Getting further towards Edinburgh, the roads were quite thick with slush and snow, but Bobby never slowed his pace, 50-60mph, the car often slewing all over the place, he was a good hand at controlling the car but very vicious on the throttle, I thought, whoever buys this car doesn't know that it had a thrashing beforehand. This was its running-in period, but we got to Edinburgh in one piece, arriving at one of his friends where we were to spend the night, this was William Stuart, whose first name was known by all others as Willum, so its one or the other, he was a super chap, very kind and good manners and his wife as charming, William was I think, head of the wool board in Scotland. Bobby decided I needed hair cut. I was inclined to grow my hair too long, so I agreed and had it cut, after this, we set off for the golf club, which I hadn't a clue, I met a few people who were to become friends, Mickey Gillespie whose father was a tobacconist in Princes St and Jack Glass who also had a large shop in the same street. Mickey thought his father would let me have Burma cheroots cheaper than Murray Frame in Ayr, but I did not carry this further. We adjourned to an excellent restaurant in George St, Bobby was an excellent host, too good in fact, paying for everyone and everything, which I did not particularly like as I liked to pay my own way, we had an excellent meal, good wine, the restaurant had some very good Cuban cigars which I was quickly into. We finished the night off at the Double Century Club at about 6 am, having my last cigar of the day, I counted up the early panatelas and cheroots and realised I had smoked practically no stop eighteen cigars and cheroots, I have never ever smoked so many in one day before, I felt non the worse for it either, having had a good teacher in my father, twelve or thirteen years ago.

We went to bed but were up again by 11 am to a big breakfast made by Williams, wife of bacon, eggs and sausages, Bobby was almost green looking at it, he left the table with a cup of coffee, so I ate his breakfast too, this was really my first long day and night of eating, drinking and smoking and I had enjoyed it. The day after, I was back cutting turnips for the fat lambs. I had put my first broodmare, Bodo, after she had her first foal by George Here, to Merely-A-Minor; the result of this mating was a bay colt which I broke in as a full colt, did some shepherding on him as a two-year-old, he was an armchair ride, good bay and very like his sire. The trouble was on the farm, he would worry the cows like a lion and try to mount them, with the sheep, he would pick them up in his mouth and shake them like a dog shakes a rat, yet in stable and to ride, he was a gentleman, I could canter for miles on the grass verge, only maybe a foot wide, a lovely mouth too, I sold him in the bar of the George Hotel, Penrith, to a young man from Culgaith, the next village to Skirwith, he was Brian Lamont, for 300 pounds. He put the colt, now named Carmoor, with Tommy Dent, who was training at Clifton Hill stables which were owned by Lord Lonsdale. A little later, Tommy moved down to Dringhouses near York, Carmoor won his first race at Pontefract as a three-year-old, I think this was 12th May 1950, this was a selling race of which the winner got 287 pounds, he was sold to a W.D. Markham for 220 guineas, so here was my first winner as a breeder which quite pleased me.

1952 turned out to be a very black year for my family. My brother Adam, the brains of the family, went to Spain on holiday with Airlie Hindley, whose family of cotton spinners had bought the Edenhall Estate near Penrith, then Adam had sold them 60 poultry fold units plus the breeding blood-tested hens. Airlie took the major domo, Simpson, along, West Tinniswood, the owner of the Crown Hotel Eamont Bridge, went with them.

All four went by car through Spain and France, they were away for four of five weeks. Adam, on his return, said Spain was the filthiest place he had ever seen, of course, in 1952, there were few tourists in Spain, it was not too far a distance from their civil war. The four stayed on the French Riviera for half of their holidays playing at the Casino in Monte Carlo, Adam had played at the next table to King Farouk, he said he was very fat by then, Adam had sent me a postcard from Monte Carlo.

Adam arrived home on 1st October 1952 and set about seeing to everything on the farm, from the milk cows to his small hatchery.

On the 7th October, he and I were in the bathroom together, stripped to the waist to wash, I happened to see his back and was surprised to see it was clean and bronzed before he had been plagued by a mass of fairly large pimples on his back, now there was not one left only a clean muscular back, he was extremely strong and well made so it must have been the sun and saltwater swimming that had done the trick. I made no comment and he was off to Carlisle to catch the 11 pm train to London to an N.F.U. meeting, he was on many committees, in Dad's opinion, too many. I was getting myself ready for a night on the town in Penrith, Adam had some paperwork to see to and prepare before he set off, this made him a bit late, causing him to miss the earlier train, so he had to take the next, at midnight. That morning of 8th October 1952, the midnight express from Scotland to Euston, with Adam on board, crashed into the back of a stationary passenger train at Harrow and Whealsdon station at approximately 8:20 am, it was late due to fog, a few minutes later, an express leaving London for the north, crashed into the wreckage of the first two trains causing a terrible carnage, there were over 120 dead and Adam was one of them.

I was driving through Langwathby village when I met Robert Jackson coming in the opposite direction, this was at

3:30 pm on 8th October, he stopped, I thought just to have a talk, but he opened with 'I hope Adam is alright', for they were the best of friends all of their lives, I asked why, he then told me about the train accident which he said seemed quite a big one, that day the radio was never on in the house, Dad always liked the news at midday, but somehow we must have been busy, I went home and told Dad and Mother what Robert had told me, then we all started to think, 'oh it can't be Adam's train', sort of it can't happen to us. By now, it was about 5 pm, Adam had about 40 poultry-rearing houses to shut in for the night, to prevent the foxes from killing the blood-tested young breeding stock for the next hatching season. I went to close these houses in, it took about ¾ of an hour when I got back, Mary, grandmother's old maid, met me and said, he's dead, tears streaming down her face. I went through to the morning room, the vicar and policeman were there, it was them who had brought the sad news. Mother was in a state of shock, unable to believe that her eldest son had gone, in fact, none of us thought it could possibly be true, we all hoped a mistake had been made.

Dad made plans to go to London to identify the body claimed to be Adam. He, Robert Jackson and I drove down to Leeds early on 9th Oc- tober to pick Uncle David up and off straight away to Edgeware Hospital, where many of the crash victims were. I drove so far, then Robert took over, I was not concentrating enough on my driving, thinking of Adam. We arrived at Edgeware and were shown into a room, the floor covered in bodies wrapped in sheets, Dad, Uncle David and I went in, a body's face was uncovered, and yes, it was my brother Adam. All he had was a bruise on one side of his forehead, we were told his neck had been broken, we left the room and Dad asked Robert if he would care to go and see his friend, Adam, he said yes, he would and said goodbye to his life long friend and neighbour. We left the hospital in great sadness and a great silence. We booked into the Russel Hotel for the night, had a light meal, none of us had much of an appetite. Inwardly, I must have been more upset than I thought as I became violently sick when going to bed.

We arrived back home on the 10th, to find Mother still couldn't believe what had happened until Dad told her it was true. Ma was devastated, many of her friends came to console her, among them Mrs Hindley from Edenhall and Mrs Brennand from Penrith, whose only son Chuck was killed, shot as a young Captain in the final moments of the war, Adam and Chuck had been great friends.

Dad had made arrangements for Adam's body to be brought to Skirwith Church by road on Sunday 12th October, Ma wanted his body to be brought to lie at Skirwith Hall, the vicar persuaded Dad that it would not be a good idea as he thought Ma would weep and grieve beside the coffin day and night, she wished the coffin be opened up so that she could see for herself that it was her son, this also was denied her, on Vicar Wilson's suggestion, perhaps the vicar was right, myself, I thought it Ma's right that she should see her son for herself.

The hearse arrived at the church at 2:55 pm, having waited at the main road at White Gates near Culgaith and Temple Sowerby, from there, I met them and showed them the way. At the church, a handful of Adam's true friends from Penrith were there to pay their last respects, I mention them here as I think it only right to do so, they were all close to Adam, they were Uncle David, Aunt Kate (mother's sister), John Barr (vet), Alan Forteath (vet), Eddie Walsh (a worker of Adam's), my family. Bearers into the church were Arthur Durham (Dad's foreman), Frank Stockdale (tractor man), Harold Metcalfe (poultry man), Edwin Kilching (village joiner).

The funeral was held on 13th October, it was a most distressing day, especially for Ma, she was comforted all day by Mrs Hindley and Mrs Brennand.

The bearers out of the church were Adams' most intimate friends, Robert Jackson, Eric Lowthian (banker), Bobbie Dickson (of car fame), Tom Park (manager of Fairbains Hatcheries and old school friend), (Jack Brown, whose father had brought my Shetland pony from Penrith many years ago dug the grave). More than 500 people attended the funeral, for he was well known and liked by many. He would have gone far in life if he had been spared.

A small reception was held at Skirwith Hall (in which I think I have mentioned before that Mrs Hindley said to me in front of a few people, 'now Joey its time you and Airlie were friends' seeing the Hindley had ignored me ever since their arrival in the district, I replied 'friends cannot be made in five minutes Mrs Hindley'). It is all I could think of to say on such a day. I never was invited to any of their functions or shoots before or after this.

Adam had more or less been unofficially engaged to a girl from Dum- fries, a girl he had met at one of the farmer's balls, after this ball, he wondered what his girl's legs would be like because of the long dresses at the time, legs hidden. They must have been alright because the girl, Pat MacGeorge and he became very close, at the funeral, she was most distressed. The following Sunday, the 19th, Pat came over for the church service, the church was almost full, including Adams' friends from Kent, Mr and Mrs Mike Young, whom I've mentioned elsewhere in these memoirs. Pat stayed the night and left the next day at 5 pm.

11

Now the question was what to do with the mass of poultry, the hatcher side of the business. Adam had just sold his small 6000 egg incubator and installed a 24,000 Stephens one. Old Mr. Stephens himself came to see Adam in his Rolls Royce and gave him expert advice on running the incubator. Dad always worried though never in a flap, when it came to biggish money matters. Although he was very clever with figures, he sent for Uncle Alex, who had married his sister—Hilda, the sergeant major. I volunteered before Alex arrived to try and carry on the hatchery business even thought I knew absolutely nothing about hatcheries as such, but I knew quite a bit about poultry in general. Dad waited until Uncle Alex arrived, not committing himself, Alex duly arrived at Penrith railway station on Tuesday, 21st October, Dad and he had lunch at the George Hotel. Meanwhile, I had made it my business to see that the poultry side was looked after, quite a few culls I got rid of on Wednesday, 22nd October, to Jack Pears of Culgaith. I looked into the feeding side to see what was needed and ordered 7½ tons of various feeding stuff from Monkhouse's warehouse in Langwathby. The Monkhouse family were big friends of all members of my family, starting firstly as butchers and old Mr Willie Monkhouse, taking an agency out for Bibby's farm feeds from a wooden hut in Langwathby village, building it up to a very big complex at the end of the village, by his two sons, Jim and Arthur.

Adam kept things close to his chest, I think originally, as at the age of eighteen, Adam had his possible true girlfriend, her name was Dulcie Groves and she was indeed a very lovely girl, she and her two brothers, Basil and ? used to come to see their Uncle Willie Groves who was head groundsman cum joiner to old Mr Parker of Skirwith Abbey. Adam had his first car then, a Morris 8, Dad saw or heard of Adam and Dulcie going out together and told him to stop as the family were not good enough. This was possibly more heated than I describe it here.

Mother had told me.

Adam stopped seeing Dulcie, but I think Dad's intervention had hurt him far more than Dad knew, Dulcie was a very good-looking girl and sophisticated also, from then on, Adam kept everything to himself, down to his girlfriends. I never knew him to have another until Pat MacGeorge at Dumfries because I was there and knew he saw Pat from then on. I told Ma, but it was a secret between her and I, Pat's father, Robert, owned, with his brother David, the Cashmere Mills in Dumfries with sales worldwide, Robert travelling to America and Australia promoting his products.

By now, Dad and Alex had come to the conclusion that Adams' poultry and hatchery were making more money than he, Dad, himself, he was rather amazed. He came to me one day to see if I would take the whole business on and I told him I would if he would pay me last year's wage of 2 pounds per week for 52 weeks came to 104 pounds. I had worked the whole year so far for nothing, the reader may think, but this young fellow had been playing all year. I did play but worked hard, often not even going to bed but straight from dinner jacket to work clothes, many times I had no more than 3-4 hours sleep, we thought, most of us young ones in those days, nothing of it, we enjoyed every moment of life. I also wanted pay going back year by year for my turnip hoeing, Dad said he would, but it turned out he never did.

Getting money, i.e. wages etc, out of Dad was very hard work, but I never held any animosity against Dad because he was a grand and gentle man and kind, nothing seemed to ruffle him. Alex and he were talking in the smoke room one day and I was in the next room, the morning room when I overheard Alex say, "You know Guy, it's too much money for Joey, the hatchery business, best had put Cathie (my sister) in as a partner." I thought to myself, *the bloody sod that Alex had*. The next day Dad put the question to me that Cathie to be a partner. I told him I would think it over and said that I did not like the idea, I let the thing simmer for a week then I approached Dad and said I suppose I had no option but to take Cathie in but not on a 50/50 basis and he had to give me all of my back pay, he agreed so it was drawn up, myself 75% and Cathie 25% but I never got my back pay.

On November 1st 1952, I brought Adam's new Vanguard saloon car back from Carlisle, where he had left it in charge of his friend Bobby Dickson (the only one to offer me lifts when I lost my licence).

Cathie went to London on 5th November 1952 to claim Adam's holdall and clothes, Uncle David went with her.

I had to know now about how a hatchery worked, how many eggs to set for, say, 100 pullet chickens. I knew the temperature of heat, but not the humidity temperature in incubators, also the hatching machines. Tom Park came to my assistance, he knew the job inside out, he explained all I wished to know with great patience. He had been at school with Adam, I had not known him until now, I found him to be one of the nicest men I had ever met, charming and kind, I still think the same today. I had to gauge how many eggs each section of hens would lay. Tom put me right on this, of course, there were variations, i.e. the weather may be too wet, then the snows in winter, hatcheries produce most of their chicks in the winter and early spring months.

Adam, for delivery, had an 8 hp Morris and ex-post office van, the first season when I was delivering, the van used to wander all over the road, its track rod ends were worn out, but I let it do. I will say, in deep snow, this little van was a wonder, that winter of 1952-53 was a devil for snow, with many roads being cut off. I used to take a shovel, the van and I always got through.

Jakob, Adam's replacement for Heinz, had been helping in the hatchery with Adam, so I gave him the job of looking after the incubator and the hatcher plus the rearing room while I looked after the rearing of the outside chicks up to various ages to be sold, plus my own breeding replacements for the following year, I had 110 rearing houses to feed and water and move onto the clean ground each day, Harold Metcalf looked after the 60 fold units plus the 400 in the hen houses, free range. Thursdays, I put aside for all of the paperwork of orders, receipts, bills etc. Saturdays, Jakob and I tested the egg trays over strong electric lights, set in a drawer under a large 10 ft long table, under a blackout canopy to see which eggs were clear and which were fertile, some were good and some rather low in fertility. The fertile eggs were then placed in the hatching machine in a different tray as the eggs were already in but with a large cage just fitting snugly over this tray to stop the chicks, when hatched, from jumping out.

So progressed the first season, but the hatchability of eggs was getting rather poor, especially in the pure breeds, this meant too many dead in shells, not having the strength to peck their way out of the eggs. I had Mrs Gibson, from the M.A.F poultry section over, she was head of the Cumb & Westmoreland accredited poultry world, she advised more riboflavin in the feed. I was making my own feeding stuff up by Hammer Mill to the same recipe Adam used, Jakob doing the mixing, I duly got more riboflavin, but things seemed to get worse. I was getting behind in some orders as too many chicks were dead in their shells, so I decided to read up the book of instructions on the incubator running. I still have the little book produced by Mr Stephens for his product. I knew the heat temperature but decided to inspect more closely, Jakob had it running at 100%, which was right, but the humidity he was using was 80%, miles too high. It should have been at 45% maximum, here lay the fault, the chicks were drowning more or less in their shells. I immediately told him to reduce the humidity to 40-45% but had to wait two weeks before the results showed a change and it was a very good chance, too. Hatchability was very good at 85%. Of course, when the eggs were placed in the hatching machine after testing for infertile after 17 days in the incubator, the humidity was then raised to 75-80% to make the shells a little softer for the chick to peck their way through and out into the world.

I forgot to mention in the interim period from me taking the business over to the start of a collection of eggs for hatching. The weekly egg cheque for eating eggs, as they were going for, came from the Express Dairy Appelby, collecting once a week and paying at the same time for the previous week's eggs. The Kirkdale Chicks bank account ran in Adams' name as to keep things as they were, Cathie could draw her own cheques as she wished.

Six weeks of eating eggs went to the Express Dairy after I had taken control, approximately 700 pounds or more. Dad had intercepted these cheques and put them into his own bank account when by rights, they should have gone into the account of K.C. This, for a start, left me to pay for feedstuff bought four weeks earlier and no income and as I took over, feeding stuffs were deregulated by the government and from 13 pounds per ton shot up to exactly double—26-27 pounds. This episode of Dad was quite uncalled for, he would not repay the money taken once in his pocket, that was the same as my turnip hoeing and working for a year without being paid, though he claimed he paid me double for tax purposes. I had my few ewes and six or so pigs, though, for the latter, I paid for the feed or fed them on hatchery waste.

By now, Cathie, snob as she was, sent her daughter to Harrogate College for girls, a very expensive school paid for by the hatchery—all new equipment and rewiring coming from my pocket, she worked only on Mondays setting the eggs in the trays.

Into the second season of 1953-54, Arthur Monkhouse came to see me and mentioned a new feed supplement had come onto the market, this supplement was named Nitrovit and was to mix with my own cereals, bought in maize etc, and was put on the market by two brothers, Eric and Guy Reed, a little later I came to know them well. Arthur, I have said before, was a very honest man, he had been a policeman at the start of his manhood with the Manchester Police but after a few years left them in disgust, this was due to the dirty tricks they played to trap people and the lies they used for that effect, he told me this himself. I told Arthur I would give this new stuff Nitrovit a try and also their ready-mixed chick feed. After I had used this new feed on the hens for a month, fertility was 97% and often, hatchability in the trays would be 100%, perhaps averaging 97-98%. It was amazing and the chicks were extremely healthy chicks to be sold at one month old because they had grown so fast. I sold them at three weeks old, one of the secrets of this feed was there was a good dose of arsenic in it. These two brothers, Eric and Guy, also had Yorkshire Poultry packers processing broilers etc. At one stage, they had to discard the livers from certain batches of processed poultry as there was far too much arsenic in them, making it rather dangerous for human consumption.

Dad, by this time, thought I had too many horses on the place, I had three mares in foal and a few young ones running about, so in January 1952, I sold Bodo for 32 guineas at York Horse Repository to a Mr George Wright, I believe she was empty, that was one less. I had Reva, a mare I had bought at the Stockton bloodstock sales, she was by Winterhalter and carrying her first foal after being mated to Brio II, this is the mare I had to sit up with for ten days, and a week of dripping milk, the result, a foal which was dark liver chestnut, a good foal, a filly, I sent this foal as a two-year-old to Harry Kitching who trained near Stocksley in north Yorkshire, I took her over to Harry's on Saturday 9th February 1952, the fees were 5 pounds 10 shillings per week, I sent her here because Uncle Bob, the Lamento one, had had a horse with Harry and had done well with it, his horses were always well turned out. He had a knack for getting a horse ready for a certain race, the filly I sent was named Betty Bayne, after a cousin of mine, a bit silly, really. In a soft moment, I had told my cousin I would name my next filly after her and this was it.

Harry was rather a peculiar character, I remember taking him to Ayr races, where we stayed three days for the western meeting, we stayed outside Ayr at a hotel beside the airport, the place was named Towans Hotel, it was a nice little place, very sunny and homely, good food and as we were leaving, Harry wanted to steal a whole lot of flowering plants from the garden, I told him strongly not to do so, there was a kind of gypsy side to him. I ran him home to Stocksley, calling at the George Hotel in Penrith to have dinner on the way. I stayed the night at the Black Bull. I think they called it in Stocksley. Uncle Bob asked if I still had a horse with Harry. I told him I had, he told me to take it away because Harry was not going to have his license renewed by the Jockey Club, he had heard this through a friend of his who had good contacts with the Jockey Club. I asked Harry about him getting his licence renewed, he told me it was only a matter of days before he got it, so I held on and waited, however after five more weeks, I again asked Harry about it and he still had not received his renewal, I decided to take my filly away, so on 5th April, I took the land rover and horse trailer and removed her. Harry was not there when I arrived, only a young stable boy about seventeen years old. He gave me a hand to load up, his name was Taffy Williams and hereby lies a rather strange tale as to why Harry had not and never would get his license to train from the jockey club. He had a woman client, and this woman had two horses in training with Harry, it turned out this woman was a nymphomaniac, and it was very possible through this that she and Harry fell out. She demanded the return of her horses. Harry duly sent them back to her in a horse box. I'm not sure if the horse box was Harry's own or a hired one. The box arrived at the woman's premises and lo and behold, one, if not both, horses were dead on arrival. There was no court case, but this woman must have reported the case to the jockey club. Though positive proof was not pointed directly at Harry, circumstantially, it did, and he never got his license, and for kidding me for a few weeks that his license was on the way, I did not pay my last bill of 25 pounds. The woman involved, i.e. the dead horses, was headline news about six months later in the News of the World. She was strangled by her solicitor while making love on a carpet in her own kitchen.

Taffy Williams, the stable boy, he later became a very successful young trainer told me himself that while he was a stable boy with Harry, used to make love to this woman in the stable's loose boxes, he said she could never get enough sex.

With Betty Bayne the filly, I put her away until she was three years old and unofficially leased her to Tot Kelso, to whom I had sold Prince Ahmed, the trainer then was an ex-jump jockey named Tommy Cook, he could get a horse fit and ready, he started training at Clifton Hill Stables, Penrith, the stables left behind by Tommy Dent. Cook never got very far, his downfall was beer, once he started in a pub, that was it. He got Betty Bayne fit, raced her at Beverley, she finished about fifth or sixth after trailing along almost last for most of the way, then at Haydock beaten a short head the horse that beat her, I think was Black Strap, quite a good horse, after that, it was decided by Tot Kelso to run her in the three-year-old hurdles, she was schooled but not too well over hurdles at Penrith, then ran in a three-year-old hurdle at Carlisle where she ran fourth taking it 'easy', we knew after the jockey got off that we had rather a good thing and that in a re run, she could easily beat the other three and go on to top three-year-old hurdle races. Unfortunately, as Robbie Burns said, "The best-laid plans of mice and men gang oft algae."

For the next day, the filly was lame on her near fore, her knee slightly swollen but not really bad. I took her home after a few days and had her x-rayed by MacMillan, the vet. The plate came up very clearly, showing a piece of bone chip floating just on the front of the knee, I thought that looked easy to take out and asked the vet straight away to operate and remove the bone chips. He said it was impossible to operate on a knee, all the joints, oil would come out, etc. I decided to send her to Alex Tully, the vet near Kelso in Scotland, Alex was supposed to be the ultimate in horse vets, off I set with a land rover and trailer. Alex looked at the knee, I explained about the x-ray plate, he said to leave the horse to me, so I left the filly at Alex's place and came home. A week or two afterwards, I phoned Alex, he told me the filly was ready to come home, so I set off again with the land rover and trailer. I had a look at the filly and was tremendously disappointed to see the same knee had been pin fired, with no operation to remove the bone chip at all. I tried the filly again after a year layoff and put her with John Dixon of Wigton, but after two weeks of training, she became lame again.

12

Bill MacGillevray and I decided to go to the motor show and dairy show in London in 1954. These events coincided with the running of the Cambridgeshire at Newmarket, which I had been to a few times before on similar trips to the motor show. We set off on 26th October after seeing a few friends and having market day drinks at Penrith, staying as usual at the George Hotel, Stamford Bridge, a lovely old place and well-run with good food. Some friends from Kent who had been racing at Kelso were also staying. We had a merry night, setting off after a big breakfast to Newmarket, this Cambridgeshire meeting was always well attended, a horse named Minstrel won. I didn't back it but made a little money in the crowds and hurrying at one time, I collided with that portly actor gentleman Robert Morley, he was not amused, I apologized, he grunted.

After racing, we collected my car, which was the Morris Oxford chick van, I did not own a car, from the car park and set off for London, we had gone only perhaps half a mile when there in front of us was Prince Ras Monolulu, whom we had talked to earlier in the day when he was selling tips, but we did not buy because he was asking too much or so we thought. There he was, ostrich head feathers still flying on his head, he was hitching a lift so we stopped and picked him up and started talking, he was a colourful figure, the first time I had heard about him was when he attended the funeral of Lord Lonsdale, the Yellow Earl. In the car, I found he was very coarse and vulgar, talked most of the time, for some reason, about his wives, how he had always kept them well fucked. He said that was the best way to keep wives quiet, he was possibly right, but I did not like this man's mentality at all, I cannot remember where we dropped him off, which we eventually did and then went to stay at the Russel Hotel, parking the car on the curbside, going round the little park-like place in the centre of the square.

That first night we dined at Scott's with our friends who

had been racing with us at Kelso, Mr and Mrs. Mike Young, Mike was one of nature's gentlemen, he had been a shepherd in New Zealand and was now a tenant farmer with a large concern at Littlebourne in Kent, his wife, Vida was alright so long as she was the only woman in the party, Mike had made a tidy sum at Newmarket so treated Bill and I to dinner, I note we had oysters and a magnum of champagne, what we had in between, I did not make a note of, except we finished with liqueurs, myself having a Drambuie, the total cost was 17 pounds, those were the days when money was real, we often dined at Scott's because it was always excellent, a friendly atmosphere and staff.

After dinner, Mike and Vida went to the Russel to imbibe with more Northeners. Bill decided he wanted a girl to have sex with, so he and I went up Old Compton St, Soho, to see what we could find, sure enough, there were plenty of girls in doorways, I thought, what do we say, I had never faced a prostitute before, in the end, we decided to be bold, so I went first to ask the nearest one, "how much dear," she said 3 pounds, I was amazed at such a high price and told her she was asking too much, in any case, I did not care for her looks. Bill asked if the next one, she too, was 3 pounds, he thought it a bit steep. We persevered and asked more girls, then we thought, what if we get one each at the same time and go in a different direction, where would we meet, we decided outside a nearby restaurant called Beguinos, by now, we had got around to girls charging 2 pounds which was better. We thought 1 pound would be a fair deal, so we now tried bartering the girls down, we succeeded almost simultaneously and off we went with our sex mates, my girl was perhaps twenty-one years old, with my friendly chatter, she seemed to lose a bit of that hardness that is in a prostitutes makeup, she told me she had a little girl of three years, condoms were issued by a 'maid' in a back room. The girl's room was only about 100 yards from where I'd picked her up, we had sex on her divan bed, taking my time. When we had finished, I said I would see her tomorrow night as my friend and I were staying a few days, she said she would be in the same place, then I set off to find Bill. There he was outside the Beguinos, waiting impatiently, he said he had finished quickly, too quickly, he told me his girl had been so-so and had offered oral sex for a pound extra which he declined. Before I forget, my girl also promised oral sex for one pound extra which I also declined, I told him my girl had been quite a friendly one.

The next day we went to the dairy show, this event was always a splendid well-run affair. Mike and Vida knew many people and exhibitors, so once again, it was a vast round of drinking with all of these newfound friends. At night Bill and I dined at Beguinos Restaurant in Old Compton St, I had previously dined here in the year Airborne won St Leger with Father Wilson and his boyfriend, Jim Peel, that then was my first visit to London, Beguinos then was old-fashioned French restaurant, very good food, in those difficult years where one could dine at the long communal tables which we chose, or a usual table to seat four, the waiters were oldish but good, they had aprons down to their toes, the vicar he'd known the restaurant from his student days.

Now next door to Beguinos, either due to bomb damage or demolition, were small hut-like places, two of which were used by prostitutes, I know because I was in one of them three days later.

Before we dined that night after the dairy show, Bill and I decided we should hunt for our prostitute friends, sure enough, there was my girl. I asked if she was free, she replied she was and off I went with her, she was more friendly than before, she said I could take my time which I did, she told me more about her life, then she had to go back to her 'patch', I waited for Bill for maybe fifteen minutes, I thought he must have got lost, then he turned up, it had taken him a little while to get a girl, he said she was not bad, I told him mine was just right, then he asks me, did I mind if he could have her after we dined, of course, you can, I said, what a friend gets is never lost. We had a good meal with a good bottle of Bordeaux, finishing off with a couple of large brandies, then we went for the girls, my usual one was quite pleased she now had Bill. I looked about and saw a very large girl built like an Amazon. I thought, *try her*. I've never had a big girl like this one, I approached her, she wanted 2 pounds. I thought, *well, we are in holiday, it would save me hunting further afield* and I agreed and followed her to her room. She stripped off, my word, she was a strong one, her legs were as thick as my waist, she put the condom on me then we got down to work. All of a sudden, there was laughter behind the far room. I asked who it was, it was her 'maid', as all of these girls called these women, myself in full work on top of this woman Tarzan, was put right off. I was no longer interested, I stopped and dressed, said nothing and left. For five days, Bill and I had one girl before dinner and one after, coming home on Sunday, we knew we had thoroughly enjoyed ourselves. The final full day, Saturday, I went to see my Aunt May Lancaster, her husband, Uncle Joe, had been managing director of Harvey Nichols, Aunt May, in the war years, came to live with my grandmother (fathers mother) at Hayton near Carlisle bringing with her, her personal maid and her own cook, they were now living with grandmother, three maids to look after two old women, to escape the bombing. Just as well because, in her absence, a bomb demolished her house and the whole of the contents.

Her maid Rose and the cook, whom we always just called 'Cook,' were still with her at St Mary Abbots Court, London, they stayed with Aunt May all their lives until my Aunt died a good few years later.

I was always amazed at Aunt May's bed and how she got into it, as the bed itself must have been about four feet from the ground, I thought if she fell out of it, she would surely break her neck, it was an old fashioned iron framed one when she died she left me a push tie pin with opal on top, and a ring, together with a huge silver rose bowl, my sister collared the rose bowl, I gave Mother the ring and the pin who in turn gave them to my sister who in her turn gave them to her son and daughter, they 'lost' or sold them.

I have mentioned Kelso races before, the highlight was the big race dance held in one of the halls in Kelso, that was when there was a Friday and Saturday meeting, the dances were held on Friday nights, I remember one such meeting and dance, Jimmy Power had that year won the Grand National on Freebooter, I think the owner was Mrs Brotherton in 1950 with Wot-No-Sun second with AP Thompson up. They were all at the dance, I was friendly with and knew most of them, another was Tommy Foran, who rode the odd one for me later on. We all congratulated Jimmy Power, many thought his legs were too short to make a good Grand National jockey, but he rode and won. He was a very nice young chap and a good rider, but of them all, and I would rate him better than most today, was Arthur Thompson (A.P.). He was an extra super jockey, an extremely strong jockey, and fearless. He rode a lot for Neville Crump and Stuart White. I have seen Arthur from one of these dances take and carry bodily two girls, one under each arm, no legs touching the ground, to bed. He was as strong as an ox and a tremendously kind and likeable man as one would ever meet, he rode many winners. Many of us were staying at the Cross Keys Hotel, the manager then, I think, was a man called Staples (or Stables), a very nice chap.

The night wore on, Tommy Foran and I had palled up for the night; however, after seeing our respective girls off, with kisses only, he and I set off to walk the short distance across the square to the Cross Keys, I pressed the bell for the night porter, waited a bit, rang again—no reply only silence, so we took it in turns to press the bell for minutes at a time. I decided then, while Tommy was ringing, I would kick the door as hard as I could, which I did, kicking backward with my slender shoes. After half an hour, a voice from the other side started shouting, an Irish voice, a voice as drunk as only the Irish can get. He would murder us if we did not stop ringing. We told him as calmly as we could (we did not fancy facing a ferocious drunken Irishman at this time of night) that we were staying in the hotel, it did not seem to register with this monster behind the door, the more we explained, the worse he became, so I decided to continue kicking the door and Tommy to keep ringing the bell, we now had had enough, and were ready for him if he decided to have a go, this went on for another fifteen minutes or more, then amidst the hullabaloo, a female voice came through to us, asking what we were doing, we explained and thanked goodness, the bolts were withdrawn and the door opened, it was the receptionist/secretary in her nightdress, she had at long last heard the commotion, the night porter, could hardly stand up, yet he still kept uttering threats, he would have been easy to overcome, the trouble was, he kept the door between us closed. After, we went to our rooms, and in the morning, we were both served a huge breakfast in bed, with the compliments of the manager, who apologized for our ordeal at the hands of his Irishman.

There was, during racing then, a whisky distiller called Campbell, he had a horse named Eastern Way, I have not made a note in my diary of the name, but it is near enough, this horse almost always won at Carlisle and always at a decent price on the books. For myself, Eastern Way was a good money maker. Mr. Campbell was or really had been a character, he was an old man when I got to know him.

One day when he was ill, his doctor asked him how many bottles a day of whisky did he drink. One look at him and anyone could tell he was a big drinker, Mr Campbell replied four bottles, the doctor then said, you must cut it down by half, his patient said he would do so when the doctor left, he chuckled and boasted to his friends, recounting the doctors' visit saying he had never drunk four bottles a day that was for the doctors benefit, he was now drinking as he always had, two bottles a day. Towards the end, when he went racing, he had a nurse with him, taking his arm most of the time, he became very frail and the nurse had to go with him to the gent's toilet to help him, even to take his dickie out for a pee. To drink two bottles of whisky a day can become very easy, as by now, 1950, I could and very often did consume two bottles in a night, a long night drinking and dining, I could outdrink most men those days.

Bridget's father was hard to beat, but halfway through a Tuesday or Friday's hard-drinking session, he would go to sleep, wake up an hour later, be refreshed and start again. I was never rolling on the floor drunk or falling off my chair, I was sober, but I suppose pickled. Bridget's father possibly saved the rest of my life for me when one hard day drinking, he said to me, Joey, you like whisky, but you want to do as I do, take plenty of water with it (he himself really drowned his whisky) otherwise you will not reach forty, I thought of this and decided to do as he advised, adding more water to my drinks as before I had added very little water, over the next few months, I put as much water in my whisky as he himself, though when I married, I cut down on drinking quite a lot. I remember going to Llandudno with the Carlisle Cricket Club to play as a reserve. My friend Tom Park invited me to stay at the St Georges Hotel. I knew many of the team. I drove four of them down in an old Ford V8 coupe I had bought a month or so before, rather a smart car too, but hard to start sometimes. Quite a few of the team were reckoned to be hard drinkers, I found them not too strong in this line and on the second night, I offered 5 pounds and then 10 pounds to any of them who could out-drink me. This was when I could knock two bottles back without trouble. I had no takers at all. This was all done in a quiet way, no noise and shouting like the young of today who seem to do little else but shout and cause trouble, if they smell a glass of beer today, they are drunk on the smell.

The barman in St George, on our final day there, said to me, Mr. Slack, I have never seen a person drink so much as you and remain a perfect gentleman, I thought this to be most kind, after breakfast when we were leaving, the manageress came to me and in front of all the team and residents, planted a big kiss on each of my cheeks, she said that was for being her perfect and favourite guest, these were her very words, again I was most pleased, yet taken aback, for I was not acting, I always played myself as I was.

Some of the nicest trainers I have had contact with then was, besides the ones already mentioned, Kenneth Oliver from near Hawick, we used to call him the Benign Bishop, he had a beaming pink face and was always ready to crack a joke, a very good amateur rider, tremendous drinker and a very good trainer, I remember when he had ridden the winner of the Heart of All England hunter chase at Hexham, he gave a dinner which he invited me to (at the George Hotel, Chollerford, this then was a Swallow Hotel owned by Wing Commander Peter Vaux's family). It was a super place to go after the races at Hexham, all the racing crowd went there, the food was good and the staff were excellent. Ken had won the race and a beautiful big silver cup went with it. The cup was duly filled with brandy and champagne, Ken having a first drink at the head of the table, the cup being so large a rim, much of the contents ran down his neck, the outside that is, I well remember the second man to drink was Arthur Elliot, Uncle Arthur as he was known by all and sundry, a sheep farmer in a big way, now he would be 70 years old, at his age Uncle Arthur was a fearsome whisky drinker and could knock two bottles back as if it were milk. His wife used to drive him, I once had a lift with him to Chollerford from Hexham and I was rather scared, his wife, an extremely nice person, could also knock a few whisky off, but she trembled terribly, especially her head, in fact, shook like a leaf. When I saw her take the wheel this particular time, I couldn't believe my eyes, I thought, if Uncle Arthur had no qualms, who am I to say so, we arrived very well. Now it was Uncle Arthur drinking from the silver cup and we all had to shout at him to stop, he was intent on draining it, outside as well as inside, he was wet to his navel and the cup held five to six bottles, there were twenty of us at the table. I had seen Ken Oliver like this the night before a race meeting when he was riding. Get up and ride a couple of winners and start again.

Ken was also an excellent auctioneer of livestock, at his auction mart at Hawick to the bloodstock at Doncaster, I and many others preferred their horses to go under his personal hammer.

At one of these bloodstock sales, I arrived and had forgotten to reserve a room at Punch's as they were all filled up, my friend, Tony Collins of the book publishing firm, was there with his greyhound, Murphy, the latter seemed to go everywhere with him, Tony heard of my predicament and offered me his room but to sleep on the floor with Murphy. I agreed and the management gave me plenty of bed clothes and pillows, as the night wore on, Tony suggested we turn in, so we did, I bedded down between Tony's bed and the wall with the door at my head, Murphy beside me on the bedside, but on the floor.

I was most comfortable but had a rude awakening in the morning when a room waiter knocked (I heard nothing) and opened the door with too much flourish and got me on the back of my head, at the same time almost falling over me, sleep or lie in were then off the agenda, Tony then took Murphy for his walk. I remember a hilarious night also at Punch's, on this particular day at the sales (Doncaster), it was an N.H sale of jumpers and potential jumpers, the Irish had quite a few to sell and there was judged to be done, also by the Irish, many of the top trainers, I cannot recall all of their names.

The day opened very wet. Indeed, my friend from Newmarket, Di Haynes, was there with a very good-looking mare, a four-year-old I think it was. I told Di she would win first prize and she did. Di herself was and still is, a very beautiful blonde, full of vitality in more ways than one, she was the daughter of Thompson Jones, the Newmarket trainer, I could never get her on her own. Someone was always in the way. With me, it was Hamish Alexander who bought foals and sold them as yearlings, he started buying in his career, foals for

300-400 guineas, he was her present bedmate. The rain poured down in torrents, I lent Di my waterproof overalls, judging by the Irish of the various classes was put off for an hour, everyone retired to the bars, which made a roaring trade, whisky going down in bucketfuls, one of the top Newmarket trainers Fulk Walyn I think it was, wanted a puff or two on my Scotts No.1 Burma Cheroot, which I let him have for a while, until looking from a veranda, he said the trees in front were leaning over too much, then he was pleased to give it back.

The hour for judging came up, still it was pouring, so the judges put things off for another half hour, again everyone retired to the bars, by now, the judges were beyond the point of no return. Drink had taken over, however after the latter half hour, still pouring, they realized they would have to get down to it, which they did, in a very intoxicated state but full of good humour. As the day drew on, more and more whisky was consumed at the end of the sales, trainers, owners and old Tom Cobbley adjourned to the Punch's Hotel. Dinner time came, Hamish, Di, myself and a few trainers, perhaps eight, at our table, our neighbours the Irish judges and trainers were in tip-top form, rather too much so for the manager, whom all and sundry regarded as a no-good wimp, decided the Irish table of about twelve, told them there was no food for them that night and took the table cloth at its four corners and whipped it off, with all of the cutlery and side plates in it like a sack and off with it to the kitchen, but he had not gone two yards before one of the Irishmen picked up their table bodily and threw it on top of the manager. Everyone, including my table and others who had witnessed all of this, thought the manager deserved it, however, the table throwing really put the cat among the pigeons, in no time, the place was full of police, the manager threw the Irishmen out of the hotel although they had reserved rooms for another day and night, anyone who muttered loudly as we did on the Irishmen's behalf was threatened with the same fate.

The behaviour of the Irish was only a bit of loud joking and bantering and was in no way upsetting for the other guests, in fact, all or 99% of the guests were friends of the Irish, who included the most famous names in the horse world, they spend many hundreds of pounds in Punch's, it was the manager at fault with a big F.

By now May 1950, Star had her second foal to the local stallion What-a-Lad, a big bay colt too big for the little mare, an ugly foal, he would not lead for a long time at weaning, he would plant his feet four square, neck outstretched and squeal, the more we would pull him the more he squealed, he eventually did lead in a fashion. Reva had her second foal by What A Lad, quite a nice sort but not the best of movers when at a canter, so I decided to sell them both as foals at Stockton sales in 1952, I duly arrived as usual, with a land rover and Robert Jackson's horse trailer boxed the foals and booked myself in at the Corporation Hotel, Middlesbrough where Esther was the receptionist. A friend, George Bate, was also staying there. George was a top man of the Rubbery Owen organization, whom were the biggest sponsors of the British Motor Car Racing team, Formula 1, I think it was.

George had a bottle of rum with him, so in retiring for the night, he brought his bottle with him. I had hardly tasted rum before, in any case, George and I finished the bottle off, in the morning, I had a terrible hangover, a few big hammers in my head going at it fast and furious, firstly I had to pick Esther up at her house then on to the sales complex, i.e. the racecourse.

Esther's mother opened the door to a bleary-eyed so-and-so. Esther hesitated before she made her mind up to come with me, we arrived at the sales, I was by now more hung over than ever, so I hired two men to walk and show off the foals in the sales ring after I had hired the men, off Esther and I went for coffee, this did me a lot of good and an hour later I was back to my old self.

The first of the foals of mine into the ring out of Reva made 25 guineas, it was, on the whole, a poor sale, but I let it go, then the foal out of Star came in, he was like a little mule to look at, he was bid to 5 guineas, I could not let him go so I took him home, later I took Esther back to the hotel for her duty roster, put the foal in the trailer and set off for home.

Three weeks later, I was in the Crown Hotel at Eamont Bridge, there was a farmer I knew quite well, Jos Bowness, who was keen on N.H. racing. He had, I think, his permit to race under N.H. rules. He had a few horses and a few wins and was a gambler. Over many whisky's I described the foal out of Star, Jos by now was well on the way, he knew Star from flapping days and bought the foal for 35 pounds, the date was 28th April 1952, I delivered the foal to Jos's farm, Low Wool Oaks, outside Penrith by the land rover, I saw Jos one week later, he exploded with, "What the bloody hell is that thing you left at my farm last week." He shouted, "You've bloody done me."

I told him, "Well, you bought him and paid for him, so now he's yours," then Jos laughed.

He said, "You, sharp devil, I'll not forget this." He never did forget either because in a short time, the ugly duckling turned into a beautiful swan as a three-year-old, Jos entered the, by now gelding, I think he named the horse Cliburn Lad thought I'm not certain, not having made a note of it, in a three-year-old hurdle at Sedgefield, the horse was only out for a 'feeler', as Jos was a gambler, the jockey could hardly stop the horse from winning and managed to pull back to finish in fourth place. Jos was beside himself with joy after the jockey had told him how good the horse was, and to cap it all off, Verely Bewicke, one of the north's top trainers, came up to Jos and offered him 1000 guineas there and then, Jos refused, not bad for Star's foal, from 5 guineas to 1000 guineas. Jos entered the horse three weeks later, again in a three-year-old hurdle and had a bet of 4000 pounds on him, halfway through the race, he took a hurdle wrong-footed, put a leg through the hurdle, came down and finished up with a broken shoulder and had to be put down, it really was extremely hard and bad luck for such a promising young horse.

Jos himself was heartbroken for the horse's sake, not his lost bet, Jos was a good loser as far as bets went, he never cried over them but invited all of his friends for drinks as if he had had a big win. The next time I saw Jos, he said, get that mare Star in foal and I'll give anything you ask for the foal, sadly Star would not breed again, she remained barren. Esther went on to marry her footballer friend, Ugolini.

I had lost my driving licence in 1953, just coming out of the entrance to Newcastle races. I had Marilyn, my current girlfriend and an elderly retired farmer, whom I had given a lift from the races just to the main entrance where he got out, I was about to drive away when a policeman came out of nowhere and told me I was booked for driving under the influence, I was most surprised because I was not drunk or wobbling about, in any case, I had to go to the police station where I was told I could choose my own doctor, I knew no doctor in Newcastle but chose one at random from their list, I chose a Dr Kopelwitz, he came and gave me various things to do which I did, he thought for a moment and then said don't drive for an hour or two, with that I was put in a cell, Marilyn in the car outside.

Three hours later, the policeman in charge came for me, let me out and we had a bit of a chat, he gave me a mug of tea and then I got in the car and drove to Marilyn's home. I was not charged with drunk driving but with having consumed alcohol while in charge of a car and was banned for a year.

I made friends later with a few of the police and they told me I had been shopped by a racing man, I cast my mind back three weeks before the incident at Newcastle and came to the conclusion that a chap I had met once or twice before was the one to blame. This man, he called himself in the racing world, Lord Harkess, which was a complete fabrication. I had given this man a lift from Stockton races to the Corporation Hotel in Middlesbrough. I had Marilyn with me, we had one drink in the place, but 'Harkess' was well in his cups and starting to be nasty, I told him I was going now, but he wanted me to take him to the station in Stockton, I said I would as it was not out of my way, outside the hotel my car was in a side road just beside the hotel, 'Harkess' went first, there was a policeman passing, 'Harkess' pounced on him and pointing at me said to the PC, "This man is drunk."

The policeman looked at me and asked what is the number of my car. Like a flash, I told him JRW 201, he looked, then asked me, looking at 'Harkess', "Do you want me to book him?" I hesitated, then said, "No." We got into the car, turned toward Stockton, and halfway over the causeway, 'Harkess' became very nasty and vulgar, so I stopped the car and put him out onto the road.

The next meeting where I saw but ignored him was in Newcastle, where I was 'shopped'. I am sure it was him, especially after the police had told me, "I was shopped by a racing man."

In 1953 there was held at Morecombe in Lancs. the big annual hunt ball and Miss Ullswater's title, proceeds to go to the Ullswater Foxhounds, one joint master was the Hon. Anthony Lowther, whom I got to know quite well, he was the brother of the Earl of Lonsdale. When he was in the army and stationed at Barnard Castle, he and a few of his officer pals, one was Captain Sam Simmonds, who became well known by the farming community, used to come at weekends to the Crown Hotel Eamont Bridge, we used to play 'spoof' five or more would gather around a table and each could have in his hand a maximum of three coins or none, then all hands with money or none were placed on the table, each person, in turn, would guess what he thought would be the true number of coins shown, when all had guessed the call, show hands was made, all hands open to show the number of coins. The one to guess correctly dropped out and so on, until only two players were left. The one to lose of the final two persons paid the full round of drinks for the rest of the players.

West Tinniswood, the owner of the hotel and I were the

best players by far, he and I always dropped out early in any play, one Saturday night Anthony Lowther and three of his officer pals sat down with us to play, West, myself and four others, six players all up, West and I drank free up to midnight then Anthony said, "Let's play for a bottle of champers!" We all agreed and by 2 am, West and I had won 8 bottles of champagne then play stopped. The champagne was to be drunk at 10 am, by now, that day Sunday, I got home, went to feed the turnips to the sheep after just three hours of sleep, I was cutting and feeding the turnips by myself as Len, the shepherd, was off ill, I never got to help drink that champagne, West told me it tasted very good.

The Miss Ullswater title was for the prettiest girl, as I had no licence to drive and the local villages had organized a coach, I thought for a bit of fun I would go on the bus to this hunt ball, which I did, getting on outside the Skirwith pub, the Sun Inn, I knew most of the lads and lassies who were also going. I hadn't been on a bus for years, it was grand fun, we arrived at Morecombe, I believe the ball was held in the Winter Gardens, a big crowd was already there. I headed off with three or four lads I knew well to the nearest bar, we drank steadily then went dancing, there must have been 3-400 people there, the Miss Ullswater girl was chosen. I did not know her, but she was very pretty. In no time, it was home time, we loaded onto the bus, as we go on, I spotted a rather pretty girl with a woman which I took to be her mother, and she was, I introduced myself and asked for the mother if I may sit with her daughter, sportingly she said, of course, I could and mother moved to another seat with friends of hers, this girl whose name was Pat, Pat Woodrow and I got on well, in fact, I kissed her all the way home, made plans to meet for the following weekend, Pat lived with her mother in a large house they were renting at Melmerby, her father was a ship Captain in the Merchant Navy and was away for long periods.

The next Sunday night, I had made a rendezvous with Pat to meet in the George Hotel. She had a job in town, Penrith, as a dress shop assistant, I had to ask one of the farm men to act as chauffeur to take me into town and if I could get a lift to the girl's home with friends okay if not I would get in touch with, it was usually Joe Frith, Dad's tractor driver, he was a grand solid chap, always obliging, this sort of thing in transport worked well over the next few months. The strange thing was, with close neighbours and friends like Robert Jackson, etc., not one of them over the next twelve months even offered to give me a lift or phone me to ask if they could help out, if racing or going to hunt balls, it was only Bobby Dickson of motor car fame, who phoned and offered at all times, I did not like to bother him as he lived at Carlisle which was 26 miles away. Such are neighbours and what one thinks are good friends, when wanted, they turn away. Dad's farm men were wonderful.

I was many times at races and even the hunt ball at Lockerbie, of which I took the train, Carlisle and Hexham races also where I would meet various neighbours including Robert Jackson, of the latter, I would have thought better, no apologies were ever offered.

I courted Pat for a month before I made a move to make sexual love to her, but she would have none of it, I could barely put my hand on her knee and that was as far as I got, I respected her for this, but it did not stop me from trying, still always the same response, I treated her always very gently. We got on fine together and nearly always being driven by Joe Frith or others of Dad's men. At the County Hotel, Dave, who was one of the chief waiters and then had charge of his own bar at the hotel, of which Pat and I were his first customers, he called her The Pocket Venus as she was only 5ft 2in and very well proportioned.

On Friday, 20th August, my Aunt Hilda came up from Wales, she is the one built like a tank. A huge snob, wife of Alex, sister of my father, a very bossy woman, she and her sister Connie had tried their best to ostracize my mother when she was newly married (they also looked down on mother), for this,

I was never in love with my father's sisters, Aunt Hilda was staying at the George Hotel in Penrith and on this evening father, mother and myself went to the George to have dinner with her, after dinner, we retired to the resident's lounge for coffee, during coffee, my thoughts were just idling along, taking no part in the conversation when of a sudden my eyes went very clear. My ears pricked up, my thoughts changed from idling into a surge of blood—hot blood; a small group of six young foreign students entered the lounge and took seats 3 yards away, my eyes were entranced by one of those students.

She was superbly beautiful, dark-haired, slim, a face of sculptured symmetry, perfection, beautiful, aristocratic, slender nose, I could not take my eyes off her. We sat facing each other; I raised my eyebrows and slowly winked at her. She responded by putting her tongue out at me, I could not help but smile, I tried again, she responded again by putting her tongue out, but this time pulling a rude face at me. A few minutes later, she left the room, I thought perhaps for the powder room, I waited a few seconds, then made an excuse to my parents and followed after her, she was nowhere to be seen, I bumped into Leslie Walker, the manager, I asked, Leslie, have you seen a very good looking young girl come out of the Residents Lounge, he said yes, he had, adding that she had gone to bed, he laughed adding I know what you are after. I asked him who and what are they, he told me they were French students from Oran in Algeria and that they were here for only the next day and night, leaving for London on Sunday 22nd. I returned to my parent's table then started thinking about where Oran was, when I got home, out came the school atlas. I soon located it and realized this was where Winston Churchill had ordered the Royal Navy to sink the French fleet in the war, it seemed a long way on the atlas, north Africa, Beau Gueste country.

The next day I realized I had some growing pullets to be delivered at about four different farms in the Lake District, I was determined to meet this beautiful creature on the morrow.

I was up at 3 am, drove the delivery van (the new Morris Ox) to the rearing field, caught the poultry, 200 at 8 weeks old and back to the farm, changed into some clean, decent clothes and set off to deliver at two farms near Ullswater, two farms in Keswick, in fact, 6 miles the far side of Keswick. I got these jobs done and headed back to the George Hotel to find Leslie, the manager, and Bridget's father, in the cubby hole lounge having coffee and sandwiches for breakfast, they were surprised and said so at seeing me so early, it was only 7.30 am, Bridget's father asked what I was doing so early, Leslie said I think I know why and they invited me to join them for coffee which I did, now the little lounge faced looking up the main staircase, I could see everyone coming down, we three having coffee, started conversing when my heart took a big jump. There she was, descending the staircase alone, I did not waste a second, in mid-conversation, I did not even excuse myself to my two coffee drinkers, I got to the bottom of the stairs before this beauty, who made my blood run wild, I know only one or two words in French, my first being 'excuse moi mademoiselle' could I talk a few moments with you, she said oui, pouqoi's pas, I motioned to a settee in a quiet corner, I studied this wonderfully beautiful face for a few moments, she had soft brown eyes that during our conversation I could see also held a lot of humour, her facial bone structure was classic, her mouth generous and wide, showing beautiful white even teeth, her lips were like the rest... perfect, what had I discovered, I invited her for a day round the lakes, she said she was unable to do so as she had to go with the group and they, were going round the lakes. Our conversation was in schoolboy French and she the same in English, however, progress was being made. I asked her her name, it came from her tongue like liquid velvet, Monique—Monique Salcedo, I told her, like the old pattern, but meaning it from my heart, a beautiful name for a most beautiful girl, a hint of a smile only. I asked her her age, seventeen, she replied. I then asked Monique to dine with me this night, she said she was unable to do that as she had to dine with the group, I told her I understood, but after dinner, could I take her up the lakeside, UIllswater, for a drink, she said she would like that very much. At that moment, the group leader and chaperone combined were calling the students together for their tour of the lakes and in minutes, they were off in the longest bus seen in Penrith, the local rag, the Herald, did a big write-up of it.

When the students had left, I went to look for Leslie, the manager. I told him that this young lady that I was interested in was unable to dine with me as she had to dine with the group in the hotel. I asked him to reserve me a table immediately beside theirs so that I had her in my eyes at all times, I was taking no chances.

I now had the day to myself, I went home and saw that all was well, cleaned the Morris Oxford van out until it was spotless inside and out, it had a bench seat which made it better for courting, no—not for sex, as the reader would immediately jump to, but to hold and sit near one's girl, instead of two seat miles apart.

I was in the George Hotel at 6 pm, the French students had not returned, they were due about 7-7:30 pm, I chatted with various people until Leslie came and told me they had arrived, I presented myself to Monique to let her know I was there, we sat for a while on the same settee, while she told me of her day's outing, at that moment, Pat Woodrow and her mother passed by, Pat looked me straight in the eye and carried on, confound me I had arranged earlier in the week to meet her this night in the George, I apologized later for this ungentlemanly act.

Monique then went upstairs to shower and dine, by the time I went upstairs, the students were at their places. Dolly, the head waitress, had had her orders from Leslie, she had a table for me to perfection, only feet away from this thoroughbred creature whom I was determined to be with. I was also determined that this lovely young woman would be my wife. Some of the students were now quite openly whispering and casting glances over to me, they had seen me with Monique twice and now here I was in close proximity to all. They sensed something was in the air, Dolly herself served me as she had done so many times, her eyes were sparkling with amusement for she knew what was in the air, one could say it was hunting. After dinner, Monique joined me for coffee in the main lounge, then we set off in my chicken van for Pooley Bridge, this village lay at the foot of Lake Ullswater.

Monique did not say a word about being driven in a van and I made no false excuses, I was me and that was enough.

We went for drinks at the Sun Hotel in Pooley Bridge, Monique ordered a lime juice and asked if she could have a cigarette, as I had only cigars, I asked what sort she preferred, she replied, Craven A, I bought a packet of '20s, Monique took one out, I studied her for a while, I gave her a light and realized she had never before smoked anything, after two or three puffs the cigarette was stubbed out in the ashtray, my lovely companion, I thought, was trying to be a girl of the world, sort of thing–growing up—so the cigarettes. We started to converse and bit by bit, things fell into place for both of us.

Monique's mother had died when she herself was three years old, also she had a brother aged two years old who had died in Tunisia. Her mother had followed her soldier husband to barracks in Tunisia, where there were no proper facilities for illnesses. Monique herself was brought up by her aunt, her mother's sister and it was the husband of this aunt whose bus had brought them to England. She was at school in a convent, failed her exams so they packed her off, as punishment on this bus tour of Spain, Portugal, France, England and Scotland, I thought to myself, some punishment, she told me of Portugal, how poor the populace looked, but Lisbon I was told, was very nice. When at school, she being a day girl in Oran, lived with her aunt and uncle. They had two children of their own, a boy Paul, aged twenty-five and a daughter Rene aged twenty-seven, I was to meet these people later on. We finished our drinks, up to now, I had had only one whisky, I was being a good boy and drove to the Queens Hotel at Tirril, this was always a popular place for the young set, but the hotel owner was rather a sour puss, I forget his name, always at closing time at 10:30 pm, this was Westmoreland, Cumb was 10:00 pm closing, he would come amongst the customers—dead on time, with his glass collecting tray, and demand one's glass—on the spot, once, for some reason, I had an almost full pint of beer—I must have been thirsty, for I seldom drink beer, and he demanded the glass of beer, or drink it in one second, I gave him his beer—poured it into his tray, it almost floated, he could not believe what had happened, I turned and left him—he never uttered a word, and neither did I. This is where I took Monique, she wished to have a coffee, I could scarcely believe my own voice when I asked the barman for two coffees, he even repeated it back to me, I suppose to make certain he had heard right.

We had a small table for two in a corner, at one stage, my left hand and her right hand were at the same time on this little table, all at once, as 'if our hands had thoughts of their own.' They met and clasped simultaneously, we looked directly into each other's eyes. I think from that moment, we both knew we were meant for each other, the unspoken word of great love. We left the hotel bar at 10:30 pm before old sour puss came round to disturb my mind, got into the Morris Oxford and started to drive towards Penrith, which was now only 4 miles away.

I pulled into a quiet small roadway place, switched off the engine and took Monique in my arms and kissed her passionately, I had never been more passionate than this night, Monique responded in a more restrained and quiet way eventually, as young bloods do when passion rules, I moved to seduce Monique, she restrained me in a gentle and ladylike way, I immediately respected her feelings then we talked of love, I asked her to marry me, she said yes she would, but at the same time she had to prepare her aunt and uncle as she was only seventeen years old, I said I understood perfectly. I took Monique to the main door of the George Hotel, rang the bell for the night porter and we parted, but before we parted, Monique had given me a list of the stops they would make en route back to Oran and for how long at each place. These I noted down.

The bus was leaving at 7 am the next morning, so I was up at 5:30 am and at 6 am I rang the main florist in Penrith, Mr Hird of Hird Bros, and by chance, I got him. I told him I wanted him to pick 17 pink carnations, that was Monique's favourite colour she had told me, and to deliver them to the George Hotel before 7 am to a Miss Monique Salcedo, with all my love, Joey. He said he would, Leslie the manager told me later the flowers had been delivered as the bus was just starting to move out of the hotel garage, he himself jumped into the bus and presented Monique with my bouquet, I was most pleased.

Here I was. I had known a young woman—still at school—known her for a maximum of four hours, proposed marriage and been accepted, had I gone mad—no it was reality and another thing that did matter, I was madly in love at twenty-seven years of age, love had come to roost in my heart.

Monique's next stop was in London, for three days, the group were staying at Halliday Hall, Clapham Common, I ordered a bouquet of 17 pink carnations (one for each of her seventeen years) to be sent each day to Monique, adding all my love, Joey, this was all taken care of by my good friend Mr Hird, the florist.

I decided that I had to see Monique once more before she left England, I wanted to take her into London and let her choose an engagement ring, I set off from Carlisle on the Midnight Express to Euston, the same time and line and stations my brother Adam had taken, I called on Bill MacGillvay at Scotby for a chat, had a quiet drink with him and his wife, told him of my plans, he thought I was crazy. I caught the train, my pockets stuffed with wads of white 5-pound notes and sat back, dozing off now and then. On arrival at Euston on

Wednesday morning, 25th August 1954, I hailed a taxi, told him where to go, it was a good distance from Clapham Common, costing a pound. When the taxi drew up at Halliday Hall, the big French bus was outside ticking over, students were going in and out of the building to the bus. I inquired about Monique from one of them and waited for a couple of minutes, then there she was, I asked her to come with me into town to choose a ring, she explained the bus was leaving within minutes and that it was impossible to do so, we had perhaps ten minutes together before the students were called on to enter the bus. I kissed Monique lightly and they left, she told me she had received the carnations each day, she also said she had quite a lot of leg pulling from her companions on the bus. I was in two minds to go to Paris but thought better of it, I had work to do, also my passport was at home in Cumberland.

In 1954, I decided to go and see Heinz in Germany, we had written to each other at least twice a month since he left England as a prisoner of war, he in his letters begged me to visit him to give, as he put it, some measure of the hospitality he had received at Skirwith Hall. As I had no car of my own just then, only the post office chicken delivery van, I did not take delivery of the Morris Oxford until later. Mother lent me her Standard 10 Saloon, which was named Henrietta, I asked the AA to give me a route map to Lymne airport in Kent, where I booked a flight over to Calais, I wish I had now not done so because I considered on afterthought, the AA had given me a very roundabout way or very zig zag way to go. I set off on 14th September 1954, being directed to Tilbury through a maze of little roads arriving there at 5 pm. Then to take a ferry over to Gravesend, when I got to within one mile of Lymne airport, I booked into a little roadway café at 7:15 pm. The woman owner was very homely and kind, everything was spotlessly clean, I asked if I may have a bath and she said certainly, I had a good soak feeling much refreshed after the long journey in a small car. I had not pushed it at all, in those days the roads were all just two-way traffic, the old A1 going through every village and town, no by-passes these roads of old plus the ancient villages and old towns, countryside unspoilt, made travelling by car most interesting, no one was in a hurry.

I drove to Lymne airport fifteen minutes past noon on 16th September 1954, an official drove the car up the ramp onto the plane, there were only, I think four cars on board. The plane dropped down at Calais at 12.45 into a grass field and went over a pool of water which splashed mud over the small porthole window I was looking out of, it was very windy I remember, but I have no recollections of customs at all.

I had an AA road map from Calais to Telgte, Heinz's town going through Dunkirk—Ostend, Antwerp, at Antwerp, Belgium and Dutch customs, Hertogenbosch, Arnhem, Hengelo, to Dutch and German customs at Glanerbrucke, then onto Langethorst, then Munster—Telgte—a distance from Calais of 334 miles, passing through Antwerp at 5:30 pm which I found to be very busy, driving on the right-hand side of the road I found was no trouble, in fact, I was beginning to prefer it to the English left side. I stopped about 8 miles through Antwerp at a small village, St Antonus, Brecht, the hotel was called 'de Witte Merel' the white blackbird, I had not eaten all day, but I had not been hungry, now I had stopped, I was feeling a bit peckish. I found the owner and his daughter quite kind, speaking some English. After a hot shower, I was more relaxed and lit a Burma Cheroot and settled down at the bar for a few whiskies before eating. My host and his daughter were very talkative, I invited them both to have a drink, my mistake, out came a bottle of champagne for themselves, I think I had eight whisky's before dinner, eating with a bottle of wine, I finished my meal and was bidding goodnight to the owner and his daughter when I was presented with the bill which in sterling added up to 25 pounds, I told the owner this was scandalous and would not pay such a large sum, we had some heated words, then he sent the waiter away, he, reappearing with my suitcases which would be confiscated if I did not pay, this was the first time I had been swindled and since then, I have been swindled by most foreigners, the worst being the Belgium's and second, the French-Italian cross breed, never by the English, I had of course to pay the hotelier the 25 pounds, it was fortunate that I had quite a large sum on my person in 5 pound notes, white notes, and was able to pay, others might not have been so fortunate, I thought pity the English soldiers never shot the sod when they came through in 1945.

I set off in the morning, I did not bid any goodbyes to the hotel people, I had taken quite a dislike to the Belgians. Henrietta was running well, petrol was also lasting very economical, I thought, having tanked up outside Lymne. We, Henrietta and I, passed through Jachtlust and Nijmegen. There had been rain in the night and most of the streets, being cobbled and very uneven, could be quite slippery, so I took care. These streets being so slippery brought me in mind Lord Lonsdale's sister, Anne, being killed about a year ago in a car accident on streets like this, her car, or the other, had skidded into one another, she was a lovely girl, a good sport, blonde, tall and slim, she more like her brother Anthony that her other brother, The Earl who was short and dark.

At about 11 am, I entered Germany at Gronau, I thought to myself, now I am in Hitler's Reich and could visualize his soldiers and tanks rolling over the plains here. Though I passed quite a few wooded sections, many or most of the houses were pockmarked with bullet holes, most likely machine gun fire and, in Germany, signs of utter demolition in the towns and villages. I thought our boys had done a good job of knocking the Nazis about a bit, I passed through Munster, the town before Telgte, this place had really taken a pasting from both bombs and artillery. I noticed hardly any motor cars in Germany and what vehicles there were, were military. I drove along quietly at 40-45mph taking stock of the countryside, the farmers were at work in the fields ploughing with horses, one farmer had a horse and oxen yoked together ploughing, it was horses all the way, they seemed to have plenty of these and quite a few oxen pulling their old fashioned wagons with high sides and very large iron-clad wheels.

All of a sudden Henrietta cuts out, she had run so well, I looked at the petrol gauge I had forgotten, in my interest in the countryside, to think about petrol, the tank was empty, I thought, you silly fool, I was on a longish straight section of road, only 3-4 miles from Telgte when the engine cut out, I had automatically pulled onto the roadside, I saw a small military car coming along, only perhaps a couple of minutes from Henrietta's cutting out, heading towards Telgte, I waved the driver down, two young English officers were inside and I explained what had happened, one of them said hop in, we'll take you to a petrol station in Telgte, and they did. One of them explained in German what had happened to me, I could speak no German, hardly one or two words and that was it. The garage man was busy with repairs to an old tractor, in the meantime, I asked where Einener Str was from an oldish woman and gathered that this street where Heinz lived was over the river and on the right-hand side. After this piece of information, I could understand no more. I waited half an hour for the garage chap to make his mind up to take me back to Henrietta, he was making no move, so I tried to explain I had to go now, not later, he understood so he got a gallon tin, filled it with petrol and drove me out to give Henrietta her drink, I had no German money on me and told him who I was staying with, he again seemed to understand, said I would pay him tomorrow, he saw me started, off I went, so did he. Heinz had not had the phone installed then; otherwise, it would have been much more simple to have phoned him from the garage. When he used to phone me, he always rang from his local pub.

I drove into Telgte, past the symbol of the town, a large oak tree just inside the entrance to the town, it had survived the shells and bombs, I stopped in the town centre and tried asking the way again, I had the same directions as before, but this time I was pointed towards the river, then I know I had to turn right after that take pot luck or ask again and show the name and address of Heinz on a piece of paper. I duly came to the bridge over the river Ems, this is a very slow-moving river, the land for miles being very flat, the flatness was broken by many pieces of woodland. There was a road to the right about 200 yards past the bridge, I thought that must be it and bull's eye, there was the street name Einenerstr. Now only to look for the number, I now realized I was on the other side of Telgte in a suburb going out into the country, quite a nice country-looking street, I was very near Heinz's number 25, so stopped the car and got out. I had gone maybe 15 yards when I was met by a bald-headed, thin man with a little girl holding his hand, it was Heinz.

We had a big hug together, the blood brothers had met at last, it was good to be together again, I parked Henrietta in his driveway beside his house, which was really an apartment in a block of seven or eight others in the same building, his being in the second floor, the third floor was the top, he showed me to my room which looked right onto the pub thirty yards away, this was fine, couldn't be better. I met Maria, Heinz's wife who could not do enough for me, this little daughter of four Margaret and his eldest son, just a few months old, Ludwig, Heinz filled me in what had been happening, how he was so thin because of so little money for food, different to Skirwith Hall, with all those eggs and milk and the rabbits, he sighed, he had become a master electrician, the exams he had to pass were long, hard and exacting.

He was at the same time working very hard as an electrician for a small firm, these two things coupled together made him collapse at his work one day with a suspected stomach ulcer and he was hospitalized, the burst ulcer was a false alarm fortunately, the crux of the matter was very long working hours, doing overtime for more money plus his exams, he was completely run down. Now he knew I was coming, he asked for his annual holidays and got them. His flat was very small but Maria, like most German house fraus was, and everything was spotlessly clean, she was also a very good cook, there was no running hot water to wash in, only cold taps. To heat the water for drinking, there was a big metal jug. One had to place an electric screw-shaped element in it and switch it on to boil, the cooker was like a pot-bellied stove, fuelled with wood and you cooked on the open top. So to shave and have hot water for the coffee, the jug and an electric plunger.

Heinz that night played his zither, we had a few bottles of beer in his little living room and we talked and talked, of old times, of dancing at the Drill Hall, Penrith, the old blue girl (Ford V8) now converted into a school taxi, Father Wilson and old Joe Varty. He had fallen in love with life at Skirwith and of the English themselves, but he said his place was here in Germany to help build it up again.

Next day Heinz said, "Let's leave the car and go on bicycles." He had two of them, off we went through tracks in the woods, where I saw quite a few roe deer, calling at a hotel in the middle of these woods called the Valdhutte Hotel very luxurious and rustic inside. We sank a few beers, then on again to our local, the one I could see from my bedroom window and was introduced to my host, Emil Koling and his wife, Mitze. They were to be my very good friends for many more years, also their two sons, Hans Joachim and Wolfgang, especially the former, as the latter was a schoolboy when I first knew him. I was that little bit too old for him, here, Emil had heard of me, Heinz had given me an exceptionally good pedigree.

Emil was, like other publicans, I was to discover, to hold a good supply of cigars of various sizes and prices from 20fg—80fg. I tried them out and found the 40 fg black Sumatra ones were very good value. Indeed, Heinz liked the 25 Fenning ones, but they had quite a lot of yellow powder on them, which was not nice. I did not care for them. Emil soon discovered he had a cigar smoker in the house because I was never without one, he was most surprised at the quantity I got through. I think in English money, my 40fg worked out at 7d each, I was in Clover, beer per glass was the equivalent of 6d, schnapps,

Emil kept Heinz and I supplied free gratis after taking us into his cellar to drink straight out of, what we would in England call, a grey hen, a grey hen is a stone jar holding anything from a gallon to two gallons.

Before I had left England, Heinz had asked me to bring some coffee beans for his parents. I bought 14 pounds of black beans, the best, from J & J Grahams of Penrith, putting them into a small Air Lingus holdall bag. We went round to his parents who lived in town to say hello and present them with the coffee beans, when I opened up the holdall, the poor old people could not believe their eyes, it seemed good beans were very scarce and very expensive, for these oldies it was Eldorado, myself, I was most touched at the tears in their eyes, out came the beer and schnapps, all German houses seemed to have cases and cases of beer. I had heard from Heinz that his father liked cigars and smoked on Sundays, often 15-20 (the German cigar burns more quickly than the Havana's). I presented him with 50 Burma Cheroots. I had brought a 100 with me for my own use, not knowing that cigars were two a penny, so to speak, in Germany.

The parents of Heinz, I suppose, like many others in town, had worked it to the full, a large allotment of an acre or perhaps more, they grew a great many potatoes also for other members of the family. Heinz had two brothers living in Telgte, one had been killed in Denmark in the war. Also in the allotment were apple and cherry trees and quite a lot of various vegetables, all dug by hand and the potatoes and fruit, all carted to the home by a hand cart on foot. Heinz suggested he show me a little bit of his country, so one day, we set off in Henrietta, himself, Maria and Hans, one of his brothers, and myself. Hans, Heinz had warned me he was anti-British, he had to be dropped off en route at a place near Koblenz, on the way, we called in at Cologne to see the Cathedral, a really magnificent place only slightly damaged by bombs, in photos taken at the end of the war this building seemed to be the only place standing—even now the devastation was terrific, I, to myself imagined the terror of these raids on the populace, it must have been hell on earth.

It was this Cathedral, quite a few years later, when my wife and I were looking through this magnificent building, she said to me, look there is Ritchard Dimblby, I went over and introduced ourselves and had a long chat together, he was a charming fellow, I think he would have been most displeased with his son, trapping Prince Charles into making that 'infamous' interview on tape.

After Cologne, we motored on to Bonn to see the Bundeshaus of Mr Adenhauer, who was president. Then, I found Bonn to be a charming little place, sitting on the river or Fatti Rhine, as the Germans call it. We went into the Bundeshaus, very simple but at the same time precise, with a huge German Eagle on the wall looking down at the members of the German Parliament.

The Rhineland here is very beautiful with its vineyards and the vines heavy with grapes. We had travelled, mostly on main and country roads, taking the autobahn only for a short time. There were quite a few stretches of the autobahn under repair, I should think, due to bombing or the severe strain on them in the war years. I was amazed at the thickness of the base of them, looking to me as if it was 3-4 feet thick before the tarmac or cement was laid.

We headed for Bad Ems on the Lahn on the 20th of September which was not far from Koblenz and hunted for a place to stay the night. Heinz chose a B&B owned by a war widow, she was a very kind soul, big and busty, she made us most welcome. The trouble was she had only one room and bed, but the bed was so large it would have held five people. So we decided to take it. The room looked over onto an orchard with a few hens running about, she gave us a key in case we were late in. She had a garage for Henrietta, so I put her in and we went on foot around the town. We quickly started sampling the wine and very good stuff it was, Heinz would ask the Kellermeister in a few of the places to bring us his recommendation, this way, we had some really good wine if we asked for a glass of wine, a huge glass was presented.

We were in bed by midnight; our landlady must have gone to bed because all was quiet, only the hall light beaming for us, which on our way upstairs, we switched off. We had brought two bottles of wine to bed and proceeded to polish them off before sleeping. When we did get to bed, Maria was on the outside, Heinz in the middle and me beside Heinz, after about an hour, I felt not too well and was going to be sick. I did not want to start looking around the house for the w.c. Anyway, I had forgotten where it was, I was by now very ready to be sick, so I opened the window and vomited into the orchard, in the morning, we all awoke feeling quite fit and ready for another day, it was sunny already, a nice day ahead weather wise, I opened the window and leant out taking good big lung fulls of air, looked down below and there were six to seven hens having their breakfast on some of the remains of my supper, I said to Heinz the eggs here would taste a bit funny this week, Maria pulled a face as if to say, no eggs for me downstairs, and she didn't either.

Our landlady made us a breakfast of all sorts of different meats including black pudding and eggs, I had never eaten black pudding for breakfast before, but when in Rome, sort of thing. We said our goodbyes and left in Henrietta, driving through the Westerwald and then through the Sauwerland. Heinz knew of a cave into the hills that had stalagmites at Iserlohn called The Dekkenhole, this was most interesting for me, a guide took us along with a small party of about twelve people, it was quite a long cave.

We arrived back at Telgte on 21st at 7 pm going straight to our host Emil to quench our thirst with his beer. Emil sold "Thier" beer, brewed in Dortmund, why his beer was so good, better than any others in Telgte and of the same name, was that his beer pumps were cleaned out scrupulously every night after the last customer went then in the morning he would swish through it at 7 am, his whole family was cleanliness itself, even Heinz said in all the town of 40 odd pubs, Emil's was by far the best. We left at 1 am after Emil had played for me many times on the piano, one of my favourite pieces, The Bacharolle from The Tales of Hoffman, he was quite a gifted pianist and played this piece beautifully.

The next day we visited the British and German war cemeteries, Heinz laid a rose on the grave of a British soldier, myself, a rose on a German one. The German military war dead were buried in a complete place of nature, under the trees in a wooded area, here and there, with a multitude of red squirrels playing in the trees overhead, it was indeed a peaceful but sad place.

Afterwards, we went to the canal to see barges going through the Locks near Muntser, a most interesting place for me, I had never seen this sort of transport before, one or two of the barges had a small car on board, but mostly they had two or three bicycles on deck, their small living quarters nicely curtained. In the evening, we went to the British NAFE for some English beer Heinz wanted to try again, in we went and Heinz said to me to try and pay with a five-pound note, I did, but they would not or could not accept the note, I believe I finished up paying in small change or small notes, we had about ten beers then went to the British cinema, Heinz wanted a taste of England I suppose. On the way home, we stopped off at Emil's and stayed there until 3 am, Emil was busy on the piano, he used to lock his doors at midnight, stopping more customers coming in, but those in could stay till morning if Emil was in the mood.

The English one pound went so far, the goods were so cheap that I could live like a king, we later bought bottles of German champagne to mix with our Pils, we seldom drank beer as such, always Pilsner, the champagne mixed well with it at only about 3 shillings per bottle.

On the next morning, Heinz wanted me to go to a place called Rhotenfelde, to see the salt hedges there, these hedges were hedges, as such, about 30 feet high with salt water dripping continuously through them, with this, the twigs and branches were coated in salt, one might almost say, like Lots wife, instead of pillars of salt, they were solid hedges of salt, the air also smelled very clean and healthy. These hedges, I cannot remember if there were two or three lines of them, but in length, they must have been 500 yards long. There were ponies and traps trotting around the length and down the other side with visitors, quite a busy place.

In the afternoon, we motored over to Detmold to see the Statue of Herman, Hermanstenkmaal—he was the one who defeated and drove the Roman Legions out of Germany, it was very big indeed made of bronze, the figure of Herman, being 27 metres high and his sword 7 metres long. The RAF must have had a few shots at him because he had quite a few bullet holes in him, then it turned to heavy rain. We set off for home, calling here and there for a few beers and, later, a good meal of pork cooked by Maria. This was the 26th. On the 27th Heinz had to be back at work, a little sooner than he intended, I went over to see Emil at 10 am after breakfast of two boiled eggs and newly baked Brodschen's with coffee.

Emil knew that Heinz had gone back to work, so he took over to be my host for a day, we set off in Henrietta, he and I then went round to numerous villages, tried all the pubs. Emil would not let me pay for a single thing, at each pub, he would tell the landlord to get his best cigars out, schnapps and beer, they flowed freely. Emil would have a drink for a drink then he had an idea, in one village he had known it must have been either before the war or during it, this particular village had a house of prostitutes, all inspected by the doctor once a week, he asked if his idea was good, I told him it was a first-class idea so off we set for this particular village, the name I forget, but we duly arrived travelling about 20 miles, into the nearest pub for refreshments, Emil asked where exactly the girlie house was, the landlord being very new in the area didn't know. We went outside and Emil asked a few passers-by, even young women. Eventually, we learned the place didn't exist anymore,

Emil was most disappointed. We set off towards Telgte, calling at every pub on the way. By the time we reached our destination, we were quite happy, Frau Koling was rather stern, but Emil was past caring.

Heinz's parents came to say goodbye to me on my last night together with his brothers. Bernard, his other brother, the anti-British one, Hans, did not come, the one I gave a lift to Koblenz. Bernard was a nice quiet chap, he had been taken prisoner by the Russians and had only been freed in the previous six months, he had not been well treated with the result he had to have an operation to remove some ribs that showed signs of TB, it took him a good few months before he got his strength and health back.

We smoked a few cigars, drank many bottles of wine and when I said goodbye to Heinz's father, he had tears in his eyes, he himself was an old soldier from World War I. Heinz's mother was of another character, kind but severe, I remember Heinz telling me that once when he went home on leave from the Russian Front, his mother would not let him enter the house, she smacked his face and told him to disrobe outside, she suspected lice in his clothes, asked him to change (is one thing I thought but to slap his face was another) his clothes, she was the strong one of the two, her doing most of the digging and work on their big allotment, the year after, Heinz's father died.

On 1st October, I left Heinz and Telgte, before doing so, I bought 500 cigars from a man who also became a good friend over the years, he was Sepple Poppenborg, his real first name was Joseph, but to everyone, he was Seppl, he supplied all, or most of the cigarette machines in pubs and hotels for miles around with cigarettes, filling them each week, or on demand, empty the machines of their money, this seemed to be all in one DM piece coins.

Seppl would sit at the table with a pile of money in front of him, he would never look at the money he was counting, he grabbed a handful of coins and slid so many between three fingers and thumb of his left hand, and put small piles, each of 10 DM at one side, at the same time carrying on a conversation with anyone, he never made a mistake, his hands were almost machine-like, he also supplied pubs and hotels with cigars. He always had a beaming smile, at this particular time, he had not a tobacconist shop, all his stock was in a room at his house, where I went to choose my cigars. I had a pleasant surprise, for this room was stacked around the four walls to the ceiling, I chose 200 Schwarze Weisheit, black ones, 200 Sumatra Felhfarben and 100 others of light brown leaf, all at 40ph. Seppl gave me 5% off, and for luck, he gave me 25 cigars of his best at 50ph. This was the start of a long association with Seppl and his cigars, I put them in the bottom of my suitcase except for 100, all of these were in boxes of 50, except for the present from my new friend, Heinz and he had been schoolboy friends in Telgte.

 I arrived at Calais Airport—if one could call it that! To find that the plane ferries had stopped ferrying cars over, either for a few weeks or for the rest of the season, I was informed to go back to Le Touquet, which was 50 miles away, the Calais people said they would phone Le Touquet for me, to let them know I was on the way, I got to Le Touquet in the hour and asked a young boy where the airport was, he gave me good direction, and I was quickly there. The authorities were most kind, Calais had phoned them, so they had very kindly kept the ferry plane waiting for me, in minutes I was aboard and off. We landed at Lymn, formalities were non-existent, I was out on the road with Henrietta and my 500 cigars within minutes, I stayed the night halfway between Lymn and London, had a good meal, no wine, coffee and a cigar, then bed, I was ready for a good sleep. I was up at 7:00 am, but had to wait until 8.00am for breakfast, and was back home by 6:00 pm 6th October. This little holiday, meeting my blood brother Heinz, and seeing how the foreigners lived—quite a different style of life, the countryside, food etc. had been a most interesting one, I had enjoyed myself, now it was time for work again.

All of this time, I had been sending Monique, three times a week at her home in Bd Magenta—Oran, a big bouquet of pink carnations, through the hands of my friend Mr Hird, her Aunt Josephine and Uncle Pineda, were still on holiday in France, where they went each year for three months, the Aunt to take care of her varicose veined legs which were terrible. In the meantime, Monique was boarded out to another Aunt in Oran, the apartment in Bd Magenta was locked up, but visited a few times a week by their daughter Rene, whom, later on, I arranged for her to be shot. However, all of the carnations sent to this apartment, it turned out later, finished up in the dustbin, thrown there by Rene until her parents came back from France, and when they did, Monique moved in once again to live with them, it was only then that Rene boasted to her parents in front of Monique, that "all these stupid flowers coming for her"—meaning Monique had gone into the bin. That was the first Monique had heard of flowers for her, had been arriving, and had never been told about it for three weeks. This, I was not to know until later, so the bouquets continued to arrive, but were treated properly and arranged around the apartment. Monique, after her 'parents' had arrived back from France, had told them about me, that we wished to marry, she told me they could not believe her, asking—Why him? As they had an eye on a young up and coming motor car salesman with his own small garage, I met this person later that year, he was indeed a nice young man—but Monique was determined, it was me she had chosen. We started to write to each other, my letters to her, of course, were in English, hers to me, in very quaint English, by studying the English-French dictionary, I still have them all.

In the beginning of November '54, I had a letter—in English, again rather quaint, from her 'parent uncle' to ask my intentions, and if I was serious—to give him some background of myself. I replied immediately, keeping the carnations flowing. I think it was this flow of flowers that helped the day for me, especially when they (parents) knew the flowers had been arriving for many weeks.

On 24th November, I had another letter from Monsieur Pineda (uncle's parent) saying he gave me his blessing for our marriage. Monique told me later that her uncle had also made enquiries through Barclays Bank about my family, he received a favourable reply, so this was it—Marriage! I told my parents, Dad asked me if I was sure of myself, I let him know I was, Monique's letters now came to me at the rate of three to four a week. I asked Bill MacGillvray to go with me as best man, he said he would be delighted. The next day he phoned me to tell me his wife, Sylvia, would not let him go. He was as disappointed as me because we were really good friends.

13

I now had everything ready to take off to Algeria, including a return ticket booked form the little travel agency in Binns shop, Carlisle, for the cost of 60 pounds on December 6th, I set off by train from Carlisle for London on arrival at Euston. I went straight to the Russel Hotel and asked for a room, but all rooms were taken. It was Smithfield Show Week, and the Russel was full of farmers from the north of England. I went to the dining room for breakfast and ran into Willie Lancaster, a farmer and sheep grader for the M.A.F. he came from Culgaith, the next village to Skirwith. I knew Willie well, so did my father, Willie, like all members of his family, was a fair and straight man—honest and well-liked by most who knew him, his first words to me were, "What are you doing here, Joey? I didn't see you last night." I did not mention marriage, only that I have a little business to see to. I mentioned that I had just arrived that morning and that the hotel was full. Never mind, he said, one of my friends had not come with me, you can have his bed in my room. I thanked him, we ate breakfast together, then we both left for the show after telling a porter to take my suitcase to Willie's room.

Later in the day, I took a taxi to London Airport, it was the first time I had been to so big a one, the plane left late, arriving in Paris at 11:00pm after a bumpy ride. The officials after I had asked what my connection was, where and when I was told I would have to spend the night in Paris, I thought—good heavens, how am I going to get there and back the next day for the flight, don't worry I was told, we will take care of everything. I was put in an Airport taxi by myself and taken to a decent-sized hotel, the taxi driver told me he would pick me up at 7:00am the next morning and I was given a first-class room, the hotel staff looked after me extremely well, at that late hour, I had an excellent dinner, a bottle of wine, followed by coffee and cognac, I did not smoke, as by now it was late indeed, and I was now tired.

At 6:00 am, I was downstairs and surprised to see the odd waiter about. One of them asked if I would like petit dejeuner. I said, Oui merci. I was given and enormous cup of café au lait and croissants.

Promptly, at 7:00 am, the taxi arrived for me. I thanked the staff and left—I thought Air France provided a very good service for its passengers; England to North Africa, taxis, food (all paid for) and the cost re- turn 60 pounds, these were the days when money had real value—no plastic cards! Either hard cash or traveller's cheques.

In the airport, I listened as hard as I could to the tannoy on plane times and places, nervously realising I could not understand it with the rest of the noise of the airport hustle and bustle. Everyone I asked did not seem to understand me, and as far as I can remember, I saw no flight boards anywhere. I decided to try and 'train' my ears once again to the tannoy. I tried to shut out all other noises. It seemed to work. After a little while, I began to pick out place names, times and gate numbers. I could not hear the name, Oran, as the English would see it and pronounce it. All of a sudden, I had it! The French pronounced it Orong, of this, I was sure. I made a mental not of the gate number, and went along, presented my ticket, and put it with a small group of people. I must now be okay, I thought. After a while, the group, which had grown bigger, was ushered onto a bus on the tarmac and taken to the plane, where we all entered.

Crossing over the range of mountains to the south of France, we were heading and landing at Marseille. The flight became very bumpy indeed. A woman opposite me, over the aisle, took hold of a paper bag and started to be sick into it. I looked away myself, watching her, was becoming a bit queasy! I thought of worse things and the feeling started to go away, but the bumpy ride seemed to get worse!

We landed at Marienanne Airport, Marseilles, somewhere about 10:30 am, all passengers had to disembark, the weather was, I thought for December, quite warm and the smell was quite different from the one at Paris, and here the people were Latin, with quite a lot of Arabs. At about 11:00 am, I had (with others) to board another plane. I heard passengers (handing their passports and papers to the ticket and police office) say, on being handed them backrest tout, the officer would reply—oui, I thought I would follow suit when my turn came, and I had my passport returned, I said, cest tout, and had the correct reply—oui. A few buses were being loaded up to take passengers to the plane, which turned out to be a massive one, shaped like a great whale, with four enormous petrol engines, the passengers entered this massive construction, which turned out to have two storeys, downstairs, where all the Arabs were directed—except for, what seemed to be, the well dressed and rich ones—all Europeans on the level deck as we walked in. It was a most comfortable place, with big seats and plenty of legroom. In no time, the plane was full, I do not know how many it held, but it seemed like quite a lot! The pilot taxied to the take-off end of the runway and waited a while for orders, the huge engines pulling hard. It took quite a while to reach her flight path height (which did not seem high compared to modern planes). I had a window, watching the last bit of land pass by, then the sea, meal time came, and the food was excellent—with a small bottle of wine thrown in.

At 3:00 pm, the plane landed at Oran Airport, and there waiting for me was my future bride Monique, looking absolutely radiant. I thought—I have chosen well! Her Aunt 'mother' was there with her. I was ushered out to the car, a Plymouth, with the family chauffer—Antoine Padilla, and off to Bd Magneta. Monique explained that I first had to go to the Grand Hotel in Oran, where a room was reserved for me. I dropped my suitcase off and went with her to meet the rest of the family. Monsieur Pineda was a nice gentlemanly sort of chap – small, his wife Josephine, seemed to be not a bad sort, Paul, their son, also seemed to be alright, a bit big headed I thought, his wife Odette, or rather, at that time his mis- tress, with his child – a boy. Paul had been married to Lillian Savelle, the heiress to the Courvoisier Brandy fortune, but the two divorced. I was also introduced, that night at dinner, to the Pineda's daughter Rene and her husband Raymond (but was known to everyone as Gaby). I did not take to. She had a bitter look on her face. Her husband, I took to right away, he was an extremely nice man, but his wife, I could see, wore the trousers.

The dinner was a superb affair, the ladies of the house had prepared a sumptuous meal with many bottles of champagne and excellent wines, and cognac. I think they were surprised at the quantity I drank without moving a hair! Rounding off with my big Havana cigars, only Gaby smoked one and soon gave up, as it proved too big! The men were cigarette smokers, especially Mr Pineda—almost a chain smoker of Bastos.

I was driven back to my hotel by Gaby after midnight. I was now ready for a good sleep. I woke pretty soon, 7:00 am, to another hot day and went out onto the balcony, which looked across the road into a square where a few Arabs were lounging about. A few children (Arabs) started to look up at my balcony, which was on the first floor. I threw them a few French coins, in no time, there were about fifteen of them, so I threw them some more. Cars were unable to pass, the drivers getting really angry—horns blowing like mad! I thought I had better stop the coin game, but the children thought otherwise and shouted for a long time for more.

Monique told Padilla to take us to the family villa at Bousfer, a pretty big villa where the French windows spewed onto the beach and sea. Later, it was here that I learned to swim. I used to see the children at three or four years old, swimming like a fish—and myself, at twenty-seven years old, couldn't do a stroke! I thought—you stupid article! And started to teach me. I pretty soon got the hang of it and became reasonably good.

After lunch, Mr Pineda—with Monique and I were chauffeured to one of his garages of S.O.T.A.C. in the town, where I met two of his partners, Mr Journot and Mr Ferrara, the latter also an Algerian member of the French Parliament. The garage was quite a big one. Then I was taken to see his new garage being built on the outskirts of the city, an immense affair, self-contained, except for the manufacture of engines, planned by him personally, within a solid wall 20 ft high. At the moment, he ran about 130 buses, his main route being the Corniche, worked for Air France and one of his main money spinners was a convoy of from 12 to 15 coaches full of Arabs going to pray at Mecca, the coaches going the whole way with a lorry in the convoy of with spare parts for everything, engines, etc., going by way of Suez, and other coaches doing tours of Europe, similar to the one Monique had been on, above the new garage, with a bird's eye view over all below, he had built for himself and family, a penthouse flat of great luxury—all floors laid with marble, and for the workers, he had a bar built for them next to the spare parts department, all drinks had to be bought, but at pure cost—only pennies, this was for aperitif time, and knocking off time.

There were many Spanish workers and quite a few Arabs, together with the French, Oran itself had a big influx of Spanish-speaking population, and it came quite easily to Monique—her second tongue.

On Sunday, December 12th, Paul, Gaby, George Cohen (Mr Pineda's personal secretary) and myself set off for Algiers by car. The barren countryside was interesting to me, passing small villages of Arabs with their flat-topped houses. We also passed, I think it was, Philipville, which had been devastated a few weeks before by an earthquake. The population was housed in Army tents, it had been raining the night before we set off, and some biggish pools of water were here and there en route—quite often, a single Arab, or a group, would be passing these pools on foot, Paul driving, would deliberately drive at speed straight through these pools, drenching the Arabs from head to foot, I would look out of the back window to see the drenched Arabs waving their fists, and mouthing curses in great fury! No wonder many Arabs hated the French!

Our journey to Algiers was to do with marriage papers, I cannot remember exactly what, but I had to visit the English Consul and French authorities also. George saw everything, in the evening we dined and wined very well, then went to see a film. I remember it was called 'La belle Ottero.' Monday, we returned to Oran. The same evening Paul, his mistress Odette, Gaby with his wife, Monique and I went night clubbing where I met a funny little man, Bebert, who was a photographer, he took a few photos of us, Paul drinking champagne from the open toe of Odette's shoe—which I thought a bit dirty, I didn't like the look of her shoes!

On the way back, they dropped me off at my hotel. I got out, it was 2 am. Monique was on the pavement. I gathered her in my arms and lifted her bodily off the ground. We entered the Hotel foyer and went towards the lift. The Arab night porter ran to open the lift, up we went, the lift door was easily opened, then I put Monique on her feet and said, "Come into my room, I have something for you." She hesitated, then entered, I took my sports jacket from the wardrobe, cut a little hole in the lining, and out popped the ring I had bought for her at Grants Jewellers, Carlisle, our delayed engagement ring. I slipped it onto her finger. It fitted perfectly, she was enchanted with it, and I was with her. We kissed, then I took her down to the others in the foyer. They were beginning to think I had taken Monique to bed! When they saw the ring, they realised I was quite a straight fellow. The odd one out was Rene—jealousy raised her head.

On the 15th, Monique and I were chauffeured to have a look at some more of the countryside, this time a bit inland, we headed out to Sidi bel Abbess, the headquarters of the French Foreign Legion, perhaps 4-5 miles out from this town, I saw two separate groups, a mile apart, comprising of one group of 4 Legionnaires, the other of 6—each with an N.C.O. escort, under what looked like punishment duty (or fatigues), these Soldiers were piled high with equipment, rifles, packs, the lot—under a hot sun fully clothed from head to foot, marching but a very slow march, perhaps they'd been for miles, with the weight of the equipment, plus clothed as they were, and the heat—even a couple of miles must have been awful.

The town of Sidi bel Abbess, more or less, a glorified big village, with the Legionnaire fort on a slight rise looking pretty grim, right out of Beau Gueste. I was told it was not safe to even go to the cinema, as one was almost inevitably sexually assaulted. I told the chauffeur to stop at a little bar so we could have a cold beer—himself excluded, this we did, casting my eye about, I thought Sid bel Abbess a dirty place, but there is no doubt her Legionnaires have done a lot of hard, and tough, fighting for France—giving their all.

Monique told me that she did not want me to wear my tailed wedding suit, she told me that no one did so out there. Now I had nothing to be married in. Mr Pineda sent me, with Monique, to his tailor Brougere. He was a jovial little man and had with him his mistress, an Arab woman. Monique told me Paul had seen him, at his favourite party piece, putting his finger into the vagina of this Arab woman and licking on it, on and on. None of the females of the Pineda's family would go to him to be measured for trousers, they had to at one time, but his inside leg measurements were an embarrassment. I picked a soft, dark brown cloth with a stripe of soft black in it—not really my taste, but for me, he had not a lot of choice. I was measured, and in between this and that, Brougere asked what I would like to drink. I told him I would like a whisky, which was soon produced, we drank each others health, he told me to come back later that afternoon for a fitting, which I did. All seemed well with his measurements; he said the suit would be ready in the morning, and it was.

A knock on my bedroom door at 7:30am—there stood Blas, the little odd job man at the Pineda's, he had a lame twisted foot—Blas, he did the shopping at the fish market and ran errands, etc., and he stank! It was no good getting too near him. I should think he had never washed for the last few years. But he was a happy little chap and doted on the family, he was married and also had an Arab mistress. I never met her, but it makes the mind boggle!

December 16th was the big day for Monique and I. At 8:00 am, Paddilla came to pick me up. I was dressed in my new suit made by Mr Brougere, I mounted the stairs to Pineda's flat—where all members of the family were present, I did a lot of handshakings, kissed my bride-to-be, she looked absolutely beautiful in a powder blue costume with a full pleated skirt, and a little blue hat, shaped rather like a butterfly, we had some champagne and descended to the cars.

We both entered the Plymouth car and drove to Marie, the others followed behind. For best man, I was asked to choose, if I so wished, either Paul or Gaby; I chose Paul. It seemed by French Law, it was obligatory to be married by the Mayor in the town hall (Marie)—a civil ceremony.

At 10:00am, we were ushered into the presence of His Majesty the Mayor, we shook hands, everyone arranged themselves, and the ceremony began. I was rather surprised at the shortness of the whole thing, I cannot remember exactly how long, but it seemed no sooner that it started than it was over. We came out of the Marie after signing the register etc., and there was Bebert, the photographer who spoke little English, he was another happy little man, always in the same baggy brown suit, he arranged the family and Monique and I for photo's, then said to me, "Take your weef." He meant to put your hand around your wife's waist. I did as he said, he also had, without me seeing, had taken photos of the ceremony with the Mayor, which turned out to be quite good.

From the Marie, the cavalcade drove to the Church, Mr Pineda had, with great understanding, asked me the day before which denomination of church I wished to be married in—Catholic or Protestant. I had seen enough in Ireland how the Catholic priests preyed on their people and lived on the fat of the land to distrust them emphatically, I had replied that I preferred Protestant and thanked him for giving me a choice, and that is where we went.

Arriving at the church, I went first with Paul to the Alter steps, Monique came a few minutes later on the arm of her Uncle. It was he who gave her away, we both sat in chairs before the priest and were married. Bebert is taking photos right and left! The register was duly signed by those concerned, then guests, about 30 or 40, I think, drove to Le Belvedere, the best restaurant in the area, I was told. Monique and I were chauffeured there by the faithful Padilla.

A scrumptious wedding breakfast was served, with champagne for guests as they arrived, dozens of bottles and very fine wines for the meal. Various speeches were made by various guests. I did not reply, except to thank them, as no one could speak or understand English! Later in the day, I sent my mother a telegram in our pre-arranged code that Monique was now my bride, Ma then telephoned the local newspaper, The Weekly Cumb, and West Herald, for the marriage to be in their marriage column for Saturday, which the Editor did on so short a notice.

At five in the evening, Monique and I decided to call it a day, it had been rather a hectic week for quite a few of us. I shook hands all around and bade everyone bye-bye. Padilla was waiting to take us to our hotel, a suite being reserved for us, arranged by Mr Pineda—and paid for by him. The hotel was the Windsor (or Winsor), a good hotel, we went straight to our rooms. Monique was so shy, she went into the bathroom to undress and locked the door! I smiled to myself. I was in my pyjama trousers, a very light pair, when she came out in the see-through nightdress that reached her ankles, she had, I saw, kept her panties on, she was extremely shy, I looked and saw how lovely she was, and also, what a beautiful figure she had, like a slender young deer just into maturity, she got into bed quickly, I followed, we kissed and cuddled, I made to move to make love to her, but she said she was frightened— would I wait, I said, of course, I would, my bride was a virgin, a great rarity these days, and practically nonexistent at marriage nowadays!

I was enchanted with my little dove, as I was to call her over the years, we talked, and kissed, and held each other and fell asleep. In the morning, we had breakfast on the bedroom balcony in wonderful sunshine. After this, I sent down for a bottle of champagne, which we drank slowly until 11:00am. Padilla arrived at 11:30am to take us to lunch at Bd Magenta. Paul and Gaby dropped sly hints about lovemaking last night. Monique put everyone right, saying I was not a brute like... she named a friend of the family, who had been married two months previously... he had forcibly made love to his new bride, frightening her to death, that gave them room for thought!

In the afternoon, Padilla drove my bride and I to the office of Air France, where I paid for Monique's ticket to England—ordered two or three days before. Mr Pineda would not pay for her going away, I understood this, but he gave me 50 pounds in French money to spend in Paris on our way home.

On December 18th, a Saturday, Monique and I said our farewells to all members of her family, who came for this purpose to Bd Magenta, and off we flew, landing in Paris just after noon, booking into the Hotel Luttecia. I had heard of the Lido as the best cabaret in Europe, so I phoned and told them I wanted the best table they had, as I was on my honeymoon. They said, of course, they would, and on arrival at the Lido, they had set us on a raised table three rows back, which I found perfect as I realised too near, or at the very front, one can see too many faults in the costumes, as we had seen this on a later occasion.

I ordered champagne, by now, I had become quite like the stuff, which by present-day price standards, was given away, the show. It was a superb piece of artistry and workmanship from beginning to end. I, or should I say Monique, and I, have returned many times to the Lido and have never been disappointed, the spectacle seems to get better.

Sunday 19th, we took the plane for London, arriving late afternoon, and went straight to the Russel Hotel, where the receptionist and porters—who knew me, remarked about my visit so near to my last one. I told them I had just been married three days before, he insisted I had the bridal suite at no extra cost. I accepted, and up we went. In minutes, a knock on the door. I went to open it, there stood a porter with a tray, on which stood a bottle of champagne and two glasses—with the compliments of the manager, the porter said. A few years previous, I had been to the Russel twice to find them full, but the manager had sportingly offered me a 'cot' as he put it, in one of the bathrooms, I always accepted and always the charge the same. At one pound per night, a large difference to the little Italians, ruiner of good hotels, charges today, I call it robbery without violence!

Our stay in London was short, as we took the midday train to Carlisle, arriving there at approximately 7:00pm. Dad and Cathie were there to meet us, as we had nothing to eat since breakfast. I suggested we had a light dinner at the Country Hotel, which we did, introducing my new bride to the management of the staff there. I had many congratulations all around. They, I think, were genuinely delighted with Monique, and for my choice of such a lovely girl, I think Dad was very pleased with my choice, he only could remember a nice young girl in the George Hotel, putting her tongue out at me, he had seen this much, Mother had not seen her, Cathie I think, a bit reserved.

Now, I did not have a house of my own, never thinking I would be married so quickly. In fact, after June Haigh, I had never given marriage a thought. Now here I was, after seeing a girl for four hours—married! Ma had bought a house at Silloth, on the Solway Bay, on the other side, was Scotland, the house, a two-storey one, was faced up with pink, a small front lawn, looking onto the Solway, a large garden cum orchard at the rear—plus a garage. Ma suggested we live there for a while, wisely thinking Monique would prefer, for the time being, a house where she was her own mistress. Mother had, I thought, though she never mentioned it, a certain reserve toward Monique. She became very fond of her, and Monique very fond of Ma—whom she always referred to as Ma, as I myself did. Monique never tried hard to be friends with my family, it just came naturally. She had good character and bubbly good humour. She loved them all, including Cathie—who, at times, could be rather cold toward her.

Of course, Monique's English was practically nonexistent. I, somehow, was the only one to understand her wants etc. and had to act as an interpreter at home, at the table, and in the shops. It took Dad years to understand her accent when others understood all. Within six months, Monique's English was almost 100% and she was also able to write the same, grammatically, better than I.

On the 22nd, Monique and I set up house—at Ma's house in Silloth, named Kirkdale. She was delighted with it. It was fully furnished throughout. Ma had had it leased for the previous six months to an Air Force Officer who had kept a large dog, this dog had spoiled some antique furniture by chewing chair legs, etc., and the lovely pitch-pine doors were badly scratched. However, that night I lit a big fire in the living room overlooking the sea. Monique had never seen an open fire in a house before and thought it was a wonderful thing. This was December and very cold, especially at Silloth, perhaps the coldest place in Cumberland. I had bought some wine from my friend, Leonard Bendelow, manager and blender of Whisky's at Glassons Vaults, Penrith, the wine was Volnay, the year—I forget! But a full-bodied wine at 9/- per bottle, we had this with bacon and eggs, followed, by the fireside, with two tins of shrimp. It was fun, and in the flickering firelight, my wife looked more lovely than ever, we still had not consummated our marriage, I never pressed her, as she was so innocent in the physical side of lovemaking, and I was patient.

The mornings were very cold indeed. There was no central heating, the cooking was by town gas, but from 7:30am to 9:00am, all and everyone in Silloth was cooking breakfast, with the result—the pressure of gas was extremely weak, only one ring on the cooker giving a small display of gas. A few days later, I bought a gas fire to put in the kitchen while we were having breakfast, but again the pressure was so, we hardly had any heat—the thing itself, like a dying match, these things mattered not at all, we had each other, we were in love—gas or no gas.

I had to travel back and forth from Silloth to Skirwith Hall as the new chicken hatching season was starting, eggs to set and collect by van, incubators to run, and temperatures to keep an eye on throughout the day.

Silloth was a wild place in the winter months of January and February, possibly the coldest for many years. One morning, getting ready to leave for the hatchery, I looked out, it was a bitter morning, and surprise, the snow was about a foot deep. Fortunately, the snowplough had just been through. Monique went with me this morning in the chicken van, the roads in and out of Silloth were piled high with snow, pushed aside by the snowplough. Otherwise, we would never have gotten through. We travelled well until we were on the Langwathby-Skirwith road, halfway along, at Appleside Lonin. There was a snow drift about two feet high but 50 yards long. I thought I might... could... charge it, I did so, but the drift was too long, the van too light—with the result—the van got stuck in the middle. I could not get it backward either. I told Monique we would have to walk the last two miles, she was excited at all of this and jumped out of the van but got a surprise as the snow went over her knees. She only had ankle-top, fur lined bootee's—snow soon began to find the way in, a hundred yards further on, there was another drift about three feet deep and quite long by the time we got to Skirwith Hall, Monique's feet were like ice, a massage to get the circulation going, and in front of big morning room fire, soon had her going again, I got Jakob to take a tractor and chains, we had to go into fields off the road, to even get the tractor to the van, and pull the van through two fields, then back onto the road at the far side of the drifts—then, I was able to drive away, we stayed at Skirwith Hall for two days, and nights, till the snow melted a bit.

In the middle of February 1955, Monique and I consummated our marriage, after about seven weeks or more, husband and wife.

Towards the end of February, I decided to live at Skirwith Hall with my parents because of the increase in hatchery business orders; temperatures had to be constantly surveyed. Many mornings, I had to start at 5:00am, so Monique and I took up residence with my parents. We had my old bedroom, a large one, Mother was quite pleased, but on quiet weekends we went to Silloth, where we entertained friends with tea. It was no good asking friends to dinner because Monique could not cook, she was still a schoolgirl when we married, but she was trying hard. I bought her cookbooks in English, which she mastered quite quickly, sitting by the fire between my knees—reading the cookbooks, she would ask me what was the meaning of this and that.

After perhaps a year of experimenting with me, the cooking improved, and after two years—very good; after three years—excellent. We had many laughs over some of her dishes, sometimes Monique tried so hard, and the result—catastrophic! She would cry, but I would console her, take her in my arms—then soon she would laugh it all off, then, out would come a couple of tins of shrimps, a bottle of Volnay, get the fire going, and eat by the flickering flames.

Regarding the open fire, Monique, for weeks, could not light a coal fire. I would come back from work, it would be as cold as Siberia, but the fire as black as the night itself, a box of matches would be struck, to no avail. I showed Monique many times how to go about it with me—I had a blazing fire in minutes. It must have been six weeks before Monique mastered the art of fire-making.

As I had not a motor car then, and now I was married, a chicken van was not quite the thing to go hunting balls or dinner with various friends, so I looked around for a good-looking car, with really, nothing particular in mind, one day, while shopping in Carlisle, I parked the Morris Oxford van in Payton's garage at the viaduct, I knew the Payton's, they were agents for Volvo and Mercedes cars, and quite nice fellows to deal with. In their showroom this day, as we were passing, I saw a rather elegant sports car, second hand, it was a Jaguar XK120, in silver metallic paint. I thought, *Just what I want.* I went back inside and had a word with Bill Payton, the car had had one owner and was priced at 800 pounds. I bought it on the spot, as Monique did not know how to drive. I told Bill Payton I would pick the car up in a couple of days, which I did. There were 11,000 miles on the clock. Monique was delighted with our 'new' car, so was I. It was a dream to drive, a lovely long bonnet to gaze down, rear wheels half covered in. I kept this car for about eighteen months, then I sold it, as by then, our firstborn came along, and we could not get his carrycot in the car, purely a two-seater, but during 18 months or so, I had a lot of fun driving this car, I even was fined 5 pounds for speeding in Oxford town.

1955, Monique was pregnant, one would not have thought so, as she wore trousers quite easily, she never had a great bulging belly, she was quite elegant. Wednesday, January 11th, 1956, at 3:00am, Monique woke me saying she had pains. I told her to go back to sleep, as before, she had complained of 'pain.' I had phoned the Doctor, Frank Eddington, in Penrith. He had come out 8 miles to find nothing wrong quite a few times. I thought this was another of these 'pains' I dropped off to sleep, as I had to be at the hatchery at 5:00am—hatching day. Ten minutes later, Monique was quite adamant these were the start of birth pains. I got dressed, not knowing quite what to do, and off we went in the chicken van, arriving at Kirkland a few minutes later. I shouted up to Mother's window, in seconds—Ma was there. "What is it?" she asked. I explained she was down like a shot, she asked Monique a few things and got the replies.

Ma said, "Take Monique straight to the maternity home and I'll come too." We all piled into the chicken van and set off for Penrith. Within fifteen minutes, we were at the maternity home on the outskirts of the town, on Blencow Road. The nurses there soon took charge of Monique, put her in a little private room, we saw she was in good hands, kissed her, wished her well, and left.

At Blencarn at 10:30am, I had a customer drop some chicks off. I used the phone kiosk on the village green. I dialled, got through, and all of a sudden, I received a sharp electric shock from the receiver. I dropped it like a hot cinder and phoned at midday from another village. This time, I had good news, Monique had had a little boy at 11:45am, weighing in at 5 ½ lbs. Dr Frank thought he—the baby, might have been a little premature. Both Mother and baby were doing well. I was over the moon!

That evening, I washed, dressed, had myself a very good—and very large Romeo and Juliet Havana, and set off to see my new son. I arrived and parked the XK120, with a good roar on the exhaust, outside the window where Monique was, she knew it was me, she said—by the car noise, in I strode, cigar and all, kissed my wife, congratulating her on her fine effort, she had been in labour, and labour pains, for eight hours, she was tired but looked radiant, I was invited to go to the baby room to see my son, so off I went—my large cigar accompanying me, I was shown to a cot, and there he was, a lovely pink baby, with beautiful blonde hair, with features as perfect as an angel or cherub, it was amazing how perfect he was, I was delighted, I went back, and told Monique, she was pleased.

The next night, I rolled up again at visiting hours, again – with a grand Havana! During our talk, Monique said Matron had asked her to ask me not to smoke in the home. I did as requested. After a fortnight, Monique was home with the baby, whom we named Adam Guy. He was admired by all.

Monique's Uncle Pineda had sent us from Oran a barrel of

red wine, about 10-11 gallons of first-rate quality. The wine had arrived at Liverpool, and after customs, to Penrith Station. My friend, Len Bendelow—manager and blender of Whisky from Glasson's Breweries, sent his head bottler, Albert Currie, out to Skirwith Hall to bottle it for me. This was the second barrel. I paid customs 2 or 3 pounds, which made it very cheap for me. My friends liked it very much when they came to dinner, so did Dad. Leonard Bendelow had in his cellar some excellent Port. I love a good Port, especially after a good dinner of pheasant or a succulent wild duck, we always had a duck per person, the Port was Crofts 1927, which he decanted and rebottled for me. The price per bottle was one pound, an absolute gift. I shudder to think of the price of that year now.

Monique, and baby Adam, came home on January 26th. The baby was being breastfed, the trouble was, Monique had milk for three babies, it poured out of her, he was a good feeder was, Adam, he thrived well, slept well, did not cry—even when cutting his teeth, as soon as anyone looked at him, he would laugh, and gurgle right away, he was the happiest baby, as beautiful as a cherub—little were we to know the heartache later on in life.

The workmen got a raise in wages in January 1956. Harold Metcalfe married, living in a council house, now receiving 7 pounds 13/- per week, but paid his own council rent, Jakob, living in a single, 5 pound 7/- per week. Eddie Walsh, single, living in his own house at 5 pounds 1/- per week, these three men were on Poultry work but getting the full agricultural wage, three women were on part-time. We all thought these wages were excessive, but to look at the farm dairyman today, at 300 plus pounds per week, it nearly makes one ashamed to say wages in 1956 were excessive, but the money went a long way then. A good dinner at a very good hotel was 30/- for two, Havana cigars, at 5 pounds for 25, compared with now for the—same size, 175-200 and plus pounds, and look at Crofts 1927 Port.

Friday, July 6th, Maria Bianco from Italy, came to work as

a Nanny—and housework. Monique got her from an agency that supplied foreign workers, she was from Benevento. Later, she told Monique, she had had a baby girl and little or no money, her mother looked after the baby—Maria was short of stature, stoutly built, strong, and willing, in very little time, she was into the routine of the house, she was absolutely great with our firstborn, Adam, like a broody hen looking after a brood of chicks, forever clucking to them, always giving attention, she doted on the wee one.

She arrived with one suitcase, which seemed very heavy, this surprised me, as she had very few clothes. Monique soon found out why, the obvious heaviness under her bed was about five stones of cheeses from her homeland – big round solid ones, she came at 6:30am and wished to start work at once, at 3 pounds per week.

We had Adam christened at the little church at Kirkland—reputed to be over 600 years old, where I was christened. The local Vicar had fallen out with all of us at Skirwith Hall, the Vicar then—was Rev. J.C. Wilson, lived with his boyfriend, Jim Peel.

The Vicar was a great tittle tattler of gossip, the trouble was, he could not keep it to himself, being a priest—people confided in him with their innermost secrets and thoughts, he would be in one house—be told all, go next door, and spill the beans—all the first house had told him. How it came about to fall out with my family was this – he reckoned, a certain lady had told him, Joey Slack (me) was at the Crown Hotel every night of the week, and always drunk, and could scarcely drive his car back home – this, he told one afternoon, to my Mother, Dad and Cathie, in the morning room, Cathie immediately jumped to my aid, in my absence, and told him—"it's not what people tell you, it is what you add on to what people tell you," he was completely taken aback, jumped up and left—saying as he left, there would be no more help from him, or Jimmy, for things at Skirwith Hall.

What Cathie had said to him, in my defence, in my absence,

was perfectly true. He was a gossiper and an adder on'er! To say things like this to my mother, and behind my back, hurt my mother quite a lot. As I've said before, he was a homo, and so were all his priestly pals, so when we decided to christen Adam, it was not by J.C. Wilson's, in Skirwith Church, I decided to get Jon McClintock, the Vicar of Fleetwood Lanc's, I had known Jon when he was a priest at Carlisle, and had been to his inauguration, I called to see him at his Vicarage in Fleetwood, he said he would be delighted to do the christening, but first, he would also—for etiquette, have to tell J.C. Wilson, as he and the latter were also friends, Jon was another Homo, his boyfriend Bill, was a headmaster at a school in, or near, Fleetwood.

The date was agreed upon, August 3rd. The Pineda's had arrived three weeks before with a new Mercedes and Padilla, the chauffer, bringing three cases of champagne with them. The morning of the third, I set off at 5am to pick Jon up, getting back with plenty of time to spare. The christening was a family affair. After the ceremony, Adam—as usual, had treated the whole thing with laughs and chuckled all through, we repaired to Skirwith Hall, where Monique had prepared a marvellous buffet, and with the champagne, all went well.

A few days later, Monique left for a holiday in France with her Aunt and Uncle, plus baby Adam, with feeding the baby plus running a large house had taken it out of her, she had lost quite a stone in weight, they were heading for Savoie in the French Alps, a place near Albertville, the hotel, Le Grande Arc, St Paul, Sur Isere, Cevins.

Then, when I was planning to join Monique (we phoned each other every other day), I had word from Heinz he was now taking his holidays and bringing his wife Maria with him. This was going to be his first visit to England since he left it as a prisoner of war, he arrived at Dover on the Ferry on August $23^{rd,}$ 1956. I went down to pick them up in the Jaguar Mark 7, Hubert Dyson, the local butcher, went with me to take turns driving because it was there and back, straight through, a drive of 300 miles to London and approx 80 miles to Dover—760, and no motorway, travelling the old A.1., in which there were 33 roundabouts from Scotch Corner, to London passing through the villages and towns.

Hubert and I arrived an hour later at Dover than I had stated to Heinz—at the Western Docks, no one there! Off we went to the Eastern Docks, again – no Heinz, we drove slowly back to the first docks, and there they were, having a look around, Heinz's face lit up when he saw us. I think he was getting worried, we collected his suitcase and left on the long drive home, I don't know the exact time we went home, but it was late, and I was very tired. I had been up at 4:30am to feed 6,000 head of poultry in the fields, as Jakob was on holiday.

Now, I had my 'blood brother' back in Skirwith Hall—it was like old times. Heinz wanted Maria to see all the places and meet all the people he knew when he was a prisoner of war, he himself, was still an employee and had no car, my parents were very pleased to see him, he was proud, and pleased, to walk into Skirwith Pub and order drinks without being told to get out by Fred, in fact, he and Fred became very good friends.

We shot pigeons, ducks, rabbits, etc. and had our fill of drink, his favourite place was the George Hotel, though he liked the Shepherds Inn at Langwathby. Later on, he named his own cellar bar 'The Shepherds Inn' together with a huge plaque of the shepherd, and dog, on the door. The name seemed to tickle his fancy somehow. Another thing that always made him laugh was the term in England 'lighting up time.' This tickled him pink, so did 'dual carriageway.'

August 29th, we started to cut corn, harvest time was here, and Heinz and I helped with it. Monique said she was putting on weight, the weather was hot, the food at the hotel was excellent, Baby Adam spent his days being driven about by Paddilla and nursed all day by Mr Pineda. I think they thought he was an angel on earth, with his golden locks and beautiful face—not like the Latin babes who, when very young, look like monkeys! Everyone fell for Adam, people would not leave him alone, all wanted to nurse him—and he revelled in it all! Laughing all the more—and could he chuckle?

Heinz's holiday came to a close, he wished to leave on September 10th, a Monday. I also had made plans with Monique for her to be in Paris on that date—she booking into the Hotel Lutecia where I would meet her, leaving Adam with the Pineda's, I drove down to Dover with Heinz and Maria and set sail for Ostende—where Heinz had his rail ticket to return to Munster, the crossing was calm as a millpond, so Heinz and I, saying our goodbyes all the way over, got through quite a supply of Whisky on the ferry!

We docked at Ostende at approx 6:30pm. I took Heinz and Maria to the railway station, said our last farewells. I am sad to leave my great friend; however, he had his work to attend to—I had my wife to meet. I, therefore, set off for Paris at 7:00pm. From Ostende Railway Station, it was good driving to start with, but when the evening closed in, early fog started to form. The first fog patch I hit was so dense, coming on it all of a sudden, it startled me, breaking sharply. As quickly as I had hit the fog, I was out of it the same. It was a pocket.

After this, I drove a little more steady, then I was hitting pocket after pocket of fog, some very dense, others not so bad, but it was slowing me down a lot—I wanted to be with my wife. Eventually, I entered Paris, not knowing which direction—or even where the Hotel Lutecia lay, I just drove centre ville for quite a long way, the traffic was very thin, thank goodness. When the traffic became more plentiful, I thought it was better to seek help. I had no sooner thought this than I spotted a taxi, pulled into the pavement side, stopped in front of him, got out, explained my predicament, and asked him if he would lead me to the hotel, he was a most agreeable gentleman, and told me 'oui bien sur monsieur' I hopped back into the Jaguar, and followed my new friend, it did not take long, perhaps 3 or 4 mins to be in front of Lutecia—so I had been right on track all the way! I parked beside the pavement outside the hotel, thanked, and paid my taxi friend—the time was 11:30pm. I got my case and went in. I told the night porter who I was, he said I was expected, told me Monique's room number, and up I went in the ancient lift. I knocked on the door, a voice on the other side asked in French, "Who is it?" I replied, also in French, 'cest moi'. The door opened, and we fell into each other's arms, we both had missed each other a great deal.

The next day, September 11th, we got up late and had coffee and croissants nearby. I asked for directions out of Paris, towards Versailles. I wanted to see the Sun King's Palace there, it was quite easy to follow the directions given. Also, it was quite a revelation to see the Palace and to visualise the rabble storming in, in the days of the revolution. I had read and digested this history, we must have spent three or four hours there. After this, I drove steadily, I had all the time in the world! From there, we headed for Foutainbleau, and from that place, we stayed the night near Salieu at a little Auberge in a quiet corner—on it's own in the countryside, we had a delightful bedroom with a balcony overlooking a beautiful stream—only perhaps, five yards from us, we had our aperitifs on this balcony and watched the trout rising to the flys. This place was ideal for a honeymooning couple to stay at, tranquil and away from the madding crowd, a strange thing—I did not enter the place name in my diary, it was a pity.

On Friday 14th, we nosed the car along the road beside Lake Annecy, it was a lovely hot sunny day, the crickets were making a lot of noise—the sign of good weather. Many people were swimming in the lake. We stopped at a café, which had a fairly large terrace platform jutting out over the lake, and had a nice cool beer as we relaxed. I thought it just the right time and place to have a good Havana, which I did, a beautiful wife, a beautiful lake, a beautiful day, good beer, and a splendid cigar—what more could a man want—which reminds me of a saying my mother taught me "When has a man enough—when he has a little more than he already has." The meaning is quite clear. But for myself, I had enough.

Later in the day, we drove through Albertville, nestling in

between the high mountains, the river Isere passing by, the locals told me it was good for trout, we arrived at the Hotel du Grand Arc at St Paul sur Isere. It lay approximately halfway between Albertville and Moutier. It was tucked away in a corner, quite a nice small hotel of, perhaps, one star. The rooms were rather run down, but the food was second to none. It was worth a good detour just to eat there. It was run by the owners—Monsieur and Madame Genet. They had two daughters, Aimee and Jeanette, quite young and quite good looking, they used to wait at the table when not at school—the reason, perhaps, the hotel was rather run down was that Madame Genet was an alcoholic, but both she and her husband were most kind, the hotel was mostly full.

As we entered the courtyard parking, we were met by the Pineda's and Adam, together with the ever-faithful Paddilla and a host of other guests, having their aperitifs outside, I had arrived nicely in time for mine. I was made most welcome by the Genets who, with the rest of the crowd, won- dered why it had taken so many days to come from Paris, in a Jaguar, I told them, the best things in life are never hurried even when making love! That seemed to satisfy them all!

I enjoyed my dinner, it was the first time I had ever eaten Calves Head, I was a bit apprehensive about it, but it was one of the house specialities, and I was told it was extra good—and it was good! Mr Pineda saw to it that at all times, there was plenty of wine on the table, they, the Pineda's had been here many times, so I was well looked after. He, himself, had thought seriously of buying the hotel—owing to the mounting troubles in Algeria—but he was going to leave this until next year.

A few days later, the Pineda's, and Monique and I were invited to dine at a lovely little chalet, on the high slopes of Courcheval, by a family from Albertville—the Bardasier's. This was before Courcheval became the famous ski station that it is now.

The chalet was at a tremendous height, and just like a doll's house, with a view as far as the eye could see, magnificent. The day was hot and sunny. Even where we were, I cannot remember the altitude. It was just right, we dined in the garden, about ten of us—again, I had eaten something I had never tried before—tripe! I thought, *Good heavens—what next! Can I get through this meal?* The long and the short was—it was excellent! I was most surprised, again, I have eaten tripe many times over the years—as long as the cook is French, there is no doubt at all in my mind, no one can beat the French at cooking, many try—and possibly try hard, but they (the French) stand alone in this field.

The wines were also excellent, the sunshine, a blue blue sky, the panoramic view, and the company of Mr and Mrs Bardasier were superb. After the long meal of five courses, with three different wines, the day was so warm we lazed back in our chairs and just talked—over our digestives! Me, with my Havana, Mr Pineda, and others, with Bastos cigarettes. Later in the day, we drove down the mountainside, Monique and I in the Jaguar, the Pineda's, with Paddilla in their Mercedes (with Adam), back to the hotel for another big evening meal prepared by Mr Genet… and bed!

On September 26th, Monique and I packed our cases into the Jaguar, Adam, in his carry cot, waved goodbye to everyone at the Hotel du Grand Arc (all the residents and staff were outside to wish us bon voyage). Mr Pineda, with tears in his eyes and not looking too well. He wanted us to stay for another week, but I had my work to attend to—little did we know that this was the last time we would see Mr Pineda alive, seven months later, he was dead.

We drove straight for Calais and took the ferry boat on the 27th, late afternoon. The sea was enormously rough—so rough that ours was the last to leave that evening. The others were not allowed to sail, for the first time, even in port. I started to feel queasy, and as soon as the ship left the shelter of the port of Calais and hit the sea—I felt decidedly sick. I went down to the toilets, no sooner had I entered than I started to be seasick with a vengeance—probably was a bit selfish—but I locked the toilet door, and just continued to be sick—or just wretch! It's a wonder my shoes did not come up on and on my retching went, but I had no food left to bring up – my, was I ill! I heard people all over the other toilets—behaving as I was, the ship just nose-dived, tail sky high, in and out of the huge troughs. As the nose went down, the screws seemed to pick up a great speed, as if they had no water to work in. Eventually, I seemed to get slightly better, so I sat down on the toilet, then the ship seemed to sink into an abyss, and all the water in the toilet shot up and over the edge, soaking the backside of my trousers like a wet rag in dirty water, that sort of brought me to my senses, I was now angry, seasickness was forgotten—what was I going to look like walking about with the whole of my trouser backside soaking, and also, it felt awful!

We were now in the lee of the cliffs of Dover, so I ventured upstairs—there was vomit everywhere! And calm as a cucumber. There was Monique, serene as a queen. She had not been seasick then or at any time. She and the baby were fine! She looked at my backside and started to laugh her head off. By now, I saw the funny side of it and laughed with her.

November 15th was a sad day, the shepherd, Len Bellas, died in his sleep. He had never been really robust had Len, but he was probably the most conscientious shepherd we ever had. I have seen him tramp six miles or more to find a missing sheep. There was one time he and I were shepherding the big enclosed allotment of 265 acres above Ousby. The ground was steep and ridged, one would mount one ridge, thinking the top end of the allotment was only a hundred yards away, only to find another and another ridge. This day, we had done our work, Len had gone to check on something to one side, I sat down and waited, he had said he would be back in a minute, I waited, and waited, then I became anxious—perhaps he had become ill, and lay helpless somewhere.

He had been off work ill quite a few times this last twelve months, odd times, being sick as he and I shepherded. The more I thought now of him, the more I became alarmed, I jumped up and set off to look for him in the direction he had gone, 265 acres—if completely flat, it is very easy to scan around, but when of ridges, gulleys, peat bogs, ridges, it is no easy task—and steep, there was no Len, I started to shout for him—no reply, I thought, I will have to go higher up, I climbed, my dogs beside me, calling, and looking in various gulleys, I was now certain something must have happened to Len, I was on the second to last ridge from the top, when he appeared on the skyline, half a mile away, when he had left me, for a few minutes, he had discovered 4 or 5 sheep of other farmers, in a small gulley, that should have been on the open fell, Len thought he would drive them out, there and then, entailing two hours walk to the fell gate, and put them out. I was most relieved to find him well, for he and I had been good workmates before I took on the poultry for about ten years. Dad and I went to his funeral at the little country church in Mungrisdale, nestling in the heart of John Peel's country, the Lakeland hills Len loved so much.

The first eggs for the 1957 season went in on December 11th, I posted 3300 chicken catalogues on the same day to farmers all over the country. Christmas Day, Monique and I passed it at Skirwith Hall, as we had Maria and Jakob to cater for, passing an enjoyable day. At night, we went to Kirkland to Mother's for dinner. It was a nice Christmas.

Dad's foreman now was Arthur Durham. He had been with Dad for forty years, a nice fellow and most conscientious, a good friend of Heinz. Arthur had a greenhouse and was an expert in growing tomatoes, and flowers, among other things. He used to bring Mother at least three bunches a week of his best blooms. When Mother and Dad left Skirwith Hall to live at Kirkland, Arthur carried on his tradition and brought Monique three lovely bouquets each week. She was always pleased, and always thanked him and had a little talk, it was one day when he handed Monique more flowers, he told her that there was a new programme on TV—just started, he said it was a good one, and that she might like it. Monique, the same night, switched over—onto this new programme, and indeed, she and I liked it so much we had watched it ever since (except when we were in France). It was called Coronation Street; need I say more?

Arthur loved fishing, and when the Briggle Beck became coloured with the rains, after work, he was out with his rod, he was not a really robust man either. Sometimes, at work, he was not well. I would ask him, if I saw he was a bit lethargic, "Are you okay, Arthur?"

He would say, "Not the best," but he would not give up and tell Dad he was not well.

I just told him, "Drop tools, Arthur, and go home to bed, and take a day or two off." It was a relief, I think, for him to be told to do this, his wife, Hilda, was a frail, nice woman. She had, I think, six children, she always had a most yellow complexion, one year, again she fell pregnant, and had twins that died almost at birth. This event put poor Hilda at rock bottom in her health, a short few years after this, she took ill, this time, with that wolf at everyone's door—Cancer. Arthur used to give her a little Brandy to keep her going, as he put it, but she was, in the end, heavily sedated with Morphine and died a painful death. Poor Arthur was most cut up. Thereafter, his eldest daughter, Dora, looked after and kept the house for him. Very sad, these episodes of one's workmen—because for me, they were not just workmen, they were my friends and workmates—such as Arthur, he had seen me grow up from babyhood, he and I, when I was a youth, had worked side by side over the years, I felt for him in his grief, the same I felt over Len's death.

Mrs Bellas, Lens widow, to make ends meet, asked if she could do some work in the hatchery. I said, "Yes, of course." So for the season 1957, Mrs Bellas was employed by me four or five hours daily, myself, all the men's wives, I, when greeting them, always used the title 'Mrs' never their first names, as a matter of respect to my elders, also, because they were of the gentle sex.

It was in February, unfortunately, Mrs Bellas, while dusting the big in-incubator and hatchers, caught one of the thermostat knobs with her duster and put the thermostat to full heat, to over 120% on one incubator—it should have been 99 ¾ % I discovered a thread from her duster caught in the knob, the result—many hundreds of pounds down for two weeks, customers to be set back, and not satisfied, I had to reprimand her, gently of course, and explain fully about these fine thermostats, for the future dustings, she continued working for me until she moved away from the village later that year.

(The old Dovecote in the stackyard had no pigeons for very many years, probably since Lady Le Fleming's days at Skirwith Hall 400 years ago). Pigeons in these medieval buildings were part of the source of food for the Lords of the manor in olden times, also fish ponds stocked with either trout or carp, Skirwith Hall had four of these fish ponds, dating from the middle ages, the Dovecote was anything from 500 to 600 years old, possibly more. Anyway, I thought, bring the old stones to life, let them hear the cooing of doves, so in mid-winter, I purchased two or three pairs of White Fantails. I have always thought Fantails were lovely, beautifully elegant birds. I put them in their new home. The Dovecote barred the exits for a week, then let them fly at will. At first, they flew round and round, inspecting their new home from the outside. They seemed to like what they saw because they soon settled on the roof, then flew in and out.

In February, the actual date 22nd, the first young fantails were hatched, like fluffy, downy things, with big beaks. Their parents were very proud of their new offspring, I thought February would be too cold for them, but they survived—and thrived. Two weeks later, a second Fantail hatched two more chicks, and they did well too. In fact, that summer, it seemed the Fantail parents, and eventually their young, continued to breed like rabbits. The old Dovecote stones must have been very happy because, inside, the melodious and gentle sound of cooing was non-stop. I was pleased with my effort! In time, the Fantails got to know my presence. When I opened the house door into the courtyard and let out a coo- ing whistle, many of them would fly down to my feet and wait for a favourite titbit of theirs—peas or tick beans, it was a nice sight this, but eventually, the Fantails had baby chicks that were multi-coloured. Racing pigeons used to stop over for a feed and rest but found these exotic white ladies too much of a temptation! An overnight stop was to become married bliss for many, and, over the years, once a year, I had to cull them out; otherwise, my white Fantails would have been no more.

On Friday, April 19th, 1957, I was working in the hatchery when a loud knock on the door. The hatchery was always locked—at all times, only myself and Eddie had keys. I opened, there was Monique, tears streaming down her cheeks. She had received a telegram that her Uncle Pineda was gravely ill, she was most upset. I asked if she wished to fly out to be with him, as he was so ill. She said yes, as it was he who had acted, since she was three, as her father. I booked two seats to fly out on Sunday, travelled by midnight train from Carlisle to Euston, flew later that day to Paris, whereas our tickets were for Algeria, the airport police would not allow us any further, as we had no visa, it seemed the Guerrilla war was at its height with both sides giving no quarter, I had a violent row with one of the senior Police Officers—in fact, we both almost came to blows, Monique had to step in between us, then, when I had calmed down, I thought, right, we will phone Mr Ferrara, one of the partners in

S.O.T.A.C. was also a member of Parliament in the French Parliament for Algeria. Monique got through to him, he quickly arranged things for us, put the police in their place, and we were off, the Police Officer I had the row with had a very black face on him. As we were cleared, I gave him a smirky smile—I had won, he had lost, and he did not like it!

We dropped down at Marseilles for a short while, arriving

in Oran at 2:00pm Monday, April 22nd, just missing the funeral by two hours—it was all over.

Oran, at this period, was in turmoil with the Arab and Guerrilla War. Garage men, plus Soldiers, were patrolling the big garage walls at night with machine guns and rifles. It seemed no quarter was given by either side. I was told firsthand that any French Soldier or civilian captured by the Arabs were strung up by their hands, a needle stuck in a main vein in the leg and bled to death—the blood being used for transfusion for their own Guerrilla, it was not really safe to venture out at night on the streets, all windows were covered with wire mesh.

Gaby had started to transfer his money over to France. One of his ideas was to buy a farm near Sennas, the Domaine de Duneau. Mr Pineda was about to do the same, transfer his money to France. One idea was to buy the Hotel du Grand Arc. Unfortunately, he died before any of this was achieved, Paul always – not too clever (except for girls and fighting) said, this is my country, I am keeping my father's business going, and no money is leaving Algeria, spoken like a fool because most of the French, of any means, were busy transferring their loot to France.

On Monday, the 29th, the garage workers gave Monique and I, one of their big dinners at the garage. As usual, it was the rabbit as the main course, with a multitude of other dishes, of hors d' oeuvres etc., wine flowed freely, the whole evening was well done, the food very good, and the workers most kind—there would be twenty-five of them at dinner, they were a grand lot, always extremely polite, and well mannered, and always most kind toward me.

Monique and I flew home the next day, arriving on Wednesday, May 1st, to a cancellation of 700 chicks that were due to be delivered on May 2nd, I had to find room for them. Cancellations were sometimes a headache if the cancellation was one or two days, or even on delivery day; if cancelled two or three weeks, or even a week before delivery, it gave me time to sell the chicks to others. I remember the case at Caldbeck—John Peels country, it was a first time customer, this one had three dozen (a small order) three moth old pullets ordered, on the delivery day I was not sure just where this customers farm was, but as I had others in the same area to deliver to, I asked directions as to where this customer's farm lay, the reply—Oh, you have just passed his farm half a mile back, three Clydesdale horse in his front field, I had seen the horses a few times, and had always admired them, as soon as I had finished with the farmer I was now with (only ten minutes), I drove straight back to the farmer with his horses, his wife came out, all smiles expecting her new pullets, I was just taking one of the crates out of the van, when her hus- band came up, full of abuse, cursing me for passing his farm (my van had the hatchery name on the outside), and going to someone else first, I explained that I had not known exactly where he lived, and had asked at my last customer further on, the verbal abuse continued, his wife was most embarrassed, and said nothing, I was sure, thinking about it later, she was afraid of him, by now, I had had enough of his impudence, I slid the crate back into the van, closed the door, turned to face the man, and told him I did not deal with people like him, he was speechless, I got in and drove away.

Another time, a customer phoned in to say that his chicks of the week before were dying. He also was abusive, telling me my chicks were rubbish, that he should have got them elsewhere. I told him I would be along to see the chicks the next morning. I duly arrived at the farm, a small holding of about 20 acres. I inspected the chicks, which indeed were in a bad way, all droopy-winged and sad. He, again, clearly told me that my chicks were a bad lot in a tone that meant it! I asked to see what he was feeding them. He showed me the sack of 'chicken feed." I said to him immediately, the chicks are not at fault, you bloody fool—my anger got the better of me. It is you that is at fault. This bag is a pure fish meal which it was, poor little chicks. They had no chance, this fellow never apologised or even acknowledged that he was wrong. People like this, and there are quite a few, spread false rumours all the time—"Hey, do you know Slacks chickens are no good, they all die," bad news always travels faster than good. I was fortunate to have good healthy chicks, and breeding stock, strictly looked after, and 95 % of clients were really good people and kind.

Another episode was with a Farmer's wife at Plumpton, Penrith. I think it was Mrs Mounsey. She had an order in for 300-month-old pullets. I duly delivered them. They were at 25 pounds per hundred, Mrs Mounsey came out, I unloaded them, then she piped up, I want these for 20 pounds per hundred, I told her she had had the invoice a month before, and the price was there for her to see, why had she ordered if she thought the chicks were too dear, "I want them for 20 pounds, or I don't take them." She said, I just put the boxes back in the van and told her I did not do business like that, and drove out of the farm. Fortunately, I had not many like this.

A customer I gave a good discount to was a blind man. He used to get 500 each week and settle up at the end of the season. His name, many will know in Cumberland, is Jonathon Fisher, of Ivegill, halfway between Penrith and Carlisle. Jonathon had won 600 pounds on the football pools, he was completely blind from birth - and decided to put it to good use and go into rearing poultry, buying pullets as day olds, and selling at various growing stages. He bought brooders heated by gas for his day-olds, a big range of haybox-rearing brooders for the month-olds and upwards.

Mrs Fisher, his mother, was an extremely hardworking woman, she had another son, Joe, completely blind also. She scrubbed and washed all Jonathon's brooder equipment each week, ready to take the day-old chicks, she often invited me to eat with them at lunch or tea time on my deliveries, I remember one tea time, at her big kitchen table, there was a big bowl of, what I took to be rum butter, together with a whole array of homemade tarts, scones and cakes, she was a good baker Mrs Fisher, all tasted excellent, well, rum butter is one of my favourites, I helped myself to a large slice of homemade bread, almost an inch thick, spread it thick with the rum butter, took a big bite, and to my astonishment and dismay, now realised that it was pure pig fat! Stuff I cannot stand! I was in a quandary, what should I do? Mrs Fisher was always so kind. She, when we were alone, would tell me of her problems and troubles in the family over huge mugs of tea. I put all my thoughts about pig fat behind me and ate on! My rich, thick slice of bread seemed now as big as a whole loaf! I finished in due course, but it is a mistake I have never repeated!

14

The rains started in August, the Briggle Beck came up nice and coloured, just right for fishing. I got the rod out, Wellington's and waterproofs on, and set forth on Sunday 11th. The Trout were biting well. I finished the day with 20 nice ones, throwing 5 or 6 others back. Monique cooked them that night, in the Papillote style, for perhaps 8 minutes, then onto one plate with a squeeze of lemon and a pinch of salt, I opened a bottle of Volnay, and we slowly—with great pleasure ate these freshly caught brook Trout, fish like this is at it's best, eating slowly enables one to really get the taste of such a delicacy, deep into one's taste buds, one gets up, and leaves the table with deep satisfaction—regarding the wine, Monique liked white wine, but her body system did not! If, and at first we did, with fish, drink white wine—she would come out with large, deep bruises on her legs and arms. She, or rather her system, was rejecting it—that is why we eventually drank Red wine with everything, including Lobster, and for me, I have—and quickly, I must say, have gotten used to eating all meats with red wine, and it really is mostsatisfying.

I was out the next day fishing and brought 12 home, all good sized Trout, and two days later—I brought 10 home, the Briggle really was a good little Trout stream, fast flowing—kept the Trout fit and firm, and there was plenty of natural food for the fish—in abundance. Monique did a beautiful job of cooking them. By now, Monique was becoming quite accomplished with her cooking. She was genuinely interested in the art, buying herself cookbooks of French, Italian, and English cooking and spending hours reading them—and trying them out on me. I was vastly amused and also highly delighted with her various menus. At baking, she had not much interest, tried a few times with no success, but the culinary arts were another thing, and in time, became very fine—and accomplished at Haute Cuisine, she had developed a flair for fine food, and at our dinner parties, received many compliments.

At knitting, we had an enormous laugh, she made Adam, when a baby, a little wool jacket. Monique made it alright, but when it was held up to see the size, it would only fit a small doll. We both laughed till tears rolled down our cheeks—as I write this, I can see her holding this little jacket up, and a puzzled look on her face, saying to me, 'Cherie, I think I've made it too small' realising in seconds, how small it really was. That, I think, was her only foray into knitting!

Dad had decided, all of a sudden, to buy Kirkland Vicarage in the hamlet where I was born. He had heard it may be for sale from the owner, a private man, I believe, of German origin, who had been interned during the war. In the war years, it had been converted into two farm worker's quarters, it was an immense building of 25 rooms, and inside was in a poor state of repair, but the building itself, was like the Rock of Gibraltar, built of Freestone—exterior wise, all was in good order. I believe Dad gave me 1200 pounds for it. There were good lawns, an orchard, good outhouses, and a perfect cellar.

I thought it was a bit crazy really, for Mother and he to go to such a big place, for Mother was not too strong, but he thought Cathie was there also to help, he bought it, and moved in on 3rd June 1955, every stick of furniture in Skirwith Hall, every carpet, and curtain—except the carpet and curtains in the smoke room—cum office.

Monique and I were left without a curtain or a carpet, only our bed and a chest of drawers that Cathie went with; within two or three weeks, we were on bare boards throughout the house, not even a table or chair, the aga cooker was left, I could not believe my parents would go out like that, and leave us without a thing, straight away, we attended furniture sales from either people deceased or furniture collected up by the auctioneers—and sold at a special sale day.

To start with, we put the Garden seat in the hallway, it looked lonely on its own. Here it was—Sandstone Flags for flooring, we had no pictures at all. Monique bought from a friend of hers at Carlisle a kitchen table in semi-plastic and four chairs to go with it. This friend of Monique's had also lived in Oran.

One week, there was a house sale of a deceased person at Temple Sowerby, there was a Queen Anne dining table and four chairs, plus a carver, to be sold. Monique and I went along to see what it was like on the sale day. We liked it, so did Jack Pears, the poultry merchant, he wanted it for his daughter Jean, who had just married a vet. When Jack knew I would like to buy the table and chairs, he said to me he would hold off himself unless I dropped out of the bidding, this was most sporting and kind of this nice man, the crux of things were, I got what I wanted at 84 pounds, Jack was prepared to go to 150 pounds he said I had bought a bargain of a genuine article, the same week, I bought a huge sideboard, a lovely piece, from Tom Park, for 25 pounds.

We had 18 rooms to furnish and we could have bought modern junk, but Monique preferred to buy good quality antique furniture at house sales and good odds and ends at auction sales of furniture gathered together by agents for a one-day big sale, many times she would wait nearly all day, for one piece, Mother eventually took pity on us, and bought a threepiece suite in red damasque, which we still have today, albeit recovered in France after twenty-five years of everyday use.

Dad had gone out of Skirwith Hall and left us the electric light bulbs, he did not offer a five-pound note to help to buy furniture of any kind, though he owed me approximately 1000 pounds for work and six weeks egg cheque, he had collared. A strange behaviour, I thought, my brother Adam's car was sold to Pat McGeorge, a car I could have done with, even Adams' gold watch was given to Pat, and when I offered to keep Adam's poultry business going, I think Dad thought it was a good thing so that he need not pay me a cent. They foisted my sister from his back onto mine, together with her two children, by now Cathie had a cheque book, and had sent her daughter

Josephine, to Harrogate School for Girls, at my cost, for when Cathie saw me arrive with a very beautiful wife, who had a great sense of dress—Monique could put something very simple on, and wear it like a princess, she—Cathie, started to spend on clothes, handbags, shoes, all expensive stuff from Harrogate or Leeds, with her school bills, and excess spending, most came from my ¾ share in the hatchery.

The doubling up of the hatchery all came out of my pocket, and three years after marriage, on Tom Parks' advice, I built a new poultry house of wood on a brick base. Asbestos roof, 136 feet long by 25 feet wide, to hold breeding birds on the deep litter system, the litter being wood shavings, Jakob and I built it ourselves at ¼ of the cost of buying one ready-made. I bought the ¾-inch boarding tongue and groove, the purlins and rafters of 6x2 ½. It was made in sections of 8 feet. Eventually, all joined and bolted together. The ends we found a bit difficult to handle, being made in one piece, but we managed. When erected, it did not take long. I was most pleased at first. I put 600 birds in to supply hatching eggs, they slept on a raised platform of solid wooden sides and a slatted floor on top, keeping all of the night droppings enclosed in, and cleaned out at the end of the season, electric light was installed by a local tradesman.

Three years later, in 1959, the success of the big deep litter house was so good I decided to build another one, of 300 feet long. The timber of Finnish Red tongue and grooved boards at 5" x 1" 6500ft planed cost 150 pounds 9/3. I bought from Tom Hartley, the timber merchant. He was an extremely nice man. I used to play cards and dominoes with him; sadly, later, he went bust. Built on the same lines, wood on a brick foundation, I had another German worker to help me. I had sacked Jakob, the new German was Kurt Witteck, who had worked for Dad for a few years. Kurt had been taken prisoner by the Americans near Casino, his hometown was now in Polish hands and he had no wish to go back, he had married Margaret Fawcett, the daughter of Albert, the shepherd who used to hang his dogs from a tree, both he and Margaret worked for me until 1977, when I left England. Kurt was a most versatile man and could turn his hand to anything, it was he and I who built the brick foundations. Looking at this from one end to the other, it seemed as though I might have been thinking rather big. The foundations seemed enormous. Dad thought I had gone with too much land, though I built this poultry house close behind a hedge and at the far end of the first one, leaving a space between tractors and trailers, etc., of 15 yards. The new building was so long I had a store room in the middle, full width, for foodstuff and egg collection storage. Once Kurt and I started on levelling for the brick walls, we used just over 3400 bricks as such—not blocks. We went from 3 ft to level in the 300 ft, taking a side each.

The weather was good, and Monique (being in her eighth month of pregnancy carrying our second child, one would never have guessed she was pregnant—unless under close scrutiny, Monique carried her babies light, she could still wear elegant clothes) used to bring us sandwiches and beer quite often, one evening she brought, I don't know why, perhaps she thought as a treat, a large jug of iced cold Martini, it was very nice, but I had been sweating at work, with the result—I may have taken the drink rather quick at first—it gave me colic, and a runny tummy for so long, Kurt and I stopped work for the night. We never had any more Martinis!

When it came to fitting the sections together and, at the same time, the trusses and purlins, just the two of us worked so hard in two days. We had them all up; only the asbestos roofing and spouting remained. Now in the middle of my building program came a catastrophe. Dad and Mother had gone to Silloth for a short holiday. I was looking after the farm when all of a sudden, the Foot and Mouth disease loomed up. A farm at Ousby—dairy and pigs, went down in a big way with the disease, when I say went down with a bang, it turned out the farm had had the disease for weeks in the pigs to start with, the farmer was Jack Savage, nicknamed 'Hellfire Jack' because he worked himself hard, always in a hurry, and made his men work the same, a very successful farmer.

The Vet from Penrith, John Barr, and his staff had attended Jack's farm, and whether they had tried to cover up because Jack could be very persuasive, no one was quite sure. In any case, the vets were fined at a court action for great laxity in not reporting the epidemic right away. The Ministry Vets found so many Pigs that had been hidden and buried. Jack was also fined. He had been getting the Army food waste from the military camp near Carlisle, plenty of meat and bones from Argentina, etc. He, Jack, had not been boiling the waste, as Ministry rules had laiddown, it should be, but feeding the stuff straight to the pigs, the inevitable result, playing with fire, meat and offal from Latin America where it was Foot and Mouth endemic. His dairy cows have also contracted the disease, the milk lorry came direct from Jack's farm, right into the middle of Skirwith Hall courtyard, for the churns of milk.

Foot and mouth were confirmed at Jack's farm on 21st September 1957 after an investigation. His farm had had the disease for at least two weeks or even more. On 25th September, I had a look at our own milk cows. They had come into milk—one was lame. I told the cowman to keep it in—tied up after milking, then I would have a close look at the beast, which I did, I discovered that three of its feet were sore, and the cow was salivating in its mouth. I thought, *Good grief, it's most likely to be Foot and Mouth*. I told the cowman to keep the cow inside, and tied up, to give her plenty of hay, and to say nothing to anyone until I had seen Dad, I set off at about 6:30 pm, called at Kirkdale, but no one at home, there was no phone in the house. Otherwise, I could have got in touch that way. I thought perhaps he and Mother might have gone for dinner at Skirburness Hotel, only a mile away. Sure enough, Mother and he was in the bar having a drink, and there were a few people in there who knew me, so I had to ask Dad to come into the hallway, which was pretty quiet. I told him I suspected Foot and Mouth, and the beast was isolated and tied up.

Dad and Mother came home that night, he had a look at the cow first thing the next morning. Dad reported the suspect cow to the county Vet. Mr Steele, who came right away, had a look at the animals' feet and inspected inside the mouth, he burst one of the blisters inside the mouth, and pus squirted out onto his spectacles. That was that Foot and Mouth were confirmed at Skirwith Hall.

The next day, Friday 27th, Laing's—the building contractors, came with huge diggers and dug six enormous long, deep, trench-like holes in the little field named Leicester Square. Also, the shooting of the stock started on the 28th. All of the cattle and sheep, those with cloven hooves—my horses were spared. The shooting went on, and on the 29th 450 sheep, and 274 cattle, the sheep were penned and shot by humane killers, then, a wire was shoved right through, by hand, into the brain. I suppose to make doubly sure they were dead. Myself, I did not see any cattle shot. It was too sad an affair as the cattle were shot, they were chained around the neck, and dragged by tractors to the big graves, and pushed in. The sheep were loaded onto trailers and then up to the graves and thrown in, lime was heaped in with them, and the whole was covered in soil.

The small number of cattle and sheep at Kirkland Hall, 2 ½ miles away, were also targeted. The vet would not let them off, so they had to be trucked down to Skirwith Hall. Monday 30th, October, the big cleanup started. All of the loose boxes, which had had nothing in them for months, and all other buildings, sheds etc, had to be thoroughly cleaned, or scrubbed, and hosed or sprayed with strong carbolic, and in some cases, formalin. The vet consigned to Skirwith Hall on a daily basis until the crisis was over was Hamish Watson, quite a nice chap. Myself and Monique were—so to speak, confined to barracks. Hamish would not allow either of us off the farm, whereas the farm men and Dad were allowed in and out at will, granted, they had to dip their feet in disinfectant, cars were left at the entrance, i.e., Dads, also, there was a policeman on duty day and night at the main gate, I used to take them a few beers, and a bottle now and then filled up with ¾ whiskey, and ¼ water, because it was a dismal job for them, the night police got a cigar to keep them company also.

We were lucky in one way. There were 400 grey-faced ewes, 250 black swale dale ewes, plus 100 wethers on the enclosed allotment above Ousby. Dad wanted to send the shepherd, a young man—David Winter, a bit of a harem scarem type, up to shepherd these sheep. I told Dad if he did send David, the vets had an excuse to put them all down and not to send anyone else from the farm, better get a friendly farmer from Ousby to do this shepherding—which he did, Bobby Little, of Ousby Town Head, so thus was saved most of the breeding ewes. However, I found out that David Winter, Dad's shepherd, had been to Jack Savage's farm the week before we had Foot and Mouth at Skirwith Hall. He had been in the cow byre and farm steading—now we had the prime suspect of who and how we got the disease. David denied he had been to Savage's farm to Dad, but a few days later, I squeezed it out of him—yes, he had been to the farm in question.

Monique's 21st birthday on 18th October came up, but the vet would not give permission to leave the farm, yet, all workers, and Father, could come and go through the disinfectant. By now, I was getting fed up with Hamish Watson, the ministry vet, I did not do any work with cattle or sheep, only the poultry, and in the hatchery, I had three weeks' supply of eggs held up, under the vet's orders, nothing had to leave the farm, I accepted this. Somehow, on 21st October, I got the green light to sell my accumulated eggs for consumption. These were all fumigated, boxes and all. I myself took them down to the entrance gate to be put on the roadside for the Express Dairy Co lorry to pick them up. Dad was there talking to the vet, Watson. I arrived with a tractor and trailer. Now, the Vet Watson refused to let the eggs go through. At this time, I saw red, I had had enough of this civil servant, a namby-pamby fellow, and jumped off the tractor to fell him. I was just about to put him on theground when Dad got in between and stopped me, I did not send the eggs that day, but I immediately got on the phone to the chief county vet, Mr Steele, a gentlemanly sort, and explained the position—which was overruled. I mentioned that I was unable to take my wife out for her 21st. At this, Mr Steele said at the long lapse of time, I should have had no trouble going outside the farm, having disinfected our shoes.

On 22nd October, Monique's Aunt, the one who had brought her up, flew into Manchester with her son Paul. I did not bother asking Watson. I drove over the straw 'mat' and set off to pick them up. By now, I had sold the XK120 and had a Jaguar Mark 7. I had bought it second hand, again, through Paton's. It had belonged to the Swedish Consul in New-castle, Jarl Trapp, and was in perfect condition.

In the middle of the Foot and Mouth epidemic, I had not finished my big new 300 ft poultry house, the trusses and purlins were all up, ready for the roof, this was delivered, quite a few tons of asbestos, but not allowed into the farm, so we unloaded the whole lot over a stone wall at Newtown, on the Langwathby road, only Kurt and myself, so he and I got busy loading the whole lot up again, on tractor and trailer to the site where he, Kurt, laid the slabs, while I cut the corners off so that all slotted and fitted in, the hand saw was to sharpen quite often, as the asbestos quickly blunted it, we finished the roofing in just 2 ½ days, then we started with the spouting, Kurt himself, fitted all the electric light cables, just continuing the cable from the first house, but independently lighted, all with fluorescent tubes for more of a daylight effect, I fitted these into the first poultry house too, they were excellent indeed, as when I wanted more eggs for the hatching season, peak chick time, these lights would be automatically switched on at say, 6.00am (winter months) 5.00am until I had them coming on at 2.00am. By our breakfast time, most of the hens had laid their eggs.

On 21st November 1957, Arthur Monkhouse and a friend came to see me in the late afternoon, it was also he who had put me on to that excellent poultry food 'Nitrovit.' They sat and had late afternoon tea in front of the fire in the morning room. We talked about shopping, the price of foodstuffs, etc. I sometimes used to ask Arthur to shoot with me, just the two of us—rough shooting walked up birds from pheasant, duck, pigeon. Arthur always enjoyed these friendly days. At about 6:00 pm, Monique asked me to see her in the breakfast room, she told me the baby was on the way, she had started her pains. I went back into the morning room and said, "Gentlemen, I am afraid I shall have to ask you to leave," Arthur had a surprised look on his face until I told them why! They could not believe what I had told them because Monique was so 'light.' They wished Monique all the best and left.

Monique hunted her things up, and I drove her into Penrith. Her Aunt accompanied us. I saw Monique at the hospital, told Matron to send for the family Dr, Frank Eddington, to come, and left. Monique later told me no sooner had I left than she went into the delivery room, the nurses had no time for anything, and Frank Eddington arrived just as the baby was born. Monique said she did not feel a thing. There was another boy, Joey Jnr, who came in, I think, at 7 ½ lbs. Monique was relieved it was a boy, as at the outset of our marriage, I had said that I would like two boys rather than one in case something happened to one, then the family is left with none, and that they were to be brought up in the protestant faith if girls arrived, they could take Monique's faith—Catholic, and she could give them the names she wished. She agreed to do this, therefore, that is why she was pleased two boys had arrived—she did not wish to have any more babies.

Maria, our Italian nursemaid, did not get on with Monique's Aunt. Maria was devoted to our first baby, Adam. She would gather him in her arms and off with him for long walks in the fields, telling him he was 'fillio mio.' It was now that we learned that Padilla, the Pineda's chauffeur, and Maria had been sleeping together for the month. They had been with us the previous year. I had little furniture for guests and for chauffeurs—even less with regard to bedroom furniture. Padilla was put in one of the main bedrooms, one of the biggest, with a single bed only. I had nothing else. This room was next to Maria's, also one of the main bedrooms. We suspected nothing and heard nothing—but we could not. Monique's, and my bedroom, were 25 yards away, at the other end of the long corridor. It turned out that when the family left Skirwith Hall on their last visit, Padilla confided in Mr Pineda he had slept with Maria on a regular basis—and Maria had a double bed—so they had plenty of room! We suspected Maria of being fond of the men because last hay time, in fields next to the house, she would be out with a fork or hay rake and love to work beside the other workmen. She knew how to handle a fo rk or a rake, as good as any of the men, but as far as I knew, nothing happened between her and them.

On Friday, 22nd November, I visited Monique at the Maternity Home in Penrith, visiting hours 7:00—8:00 pm, and saw our second son in the babies' room. He was an ugly article, with a jutted pointed chin, with a cleft in it—bald as a coot. I was disappointed when I saw what I had got as a sire. I returned to Monique, she saw right away my disappointed look. She told me herself he is an ugly one, but she told me because of his ugliness—I love him all the more, such is the female of all species with their young—the male will perhaps never comprehend. I left Monique after hours of visiting and went to the George Hotel for a celebratory drink. I went into the little cocktail bar behind the reception—no one in at all, I said to Tony, the barman, quiet tonight Tony. What's happened to everybody this Friday? He replied, "They are all upstairs dining."

I asked him what function it was, he told me it was the Golf Dance. I had forgotten all about it. In any case, Monique and I would not have attended, being as she was pregnant, now with a newborn.

I bought Tony a drink and had a double whisky myself, had a small talk with Tony, then people came from the dining room in driblets. I knew most of them. In a few minutes, the bar was full, all in dinner suits, me, in a loud checked suit by Bernard Weartherill, all helping me to celebrate my newborn, Leslie Walker. The manager came in, I told him the news, he was delighted, and invited me to join the dancers for the evening. I said, "What about my suit?" Never mind that the occasion merits a celebration! I danced the night until 1.00am—Monique would not have approved! Then, I was invited for drinks by Mrs Stamper of Brooklands. On my way home, I accepted, and when I arrived, there would be fifteen others. One would be Hubert Dyson, the butcher from Langwathby, a nice little man. I stayed there drinking until 4.00am, then Hubert asked me to call on him on the way home, as he was leaving. I left Mrs Stampers at the same time, calling at Hubert's on the way home. I was now only three miles from home, and I arrived at Skirwith Hall at 5.30am, slightly the worse for wear.

Monique's old Aunt was at the top of the stairs, with a black look on her lined face. I bid her good morning and went to bed. Saturday 23rd, I was invited to a pheasant shoot by Arthur Sowerby, the shoot was not far away, at New Biggin Temple, Sowerby, an estate that had belonged to the Crackenthorpe family of New Biggin Hall, but the last young member had sold the whole estate. Bridget's father had bought the hall, a large country mansion, but lived as he had done so latterly at Skirwith Abbey—in the kitchen; furniture was just piled in various rooms.

To get back to the shoot, as I say, we all met up at the gamekeeper's house, then some guns and beaters got into Jack Pears' (the stubs collector) half-ton van to go the two miles across fields, and an old track, to where we would start the shoot, the two miles were very bumpy, I was sat on the floor, with my legs hanging over the end, with the doors open. It was like being on the stern end of a ship.

Halfway there, I started to feel decidedly queasy, when we reached destination, behind a stone wall with a wood at the other side, my face must have been green because I certainly felt that colour. The van stopped, I ran for the wall, to get rid of some stale whisky when Arthur shouted like a bull 'keep off that bloody wall' his shout fell on deaf ears, I had one thing in mind—to be sick, two miles of the van ride had beentoo much, I reached the wall and was sick, I looked over the wall, Arthur had also shouted 'pheasants other side' I could see none, after this, I felt much better, Arthur did not hold it against me, because on shoots, he could be a Sergeant Major—but he ran things well. Feeling better every minute, I had an excellent shot, killing a pheasant stone dead at 70 yards, crossing me at about 40 yards high—going like a rocket. Arthur was next gun. He saw it all and shouted his congratulations.

The day after I took the Aunt to see Monique, she had an hour alone with Monique, and I think in that hour, the Aunt had pulled me to pieces, telling Monique of my coming in 'at all hours.' The day after, our family Dr, Frank Eddington came out to Skirwith Hall to see me and told me that Monique refused to breastfeed the baby and was going to discharge herself, he said she was upset at my outing, then I knew who was responsible for this, the old Aunt, I told Frank what my 'outing' had been, he laughed and told me to come up and calm Monique down, which I did, like, I suppose, many young women newly married, she thought my late nights out might involve girls, poor little chicken, she need never have worried on that count, but the old Aunt had sown the seeds of doubt, and when one starts to doubt, one starts to think, I should have gone to see Monique after the shoot, but when men get together and discuss the day's highlights, time just races ahead.

However, all was well, Monique decided to quit the Maternity home after one week. In those years, the usual stay was two weeks, which even I thought absolutely stupid even a week was stupid for a woman to stay in bed after the most natural thing in the world, George Davidson of Gamblesby, whom I used to buy sheepdogs from, told me himself he was born behind a hedge, while his mother was hoeing turnips, after 'I slipped out' he said, Mother just wrapped me up, and kept on hoeing—his parents lived at Skirwith, his father had the nickname 'Tito' who had a reputation for opening his neighbours gates at night and letting his own stock graze these till the early hour, then put the stock back in his own field.

Monique came home on 28th November 1957, already bottle-feeding little Joey, as we called him. He looked a little better after a week of age on him, his cleft chin had almost disappeared, Monique's breasts were huge and full, as with our first, they were uncomfortable for her, but she was determined to do away with breastfeeding. The new baby was very good in the daytime but a menace at night. He cried and continued to cry night after night, all night. I suggested we put him in the end bedroom, 25 yards away. This was a very large room, but I had fixed a fan heater—the same big strong ones I had in the hatchery, on one of the walls, the room, when we put the baby in, was nice and warm, Moniquefed him about midnight. That was his last feed till morning.

Monique went to see him, and gave him a change, and bathed him at 7:00 am. I heard a shout from her, she came out of the room with the little one wrapped in a shawl. Monique was beside herself, the baby had been sick all over, diarrhoea, he was as cold as ice, the heater had gone wrong and was blowing cold air, and this was the end of December, the weather was ice cold, poor little chappie, Monique gave him a warm bath, fresh woolly warm clothes, and nursed him for hours in her arms, she was distraught at what had happened. Little Joey, no matter how he cried, was with us or just next door 3 yards away. From then on—at six months old, he stopped crying and was good as gold. His looks had changed—and for the best, he no longer looked like an old college professor. His cleft had disappeared, he was now a handsome little man.

On 13th January, Dad and I sailed to Belfast from Morecombe with a view to bringing some bulling heifers (that is, two-year-old females) Angus Shorthorn X to start a beef herd. The crossing was smooth, we arrived in Belfast early on the 14th and took a taxi to the auction mart, but there was nothing for us there, we decided, therefore, to go to Dublin, which we did, and took a train forthwith, arriving late afternoon—booking into the Gresham Hotel, here, as always on later visits, the food downstairs was excellent, and as usual, there were many of those black crows—or should I say, Vultures, the Catholic Priests guzzling their hearts out on their poor parishioner's money.

At the auction, when we had bought what we wanted for the moment, the question was, to get them to the ships bound for Liverpool, a small, thin man came to our rescue and said that he would see to everything for us, and not to worry at all. His name was Christy Collins. He was to prove a good friend over the years. As poor as a Church mouse, Christy lived each day on its own. On later visits, he seemed to know we were there because, without fail, he was the first to greet us on the quayside when docking in Dublin from Liverpool. Dad never let him know we would be there on a certain date, but he never failed to meet us, and when we left for the return, he always escorted us onto the boat. One time, Mother went with us. She was rather shocked but also rather pleased as Christy kissed her on the cheek as he bade us farewell on the boat. When business was done and finished, Dad would invite Christy to the nearest Pub to Ganly's. It was a good pub, too, full of farmers, drovers, and buyers, it was a nice place to be in, most friendly. There, we would drink Guinness. At first, I used to think the barmen had forgotten our orders, it took such a time before the glasses were handed over, but when they were handed over—what goodness it was! The Guinness was like Jersey Cream, as smooth as satin, and it went down like satin— this, I learnt, was the secret of a good Guinness, do not hurry the pouring of it, little by little, slowly, until the glass has been filled, then there is the glass in front of your eyes, your tongue passes, without one knowing it, over one's teeth, watching, as this black beauty gently settles, you lift the glass to your lips, then one realises—the wait, was very much so, worth while.

Guinness poured like beer, out of the tap into the glass, is not a true taste. It is as different as day is to night. Another thing that is a must for Guinness, it should not be served ice cold or chilled. It must be at room temperature—but decidedly also not warm, Christy told me, on a Saturday night, he could down 20 to 24 pints—looking at him, he must have had hollow legs!

Once again, Dad wanted me to go with him to Dublin on 4th February. I did not want to go, as now, I was at full stretch—or almost with full incubators, brooders full, and month-old chicks to deliver on the afternoon of the 4th. Day olds—quite a lot. On the 5th, I gave Jakob a paper of customers to deliver to. For both days, the frost was back again, the ground like iron. I gave the chicken van key to Monique to give to Jakob. I had taken it out because the present shepherd, David Winter (of Foot and Mouth fame!), had a habit of 'borrowing' any vehicle with a key in it. This time, I gave it to Monique for safekeeping, telling this to Jakob. Dad and I set off after lunch because of the frosty conditions. There was no motorway then, having to pass through all of the small villages on the way. On arrival, as usual, there was Christy, with a welcoming, big smile on his face—cattle stick in his hand, it was nice to see him—this time, it was not so cold, in fact—it was colder at home, we had a look at quite a number of cattle before the auction started, cattle trucks were bringing cattle in nonstop, the Black Crow's were also gathering.

Dad wanted both heifers and bullocks today. He bought seventy head of bullocks and a twenty-two-year-old heifer—a nice bunch, as usual. At the drop of the hammer, they were in the hands of Christy for marking with scissors. He never made a mistake—all of the cattle we bought had veterinary papers of clearance for T.B. and Brucellosis.

We got home on Thursday the 6th to a very cold, hard frost. I had complaints from three good customers that on Tuesday the 4th, the month-old chicks had been delivered in the dark, and the cold conditions had killed quite a lot of these chicks. It turned out that Jakob had been very petted and refused to ask Monique for the key to the chick van until Eddie, the egg incubator and brooder cleaner (plus many other jobs) had told Jakob to get a move on and delivered chicks that had been boxed hours before, he told Eddie, he was not asking for the key, Eddie went and told Monique, so she told Eddie to tell Jakob to come straight away, and shewould hand over the key, he eventually did, with great surliness, and impudent to boot, these chicks, no matter how cold the weather, if put in their hay box brooders at the customers place in the day time, would have taken no harm at all. But, at night, taken from their warm dispatch boxes and put into outside hay box brooders, with the frost as hard as iron, they could not generate enough heat on their own quickly enough, so cold overtook many during the night and died. One of the customers, Jack Metcalfe, lost 75, and the rest risked a chill and perhaps would not grow and develop for a long time. I had to apologise and replace 200-month-old chicks from this episode, and—to boot, it is very bad public relations, as bad news always travels fast.

On his return from delivering the chicks, Monique was in the kitchen when Jakob returned—he lived in and slept in the men's quarters above the large kitchen and again was in an impudent mood. He threw the van keys at Monique, whence they dropped to the floor. I stopped him at his work and asked for an explanation. I told him I had customers complaining about his delivery—far too late in the day, and of his attitude when delivering, and that I was most displeased. We had been friends when I was just a farm boy—now I was his boss. I think it rattled him, though I had always been fair to him. He could give none—I told him he best return to the house and apologise to my wife, there the matter would end. He said he was apologising to no one—with that, I had no alternative but to sack him on the spot, I got someone else to finish his work. He packed and left. Within the hour, I was in the kitchen, talking to Monique, when I heard him starting to descend the boxed-in, rather steep staircase from the kitchen to his room. All of a sudden, he lost his footing. And fell from top—to bottom of the stairs with a great crash. Monique and I looked at each other and smiled. He'd been asking for this for a long time. Monique of course, could not cook at first, but after a year, was quite good. This is when after a year with Jakob living in, she cooked for him—as for me, the same food as I ate, and for the nursemaid Maria, in his pique, he, at mealtimes, would take a look at his plate, and throw it to the other end ofthe long kitchen table, that would seat twelve people, I told Monique, if he can't eat the same as you and I, he must do without, Monique was rather demoralised by all of this—perhaps I should have got rid of him a long time before.

15

The hatching for this season of 1958 was very good, except for the hiccup during the extreme cold spell, finishing hatching on the last day of April. Monique thought she would like to go to Oran for aholiday with the baby, Joey. I took them both down to Manchester Airport. I applied the same day Monique left for Oran for a visa for myself to go out at a later date. Visas had to be had now to enter Algeria because of the troubles and Guerrilla War with the Arabs.

Mother was looking after Adam, our firstborn. She absolutely adored Adam but took little interest in baby Joey—whom she and Dad always referred to as Charles, he, the baby, was also named after the family's famous great Uncle Charles of Klondyke fame.

I phoned Monique two or three times a week. We missed each other, the phone lines were not very clear in those years. Monique said she would come home if I have no Visa by Monday 16th. She says she is missing me too much. However, on a Monday, still no Visa in the post, so I phoned the French Consul in Liverpool, they themselves couldn't understand why I had not received one, the girl on the phone knew me by now, and said it was just awful, I phoned Monique at 11:00 am. I told her I was on my way, with no Visa, but I would stop off in Marseilles and try the authorities there. With that, I set off for Manchester Airport in the Jaguar Mark 7. On the 17th, I left the car beside the entrance to the terminal—Manchester, those days, was only a small provincial airport, not like the giant it is today, like a few more parked there, walked a few yards, and got a ticket to Marseille, but the plane had to drop down in Paris—where I had to take another plane, I duly arrived in Marseille at 9:00 pm, and went straight to the Continental Hotel. The airport bus very kindly, dropped me at the door. I thought 'always good service, these French Airlines' they looked after their passengers.

I phoned Monique to say I had landed, she was delighted

and told me she herself would take a plane from Oran and be in Marseilles in the morning (next day, 18th). I was pleased, and so—even at that late hour, the hotel was still serving dinner (not like the English finish serving dinner at 8:00 pm). I sat down to a meal of huge prawns, followed by ½ a guinea fowl, brie cheese, and wild strawberries to follow, all washed down with a very good red wine, a good Havana in the lounge—accompanied by a Courvoisier grad lux, and to bed bymidnight. The French never hurry over meals, and since I married Monique, neither have I and when we are together on holiday, we often take four hours over a meal. This, I think, is the spice of life. It is a lovely partof living and also good for the digestive system, but, of course, on the farm, I only have an hour for lunch, but dinner is another thing! Once the babies have their bath and put to bed by 5:30 pm – 6:00 pm, we can eat at leisure, taking an hour and a half to two hours.

I went to Marignnane (Marseilles) Airport on the 18th by taxi to meet Monique. She arrived near midday, looking beautifully sun tanned, we fell into each other's arms—together at last. We both had been lost without each other. We lay, the night long, in each other's arms, contented to be together. That evening, we dined at one of the many small restaurants surrounding the little old port. We had a table on the pavement, which I liked. One can see the rest of the world go by. The weather was sunny and hot, I cannot recall the name of the restaurant, but the owner was a large, jovial, beaming man. We both had, for starters, the extra big gambas, then Monique said she would like the speciality of Marseilles, Boul-labialise. I had never had it, so I decided to follow suit myself. I like to try everything once! The Bouillabaisse arrived, a grand, large bowl of fish—in their own special soup, there was enough for six people. We had, from the start, two bottles of Bordeaux! We quietly waded through this speciality of Marseilles, but after two servings of the soup—while on my second plate—I realised that I had had enough. A little man in my stomach said, "No more." The food was, no doubt, excellent, but my system wanted no more Boullabaise. Monique went on to have three servings—until the large bowl was empty. It was her favourite—fish soup or the like. Since then, I have never touched Fish soup, or Boullabaise. If I did, I know I would have to leave the table and possibly vomit—it is very strange. It must be some allergic reaction to the concoctions; otherwise, I love and eat all varieties of fish.

The restaurant owner was delighted that his speciality had gone down so well. It showed on his beaming face. Next, we had a cheese board with at least a dozen cheeses on it. Over this and the second bottle of wine, we went very slowly—sampling these lovely cheeses, looking into each other's eyes with love, and holding hands—not like the English, but openly on the table, by gosh, I thought life is good. Our host, the large beaming man, saw we were in love, and of course, the French love a couple in love. He would watch us, and when I caught his eye, his smile would get bigger. He insisted we have wild strawberries from the countryside—picked that afternoon, he said. I obliged, so did Monique. She had hers with a touch of wine, but I love thick cream on my strawberries, so the host brought mine in a small silver jug. We thanked our host for the taste and freshness of our strawberries, going on to congratulate him on his excellent cuisine—which, in truth—was an excellent meal, he was absolutely thrilled by our compliments and, I think, captivated by Monique's beauty. When I ordered coffee and cognac for myself, Monique stayed with the wine, he insisted they were on the house—with that, he brought a bottle of Biscuit de Bouche to the table and poured such a large one, we sat another ¾ of an hour while I cut and prepared, and smoked a beautiful Ramone Allones, by the time we left, after thanking our kind host, we had been four hours at the table, it did not seem that long, but I suppose when two lovers are together, and a superb meal, time is forgotten.

After our meal, we strolled, hand in hand, around the little port, watching the fishermen preparing their boats to go out a little later and be back into port in the early hours of the morning with their catch. We had another drink at a pavement bar and just watched this sitting, and browsing quietly at a pavement bar, is a fascinating thing, watching all the different species of human nature go by. Then, in 1958, there were not many Arabs here.

At the turn of 1.00am, we turned in for the night; though the place was still a beehive of activity, I wished to have a clear head in the morning, for I had to visit the Police. The morning of the 19th, we both went to the Gendarmerie for my visa, it was a special office, I explained, and hey presto, within the hour—I had a visa, all that hookery-pookery with the consul in Liverpool, what a load of nonsense they were. To celebrate, we returned to the restaurant where we had dinner the night before, for lunch. Our beaming host beamed more than ever. He was delighted we had returned to him. This time, we started with foi gras, possibly not the thing—in hot weather, but it was perfect. Our host was pleased; he told us he made his own. It was a lengthy job, he said, taking all the little veins out of the goose livers. In any case, he made a good foi gras. Then we had Lobster; they were good-sized ones too and tasted excellent with our host's own made ioli to go with them. I had the wild strawberries again. Monique had eaten almost too much, so we finished off with ice cream. The cheese board was placed in front of us, all varieties, completely new cut, and fresh. We had gruyere, and a brie. Again, we had two bottles of superb wine—and with the cheese – better still. We had coffee, those small cups, and excellent black coffee only the French or Italian can make. Once again, our host insisted on my having an extra-large bisquit de Bouche—on the house, I accepted quite willingly—he never needed to twist my arm on things like that! Monique stayed, once again, with the superb wine—and once again, I cut a grand Ramone Alones, and once again, we had taken four hours at the table! I think our host must have been thinking it rather strange—here is a young English man who seems to know and love his food—but then, he would think—yes—but look with whom he is with!

On 20th June, we flew to Oran in one of those enormous, four-engine, double-decker planes that I had flown over to be married in 1954. The service and food were as usual—excellent. Arriving in Oran, the weather was boiling hot. Paddilla was there to meet us with Monique's Aunt, Josephine.

We have whisked away in the Mercedes. I noticed all of the buses had their windows and windscreens covered in heavy metal grills and Soldiers everywhere. The rebel Arabs war was hotting up. We entered the new garage, the guard raised his barrier pole, saluted, and we were in the vast courtyard of the garage, with its workshops for leather, diesel, metal repair, washing, and greasing departments—all separate from one another, at full work. In the middle of the courtyard, there were petrol and diesel pumps with the S.O.T.A.C. flagpole. Surrounding all of this was a 20-foot high wall with a 3-foot walkway on the top. This, at night, was patrolled by some of the garage men, plus a handful of Soldiers, all with Sten Gun type of Machine Guns. The outside grounds were always floodlit at night, making it impossible to approach any part of the wall without being seen. The whole garage was on a war footing.

However, here we were, I was made most welcome by all, and when I went for my beer to the bar, at the end of their days' work, dozens of the garage hands gathered around to say hello and shake hands—from Arab to French and Spanish. They told me to be free for the next night, for they were going to give me a party, a meal for Monique and I, and to wet our little Joey's head. They were going to hold it in two or three of the bus bays, tables and chairs—everything! The next night, the garage hands had made a rather splendid effort, there were bottles of everything—in abundance, all paid for by themselves, and in our honour, I was really touched by this kind act.

The meal was mostly of rabbits that the workers had reared at one end of the garage in cages. About 15 huge rabbits, as big as hares, had been reared and fattened. They usually reared the rabbits for some holy Saint Day, or Bastille day—now, they had honoured Monique and myself. The rabbits were cooked as Lapin Provencal. I loved it, Monique so—so, she never has been a lover of rabbits, but she made a good effort, as all eyes were on her, most of the workers had seen her grow up, now they saw her blooming into young womanhood—in all her beauty. The party finished at midnight, and everyone thoroughly enjoyed themselves. I thanked all assembled for their great kindness on behalf of Monique.

The garage workers to a man if Monique walked around the garage courtyard with baby Joey, they would down tools and run over to see him, by now he was like a chubby cherub, pink-faced and blond hair and blue eyes. They had never, they said, seen such a beautiful child. He washeld and nursed by many. The Latin race loves babies and small children—men and women, and to them, here was the eighth wonder of the world!

By now, since we had married, Monique told me a little about her childhood and her family members. Her maternal Grandfather had started the bus business—at first, with horse-drawn buses, then petrol-engined ones, becoming very rich in the process, owning a large mansion in the Rue Gambetta, in the middle of Oran—named La Remise, a string of racehorses behind the mansion, grooms and servants. He lived in grand style. He had two sons and five daughters, the mother of Monique being one. Over the years, the world slump of the 20s hit him also, and his fortunes declined. When Monique was a small child, she could remember him driving up with one of his ponies and gigs, picking her up, and going for long drives. When he died, he did not have much liquid cash, but he left Monique 20 big Luis D'or, which Monique's Aunt Josephine immediately gave to that witch Rene. A little later, her Grandmother died, leaving Monique most of her jewellery, of rings and earrings. Quite a selection of the very best, the other members of the family dipped their fingers in, and Monique was left with very little. They, the family, said they wanted mementos – some mementos!

It was only in the last two weeks before we were married that Monique ever went to a hairdresser—which reminds me! Paul had seen Monique talking to a boy on the pavement after school one day, she was fifteen years old, he went home, told his mother, and when Monique arrived, she got the usual hard slaps across the face, then the Aunt called out, and a strange woman came out of an adjoining room with a pair of scissors, Monique was held down, and her hair—all of it—was cut off, almost to the scalp, this completely demoralised her for days, then, being determined, she tried to put it behind her, her hair had been long, it must have been an awful shock for her, the worst thing, Monique told me, was facing her school friends. If I had known any of this when I was over there getting married or on holiday, I would certainly not have been too friendly to the family Pineda. It was also the first time she was allowed to choose her own shoes or dresses, even on holiday with Mr and Mrs Pineda, and Rene, when staying at hotels where dining and dancing was the regular thing. If a person at an adjoining table wished to dance with Monique—at fifteen or sixteen years old, Rene would then insist that Monique be sent to bed, and of course, the old Aunt would. It can not have been a very nice life for her.

It was a hot summer in Oran, Monique and I adjourned to the family villa at Bousfere. From this, we walked across the sand, which was red hot, into the sea. We had baby Joey with us in his carry cot, and before it got full heat of the day and evening, we had him on the beach under a huge umbrella. This was very necessary—for me as well. Even so, I got so badly sunburned my shoulders were raw, almost to the bone. It was painful sleeping for a few days. It was now that I learnt to swim, the sea was very warm and clear as crystal, and I saw no signs of pollution at all. I also had a nasty bout of the flu and craved Lemon drinks. I was in luck, as each day, an Arab would call at most villas with his donkey and cart, loaded with fruit, melons, and lemons. I bought about two stone lemons for very little money. Now I had my drinks, each one like nectar. In a few days, I was back to my old self.

Talking about Arabs, there was one old Arab farmer who would call at the S.O.T.A.C. garage with his little cameonette loaded with fruit for Mr Pineda as a gift, I met him many times, and we always had a little chat. He was a most charming and delightful old man, with a smiling open face, he had two sons working at the garage, it turned out, his gifts of fruit were a gesture of thanks for the past, Mr Pineda had helped him financially in his younger days, to start a small farm, in which he was quite successful, but by his open friendship with the Pineda's during the Guerrilla War in 1959, the Arabs—his own friends, cut his throat, when I heard the news, I was extremely sad at this terrible thing, for Belle Arbi was a gentleman.

On Tuesday, 1st July 1958, Mother phoned me in Oran to tell me—over a lot of static noise which made it difficult to make out, that Frank Stockdale had been killed in a tractor accident. He was one of Dad's tractor men, he was a good worker and had been at Skirwith Hall for fourteen years. It seems that he had been grubbing land for potatoes. The grubber, not being on hydraulics—but on the drawbar of the tractor, had hit what we call in Cumberland a set fast. This is, or can be, a very large rock or stone just under the surface of the ground, Frank struck one of these set fasts with his tractor, a Massey Fergusson 135. Joe Frith, one of the other tractor drivers, was working in the same field, 50 yards farther away. Frank tried again to pull the grubber away, with some force—still no result. He backed the grubber a yard or two. To the rear, he put a heavy snigging chain onto the grubber's drawbar and then onto the top link of his tractor. This link is way above the back axle and charged the set fast at full power. As soon as the grubber hit the stone or rock, the snig chain being so high above the axle pulled the tractor quite easily backwards and upside down on top of Frank—killing him instantly. Joe Frith rushed over and was there in seconds, he could do nothing himself. This happened in a field on the roadside between Langwathby and Skirwith. Joe stopped the first car to come along and, between himself and the others, managed to get Frank from under the tractor, it was too late, only a few minutes had passed since Frank was freed. At the autopsy, it turned out that a rib had gone through his heart.

Mrs Stockdale is still in the village of Skirwith, and Frank's daughter becomes a housekeeper to Robert Jackson, a certified bachelor. She also is still keeping house for Robert in 2008.

While I was in Oran, Monique and I thought it a good idea to have baby Joey christened there, at the same Church and the same protestant parson who had married us. Monique and I went to see him. At our request, he was over the moon with delight. Forthwith, we had him christened in June, a big lunch was laid on in the penthouse apartment for thirty-five family and close friends.

On 20th July, our holiday came to an end. We took the plane to Manchester—via Paris. On the plane were quite a few French Soldiers going home on leave. Many of them, including other passengers, were taken with baby Joey. He spent more time being nursed by them than us—especially by a Sergeant, a large, kind chap, going home to his children, he was a hit wherever he went, our baby. We landed in Manchester in the afternoon and walked out of the airport building. The Jaguar was still there, in the same place. A uniformed chap passing said, "We were wondering who owned this one"—the trouble was, the battery was flat! So, I asked a taxi driver to give me a tow to jump-start her, which he did. It took a good pull before the car would fire, and then she caught it. I gave the taxi driver one pound, thanked him, and we were on our way. I thought we would go home via Leeds, see Auntie Kate and Uncle David, whereas, usual, Auntie tried to kill us with kindness and stayed the night. 22nd July, the Jaguar nosed into the drive leading to Skirwith Hall. It was nice to be back home. I went around my breeding birds for the 58-59 hatching season to find them in 1st class condition—(note in my diary to this effect!)I remember, as a boy, following the binder on foot, with a stick to knock the rabbits on the head—as they squatted flat and let the binder pass over their heads, it was the same field that poor Frank Stockdale was later killed in. John Dixon—the head man, was on the binder pulled by three horses. The day was sunny and hot. John was a great pipe smoker. It was he who gave me a chow of black twist when I was in my teens hoeing turnips and had to sit down. John lit his pipe while driving the binder and threw his still-lit match over the back side of the binder into the ripe oats. At once, a blaze started—small, but spreading every second, quick as a flash, I started to stamp out the fire. John stopped the horses at my shout, he had not noticed what he had done, we both managed to stamp the fire out within seconds, poor John, he was most embarrassed and more or less, implored me not to mention the incident, I never did, either to Dad, or the other men, but for me jumping into the fire, the field—in seconds, would have been out of control, all 18 acres of it. I was, perhaps, twelve years old.

On 20th January 1959, Dad and I went down to Hereford Bull Sales to buy a bull by car. We ran into the fog in patches, and on approaching Warrington, it got denser and denser until I was unable to see more than two or three yards—quite unable to see across the street in Warrington. Dad got out and walked beside the front of the car—his Alvis. On the pavement side, I just could not see even the pavement, a crossroads came up, but all we could see—when we were on top of them, the traffic lights. We managed to cross with Dad leading the way, over the crossroads, we realised it was no good going further, it was impossible. Dad was looking for a hotel while walking beside the car, by luck, in a few minutes, there was an illuminated sign—hotel, in we went, and by chance, they had a room, thank goodness, they, the hotel, were full, everyone had done what we were now doing—but much earlier than us. In any case, we were now easy for the night. The hotel was the

Pattern Arms, it was quite a cozy hotel, we both had a good stiff whisky or two, sat back after a good dinner, and lit a Havana each, we were good company, Dad and I got on well together, all the bits of money he owed me was really nothing, he had reared, and looked after me well, in childhood and adolescence, we shot, and smoked together like old pals, we had a nightcap, then to bed.

In the morning, there were only patches of fog, which soon cleared, and we were on our way to Hereford after breakfast, arriving there just in time for the judging—First went to the Green Dragon Hotel to book in, but they were full, the receptionist tried the Graftonbury, and others, eventually getting us a double bedded room at the Kerry Arms, the room was small, but seemed not bad, at the same time—not what we were used to. We left our bags in the bedroom and off to the sales. Dad bought a very nice sixteen-month-old Bull for 230gms, the top price was 5,000gns, the Champion made 1900gns, and the Reserve 1000gns. After dining at the Green Dragon, we left to sleep at the Kerry Arms, when I got into my bed, I thought, *By jove, this is damp*, so I put my raincoat on top of my pyjamas and slept in that, in the bed—which was a mistake, I should have slept on the top of the bed or, better still, complained to the manager, because four days later I came down with bronchial flu, I had to take to bed for ten days, only getting up a week later on the 11th February, to go with Dad to Joe Varty's funeral at Ousby, Joe had had a fall, and had to go into Penrith Cottage Hospital, where he died a few days later, he was eighty years old. Joe had worked at Skirwith Hall for forty years or more, bouncing Adam, Cathie, and me on his knees when we were babies, I was sad, it was as if part of our family had gone, indeed, part of the past we look back on had gone, then, I went back to my sick bed.

In June, I helped Dad castrate the bull calves. These were seven to nine months old and very strong young things. We would drive a dozen of them into a loose box, which had a gangway (corridor) leading into the box, the men would cut two off into the gangway, catch them with a rope around their neck, bend the heads back until the calf would fall over, quickly sit on its head, tie its legs, and put the animal on its back. Then, with a calf each, Dad and I would set to with red hot gelding irons—specially made irons, green salve and clamps, the irons heated in a brazier outside. Some of the bull calves were either Angus X or at this time, we had some Galloway Xs. These youngsters could be hard to handle. They had a lot of bad tempers in them. When they knew they were cornered, they would charge us in the gangway, letting off a mighty roar in the process. Men would dodge, grab hold and hang on to them. We had some savage tussles, and inevitably—at the end of the day, most of us would have our trousers torn from hip to ankle with their flying hooves—sharp as razors. It was hard but exciting work.

One-eyed Willie Chapelhow always asked me to save the testicles for him, which I did, he seemed to love them so much that I asked him how he cooked them. He told me, so the next time I gelded bull calves, I kept some myself, followed One-Eyed Willie's instructions, and found the testicles to be delicious! After this, Willie got very few of them, and later in life, I ate wild boar testicles—and educated the French to do so. Red deer stag, lamb—of course, and to finish, horse's testicles—all are extremely succulent and delightful to eat. Later, in Cannes, I asked our butcher, George Brouger, to keep the young bull testicles, thinking they would be eighteen months or thereabouts. George kept me about a dozen the first time I asked him, they were huge but far too tough, they must have been from beasts three to four years old—and from Charolais, which George specialised in. The Charolais itself is a magnificent animal, but as far as the meat taste is concerned—zero!

My Jaguar Mark 7 had been drinking petrol as I drank whisky, far too much! I almost needed a Petrol Tanker towed behind! She had two tanks, one on each side, so I had an element of safety from being stranded, as one tank emptied, I filled the other up at the next Petrol Station. I had the car over at Studholm, Dixon's garage in Whitehaven, the mechanic there was Bobby Dixon's own racing mechanic. Bobby, of my school days—this garage could find nothing wrong. I had County Motor's, Carlisle, take a look, they could find nothing wrong, I was at a loss when Dad told me his Alvis had been serviced regularly by old George at Arm- strong and Flemings garage, Penrith. As a last resort, I took the car to George, he would be sixty years old then spoke a broad Cumberland dialect, I explained to George my problem, the car only did 8-9 m/g. He said, leave her with me for a couple of days, which I did.

Two days later, when I was in Penrith, I called to see how George was getting on with the car, he seemed pleased with himself, then elaborated, ' She's had a bloody rotten petrol pipe, that's the trouble' Sure enough, George had found the root of the whole problem—a rotten petrol pipe carrying petrol to the carburettors, he told me he had tuned it up, he used only his ears when doing this, listening intently—No new-fangled instruments, I realised then, that George was unique, he was a natural, a born mechanic. He went with me for a short run, the car ran for the first time since new, absolutely perfect—as smooth as satin. I thanked George most profusely and slipped him 2 pounds, he was pleased that I was pleased. Two days later, Monique and I set off for the Dairy Show in London—on 26th October. The car ran like a dream and made 24 1/2 m/g—a tremendous difference. We stayed, as usual, at the Russel. Most of the management and staff knew us, and of course, many Northerners were there that I knew.

22nd November 1959, an old shooting and drinking friend died, he was Tim Parker of Skelton, he was a cousin of Major Parker, Bridgett's father. Tim took a lot of land around Skelton, a few miles outside Penrith, where he used to invite me to shoot together with other friends of his. The trouble was before Tim invited anyone, he made sure he, himself, had shot the land well before any invites came. He was an excellent shot, he had only one eye. That, he told me, had been damaged while riding over the sticks on Manchester Racecourse, for which he claimed compensation and received 500 pounds from the racecourse committee there. In reality, Tim said, my eye was badly damaged by a friend's catapult, which accidentally hit Tim in the eye. He rode at Manchester two days later and put the blame on that racecourse.

He, in his young days, was a great 'point to point' rider and rode the whole of the winners in one day. I believe it may have been the Cumb and Cumb Farmers, then, of course, there was no lady's race, he had the physique of a boxer, tremendously strong, and broad shoulders, his face strongly resembled Hugh, Earl of Lonsdale—the Great Yellow Earl, it was acknowledged by those 'in the know' that the Yellow Earl was in- deed, his father, and like his father, he liked to fight or box, it was all the same to Tim. One day at Skelton Agricultural Show, he fell foul of the police, knocking three of them unconscious. He jumped in his car and went home. Of course, in no time, the police had him arrested, but because of his family's connections, little more was heard of it.

In his later years, he used to be at various local Agricultural Shows, he had many friends from the town head, potters like Bowmans, Lowthers, and Jackson. He would get a lot of drink into these chaps, and encourage them to get into a row that would turn into a first-class fight. Tim would stand and watch all of this in great delight, laughing his head off! His parents could keep few housemaids for very long because as soon as they ar- rived, Tim would bed them down, whether they liked it or not. At one time, he had chauffeurs, or rather, the female side of the chauffeurs. Tim would sit in the back, behind the driver, with his feet on the chauffeur's shoulders—nearly always full of drink in the evenings, he was a colourful character!

His father thought he would settle Tim down, so he put him on one of his own farms near Skelton, where Tim started farming. The trouble was, Tim was always short of money, so he would sell a couple of cows or a dozen sheep to tide himself over, his father went one day to see how Tim was farming and to see if he had settled down, he asked to see the stock, but had rather a surprise, there were none! Tim had sold the lot, that was Tim's venture into farming!

When his father died, he did not leave Tim a large lump of cash, he had tied it up so that Tim received the interest either three monthly or yearly. That was the best thing he could have done. Cash would have been water in his hands. Tim always wore a bowler hat and his best-checked suit for Carlisle Races, arriving back at the George Hotel absolutely full but ready to take some more. One of the last days I shot with Tim would be just two weeks before he died, we shot not much game but had a good lunch in the 'Dog and Gun' pub in the village. There were four more Guns from Lancashire, it had been a wettish morning, Tim in knickerbockers—had no coat, so he stood in front of the roaring log fire drying himself, in minutes, we could hardly see him for the steam. The last day he shot was a Saturday, I was invited but was unable to go, it was again a wet day. Tim—again no coat, he liked his arms to be free for his gun—once again dried himself in front of the fire, downing seven or eight large gin and waters; during the drying process—steam rising in clouds, he sat down for a meal in the 'Dog and Gun' of 6-8 eggs and bacon etc, downed another 8-10 Gins before going to bed—where he lay down and died.

I remember one day shooting with Tim, his big friend from Lancashire (I forget his name) had come, together with two others—all buddies, at Tim's request. This day, we had quite a nice sample of the game, and a good lunch was consumed in the pub. At the end of the day, we adjourned once again to the pub—only for ½ an hour, it turned out today was the birthday of his big friend, who was going back to celebrate and stay the night at Shap Wells Hotel. In a short while, Tim's friends left to return to Shap Wells Hotel. When they had gone, I stayed talking to Tim—he was not responsive at all. I asked him what the matter was, and he replied, "My friend for years has just left for his birthday celebration and never even asked me." He said this with a heavy heart. Of course, Tim had no motorcar, his friends would not want to run him there and back again—such are friends. I asked him he would have liked to have gone to this dinner with his long-time friend. "Of course, I would," he replied, I then said, well, come on then, we will gate crash them, at this Tim is always ready for mischief, his face broke into a big grin, right, he said, come on, so into the chicken van we got, and set off for Shap Wells Hotel, the old shooting lodge of the Yellow Earl, which in the war years, housed the high ranking German Officers Prisoners of War, now a Hotel.

It was not too far, perhaps 15-18 miles. I put my foot down, each of us in our shooting togs, boots, etc.! We arrived as Tim's friends were just sitting down for their dinner, the surprise on their faces were something to see! Two more chairs were added for us to dine—which we did! The oth- ers were in dinner jackets and black ties, Tim and I in our shooting clothes and boots. We passed a good evening, the food was good—and better still, Tim's friends paid the bill. After treating the manager and chef to drinks, we left the hotel at 1.00 am I had to take Tim home first, then made my own way back to Skirwith, passing Carleton, a suburb of Pen- rith, a rear tyre burst, my spare was at home for some reason, so I ran the car slowly about 20 yards into someone's front garden, a telephone box was handy, so I phoned Monique—she was not very pleased, but she came to pick me up, this was the time she was breastfeeding Adam, her breasts were so full of milk, she could hardly steer the car for it was painful for her, it was a beautiful full moonlit night, and before Monique picked me up, I had walked three miles with my Westley Richards 12 bore over my shoulder, I got a ticking off from Monique—which I deserved, as she had never liked Tim, he was too rude for her.

Christmas came and went, but it was a very pleasant Christmas, on Boxing Day, we were invited to dine with my parents at Kirkland, where it was Christmas feast once again, whisky and cigars. The year closed down on Wednesday, 30[th,] to the first Chicken hatch for the 1960 season. My main egg and hatchery cleaner, Eddie, was off work with housemaids knee, Elsie Frith, the head tractor man's wife, took over temporarily from him, Elsie was a former school friend of ours from the local village school, a pretty blond, and a good worker—always pleasant, her mother, Alice Robinson, kept the Post Office in Skirwith, she was a little dynamo, delivering telegrams to people miles away, on her bicycle, anyone died, Alice used to 'lay them out' but, one-day delivering telegrams, she fell off her bicycle going down a steep hill, something jammed in her front wheel, and she came to a dreadful Clopper, cutting her head open badly, and I think, broke her arm, I don't think she ever recovered from this, because about two years later she had a stroke, and was paralysed down one side, she recovered slowly—but only partly, and had to give up the Post Office. Monique used to call on her to perk her up with a little chat. Strange, at one time, there were three Alice Robinson's in the village. I often wondered whether they received each other's posts!

On Saturday, 30th January, I was invited to shoot a duck with Major Ritchard Burton of Brackenbank Hotel, Lazonby. Ritchard Burton was a character out of the old school, he lived for his dogs and shooting. Having his own moors on the Pennines, he would, in the auction, ask farmers from quite far afield if he could shoot pigeons with a few friends off stubble or rape turnips. Consent would be given, but then Ritchard would arrive quietly and begin to shoot the whole farm until hardly anyone would consent to give him anything. He was, though, always a gentleman. He kept a fine table, served in the old genteel style—himself doing the carving, he had invited Monique and I twice, and again on 1st January, with excellent food and drink, Monique was quite impressed. My hatchery man Eddie had worked as a part-time cook for him, and he—Eddie, had spotted Ritchard in the bath with his secretary—he was also a lady-man and quite charming with it. More of Ritchard later!

July 18th Monique flew over to Oran for a holiday, she felt like a good rest, she had lost quite a bit of weight, the children were pulling her down, and running an 18-roomed house, buying furniture bit by bit, my drinking habits with my shooting friends—when I would be away shooting, which was once, sometimes twice a week, I would not return home until the early hours—quite innocent, only Men's world—the world of shooting, but Monique would think sometimes there would be a woman about, of course there never was, and never has, Monique has been my sunshine for now fufty-eight years, and we are still in love, and still lovers. (We had plans to meet up later).

I landed in Oran at 9:30 am in a sizzling heat. Monique and Padilla were there to meet me, it was good to be with my wife again, we had both missed each other. On my car trip with Heinz, I had sent Monique a postcard every day, telling her exactly where we were—she still has them!

By midday, I was at the family beach villa, swimming in the very warm sea, the sand was so hot on my bare feet, I had to run across the sand to either our umbrella and straw mats or into the sea, one could almost cook an egg on the pavement, it was so hot. I swam, and rested, and got my shoulders so sunburned, they peeled and peeled and became almost raw, it was, for a few nights, painful to lie in bed on my back.

The following week, the garage men gave Monique and their—by now, usual big dinner party held at the main S.O.T.A.C. garage. They were a good, kind lot, of course, most of them had seen Monique grow from a small child into womanhood. And, they all thought a great deal of her and I like to think they seemed to have taken to me also. The meal was, once again, as a main course—Rabbit, but beforehand, there was a variety of knick-knacks, especially the spicy sausages—merges, these are excellent indeed, aperitifs were Ricard or Anisette, I kept off the latter because it made me queasy if I had too much, I took Ricard, which I could down like water, a good selection of red wines was also on hand, the party went on till 2:00 am. The soldiers and guards were still patrolling the garage walls, flood lights were on to prevent against surprise attack by the rebels. However, all—for the moment, was quiet.

One of the nights, Gaby invited us to dine and play at the casino. I played—won and lost. Gaby was always a perfect host, in all ways, very well-mannered and polite. By now, he was making so much money. It was incredible, and he was putting it all into his bank in France as it came in. Gaby had been in the French air force, learning flying in the U.S.A, and spoke some English, not a lot. He introduced me one day to Robert Tabereau—of whom, more later. This man was wanted by the De Gaulle Government.

Monday 15th August, Gaby and Rene invited Monique and I to a fancy dress party at a large beach house, Gaby had rented. Monique and I had news of this party ten days previous, so we both bought materials for our fancy dresses. Monique was going as an Eastern beauty princess, as Maria Montez in the films used to dress like, Bra all done in jewels and sequins, with baggy—almost see-through trousers worn from the hips and clasped at the ankles—plenty of sequins, leaving her with a bare midriff, she looked the part very much if Sam Goldwyn had have seen her, he would have had her in films without more ado.

Myself, I was dressed like either an Indian gentleman or an Arab well-to-do, with Fez, a white tunic jacket, and long, very slim, white trousers, with long curled at the toe, Turkish slipper-type open shoes, was very good affair, with many of the French well-to-do businessmen and their wives, and plenty of youngsters, married and unmarried—perhaps seventy people. Aperitifs flowed in abundance, champagne flowed like a river, followed by an excellent meal prepared by a top restaurant chef, the wines were excellent and in no shortage. Gaby, always, when he gave a party or dinner, always had the very best of wines—he knew them well, then, we danced and drank till dawn, then to bed—for Monique and I, only two hours, for we had to catch the plane for Düsseldorf via Paris, we were going to call on Heinz again.

Tuesday 16th, Monique and I left Oran by plane for Paris, we had little time to pack clothes—all was a rush at the last minute, and we were still tired from the party. Monique had been left some jewels from her Grandmother. These were taken from the bank and put on top of the clothes in the suitcase in a small wallet—and off we went to the airport, chauffeured by the faithful Padilla.

We arrived in Paris mid-afternoon and went straight to the Grand Hotel, which boasted a thousand rooms, as we had no connection to Düsseldorf that evening, we went straight to our room, leaving the suitcases with the porter to be sent up, tiredness was now taking over, so we thought to have a couple of hours rest on the bed, but before doing so I phoned the Lido and booked a table for two for the cabaret later that night—then I thought, the porter is taking a long time to send the suitcases up, I phoned downstairs and told them to get a move on and send them right away, ten minutes later, a knock at the door, the porter was there with our bags, I thanked him, and gave him a tip. Then we lay down and slept for a couple of hours, in readiness for the night's frivolities.

After our rest we showered, Monique opened her suitcase and after a pause, she shouted—my diamonds have gone, sure enough, the lot had been stolen. I put the blame on the porter's room downstairs, they had had the cases for ¾ of an hour—far too long for comfort, I rang and asked for the manager. When I explained, I was told the manager was away, I asked for the under manager—I was told he was also away, I asked for the hotel detective—he was not available, I had absolutely no help from the hotel whatsoever, so much for a Parisian 1000 bedroomed hotel.

Monique and I decided to go to the local Gendarmerie, I hailed a taxi, and it took us there. It turned out the Gendarmerie was only two or three minutes away by taxi. We explained our predicament, Monique gave a description of her jewels, and within minutes the police were in the hotel questioning the porters and other staff, but nothing turned up. Whoever had taken them in the hotel had had ample time to get rid of them. The police were very good and kept in touch with us in England. However, nothing ever turned up. The hotel refused to pay compensation, and Monique lost her jewels, it was a sad moment for her, but—in the first instance, they should never have been put on top of the contents of the suitcase.

Rather than cry over spilt milk, I insisted we carry on with our plans and go up to the Lido later that evening, which we did, and as always, the spectacle was superb. I reckon that the Lido floor show, or cabaret, is unsurpassed, it's the best in the world and still is—thirty-five years on. Whenever I or Monique and I are in Paris, the Lido is a must. Any of my friends whom I know are heading for Paris, I always tell them, for heaven's sake, do not miss the Lido.

The next day, Monique and I took the evening plane to Düsseldorf, it was still bright daylight when we landed. Heinz was there to meet us and took us quickly to 5 Milterweg, Telgte.

That same week, I bought in Munster a small gold watch for Monique, costing 42 pounds. Monique later incorporated it into a gold bracelet I had bought her for our first anniversary of marriage, when she did this, it looked to be worth a million dollars. I, for myself, bought a Leica camera for 50 pounds, and a very flat fob watch, a Swiss Pronto, also of gold. (Robert Jackson was the only other I knew who had a Pronto). I gave 50 pounds for the Pronto, and fifty years later—still have it. It is as good as new, never causes any trouble. Monique, for one of my birthdays, bought me—to go with the Pronto, a solid gold antique chain. I've had a lot of people admire them both when I look for the time.

After we had been with Heinz for two weeks, Monique and I drove home. Back home, all was well with our little boys. Mrs Metcalfe told us she had smacked Joey's bottom—not hard because he had wet his pants. She was too kind, we knew, to smack him hard, she had a good cry to herself when Monique called for him. Adam was, as usual, full of beans, but Cathie—my sister, was glad to see the tail end of him, Mother used to let him do anything he wanted, he used to like to use the Hoover carpet cleaner—so she let him, he was in his element, so was his Grandmother, she totally loved him. I think this put Cathie out of joint a bit!

16

4th October was blood testing time for the hens. At the moment there were 5000 to do. I was told a Mr Ted Sharman was coming. I had heard of this man at M.A.F. He was one of the men in command but sometimes liked to be out in the countryside himself to see how things were. Everyone at M.A.F. at Carlisle was afraid of him, he, so I was told, ruled with a rod of iron, and stood no nonsense, my word, I thought, if I have one hen react to the test we—with him, will have to go through the lot again, if a doubtful test of one hen came up before, with the girl testers, I would pull that hens neck on the spot, I myself, took no chances.

The morning of the 4th arrived, and I had all organised to receive Mr Sharman—I had engaged a man out of the village for the next three days, as Kurt was still on holiday, and my men were all versed up in all aspects. The ogre arrived, he got out of his car in the courtyard, shook hands, he in- introduced himself as Ted Sharman—I liked him right away, into the house we went, Monique made us coffee and a few biscuits—then to work. Midday, we stopped so that the men could have lunch. I also. By now, Sharman told me to call him Ted, before lunch I gave us both two very large whisky. I was taking no chances with Ted, in case of the odd hen—I was surprised, his whisky went down like cream, so I had no alternative but to do the same, and recharge our glasses with an equally big whisky. We had lunch of home-killed milk lamb of three months old—a succulent leg, it melted in one's mouth, we washed this down with some of the wine Mr Pineda had sent over in barrels, quite good wine too. I realised Ted Sharman, after we had finished testing that day, had to drive back to Carlisle—and return the next day, also the day after that, we had three full days to do blood testing. I mentioned to Monique, we should ask him to stay the two nights, I put this to him, he accepted right away, I said I had a new toothbrush, and if he wanted pyjamas—I had none! As I always slept nude, he laughed and took me up on the toothbrush, after the day's testing and a wash to freshen up, we retired to the morning room where Monique had a roaring log and coal fire going. By now, she was an expert in fire lighting. Ted and I settled down in the deep armchairs, Mother's gift to us, out came the whisky bottle, Dewar's White Label—my favourite for quite a time, I poured a couple of large ones, and a small one for Monique, who had joined us before preparing dinner, I lit one of my German cigars, Ted lit his pipe, we sat back, and had a good long crack, in front of the roaster, in no time, Ted had to move back, he said it was a bit hot for him, he had finished his pipe, and I pressed him to try a cigar, he did, and liked it immediately, by now our glasses were dry. Monique was busy cooking a couple of wild ducks I had shot,

I refilled our glasses again—twice over. At 9:00 pm, we sat down to dinner, the duck proved to be two young ones and were very good—once again—with some of our 'house wine.'

After dinner, we sat and talked and drank until midnight. We were well on our way to finishing our second bottle of Dewar's, by then, Ted was well on the way to Mandalay. I showed him to his room and went to bed myself. The next day was a repeat of the day before, except that for lunch, we had cold lamb, and at night we had a brace of pheasant I had shot on the opening day. Once again, we sat up till midnight, and once again, Ted was seeing double! The third day was a repeat of the first two, except for lunch, we had a farm chicken and, at night—beef. We ate much earlier, as Ted had to return to Carlisle, we had consumed quite a few bottles of wine, and a nice few whisky's had gone down, by now, Ted was getting quite used to this way of life, I sent him away with a couple of large ones. After dinner, he left—reluctantly, he said, and I think he meant it, I wish you had some more hens to test tomorrow.

One day I met Arthur Monkhouse, whose firm supplied Nitrovit foods in Skirwith village, he asked me if the Reed brothers owed me any money (it seemed they had overstretched themselves cash-wise), I told him they owed me just over 2000 pounds, he said, "You had best get in quick because they are going to go under." He also added, "Or by a miracle, they might survive." Well, I said, if that's the case, I will risk leaving things as they are, and hope they go ahead. They, the brothers—Eric and Guy, with their right-hand man Richards—who was also an extremely nice chap, are very capable—did clear the financial hill, and went on to become multi-millionaires. In those years, multi-millionaires were rather rare—not like today in the 90's, where they are a common thing.

The money the brothers owed me came in dribs and drabs, I kept send- ing them day old cock chickens each week, I kept getting cheques now and then—always quite a sum was in arrears. Then one day, the debt was cleared. Later on, I told Guy that if I had demanded payment immediately of my 2000 pounds plus, it could have been the straw that broke the camel's back. I don't know if he saw it this way, as by now they were on a roller coaster, but I did, so did Arthur Monkhouse, the two brothers went ahead with Yorks poultry packers, producing broiler chicks in millions. Within a short few years, Imperial Tobacco bought the two brothers out. At this time, they owned the biggest house in the village, both were bachelors, on IMP'S buyout, they immediately bought the village pub—a run-down place. Guy told me the total assets inside—including drink, was about 60 pounds, they turned the pub into an extremely plush and nice place, where it was a pleasure to go for a drink, they bought an E-type Jaguar and a Rolls Royce each. The payout by IMP was 6,000,000 pounds for each brother. Eric retired to Monte Carlo, and Guy indulged in his passion for breeding and racing horses, buying Nidd Hall Stud outside Harrogate, one of his horses— Warpath came fourth in the derby, Guy must have spent a fortune, putting most of his mares to this horse, but he never really got anything of class. I used to meet Guy at most race meetings in the North, and he was, as usual, never changing—

always a nice charming man, never losing his Yorkshire accent.

Monique quite often used to deliver chicks for me if Cathie did not arrive to do the job, the trouble was Monique, by now driving—she passed the driving test while pregnant with Adam, did not quite know where customers lived, she had to ask and ask, but eventually learned a great deal of the Cumbrian countryside. One day, she delivered some chicks to a farmer's wife who lived near Ullswater, but this farm was two fields from the road, and these two fields were only grass, no hard road, it had been raining hard, and the track up these two fields was very soft and muddy, poor Monique, she got stuck, it was slightly uphill to the farmhouse, she tried and tried, so she told me, but was unable to make it, so, she broke down and cried, after perhaps, fifteen minutes, she tried again with the chicken van, this was the Morris Oxford—she succeeded.

Boxing day 1960, I went down the beck at Skirwith Hall shooting duck. I shot ten, then I walked some of the rough ground and bagged half a dozen pheasant, and four snipe, they became so heavy, I had to leave them and come later on to pick them up with the land rover.

At night, Monique and I got ready to go to the private invitation ball at the George Hotel in Penrith, Robert Jackson went with us, I called to pick him up at his farm in the village, but Robert was never ready, never once on an outing, if I had to pick him up, he was a fiddler and a faddler. My brother Adam had once told me his—Roberts, the bedroom was like a chemist shop, full of bottles and pills, and lotions—but he was a grand chap to go out with, never greedy to stand his round, in fact, most times he would be the first to pay. Off we three went to the ball. These dinner dances were by invitation only, by Frank Street and wife Dorothy, owners, and his manager and wife—Leslie, and Lucy, these ladies were sisters, they were excellent affairs, excellent food, a very good crowd of people—all run like clockwork with super staff, that knew their job to a

T.

This night, one of the dances had a prize for the best-looking couple, Frank Street was the judge, he picked Monique, and I, my prize was a very nice thick wool scarf, Monique's was a box of chocolates, we had a good laugh, but Frank was a very nice man, long before I was married, he would come and chat to me, he said he envied my life, style, and good-humour. The reader may think I am blowing my own trumpet, but these were his words to me, my lifestyle was pretty ordinary, I did not see anything unusual in it, except no one smoked cigars, drank whisky, or shot like myself—but I thought nothing of it, my Father perhaps even less, but this was Frank speaking, and he was a straight talker coming up the hard way, he often gave me cigars, and on one occasion, a very good box of five Cuban corona's, I think he must have been a sexy young devil in his younger days, because he used to like to quiz me on my current girlfriend, trying to squeeze from me things he should not know! But I never betrayed a girl I had been out with.

Frank had married Dorothy, who was evacuated—voluntarily, I suppose, to the Fox Inn, Ousby, she was then Mrs Buck, Frank used to be at the Fox three or four times a week in his Jaguar car. They were the war years until Dorothy said she would marry him, I think it was a perfect marriage because they were always together, always content together, and always worked together, Dorothy quite often saw to, or actually did, the cooking on big occasions at the George, and very capable she was, otherwise, they left everything to Leslie Walker and her sister Lucy. Both ran the George and made it the best hotel in the North of England. For food, it was excellent. Dorothy had a daughter with her first husband, named Christine, Frank later adopted this girl, who I first knew as a gangly slender schoolgirl, she grew into a beautiful young lady.

Frank and Dorothy used to take their annual holidays in the South of France, at Nice, staying at that most magnificent of hotels, the Negresco. Christine used to accompany them, it was there that Christine, on one of these holidays, met and fell in love with a young chap named Robert Sangster. Monique and I used to see Christine sitting on the same settee beside the stairs that we had sat on when we had first met, we used to pass the time of day with them, but not once would Christine introduce us, at this time, I had no idea who he was, except that he was so shy, he would hardly open his mouth, he was so quiet and shy that Monique and I wondered who had made the first move when they had first met, Christine or he. Eventually, I knew who he was, but still, no move to introduce Monique and I, and before young Mr Sangster came on the scene, Christine used to buttonhole Monique, take her to the family's private apartments and go over hit records, and general chit chat of girls.

Come the day of the big marriage of Christine and Robert, Monique and I were never invited. I, and I think Monique also, could not under- stand why her friend could not invite her to her wedding, myself, I thought it a snub uncalled for— I remember Dorothy, Frank's wife, saying to me in the corridor of the George Hotel one evening when my brother's will was published in 1953, "My word Joey, I am going to keep Christine for you." These were her exact words, of which, I thought there and then, was in very bad taste.

Throughout my life, I have been let down—one way or another, by 'friends' that eventually, when these things happened, I just shrugged them off. Of course, Robert Sangster, as the horse racing world knows, went on to do great things on the turf, then, he had about one horse in training with Eric Cousins. Robert, as I knew him then as I was eventually introduced to him, was a very likeable and rather shy young man who grew his feathers very quickly indeed.

In another episode, when Adam was four and Joey Jnr two, we had a telephone call at about 6:30—7:00 am from Alice at the post office, it was mid-winter—six inches of snow on the ground, Alice said on the phone Adam and Joey are just passing the post office in their pajamas, and the little one seems to be having difficulty walking, my word, Monique was like a jet-propelled rocket! Tears streamed down her face, what's happened to my babies, she cried. Before I could do anything, she was in the chicken van just outside and off, at full speed, to the village ½ a mile away, there she found the two boys, Adam leading Joey by the hand at ¼ mile per hour—cold as ice, the reason Joey was having trouble walking was that he had both of his legs down one leg only of the pyjamas! He could only manage four-inch steps, Monique scolded them but laughed her head off later—when the two had had a long hot bath to warm up, they, Adam had told her, were off to see Ma as they called her—my Mother at Kirkland, he loved his Ma, more than his mother, and Ma adored him.

Another time that year, in 1960, he had a little three-wheeled trike, one day a farmer from the village phoned to say Adam had passed him halfway to Kirkland, the farmer, Eddie Woof was bringing his cows in for the summer afternoons milking. Eddie had about thirty cows, he told us. Adam on his trike weaved in and out of the cows on the road like an old stager—not frightened a bit, then he went straight ahead to—again, see his Ma. Monique put the phone down and off after him in the van. She caught up with Adam as he was entering Ma's house, she told me, as red as a turkey jock from his bike ride—which was mainly uphill.

We thought it might be a good thing to send Adam to Michael's, my nephew's school, they took young ones of Adam's age—5 ½ because Adam liked Michael quite a lot, and the pair got on well. The school was Blanerne, in a village called Denholm, near Hawick, Scotland. Michael was cramming to go to Crawfordton House, a minor public school in Edinburgh. Blanerne was run by a Mr Case, he was an ex-army Officer. Monique and I went to see Mr Case, had a chat, and afternoon tea with him, discussed sending Adam there, as his cousin could keep an eye on him. Mr Case thought it a good idea, so off Adam went after the holidays, we took them up by a car, it was only about a 1 ½ hours drive, Adam was pleased to be with Michael. He had been there about six or eight weeks when he thought he would rebel, he started to break a few windows by throwing stones through them, on the whole, a naughty boy. Mr Case, the owner and principal headmaster of the school, asked us to go and see him—which we did. Monique and I were shown to his study and told that Mr Case would be along in fifteen minutes. We sat down and waited, half an hour went by, we were told once again by a woman—I suppose his secretary, Mr Case, would be along shortly, we waited, an hour went by, I thought to myself, this is not good enough, we had driven eighty miles to see this man at a certain hour, now he seemed as if he did not want to see us. We waited again. By this time, we had been in the study for two hours. I had had enough and told Monique, let us go and find Case. At that moment, the study door opened, and there stood Mr Case—his face almost purple, he became most abusive towards us, then ordered us out, slammed the door, and left, Monique and I were dumbfounded. However, we got up and left the study, and en route to the front entrance door, we came across Case tete, a tete in the living room cum hallway with a well-dressed woman. As we were passing, he was taking absolutely no notice of us. I stopped and told him very firmly, in a normal hard tone of voice, that we had waited for two hours, of which he was aware, but that his manner towards us was most deplorable, we then left, with the well-dressed woman with her mouth wide open, and Case not knowing what to do at that instance, I had given him back his own medicine. As we were getting into the car, he came running out of the school towards us, almost in an epileptic fit—face livid purple. I had heard from Cathie that he was a bit of a tiger—shouting take your son away from this school now this instance, as I was getting into the car, I turned to face him and told him in no uncertain terms—because by now I was fed up with this nasty fellow—I have paid a full terms fees for my son, and he stays here until the end of the term, and with that—drove off, leaving him fuming.

The school term ended in three weeks' time. I heard nothing more from Mr Case. I was puzzled at his attitude, at not seeing the boy's Mother and Father—whom he had asked to go to the school for a talk, he must have been at the bottle because, on casting my mind back, he did seem a bit wobbly at times. We decided to send Adam to the village school at Skirwith, we should have done this at the very start, we had to talk to the—then headmaster, Mr Pickering—who was married with a family. I explained about Adam's other schools, his not settling, he told us he would be only too pleased to have Adam at his school, Adam was much more content at the village school, but he had difficulty in reading, he was not dyslexic, Mr Pickering tried, but unfortunately he left after falling out with the Vicar, Father Wilson, it was a Church of England school, and the two could not get along together.

After Pickering came Mrs Dickinson, she was like a mother to all of the children, an extremely nice and likeable woman, she lived at Ousby three miles away, but the children—instead of being taught to read and write, were allowed to play. Whence Adam left to go to his prep school at nine years of age, he was unable to read or write, as were many of the other children. At this time, a cousin of Dad's, Roy Slack, from Liverpool, and his wife had bought a tiny attached cottage at Kirkland for holidays, Roy's wife, Peggy, was a teacher and a staunch Irish Catholic when it was holiday time, I asked Peggy if she would teach Adam to read and write, to which she readily agreed—two or three hours in the mornings, the two of them in the dining room, going through something like Green Eggs, and Yellow Bacon! It took quite a time, but eventually, all was well.

In time, Adam went to his first prep school in Carlisle—Lime House School—a country house outside Carlisle by about three or four miles, run by a Mr Ingham's (the brother of Ingham's, of Private Eye paper fame in London). Adam got on well here, the teaching staff was good, and the Christmas

Carol's and service at Church on Christmas Eve was an extremely nice affair. Lessons or Bible Verse's being read out by some of the pupils, Adam's first Christmas there, he read a passage, quite long, from the Bible, he stood up at the lectern and read aloud, in a very clear and precise manner—we were quite proud of him.

The following year, two or three of the waiters at the County Hotel told Monique and I—when they knew we had one of our boys there, that Ingham's was a bit queer, I asked 'In what way?' We were told, first by Cherry—now the head waiter, then Leo, and Horace, the wine waiter, Ingham's would bring two or three boys aged about thirteen to fourteen years for dinner and ply them with wine, and other drink, until he was told he was not to do this by the staff at the Hotel, Monique and I smelled a rat and approached one of the senior staff at the school, he was sympathetic to our questioning, and told us what we had heard was true—Ingham's was kinky with young boys. At one stage, he had taken a boy's pants completely down and whipped his bare bottom so hard and long that a few of his own staff got together and told him that if he did a repeat, they would inform the Police. I told Adam, and later Joey, who also went there, if Ingham's tried this sort of thing with them, to run away to the nearest phone—to phone me or Mummy, and we would be there within half an hour to attend to Mr Ingham's. The boys knew what I meant. I also asked the senior Master to phone me immediately if anything like this ever happened, he promised to do so, fortunately, nothing did happen in this respect, the boy's got a good schooling in the three R's—and in Religion, which I think is necessary also.

Ingham's had two Indian boys at school with their turbans, he himself paid the schooling fees, he said—out of charity, Adam came home for half term holiday. I saw him, at times, rub his head vigorously with his fingers or knuckles or a good hard scratch. After seeing him do this a few times, I asked him what it was, he said, my hair itches, I had a look at his scalp, this was in the dining room—I had a shock! Adam's hair was full of mature head lice, or fleas, they were very big ones too. I called Monique and showed her, she nearly had a fit when she saw them running about Adam's head like rabbits, and at the same time, we were both very angry towards the school, and especially toward Ingham's, and, indeed, the school had a woman who was kind of housekeeper cum nurse if and when the children were sick, this woman had never inspected the boys, Adam himself, thought nothing about it, not I suppose, understanding, he said many of the boys had these things in their hair. This was a Saturday, the boys were due to return to school on Tuesday, Monique and I drove down to Lime House on Tuesday, Ingham's was busy greeting parents, Monique and I approached him. I told him I wished to speak to him in private, he took us to his study, I then told him of the mass of fleas in Adam's head, he then astounded me by saying he, Adam, must have got them from contact from the cows, I told him not to be so damned stupid, the fleas were the result of dirt, and contact with some person/s at the school, as these fleas were the type that humans had when living in dirty, or poor conditions, Ingham's would have none of it, so we parted on bad terms.

A week later, I was having my hair cut in Carlisle at Monsieur Le Galls, where Mother had taken me when I was six or seven years old. Then, there was five or six staff cutting hair in the gent's department. Now, there were only two, I myself went on a regular basis for my hair. I mentioned to the chap who cut mine that day that my two sons were at Lime House, he knew them both. I told him of the lice (or fleas). Well, he told me, I go to Lime House once a week to cut the boy's hair, and it is the two indian boys who give the lice to the others, he said under the turbans, the lice are in abundance, now I knew, straight from the horse's mouth. I then called around to Lime House on my way home, confronted Ingham's, and told him who had told me, he did not say much then.

Ingham's himself liked mountaineering, and once a year, he would send a party of boys on a sort of hiking, mountaineering trip, accompanied by a master, or masters, on one of these trips, a boy died, I think he fell to his death. At the inquest, Ingham's was reprimanded by the coroner for not being vigilant enough. I believe on another occasion, the boys were caught in a freak storm, one boy, again, died, from exposure, Ingham's was reprimanded again by the coroner. The last I heard of Ingham's, was that he was mountaineering in the mountains of the South Americas in Winter, the party he was with at high altitude were stopped by a blizzard, they decided to return to base—or to camp—I cannot remember which, Ingham's decided to go on alone, which he did, and was never seen again, I think myself, it was the best end of him. On his part, who knows, was it a death wish—he has never been found.

Adam, at Lime House, became the best cricketer the school had ever seen or had. When he was twelve years old, he could bowl the sixteen/seventeen-year-old seniors out with the greatest of ease and accuracy, he could—if the eye of a needle had been big enough, put a ball through it without touching the sides, he just didn't knock the bails off, he knocked the stumps out time and time again, Joey, his brother, told me once Adam had broken the stumps in one game, but I do not know if this were true.

When the time came, what Monique and I thought at the time was to move Adam on to his final school. Although Lime House was carrying boys on until eighteen years of age, we were always suspicious of Lngham's intentions towards young boys, and other Masters were watching his moves, we decided to move Adam to Dunrobin Castle in Sutherland when he was fourteen years old, Ingham's came to life then, telling us it would be better if Adam stayed with him—at the same time, saying if he did move, he himself would lose the best cricketer he had ever seen. However, we made plans for him to go to Dunrobin, and we stuck to them.

17

In July, Heinz and his wife Maria came to Skirwith Hall for four weeks' holiday, where we fished and shot pigeons off the ripening cornfields, and late July, shot wild duck as they were making a mess of the ripening barley, the young ducks just, at this time of the year, were most succulent, we had some good dinners with them. Wild ducks in Germany appeared on the menus at the best restaurants there. We often went racing, as at this moment, it was a quiet part of the year, so I was able to indulge in some free time. Heinz and I had some hard drinking days on Tuesdays and Fridays in Penrith, mostly at the George Hotel. Heinz was liked and made welcome by all who knew him. However, time went very quickly, and the day came for him and Maria to return to Germany. He had driven over by way of Dover in his Opel Estate car—though this one, a newer model than the one which we had holidayed in. Monique and I decided to go to Spain to look for a quiet fishing village to holiday at.

Heinz and I started the same day and time, he led the way down the A.1. Heading for London, about 25 miles through London, Heinz started to wave me down very near a roadside cafe. He coasted into the car park. His engine had cut out and would not start again, I was in the A.A., and Heinz was a member of the A.D.A.C., so I got on the phone, rang the

A.A. In a short while, our man arrived, he tested the car here and there, but nothing happened. Then he produced a bottle of air—under pressure, disconnected the fuel pipe, connected the bottled stuff to this pipe, and blew compressed air back into the fuel tank to clear it, the A.A. man tried the engine, in a few short seconds, it fired and ran as before— possibly an air block or something else, anyway, the car ran well, the A.A. man would not take payment, so Heinz gave him five pounds. Onto the ferry boat, we drove when the restaurant opened. We had a meal, then a few whiskies, but Heinz did not want too many as he feared the German Police.

They were sending car drivers with a drink to jail, no matter who they were.

We parted after passing customs at Calais, we embraced, my blood brother to Deutschland, Monique and I on our first visit to Spain. I had the Jaguar Mark 7. I drove towards Arras, a countryside I was to know quite well in later years. I took it very easy, as we were in no hurry. As dusk started to arrive, we approached a little place called Bapaume and found a small hotel where we pulled in for the night. The hotel had a nice rustic restaurant where we had our dinner. I remember I had a main dish of kidneys. But to start, I had soup, I am a lover of good soup, and in those years, each French restaurant or hotel made excellent soup. A great tureen would be put in front of you, and it helped yourself, I used, many times, to have three helpings. However, the kidneys were just not right, they had a taste of urine, they had not been boiled enough to start with—to take the scum, and taste of urine out, I told the head waiter they were no good, which he did not appreciate, he took them away then, with bad grace, asked if I wished to have something else, I told him I would have a couple of quail which when they arrived, were very good, Monique had pate de champagnes, which again, in those years, was always excellent,—not nowadays, they put any old mush in—same with the soup, it is seldom one can get soup in restaurants and when one does, it usually comes out of a tin, times change, but not for the best.

We often saw, also in these villages, unspoilt since they were built—a few cows or bullocks housed, what looked like in one of the house rooms facing the road, the owner would be mucking them out, throwing the accumulated muck of a month or two out of either the front door or through the window making a midden by the front door to be collected up at a later date, then the hens would jump on the top of the midden and start scratching it all over the place, hunting for bugs or undigested corn.

The farmer's wife would always be there, helping, forking

the dung alongside her husband. Then there was haymaking and small fields of oats or barley to cut. We watched many times along the way, all done by hand, the farmer's wife and other women, mostly dressed in black, working like slaves, for such was the life, I'm sure, of a peasant farmers wife, from dawn to dusk, she had to bear the children, and rear them, make all the meals, the housework, and mostly the fieldwork for her husband—a complete life of drudgery. I said to Monique if I were a woman, a peasant farmer would be the last person on earth I would wish to marry, she agreed.

However, came time for dinner, we had seen some of the big brassieres in Nimes becoming very crowded with customers, but decided to seek out—if we could, some nice small restaurant tucked away that might have excellent food, we were both strolling along hand in hand when we spotted what we were looking for, a small, neat, spotless restaurant with starched tablecloths, and silver looking cutlery, we studied the menu outside, and decided to try this one out. There were no other customers just then, perhaps we were just that bit early, we ordered the meal, and also the wine, it was good wine as I remember, but the meal, as it came course by course, we sent it back—everything, it was a disaster, I told our waiter that I was so dismayed with the whole meal I was only prepared to pay for the wine, I was then confronted by the—I suppose, owner, who had the good grace to apologise, and accepted payment for the wine. While we were there, two other customers only arrived for a meal, so off.

Monique and I went to one of the big brassieres—which was like a beehive of activity, we were shown to a small table, a paper tablecloth was laid in front of us, then we had a very good, wholesome meal—with another bottle of wine. It was a lesson I had learnt, and I followed it all my life after that— Never eat in a place where there are no customers, when other restaurants are busy as bees, no matter how nice and tidy the place looks, go for the one that is almost full, and if no table is available—order one for later, and go to the bar and have a drink or two while waiting, and to be sure of service plus table—tip the head waiter!

From Nimes, we drove through Montpellier towards the coast, passing very near Sete, where ships from Oran came in. We saw many of the oyster beds and plenty of signs bidding one to drop in for a tasting of these juicy morsels, we decided to try one of these places, so drove in and parked, we were welcomed by a genial man of about 50, he showed us to a small front room with a view over the bay, we ordered a dozen oysters each, and asked our host to give us a bottle of wine which he himself would drink with oysters, he came out with a bottle of white wine, that was absolutely superb to go with our dish, I made a bad mistake of not making a note of this beautiful drink, we both congratulated him on his choice, and promptly ordered another dozen oysters each, he was delighted and sat down to chat with us, we were there a good hour. When we left, he bade us wait a minute, left, and came back with a bottle of the same wine we had just drunk. We thanked him profusely for his kindness and hospitality. I noticed he was a smoker, so I fished out a good Cuban Bolivar and gave it to him. He was most pleased, then he bade us bon voyage.

We stopped at various little cafes en route to have a few drinks and view the countryside. I was not impressed by this side of France at all, it seemed rather sad and there was, or seemed to be, an endless wind. I noticed this each time I passed through Port Bou, where the Spanish frontier was, to my surprise, quite busy with traffic going into Spain, quite a few English cars also. We passed through quickly enough, then we were in Franco's country, where my brother had had his last holiday in 1952, he had told me it was a dirty place and very backward, now it was my turn to have a look at it. By now, evening was upon us, and I thought it prudent to look for a hotel in the next town we headed for, as I did not wish to holiday on the coast just inside Spain. I wanted to be in a true Spanish fishing village, so I drove into Figuera's, it seemed quite a nice place, but it also seemed very busy—people everywhere. The trees in the avenue, in what I took to be the main street, were alive with little birds singing their hearts out, I had not heard anything quite like this, and the electric and phone wires over the streets were full from end to end with swallows roosting for the night, I thought, well, this is a pleasant start. Then we went to the nearest hotel to take a room, I forget its name, but it seemed the best looking place there—very neat and clean looking inside, Monique asked in Spanish (of which she is very fluent) for a double room but surprise—she was told they were full. We tried all the others we could see or find—only three, I think, all were full, I could not believe it. To my thinking, Spain would have to be a quiet place where tourists hardly visited, I was wrong, the place was full of tourists from all over Europe. Judging by the cars parked everywhere, foreign number plates were in abundance.

We wondered what we should do, as by now it was 9:00 pm, not knowing this hour is not at all late by Spanish standards. Monique decided to ask a couple of men who seemed to be local if they knew of another hotel that we may have overlooked, they told us that there were no others. Monique explained our predicament, the two listened intently, then suggested we try the local joiner or carpenter, who had a room which he and his wife let to passing tourists, we jumped at the chance, so one of the men told us to follow him, which we did on foot, it was only about 50 yards away, in a side street, he knocked, the door opened, and a plump, nice woman of about 40 answered, he told her our problem, and left. The woman was delighted to show us her room to let, a large double bed, and that was all, but everything seemed to be very clean, the washbasin was outside the bedroom in the hallway, where one could wash while others passing could watch—the toilet, fortunately, was inside the house, also very clean, we said yes we would take it for the night, the woman was delighted, then I asked Monique to ask her what she charged. Monique asked her and was told so many pesetas. I quickly reckoned up, it came to 5/English, I couldn't believe it. I brought the car around to put the suitcases in the bedroom, Monique told our hostess that we were going for something to eat, I left the Jaguar outside our dwelling place, and we walked to the hotel where Monique had first asked for a room. I thought it would be too late for a full meal, but that we would be able to obtain a sandwich, as it was now 10:30 pm, but the hotel was, or seemed, to be in full swing, we were shown to our table by an immaculate waiter, table cloth and serviettes all starched linen, and silver looking cutlery, I thought, and told Monique, we are going to enjoy this, we ordered a dozen snails each, for the main course, I had a tournedos when it came, I could not believe how thick it was, Monique had chicken, which she said was excellent, my tournedos was simply delicious, the best I had had in ages, we had a big carafe of red wine from the region, which was also very good—so we had a refill. Nearby was a Spaniard holding one of those carafes that have a long spout with a fine hole through, from which he was pouring the wine onto his forehead, the wine ran down the middle of his nose, down his top lip, and into his mouth, this, I realised, was expertise in this art, at it's best. When he had had his fill, I applauded him because, yes, it was an art—he was most pleased, he then picked the carafe up, held it as far as he could from his mouth—I would say three feet or more, tilted the carafe, and the stream of wine shot into his mouth—never missing, he finished with a flourish, pulling the carafe within one inch of his mouth, then holding it up, never spilling one drop, quite good entertainment. I asked Monique to ask him if he would care for a brandy, he replied he would be delighted to do so, through Monique, we had quite a chat.

By now, it was well after midnight, and we decided to go to our room and bed, bidding our new friend goodnight. I paid the bill, then realised the dinner, wine, and brandy had cost only 12/6 the lot—amazing, I thought. When we returned to our nest for the night, our hostess was still about, making us most welcome, Monique jumped into bed, I told her I was going to the WC, then washed my teeth in the hallway. I opened the bedroom door, and waiting for me on the other side was our hostess. She grabbed my arm and talked rapidly in Spanish, of course, I knew nothing at all of the Spanish language. I went to the loo, she followed, almost in my pocket, waiting to come inside with me, I managed to shut the door without her entering, but when I came out, there she was, pouncing on me again, all the time talking rapidly, I had a hard job to wash my teeth, then it dawned on me—she wanted me to sleep with her, or at least make love to her, I opened the bedroom door to go in, and heavens above, the lady tried to follow me in, Monique had to rescue me, and be firm—but not too firm, or we might have been asked to leave. Once inside the bedroom, Monique locked it. A good thing the door had a lock and key. Otherwise, I don't know what would have happened. We slept well, woke up at 8:00 am. Monique refused to go and wash in the hallway, I had to shave, so I steeled myself and unlocked the bedroom door, went the three yards to the washbasin—only cold water. Within seconds, our lady was once again on my heels. I thought discretion was the best part of valour, picked my things up, did not shave, beat a retreat to the bedroom, dressed and left, Monique thanked our hostess in Spanish. The poor woman looked very sad and disappointed. We waved and left, I dread to think of a man tourist alone with her—I think he would emerge in a coffin.

That day we headed for Gerona, the sign posts were very old-fashioned, and the kilometres seemed to be much longer than the French kilometers, we passed Gerona, then carried on for a few miles, looking at the Michelin road map, I decided to cut off from the main road, and head towards a place that, on the map, seemed to be small and quiet, this place was Tossa de Mar, we arrived just after lunch. I was amazed by the number of tourists. I then realised that Spain was now hitting it off in a big way with tourist wise, we tried hotels, and boarding houses, all were full, so we went to the tourist office, run by Jimmy and his wife. Jimmy was not there, but his wife was. I explained all hotels etc, seemed to be full up, she agreed, but something in her speech clicked in my mind, I offered a good 'present' if she could fix us up for two weeks. She told Monique and I to return within two hours—when we did return, she had fixed us up at a very nice hotel, the name escapes me, but we were pleased with it. I gave 'Mrs Jimmy' pesetas to the value of 5 pounds, she was most pleased, in fact, she was a very nice woman, so was her husband Jimmy when we met him the next day, he had chronic Catarrh, smoked endless cigarettes, and his skin was a deathly pale yellow, I realised then that Jimmy was not in the best of health, he spoke, like his wife, good English, he would in the course of our stay, have drinks with us in Pedro's bar quite often, a nice kind man.

Our favourite bar was Pedro's, where the ceiling was covered with hanging cured hams, with small metal cups stuck in the bottom of them to prevent the fat from dripping onto customers. Pedro, his last name I think, was Artigas, was the president of the local football team and possibly mayor of Tossa just then. His was the best bar in town, and about 9:00 pm, his four-piece band would play, and we would dance till 2:00 am. Pedro himself became a good friend of us both, Monique could converse easily with him, and of course—all Spaniards, this was a great asset. Tossa had a rather small beach, which shelved steeply, within three metres of entering the water, one would be up to one's chin, rather dangerous, I thought, for children four to six years old, but it was a happy place called Tossa! We grew to like it immediately and returned again in the following years.

Pedro himself became a good friend of ours. He invited us to various functions and dinners. He looked forward each night for us in his bar for aperitifs, always at this hour after swimming and swimming all day. Monique and I would retire to Pedro's. Also at Tossa, we met a family from Carlisle, Tom Preston, he was a teacher at the new polytechnic at Carlisle, they had their two daughters with them, Angela aged about five—one of the most beautiful little girls Monique and I had ever seen, she was like a doll, but spoilt to bits, the other daughter, Caroline, aged about twelve. A nice girl, Tom himself, a nice tall chap, straight as a ramrod while walking, sitting, or driving, had lent a few thousand pounds to a Spaniard to start a bar in Tossa, I thought when he told me, he seemed to be taking a big risk, but Tom had—it seemed, had holidayed in Tossa a few times before, and got to know quite a few people there.

The Spaniard he had lent money to got his bar going well, and each year on Tom's holiday, he paid his interest. At what percentage, Tom did not tell me, he said it paid for his holidays each year, and he was satisfied.

Tom's wife, Sandra, had told me one of her sisters had married a German, Willy Weiser, who was a director of the largest makers of German champagne (Sekt) in that country—situated at Eltville am Rhine. I had mentioned that when Monique and I left Tossa, we were driving through Germany to Westfalia. Sandra mentioned that it would be a good idea to visit her brother-in-law, Willy, I myself thought so too.

So after two weeks in Tossa, we said our goodbyes to our friend Pedro, his waiters and musicians, they were a grand lot and had been most kind to us. I filled the Jaguar up and set off early. We retraced the route we had entered Spain by, I thought, cutting out the mountains in the French Alps, and taking the main road through Lyons, then onto Besanson, Belfort, Mulhouse, Frieburg, entering Germany rather late the second night, we came by accident, on a little village by the name of Sexau, near Waldkirch. We decided that it was time to ask for a room for the night, I stopped at the first hotel I saw in this little village, it was the Hotel Lerche. On entering, the atmosphere was warm and snug, with a scent in the air I just could not make out, but pleasant. I asked for a double room, yes, they had a room, said the pleasant woman who, it turned out, was the owner's wife. I parked the Jaguar round the back, and took the bags in the rear entrance, took them up to our room—a simple place with a little shower box in a corner, sparsely furnished but cosy, with those very thick, pure goose down duvets.

We had not much time for a shower, as time was getting on, so we went down to the bar ordered two glasses of pills. I then noticed a few locals having glasses of yellow liquid, almost like grapefruit juice, I asked our host, who had arrived on the scene behind the bar—dressed as a chef, what it was, he told me it was called Neur Zusser, the new wine, in it's fermentation, I asked for a glass, and found it to be an excellent beverage, nice to taste, and drink, and strong. Monique tasted mine and decided to have a glass too, this was followed by another three glasses (large wine glasses), after the fourth, that is when I knew the strength of this drink! In the meantime, I noticed the restaurant part was filling up, after our fourth nuer zusser. By the time we decided to eat, we discovered the restaurant was packed. The owner suggested we eat in the bar, which we did. Our waitress for the bar, was the same for the dining room. She was blonde, and very pretty, with the Bavarian costume an extra low décolleté, showing off her well-proportioned breasts, she would be twenty-two to twenty-three years. She was so efficient, not one table or person had to wait more than 2-3 minutes for a meal or drink, of all the waitresses I have known, even to this day in 2012, she was the best, and always, she had a lovely smile, on or off duty.

We ate, I had venison, Monique chicken with spaetzle, the sauces were equal to a top French restaurant, also the desserts we both realised here, Henri Gerhi, as I later asked him his name, was thanked for the quality of his food, he was most delighted, and sat down for a talk, introduced his wife, and three daughters, I believe he had four, but three were there that night. We both decided to stay another day and night. I asked Henri Gheri if it was possible to keep our room for the following night, the whole family was pleased that we were staying on.

Later, in the bar, I invited Henri Gheri and his wife to have a few drinks with us, which they did—at the same time, congratulating him on his food. The next day, we bade the Gheri's au revoir, filled the car up just across the road, and drove off to Eltville am Rhein, we did not hurry and reached Eltville in the early evening. It was too late to go to the champagne factory (or distillery), so I booked into a small hotel in the village with very nice, comfortable rooms. We had a stroll around for half an hour. I asked where Mathias Mullers lay so that in the morning, we could go straight there.

In the morning we rose at 9:00 am, had a quick breakfast, then drove to see Willie Weiser, I drove into a parking place at the champagne place, we both got out and went up to a reception office, told the man there I was here to see Herr Willie Weiser, and to look around the factory, he got on the phone and rattled something off, within three to four minutes a young man came to speak with us, he spoke good English, and told us (in English) that Willie Weiser was in hospital, he had had a heart attack only a few days ago, I told the young chap I was sorry to hear this, and explained I had a special invitation from his sister in law, to visit, and see round the place, he explained they did not show visitors round anymore, but as it seemed we were personal friends of Willie Weisers family, he would see what could be done, and took us into a private room, he left us, and returned in about ten minutes, saying he himself, was instructed to show us round the factory—to see everything in the making of champagne.

Off we went, with our guide of about twenty-five years old. We were shown and could see inside the empty ones, glass rooms holding a ¼ to ½ a million liters of wine in many of them, thousands of racks with bottles to be shaken gently, we descended, I think it was three floors down by lifts, viewing in the gallery's, literally millions of bottles of the factory product. We were under the Rhein when our guide told us at that time (I am not 100% sure of the number of bottles) they held 25 million bottles. Eventually, we reached the end of our guided tour, which lasted in the region of three hours. Our guide led us to the private room once again, and there on the table was a bottle of their best 'Mattius Muller Private' and three glasses. We were invited to sit and drink the bottle with him, which we did with pleasure. After ¾ of an hour talking and the bottle finished, we thanked our young host most kindly, left word for Willie Weiser to get well, and left. Outside, I remember it well, it was a blazing hot day, we got in the car, I started off, the next second I had to stop, I was going dizzy and could not focus properly, I got out of the car for air, leaning on the bonnet, in no time, I felt first class. I think the continued coldness of the underground cellars, then the champagne, and into a hot sun was to blame. Within five minutes, I was off on the way to see Heinz.

We took the autobahn via Koln, Wuppertal Recklinhausen, after that, there was no autobahn to Munster, though I belive it was under construction. Those days there was little traffic on the autobahns compared with today's, it was quite pleasurable to drive. Now it is a race track, entering Munster to the streets I knew so well. It was quite easy to find the road to Telgte, only about eight miles distance. Up we rolled at 5:00 pm, Heinz and Maria gave us a grand welcome and a few beers to boot. Later while Maria made dinner—she was a very good cook, also made her own bread which was also tip-top, Heinz, Monique, and I walked down to Emil's pub, only 150 yards. Emile was most pleased to see us walk in, as was his wife and two sons Hans Joachim and Wolfgang. I always called Emil's wife to her face, Frau Koling, though she had a pet name Mitze. Emile immediately gave us the first round of drinks on the house, together with a schnapps each, sat down at the piano and played for me 'The Tales of Hoffman' one of my favourite pieces, the music would roll off his fingers, he was an excellent player, then he would turn, give me a great big smile, half a laugh as if to say 'nice to see you again.' He knew when Monique and I arrived, he could guarantee some fun and laughs—then home to dinner, Maria had prepared a leg of venison from a Roe Deer, she excelled in venison.

I had made good friends in Telgte with quite a few of the local landlords, they were Albert Greveler at Gasthof Greveler, his wife put very good, plain meals on midday and night. Albert was a rich man in his own right, without his pub. He had the smallest, red bulb end of a nose I have seen, but his face always had a fun-loving ready smile. He and his wife had two daughters, one, Margot, stunningly beautiful. She was now 16 years old, still at school, her facial bone structure was classic, with perfect legs and carriage—by contrast to her sister, poor girl, she was not, shall we say, striking in her looks, also a school girl. Over the years, Albert and I have remained good friends, we have had some memorable drinking days in his place with some of the businessmen of Telgte.

Just below Grevelers was the pub, The Wild Man, run by Joseph and his wife. We had a lot of fun in The Wild Man. Joseph was anything but wild, we used to call him the high priest because he was so quiet, he was also always in a black suit, like a priest, but he and his wife were most kind. It was here one afternoon, at carnival time, I was singing and larking with many others, when all of a sudden my chair, a normal high one, tipped completely backwards over, landing me on my head! Three or four youngsters in their teens shot over in a flash to help me to my feet and see if I had hurt myself, which, thank goodness, I had not, being full of beer at the time, they were most concerned for me, the youngsters in Germany at that time were extremely well mannered and always very polite. I saw a change—a big one—in later years, and not for the best.

The best hotel in Telgte for rooms, and food, also for fun, was the Althaus, run by Erika and Helmut Schrade. They had the place on a lease—in Erika's name, as it seemed that Helmut had, at one time, run foul of the Police. Erika saw to all the cooking, and guests could see right into the kitchens, where there were five or six girls and boys doing their various chores, there was Willy, the head waiter—a young fellow of 25, Erika ran the hotel with a rod of iron, everything had to be more than perfect in all aspects, I remember a waiter put a new starched table cloth on a table next to Monique, and I, Erika was seated with us, as the table cloth was laid, she noticed a crease in it that was nothing really, but should not have been there, she gave the waiter a dressing down in no uncertain terms, and to lay another immediately. There was no messing with her, though she was a bundle of fun and also most fair with her staff, but she would brook no nonsense, her cooking was very, very good indeed, in fact, second to none, her dining plates were immense—which I liked, I hate dining off small dinner plates, food flies off them onto the table too easily.

They knew that was a fun time. One time, I arrived unexpectedly on them, Monique was with me, we walked into Erika's dining room at mid-day, it was full, I gave a loud Sieg Heil, the Hitler salute—always my joke with them, on looking back, probably not in good taste. Helmut and Erika came up to the dining room floor at full speed. Some of the diners said later they thought Helmut was going to throw me out—instead, he threw his arms around me, gave me a big kiss on my cheek, and shouted in German so that all could hear—Thank God you are here, now we will liven the place up and have fun, then he kissed Monique on each cheek, while Erika threw her arms around me, kissing me rather profoundly on each cheek—while I in my fumbling haste to do the same, clutched her very ample left breast in my right hand, I apologised, but she saw it was an accident. I rather think she enjoyed the moment, this then was the Al-thaus.

The Bahnhof pub was another favourite—but only for drinking, this place as the name suggests, was by the railway station, run by Theo and Annaliese Bernsman, Theo was the kindest man, his wife was also kind—but a bit scatterbrained. They had a daughter of, then, about fourteen years old, she seemed sex mad and used to ogle me whenever she had the chance, she just wanted me to go to bed with her, I never did, though, because her parents were my friends. Once, when she would be about twenty years old, or thereabouts, she visited us on the Cote D' Azur with her boyfriend. On the beach, she stood in front of me while I sat in the sand, she was only three feet away, she started to slowly undress, casting each garment off so slowly—all the time, her eyes trying to catch mine, she had a good figure, and would be 5 foot 9" tall, then, her last garment came off her scanty panties, she dropped them to her ankles, and there she stood—completely starkers, with a nice bush of pubic hair, I looked up, her eyes were on mine, then she smiled a whimsical smile, I returned with a smile of amusement, then she stepped out of them, put her swimsuit on, laughed and went swimming.

One of the habitué of the Bahnhof was Joseph Tunte, he had been a prisoner of war in Russia. He told me that the conditions there, as a prisoner, was grim indeed. At various coal mines the German prisoners had to work in, they were allowed to surface once a week or once a month, as the mood took their masters. Once outside, the prisoners would run to the nearest birch trees and strip them of bark, boil it—they would eat the bark and drink the liquid. Very few came home, but Joseph had been a trusty, they treated him fairly well because he was an expert at vulcanising tyres or similar stuff, the Russians put him to work vulcanising, fed him fairly well, and finally—seven years after the war, they let him go home, he was a great drinker and cigarette smoker, we used to sit together quite often in the Bahnhof. I would give him a large German cigar, and he used to puff and puff the thing so fast— and also inhale until, within minutes, no one could see him for clouds of smoke, it was an incredible sight to see a man in the middle of a room surrounded by a smoke screen, but cigars were too strong, and he inhaled so much, it was not long before he was cross-eyed.

Whenever I left Telgte, over the years, Joseph would always give me a litre stone bottle of schnapps, the latter was a bit like miniature grey hens of olden days, nowadays collector pieces, and, one time, he gave me a framed photo of himself, he was an extremely kind soul.

I bought a thousand cigars from my old friend Sepple Poppenborg, he gave me a 7 ½ % discount and a very good box of 25 for luck. The next day I took the door panels of the Jaguar, and put them nicely inside, except for 200 that I was going to declare. We were allowed 150, 75 for each person, and declared 50 to pay for to avoid suspicions.

The following week, we left for home via Dover, I had no bother with customs, acting a bit simple and innocent. We were through and passed through the middle of London, onto the A1 heading North, and home the night of 9th September. I was a little tired. It had been rather a hectic holiday, but one which we both had enjoyed.

While we were on holiday, my little Dachshund 'Bonzo' had died, one of the tractors had run over him with a front wheel three months before, he was his old self with no effects from his accident for ten days, then he became not well, the vets could not save him—telling me they thought his spleen was damaged. The little fellow was extremely brave, he would stand up to angry cattle and ewes with lambs, but he was also a great little dog in the turnip fields—and rape flushing pheasants out for the walked up shoots. He could go with ease up the fields, under the turnip leaves, never going too far in front. If he did, he would come obediently back when called. He was also a popular little chappie with the barmaids at Sedgefield races—always on a lead, of course. At the races, they used to give him whole pies, which he devoured with great zest—now he was no more.

The year before, Tommy Hudson 'borrowed' a T.Y.O. from me -to get his horse numbers up for his training licence just before I went on holiday. On my return, Tommy Robson now trained a three-year-old by Darra, named Coquino—full brother to the one Hudson had, I duly signed the authority to act form for Robson. About three weeks later, a letter arrived from the Jockey Club in Cavendish Sq—why were my signatures different on two authority-to-act forms? At first, I could not understand what they meant, then I thought, what must Hudson have been up to, I phoned him and told him of the Jockey Club letter. He then told me he had named the horse himself and forged my name on this form. I thought what a damned stupid thing to do, he had named the horse Darwinian—he was by Dara. I replied to the Jockey Club, telling them that I had only lent this two-year-old as a favour to Hudson and also that I had no idea he would even race the horse—of which he had done so.

I received a letter from them requesting me to visit them at Cavendish Sq on a certain date. On the date requested, I had to go to Dublin with Dad, I wrote and explained this, at the same time apologising. The stewards then asked me to appear before them at Liverpool when the next meeting was on. I thought I had better see them this time, so on the appointed day, I motored down to the Liverpool meeting, I was early, so hung about. Eventually, a few Jockeys and trainers arrived—whom I knew and passed the time chatting. In due course, Mr Weatherby—I think his first name was Bill, an extremely nice man, he put me at ease right away, a few moments later, I was shown into a room with four or five stewards.

I cannot remember exactly who they all were. Bill Weatherby was one, but in the chair was the Duke of Roxborough, a big chap, always wearing a permanent scowl, his complexion always reminded me that he must have some black blood in him. I believe some of his ancestors had American Blood. Anyway, I was asked to take a seat, an upright kitchen chair facing the others who were roundabout—the Duke behind a table. He opened with—It has taken a long time to get you here, I replied—Yes, I have apologised for that, he did not seem to like this reply, I told them at the time that Hudson signed these forms himself, I had been in North Africa, and had no knowledge of faulty signatures until the Jockey Club had written to me on the matter, I was straightforward with my answers. As far as I can remember, the Duke was the only one who interrogated me, I could almost feel he wanted me to eat humble pie—or squirm a bit in his presence, but I was innocent of all and had no intention of being intimidated by his presence, he might have been better if I had called him by his nickname, Bo. All of his friends—if he had any, called him this.

Eventually, I was asked to leave the room while they deliberated the matter. A few minutes later, Bill Weatherby called me back in. I was then informed that I could not enter or run, any of my horses until further notice and was dismissed from the room, I had no appeal, there was none those days. They fined Hudson a few hundred pounds, this all appeared in the Racing Calendar, which did not look well to me.

I had, next winter, two horses in, Darwinian and Coquino, for the N.H. season 1961-1962. I had them boxed at Kirkland and Kurt and I exercised each morning, doing quite a bit of slow hill work. I had by now, written a few times to the Jockey Club requesting permission to run my horses, this was always refused, I had the horses by now, quite fit, but it seemed that my work with them in vain. One day I thought I'd approach Colin Parkhouse to see if he was interested in running them in his name, I would train them, he agreed, Colin was a small poultry farmer at Penrith, he duly applied for his permit, this was granted—I thought right, I had been treated most unfairly, I would get my horses in the back door, so to speak.

The road to Kirkland was blocked by drifts of snow 100 yards long and very deep. We could not get through to exercise the two horses for a few days, my nephew Michael fed them for me, he was on holiday from school, there were drifts 10 feet deep in front of the loose box doors and walls. He had to tunnel through with a shovel, the horses did not get out for a full week.

I shot literally hundreds of pigeons that wintered off the turnips and raped them. There were so many thousands, if not attended to, could strip a field of turnips of their leaves within a few hours, I never tired of eating these delectable birds. To me, they were delicious, always devouring three each time I had them for a meal, Monique, however, did not like them but prepared them for me with loving care.

18

It was about 1962 when Monique and I—one day at Carlisle races (possibly the Cumb plate, three days meeting), met two young blond men who, at the member's bar, were it seemed in a happy way, this was before the first race, the two were speaking pretty loud, eyeing Monique and I on our entry. Monique was very beautiful and elegant, two or three newspapers had photographed her at previous meetings and put her in their papers, one wanting her to pose for the front page picture of their paper—the Sun or something similar, but she refused. The reporter pestered her for quite a time for this. I could see these two young chaps were dying to talk, edging nearer and nearer to us in the bar. Eventually, one of them spoke to Monique—who, by this time, they were beside her. Within a few minutes, they introduced themselves, one was Phillip Johnston whose father was a steward at Carlisle and other Northern race courses—also a farmer near St Boswells in Scotland who had married a daughter of Carr's, the biscuit makers of Carlisle. The other was Sandy Taylor, whose father, Col Ritchard Taylor of Chipchase Castle in Northumberland, he was a steward of Newcastle, of which course I was a member, Sandy's mother was a daughter of Lord Joicy.

In any case, when we first met these two wild young men, Monique and I met them many times racing. We had dinners, dancing at the nightclubs after racing at Newcastle. There was one nightclub in Newcastle, which was the 69 Club, named because it was on the A69 road out of Newcastle, towards Hexham and Carlysle. This club was run by Lucky Joe Lysle. Joe had become a good friend of mine, he was called Lucky by the media, because of his amazing luck with his horses, he was a great racing man and a fearless gambler, but the taxman must have been reading the racing pages in the papers because they thought to have a go at Joe. He up sticks, put his money in a suitcase and quietly went to the Isle of Man where, also quietly, he started in real estate—and did very well, returning after a few years to the racing scene in England in person.

At every Newcastle race meeting, a few of us, like Phillip, Sandy, Robert Jackson, Tommy Robson, would all dine at the new hotel built on the race course grounds, the Park Hotel. This was an excellent watering place as well as the food, except the time at dinner when Humphrey Cotterill and Robin Terry of the chocolate family were dining with us. When I ordered Veal Cordon Bleu, this was served, but I found that I could not cut through it, the ham in the middle was still enclosed in its plastic jacket from the packaging factory. I called the head waiter over—he knew us well, I showed him what I had been served with, he was taken aback, I told him it was quite disgraceful, and that I hoped he would not charge me, he said—certainly not sir—I was given a fresh serving of the veal cordon bleu, I then asked the head waiter to put dessert on for the whole table, a soufflé Grande Marnier free, which he agreed to, the soufflé Grande Marnier was served, with it risen to great heights—a beautiful sight.

One day, at Newcastle races, Tommy Robson came to me and said the police (at Newcastle) were going to raid Joe Lysle's place next Thursday. Tommy knew, with his training activities, many people in many places. I thanked him and went in search of Joe. I soon found him and told him the news, he thanked me and said he would be prepared, sure enough, the police raided Club 69, and sure enough, Joe was prepared. The next time we met at the races, he again thanked me. He never forgot that tip-off, as I will explain later on.

1962 was the start of the decline of the traditional hatching business, with the old established laying breeds and crosses of them. The reason was the craze and the propaganda of the American hybrid hen. Big sums were being spent on advertising these newcomers, supposed to eat half as much and lay twice as many eggs as the old breeds and crosses. At the same period, prices of eggs were dropping; feeding stuffs were on the increase. A few people saw that the laying hen was, and had, been a nice money spinner. When I took over Adam's hatchery in 1952, 1000 laying hens, free range, would keep a family—Husband and Wife, and three or four children in relative comfort, but not now in 1962—These few people, there were three or four round Penrith, decided to install large poultry houses, air-conditioned, and install batteries—or cages. Each of these houses would hold 15,000 or 20,000 hens. With this new hybrid hen, the shaver, the early birds, as a figure of speech, made a lot of money out of this, egg prices dropped, more of these battery houses went up, the result—my customer, the farmer's wife, and small poultry keeper were dropping out of poultry keeping altogether. This started the end of the small hatchery, and there were quite a few in Cumberland as, by now, the men who had built the first battery houses were now building more, keeping 30,000 plus hens.

However, I struggled; the school bills were still to pay—and getting heavier. Last season—1961, I had decided, due to the hybrid coming to the fore fast, to try the broiler bird, breeding the bird for the table. I bought 3000 broiler pullets from E.F. Fairburn through mine and Adam's old friend, Tom Park. These birds were as day olds. They were reared in the brooders at Skirwith Hall, then on the free range until four and a half months old, then put in one of my deep litter houses. These, as it turned out, were a bit of a disaster. These birds, after laying for about six—eight weeks, started to die. Eventually, twenty or thirty a day would die. It looked like it was leukemia. I phoned Tom Park and told him what was happening. He then told me the bad news, that Fairburn's hatcheries were having big trouble with their breed of broiler, theirs was dying in thousands.

I called Mrs Gibson, the chief M.A.A.F. poultry woman in Cumberland, all the poultry men and hatcheries in Cumberland were frightened of her, as of Ted Sharman, but she and I got on well together, she was straight and stood no-nonsense, and would go out of her way to help one, Mrs Gibson looked at the hens, quite a few eggs—of which many were deformed, a sign of fowl pest, green droppings, she had

P.M.'s done on a few hens, but no, the hens were clear of fowl pest. During that period, there was a big outbreak not far away in Lancashire of fowl pest. I thought that if my hens had fowl pest, I would get in the region of 20—25 thousand pounds in compensation, which would enable me to fit the whole place up on the battery system, as I could see only about two or three years left for the hatchery as it now was. Alas, no foul pest was found.

That hatching season of 1962 was not a good one at all, many farmer's wives stopped keeping poultry altogether. The only holiday we took was to go to see Heinz for Karnival time, staying ten days, buying 2000 cigars, drinking and dancing the nights away, in general, having quite a time. It was on this trip that one night, at midnight at Emil's pub, a very tough-looking man came into the bar, he was very solid, about 6'4", a battered face—he reminded me of Max Schmelling, the boxer, Emil brought him over to our table to introduce me, which he did, I invited him to have a drink, he accepted, he was most polite, seemed to have very good manners, extra polite to Monique, his name was Willy Hessellmann, a farmer in a biggish way, his farm only five miles away at Vertrup.

Willy spoke no English and never tried to learn it, we conversed until almost 2:00 am and drank an enormous amount of beer and schnapps. Willy could drink, and without being big-headed, I could just better him, he had turned to drink during the last six months, we learned he had been married the year before. Willy would be 35ish, a love match, but within six months, his big love—his wife, contracted cancer and died. Willy had been brokenhearted and still was—taking to the bottle for comfort. He invited us all out to his farmhouse for the following evening at 8:00 pm for drinks, which included Emil and his wife Mitze, Heinz and Maria, Monique and myself, and Dieter the part-time barman of Emil's.

At 8:00 pm the next day, we set off in two cars to Willy's farmhouse, none of the others had seen it before and were agog because it seemed that Willy's family were big shots in the area. We turned into his driveway, passing before we got to the house, huge barns and silos. His house was a very large one and built to last. Willy welcomed us into his living room, quite large, with an enormous open fire as laid, but as yet unlit, he had central heating all through. Willy put a match to the brushwood, and within minutes, we had a bonfire, out came the champagne, schnapps, and beer, a full box of excellent German cigars was open on a side table help yourself Joey, he said, which Heinz and I did so.

Willy put some records on, and we danced, and drank, and talked, and danced, then Willy asked Monique if she would like to see his wife's things upstairs, Monique said she would. She told me later that night Willy had shown her his wife's new dresses, her perfumes, and little personal things while tears poured down his cheeks, for him and his wife, they had an enormous en suite, the bathroom and dressing, all done out in marble—most tastefully done Monique told me.

Willy showed me his wine cellar, it was good and big, he had in the region 5,000 bottles of French red wine and almost 3,000 German white, including champagne. By now, the time was 3:00 am. Emile and Mitze, and the others wanted to go, so I thought we had better follow suit. We had already drunk 15 bottles of champagne and a fair quantity of Pilsner beer, smoked quite a few cigars, we said our farewells to Willy, him saying he would see us the next evening at Emil's. In a few minutes, we were in bed, tired.

At the moment, there was a difficult patch in their marriage. Heinz and Maria were not sleeping together, he was relegated to a small single room, when I asked why, she told me that she had discovered he was making payments to a nightclub girl—for a child she had had, claiming Heinz was the father, I had a good laugh at this, the old dog had never told me this episode in his life! I could not really believe it of him, he rarely did any nightclubbing, in fact, I had tried to get him into one or two in Munster, but he was always reluctant.

I told Maria that the girl who claims from him could have

slept with twenty men, and no doubt she has—and perhaps she is claiming from the other of her nineteen customers, but she would have none of my explanations. Forthwith, Maria now made Heinz sleep in the smallest bedroom in the house. In it, there was a small single bed, a small chair, and a small wardrobe. Maria herself kept to the very large luxurious bedroom she and Heinz had shared. Maria's language toward him was vulgar, calling him a pig and filth. He took it all quietly, but he told me more than once he—in marriage, had taken Maria from the gutter, she had been nothing. Two days later, Willy asked Heinz, Maria, Monique and myself to go nightclubbing to the Kakadu Club. Heinz said no. The Kakadu was also a well-run club—soft music, beautiful girls—all very young and all to be had, the place was full of, it seemed, well-off and well-dressed businessmen. Monique and I enjoyed the place very much, one was never pressured into buying drinks or by any of the hostesses, but at the sight of Willy, they would flock around him, we had not been there more than twenty minutes when Willy asked me quietly if I could lend him 300DM, as he was a bit short, he would pay me back tomorrow he said. Now we had only just got to know Willy, I thought, is there a catch in this? A quick second thought: I gave him the 300 DM under the table. I never like lending money.

 We left the Kakadu at 4:00 am and went to the nightclub opposite the Haouptbahn hof called the Casino, I parked the Jaguar on the Bahn side, we walked over, by now, Willy was showing signs of wear, in we went we had no bother with this, there were perhaps ten people all together in the club, as customers, plus half a dozen hostesses. I ordered drinks, then two hostesses came over to bother us, I asked what they would like to drink—it was always champagne, this was cheap enough, as the champers was always German, in came a bottle of Matheas Muller.

 Two of the hostesses told Willy they were hungry and were going to have some rag-o-fin. Willy dismissed them with a wave of his hand and fell asleep. Monique and I kept on dancing, then at 5:00 am we both thought, let's call it a day and go home. I asked for the bill, which was produced quickly, by now, we were the only ones left in the club. I studied the bill, the drinks seemed in order, but there was quite a sum for rag-o-fin, which I pointed out to the manager, or owner, who had presented the bill, it was his girls that had asked for—and eat the stuff and he, himself, should pay.

I tried to wake Willy up, he did so, but in a drunken stupor, he was lost for the moment. I tried the owner—or whoever he was, again. This time, he started to get angry, and I took an instant dislike to his new manner and told him, in no uncertain terms, that I was not paying sous for the rag-o-fin. At this, he threatened to call the police. His attitude now made me angry. I had my temper up, I told him to hold on a minute, at this, he probably thought he had won the battle, I again tried to get Willy awake, I was greeted by a few grunts. But he seemed to be coming round, I asked Monique to get the Jaguar, bring it round to the door of the club, and keep the engine running for a quick getaway. I went to the pavement side—by now, it was full daylight at 6:00 am, to see if any police cars were about, There were none, I went back inside the club, Willy was now awake and taking notice. I explained to him what had gone before, I then approached the owner, offered once more to pay for all the drinks bill—which was quite high, he again refused, and again said he would call the police, and went towards the phone, at that, I went behind his counter, grabbed him by his shirt front with both hands, shook him hard, stared at him in the eyes—about six inches from his face, and told him if he insisted on this he would get nothing at all, at this, he took fright, and bab- bled yes, he would accept, at this, I flung the money already prepared onto the counter, told Willy to get going, off he went into the hallway leading to outside, I told the owner—Why couldn't you have settled like this before, it would have been much more pleasant, with this, I left to follow Willy in the hallway, the exit doors were two very tall thick glass doors opening onto the pavement outside, I could see

Monique in the Jaguar nicely placed outside. I thought, well, all is okay, we can go quietly. But I was wrong, the naughty owner had locked the big glass doors—possibly by electric impulse from behind his counter, now I saw red. I stepped back 3 or 4 yards and charged the double doors full blast. With one huge kick with my right foot straight in the middle where the locks met, I nearly fell to the floor but regained my balance—to the music of shattering lock and glass, and hey presto, the doors were open, into the Jaguar we jumped, Willy now was his old self again, we had the last laugh on that greedy bug at the Casino!

19

On 24th February, 1963, my old favourite pony, Helm Star, died. She was twenty-two years old. In her later years, she had developed a very stiff hind leg due to an accident in her younger days until she was unable to bend the leg at the hock—carrying it stiff and straight, it had been an extremely hard frost for quite a while, the ground was like iron, when I went to feed her on the morning of 24th February, she was lying flat on her side, I could from 50 yards away, see no movement of any breathing, I called her name, with that her head came up, bent round to look at me, and whinnied a greeting, but I realised it was also a whinny of 'please help me my friend' I ran to her, she laid her head down on the ground, too weak to hold it up after the big effort to greet me, with a lump in my throat, and tears in my eyes, I realised she was going, I rushed home got the land rover with two or three bales of hay, and some empty sacks, hurried back to Starry, once again, I called her name, she tried to lift her head and whinny, she tried but the last effort seemed to have been reserved for my visit to feed her, she had reserved her call, and the little strength she had for, I think, her farewell to her master and friend, I wept, I weep now for her, as I write this, her last farewell is crystal clear in my minds eye.

I took the bales of hay and got her head and shoulders up. She was too weak to try and stand, so I propped her up with two bales, but I was unable to get her hindquarters up properly because of her stiff hind leg. I put some thick hessian sacks over her to keep her warm, stroked her, and talked to her in a soft voice, telling her of all the good times and fun we had had in our younger days. I stayed with her for quite a time, she tried to eat a little hay and soon gave up the effort, she knew that she would soon be in heaven. I drove slowly away to home for lunch, it was a Sunday, after lunch, I drove straight to her field—Springfield, it was called. I left the Land Rover by the roadside and walked the 100 yards to where Starry lay.

She was again flat on her side, the bales of hay pushed back, I looked down upon her and saw that my best and dearest little horse ever had died. I sat on a bale of hay and wept. I stayed there for a long time. I never did have a horse like her in any after years. She was clever, a splendid galloper, winning dozens of first prizes at the local flapping meetings. She loved to gallop, she could jump like a stag, knew her name, and would come at full gallop on hearing her name called—even from half a mile away, it was a sad day indeed—as sad as when my dog Spot was killed, Spot and Starry were great pals, she loved it when at full gallop, Spot would be, or try to be, running beside her and would let Spot jump on her back for a trot round, now both my animal friends, the best I could ever have—had gone.

Monique and I were invited to shoot with our friend Archie Glendining of Nethercassock, Eskdalemuir, over the border in Scotland. This was on 17th January. At Archie and Pat's, shooting lunches and/or dinners always consisted of before and after copious quantities of liquid—especially whisky glasses were never seen to be empty. They had to be refilled immediately after one took the last gulp—mostly, Archie's brand was Gloags famous Grouse.

This particular shooting day was a very cold but dry and frosty one, snow had fallen and lay six to eight inches deep. We were walking up the game through rough ground and small copses of pine where the hunters went in, and Archie had five acres of oats that he had been unable to harvest at all. Now it lay either flat or mostly crippled—ideal for winged game or hares. Pat, herself, was shooting; she had been taught by my father and myself at Skirwith Hall and she had turned out quite good. Monique walked beside me, and it was tough going in the snow, one thing—it kept us warm. Archie's hip flask kept him warm; he gave me a slug or two, but it was pure whisky. I liked mine with water. When we adjourned to the house for lunch at midday, the snow had entered Monique's wellingtons, they being rather on the short side, the snow had become so hard pressed inside the boots I was unable to pull them off, the snow had gone to the bottom—round her toes, and was packed. Archie got a large bucket of hot water to melt the hard-packed snow, and before long, I was able to pull the Wellingtons off together with icy snow and socks. Monique's feet were as white as the snow outside and stiff with cold. She could scarcely move her toes if we had not stopped for lunch or even just had a picnic outside, there is no doubt Monique would have lost some—or all of her toes through severe frostbite by luck, we had been in time—just to save them.

Well, morning came—surprised, I woke up as fresh as a daisy, no headache, head clear as a bell. I thought, if that is Gloags Grouse, I shall drink it from now on!

A few days later, I asked the local off-license in Penrith if he had any of the famous Grouse in, he told me they had never stocked it. I asked him (Mr Bryan) to get it in as soon as possible. Stuart Coulthard, the new manager of the George hotel, had never stocked it, but he said he would right away, from this beginning of the Grouse whisky in the Pen- rith and surrounding districts, I claim to be the one that put it on the shelves. In Cumberland, wherever I went, I asked for Grouse and, at the same time, gave it a pedigree a mile long. Within two years, the famous Grouse was all over Cumberland.

1963, it was getting harder to make a decent profit from the hatchery.

Quite a few small ones all over Cumb and Westmorland, like myself had closed down, and as Cathie's children, and also mine, grew older and bigger, like the latter, so did the school fees, Dad so far, had refused to help or to shoulder the burden for his daughter's fees, it still was left to me and the hatchery. School clothes were an expensive item. It seemed the better the school, the more luxurious a shop one had to buy from.

Kurt and I were up at 4.30 to 5:00 am to exercise my two N.H. horses, Coquino and Darwinian, the latter who became the problem of me being refused a trainer permit by the Jockey Club, we would saddle up and be off in darkness, one soon got used to seeing pretty well before the dawn, as did the horses.

On many exercise mornings, I would choose a different route, it did the horses good—a change of scenery (at least when it was light enough to see). One of these mornings, we were exercising up the old Roman road starting at the end of Skirwith Hall on the Langwathby road running through to the Culgaith Skirwith road, with only one slight curve in it, the length of perhaps 2 miles. This road was all grass, being used only for stock driving and farmers getting to various fields with implements, the road was about 40 feet wide from side to side of fences or stone walls, the middle was grassy and quite good for a good canter up most of its length and/or trotting, the sides were overgrown with bushes, and quite often we, when cantering along, would startle one or two Roe deer, which would for quite a distance run beside, or just in front of us, before darting to one side, pheasants would startle the horses quite often, flushing from the bushes with a clattering din.

One morning, Kurt and I had just entered the Roman road and starting to trot, we were taking it easily, talking, we had only gone 200 yards when all of a sudden, all hell broke loose, just above our heads, a large, very branchy tree, which must have had 200-300 wood pigeons sleeping in it for the night, suddenly, in the gloom of dawn, they took fright,—I suppose at our voices and took off all at once together just when we were underneath, their wings making a terrific noise, I was riding Coquino, who had a mouth like iron, he would not bend at the poll, just stuck his neck out in a straight line, he took some holding. Well, these birds frightened him out of his wits, he took off like a bat out of hell so fast I nearly went off his behind, I regained my seat, but pulling him up was impossible, no matter how hard I pulled, there were—so Coquino thought, a thousand demons behind him, and he was determined to leave them behind.

We had gone a mile like a rocket, and by then, I was almost exhausted from using all my strength to no effect. Kurt was not far behind on Darry—as we called Darwinnian, he was in charge of his mount because he had a good mouth on him. Kurt shouting advice towards the end of the Roman road, we arrived where the stonework started, the clattering of Coquino's shoes on the stones seemed to startle him further. But then, I knew he had had enough. I felt his speed slacken, I made my last feeble effort and got him stopped, he must have thought the demons were far behind now. Myself, my legs and arms were like jelly, Coquino was sweating from fear and exhaustion, he had had his exercise over quickly that morning. We cut across some fields and passed the lake and small country mansion where Bridgett used to live; her Mother and Father were there now.

Coquino was a grand horse to ride at no more than a decent canter, any faster and it was impossible to pull him up when I broke him in as a two-year-old, he was gelded but had the neck and bearing of a full-blown colt, he was good to deal with, to lunge and drive, but one day when I was lunging him, the ground was stone hard with frost, I had my Lotus Veltschoen boots on with metal studs in the soles, my lunging rope was too long and too thick. As he went round and round, I gave him a little more rope, and as it was too thick, I could not hold the whole in my hand—there being a good few coils on the ground at my feet, all at once, Coqino pulled just that bit harder, I pulled to restrain him, my boots sliding on the hard, short grassed soil, making a loud scraping, rattling noise with the metal studs, this frightened the horse, he pulled harder away from me, I pulled—or tried to pull him in, to no avail, by now my studded boots were making more noise than ever, he got his head and body away from me, and took off.

The next second, I was flat on my back with the rope twisted around my left foot, going at 35 or 40 miles per hour towards a small wooded corpse at the end of the field 300 yards away—the ground flying past like lightning. Just before all of this, I had waved to Monique, she was taking baby Joey in his pram to the village to go to the post office, she was halfway down the drive when Coquino took off with me on the end of his lunging rope, I did not hear her screaming, she told me later she had done so, loud and clear.

At the end of the rope, I thought if the horse entered the wooded corpse, I might have had my chips. I visualised swinging into a pine tree at full speed, thinking it would be rather nasty. Then, twenty yards from the trees, Coquino skidded to an abrupt halt. He could easily have swung round in a wide circle and continued in his wild burst, but no, in a straight line, there he was—stopped dead. Before the blink of an eye, I had the twist of rope off my foot; relief in being free was almost instant, and in a flash, I had the rope—and Coquino under control, he never moved and was quite docile. He had had a fright. By now, Monique was beside me, tears streaming down her cheeks with anxiety—a relief to see me on my feet, she had left the pram on the driveway, I was perfectly alright except for a few bruises on my back due to the hard, bumpy ground.

The next day, I mounted Coquino for the first time, I got on him in the same field as we had used the day before—the Croft. The first one leading up to Skirwith Hall. He stood perfectly still—I edged him forward with my heels and voice, he responded with ears pricked, and within minutes, I was trotting him around in figures of eight. He never put a foot wrong. The trouble was, though, that he would not bend at the poll.

In the hunting field on his first day with hounds, I could feel he liked the atmosphere of the whole thing. At his first hedge, taken at a slow canter, he—when only a few yards from it, suddenly realised that he was supposed to jump this thing, he put on a spurt that had him up and over, landing a few lengths the other side, landing beside Anne Tinniswood—now Anne Robson, wife of Tommy RCVS—horse trainer, she laughed, saying well, at least he can jump Joey, I also laughed and replied ' yes it seems like it' Anne herself was a first-class horsewoman, riding out every day at exercise with Tommy and staff, and hunting twice a week, she was a fearless rider, as were husband Tommy, and sister Mary, all was quiet for a while in the hunting field, then a fox was found, all was excitement, horses, and riders got ready for a run.

The master at this time was Jim Tinnswood, Uncle of Anne. The horn was sounding the away, and we were off. Coquino, it seemed loved the sound of the hunting horn, it seemed to stir his blood. I was side by side with Robert Jackson, we were going just a bit too fast, I thought, he shouted—maybe get a good run this time. A fair-sized hedge was in front, Coquino's ears were full forward, he was eying this hedge. I could almost read his mind "I am going to fly this one."

The hedge loomed up. Coquino thought he was going too slow, he took hold and bolted it—taking off far too soon, he had me in mid-air, my legs not even connecting with him. I wondered for a split second what was going to happen next. His jump was spectacular, he cleared the hedge by a mile, landing with a mile to spare at the other side, myself, just regaining my seat by the skin of my teeth, as we landed I was miles ahead of Robert, who seconds before at the other side of the hedge, was beside me, but Coquino now had stuck his neck out, and more or less had control of me.

The next hedge was vastly overgrown, it came towards me in seconds. I could only steer Coquino in a straight line, and in seconds we were airborne again, another enormous jump by Coquino, I thought quickly that he really loved this game—but thinking in split seconds. This was a bit frightening, I had little control over him, at this rate, we would quickly overrun hounds, then we landed, everything perfect.

I saw a few horses in front pulling up, not jumping the next hedge. Someone shouted 'wire'. In a flash, I realised no way I was jumping the wire hidden in the hedge, even if Coquino had, so far, cleared everything by miles, I could not stop him by direct pull, so I pulled him in as tight a circle as possible, going twice round this field of about ten acres—almost colliding with a couple of other riders, at length I could stop him, but by now, I myself was exhausted. Robert Jackson came up and asked if I was alright. I asked him right away if I would swap horses for a while until I got my strength back. Robert was riding a mare—Cool Cop. I think she was out of a daughter of his mare Miss Fitz—a close relation of Helm Star, my pony who had given me years of fun. She was a good ride, Robert quickly agreed, I thought now, my boy, you'll realise what a puller this one is, at this point, we were wired in, so the field of about twenty horses filed through a gate into other fields that were also wired—either inside hedges, or of wire fences, due to this we lost the hounds, and the hounds were soon off the fox, by now, we were travelling on hard tarmac roads, the horses were calm.

On 16th March, I ran Coqino at Ayr in a 2½ mile chase, he jumped very well, but ran sluggishly, finishing 5th out of 8 runners, perhaps he had not travelled well. A week later at Sedgefield, I had entered both Coquino and Darwinian, the former in a chase with Nevin up, the start was opposite the stands at the far side of the track, and just outside of the horses was Sands Hall, where our friend John Cummings lived, with his bad-tempered wife Valerie.

Watching through my glasses, the horses lined up. Coquino, on this day, was on his toes—he was last to line up, and as he did so, I saw the starter, assistant, curl the long thong of his whip around Coquino's rear end, the same instant that the starter flagged them off, Coquino must have felt like he had been stung by a wasp because, in a flash, he was in the lead, going at full throttle, at the first fence, only 100 yards from the start, he was going so fast he did not have time to pick his legs up, crashing through, and falling heavily, sending Tommy Nevin for yards, the ambulance had to go and pick him up, I went to see him in the first aid room, poor Nevin, he was badly shaken. He, for one thing, had pulled his shoulder out, then they carted him off to the hospital for x-rays. He was discharged, I think, the next day.

This was the Carlisle Easter meeting, on a Monday, I ran

Coquino in a 3-mile chase with Charlie MacMillan up, Charlie was an excellent amateur jockey and strong, he was from the Lockerbie area and hunted with the Dumfriesshire pack, he had plenty of winners to date and was much sought after, Robert Jackson had told Charlie that he was an excellent jumper and could look forward to a splendid ride, the going was soft, the horses started at the end of the parade paddock, to one side of the stands, so spectators had a good view of the start. Off they went, Coquino with them and to my amazement, he made a bit of a hash of the first jump, going through instead of over it, in fact, he made a mess of all his jumps, doing well only to stand up. It seemed he had not only given Tommy Nevin a shock but had given himself a bigger one, in the end, Charlie pulled him up, this was the best thing he could do. I was disappointed, so was poor old Kurt, Charlie on taking his saddle off, remarked dryly. I thought you said this thing could jump, and with that, strode away. He had every right to do so.

We spent a nice, quiet Christmas at home at Skirwith Hall, as my sister did not want us to dine with Dad and Mother at Kirkland because of young Adam. They were always good to put to bed, never sulking or wanting to stay up, and on Christmas Eve, they were hard to tell. Now, boys, it's bedtime. They raced to bed.

At about 11 pm, Monique and I filled their stockings with all sorts. The boys were deep in sleep, and all was well. At 6 am, we heard chattering and shouts of delight, we smiled and dozed off. It was a Christmas we both enjoyed and by now, Monique was a fantastic cook.

We were unable to go racing on Boxing Day. I had too much work to do on the hatching side of things, but on New Year's Day, Monique and I went to Catterick races. I had a good betting day. On the way home, we made a slight detour and called at the invitation of Doug and June Simp- son, they lived not far from Catterick. June's mother was Mrs Blow, she had a few horses with one of the Easterly Bros, we had run into them at the races, June was great fun, Doug was of a more serious nature but both were charming people. June liked her whisky and spoke her mind, which sometimes made Doug wince. We had consumed a large amount of barleycorn with them that day, but before I forget, at Catterick, they sold in the members bar a very, very good Cuban cigar by the name of Cydrax de Luxe, Kohinoor, they were almost 8 inches long, a beautiful smoke, lasting me for 3 hours, costing 10/-, I had bought four of them. Now, June's big boast was that she never wore any knickers. I asked her at the races, "No knickers today, June."

"Not bloody likely," she said, and later at her home, right in front of me, she lifted her skirt to her waist and said, I told you so. I had an eyeful at 3 feet distance. I was sitting on the sofa in her living room. June was almost in front of me, standing up. She had very few pubic hairs, in fact, getting rather bald, but she was beautifully formed. Monique, sitting beside me, was looking in the opposite direction, talking to Doug and missed the show. June was always a nice, bubbly person, always full of fun and when she gave a party, it was a grand affair. We had spent an enjoyable New Year's Day.

The snow started to fall on 13th January and quite a lot. The farm school Poultry Manager at Newton Rigg Farm School had asked if I could take a West Indian young man as a student. I told him no, visualising him living in more meals for Monique to prepare, but Mr ? said no, this chap would live in digs in Penrith and catch the bus each morning and evening and bring his own meal for midday, so I relented. The West Indian Roy Copeland came on Monday, 13th January, together with the snow, poor beggar, he looked absolutely starved of cold, his clothing was thin and he himself was as thin as a stick. I asked him if he missed the sun, he said he did. I then explained a few things to him and put him to work with Kurt, who took Roy under his wing in a kind way. It turned out Roy was not very strong. He would be about twenty-two to twenty-three years old—one day, a load of oats came to be unloaded from Monkhouse in 10 stone stacks. These loads were put from the lorry onto an elevator to reach a landing leading to my storage loft, where whoever was doing the unloading on the landing would put his shoulders just below the elevator end and accept the sacks on his back and shoulders. No sacks were allowed to fall to the ground from the elevator, the man on the lorry spacing the sacks to suit the unloader. This day, I was there when the lorry load of oats arrived, so decided to give Kurt and Roy a hand to unload. Kurt and I started first to let Roy see what was needed of him, I watched when he was getting himself tensed for the sack of oats to slide onto his shoulders, which it did, but the next second, Roy hit the floor with the sack of corn on top of him, his legs just gave way, Kurt was quick to rescue him from under the lost sack, he was none the worse, I thought the sack had probably caught him off balance and asked him to take the next one, I told him to steady himself, the sack was almost at the top of the elevator, next few seconds it was on Roy's shoulders and the next thing, Roy was facing down on the floor boards, his knees just buckled under him, I realised that he was not strong, and told him to help the driver of the lorry to put the sacks on the elevator, but he could hardly do this. The next day, 20 tons of baby chick meal arrived all in 4 stone paper sacks, this was a piece of cake to unload. When these big loads arrived, I positioned the elevator at one of the loft windows, where to store and pile them up was only a few feet away, not like the maize and oats where once on one's back, they had to be carried 20 yards.

The four stone sacks were put on the elevators at a continual rapid rate, sack touching sack on the way up, Kurt throwing them to me where I would pile them up as neatly as possible. I put Roy in my place to see how he could manage, to my surprise, he could scarcely lift the small sacks. He just had no strength. I felt sorry for the poor sod, so after this I put him on very light work looking after the young chicks under the supervision of Kurt. Roy was a nice young chap, always willing to try, after his stint with me, he told me he was going home, I think he said to Antigua to be the manager of a poultry farm there. He invited me to visit him if ever I was in that part of the world, but I have so far never been out in that part. I often wonder how he was, I hope he did succeed.

Later in January, I gave shooting party Robert Jackson, Pat and Archie Glendinning, and Hamish Alexander, a small party, but the game was not plentiful, bagging only 32 pheasants, 3 hares, 4 mallards. I had kept the pigeons in the dovecote for the end of the day, perhaps 60 of them. There were too many of my white ones crossed with racing pigeons that decided to stay on. I thought it a good time to thin them out, The guns surrounded the dovecote while Kurt opened the wire at the two outlets in the roof, then went down, in at the entrance and put them to flight, this was the best sport of the day, the birds getting higher and higher, I had given instructions no white birds to be shot, only coloured and multi coloured, I happened to look at a white pigeon at a tremendous height, thinking, well at least you're safe, when all at once, it started falling, shot dead, I could not believe it had been killed at that height, but it was and it hit the courtyard with a loud thump. The culprit was Robert Jackson, it was a marvellous shot, even if it was a lucky one. The pigeon shoots lasted about half and hour and proved to be the most popular of the day. Afterwards, all came into the house to wash, clean up or take a bath, then drink in the morning room where Monique had blazing coal and log fire going. At 8:30, dinner was ready, a great bowl of hare soup made from two hares by Monique. This was followed by roast pheasant, our own, of course, absolutely succulent, even the aroma of a roasting pheasant was enough to make one's taste buds drool, this was washed down by bottles of Volnay with Crofts 1927 port for after dinner, the sweet was Xmas pudding with rum sauce, with plenty of rum in it and crème caramel of which Monique made beautifully. The meal lasted about three hours.

Later the same week, I took Coquino and Darwinian to Tommy Robsons to put them over Tommy's big steeplechase jumps. I rode Coquino and Robert Jackson Darry, both went very well. I had prepared Coquino for the point-to-point of the Cumb and Cumb farmers held at Holme Hill, Dalston. The day arrived and Monique had spent hours preparing a picnic of royal proportions. I cannot remember all that she made, but the size and quality of the large hamper would have put Fortnum and Masons to shame. For drinks, we had everything plus a case of champagne, the day started rather overcast; I helped Kurt put Coquino in the Bedford lorry, saw him off, got myself ready, helped Monique put the big food hamper in the Jaguar, plus all the booze and cigars, and set off, we were halfway there when it started to snow, gently at first, then so fast and thick, visibility was down to 25 yards, we carried on then we met cars coming towards us, too many cars, they were crawling, Mary Tinnis- wood, Anne Tinniswood, now Tommy Robson's wife and Tommy were among the cars coming back. They waved us down and told us the Point to Point was off for the day. I told them to come on with us to the P & P grounds, at least the bar would be open, and help us to eat our hamper of food. They laughed and tried to turn their car around but got stuck in the snow at the roadside, we all piled out to push and got the car out for Anne, she was driving. We carried on entering the by now snow-covered field, the bar was open, so drinks started to flow, we had an hour of drinking and smoking, the atmosphere in the large tent was one of mellow, good comradeship and laughter, then we took Monique's hamper and champagne, plus all the hard stuff, into the committee tent, smaller and more intimate, Monique opened the hamper lid, undid many packages, there were gasps of wonder and delight, amongst these goodies were roast pheasant and wild duck and grouse, a whole salmon from Pow Foot, a leg of suckling lamb, etc, etc. We invited many of our friends, and quite a few we did not know to join in the fun, we were there in that tent for four hours eating and drinking, the food was eaten to the last crumb, the case of champers finished and most of the spirits, a box of 50 Burma cheroots was also smoked, Scotts No 1. when we came out of the snugness and smoke filled tent into the cold outside it was almost a shock, one's lungs had to adjust all at once, the snow had stopped falling, the wind had dropped but the snow had fallen thickly, there was 6 inches on the ground, as we said farewell's to all of our friends, everyone said it had been the best P & P that never was. We had to drive home most carefully because the roads were treacherous.

The Point to Point was postponed until Tuesday, 31st March when I rode Coquino in the member's race. Unfortunately, there were only two runners, Coquino and Robert Jackson, on Cool Cop, I think it was. I took the lead, as Coquino still took a fearsome hold. Two fences from home, I heard a voice from behind, take it easy a bit. I let Robert draw level, then the last Coquino hit a rail in the fence very hard, checking him, though not much, on the run-in, I gave him a stroke of the whip on his backside and it was as if I had have hit him on the side of his face, he shot off, left-handed like a bullet before I had him straightened up, the race was over, won by Robert, I had never used the whip on Coquino before, and to my regret wished I never had. Otherwise I would have won easily, I had let Coquino down—that cost me another case of champagne, which we drank with the master, Dennis Wybergh and committee members, not long after this, I was invited to be on the committee of the hunt, at the same time also asked was Anne Robson, Tommy's wife, we both accepted.

I ran Darwinian in May at the Kelso meeting, the sunlow hurdle of 2 miles, he finished 4th. I always liked Kelso races. The farmers and others in that area and district were great people, kindly indeed, the likes of Bob Forrest and Alistair Payton. These farmers used to open a bottle of whisky and, before pouring, throw the cork into the fire, which meant the bottle had to be finished before one left, even if you were the only one present.

Darwinian was entered at Cartmel on Monday, the bank holiday. He was fit, but again, unfortunately, a few hours before the first race, there had been a thunderstorm and a tremendous torrential rain, turning the track into a bog and that is what happened to Darry, he was completely bogged down. Cartmel is rather like a flapping track, with the grandstand in the middle of the track going around it. Spectators would see the horses at one side, all would then rush to the other side, almost in the process, tipping the whole thing over, like capsizing a ship. We had a marvellous time, it was my first visit to Cartmel, it was a picnic affair and I was fortunate to be invited into two or three of the tents, where nothing but the champagne was drunk, the atmosphere was most friendly all around. It was years later that my friend Tony Collins and associates from Ireland tried to pull a ringer on this same course, almost pulling it off. Tony was banned from racing for a few years, a pity because he is such a great sport and gentleman. He may be back now, and I hope he is. I have lost contact with many of my old buddies, living abroad most of the time.

I entered Darwinian next at Sedgefield in a Novice hurdle of 2.5 miles with Eric Campbell up. Unfortunately, we had to meet one of Arthur Stephenson's good hurdlers, Dashing White Sergeant, Darry, finishing second to him. I had a nice bet on the winner and a 5-pound place bet on Darry, which turned out to be very good at odds for a place of 80/1. The day turned out to be a good one, so we celebrated with John Cummins and his wife Valerie.

At one of the Newcastle race meetings, we were invited to dine at Mr and Mrs John Cummins Sen house near Newcastle together with Philip Johnston, Sandy Taylor, Dr Ken Stroughan and Nancy, John Cummins Jnr and Valerie. Cummins Sen was a grand sort, always full of fun, and always the first to buy drinks, he had an infectious laugh and was well-liked by all, his business was in building in and around Newcastle, John Jnr taking over from him at this period, and Valerie had to spend, spend to prove it. John Sen just laughed, he was like that. Another time he bought a new Rolls Royce—

he always had one—he had been celebrating before and after taking delivery, took the car home, where a few friends were waiting for him, he stopped the car at his front door, put the car or so he though in a park, fell out of the car, he had imbibed too freely, the car though was not in a park, it was in drive, and as John Sen fell out the car started off on its own, there was a circular gravel drive cum parking at the front of the house, and low and behold the car followed the path turning in the large space at the far end, and as if a phantom driver and came straight back to its owner, who was still lying on the pathway mesmerised at his new car driving itself straight towards him, he would have been run over, if it had not have been for the prompt action of Dick Coleman's headwaiter Eric—Eric was headwaiter of another of Dick's hotels, John laughed at this one, "almost run over by my own car".

However, to get back to the dinner, we dined for over four hours, quite a few had left the big dining table, including Cummins and his wife, then Ken Stroughan, who was sitting beside me—Ken had terrible trouble with his hips, only young, he, later on, had replacements done on both of them—he decided he wanted a pee, I moved my chair so that he may get out from the table easier, don't bother he said, with that he jerks out his John Willy and commences to pee from his chair under the table onto the lush dining room carpet, I could not believe it, neither could Monique, his bladder must have been full, because in seconds it sounded like a waterfall hitting the carpet. Ken was a peculiar fellow, a nice chap, but many times, he was extremely rude and vulgar. A likable chap also, he got a bit hard up at his practice in Newcastle, so went off to Saudi Arabia for a spell. When he came back, he had quite a handful of Cartier gold cigarette lighters given to him by the rich over there. How he came by them was, so he told me, he would have an old or plastic tin lighter with no fuel in, and in the company of his rich clients, would bring it out, flick it a few times, of course, it would not light up, and he said without fail, his Arab friends would straight away give him a gold Cartier, worth a few hundred pounds each. He was a sly monkey, good company, but a bit dangerous to go to restaurants or clubs with, as one did not know what trouble he would bring on his or our party because, for one thing, he would bring his penis out of his trousers at the drop of a hat. He eventually, before I left England, applied for and got the part of Doctor for the factories of Ever Ready batteries.

20

In the middle of June, I decided to have a poultry sale of all the surplus stock, as a business, I could see it was not going to improve. On 26th June, I sold at auction on the farm in the region of 5,000 head of poultry of various ages, the weather was and had been for a few days, sunny and hot, the attendance was poor because nearly all farmers were haymaking. The sale was conducted by Penrith Farmers & Kidds Auction Co. 20-week-old pullets ready to lay made 10/- each. A year or so back, I would have asked 30/- to 2 pounds and got it with no trouble. Eight weeks old at 5/-. For me, it was sad and a waste of time, energy and money to have reared the birds to be sold at less than cost. However, it was no good keeping them on and feeding them stuff was costly.

We met up with our friends, the Cummings, including Sen & Jun, Sandy Taylor, the Dr Ken Stroughan, Charlie Brown, who had a large farm just outside Newcastle. Charlie had a few horses with Tommy Robson at Greystoke. He was at all the dinners given by Ann and Tommy and many weekends, he was also very keen to bed Mary, which he eventually did, the one Robert Jackson was keen on, but Robert always was very slow when it came to women. A little later in the year, after Hexham races at the County hotel there, Charlie was dining at an adjoining table with other friends. Robert, Monique, Sandy and I dined at one another. I left to go to the toilet, a second or so later, Charlie came into the toilette, we chatted, then in came Robert, and started to verbally attack Charlie for seducing Mary Tinniswood. I tried to pacify Robert, who then turned and gave me a hefty wallop across the face, I thought at this stage discretion was the better part of valour and left to return to my table, shortly after Charlie returned with a bruised face, and then Robert all disheveled. They had no doubt been at blows, Robert later apologised for striking me. After this incident, Mary, who had for years waited for Robert to pop the question or at least take her to bed, would not suffer his presence any longer and avoided him. Silly fool, he missed a nice, kind, caring girl in Mary, a very capable one also.

At the end of July 1964, I sold Coquino and Darwinian to a butcher of Whitby, North Yorks, Mr Richardson, he wanted them for his son to hunt and point-to-point. He drove a hard bargain, I sold for 300 pounds a pair, they went to a good home. Coquino, without his market har- borough bridle, was, as usual, a tremendous puller, and as far as I learned over the next year or two, Coquino was second in almost all, if not all of his p-to-p, taking a hold, leading the field, but beaten on the post.

Darwinian, I believe, won about a dozen p-to-p, so Mr Richardson and son had a lot of fun with them. I sold because of the hatchery slowing down, school fees for my sister's children were becoming a burden, and thirdly my father hated racehorses, and I could see the day I may have to ask him a favour.

The next day, the 13th, dad's dachshund Pluto died, he was twelve years old, he was a solid dog, probably the best specimen of its breed I have ever seen, a great putter up of birds in the turnip fields, a bit short-tempered, he adored dad travelling day after day and year in year out in the land rover, now he had gone to the happy hunting grounds, Dad was sad.

August 17th Kurt set off for his holidays in his van to visit his mother in Germany. She was in a place called Mellor, about an hour's drive from Telgte, my German stomping ground. I gave him money to buy me 1,000 cigars and told him to get them from my friend Sepple Poppenborg directions to visit Heinz and Willie Hesselman, which he did. He got on well with Willie, in fact, rather too well. Willie got the big schnapps bottle and a few beers out, with the result, Kurt had to stay the night at Willy's place. Heinz reckoned he, Kurt, was Polish and not German. Kurt did come from Frankfurt-on-Oder, the town or city right on the Polish border, and the German people did not like the Poles. However, Kurt did visit Heinz and the latter made him welcome; also, he went to see Sepple Poppenborg and bought my 1,000 cigars, stuffing them behind partitions in his van and bringing me a stone bottle of schnapps, a present from Josef Tunte to me. Josef is the chap whom, when I gave him a cigar, you can't see him for the clouds of the smoke screen he puts out.

Also, in August 1964, Auntie Kate died, This was her mother's sister, whose husband David lived in Leeds, where he was a city engineer, there are some playing fields named after him there, "the Currie playing fields". David had retired two years before and had bought a lovely bungalow near Armathwaite village on the banks of the river Eden. David was going to indulge in his passion for the sport of fly-fishing and golf, but Aunt Kate's health started to be not so good in her last two years in Leeds. When Monique and I visited her each month, she complained of pain in one of her legs. On going upstairs, she would take one at a time. She put it down to rheumatism, but the year after, she started to lose the use, firstly of one leg, then the second year of retirement in her new bungalow Eden Brae, she lost the use of both legs, becoming paralysed and unable to use her hands and arms properly, I used to lift her in and out of the car when she came to see mother, as mother and her, were as close as sisters could ever be, they were absolutely in harmony with each other, it was absolutely incredible, all of a sudden Aunt Kate died, Mother was devastated, she still had not recovered from Adam's death, now her closest sister and friend had gone, at the early age of 62, on 1st September.

Kate was buried in the cemetery in the little town of Annan on the banks of the river Annan, where her parents were buried, I was one of them who lowered the coffin into the grave, it was a sad day. I felt extremely sad for my mother. Uncle David was devastated, for he and Kate had been boy and girl sweethearts, they had been in love all of their life together, he could not bear to be anymore in Eden Brae and sold it within two or three weeks and retired to Annan to live with his sister. He had passed his schooldays there at Annan Academy, where he had met his sweetheart.

Monique and I had turned mother's drawing room into a party room, it was done on the cheap but looked good and was good, the walls were lined to a height of 7 feet, with thick canes, the floor was tiled in black and white squared floor tiles, the wall lights were ordinary bulb holders, with a frame of wire from the farm, covered with a thatch of straw, giving a very good effect, the middle light was a large wire ball covered with a Hessian chicken food sack, the bar front was of birch tree, largish branches split and placed end on end with the silver bark to the outside, the top was of planed sycamore, with a corner of the front of the bar a thick hazelnut branch from floor to ceiling, behind and at the sides be- hind the shelves were silver birch branches split, the flat side up, for bot- tles and glasses, the bar roof, thatched with straight out straw, the tables were wine barrels, that Monique's uncle had sent over, full of wine of course, but now empty, these were placed in front of bales of straw round the walls of the room, it was a cosy night club affair, very snug. On 12th October we decided to christen the new party room, it did not matter here if drinks were spilled over the place, not like our other rooms, when on various occasions we had furniture burnt with cigarettes and sofas, carpets, etc. stained by careless guests.

We invited 35 guests and they all came, we had a 22lb turkey, a large ham, and 6 lbs of the tongue. Besides other things Monique had made, everyone enjoyed themselves. The last guest left at 4:30 am. On looking back, not one guest invited us back, except one near neighbour. It is strange how some of these so-called friends can be, like Tim Featherstonhough, whose wife tried her best to rape me on the dance floor when not long married. Tim used to be the first to arrive and the last to leave, making sure he had his fill of drink before the start.

In October, my Jaguar MK 7 had to be sold. The valves were burnt out and it needed quite a bit of money spent on it, so I decided to go for something smaller, seeing the sale of chicks declining. I got an 1100 MG from Howard Lace of Lazonby, it was a nice little car to drive, the only thing I did not like was that the steering wheel was slightly offset from the centre, but I eventually got used to it. The first trip in the new car was to Leeds, where Monique got her hair done. The Penrith hairdressers were a useless lot, also to visit Marchall and Snelgrove, where Monique used to buy her dresses, there, the head fashion buyer Mrs Morris, had taken Monique under her wing, realising what Monique wore, she wore it well, not only that, but Monique had for quite a few times, been mistaken for Sophia Loren. Mrs Morris always had the top dresses put away. When Monique called, out they came, all models of first-class material, all very pricey, Mrs Morris probably thought I could not afford the price tabs, she probably thought right, but a dress or coat with a price tag of 150 pounds would for Monique be reduced to 40 pounds. Monique dressed herself for years through Mrs Morris, who, without the reduction in the price tags, was a lovely and charming woman full of character and bubbling with good health. Mrs Morris, after a number of years, retired, then the middle was knocked out of Leeds, building after building was refurbished or pulled down. The character of Leeds, for me, had gone. Gradually, Monique and I stopped going there.

Kelso Races was our next trip, this lovely little town sitting on the banks of the Tweed. I was very fond of Kelso; this is where Jimmy Goldsmith married his Isabella Patino, a great love story then, and sitting back in the parkland, that fairy tale beautiful castle floors, the home of the Duke of Roxborough, the racecourse was a little gem. One could always have a good lunch in the member's restaurant. I always knew a lot of people there, and this day, old Major Parker had driven himself up the 100 miles in his old Rolls (this was Bridget's father). On the way home we called as usual, at the pub in Denholm, the Major was in before us, a fair sized drinking party was in full swing, all farming friends, we joined in, then on to the Tower in Hawick, here, rather quiet, so after half an hour, then on to

Mosspaul pub in the middle of the hills, this was always a good watering hole, we found Uncle Bob and my Aunt Jean, Bob was my favourite uncle, mother's brother, the Major arrived, he knew many of the people there, and could more than hold his own, but when seated and fairly full had the habit of dropping off, for 40 winks with a glass in his hand, waking up as if nothing had happened, and starting again, with great gusto, well at Mosspaul he dropped off, on our wishing to go to Langholm, we could not wake him up, so we left him, I heard later on he had woken up at 2 am, the bar still going strong, himself not knowing how late it was, started all over again, eventually arriving home at Skirwith after six in the morning, none the worse for wear and he was about seventy years then.

The weekend after, races were, I think, at Catterick. Monique and I decided not to go, so I had a little bet with Willy Whiteman, a 2-pound acc winning 150 pounds. Willy was not amused, he even tried to say I had put the bet with his clerk, too late for the first horse, but he paid.

In Nov I decided to go for the new breed of poultry, bred for the table, Cobb, they were called, I ordered 1,000 female chicks plus 140 cocks. They were flown from Sweden to Glasgow, then delivered to me, almost 100 were smothered on delivery, otherwise they seem good healthy chicks, very thick set ones, into the rearing brooders they went, where they would remain for four weeks. They reared and did well.

It had been a busy week so far, two weeks later, my sister Cathie, Monique and I were at the wedding of my cousin Walter Tinning, Uncle Bob's son and Laura Johnstone from near Lockerbie, the reception was held at Carlisle, in the Central Hotel, rather a private affair, but quite good, young Walter was a grand young man, hard-working, a ready smile always. The same week, I saw an advert in shooting times, Labrador bitch for sale at Beatock, just over the border in Scotland, it was 11 months old and was trained to the gun, I phoned the number given, a Mr. P Jolly. I set off alone to have a look at the young dog, I liked what I saw, it was a friendly little bitch, but seemed rather nervous of its owner. I told Jolly I would take it, as he said it was fully trained and retrieved well.

I gave the dog two days to settle before I took it with the gun, but when it saw the gun, it did not want to go with me, deciding to go and hide in the stable, I thought, that's strange, so I put a lead on her and even then with the gun, she did not want to go. I insisted and dragged her along, eventually, she decided to behave and trotted by my side—though on the lead—I knew where I could put a few pheasant up to try her out for retrieving, as I approached this particular rough acre or so, I let her off the lead, within a few short minutes 3 pheasant got up simultaneously. I dropped two of them, both fortunately dead, I turned to urge the bitch to retrieve and could not immediately see her, then I spotted her, hidden in a large clump of reeds, petrified, she was scared to death of the gun, I calmed her and spoke kindly to her, petting her up, letting her smell the pheasants, but I could see, no matter what, she was just too frightened, I tried again walking on until a solitary bird got up, I shot, killed it, the dog ran away and hid in another clump of reeds I could now see, as I approached the poor dog, she fully expected to receive a good beating. No doubt our friend Mr P Jolly, gamekeeper of Beatock, had done just that on many an occasion.

I had no option but to take her back. I did not want to purchase a dog scared stiff of the gun, I phoned Jolly telling him I was returning the bitch and giving the reason why, all I got was a lot of abuse over the phone, so next day, I put the little dog in the 1100 and set off once again for Mr P Jolly, he certainly was not living up to his name, I arrived there he was in his gamekeeper's plus 4's. Out came a stream of abuse, saying he knew all about buggers like me, what he meant by this, I do not know. When I asked for the return of my money, I thought the man was going into an epileptic fit. I did not get my money back just then, but a letter from Quentin Little, my solicitor brought instant results. The strange thing, though was when I took the poor little bitch out of the 1100 and she saw Jolly, she took one quick look and tried to get back into the car, I think she was probably more frightened of Jolly than the gun.

Sunday on, 13th December, Arthur Durham, Dad's old foreman, died, he had been very ill for a month but had not been in good health for quite a while, he had been at Skirwith Hall for over 40 years. His wife Hilda had gone before him, she had had dead twins the year before she died, herself a rather frail woman, always with a rather tragic look on her face and always a very sallow complexion, she died of cancer, poor Arthur trying to keep her going with sips of brandy, he could ill afford. Now it was his turn, he died of cancer with his eldest daughter Dora keeping house for him. I used to visit him and take a fat hen and eggs, but Dora said he had little appetite. His face always lit up when I went to see him and have a chat, he had seen me grow up from a baby. He always two or three times week took my mother's flowers from his little greenhouse or garden. Now Mother was 2 miles away, he did the same for Monique, the kind gesture was appreciated by Mother and Monique and also by me, I thought it most kind, now poor chap he was gone.

The week after I bought a 12-week-old yellow Labrador bitch puppy from Mrs Hilditch of Appleby, she and her husband ran the Royal Oak Hotel there. They had two lovely daughters, one of whom I was rather keen on a few years ago, they ran a good hotel, good home-cooked food and a good bar, her husband Pip, a big jovial man, I liked the puppy and I knew the mother of the litter, so I bought it there and then, I told Adam he could be the owner, he was overjoyed, Lassie was to become probably the best gundog I had had—with the exception, and he was not a gundog by breed, my beloved Spot, Lassie was to never lose a bird, very obedient to the whistle, quartering 20yds ahead when walking up, unfortunately when she was about 5 or 6 years old she started to go very short-sighted, she had likely inherited the malady "eye dislepsia" from one of her parents. Also, she was to come to a very sad end due to the idiocy of a neighbor, an invite to one of my shoots at Skirwith Hall. However, in her early years, we had some great times down the beck after duck, in deep snow, and wild days when I was invited to various shoots. I always took her and without fail she was the most obedient of all other dogs there, Arthur Sowerby, who always had Labradors used to get wild at his dogs, he would give them some thrashings and let off a lot of steam at them, shout his head off, as did most of the others, Lassie had only my whistle, I never shouted to her, or at her, as the human voice in-game shoots is not a good thing, birds are scared of it, I like silence. I took the new puppy Lassie, she was now 14 weeks old, rather young to go shooting. I downed a pheasant after half an hour, letting Lassie have a good smell at the bird, she was highly interested in it, I asked her to fetch—because she had learnt to fetch tennis balls and slippers thrown away for her, now on command she tried hard, to carry the bird, getting hold of a wing, and drag- ging it, she tried another hold, but her mouth was too small for the large cock bird—she had tried hard and had learned what to do, that day, so I would put her for more training later on in the year.

Harold Metcalfe, the 1st poultry man, went to work for Dad as shepherd, he was offered this post and took it. I was pleased he was staying on the farm—I kept Kurt for he could put his hand to anything, and he could ride the horses. At the closing down of the hatchery, I was now losing money, etc.

Adam went back to school at Lime House on 14th January. On Wednesday, my long-lost cousin Peter Bayne came from Canada to stay with mother and father at Kirkland. They were all excited about him coming, the mother saying he, Peter, was a well-travelled man. All I could remember of him was that he could not pronounce his R's, such as in cracker, he would say quacker. I always thought him so, too—I remember I did not like him, he was a nasty snob. He had run away from Hailebury

School on his bicycle, travelling all the way north to land up at Skirwith Hall. He was on the news bulletin on the 6 o'clock news, as lost, but he had the guts to travel all that way, knocking on a house door on his first-night escapade, the people taking him in for the night, on a plausible story from him, giving him a big supper and breakfast. The next stop was Skirwith Hall. Now here he was again, I was busy dipping new sawn fencing posts into a barrel of creosote when I heard a voice behind me, it was him, I turned and there was the marvellous, "well-traveled man," I was amazed, he was only about 5ft 2 or 3 and quite insignificant, I had not seen him since I was 12 or 13 years old. He still could not pronounce his R's and one look was enough for me, I still did not like him, however, I shook hands, made myself say pleasant things, etc. It started to snow hard. Whenever any of us, including Father, asked Peter's father, Alex, what sort of work Peter did in Canada, all we got was, "oh he's in banking, you know", nothing more. I suspect, yes, he was in banking but behind a counter as a clerk.

Monique and I took him, with my sister Cathy to dinner at the country club near Armathwaite called Heather Glen. Ossie Partington was the owner, I was a member when we arrived, there was a wedding party going strong given by a chap called Peter Vasey, I knew him fairly well, a very nice young man, he invited my party to join his daughter's wedding guests and all drinks and eats were on him. He told Ossie this, but at one stage, Vasey saw Ossie charging Peter, my cousin, for drinks and made Ossie refund the money after that Ossie complained to me about my cousin's behaviour—as far as I could see, it was sour grapes, at being made to refund the money.

Later in the week, I took Peter Bayne, Cathy, Monique to the same club for dinner, which was quite good, after dinner we sat around, having a few drinks, when all of a sudden, my cousin told me Ossie had refused to serve him, this sort of thing had happened between Sandy Taylor and Ossie a month before, Ossie complaining that Sandy had insulted his daughter, Wendy, on this occasion, knowing Sandy, I apologised for Sandy and poured oil on troubled waters, but it seemed that with Ossie, things always rankled in his breast, I went up to the bar, where Ossie was behind serving. I was getting fed up with his stupidity and asked why he was refusing to serve my cousin, as this was the third time in 4 weeks this sort of thing had happened to people I had taken to the club.

Ossie then told me that without more ado he would not serve me either that was enough I thought, I was no more than 2 feet from Ossie, he was behind the bar, and 16 stones in weight, I gave him a tremendous right to the jaw, down he went poleaxed, at that moment as I made contact with the bar, as my momentum had carried me against it, I felt it give, I gave it an almighty heave, and over it went with dozens of glasses and bottles cascading onto Ossie lying on the floor behind, then some two chaps grabbed me from behind, and held me hard, I shook them off, for now my temper was up. Mrs Partington and daughter Wendy came running, who was a charming woman, so I calmed down, at that moment, Ossie started to surface, holding his left jaw with one hand, it must have hurt him, I told Mrs P that I had had enough of Ossie, insulting my guests and I forthwith resigned from the club, and to refund my club fee, which to my amazement she did. That was my last visit to Heather Glen.

A day or two later, I was moving chicken hay box brooders in a field next to the farm buildings when dad came walking up, I thought he looked rather serious, he bid me a good day, then came out with, first clearing his throat as he always did—you he said, addressing me, will have to get rid of Peter, I laughed and said why me, he's staying with you, well he said we'll have to get rid of him, I asked why the hurry, but knowing at the same time, one or two days was enough of Peter, he got on one's nerves, he was a human being—but an empty one. Dad then told me at night, when all were sleeping, Peter would go to Cathy's bedroom, and stay there for quite some time, well it did not take much imagination to conjure up what that meant, I told Dad to give him his marching orders right away, saying it was his place to do so. The next day, Peter left, I have never heard of him to this day, 2012. I thought when Dad told me he had gone, good riddance.

Me at approx 18 months

Petite Joey aged 8 years.

(Above) My first true love, Bridget. My age then 13 years. (Below) Monique with my own personal sheep dog, Maid, with Skirwith Hall buildings in the background. The field, The Croft.

Me at a young age with Don, who killed most of the ducks in the neighbourhood and two pups.

Monique's mother, aged 18 years.

My father with his two grandchildren at Kirkland, L to R Adam, Joey Junior.

Monique in my Jaguar 120, with Cross Fell in the distant snows.

My mother 1947.

Me, Spot and Sammy rolling corn fields with Blossom in Black Wood, aged about 13.

Kurt with Cocquino, Sedgefield Races

My great love putting the ring on my finger, at last. 16th December 1954.

August 1962 at Kirkland House. L to R, Little Joey, Ma, Dad, Michael (behind), Adam, Cathie.

The Dovecote reputed to be 600 plus years old.

Me with Helm Star (or Starry) at Skirwith Vicarage, about 1942-43.

Just married outside the church, Oran. Isn't she lovely?

After our marriage at the Town Hall, Oran, 16th Dec, 1954. Ma cherie.

Karnival, Althaus Telgte

Monique

Lassie 2nd, 12/8/73.

Monique and I on one of our travels on a river boat, Bangkok.

Me at Horse Fair inspecting the teeth, Telgte 1953.

Monique in a dancing mood at Muska.

Adam my brother, the brains of the family, at possibly Mary Jackson's wedding aged 27 years.

At the Horse Fair, Telgte inspecting a piglet, Maria watching 1953.

Function in Hotel Hermitage, Monte Carlo.

Adam and Bronco.

Grouse shooting on my moor, 12th August. Standing L to R:, Adam, John Frith (beaters) Hamish Alexander, Heinz, Willie McCauley. Front row L to R: Kurt Witteck (beater) Me, Alfons Ludkehaus, from Telgte, John Cummins and the dog Lassie.

Skirwith Hall.

The new courtyard of Skirwith Hall.

Me with a nice bag of duck and pigeon and pheasant with my faithfull Lassie and Sammy.

Heinz and I at the Horse Fair, Telgter, taking a breather.

One of the oldest retainers at Skirwith Hall, Joe Varty, pigman and general factotum, a true gentleman of nature.

At Newcastle races with John Cummings and Vallerie.

My great friend and blood brother, Heinz Uekotter from Telgte, Munster. Heinz died 1978.

In the night club, dancing, L to R: Gaby, Réné, me and Monique, Beber (the photographer), Oddette and Paul.

Getting of the plane from Paris from Oran at Dusseldorf, August 1953, to visit Heinz and Maria.

21

By now, the poultry were in their various quarters, outside and in when Monique and I decided to have a holiday in Spain, on the Costa del Sol, where, according to brochures, it was always hot.

This was Feb 1965, Kurt knew what he had to do, straightforward work and it would probably be the last holiday for quite a while with the hatchery closed.

We set off in the little MG 1100 on 4th February 1965—starting at 1:40 am got to Dover at 9:30 am. I onto the ferry boat at 10 am and arrived on the French side at 11:30 am, where I sent Mother a telegram saying we had arrived there safe at Calais, we drove on to Beavois and booked into a small hotel Le Croix d'or for the night, not so far from Crecy. For dinner, we both had snails, I had wild boar, Monique had veal all very good, washed down with a good bottle of Volnay, it was like a second honeymoon for us. Mrs Metcalfe was looking after little Joey, as mother was and looked tired.

The next day Saturday 6th, we set off at 8:30 am. Had breakfast in Limoges, which was very good, then driving towards Toulouse, we pulled up in a small village. Monique bought a couple of baguettes, some charcuterie at the butcher's shop, which looked so good we would have eaten it on the spot, a large chunk of gruyere, with plenty of holes in it, a bottle of decent wine and not far from Toulouse we had our picnic. The weather was nice and warm, for Feb. Then on we drove, where we entered Spain at Port Roy at 4 pm. Here, things changed. We were entering snow country and at this moment, there seemed to be plenty. We were in the middle of the Pyrenees roads covered with snow, though quite passable. We drove through a tunnel, it seemed a very old one, I clocked it to be about 4 miles long, I think it was named Villa, at long intervals, a small electrical light bulb hung from the wall side, it was cold inside the tunnel, with icicles 5-6ft long hanging from the roof, it was quite fascinating, but was pleased to be at the other side, where we stopped at 7 pm at a place named Pablo de Segur, Monique could now use her Spanish vocabulary, she went into a small place which looked quite nice and clean to ask for a room, they had and this is where we bedded down, it was called Pension Martin, it turned out to be quite good, the food as well.

Sunday morning we set off once again—at 8 am after having a huge cup of cafe au lait each, fresh bread, butter and jam, plus the croissants, it all tasted delicious. We were ready for driving. Outside the frost was as hard as iron, but a crystal clear day, the sun was shining bright, but thank goodness the MG had an excellent heater, we drove on to and had lunch at Zarragosa. Driving towards Zarragosa was a very wild and picturesque land, I think it was the Sierra de la Pena, but I may be correct on this; it was fascinating. Some of the villages, if one could call them that, consisted of cave-like dwellings built into hillsides, with only chimney pots sticking out of the ground. I would have liked to have stopped and investigated more, but I did not like to intrude on the people's privacy, at the brassiere La Maraislla, where we had as a main dish quail, three each, very plump ones too, the wine, I have not made a note of it, but it was excellent equal to good French wines. After being fortified with lunch, we dallied over coffee, where I had a good Cuban cigar and a large brandy, which I think was Fundador, I found it rather fiery.

We then took our time driving to Alicante. We came across a small village and stopped at the local and, I think, the only bar. The bar room, pretty large, was packed full of locals and cigarette smoke, one could have cut it with a knife. Monique and I made our way to the bar, the peasants for that is what they were, made way on each side for us being most polite towards Monique. I ordered two beers, saying good morning in Spanish to all and sundry, in no time they were all wanting to talk with Monique, on hearing her speak Spanish, we stayed for an hour, I myself could not speak the language, but Monique did a lot of interpreting in that hour, they were a kindly lot those peasants. I think if one was stuck on the road, there would be no trouble seeking help or a bed for the night, it would be gladly given.

We drove to Valencia, where we stopped for the night. It was rather a poor place when we got in, but we made do. We slept well, though.

On Monday the weather was very cold and at night colder than ever, I was beginning to wonder when the heat was going to start, because according to the English travel bureaus, it was always warm in these parts, even in mid-winter, so far all we had had were very hard frosts, yet again we were enjoying the trip calling at little country taverns, Monique speaking to the locals, we had met great kindness from these people, poor as they were, also they seemed a happy lot. Alicant itself seemed deserted, hardly a tourist in sight, in winter, it was sad and cold. I drove 25 miles outside of the place, asking the price of hotels to stay, two or three hotels were far too expensive, but as I say 25 miles out, I stopped at a place on the seafront, beside the main road, called Berlin. The placard outside had the Berlin bear on it, I suspected it was German-owned, and it was, there we thought we would stay a day or two, allowing us to have a look round, the Berlin was quite a nice cosy, very clean small hotel, we soon discovered the drinks were double price here to what they were on the Costa Brava. However our first night, we slept badly, my hips and back seemed full of rheumatism, I thought the beds must be damp, for the place was empty, with no tourists to be seen.

The following morning turned out to be a bright and sunny one, we surfaced at 9 am and had a good breakfast, then I thought, it's a grand day for a swim, off we set in the MG. We drove to a nice wide bay, the sea was calm, the sun was shining but giving no heat. A square-hatted policeman was coming out of his little sort of guard hut, very like the AA telephone huts but twice as big, he said Buena's dais as we approached him— he then realised we were going for a swim and tried to dissuade us, he said the water was too cold, I scoffed at this and told Monique to hurry and get in the water. The policeman I heard use the word Loco, which means crazy, Monique and I were ready to now run in, which we did, but soon stopped running. The water was indeed cold, I thought it would be better if we started to swim, Monique started or tried to swim, but the water was so cold it took her breath away, she could not breathe, I told her to have another go, she tried, but once again she could not breathe, I got right in and started swimming, but it was like ice, so discretion being the better part of valour, gave up. Monique was by now blue and goose pimples of huge proportions, the policeman still watching and calling us crazy. English lost no time in opening his little hut and shepherding us inside to change before he said, "We die." He was most concerned but did not turn away when we changed, getting his eyes full of Monique's nude form, she was shaking so much, once her clothes were off, she could hardly put them on. After the swim, I had to towel her down as hard as I could, rubbing hard to get the circulation going, the policeman giving advice at the same time—probably wishing he could have done the rubbing down, however, I shall not forget, he was most concerned and kind so much for the holiday brochures.

On Wednesday the 10th, I was fed up with the cold and frost, almost everywhere was closed in Alicante, there was no hustle and bustle that holidays are all about, so we left the hotel Berlin at 8 am in very hard frost, stopping at a village store, buying bread, cheese and pate and a bottle of wine, for a picnic lunch, which we had in the Sierra de Nevada. I took the inland roads, not wanting to follow the coast, it was much more interesting, a few workers here and there on the road had little fires built for warmth when they ate their coffee break or lunch. We were heading for Seville to catch a boat to Fuerteventura. I had read an article on this island by Lewis de Fries in one of the Sunday papers, it seemed an interesting place and was supposed to be hot, being in sight of the Sahara desert, after our picnic, we thought to call at Granada to take a look at the Alhambra, the Moorish Palace there, it was a very interesting place, beautifully built, the mosaic wonderful, and the harem end, the bathrooms or bathing pools. The Arabs no doubt could build beautiful palaces, swords, guns, and knives, but it seemed as if that was all they could do. However, we enjoyed our visit to this ancient place, lingering for quite a long time. Monique suggested visiting the caves of the gypsies, but then we thought to push on to Seville, where we booked a hotel, a fairly large and good one, its name I must have forgotten to enter in my diary, it was very comfortable, we parked our car outside, took the baggage up, had a bath each. We always bathed together—went outside to explore, having a drink here and there, in some very nice old-fashioned bars, many with sawdust on the floors, for the Spanish seem to be full of catarrh and thought nothing of coughing it up and spitting it out in large lumps direct onto the floor of the bars or in front of one on the pavement, it was a disgusting habit, I thought, but had to put up with it. I was very fond of one of their good habits though, this was on ordering one's drink or drinks, summoning the waiter with a loud clap of the hands—another thing I liked was the offering of Tapas, usually, a few shrimps or some other little delicacy.

At about 10 pm, after numerous drinks, we decided to dine, hunted up a very good restaurant where we had a very good meal and a bottle of excellent wine. On Thursday, I enquired where the shipping office was, which was right on the river Guadalquivir from which the boat sailed, The clerk told us the ship sailed on the morrow Friday, at midnight. I bought the tickets. Then I drove towards the middle, or so I thought of Seville, and seeing a large number of cars parked, I parked the little MG in one of the parking lanes, Monique asked where a good hairdresser might be, and was given directions, it was 5 minutes walk only when Monique went to have her hair shampooed and set, I retired to a nearby bar, where I had a few of the local brandy Fundator, I was getting used to its fire by now. Also nearby, I bought a few Cuban cigars and a few of what the locals seemed to smoke, panatelas, which turned out pretty good, but the Cuban cigars, good large ones, were very damp and smoked too strong. I did not enjoy them. This bar was situated on a corner of a crossroads of a busy thoroughfare, one young policeman directing the traffic. When Monique joined me, we somehow just watched the young policeman, he was kept quite busy, he noticed we were watching him, so we raised our glasses in the sign of cheers, he bowed and laughed, which seemed to set him off, he stopped traffic, for the fun of it, looked over at us, we laughed with him, this went on for half an hour, then he stopped a woman on a bike, she was alone in the middle of the road, and at that moment, no traffic. He held her there for a good five minutes, then, with a flourish, waved her on, looking over to us with a big laugh on his face, we raised our glasses once more to him, then I thought it better to move on. He might become over-excited and do something he should not. We waved him goodbye, he saluted, and off we went to find our car, as we approached where we had left it, I thought, it was strange, the scenery had changed, I had to look hard, I thought this couldn't be the place where we left the car, but it was, there the MG was, all on her own in the middle of what was now a very wide busy street, all the other parked cars had gone the everyday traffic passing on each side of our little MG, it was nearly a nightmare, and to make it worse there standing beside our little car, was a square hatted policeman. There was nothing I could do but march up to the car and face the music, he asked why we had left the car in the middle of the street, Monique explained the situation, that in the first instance, we had parked in what we had understood to be a public parking place, now it seems it was not.

The policeman listened, then with a smile, he told us that this was a park for cars, doing local market on certain days and a certain time limit, he told us to be more careful in parking next time, Monique assured him we would, I then asked Monique to ask him if he knew of a garage that would take the

MG for a month, as we were taking the ship to Fuerteventura at midnight, he gave us the name of a garage near the docks, called the Torre del Oro, and directions to get there, we thanked him, he gave us a big smile, saluted and left, he was a kindly man with a kind face, thank goodness. I thought it a good idea to go and see the garage owner about the MG and, following instructions, drove there without any problems. It turned out the garage was situated at the other side of the river just across from the ship, crossing by a bridge very nearby, nice and handy. On explaining to the garage owner, he said it was no problem to garage the car for as long as we wanted and pay when we collected the car, he mentioned the cost per week, which was low enough.

That night at 11 pm I garaged the car, walked over the bridge, showed our tickets, which were second class, and were directed to our cabin on the ship Plus Ultra, it was not bad, but not good either, I wished I had taken first class instead, however, here we were. We were tired, being on the go all day, so went straight to bed, or rather to our bunks. Monique did not like sleeping alone, so after a few minutes, she joined me on the top bunk. There was hardly any room before, now, we were like two sardines, side by side. Nevertheless, we slept well, in the morning, we surfaced at 11:30 am, and breakfast of course, had long since finished, we went to the first-class bar for drinks, it was quite a roomy bar, nicely decorated and cosy, the barman was a nice little fellow called Jesus.

We had lunch in the 2nd class dining room, which was a dump, about 8 of us all at one table, an extremely bad lunch, and our table companions had very poor table manners, for me, was quite disgusting. I told our waiter there was only one, I wanted a table for ourselves for the evening meal, adding that the food here was terrible and gave him 100 pesos, for which he thanked me profusely.

We spent the rest of the day looking out to sea, having a look round the ship, which took only 5 minutes. The ship was very small, carrying cargo in her holds and three cars on the open deck, together with a few open deck passengers, perhaps 7-8. The rest of the day we spent in the bar, and as I got the drinks, I asked each time if Jesus the barman would like one. he always declined, but in asking him to partake, I could see thought I was a nice chap because the Spanish never ask barmen anywhere to have a drink. He, with this, kept me supplied with Spanish panatelas all the way to Las Palmas at no cost, they were pretty good, too.

Night came along, and dinner time, we went to our 2nd class dining room, the steward showed us to a table for two, flashed us a big smile, then served us before any of the others and low and behold, the food was very good, I took a look round, and whispered to Monique the other three tables were having quite a different meal to us, she glanced round casually, she could not believe it either, it seemed the 100 pesos had done the trick, on the way from Seville to the open sea, the ship called in at Cadiz. This stretch, as far as I can remember, was all done at night. We went to bed quite content that night and once again slept as lovers do, close together.

On the morning of 14th February, Sunday, we had a good breakfast, and once again, our steward gave us a big smile and a Buena's dais senor and senora, then we stopped on deck for a while, watching the sea. it was as calm as a millpond, and the sun was shining, the day was quite warm. I smoked a good big Cuban Bolivar, it tasted good. After an hour and a half, we retired to the first-class bar. There were I think only two first class passengers, I thought we would ask to be moved from second to first, but thinking about it, it would mean having first class only for one night. The barman Jesus was outside on the promenade deck, he came running into the bar shouting for me, senor, senor, big feet—big feet, pulling my sleeve, and dragging me to the bar door and deck, the little fellow pointed excitedly, still saying big feet, on and on, I looked out to sea and there were the big feet, 30 or 40 of them, dolphins keeping pace with the ship, only 50-60 yards away, jumping in and out of the water, it was my first sight of such a thing, and it was a delight to see, the dolphins stayed with us for about 10 minutes, then went out of sight, I thanked our new friend Jesus, and asked him to have a drink, instead he gave me another panatela.

When we docked, we were sleeping that night on the Plus Ultra and sailing for Fuerteventura, the next night, Thursday the 16th. Monique and I decided to have a look around a few of the streets and shops, so off we set, down the little gangplank arm in arm, we were disappointed with what we saw, all seemed very sleazy and dirty, we had one or two beers

in sleazy bars and brassy lights, then back to the Plus Ultra for bed, for tomorrow, we had to change ships.

On the morning of the 16th, we were woken by the cabin steward at a very early hour, his noisy knocking on the door with his keys woke us up, it was 6 am, Monique asked what he wanted, he said the bedclothes for washing, I told Monique to tell him to get lost, we were not getting out of bed at this hour, off went the steward and we heard no more from him.

But now Monique and I were wide awake, and neither of us could go back to sleep, we chatted a while, then we got dressed re-packed our baggage, for we now had to leave the Plus Ultra and purchase tickets from Las Palmas to Fuerteventura. We surfaced, did not bother with breakfast on board, said our goodbyes to our new friend Jesus the barman and our table waiter, giving them 100 pts each, causing them to break into big smiles and many gratze's, then off we went to the booking office for our forward tickets and this time book into 1st class.

After all the, postcards had been written, we lingered a while longer, when a Spaniard came over from a nearby table to ask what cigar was I smoking, because it had a very different aroma to what he knew of cigars, I told him it was a Burma cheroot, explaining a little about the tobacco, he then invited Monique and I over to his table, to join him and his wife for drinks, which we did, it turned out he was an officer in the army of Spanish North Africa, he was a cigarette smoker, and when he lit up, he pulled what looked like a piece of metal with a rope attached, out of his pocket, it was a Sahara desert lighter, a flint and wheel, and fuse rope, when the flint sparked onto the fuse rope, it would glow a little but when gently blown upon, one could get a red hot glow, to snuff it out, pinch it with the fingers, I suppose a very good thing in the desert, whence a gas or petrol lighter would be dry in a day with the heat, this type of lighter could last 6 months or a year, though not too good for cigars, it would do the trick if one had nothing else. I expressed interest in this chap's lighter; I had never seen one like it and without more ado he gave it to me. This was in 1965 and I still have the lighter plus fuse rope, and it still works perfectly.

Monique and I boarded the little cargo cum passenger ship at 5 pm and were shown to our cabin, my what a difference the first class was, it was grand, but, it was as big as almost any bedroom, with a bunk at each side, one only which was used, we both always slept together side by side holding hands, a thing we still did in 2016.

The dinner was very good, with spotless starched linen and silver plated cutlery, the wine also was very good, the dining room spacious and spotless, as were the stewards. After our meal we had one drink, myself a cigar, which we lingered over, then to bed, once again the sea was calm, and we were soon lulled to sleep by the gentle thud of the engines. I was awake early, looked out the cabin porthole to see that we were passing the tip of an island. I took it to be the island we were going to land at, the ship kept gliding on up the coast of what seemed a desolate, deserted land. We were not sailing fast. The water was completely still. Monique joined me on deck. It was quite warm we noticed at this hour, by now 7 am, we glided on. We were near the shore, and in time saw the odd house or two, very ordinary things. Then, nearer our base, we could see the inhabitants, looking like ancient peasants of some ancient land, the men wearing large trilby-type hats but completely round and high domed, I began to think what have we landed in, the houses were all dirty white, small, square, and flat-roofed. We docked at about 10 am at Puerto Fuerteventura to find the place quite packed with officials. They had come from the mainland and other islands for the grand opening of the first tarmac strip of 50 yards of road laid in the town, or so we were told. We were directed to the one and only hotel on the port side. Monique asked for a room, only to be told they were full by all the government officials here for the road opening, we were told there was nowhere else except at the other end of the island, Puerto Rosario.

We were now at a loss and had no option but to take a taxi if there was such a thing on this deserted-looking dump that we had landed at, Monique asked if there was a taxi; yes there were, I think two of them. We were told where to go to procure or try to procure one of them, we had only gone 20 yards and low and behold, there was one parked at the roadside, Monique asked him if he could take us to the next Port, he quickly obliged. Thank goodness Monique could speak fluent Spanish otherwise we could have gone crackers, we got in the taxi, it was an ancient model as old as myself I thought at the time, pity I did not memorise the exact model, however, we set off, it took us over an hour, through a land that grew only scrub tussock stuff and rocks. It was an empty place. I could not see anyone making a living out here, in fact, I think on the taxi journey, we saw only two or three isolated houses. We eventually arrived at the far end of Fuerteventura, a small port named Rosario. There was also only one hotel there, which looked like the rest of the village, dirty, however we had no choice. We entered the hotel cum pub telling the taxi to wait just in case, it was more sleazy inside, with a fattish greasy landlord, who had a fat sleazy smile through dirty teeth, yes they had a room we dismissed the taxi first asking how much the journey was, he charged 300pts which I thought was scandalous, took our bags in. The fat man's wife then appeared; she was quite a tidy, clean woman, and surprise of all, she spoke good English and had worked in London as a maid at Swiss Cottage, I thought, well, perhaps all is not lost.

Up we went to our room, it was very bare, with nowhere to hang our clothes, the washbasin had a jug of cold water to be poured into it and a bucket underneath to empty the water into, there were taps but no pipes, the toilette was in the same room, so one's partner could watch the other sitting perhaps having a very smelly crap, this toilette had to have no paper put in it, but when one had finished cleaning one's self, there was a bucket beside the toilette to put the soiled paper in, and a bucket of water standing beside to flush the thing with, I thought what a mess, flies and big ones were everywhere.

We did not unpack the two suitcases one because there was no cupboard or shelf or hangers, two I thought to move on or away from the island, but first let us explore this paradise, as Lewis de Fries had described it, I think he must have had rose tinted specs when he wrote about this place because he had been here in this very place—I heard later from the Spanish, that the authorities had given him a good backhander for the article—off we went outside, but before doing so, we had to pass through the bar, which was thick with flies, and now guarded by two very large Alsatian dogs, who got up and had a good sniff at us.

First, we walked up the beach of blackish sand, debris had collected for months on the tide mark, and amongst all this were two dead cats. When our beach walk was over, I had another look at it (the beach) and decided there was no swimming here for me, Monique had taken the place in disgust.

We had a walk along the two or three small streets when at one open door, we looked in and saw a number of thick black round rings, the next second, realising what they were we both let out a cry almost of horror, they were big round cheeses absolutely, thickly covered by huge black flies, it was unbelievable. We had to have another look before we could even believe our own eyes, we thought this was too much, things were getting worse instead of better. We returned to our room disheartened then decided to leave as early as possible the next day, we thought of the taxi, I did not feel like paying another 300 pts. Monique then said perhaps there is a bus, I thought what a good idea so off we went out again, we were not going to ask our greasy landlord. Once more, the big Alsatians came very suspiciously to look us over, following us to the door right on our heels. Outside Monique asked about a bus back to Port Fuerteventura from one of the local woman, she told us the bus left at 7 am from a place called Toragel, a place in the village which looked like a waiting room, a stable and hen house all rolled into one.

We returned to the pub hotel for dinner, which we had in the bar, we were the only ones eating and no one was drinking at the bar, the flies were thick all over, they did their best to land on any food or on one's plate on the table, but when the food was served we both thought the flies are welcome to it. The first course was a thick, greasy soup, now I love soup, but this was awful, Monique had one taste and left hers, I plodded on for a while, then gave up, next course was thick, very fatty and also very greasy sort of stew, the sight of it put us both off, we tasted it and left it I had to tell our greasy landlord what I thought of his food and his hotel, a glorified one at that, the whole of the place was like a back street, sleazy (I am using that word quite a lot here, but it is necessary and true) joint in Macau or Hong Kong, as one sees on the big screen, I told him the place was filthy and his food also and that we were leaving in the morning, and that I would report him to the Government Tourist Bureau in Spain, at this he became very quiet. (I never did report him though I felt like doing so). I asked how much for our stay overnight and was told 250 pts, one day and one night, this indeed was expensive for what we had got, however, I paid without more ado, we were sick of this filthy place, there were no other pubs or hotels in the village, we had to wait until morning.

We were both awake at 5 am, we chatted wondering how we were going to get past the two big Alsatian dogs left to guard the bar downstairs. At 6 am we left the bedroom, quietly went downstairs, and into the bar, the two dogs growled and came forward. Well, I am used to dogs, but I was rather nervous about these two, whose looks were fierce enough to deter passing them, but we were determined to get away from this village. I don't think we could have spent another day there, and if no bus or taxi, we would have walked all the way back to Fuerteventura, however, I thought it's now or never and strode boldly to the door leading to the street, the two dogs circled me while Monique watched from the staircase door, however I crossed the room the dogs wondering now what shall we do, stop him or let him go, one could almost read their thoughts, I reached the door and turned the key but it would not open, my heart sank then I noticed a slide bolt, gave it a tug and hey presto the road was in full view, I then told Monique to cross quietly but firmly, which she did, and there we both were, free, or at least it felt like that, I thought it must be like a prisoner escaping from Alcatraz.

We waited in the dirty hall, come hen house, dog house or whatever, about 8 or 9 people were also waiting for the same bus, dressed as if they were still in the Middle Ages, but kindly faces on them, the women older than their years, I suppose worn by trying to till this barren land.

The bus came on the hour of 7am and off we set, the bus would stop here and there at some post on the road, to drop a parcel or letter and pick one up. I saw only one person handing him a parcel to take on. Otherwise, the rest were left for himself to take or deliver—to whom they belonged, picking them up sometime during the day. I thought well, at least they seem honest. The bus duly arrived outside the hotel (one and only) in Port Fuerteventura. Monique again asked for a room, explaining our predicament, but this time, there were plenty of rooms, the notables had returned to the mainland and elsewhere.

We carted the baggage inside, and we were pleasantly surprised. The decor in the main was rather rustic and well arranged, our bedroom the same, nice and airy, our landlord Andreas, a nice homely fellow, his wife did the cooking on some large cookers that looked rather like big Aga's and clean. Monique told Andreas we may stay for a couple of weeks. There were no other tourists staying or anywhere else, he said, they were rare things, we were the only foreigners he had ever had staying, this time we unpacked our suitcases as there were plenty of space, wardrobe and cupboards, the sun shone nice and hot, we retired to the little bar, for a few well-deserved beers, a few of the locals, eyeing us up, one of them very suave, very clean, spotless shirt, hair slicked back, rather like Fernando Lamas and his type, he kept eyeing Monique.

Then it was lunchtime, a nice spacious dining room, the tables clean had red and white checked table clothes to match the red of the curtains, but one thing I had noticed before was there was a multitude of flies all over the place, and about an hour before lunch our landlord Andreas, had gone over the dining room windows and walls with an old-fashioned flit spray gun, this he did every day and sometimes in the evening. It did the trick, killing most of the flies, then we could eat in peace. After lunch, we thought to explore for a nice beach that we could swim, Andreas had told us of a beach called Playa Blanca, but it was about three miles up the coast, we decided to hunt around the coast nearer than this, off we set through the small town, it had quite a bit of character. We quite liked the look of the place, noticing the houses, all more or less square concrete blocks with flat roofs, no upstairs, flat walls with a couple of windows. I thought the people here must be very poor, the older men were dressed like in the Middle Ages, the older women all in black like widow's weeds, we greeted them as we met them with buenas dias, they replied the same, they were a kind-faced lot I thought, the young girls of what we saw just then were very pretty.

We walked and walked, the shore was only rocks washed by the sea at the edge, it was hot enough and we were ready for a swim, so we decided to cross the rocks, and swim from them, which we did, the water was good and warm. After we had swam for half an hour, we soon found some flattish rocks to stretch out and sunbathe. We stayed for four hours, then started to walk back to town, I think we had gone about a mile for our swim. Once on the road off we set Monique carrying our towels in a bag. Within a couple of minutes, an old truck going our way slowed down and stopped beside us, the driver asked if we wanted a lift to town, we accepted with pleasure, in fact, within a few days, we were so well known in the town that wherever we walked, we were offered lifts.

On arrival at the hotel, we first thanked our truck driver, had a shower, then adjourned to the little bar for a few sundowners (whisky's), Andreas poured what I took to be quadruple whisky's for the equivalent of 2/6, Monique drank Tio Pepe sherry, she as yet did not care for whisky or gin, behind the bar on a shelf I noticed a bundle of Churchill sized black cigars, they would be 7 inches long and very thick just the size I liked, I asked Andreas for one and also where they were made, he told me Las Palmas, I asked how much, for at the bar I paid cash for everything, to have no surprises later, he told me the price which in English money was equivalent to 3p, I thought my word this is a place I am going to like, the price of our room and full board was for two of us 1 pound and 7/- per day, it was indeed a lost paradise, except there was no greenery in the land, never mind, for the time being sunshine, prices what they were, Monique and I on honeymoon eternal, life was indeed quite good. In the little bar, the suave Fernando Lamas type was there, once again eyeing Monique up and down and forever eating small tapas, we greeted all the bar as one with buenos tardes, seven or eight men replied as one—after a couple of stiff whisky's, we thought to see around the small town of Fuerteventura and see if there were any more bars, we found one not far from the port, perhaps 150 yards, the name across the window read Rosie's bar, on the window shelf on the inside six cats were sound asleep, in we went, a narrow room with 4 or 5 tables, fishnets on the walls, the bar and beyond the bar was a petite, good looking blonde (the bottle I think), this was Rosie, she greeted us warmly, I ordered whisky, Monique Tio Pepe. My whisky was up to Andreas' measure, which I was pleased with, the price was more or less the same, no measures were used, just poured from the bottle. I noticed beyond and at the room end and above the bar, but at least 8 feet from the floor, was a platform covering the width of the narrow room, the front opening covered by a net curtain, and approached by a ladder set in the bar floor, was Rosie's bed and/or bedroom, she had a makeshift kitchen on the ground floor, about 5 foot sq but curtained off.

The following day, we followed the same pattern but took more notice of the local people. The girls in late teenage and early twenties were extremely pretty, some beautiful, and coming out of what I would term many of the "houses" hovels, groomed and manicured to perfection, they walked well, swinging their hips and dressed very well in what they had, per- haps many dresses would be run up themselves, to suit their own tastes, for I suppose money would be a scarce item for many.

There were many donkeys pulling little carts with one or two 40-gallon barrels of water. This was delivered around the town householders, as there was only one source of this precious liquid, and the source belonged to the family of so far, our silent friend Fernando Lamas, this made the family quite well off by the islander's standards, much water was also used for the production of tomatoes.

When these donkey carts would meet each other, always at a fast trot, they would start a tremendous braying, what a noise it was, whether the donkeys were greeting each other or threatening each other, only they knew.

The day 19th February on Friday was hot, off we went swimming again from the rocks, not a soul in sight, we thought we would swim in the nude, which we did, then lay on the flat rocks we had picked out the day before, at 3 pm an oldish man passed along the beach but on the land side, about 50 yards away, with 50 or 60 goats of all ages, he could not see us, and we could only see him if we raised our heads but the goats were easy to hear because a few had bells round their necks, he passed the same time every day, when we returned to the hotel for a shower, and had just dressed for the evening, there was a knock on the bedroom door, I an- swered and standing there was a young army officer, he spoke to me in Spanish, but I did not understand and asked Monique to translate as she had heard him speak, she told me the Colonel of the army garrison was getting married this evening, he had heard there were English tourists at the hotel and would like us to go to the officers mess and be his guest for his marriage feast, we both thanked the young officer and said we would be delighted to attend, we had to be there in an hour's time, for aperitifs first. We thought it a most kind gesture of the Colonel, and so we dressed once again for such an occasion. The army barracks were only 200 yards distance from the hotel, we told Andreas we would not be dining in that evening, explaining where we would be eating. His eyes opened wide in disbelief, but it was he who had directed the officer to our room, so he had to believe he was amazed.

Monique and I arrived at the barracks and introduced ourselves—we were expected. Immaculately dressed young officers showed us great cour- tesy, as they ushered us into the officers mess bar, and introduced to the Colonel, Pedro Baena Martinez, a solid tall and kindly man, he bade us both welcome, at the same time adding that the officers mess and bar and restaurant facilities were at our disposal for as long as we remained on Fuerteventura, Monique and I thanked him for his kindness and gen- erosity, he then said, now—it is time to enjoy yourselves, and with that he gestured to a group of officers, young and middle aged, they imme- diately surrounded Monique and I, asking what we would like to drink, these were soon pressed into our hands, one middle aged officer spoke a little English so I had him to myself, in no time Monique had half a dozen young chaps round her, like bees to the honey, they were en- thralled by her, and amazed at her command of their language, I saw on a shelf behind the bar, those big black 7 inch cigars and asked if I may have one, they could not give me one fast enough—strange I thought from what I could see, most smokers there were smoking cigarettes. We had an hour of aperitifs, then came the wedding banquette, my word it was a most super feast, everything one could wish to eat was there, beautifully prepared and served by immaculate waiters, together with the most excellent wines and in abundance too, this feast lasted three hours, then came dancing to a very good 6 piece band, we were treated with great kindness all round, the army waiters or stewards continuously on the go, seeing everyone had full glasses the whole night long, at about 3am the party was thinning out bit by bit, Monique and I thought it prudent that we also should take our leave, we went over to the Colonel to thank him, and bid him and his bride goodnight and wish them all hap- piness in their marriage, Monique of course being my spokesman, the Colonel replied that he was most happy that we could be there, and then told us that we could use all the facilities at the officers mess, also at the officers club on the beach not far from town as long as we were on the island, we thanked him again for his kindness and took our leave, this had indeed been a very good day and night, we retired to bed and slept well.

The next day, we were up late, did not bother with breakfast, and went swimming from our rocks, the day was just a little cooler but quite pleasant, the old goatherd passed with his goats at his usual hour of 4 pm, he could not see us, as we always kept low down on our rocks, he was the only person we saw near the beach that day.

Andreas came over and asked if he could introduce "Fernando," our suave friend—no doubt Andreas had been asked to do this—I said, very well, the suave chappie came over and was introduced as Isidor. I invited him to sit and have a drink, he looked at my glass, then asked for a whisky, before I had noticed at other times he drank very baby rickard—now he was on a man's drink, Monique had to do all the talking and translating, it turned out that it was he who had the pure water Well on the island, this was his source of revenue selling the water to householders and for the tomato growers, in fact he was the big fish in the proverbial little pool, his family owned quite a lot of land, which of course consisted of scrub and rocks, Isidor never, from what I could gather, had never done a day's honest work in his life, his hands were as a woman's, Isidor was enjoying himself talking to Monique, he was not too interested when I butted in to ask anything, he I will say, got the next round of drinks in the second my glass was empty but leaving himself out, I insisted he also fill his glass, otherwise I could not drink mine, with hesitation he did so, I saw, or thought I saw, that he wanted me to be under the table, so that he could monopolise Monique—little did he know who he was drinking with, I thought to myself two can play this little game, and I know the winner in advance. I finished my glass without hurrying. Isidor had his glass half full, I immediately ordered a round in, and so it went on, and I will say each time my glass was empty, he did the honours, then he ran out of money and had to put the drinks on the slate—at 10 pm Isidor's eyes were getting glazed, I decided it was time for dinner, I excused ourselves and left for the dining room, the meal that night was hot and very good.

Monique and I got up at 9 am, showered, had breakfast, having a look at the bar at 10 am, no Isidor in sight, I smiled to myself, thinking, serve him right. Off we went for a morning swim, having the intention of going to the officer's mess for midday drinks and lunch. Returning to the hotel, we again showered, Monique not having a swim. We dressed rather better, then passing the hotel bar, noticed still no Isidor, we walked the short distance to the military camp and officer's mess, as soon as we entered, the few officers present came forward and made us welcome, we had met them all at the

Colonel's wedding, They really enjoyed Monique's company, they clustered round her like bees to honey, myself taking a backseat, so to speak, until an English speaking officer, to whom I had had a long chat with before, took pity on me, he was a shooting man, very keen on partridge, and wild boar in the mainland of Spain, but he told me the partridge shooting was also very good on Fuerteven- tura, I told him I had seen quite a few birds on our travel through the island, which was true. I also heard that many Spanish from the mainland go to the island for the partridge season.

We then had lunch, and a very good one at that, with great politeness, the officers showed us to the best table, wishing us bon appetite, and left us to enjoy our meal alone and in peace, the wine was excellent, we took our time over the meal, eating for a couple of hours, then a very good brandy, not the hot stuff I had become accustomed to drinking, and a very large black cigar, it certainly was a pleasant island, barren as it was—when it came payment time, I could scarcely believe it, the cost for both was only a few shillings.

We walked back into town, and as we walked, two donkey carts, each carrying water barrels, each cart with two donkeys started to bray at each other, now 100 yards apart, as they drew nearer at the trot. The braying got louder and louder, 4 donkeys, which seemed by the noise, hell-bent on a fight, it was incredible, in fact rather frightening, as they drew nearer and nearer, I wondered how the drivers were going to manage them when they actually met when 20 yards separated them, the drivers started to use their whips, and with great abandon, this seemed to take the donkey's minds off, either having a fight or having a kiss, then they passed each other and the violent noise, suddenly stopped—I suppose until next time round.

On our walks to the beach, we passed each morning, an epicerie where odd times, we would buy something for a sandwich, we were served each time by the owner's son, a short dark, stocky chap of perhaps 20-22 years old, he spoke some

English, as the days passed, he seemed friendly enough, and one day, asked us in for coffee, the shop was and had been, a room of the house, we walked through the dividing curtain into a pleasant living room nicely furnished with two leather armchairs, and a leather sofa to match, a very big television, etc., coffee was served with biscuits, followed—for me one of the big black cigars.

He was a friendly chap, in fact too friendly, all at once he had eyes only for Monique, by his manner, we both realised he had become ob- sessed by her, a very short while later I got up, saying we must now go, thanking him for the coffee and cigar, if looks could have killed, then it was now by this little squirt. The rest of our holiday there, we made a detour of his house and shop, but he was not too beaten, or at least—so he thought.

Saturday 27th February, I felt a bit queasy from possibly too many big whiskys, combined with the hot sun with the high U.V. rays in that region, anyway, off we went to our rocks, I had a long swim, Monique was still bothered with her periods—she always had very heavy periods, lasting a full week each time—sometimes longer, the swim made me a bit fresher for a while, then I started to shiver, I thought blast, it must be a bit of sunstroke, after the swim, we strolled back to Rosie's where I had three enormous gins, with a lot of squeezed lemon in each, I thought I may as well enjoy my sunstroke, then back to the hotel for lunch, it was a nice lunch, in fact, Andrea's wife was getting very good at cooking, and as always, ½ an hour or an hour before lunch was served, Andreas went round the entire dining room with his flit gun.

We had been invited to a masked dance in the Casino that night. Isidor, Monique, and I seated ourselves at a small table and, for a while, watched the dancers. There was one dancer who seemed intent on almost knocking our table over. The dancer was covered completely, from head to foot, in a full, flowing costume, and well masked, but by the hands, it was those of a man. However, Isidor asked Monique to dance— first asking my permission, she was, and still is, a great, energetic, and elegant dancer, myself very average. I then thought to cross the room to a very beautiful girl of perhaps 19-20 years, I bowed and asked—in English, if I may have this dance, to my surprise, she refused. I returned to my table and had the next dance with Monique, telling her of my rebuff, she laughed—I thought perhaps better luck next time!

The next dance some other Spaniard—masked, asked if he may dance with Monique, I gave permission, and took off again across the room to the same girl—again to my surprise, she refused, I began to think I must either have a bad smell, or they did not like me, I retired once more to our table, almost with my tail between my legs, thinking—I can't be that ugly, when Monique returned, then Isidor, I told them my evening was going very badly, and that I was not going to ask another girl to dance, Monique then explained my predicament to Isidor, who then told me that no girls would dance with a stranger unless he has first been intro- duced to the girl, or her chaperone, by a member of her family—or a friend of the family, I showed him the first beauty I had asked, he looked over and told me not to worry, it was his cousin, and the second girl was a personal friend of the family, he then crossed the room, spoke to his cousin, and a striking woman of about 40 next to her, turned out it was her mother, then he spoke to two or three more young women at that side of the room.

The next dance, I held my breath as I crossed once more, bowed, and demanded her hand to dance, this time, with a lovely, graceful smile, she rose to her feet—then, I had my arm around her, and we were dancing. I spoke my little bit of Spanish, telling her I liked her island, the people were kind, and the girls were beautiful, she had, like the majority on the island, never visited the Spanish mainland, Isidor, I remember, told me he had never been to Spain, but had visited Argentina.

My dance with this beauty went well, when it was over, I escorted her back to her seat, bowed, and thanked her. I could see approving looks from her mother; no one except one or two escorted their dance partners back to their seats, and no young man bowed.

In the meantime, the heavily masked person who had been hanging around our table had, in my absence, taken Monique to dance, she had no idea whom it was, the next—and the next, he asked my permission, the third time, I said no. He was becoming a pest, I had had two more dances with other girls whom Isidor had introduced to dance with me. I had another dance with his cousin and left it at that, not wishing to impose, Monique and I danced a few, but she was in great demand, I think it was perhaps midnight, masks had to come off, then we both noticed the heavily masked chappie, he took the mask off with a flourish, in front of Monique, he was the thickset epicerie owner—who had an obsession for Monique, this time, he ignored me, asking Monique to dance, I told him no in firm tones, his eyes grey—hard with anger, but he backed away, I thought to myself I don't trust you my boy, we had a few more dances, then told Isidor we were going to the hotel. It was 1.30am. We had had a very nice evening and had consumed a few whisky's—which seemed to get bigger the more Monique and I were known, we said our goodnights to the new friends we had got to know—ignoring the epicerire chappie and went to bed, what I did not realise at that moment, the dance—most of the people there masked, it was costume time before Ash Wednesday.

Two days later, Monique was invited to the sergeant's mess, the men there making us most welcome. We mingled with the people there, though they were not a big crowd, again, in no time, Monique was surrounded by new admirers, she could hold her own in any situation. All personnel we had contact with, in the military—and otherwise (excepting the epicerie chap) were most polite and had perfect manners at all times, we were shown great kindness all around.

Drinks were flowing nicely; a few of the girls I had danced with the week before were there, including the cousin of Isidor. Her name escapes me for the moment, so I had no trouble with asking and being refused to dance as before. Then, at approximately 11:00 pm, the Commander and his Captain came in. All soldiers nearby stood quickly to attention as both Officers moved along to their reserved table. They glanced around and saw Monique and I, they acknowledged our presence, and within a minute, a sergeant came over, bowed to us, and said the commander would like us to go to his table for drinks, we were indeed, given preferential treatment at all times, as we approached the Commanders table, both he and his Captain rose, they bowed low over Monique's hand, touching it lightly with their lips, and then shaking my hand. I thought my word they were a polite bunch, we were asked what we would drink, me as usual, whisky, and Monique—her Tio Pepe.

The evening went well, the dance went well. 3:00 am came and passed, 4:00 am came and passed—the Officers left at 4:00 am well oiled, Monique and I were the last invites to leave, only five or six soldiers remained, we, Monique and I, danced alone, no other girls remained. At 4:30 am, we realised the others present were tired and that as long as we danced, the band would remain and play, so we thanked the remaining sergeants heartily, treated all there, including the band of six, Monique and myself, to a last beer each. They were delighted as we took our leave and shook hands all around. We were pressed to visit their mess at any time during our stay, so we ended a perfect night.

The next day, we slept till midday, surfaced, showered to make us fresher, had a beer each in the little bar of the hotel with Isidor—Monique filling him in on the events of the night before, he seemed a bit jealous. Then we had lunch. I invited Isidor to join us, I felt sorry for him, he seemed a stranger in his own land, whereas we were invited everywhere. He told us about a dance at the Casino that night of 7th March—open to all, I thought, another dance and we had just more or less gone to bed.

Monique and I drifted off to the Casino dance at 10 pm, we

took a table, I had a couple of dances with Monique, at the second dance with her, I had a nasty surprise, the thick set little epicerie man also dancing, keep- ing very near to us at every turn his eyes were definitely holding anger towards me, I dismissed him from my mind, but there he was, brushing against me, too much for my liking, all at once as he was doing a sort of spin in the dance, his jacket flapped a bit open, and there strapped to his waist was a long sheath knife, I told Monique this, she kept a look on him, and verified what I had seen, I thought, this blighter's face is so lit up with anger, and he seems determined to be right up against us on the dance floor, any minute, that knife will be in my ribs, after the 2 dance with Monique, we sat at our table, Monique told Isidor about our friend with the knife, and he agreed, that this chap could be dangerous, he mentioned that when in the army, the epecerie chap had done some bad deed, I decided it was better I did not take the floor any more, but watched proceedings, and kept my eyes on the knifeman, Isidor had plenty of dances with Monique, and two or three others asked, including the English speaking officer, the knifeman knew better. On Tuesday, 9th March, Monique and I set off for Playa Blanca with a sandwich each prepared by Mrs. Andreas by now, Monique and I swam and sunbathed in the nude, when by mid-afternoon, we noticed two or three warships far out to sea but seemed to be heading straight for us, within minutes there were 8 of them, all dropped anchor, they were I suppose as far as I could make out, only a mile out to sea, and they were French, Monique and I still in the nude waved to them from the beach, quite unashamedly, thinking well they will never meet us face to face, so why worry, we returned to the hotel at 6ish pm, to find a message from the Colonel, inviting us to a cocktail and dinner that evening at 7:30 pm.

We showered and dressed for the occasion, Monique had had the sense to pack some very pretty dresses, some bought from Mrs Morris of Marshal & Snelgrove—she always looked the part and was always cool, never flustered, except possibly once. On arrival at the officer's mess, the cock- tail party was no ordinary affair, we had a surprise, for we were introduced to none other than the Captains and officers of the 8 French warships that we had been waving at in the nude earlier that day, as we were introduced one of the officers said to Monique, I think we have met earlier in the day Madame, that was one of the few times that I have seen Monique blush, but as usual she had the situation under her control, she was now speaking her own tongue of which she had full command. (Rather like Winston Churchill, with his command of the English language). The Spanish had laid on a splendid cocktail party. We were most impressed, and again Monique was like the old song "You be my honey-suckle and I'll be the bee", she had, after only a few minutes, a hive of bees around her of both Spanish and French. Amazingly, she could listen to both and switch to either lingo without blinking an eye, drinking her Tio Pepe, she should have been an ambassador's wife the way she could carry conversations.

When asked about my profession, I said I was a farmer, many did not believe me, they always thought I was leg pulling, if I told them I was a racehorse owner and amateur rider, they believed me, the cocktail party finished, we shook hands and said our farewell to many people that night, thanked the Colonel and other Spanish officers for their kindness and hospitality, tired we went to the hotel to sleep.

During our stay on Fuerteventura, and since Isidor had come on the scene, I had done my best to drown him in whisky, and to keep his attentions to himself, I had succeeded in drowning him for a few days, but he eventually surfaced, and as I had said before Isidor was rather a gentlemanly, he had made no improper moves, or said anything improper, so Isidor continued to appear.

The day after the cocktail party, I found it was necessary to cash some travellers' cheques, because we were leaving the island in a day or two and returning to Seville. I asked where the bank was, as I had never seen one with signs up indicating a bank, I was directed to an ironmongers shop, inside was full of pots and pans, plates, in fact, everything and anything that an ironmonger would sell, I thought my leg had been pulled, but no, in a far corner was the shop counter, which was also the bank counter, I knew the man in charge, we had met quite a few times at functions and in the hotel it turned out was the shopkeeper and banker rolled into one, I told him what I wanted, thinking, with tourists nil here, my transaction would take a day or so, but to my surprise, this banker was far quicker by miles than on the mainland, so in the midst of pots and pans hanging from the ceiling, cookers and plates, I received my money, quickly and at the correct rate. They were not robbers here, in fact, the people of the island were amongst the most honest I have ever met, a simple way of life they had, but most importantly, they were content, I have and Monique also, many happy memories of these kind and happy people.

This evening, we decided to go to the beach club of the military officers, this club was very well appointed, Monique and I were always made most welcome, one night, when Monique and I were having drinks at this club, Isidor thought he would also enter this exclusive place, I think he could not understand—if these two foreigners can go in why not me, he presented himself at the guarded entrance and was immediately turned away, he was not happy when he told us next day. I told him (Isidor) Monique and I were personal invites of the Colonel; therefore, I could not help him.

The 10th March loomed up, it was our last full day in Fuerteventura, we, after breakfast, swam until noon, then showered and dressed and set off for the officers' mess, where we had a few aperitifs with our friends there, a light lunch, digestives, then thanked the Colonel and other officers for their kindness to us both, there was sadness on both sides, we had enjoyed their company and tremendous hospitality, and they had it seemed enjoyed our company, we left to say our goodbyes to the boys in the sergeant's mess, more drinks, more farewells, they and ourselves were sad at parting and we left, walking slowly to the hotel. Isidor was in the little bar, Andreas serving, I asked him to get me a hundred of the big black cigars to take back with me, I always wish I had asked for at least 500, for they were too good to be true, I had smoked them non-stop during our stay, and never had a bad one, and at 3p each this was really good value, however, Andreas got me the 100 I had asked for, they were not in boxes but tied by a ribbon in bundles of 25.

On Thursday 11th March we bade Andreas and his wife farewell and thanked them for looking after us so well and promising to come again one day, they were kind people, our bags packed, cigars etc safely stored, we took off in the taxi, that we had used on our first day on the island, to the airport.

We mounted the steps into the aeroplane. There were few passengers, as the plane roared down the runway then seemed to run out of road, I thought, good grief, we've had it, but a second look and we were in mid air, we had gone over the edge of a cliff at the runway end it seemed, never mind the short runway, there was plenty of air space and depth at the end of it.

We waved the island aurevoir. It was a sad moment for us to leave these kind-hearted people, once on board, I expected to head for Spain, but no, the plane landed at Las Palmas, a short wait there, picking up a few soldier passengers I thought would be going home on leave to Spain, then we were airborne again, Seville next stop, but this was not to be, after a while we were told over the intercom we were landing at El Auin, in the Sahara. As the plane did a wide circle over the sea of sand and dunes, the scene below was typical Beau Guest, the black tents, and camels and donkeys of the nomads, plain to be seen from just a few hundred feet up. One could almost have the feeling of going back in time, the plane taxied to a halt, everyone got out, Monique and I mooched about, there was little to see, it was a Spartan airport, it was very hot also, we bought a few postcards, posted them, thinking it rather fun for our friends to have a card from the Sahara, I sent one to mother as well, we would be about an hour at El Auin then all piled into the plane again, new soldier passengers got on board, the previous chaps, staying behind for their duties, in Spanish Morocco. The plane took off and landed not long after at Sidi Ijni, again in the Sahara, and once again stepping back in time, Sidi Ijni, we were told, was the headquarters of the Spanish Sahara Army, again it was a Spartan place and hot. After a short wait and taking a few more soldiers on board, going on leave to their homes on the mainland, Monique and I had a couple of beers, then once more on board, we took off, this time for Seville. The flight was a nice, quiet one, landing in Seville at 5:30 pm. We went by bus to the city, Monique explained to the driver where, if possible, to drop us off, without more ado, after dropping a few other passengers, the driver told Monique this point where we now were was only 100 yards from the garage Torre del Oro, he pointed the way to go and with two suitcases, we quickly found our garage, the bus driver had done his job well.

22

The garage owner recognised us straight away, I thanked him through Monique for looking after our little car and then asked how much I owed him, the car had been undercover all of the time we had been away, he told Monique the price, and in Sterling, it worked out at 5 pounds 10/- 28 days garaged and 35 days on holiday so far. We put the suitcases in the car, switched her on, and at the second attempt she started, more thanks and we were on our way to find a hotel in town to stay the night, after paying for the car, I had only 12/- left in Spanish money, I would have to cash some travellers cheques in the morning. We soon found a nice middle-sized hotel in the middle of Seville, taking our suitcases inside, I left the MG outside by the kerb, we showered, then on foot, had a good look around some of the shops and bars, what I liked were the small orange trees planted at spaced intervals on the pavements in full almost ripe fruit, I was tempted to pick one or two, but this was in Franco's time, one must be careful. This was when, if a boy gave his girlfriend a kiss or peck on the cheek on the pavement, he would be jailed for 6 months, especially if he was English—so I refrained from my urge to pick the, we could say "forbidden fruit".

We headed for Alicante 400 miles away, staying the night there in a small hotel, and I thought at the time expensive at 180pts, it was the Hotel de Secunda, where we had a nice hot bath, we went out for our dinner to a good looking bar restaurant, where we sat up to the bar counter itself, I made a note of what we ate adding a note—very good, with lobster, then eggs with black pudding, sausage and beer, to me now it seems rather a droll mixture, but then we both liked it very much.

Sunday 14th March, we left Alicante, had breakfast in town at a big brassiere place, then refreshed, drove on, we meant to try and stay at Figueras for the night, so did not dally on the way, the car was running well and we arrived at Figueras, booking into the Hotel Duran for the one night, after 430 miles that day, strange to say we were not tired and before dinner in the hotel, we had a few beers, in the little town, listening to the chatter of thousands of little birds in the trees running up the middle of the main street, the hotel food was good, we had eaten here on our first holiday to Tossa del Mar, starched linen and correctly attired waiters, the room cost 120pts.

We were going to visit Monique's aunt Madame Pineda. The aunt was pleased to see us both. She had a studio, rather a nice one, off boulevard Carno, one of the main arteries running into Cannes.

Now on my return, I was given the news: the aunt wanted to see her daughter Rene, for me, the bad one, and her husband Gabby. I said a silent curse, I had just passed Marseille the day before. It was about 2 hours drive back, Gabby took us all out to lunch, a most excellent one, too. I liked Gabby, in fact, everyone who had contact with him liked him, a pity he had married a complete bitch, he was a connoisseur of fine food and wines his wife Rene, the bitch could cook when she so wished, and this night she did just that, Gabby had his best wines out, the aperitifs was crystal champagne from Louis Roederer, the wine was a fine Pomerol then later came, of course that excellent French coffee, and cigars, we returned to Cannes that night arriving at midnight, it had been an excellent day out.

Monday 22nd March, Monique and I loaded the little car up, we were leaving for home, there were tears all round as we said goodbye, Paulette gave Monique a linen set, tears streaming down her cheeks, she was very fond of Monique, she had told Monique how Josephine and her husband had stolen some of the little inheritance Monique had been left by her grandfather—Rene the bitch profiting from this by her father giving her 20 gold Luis D'or, big coins that Rene had made into a massive bangle, these were part of the inheritance together with diamond rings etc., monies that Monique saw only a pittance of. Paulette told Monique all, after this, I never had a lot of time for Josephine and less for Rene.

At Calais, we were up at 10 am, I paid the hotel and had F50 left in French money, I drove onto the ferryboat at 11:30 am, at the ferry terminal we had time to kill, so I thought it a good idea to pop into the duty-free shop, there I bought two bottles of Ricard, then we both went to the bar, sat down, I put the two bottles of Ricard on our table, went over to the bar, bought 2 glasses of beer, took them back to our table, we chatted away to each other about our holiday, when all of a sudden, a dirty unshaven man in a bomber jacket and dirty trousers came to our table, opened a wallet, with a picture in it, muttering something to us, I told him to go away thinking he was trying to sell me porno photos but as I discovered later, he was showing me his warrant card of the local police, then carried on talking to Monique. The dirty chap brought another man over to our table, but the second one was uninformed, this one told me to hand over our bottles of Ricard. I told these fellows that it was not bloody likely, I pushed them out of the way, went to the car, and locked the car doors then surprise, when I returned to our table, there was a discussion amongst the personnel in the bar room, it turned out, when we bought the bottles of Ricard, I should have put them straight away in the car, in the hallway to the ferryboat, not taken them, as they put it, out of customs area. I told the police—by this time, I knew it was them—that I had not tried to hide the bottles, they were on the tabletop for all to see, but this policeman in cahoots with the first dirty-looking bloke wanted blood, one of the others tried to tell them, that we had not tried to hide them, and he tried to calm things down, the two baddies then demanded my passport, I refused to give it to them, they then said if I again refused, I would be arrested and taken to the police station and put in a cell, this is when I thought, discretion is the better part of valour, and handed my passport over, they told me it would be given back when the cars were being loaded. When the time came and cars were being driven onto the ship, no one came to give me this precious document, I had to go to the police office there and ask for it. It was handed over with bad grace from their side, the whole thing was much ado about nothing.

Now our holiday was over, readers must have thought that I had spent a fortune. The whole holiday cost less than 200 pounds, after Monique and I were at Andrea's hotel for bed and three meals a day was 27/6 a day for both, drinks were cheap quadruple whisky at 2/- to 2/6, large cigars like brush handles 3p each, ship and airfares likewise, also petrol was not expensive and I had a car that was unbelievably economic. These were the days when travelling one did get value for money. Now one needs a suitcase full to pay for each hotel. Meals throughout France at superb places were gifts, eating like kings of old, each meal would be no more than 2 pounds each, wine often included, it was indeed a golden time to travel. We had lunch on board, which was not bad at all, disembarked at Dover at 2:30 pm. The sea had been nice and calm on the way over, thank goodness for I am not the best of sailors.

I drove to Sittingbourne in Kent to see our friend Mike Young and his wife Vida, Mike was one of the nicest and kindest chaps one could wish to meet, he was one of nature's gentlemen, he farmed at Sittingbourne, having large orchards of fruit quite a few acres of hops, together with acres of barley, oats etc, we had coffee and biscuits, then I asked Mike to cash a cheque for 10 pounds, as I was now low in cash, which he did.

Arriving at Skirwith Hall, Monique and I then a little later went to see mother, I was surprised and saddened by her appearance, she looked very tired and frail and was looking much older, she had been ill, I was told, the family doctor Frank Edington telling her she was just ageing—I did not think much of this cruel statement, the weather was cold and sleet was falling.

I now began to hear from Kurt, stories of a father meeting a woman in the village, a Mrs Page, who was known by quite a few as the village bike, her husband she said, was killed in the war. She had appeared in Skirwith in the first place about 15 or more years ago with her brother-in-law, also named Page, he had bought the travelling butchers business from WP Monkhouse of Langwathby, selling meat and sausage from his van around the villages, Mrs Page took rooms at the village pub in Skir- with, the Sun Inn she being as well as other things, the mistress of her brother in law, she was a sharp-tongued and not well-liked woman, she had each year, bought about 24 chicks from me, for egg laying.

A few months ago, I bought quite a few, sporting prints and prints of birds, from the sale of the contents of the two lions pub in Penrith, they were a nice lot, I think about 30 of them. I had sent them down to the Motcomb Galleries to sell. Now I had a letter saying they had not reached the reserve. I wrote back and told them to return them to me, a few weeks later, I wrote again to Motcomb Galleries, requesting the return of my prints, to have a letter by return, saying the prints had been lost, and sending me a cheque for 9 pounds 10/-. I suppose someone had taken a liking for them and stolen them. I had a word with Mr Amison, the family solicitor, he said he could do little about getting them back, so I called it a bad loss.

On Monday, April 5th, Dad, Mother, Josephine, and I set sail from Liverpool to Dublin.

A week later, little Joey, aged about 7, fell from a hay mow in the barn, 20 feet, to the ground and broke his collarbone, Monique took him to the hospital in Penrith, where he went by ambulance to Carlisle to have it set, Monique going with him.

The following week, on Saturday April 24th, Kurt and I were trying to catch a very wild yearling filly, we had this filly in a loose box, but it was too wild to handle inside, I had never had one like it, wildness itself—we put the portable cattle crush, a very heavy solid wooden affair in the doorway, I waited outside with the thick wooden bar to shove behind the beast, once it was in the crush to stop it from backing out into the loosebox—Kurt was in the loosebox, gently edging the yearling towards the crush, she put her head and neck into the crush, had a look round, again edging forward at Kurt's coaxing from behind, she came halfway, then she was totally in the crush, I quickly slid the thick wooden bar across behind her, but as I did so, the filly like a flash, must have sensed the trap she was in and shot backwards, her backend striking the bar I had hold of, I was in the bending position, while pushing the bar, now this solid piece came up like a flash, striking me a terrific blow on the side of the bridge of my nose, for a second or so I must have been senseless, then I thought with the pain, I must have lost an eye, I could not see properly for these few seconds, then between my hands, I saw with my left eye, a torrent of blood pouring onto the ground, I was bent double, I shouted to tell Kurt what had happened, then I trotted over to the kitchen door, went directly to the cold water tap before I put my face under the cold stream to stop the blood, I took my right hand away from my face, looked through the kitchen window, and was relieved to see that my eyes were alright, my vision was perfect. Monique came rushing in, panic-stricken at the amount of blood. I put my face under the cold water and held it there for some time, then the blood became less and less, finally, practically nothing. Monique brought a mirror for me, and there was a nasty gash on the side of my nose bridge and a nice piece of bone sticking out, I touched it, it was loose, so I gently pulled it out, the piece was the size of a silver 6p piece, then Kurt came in, and in his hand was another good sized piece of bone, he had pulled it out of the wooden bar, I had held behind the horse.

I first went to our local doctor, together with the pieces of bone, to Temple Sowerby, Dr Aniscow, he said he could do nothing, I asked him to put the pieces of bone back in my nose, he said he could not, and to go on to Carlisle Infirmary there and then, as Monique and I had intended that day to go to Hexham races, I thought after the hospital to carry on to that place, Monique saying that she would not go on to the races as

Adam was on holiday from school, I took him along with me, he liked horse racing and he somehow could pick winners. I drove to the infirmary, they took me right away. I explained my accident and gave the pieces of bone to the doctor who was attending me, he was a black one. I thought, oh dear, is he any good, but it looked as for the moment he was all I had, he got his needle and thread, and started to sew the wound as I stood in front of him, with not even a jab to kill the pain. I thought to myself, if he thinks I'm going to squeal for him, he can think again, he put 5 or 6 stitches in and told me to go home and rest, I said I was going racing and left it at that.

Adam and I duly arrived in plenty of time for the first race, where I met up with Sandy Taylor. Sandy was an extremely nice chap, except when he was in his cups, his every other word would be a swear word. When like this, he always shouted at me, where's that bloody wanker Jackson—meaning my neighbour Robert.

That day at Hexham, we enjoyed some good racing, each backing a few winners, Sandy nearly always betting like me, with Willie Wightman. In the evening, Sandy left his car in Hexham and went with Adam and I to the George Hotel at Chollerford, which was then, for us racegoers, a family club, we enjoyed a good meal, had plenty to drink, many racing people to chat to, then we decided to pay a visit to Dick Riddle, and have a few drinks with him and his wife. She, Margaret, I think her first name was, had given me a standing invitation to their house whenever I wished, Dick was a very nice and kind man, we always had drinkstogether at various race meetings, he was in shipping in Newcastle. Dick was also a big friend of Sandy's father and Jimmy Alexander. Jimmy lived a hundred yards from Dick.

In we went to Dicks, it looked as if a party was in full swing, Dick saw us and came forward to greet us, our glasses were charged, Adam had a lemonade, when all of a sudden, Dick's wife, descended on us like a ton of bricks demanding, who had asked me, she addressing me personally, in front of other guests, this outburst amazed me, as she had professed many times to be a good friend, I replied to her in a clear voice so that the others may hear, "You did Margaret, you have many times given me a standing invitation to your house, but obviously now you do not like my company, I will take my leave," before I had finished she had returned in a hurry to the far end of the room, I put my glass down, Sandy his, and we left poor Adam he wondered what was going on.

Ten days later, Robert Jackson met Dick Riddle at a point-to-point, he told Robert he was very sad at the way his wife had behaved towards him and to convey this to me. This is as it may be, Dick and I had drinks after this, but he never mentioned or apologised himself personally, I never entered his house again, neither did Sandy. His first wife had been an out-and-out sport, bubbling over with life. She and I had been great friends, but unfortunately, she died in a car accident. Margaret was his second wife—I think within two years of this party incident, she was admitted to an asylum. A week later, I went to Carlisle to the same doctor to have the stitches taken out of my nose, one of which he pulled the wrong way, pulling the knot through the flesh, I still think he wanted to hear me squeal; it stung me, but I said nothing.

From a 2-pound treble with Willie Whiteman on Whit Monday, I won 200 pound/8/2. This was well received as school bills for Cathie's two children. Josephine had left school, thank goodness, but Michael was at Murchison, a top school in Edinburgh, costing a bomb, together with my own two youngsters, was becoming hard to pay these big bills, for dad had not paid one penny piece towards his daughter's children in schooling or clothing all coming from my little hatchery.

At the end of July, Monique's two aunts came to stay for a month. Josephine, who had brought Monique up and Paulette Roman, and on 9th August Gabby, Rene and their two children came to stay, I now had ten people to feed, and seeing the French were in force, wine was obligatory, we were all getting on pretty well, but keeping an eye on Rene. Mid-

August, I took Coquette to Doncaster sales, she was bid to 230gns, I didn't sell her, two days later, Josephine and Paulette, the two aunts, had to go back to France. Gabby took them to Manchester airportin his Mercedes, it was Paulette who told Monique about her uncle swindling Monique out of some other inheritance, Josephine being in on it.

Rene became a nuisance in the house when Monique and I would be away for a few hours a day, Rene would ransack the house looking for something—I know not what, she would let her two boys play on top of the 3 piece suit, mother had given us, and break ceiling lights, pull curtains off the windows, they even killed Cathy's pet cat, snowy, and 21 of my newly hatched guinea fowl, I was going to experiment with, my plan being to let them off in the woods and rough ground on the farm, with a view for sport in later years, now the first batch had been slaughtered by these two bad boys. Monique and I were glad to see them go on September 1st. We heaved a sigh of relief.

I thought to try my hand at mushrooms to see if I could earn more money, so I thought one of the lofts where the incubators had been might prove to be a good place to start them. I had seen various adverts extolling the big profits of growing them, and I could get plenty of horse manure in the district.

The first load of manure came from Tommy Robson's stables at Greystoke. Kurt and I took the Bedford lorry and forked the stuff on, I stacked the manure on the lorry while Kurt forked it on by hand, this was hard work, as when we were at it, we thought we might as well put a big load on. When finished, the load was covered with a large canvas sheet and tied with ropes. Back at Skirwith Hall the load was forked off, and made into an oblong stack, exactly like a corn stack, except I had a large hosepipe, and when a round of about a foot in depth was forked off, the hosepipe was turned on, and that layer would be given a soaking, each layer treated the same, a few days later, the heap would be turned, that is dismantle the manure stack, and rebuild the same beside the original, taking the temperature with a long push in thermometer, special for the job, I had bought, when the heap or stack, and by the way, from the start, each stack was completely covered and tied or weighed down by a heavy plastic sheet to keep the heat in and break the straw into a kind of compost, when the heat passed 120% it was turned again, eventually reaching the stage when the manure was broken down at the correct stage for laying down where the mushroom beds were going to be, the stack was then loaded onto a farm trailer making 6 or 7 trips, unloaded onto a barrow, from the barrow onto the beds, I was doing it the hard way every turn done by hand, and the heat of the stuff, made it hot work, however I got the first experimental stack put down. I had to wait a while, taking the temperature of the beds quite often, to ensure that when the spawn was planted, @ 80%, it was just right, this Kurt and I did the day after planting the whole we covered with an inch of light soil. I should haveused peat moss, but I thought soil, for this experiment, this done we waited.

Nov the snow fell heavily and lay so, for hard frost at night, I thought it time for some shooting for pigeon and duck, it is a great sport, walking up with a good dog in the deep snow, the young Lassie was retrieving well, and enjoyed the snow, my first walk down the twisting briggle beck gave me 14 pigeons, 4 teal from the syke at Blackwood and 7 mallards down the beck itself. Lassie now was showing no signs of gun-shy. In fact, she was revelling in the sport, retrieving to hand perfectly. I was most pleased with her; she was turning into a perfect gundog and for walking up, she would work 20 yards in front, quartering beautifully. If she happened to go just those few yards farther on or too much to one side, one blow on my thin whistle by this, a whistle with a sharp thin tone, a tone that would not frighten birds in front—instantly Lassie would return, to foot and on order start quartering again, she was a natural, and with a marvellously soft mouth, I had taught her to carry eggs, for long distances without breaking them, and wounded birds would be brought back alive and with no tooth marks. The snow continued to fall quite heavily and on Monday, the 29th, it snowed with a gale-force wind, making it into a good sporting day. Lassie and I set off after breakfast, I donned my waterproof overalls and the barber jacket, cartridge belt, the latter with open metal spring clips, then the game bag over my shoulder. I set off on foot along the beck, the snow deadening any noise from my stepping on fallen twigs from the tree-lined beck. In any case, the wind would take any noise away—the first leg of the beck for 400 yards never did reveal many ducks, they preferred lower down. There was a band of rushes, 25 yards wide down the first stretch, Lassie on order started her gentle quartering of these, we had gone only 200 yards when, with a great flurry of wings and cry, a cock pheasant burst up, I let him travel a little further then shot him down, dead in the air, Lassie brought him back to hand, with what seemed to me a smile on her face and eyes looking into mine, there is something about Labradors they seem to like eye contact with their masters, especially when talked to in loving tones, and again when they have, or think they have, done something clever, and that master would be pleased with—this was Lassie on bringing the first bird of the day to hand. Into the game bag it went, a nice plump bird too, a few boggy stretches of ground in the first stretch, what was called the gang, made it rather difficult to cross, with the snow covering the too-soft places, at one point I was almost over the top of one Wellington boot. However, Lassie and I continued. The gang stretch ended, the field named the gang got its name from being a long and rather narrow field, hence, the name "gangway" was shortened to the gang.

Now we were on a 500 yards long stretch with good duck dubs andlittle sidings, plenty of twists in the beck and on either side, plenty of rushes and rough grass always good for holding pheasant and hares, this was called Scaws Gill Bottoms, proper name was Scaws Gill, I had gone only 20 or 30 yards, walking 5 yards from the beck side, when about 15 or more mallard duck got up, some flying out the other side, but I downed two of them, both of them only winged, one falling back into the beck the other on land but then it scrambled back into the beck, now wild duck, when wounded, take a lot of getting out of the water, especially a tree lined beck like my briggle, with a multitude of roots for duck to hide in beside deep crevasses under the banks—now it was up to Lassie to bring them out, I put her in where the first duck fell, she was in the water like a flash, ice cold as it was, in fact in shallow edges and over stones it was well iced, she sniffed under the banks, for a while, then she found it, going under the bank among some roots, but the duck was too quick, it had dived and was swimming under water, amazingly so even though winged, I saw it surface only 3 yards away near some more roots, I directed Lassie onto it, she tried again, she saw the duck dive again, and lunged at it, putting her entire head under water, but she was not quick enough, I could possibly have given the duck a shot as it appeared but Lassie was perhaps too near, and again, I thought it great experience for her to catch the duck in the water, after 20mins of under roots and banks, she had the duck, I pulled its neck and put it in the bag, she had enjoyed the water hunt, I could see that and had come out of it with flying colours, I immediately put her onto where the second duck fell, again we had the same problem with this one, except Lassie had it in her mouth within ten minutes, she was learning fast, on we walked, another small band of duck got up about 8 or 10, again, I shot 2 down, both dead, I stood still while Lassie duly retrieved to hand once again with that satisfied smile on her face, these went in the bag. I then backtracked, putting Lassie to work on the 50 yards width of rough, at once getting a lovely big hare, this was the heaviest piece of game Lassie had carried, at first lift, she had the hair too much by the back legs, not easy to carry, she realised this, put it down and got hold of it in the middle. She carried it to my feet, her eyes looking up into mine from 4 or 5 yards away with such a satisfied and smiling look that said it all, I praised her, and tickled her ears, telling her what a good girl she was, her face from all of this was one of bliss, into the bag went the hare, now I realised I had quite a heavy load, hares are heavy, anyway as I was returning this way again once I had shot through this stretch of rough, I left the game bag on the ground, and carried on, Lassie put 2 more cock pheasants up, which again got up too near. I let them cover some ground, then downed them quite easily, that was all in that part of the rough, carrying the 2 pheasants back, I crammed them into the game bag, swung it around my shoulders and set off again by the backside. There was nothing more for the next 100 yards, then I was approaching the bridge over thebeck about 1/3 of the way from home and just 30 yards past this bridge was a place we called the water quarry cut into the hillside of Scawgills where sandstone had been taken out for dry stone walling then left to nature, it had filled the 4 or 5 feet of quarry below ground level by a small natural spring, leaves and soil blowing in making it not too deep. 9 times out of 10, there was always from 4 to 50 duck on it, and in the winter, I used to put tailings from the threshing of oats and barley there, for the duck, I was almost on the quarry pool, Lassie to heel, I had to bend double to get near, without the duck seeing me, then I slipped the safety catch on, stood erect, took 3-4 steps when the pond, only 20 yards by 10 erupted mallard, in the flurry I missed with the first barrel but downed one with my second, I don't think Lassie was very pleased, another duck in the already full game bag, the weight now making it too heavy for comfort and good shooting.

 As I had a full bag, and I had only gone a third of the way down the farm, still plenty of sport to be had, I left the full game bag at the water quarry, the weather was still wild, with snowflakes flying, but the heavy bag and my waterproofs had made me sweat. I was pleased to have the weight off my back.

 On Lassie and I went, staying by the beck side and, for the time being ignored the rough ground on the side, within the next half hour, I had 7 more ducks, all mallard, Lassie having to hunt the water for one of them, it was a hard one for her, but eventually, she had it in her mouth, handing it over to me still alive. Now came the end of the farm touching onto Beck Mill Nurseries, run by Alf Britton, who was well known in Cumberland for his outdoor lectures and his market garden. Alf's father had worked for Bridget's grandfather at Skirwith Abbey as coachman and gardener but did something to displease old man Parker, and got the sack, he then went to Skirwith Hall to see my grandfather, crying his eyes out—so my father had told me—that he had nowhere to go with his wife and children, he was destitute, my grandfather (the one who thrashed me) let him have Beck Mill which had a deserted old house with a stone barn attached and two or three acres of scrubland at a rent of 5 pounds a year, payable at the end of the 1st year. Alf's father went on his knees in thanks—to cut a long story short, this Britton bit by bit cleared the land and started selling produce from a stall in Penrith market, Alf himself, making it better and bigger though seldom paying the rent, I think at Alf's death he was 7 to 10 years in arrears.

However, at the end of the farm, 400 yards to the right of Beck Mill, in the field known as Black Wood, ran a freshwater spring at the source crystal clear. On hot days, I have slaked my thirst there many times, as the spring ran, it grew wider to about 5 feet, growing excellent watercress—Alf used to pick it for his market stall—then further in rather boggy, the length of the spring as it ran, 60 yards. I thought it a good day to take a look at this syke, as we called it. It was nicely sheltered on both sides, lying in a hollow, so I could approach within 30 yards without being seen by any duck that may be there. The way of approach was in the open, across Beck Mill field, Lassie by my heels, we plodded over the 6-inch deep snow, getting nearer, I bent double to enable me to get nearer, when I could no longer walk doubled up without being seen I straightened up and for a second I was amazed there were easily 200 duck on the syke, another second and the area over the syke was black with duck, I chose at the same instance a quick left and right, and was more amazed when at my shots quite a number of birds fell no doubt hit by my first two shots. I reloaded instantly as I always did and sent Lassie in to retrieve, just then 5 or 6 more ducks rose out of some rushes, no doubt hiding there, as they often do, I shot two stones dead, now was picking up time, Lassie brought the shot duck to hand, one by one, I had to wring the necks of some, I now had 7 at my feet leaving them in a heap. I slowly walked the length of the syke with Lassie, I think she could not believe her luck at having such a field day with feathers, she found more and more, hiding in the rushes. At the end of it all I had downed 15 ducks, 11 by accident, they being so thick in the air on take off. I was absolutely delighted roast duck would be on the menu for quite a while. They were too heavy to carry, so I put them in a heap and would pick them up with the Land Rover later on.

Lassie and I then walked home, I dried Lassie as much as I could with a Hessian sack, then she finished drying herself by rolling in the hay and straw in the big Dutch barn. I then had a strong hot toddy, tea and sandwiches before I set off again with Lassie to collect our birds, I had the idea of flighting pigeons into Spring Field wood in the evening, this wood was a good flight path for wood pigeon. I thought with the high wind and snow flying, they would be flying low, I duly collected my bag from the water quarry, drove on to Black Wood syke, and collected these birds. I could hardly believe it when I counted the last bird in. I had bagged 29 duck, 3 pheasants and a hare. I then drove the Land Rover into Spring Field wood out of sight of pigeons, I could see they were already flighting in. I stood behind the stone wall with the wood behind me and a few oak trees in front 30 yards away, rather than sheltering this short stretch, I put a doubled-up sack for Lassie to sit on instead of letting her sit on the snow, getting cold. I shot three pigeons from here, then decided to move down the stone wall into the next field. I saw steps, as pigeons were flying in good numbers there, across the open field into woods farther on, on Cyril Parker's estate. I again took up position and on standing erect, the blast of the wind and snow was strong, keeping the pigeon low, many just skimming the wall, I shot well and bagged 33 birds beforethe flighting trickled to a stop, Lassie bringing all to my feet. Sometimes, I had no time to take the birds from her mouth. she learned to drop them, more or less together and she was off to pick more up, she never had to go far for them, but it kept her busy, she had proved a bargain dog, and had proven herself from that day as a puppy, she had fled, as the guns opened up on the lawn at Skirwith Hall in fact she deserved a medal for her work this particular day.

I put Lassie to bed and fed her well, she was now very tired after her marathon day, quite a lot of it in ice cold freezing water—she had not missed one bird, she was to turn out, perhaps my best gun dog—little did I know, sad times lay ahead.

Monique had a roasting log and coal fire in the morning room—now I was tired, she opened the bar, in the thick wall, she had asked the village joiner, Edwin Kitchen to make it—had been a biscuit cupboard before—poured me a very large grouse whisky, topped it with water and put it on the round shelf of my large standing ashtray, reached over from my armchair by the fire and took a German black Brazilian cigar from what used to be the gun cupboard, now Monique had it made into a niche 4ft high 12 inches deep with glass shelves, for my cigars, or at least some of them. This cigar niche held 1,800 and was always kept full, I lit up, put my stockinged feet up to the roasting fire, took a large (gulp or mouthful) from my glass, and thought, what a good day's sport I had had, and my little puppy, had grown into a splendid gundog, an hour passed, while I was, dreamily, going over the day's events, then I heard Monique say, dinner was ready, I was surprised time had gone so quickly, I had drunk only half of my whisky. I soon put paid to that into the dining room, and behold, there was roast pheasant for dinner, but not today's bird. Monique knew better than that, and to start, vegetable soup, made by

Monique, she was a past master of soup making, and I was looking forward to the day's hare being turned, under her fair hands, into the queen of soups.

The next day was very cold, the gale and snow had stopped, I thought to take my dog and gun out again, but not for the duck. I only shot them once every two weeks, or sometimes I would shoot the duck three times a week, but only so many hundred yards, then leave the other sections for the next day, and so on, this day, I would go for snipe to some soft places in fields away from the main estate, one and a half miles away we had an outlying field called Hungry Hill, this lay not far from Ousby, it was about 15 acres rather rough grazing and always held snipe, and hares, I took a few cartridges of No 6 shot, let Lassie out of her pen, she jumped over the back ½ door of the Land Rover, and we were off, to get to Hungry Hill, which was an outlying field. I had to drive past BurrellHill farm, now dilapidated, owned by 2 brothers and a sister, John, Donagh and Clara Sanderson. Dad had told me when their father had farmed Burrell Hill, it had been a model farm, but on their parent's death, the three had rented the fields out to various other farmers. When I first knew them, John was 6 ft 4 inches and well built, his teeth were an inch long and all rotten black and green, when Gably saw him for the first time, he returned to Skirwith Hall, telling Monique he had seen a monster, poor John, he was a kind soul, would not hurt a fly, he ran an old car, a Whippet and shot the hares on his land with a 10 bore mussel loader, which I eventually bought from him for 30/- and still have it, in working order. He was a gifted pianist and organ player playing the Church organ, at Kirkland, for his own benefit and also a good mechanic, eventually he was so crippled with rheumatism he could scarcely walk. Donagh was always dressed in a brown pin stripped suit and very shy, if he saw anyone coming, he would run to the house and hide, the only way I have ever talked to him for any length of time was—he loved to fly a kite he had made, and when he had it aloft, he could not get it down in time to hide, I got him 3 or 4 times this way, he was an excellent photographer, developing his own—he would cycle into Penrith about once a month, and could be seen many times gazing, into the window of Dixon, the chemist, at the various large glass vases or jars filled with coloured water. Clara kept house for them, there was only one water tap in the whole house, and that was cold, no bath and no inside toilette, no heating except by one open fire, Burrell Hill stood alone and isolated, facing the full blast of every gale, a very cold place, none ever married, in the end, Donagh died of malnutrition, John of pneumonia and then Clara went to live in the village of Skirwith with a widow there Mrs Ridley, a sad end too, when one knew of them as a nice family, John himself was a great talker, I had bought an old motorcycle of 600cc from him in the war years for 3 pounds.

On this morning, passing Burrell Hill on my way for some snipe, John came out as usual for a talk, usually on farming or shooting, we talked for half an hour before I moved on to the snipe, only another 300 yards. Once there, Lassie jumped down, saw to her ablutions then I went straight to the soft place in the middle of the field, Lassie was only 10 yards in front, I was not letting her go farther on just now, all at once up and jumped a snipe, but as quick he was also down, dead, I reloaded automatically another 5 yards forward another snipe, he went down, the snipe are a very quick little bird, and can be hard to hit, but these days I rarely missed, but just a bit further by a few yards 2 snipe got up, and I did miss one of them, I got three more snipe from Hungry Hill that day, a year later on with Heinz in this same field I shot 9 snipe and missed none, downing them before Heinz could get his gun up, they were too quick for him. Monique cooked them for me on a bed of toast for breakfast whenever I baggedsnipe, delicious little things. The next day, the thaw set in.

Christmas came along, the boys were home for their holidays, I had been unable to pay for Cathy's son Michael for his last term at Murchiston in Edinburgh, so dad, after much grumbling, had to stump up, Michael should have had one more year at school, but dad told Cathy, he had to earn his keep, so he had to leave at 17 years old, a pity because he was or seemed to be quite clever, at least he had 4 more years than I did. Josephine had left Harrogate College and was taking a secretarial course in Leeds, Auntie Kate taking her in.

In January 1966, I put Coquette over some small jumps with gorse branches stuck in. She did very well, I was pleased with her progress, this was to prepare her for hunting the same week. I was taking Adam on his pony Bronco to the next meet at Dalston, but severe frost set in, and hunting was cancelled.

I had laid the smaller deep litter house with mushrooms. Now I had quite an area down and they were coming well, now I had to sell them. Leo Cioli is now the head chef at the county hotel Carlisle, his father, our good friend, had retired, took some for a trial, also the Crown and Mitre, Kerr's the fruit and veg shop in Penrith, also, then dad and I set off for Hereford to buy a bull for the beef herd, while there, I bought one also, with a view to reselling at Edinburgh later on.

When I got back home, all who had mushrooms now wanted more and more, all except the Crown and Mitre, saying they were the best mushrooms they had ever had, this was good news—I must say, the ones Monique and I had eaten were excellent, full flavour and meaty, the central hotel, Carlisle had heard of them and phoned to ask about them, becoming a good customer.

On Saturday, I took Michael to Newcastle races, and afterwards, we went to the Dolce Vita for a flutter of 5 pounds, dancing, then calling at Joe Lisle 69 Club, getting home at 5 am. I let Michael drive home to give him some driving experience in any case—I was tired, he drove very well, though he had no licence.

February 7th, 1966 Dad and I set off for Perth Aberdeen Angus bull sales, Uncle Jim, from Australia, coming along too, dropping off mushrooms at the County, Central, I drove the Alvis, reaching Glenfarg and staying in the hotel of that name for the night, we all went to the bar for one before dinner, having to drag Uncle Jim to dine, as soon as he had a whisky glass in his hand, that was it, after dinner, we had a couple of drinks Dad and I, also Jim, but then he started talking to another farmer guest, drinksflowed, Jim became more boisterous and loud, so Dad and I went to bed, in the morning Jim was very quiet, for one thing, a big headache kept him that way—he was a headache for my mother this man.

It had snowed heavily in the night, at the breakfast table, I saw at an adjoining table, a sight I had not seen since I was a boy, two male guests, farmers by the look of them, had a plate of porridge each, and beside each one, was a cup of milk and instead of as nowadays, pouring the milk onto the plate of porridge, they did as they had done all their lives—taking a spoonful of porridge, then dipping it into the cup of milk—then into their mouths, this was the last time I was to see this practice.

On to Perth, where there were, I believe, over 700 bulls and so many bulling heifers for sale. Dad wanted a 3 or 4-year-old bull of big size. We were both amazed at what we saw being offered by the breeders, hundreds of bulls the size of Welsh ponies and 2-year-old bulling heifers the size of Shetland ponies, it was my first visit to these sales at Perth, I had heard a lot about them, of the Argentineans who would give thousands of pounds in some cases 40,000 pounds. These buyers stopped coming to Perth for bulls because the bulls were too small to serve the cows on the pampas, the breed had been ruined in size by the judges and showmen, who had gone off the large bull size too small, blocky, dolly sized, nice looking things but useless for the growing of meat and useless for the pampas, the bulls continuously broke their penises, the best breed for quality meat in the world, ruined, so went the same way, the scotch beef shorthorn, once the two breeds, when I was a small boy, the bulls were magnificent in size.

Judges, in all aspects of animal life, are a parasite that can be done without, at least in the British Isles. The French and Germans breed from and show bulls that are like bulls—not ponies. When I visited the Smithfield show a few years later, almost every bovine beast there had been sired by a Foreign bull, in a corner were ½ a dozen Aberdeen A, the smallest bovine there, I remonstrated with the owner on the smallness of them, all he could say was, "They eat a lot less than the big beggars over there" pointing to the foreign blood. The British Isles had put the world on its feet as far as beef cattle go; the world ate British or English beef, and wherever one went worldwide, one saw sometimes, as far as the eye could see, the English or Scottish breeds now these breeds of pure beef cattle, becoming almost in 1997 an endangered species, purely laid at the feet of the show judge, theirs is the shame of it all.

Dad and I hunted for a long time before he found a decent-sized bull of 4 years old, there were perhaps 3 others of similar quality. Dad bid and got him for 370gns, a chap from Blencarn, John Stamper gave1,100gns for the usual small, nice, blocky bull, serving his first cow, he broke his penis so badly, he was sent to slaughter.

The bull we bought was used for eight years before he became too tired to serve his cows.

Mid-February, I sold the little 1100 MG for a new MBG sports car from Howard Lace of Kirkoswald. I sold the MG 1100 for 580 pounds, paying as part trade in 461 pounds.

I got extras for the MGB, a hard top 73 pounds, an overdrive 50 pounds, a delivery charge 13 pounds, a headlight flasher 1 pound, number plates 2 pounds, an anti-roll bar 2 pounds, heater 15 pounds, perhaps not much by today's standards but plenty then.

April 1st opened to heavy snow, the children must have had ½ term or something because Monique and I took them to see Snow White and the Seven Dwarfs, they enjoyed it immensely when we came out of the cinema the snow lay thick, on the TV news that night, it seemed that the Labour Party were now in power.

My birthday was on June 2nd Mother gave me a Ritchard Dimbley record of speeches and 5 large Macanudo cigars, I still have the record. Mid June, I bought another pony for Joey Jnr, he was nine years old, his first pony, a little Welsh gelding, had been too fresh and also could kick quite unexpectedly, so I got rid of it, his second one Jimmy with whom he had had heaps of fun, and a grand character was now much too small, so I sold him on, for a child's first pony, this one I was going to see belonged to a girl who had outgrown it, into the Land Rover, Lassie in the back, the pony was at a village only 8 miles away, the girl Miss Robertson, showed me her pony, I liked it immediately, it was ½ Norwegian and Welsh gelding called Struan Gold, Miss Robertson had won prizes in gymkhanas with him, he was 10.2 h.h just the right size and temperament, I was asked 60 pounds and without argument gave it, Miss Robertson had her new saddle for sale, or practically new, for 10 pounds. I took that as well.

The next step was to bring him home, I borrowed Robert Jackson's horse trailer, hitched the Land Rover and returned to pick the pony up, he loaded with no bother, and I took him to his new home. Young Joey was delighted and got on him right away, he was quite a good rider by now, he had learned a lot from Jimmy. Joey now shortened his ponies' name to Struie, and for a long time, they had heaps of fun until quite a few years later, when Joey was in his teens, I sold Struie to the daughter of Arthur Monkhouse, ex-policeman and Monkhouse's animal foods—forher son Simon, who was aged about 7, Simon kept Struie for many years, then I lost contact with them. Strange, my father had never bought me a pony, I had to buy my own when I was very young—Patsy for 5 pounds—looking back, he would not pay the 7/- haulage, and mother had to borrow it from Uncle Willie.

For winter warmth for the mushrooms, I heard of a second-hand central heating plant for sale at Mrs Distins hatchery near Glastonbury, she had closed down and had been bigger than mine. She lived only 5 miles away, so I popped over to see her, I was too late for the boiler part, she had sold it to a scrap dealer Shocker Bowman of Penrith, Shocker was a pal of mine, he had been a boxer in the days of, when each town or nearly each, had their boxing bouts in the market halls. Shocker had been very good in his day, George Bowman, of carriage horse fame, would be I think a grandson of Shocker; those days of my youth, George and I used to compete in the flapping races; those were the days of fun and freedom. I bought all of what was left of the plant at Mrs Distins for 10 pounds, I thought I best see Shocker at once, so I headed for Penrith, fortunately Shocker still had the boiler intact, I did a deal there and then with a bit of haggling, giving my friend 10 pounds. The next day, Kurt and I took the Land Rover over to Mrs Distins picked the heating pipes up etc., with a trailer, dropped it all off at home, then on to Shocker for the boiler, without the trailer, the weight all dismantled made the Land Rover sink on her springs. The whole plant was for the long Deep Litter house of 300ft and was installed in what had been the meal house store, dead centre of the building. Kurt enjoyed himself, putting the thing together, he liked mechanics and, in no time, had the boiler and burner burning well, now was the installation of the pipes and radiators. I had to buy many new ones from Monkhouse's hardware dept at Langwathby; they were installed on each side and full length of the Deep Litter house, Kurt and I were working like niggers at this stage, as there were various stacks of horse manure cooking away, so many that almost every day, some were to turn, mushrooms to pick etc. Mushroom sales were going well, even Andersons of Scotby Fruit Importers said there were the best ever tasted and would take all I could produce, but being in one person's hands did not appeal to me, I kept my old first and faithful clients on though Andersons were very good customers and were also very straight and honest to deal with.

The year passed into 1967, the year 1966 had been a hard one for work, just too hard. The sale of mushrooms had been very good, but the work was too much to do all by hand. The central heating was quite costly but was doing a good job, I was now skinny as a rat, with not an ounce of fat on me, my trousers had to be held up with a belt, we would see what 1967 was to be.

Baycut had run 2nd at Sedgefield with Ian Watkinson up, a good performance and at a good price, second prize 40 pounds myself, making 210 pounds that day. She ran at Catterick, finishing 7th, a fast track, just too fast for her, but she was not disgraced.

Jan and Feb, the mushrooms did well, but in March, something happened to them, many became distorted and misshaped, also not growing well, I went to see another grower near Carlisle for advice, myself having little knowledge of mushroom growing, I had followed instinct and had done well, now the grower near Carlisle, told me at this moment all mushrooms had been growing badly, there seemed by what he said, that there was a disease going about, I had big areas down, with spawn, but going from bad to worse. I had tried and had done well for quite a while, then this period of disease, I thought to myself, I would finish trying more mushrooms, I had a heart-to-heart talk with Kurt about giving up, he understood and said he had enjoyed working for me, he had been not only a faithful worker, but also a friend, I paid him off on Saturday, April 8th 67. He applied for redundancy and got it, he had a few weeks off, then Dad took him on for the coming harvest as a tractor man. Kurt had worked for me for 10 years.

I explained to Dad about the mushroom disease. I did not want to work again for my father, wishing to remain independent but circumstances had to be faced—I asked if I could join him as a partner, he said yes and had been thinking the same himself, he said he would pay me 25 pound per week, which was then less than his men were getting. I agreed. I had the boy's school fees to pay for one thing. So, from the end of March 1967, I was back in the lambing field, helping to lamb the ewes, I was quite happy to be back with the sheep, I liked to work with them, the shepherd then was my other old poultry man Harold Metcalfe, whose wife was Monique's daily help, I soon saw Harold, good as he was, was much too rough in lambing the ewes, if a lamb had a leg back, he would try to pull the lamb out of its mother by the one leg showing, instead of pushing the whole lamb back into position, now I understood the three or four lambs running about with shoulders out of joint, I remonstrated with him, and explained how to push the lamb back inside the mother, he knew but for some reason, thought that he could pull a lamb out on one leg, sometimes it can be done, but when brute force is used on one leg then the lamb must be pushed back, otherwise Harold was quite a good shepherd.

I did a bit of shepherding on the higher lands with Baycut, which helped her to get fit, I ran her in May at Sedgefield with Barry Brogan up. She was 2nd to Demon beaten a neck, a fast run race. She had been struck into from behind, cutting into her offside rear tendon, though not too deep. I was most pleased Barry Brogan had been the leading amateur jockey over jumps in Ireland, just then he was riding for Ken Oliver, he had brought Brogan over, and this was his first season in England, Barry was a very strong jockey, very forceful, he could get a horse to the line, as good as the top jockeys in the land, a pleasant chap, good to get on with, he had enormous success over the jumps, but then wine, women and song took over, the success it seemed had gone to his head, going from trouble to trouble, eventually so I heard, ending in a prison sentence for some misdemeanour, a great pity a great career to end as it did.

I had another young filly I was breaking in, but she was one of the wildest I had ever broken, she was a living dynamo and had thrown me off quite a few times, she could arch her back like a cat when she bucked, reaching for the sky as high as she could, I thought to send her to a man just over the border in Scotland to finish off for me named McMurchie, I had heard he could break the wildest horse in. I trucked the filly named Champagne Suzy and took her up to McMurchie, he said he would do what was necessary. I picked her up a month later there she was standing like an old lamb, stock still, not moving, saddle and bridle on, I thought he had done a good job, which he had, but on riding her at home, I realised her spirit had been broken, she was a listless, empty-hearted horse.

Champagne Suzy showed sparks of brilliance at home but on the track proper, useless, running listlessly, so after a while, I pulled her out of training. I sold her the following year at Doncaster sales for 250gns. A young man with a very pretty girl bought her from the Devon area, I saw in Horse and Hound, over the next few years, Champagne Suzy won quite a number of point-to-points and quite easily.

Meanwhile, I had had Lassie mated with Derek Pattinson's good Labrador, Derek was the land agent for Lord Lonsdale and the brains behind the whole estate, the dog I mated Lassie with was an exceptional worker, I hoped she would have a good litter, then I would present dad one for his Xmas present, he could do with a good dog, but he forestalled me, he got himself a pointer that turned out to be a wild one.

Dad always liked the trip to Kelso Tup Sales, and prepared the day before, seeing the car tyres had full pressure, the water, petrol and oil, also if the car horn worked. I remember in the old Standard 20 as a youngster, the electric horn did not work, so he went to the garage in Langwathby, Mrs Hope's and borrowed a trumpet horn with a large rubber balloon on one end. One had to squeeze this hard, to get a good honk, honk, and dad used to blow the horn at each corner, so going up to Kelso, the window was nearly permanently open, with the horn sticking well out, we tookit in turns to blow, only when dad said blow, not once but twice and three times for each comer. That time, we, as well as mother, were fed up with that trip, at 30 miles and hour, Dad's speed, for the 202 miles round trip. This time, however, the Alvis was going, she was a beautiful car to drive, with excellent acceleration, but as I have said, the foot pedals were much too near together, and the headlights were poor.

Dad made the most of this trip of 101 miles, egging mother to nerve-breaking point by preparing an enormous picnic to have enroute, he himself would be up at 5 am, make an enormous fuss, get mother into a nervous wreck and off we would all set, at 6 am, mother, Cathie, Monique, dad and myself, I would drive, but I refused to drive at 30 miles per hour, after one episode with him, ordering me to "follow that car in front" which I did, (a previous outing) the car in front for no reason, and no signs, stopped, I missed an accident by the skin of my teeth, after that I refused to follow any car in front,—on overtaking dad would drive carefully passed the other vehicle, going sedately side by side until one could have opened the window and had a chat with the other driver, the odd time, the passing of such was left nearly too late for oncoming traffic, then dad would say, look at that damned fool. Myself when passing other vehicles, I would get on with the job, Dad sitting beside me, telling me to slow down.

After perhaps 60 miles and into those beautiful Cheviot Hills, 2-3 miles north of Mosspaul Dad would choose the picnic place, almost the same place each year, given a yard or two, when really none of us were hungry, all of us had had a hearty breakfast, however we tucked in, there was now no hurry, it was a day's outing. We arrived in due course over the rise, looking over to that most fairy tale and beautiful castle, Floors, belonging to my old friend the Duke of Roxburgh, the big dark-faced chap whom I did not like, it was about this time the Duke was busy kicking his Duchess out of Floors, but at first she would not budge, in the end, she did move out, making way for Mrs Church she was with him at the sales today, she had three sons of her own from her own marriage, two I think went to Blanerne, near Hawick, where we had sent Adam. The sales were held on parkland, belonging and adjacent to the castle, a very lovely setting, with the famous river Tweed, famous for its salmon flowing by.

There were many hundreds of tups, or to put it correctly, rams from all over the British Isles, usually Dad bought. Border Leicester tups, but this year, a Dorset Horn tup was wanted, he got one for 55 pounds, a lorry from a local firm near Penrith took the tup and delivered him that night.

On the return journey home, Dad always liked to have tea at the greencafe on the main street in Hawick, in fact, it was a ritual, not tea and cakes, but high tea, steaks or roasts, and it was always good, also very clean, and the waitresses always very pleasant. Dad would never park on the street, always parking the car at the opposite end of the main street in a garage there and paying 2/-, walking back to the cafe. The Dorset ram was put with his wives the day after, mating with one of them there and then.

The week after, to ease the money situation, I sold Baycut to Paddy Chesmore, the trainer, on behalf of Lady Moore. I did not mark the price in my diary, likely forgetting, but I seem to remember the price was about 500 pounds, I was sorry to see her go; I had had a lot of fun with her, and what is life without fun, one might as well lie down and die.

Race days to Ayr. On these trips with Robert Jackson, we would go in his car, a Rover. He was a fierce driver, but a good one, never under 80mph or more, when he was driving, I could relax and smoke my Burma cheroots, which Robert really did not like, he would open his window quite often—doing 80mph, causing an awful draft, letting the smoke out, then shut it, as quick, but he himself chain-smoked cigarettes, which I did not like, the smoke being most pungent, to my cigars or cheroots, I suppose he was right in opening the window many times, because inside the car at times was like a thick fog, and Monique herself never complained.

23

Lassie was now near to having her puppies. I was looking forward to seeing what she would produce. This particular morning, I was going to see the sheep at the little farm where I was born in Kirkland, just a walk around to see how things were. I was taking the MGB and leaving it at the farm, then walking round the farm, I thought to take Lassie, so put a thick sack in the car boot for her to lie on, she was pleased, in she jumped, for the 1 and a half mile run, on arriving at the farm, I opened the boot, for Lassie to jump out, she did not, I said come on girl, she then got out, looked into my face with a crestfallen look—as if asking what am I to do, I thought with that look, she maybe is thinking to have her puppies, I said to her good girlie, get back in, she did not need to be asked twice, in she jumped and curled up, looking at her tummy this convinced me, her babies were on their way, I closed the boot lid, but propped it open by six inches, leaving plenty of air space and light, then I set off, to see if all was well with the sheep—all was well. I returned an hour later, lifted the boot lid, and there was Lassie—now with a smile on her face; with two wet babies, she was doing her best to clean and dry them, licking the little ones for all she was worth, this was 12th October 1967, I took her home quickly and put her in her bed, a little later, she had two more puppies, a total of 4, not a big litter, but perhaps enough.

Three days later, I started again with flu, and the heavens opened, causing the Briggle beck to overflow its banks from end to end. I had never seen such a flood before, then two days later still, the fells were covered with snow.

The big sale of the beef calves we had reared at Skirwith Hall was on 19th October, the suckler sale, as we knew it, was named so that all calves sold at this sale had never been fed milk from a bucket but suckled solely on their mothers and had to be beef breeds, no dairy cross allowed. This sale was where most of the income for the farm came from.

Unfortunately, I was ill in bed with a bad attack of flu in my first year with my father, the sale was a good one, being up 6 pounds per head compared to the year before.

At the weekend, Monique and I went to Kelso races in the MGB, passing Maj Parker in his Ford V8, with him was Denholm Rowlands, an extremely nice chap. Denholm was the agent for the Duke of Westminster, who had bought quite an area of agricultural land in the area and woodlands at Whinfell, with a view to future death duties on them. I believe death duties on land was 40% or thereabouts. Denholm was a great drinker, quietly but surely, he could get through a tremendous amount, he was also a member of Market Day and Friday booze ups near Moss- paul, passing him at 90 mph, giving him a blast on the horn and a big wave, telling me later on I was driving too fast. This time at the races, I lost 15 pounds, on the way home, after having a few drinks at Ednam House with a host of friends, Monique and I set off calling at the little village of Denholm, outside the local pub was the major's car, I pulled up in front of it, we might as well have another drink or two. Sure enough, there was Cyril (the major) and Denholm, having drinks with one-eyed Willie and two of his sons, the talk was of the day betting, Cyril as usual, had plunged on the last race, "his getting out stakes", drinks also, as usual, came in like confetti, then everyone decided to move on to Mosspaul, the pub in the middle of nowhere—but in the middle of those rolling cheviot hills, it was a favourite watering hole of the racing and hunting set, a simple place but one could usually meet friends there, next call for quite a few was Ashley Bank, Langholm, where the process of drinking was continued.

A Very Sad Period

On 8th November 1967, I went early, about 7:30 am, to see the sheep at Kirkland, I took the Land Rover but first stopped at Kirkland House, mother and father house, the ex large two storied vicarage, only 400 yards from the house where I was born, I went in by the rear entrance into the kitchen, Uncle

Jim was having breakfast alone, I asked where mother was, all seemed very quiet, he said he had not seen anyone, the lights were on in every room, I shouted from the hallway but got no reply, not even dad or Cathy, I went upstairs, all lights were on, mother's bedroom empty—the bed had been slept in, Cathy's the same. Puzzled I went downstairs and told Uncle Jim there was no one in the house, his reply was they might have gone to Penrith for something—I thought that a bit silly at that time of the day.

I then went to look around the sheep at Kirkland Hall with what had been Dad's dog, Maid, she was a grand little sheepdog, after two hours of shepherding, I called in again to see if Dad or Cathy had turned up, sure enough, they were in but Cathy met me with a solemn face, saying Ma had been taken ill in the night with a coronary thrombosis, Dr Frank Edington had been called out, and they had taken Ma to the cottage hospital, she was in pain, Cathy told me, she had taken ill in the night. I was devastated, I returned to Skirwith Hall, shaved, changed and went straight to the cottage hospital, to her bedside, in a ward with perhaps 8 more beds, I was surprised the Dr had not put mother into a ward by herself, I approached the bed, ma was very pale, but breathing evenly, I took her hand and said hello ma in quiet tones, she opened her eyes, and smiled and spoke softly, rather hesitantly, saying how nice it was for me to visit her, adding she was not very well, I said, you will soon be back home Ma, she smiled, closed her eyes and slept, after a little while, I left quietly and went home. In the evening, Dad and I went to see Ma again, she was sleeping peacefully, but within a second or two, she opened her eyes as if she had known we were there. Smiling, she greeted us, speaking softly, but clearly, she wanted to go home. Dad said of course, in a few days' time, when you are better, she appealed to me, saying Joey take me home, I had to say the same as Dad said, you seem a lot stronger tonight, it won't be long before you are at Kirkland, she asked after Monique and the boys, Adam and Joey—Adam was her out and out favourite, then ma closed her eyes and was sleeping, after 15 or 20 minutes Dad and I tiptoed out.

Monique and I went at 9:30 am to see Ma; again, she opened her eyes as soon as we approached her bed. This time, she seemed stronger than ever and had a longish chat with Monique, we would stay 30 minutes, not to tire Ma out and as we left, we both thought Ma would be back home in a few days. I was most pleased, Monique and I went in again in the evening. Ma was quite perky.

Sunday, 12th November, we all went to see Ma, I was surprised and saddened to see her, she seemed to be breathing too fast and seemed disturbed, she spoke to us, softly telling us she wanted to go home, Dad told her its only a few days now, she understood and too tired, went to sleep, I went again at 7 pm to see her, and could not believe it, the TV only 2 yards from her bed, was turned up very high, so the rest of the ward could hear, ma smiled at me, I mentioned the noise of the TV, she smiled again, never mind she said, I am going to die, I held her hand, and she drifted off to sleep. I went back at 9 pm and sat with her, at moments, she would ask about Monique and our two boys, then reassured me all was well slept.

Monday 13th, Dad, Monique and myself went at 8:15 am to the hospital, Ma opened her eyes, saw dad, spoke to him closed her eyes again, she knew Monique was there, and with her eyes closed, asked Monique to help her, Monique took ma's hand in hers, saying of course she would help her, Michael, Cathy's boy, had come home and arrived at the hospital, ma was most pleased to see him and the two had quite a chat, we had taken some Lucosade to the hospital, and now we gave Ma, little sips of it, every 10 mins or so, she liked this very much, she would drift off to sleep, then wake up mins later, smile at us, have a little sip of Lucosade, then drift off again, Dad wanted to give ma a kiss but could not because of the guard rail on the side of the bed, I lowered it, and he gave her a kiss on her forehead, little Adam was at home, possibly his half term, Monique and I took him to see ma, she adored him and he adored her, as soon as ma saw him she said right away, "My little boy, come and give ma a little kiss", Adam kissed her on her cheek, she was so pleased with his visit it made her day.

14th November Tuesday Dad and I went to see Ma at 8:30 am. Ma was in a deep sleep, breathing nicely, we did not disturb her and after 15 mins left, we came back at 11 am, now ma was breathing not too well and with what seemed a lot of phlegm and could not seem to get it up, nearly choking it seemed, ma's Dr was there, Frank Edington, I asked if he could give ma something to get rid of the phlegm, he told me everything is alright, the head nurse a male at the cottage hospital had now moved Ma into a little room on her own, I thought she should have been in this room from the very beginning instead of being placed beside a blaring TV and in a full ward of other patients. We left the hospital, Ma was sleeping and seemed to be choking on the phlegm, I was inwardly getting angry at the doctor for not relieving this problem, I was later to understand more.

Dad, Monique and I returned to the hospital at 2:30 pm, I could see now ma was slipping away, dad moistened her lips with some Lucosade, she did not open her eyes, the phlegm in her throat seemed worse, at 3 pm sharp I was sitting beside ma looking into her kind face, when I saw a slight movement of her head, her eyes opened, then rolled back, and ma stopped breathing, I said sharply to dad, ma's going, yes ma had gone, I went to bring the head nurse then and sadly went out and sat in the car, Monique followed me, both of us did not speak, then for the first time in my life, I broke down, I became racked with great sobs and tears, my life's sweetheart had gone, and now all at once, I realised there was, besides the great sadness, a void, an enormous emptiness had descended on me, the heart of my family had gone, I had started a new family with Monique and my two young sons, but my old and treasured family in who's bosom I had rested for so many years—had gone, never to return. In my diary I wrote, Ma, she was a saint to us all. Cathie and Michael arrived 5 mins too late. After a while—I did not go back inside the hospital, there was no need, my sweetheart, my mother was now in a better land—God's heaven.

After a while, my cries subsided, then I drove home, Dad and Monique also in the car, entering Skirwith village from Langwathby road, there is a sharp corner where one has to really slow down, as I approached this corner, we drove in silence—there, the first person to see, was that awful woman Mrs Page, walking her dog, it was a nasty twist somehow, little did any of us know what was to follow. Here are the little things I entered in my diary, the time Ma was in hospital. I put them down because I loved my mother from my heart and, like many others—wished the rest of my life that I had told her so. Ma, of course, knew I did, but I wish I had told her, "Ma, I love you", such a short little sentence—but with enormous meaning.

One evening Dad, Monique and I took an aspirin bottle of Bovril and gave it to Ma through a little feeder for small children, ma enjoyed it, she said come on, Guy give me the soup, the soup Guy, be quick Guy, the soup, how nice it is, Dad told her the soup was Bovril, ma replied of course its Bovril Guy, she asked for some lemon and coconut sweets to suck, for my mouth its too dry or barley sugar, it you want some money, look in my pocket there might be some there, poor ma, she wanted to be tired she said, so that I can sleep. Michael and I sat with Ma from 8 pm till 11 pm. She would put her hand out and get hold of one of ours, open her eyes and smile at us. Sometimes she would say, its Joey and Michael, saying, poor wee boy Cathy's boy, poor wee Michael, he's had no father, only for a little while he's had a father—to me—be kind to him Joey, Cathy's wee boy—then to sleep again.

On the 14th, the day Ma died, Dad and I went in at 11 am and stopped for an hour. The only words she spoke that day were "Guy, kiss me, kiss me Guy", she said it so nicely, but evidently in a hurry, I think she knew she was going to die that day. Her eyes were shut all that day, but Ma knew who was there, I would say hello, Ma, it's dad and Joey, she would slightly nod her head. She knew, sometimes the day before, she would jokingly say, "You are getting old, Da" and to Frank Edington—she took off his glasses when he was bending over her and told him "you are getting old Dr, you should not be working so hard". To me and all of us, "take me home", and to Monique, she was so pleased to see, "Monique—Monique, where have you been all this time" Help me Monique". To me, "I'm going down the Swanea Joey, I'm going to die—Guy doesn't know it". A light went out in my life when Ma died, there was an awful emptiness, overall, now I felt the family was alone and vulnerable—vulnerable to what, I thought, nothing really, but the great emptiness would go away.

Ma's body was brought back to Kirkland the day after and lay in her coffin in the drawing room there. I went in a few times to say prayers and kiss her on her forehead, the best friend of my whole life lay there. I had confided all my troubles to Ma and somehow, hers to me—we had a strong bond—I never confided in my father, it was to Ma I always turned to—what a sad period it was.

The funeral was held on 17th, with a service at Skirwith church and later cremation at Carlisle. I never once heard Ma say when she passed away, she wished to be cremated, this was left in Dad's hands, the bearers

were some of the staff at Skirwith Hall, Joe Frith, Tractor Man, Harold Metcalfe Shepherd, George Walker, cowman, Maurice Fawcett, tractor man. Pat McGeorge, Adam, my brother's fiancée came to Kirkland before the ceremony, it was a cold, dry day, and as I followed behind the hearse, I was most touched by road workers and many other people of poor circumstances taking their hats off and bow their heads—it was a lesson for me, for after that, any hearse carrying a coffin I did the same.

To recap a little, if I had known Ma had taken ill with a stroke or coronary, I do not think I would have let Dad move her to the hospital, and again, Frank Edington should have told Dad to move Ma—knowing the problem could prove dangerous, movement by a vehicle, could dis- lodge clots to anywhere, as at the finish mother's clot shifted at the last day to her head the best way for such an illness, is complete immobility, completely quiet and rest, in the quietness of one's own familiar bedroom, however by the time I knew, it was too late for me to interfere.

In the days that followed, I would do my shepherding and would think continuously of Ma, tears just running down my cheeks. I would go up to the limekiln field at Kirkland, to the very place where Ma had taken me many times when I was a baby and up to when I was three years old. There in between two limestone rocks were 4-5 pieces of coal she had put there those long years ago—still there, and there in the privacy and quietness of the fells, I could cry out to Ma, asking her to forgive me for not telling her I loved her more, my heart was broken, my sheepdog Maid sat away from me these times, watching also with sad and drooping head, she knew it was a terrible time in my life.

Meanwhile, foot and mouth disease had broken out in Westmorland or further south, Kendal Auction Mart was closed, and Penrith was closed due to the foot and mouth. The number of farms so far infected and slaughtered up to 30 was 1,311 cases, the most in the country's history. Saturday, to take our minds off things, Dad and I went to shoot walking, the rough ground here and there, Lassie doing her work and retrieving so well, Dad said she certainly was an excellent dog, we shot 4 braces of pheasant, then slowly went home, they were heavy enough to carry, it was very mild. Sunday, I went to church, Monique being Catholic, I did not attend the church at Skirwith, afterwards, Mr and Mrs Johnstone invited me to the Abbey for drinks, old Major Parker—Cyril—had moved out of the Abbey two years ago and bought Newbiggin Hall between Penrith and Appleby, from the Crackenthorpe family, for the major, this place had more historical links, than the Abbey, Newbiggin was large, but at the Abbey, he and Mrs Parker had been reduced to living in the, below ground kitchen, Cyril himself never going to bed, but slept in an old armchair and had been doing this for the last 10 years.

24

A year ago, in 1966, Cyril Parker had the home farm at Skirwith to let, he had been plagued by other farmers on market day and Fridays boozy day, plying him with drink, to obtain home farm for their various sons, one-eyed Willie was one of these, one day Cyril asked me if I would like to lease the farm, but there was a catch, I had to live in the Abbey, and make it presentable, and asked if I could see him the following week, I told dad what I had been offered, and would he help me, but the answer was no. I saw Cyril the following week. I thanked him and said I could not leave Skirwith Hall to live in the Abbey, two large houses to upkeep—so he asked if I knew of any nice family of farmers—who would take both the farm—which had its own house—and the Abbey, as he was fed up with the local fraternity, who would probably live in the two rooms of the Abbey and let it go to ruin. I said yes, it is possible, having in mind a family I had met, racing, new into racing, meeting the father and son a few times at Tommy Robson's, a Mr John- stone from Whithaven, West Cumb and his son Bert a young man of about 20 or so. He Mr Johnstone, strange enough, had asked me if I knew of any farms to rent, after talking with Cyril, I got in touch with the Johnstones at their farm, Spout House—in the shadow of the atomic station Sellafield, he was very interested, for Bert's sake, I told Cyril I might have a client for both of his places, I told him, the Johnstone's pedigree, at least what I knew of Mr and Mrs seemed and were, especially Mrs Johnstone, very nice people, a cut above the locals who were chasing Cyril round Penrith. I said they would like a look round the farm and house on a certain day, would I get the keys from Kitchen the Joiner, I did this and Monique and I showed the Johnstone's round the Abbey, and there in an upstairs corridor was two pairs of Mrs Parker's knickers lying there, just as if she, Mrs P, had disrobed there, the place needed quite a bit of money spent on the interior alone, I took the two men folk on a quick Land Rover trip round the fields, I think the acreage was 210, then back to the ladies, where on the lawn, Johnstone Snr asked Bert, well Bert what do you think, I knew before Bert spoke, he wanted to live in this rather nice and imposing house, because Bert had a touch, quite a touch of snob in him—not his parents—his father adding, I think it maybe is too much to take on, Bert said quite forcibly, he wanted it, so that was that, I made sure the same day by asking Mr Johnstone if he was certain he wanted it, because if he did, then it was his—and I would notify Major Parker that evening, which I did, the Major thanking me for helping him out.

When the farm men, three of them, at Home Farm, heard a new tenant was taking over, the Johnstone's had made their presence known to them, travelling 3 or 4 times a week from their farm in West Cumb—I don't know why, but they all decided to leave, and work elsewhere, I soon got to know of this because my phone rang one night, Mr Johnstone was in a panic, he told me his workers at Skirwith were going to leave, could I help him. I said I would do what I could. I knew the men personally. They were decent chaps who seemed rather at a loss just then because, officially, Mr Johnstone was not then the tenant, he was not due to take over for another month. I went that night and visited each one of them, putting their minds at ease, I gather by what was said, thought Bert the son, had ruffled their feathers, however, I spent an hour with each and put their minds at ease, persuading them to stay on and work for the newcomer Mr Johnstone, giving the latter an excellent pedigree of reference. I phoned Mr Johnstone, giving him the news, he was most relieved and said he would not come to Skirwith that week, would I please see to his men for me? I told him I would, which I did. I reckon—I did a good job for the Johnstone's firstly, by getting them the lease of the home farm, and secondly to have kept the staff on, as they were hell-bent on leaving.

Dad's birthday fell on 7th December. He was 71 years old, Cathy told me, it was the first time I had learned of how old was either my father or my mother, regarding my mother, I did not know her age until she died. Now this day, his age was sprung on me.

On 9th December, there fell 2 inches of snow, the ewes had to be brought down from the high-lying land and fed with hay, later that day, I went out specially to shoot a hare for the Xmas festival. Monique would make hare soup, with which we started the meal with the Queen of Soups, I got an enormous hare, the size of a fox; that is all I wanted that day, and I went home.

Saturday, 16th December, was our wedding anniversary. I took Monique to the Crown Hotel at Wetheral near Carlisle; the Crown was tucked away in a corner at Wetheral, a small place, but one always ate well there. Bill McGillvray and I had had many meals and a lot of fun at the Crown and this night was no exception.

However, on Xmas day, why we did not all dine together at Xmas with Dad, Cathy and her two children was that Cathy did not want our son Adam to be there, as he was or had been a handful to deal with. I will say Adam could be rather petted at times, but Ma would give him full rein, she really adored him and her. As we were sitting down to lunch, in the middle of the turkey, figures passed the dining room windows, looking out, here without a word, saying they were coming was Heinz and Maria, with two of their boys, Ludwig and Ulrich, to stay for a few days, Monique was not too pleased, as we had nothing prepared, however, we made them welcome and laid 4 more places at the table, neither Maria or their children would take hare soup, Heinz, of course, had an international taste for everything, loved it, the turkey went okay but stuffing, bread sauce, turnips they would not have, only Heinz, the plum pudding and rum sauce they also would not eat, again only Heinz. I took Heinz and his family round and one day up to Edinburgh round the Castle, etc., which they all liked and on the 30th they left for Germany.

Pat's father, Robert McGeorge of Dumfries', had a

cashmere factory there in partnership with his brother David, Robert's wife had died a few years ago, he had 4 daughters. Pat told me herself, 2 if not 3 of them, had different fathers, Mrs McGeorge must have been a sporting girl.

Robert McGeorge would travel to America, Canada, Australia and many times to France, especially Cannes, where he always stayed at the Carlton, a French girl there was going to sue him for breach of promise until he coughed up a sizeable sum of money. Now he was courting my sister Cathy, going up to Kirkland each weekend in his Rolls Royce, over which Dad used to swoon. Cathy accompanied him many times to the USA, Canada and France, he was his own, so to speak, international salesman, all of these exotic trips he made and his Rolls Royce was paid for by the firm of McGeorge Bros, he told me once his tax-free travelling and expense account was 25,000 pounds per year, he was a man Monique and I did not like very much, he had a tendency to look upon us as country bumpkins, boasting of his money and his investments, he told me if the Distillers Co (of which I myself had bought quite a lot of shares) went up 2d he was making thousands of pounds. He used to sit—not often, thank goodness—on the large settee in the morning room at Skirwith Hall, his jacket (nearly always blue in colour) covered like snowflakes with dandruff, spouting off, the hotels he had stayed in, and no doubt they were the best, I would smoke a cigar and let him ramble on taking no notice, he had proposed marriage to Cathy when Michael was about 12 or 14 years old, but Michael did not like him, so she said no, which was a pity.

Now mother was no more, Cathy offered to look after dad for the rest of his life, which was sporting of her, in the meantime, Josephine, who now worked in Paris, was married sometime in 1967, Monique and I were not asked, and I have no exact dates of this event, her husband was Henri Gerbrier of 14 Rue de Colonel Moll, Paris, France. I saw the wedding photo; he was balding and looked to be 5 ft tall, and from what I could gather, he was in "films" and the underworld, a bit of this and a bit of that, from this marriage they had two children, a girl and a boy.

The foot and mouth disease was still going strong into 1968. When dad had word that Skirwith Hall was for sale, Michael Le Fleming, the owner, had died in South Africa and had left his wife a large sum of cash, and together with death duties, most of his estates had to be sold to provide the cash, his brother Dick was left Skirwith Hall and he wanted to sell. Dad was, as before, when he was offered Skirwith Hall, in a dilemma; his buddy and advisor, his brother-in-law, Alex Bayne, had died, now he had to think himself, but to make matters worse, he was seeing Mrs Page, openly now—however with foot and mouth Kendal auction mart was still closed and that is where the agent for Skirwith Hall had his office, he was Tony Holliday. Six months ago the middle of 1968, Michael Le Fleming had paid us a visit to Skirwith Hall with his agent Tony Holliday, whom I knew well. Dad was, of course, present, being a personal friend of Michael, in the morning room, I kept the whisky bottle going and Michael, who used to almost live on the stuff, could still knock it back, but I realised he was far from a fit man when he wished to spend a penny he was unable to go upstairs to the loo, I had to escort him to the front door, for him to pee on the lawn, but even that was too far for him, as soon as I opened the door he started to pee on the great sandstone flagstone from the doorstep, I led him back inside, then I asked him, a thing my father had never asked him, would he sell Skirwith Hall, he hesitated, then replied it is the jewel of my property, no, not at the moment, so at least he told me to my face, dad coughed and growled. Now not a year later, Michael is dead, and Skirwith Hall is for sale, and his brother Dick is the new owner. Dick was an extremely nice man, small, possibly 5ft 5inch with the clearest of blue eyes, liked jokes and shooting, a little like Terry Thomas, without the gap in his front teeth, very, very English, lived in London from an allowance from the Le Fleming estates, never rich, but spent his time at Whites Club, where I used to phone him, he used to visit Skirwith Hall once every 3 or 4 years, and he and I would go shooting, he always wanted to get a hare for hare soup, which his sister at Rydal would make him, he usually stayed with her for a week, where he told me her dog George, a fox terrier would sit and watch cowboy films on the TV and when the shooting was on, he would bark like mad, George would not watch anything else but cowboys.

One day at Hungry Hill, one of our outlying fields, on one of Dicks last visits, a hare got up 30 yards from him, I was at least 60 yards from the hare, I let Dick have first crack, he missed with both barrels, the hare now easily 70 yards from me, I thought Dick is going to be disappointed if we don't get this one, I gave the hare plenty of room in front, fired and the hare somersaulted 4 or 5 times, shot right through the head, my Westley Ritchards, had a very good pattern, I had no trouble killing game at 60 and 70 yards, and once shot a pigeon at 110 yards, no doubt a fluke, but the evidence was there—Dick was delighted.

Now I talked to Dick several times on the phone, always to Whites. Lambing time in March came along and Dad had made no move to buy Skirwith Hall, but he had told Cathy one morning in February 1968 that she had to move out of Kirkland House as he was going to marry Mrs Page, Cathy was devastated, she came immediately to see Monique crying her eyes out, Monique could not believe what she heard, neither could I when I came into the house later in the morning, father marrying a slut of a woman, the village bike, it was like a nightmare. He had told Cathy she must move out as soon as possible. The day after, Dad told me himself, adding he would like me to be the best man, I could not believe my ears, I told him it was impossible for me to do this, as I loved my mother and treasured her memory too much, myself telling him "you cannot be serious about marrying a common tart of a woman like that", "if you want sex, live with her, but never marry her". His stupid reply was—"I am going to do the right thing", his very words—then he walked away in a huff.

Cathy now got cracking, and not to my liking, but before I knew what she had done, it was too late—because after Dad's news that day, I had never set foot in Kirkland House, at least not for 20 years. Cathy gathered all of Ma's clothes, many items just one-two or three years old, and built a bonfire on the rear lawn outside the house and burnt the lot, including a complete collection of Victorian ladies' clothes belonging to her Ma's mother, our grandmother, also my brother Adam's clothes went into the flames, Cathie gave me my brothers evening tailed suit, and gave Monique ma's Canadian Squirrel coat, she had bought at Marshal and Snelgrove, Monique had it refashioned by Marshals. Bedclothes also went in the fire, including papers, including all my letters when I was at school, written to Ma, some on paper bags, torn up to make toilette paper at Grosvenor College. Ma had kept them all, now all had gone, I was angry at this, photos etc. Later, Monique told me the burning went on for a whole week, I said it was a bad mistake, all or most should have gone to the poor house or Red Cross, I could not believe what Cathie had done. I suppose with the ultimatum Dad had given her, she was not thinking straight, Robert McGeorge was now going to take Cathie to live with him at Netherwood House, at Glencaple, just outside Dumfries, marriage so far was not mentioned. Now Cathie, with the connivance of McGeorge, had two furniture vans arrive at Kirkland, then she started to empty the house of most of the best furniture, porcelain, ornaments, and pictures, cutlery, etc. So far, Dad had not said a word, he had, I should think, somehow let sex go to his head, like an elephant in musk, they lose their head. All of this furniture went to Dumfries, the third lorry to take stuff from Kirkland House was Robert McGeorge's, factory vehicle, more like a 2 or 3 tonner, in this Cathy had put pictures, silver and light furniture, chairs etc, this came to Skirwith Hall, Cathy had asked.

Monique asked if she could store some of the stuff, mostly

pictures and silver, this was stored in my drawing room, which was still bare of anything, for this favour my sister gave us mother's silver, bacon dish, a domed affair, that had been one of ma's wedding presents, she had no right to the dish, but there it was, Monique and I were never offered even a picture or a piece of furniture, not even a knife or fork from 3 wagon loads of household goods and furniture. A few days after this, Cathy left Kirkland and Mrs Page and her sister, an equally nasty woman, moved in, and within three months, they were married, the best man was my old friend from Glasson's breweries—now retired—Leonard Bendelow. Dad had bought Mrs Page a large ruby "engagement ring", I should think cost quite a lot, when he would not pay Mother to rent the cottages or as promised, to licence her car, this left a sour taste in my mouth.

I asked Dad if he had approached Tony Holliday with a view to buying Skirwith Hall. I was most surprised at his reply, he said, "I think it far better to have a new landlord, not as many headaches". These were his exact words: this was mid-March, lambing time. I talked it over with Monique, but we did not come to any clearness on the matter, we were invited on Sunday to have lunch with Pat and Archie up in Eskdalemuir, off we went, and as usual, in preparation, on these occasions, 3 bottles or more of the liquid gold were sunk. Now, Archie had had a hard time after his father had died to get his spendthrift and man-made mother together with his simple brother out of the farm.

He and Pat had got together and borrowed as much as possible from the bank. Pat had put quite a lot of her own in to help (she had her own money from the Cashmere factory) and bought Archie's mother and brother out completely, which was just as well because Pat reckoned the rate Archie's mother was spending, the farm would go in the near future, now he owned the place, 5,000 acres of splendid sheep and beef country.

Over our first few whiskys', I told our two friends of my

predicament. Dad, not wanting to buy the place and then his impending marriage to that awful woman, this conversation carried on at the table. The whisky and wine were now opening my brain to see more clearly how things lay. Both Archie and Pat how they had surmounted their problems vis a vis the Nethercassock property, their advice was to buy the estate myself and borrow as much as I could, for Skirwith Hall was well worth borrowing for, this conversation that day made my mind up for me. After the meal, round the fire and on the second bottle of grouse and my second Bolivar, things started to look much better. We stayed for dinner, finished the third bottle of grouse, and left Nethercassock at 11 pm with another Bolivar firmly clenched in my teeth and with a firm mind.

Later in the same week, on Friday 15th March, I decided to go and see Tony Holliday in his office at Kendal, just to feel the way, so to speak, Tony liked his wine, and so we talked quite a lot about our travels in France, he himself loved to motor through France, so we had a lot in common, and only 10 yards away from his office was Kendal wine merchant, Mr Yuill, who was an extremely nice man, so Tony and I adjourned to the office of Mr Yuill and sampled a few wines, myself buying two cases of Bordeaux, I mentioned the sale of Skirwith Hall only slightly, Tony said nothing had got going because of the foot and mouth disease still going strong, I left Kendal and went home, thinking.

Lambing time had started, so I was kept very busy in the lambing field, starting at 5 am in darkness, but surveyed the ewes with the Land Rover lights and torch, the ewes never stirred as the Land Rover went in and out amongst them, any ewe having difficulty lambing were easily caught with the help of the headlights.

But I realised time might be running out with regards to buying the farm if it became common knowledge in the area, someone somewhere would get in first, so after my first meeting with Tony H, I phoned him on Monday 18th March and told him I would like to see him on the morrow at noon he said it was his lunch break, I told him I could not make another hour, as I was overhead with lambing, okay he replied. I did not tell Father a thing, only Monique knew of my absence, on the morrow, Tuesday 19th, came 11:30 am—I had taken the M.G.B. to the lambing field—I left Harold in charge of the ewes, jumped into the car and hared off to Kendal, foot hard down I was in front of Tony's office in no time, up I went, now I did not beat about the bush, put my cards on the table, telling Tony the whole sorry past of Dad's intended marriage to this awful woman, and his unwillingness to buy Skirwith Hall.

Tony thought for a moment, then said, why don't you buy the estate? I will accept a bid from you, I thanked him, asked him to give me an idea of what sum Dick Ie Fleming was thinking about for the estate, but it turned out it was Dick's two sisters who now had the estate, not Dick, as I had presumed, he then gave me a rough figure of what was expected, I thanked him again and left, back to the lambing field, no lunch, I was not hungry anyway, I was too busy turning things over in my head, where to borrow the money from, myself I could only put a paltry 3 or 4 thousand pounds, I thought perhaps my friend Joe Lisle of the 69 clubs Joe was, in my opinion, a gentleman, perhaps in others eyes he was not, but to me he was, I'm sure Joe would have loaned me what I wanted—that was one train of thought—but I never did ask Joe.

I phoned Tony at the end of the week, I thought first to get a deal, then hunt the money up. Tony noted my bid and said he would get in touch with the Ie Flemings, I was in two minds about dealing direct with Dick, but on the other hand, I realised it would not have been correct, Tony had listened to me and had offered the estate to me and so I awaited the result of my bid. Two days later Tony phoned and told me my bid had been re- jected, they wanted more, I was taken aback because this was the sum I was led to believe would be accepted, I thought quickly, as Tony held on the line, I again thought if it becomes known, the estate is on the market, that is me out of it, Tony had hinted if he was offered the right sum on the street, he would sell to anyone—I quickly put in a higher bid and told Tony it was my final offer. This was the end of the week.

Tony phoned me back and told me my bid had been accepted, I thanked him and told him I would be in touch later on through my solicitor. Now I was—or nearly was—the master of Skirwith Hall and Kirkland Hall and, with grazing on the fells of nearly 4000 acres. Now I had to think—I did not approach our family solicitor, Amison and Co. I had had a small dispute with them, and so I thought the less they knew, the better, I went to see Quintin Little, whose family had looked after the Earl of Lonsdale's business for years, I had often had a glass of whisky with Quintin in the George Hotel, so I chose him, once inside Quintin's office, out came his pipe, he leaned back in his chair, listening and puffing away, right, he said, first I will prepare the papers, then we must sign and tie the sale up so that the other side cannot change their minds, I agreed, what I am going to do is not ethical, but we must do it, he said, the quicker the better. He congratulated me on such a good deal, then asked how much money I had ready I told him the truth, very little, never mind, he said, leave things with me, I'll see all goes well, then I left, before doing so, he said you had best tell your father. I agreed.

That must have been a lucky day, for I had a bet at Liverpool on a horse called Golden Duck and won 81 pounds. The morning after, I told Dad that I had bought Skirwith Hall, I told him the story so far, he asked the price I had given, I told him- strange to say—Dad never once congratulated me on my purchase. He said I had given far too much for it. I reminded him of once before, he had the chance to buy Skirwith Hall when I was in Oran with Monique, and he had his brother-in-law Alex Bayne had bid 13,000 pounds and the le Flemings closed the door, he did not reply, I asked him if he would help me out with a loan, he said he would have to think it over.

The next day, I asked Dad once again if he would help me with a loan. He said he would, I thanked him and asked if he could give me a cheque as soon as possible, as Quintin was pushing things fast. This father did, he gave me the cheque in Barclay's Bank Penrith in front of the manager, Stanley Blamire, the latter said he would put it on deposit for me at his bank, but I told him no, it was going on deposit at another bank, Blamire was taken aback, I had once liked Blamire as an under manager, but as manager, I had taken a dislike to him.

Dad's cheque went into an account I had just opened in the Clydesdale Bank, Carlisle, explaining to the bank manager there, he gave me the best interest he could, I thought the least the bankers at Penrith knew the better. I had not breathed a word to a soul, only Dad and Quintin and, of course, Monique. Time was passing on, it seemed to be going too quickly, I had been to see Quintin a few times. He had the papers prepared, so now I was a step nearer, he told me the other side could not now give back the word, however, I still told no one I wanted to make sure and that would be when a deposit was paid.

I signed the contract of conveyance on 25.6.68. Now, the estate was truly mine, two farms, plus houses and two farm cottages. That Saturday night, Monique and I took Robert Jackson and Bert Johnstone from Skirwirth Abbey to dinner at the Kings Arms, Temple Sowerby and told them the news, Robert was not very enthusiastic. The Kings Arms was then rented and run by a young couple, Peter and Brenda, they provided an excellent table, Brenda herself saw to the cooking. The dining room was small, only 8 or 9 tables. Monique and I dined there two or three times a month, this night of celebration, I forget the main course, but we had two bottles of champers, 3 bottles of Nuit St George and three helpings of strawberries and cream, an excellent dinner, our youngest son, Joey Jnr was also present.

On Monday, 1st July, I was clipping (or shearing) the hoggets and some Swaledale ewes, together with the men, on one of the great lofts. When we had finished for the day at 6 pm, I told the men the news that I was the new owner of Skirwith Hall and would like them to join me that evening for drinks at the Sun Inn, the local pub, to my astonishment, they did not want to do so, they became surly, I turned on my heel and left them. Kurt, for some reason, was not there that day, otherwise, he would have been the only one to accept. Five men I had worked side by side with as one of them, now they had turned jealous and surly.

The A.M.C. asked Mr Fleming Smith of Smiths Gore, land agents, to evaluate the estate for the loan, I knew Fleming Smith from the shooting days when Michael Ie Fleming had his guests at Skirwith Hall, Fleming Smith was one of them, I went round the farm with him and his son An- thony who was with him, he asked me how much I had given, and I told him, he immediately offered me 25,000 pounds profit, so much for father saying I had bid far too high, and also a good thing I had moved fast with the advice of Archie and Pat, plus eventually Quintin, I paid the first deposit for the estate on 12th August.

Now Quintin told me there might be a problem with the loan from the A.M.C., as he had asked for and had gone through the profits etc., of Dad's farming for the last 2 or 3 years, it turned out the profits of 2,000 pounds per annum which Dad had been making would only just cover the premiums for the loan, this was the first time I got to know what profits if any were made at Skirwith Hall, at my age now of 41 years, I still had never been confided in by my father, it was indeed a surprise, and not a good one. It was now Quintin who asked me if I would rather farm Skirwith Hall estate on my own and not in partnership with my father. I replied I certainly would, but Father was still the tenant, and as such, he could not be removed, he could, of course, give up the tenancy voluntarily, I told Quintin I could not talk to Father, he was too difficult, he said, ask him to come and see me. I passed the message to Dad that Quintin would like a word with him. Later that week, Dad went to see Quintin, and then I had word from Quintin to go and see him, which I did. Quintin went on to tell me that he had never dealt with a man like Father, he was completely stubborn, he could make nothing out of him at all, and that he, Quintin, was sorry he could not help more, so here I was the owner, and my father tenant. I offered Dad 2,000 pounds a year for a number of years for him to give up the tenancy and let me farm on my own, but he refused.

Uncle Bob, whom I went racing with a lot before my marriage, told me after I had put him in the story, hold a group, the Scottish term for farm sale of stock and implements. He told me to force it on Father, but I was reluctant to do. Dad might be a difficult one to deal with, but he had been a good father to me, and we—besides the farming deal—were good friends, so for the moment, I did nothing.

Before things went further, I went to see Tony Holliday, I had just remembered the sporting rights over Skirwirth and Kirkland Falls and wanted it. There was plenty of grouse there to shoot. Tony, on hearing I wanted the sporting rights, he said there was nothing up there to shoot, no, I said, not much really, one or two grouse only—he immediately included this side of the deal in with the rest. Now, I was the proud owner of a grouse moor. After this little deal, we went down to Mr Yuill's and spent 2 hours wine tasting, I bought two cases of Beaujolais.

The very same day I was getting the grouse moor from Tony, Dad was married to Mrs Page, by special licence at Mansion House, Penrith, with my old friend Len Bendelow, formerly of the local brewery, and Mrs Page's sister, a Miss Richards as witnesses, only 9 months after Mothers death, I remarked in my diary "We were all very sad and shocked at this event. Father had been busy keeping company with Mrs Page, and after Cathy moved out of Kirkland, Mrs Page and her sister moved in permanently. The atmosphere and that feeling of intimacy in the family had now disappeared, my father was almost a stranger to me; he was there, but he was not the man or father I had known. To mark a point, young Adam aged now twelve, went to Kirkland on his bike to try to find his and his Grandmother's cat they both shared, this was just after Cathy left, and he was looking around the garden for the cat when an upstairs window opened and there was Mrs Page, she shouted at him to get out or she would throw a bucket of water at him, he retaliated by telling her to "Shut up you old bag". This is to show what a common fish wife of a woman she was, my father's grandson, being ordered out of his own grounds.

Dad came to see me over this matter the day after, asking me to send Adam to Kirkland to see Mrs Page and apologise to her, I asked, for I did not know why or what Adam had said or done when Dad told me, I burst into laughter and said "good for him", Dad turned and walked away, now more than ever I realised what a void had been created by Mothers death. We were now a family divided.

Eventually, the A.M.C. gave me the loan, Quintin had advised me to have it converted into a life policy, this went through the N.F.U. Insurance Co. payment is made monthly. A few weeks later, I read in the local Cumberland and West Herald that Skirwith Hall estates had been bought jointly by Mr G.L. Slack and his son. I was rather surprised to read this, but Dad's new wife was making sure I did not have the accolade I deserved, I did not bother speaking to Dad about this; I let it pass. Later on, we both signed a partnership contract on the farm profits, 50% each.

It had been a busy year for me, with the buying of the estate, many times haring off to Kendal at midday so that Dad would not know what was going on, nothing to eat, but straight back to work at 1 pm, to be there when the rest of the men started work, etc.

Kurt and I cut a few good Scots pine trees down in Black Wood. I never liked cutting a tree down, I found it rather sad. I liked to see trees standing, a good tree is a nice thing to look at, but these were for fencing posts and—boards for new yard

Box doors, a necessity. Dad had neglected the post and wire fencing on the farm, and some box doors in the courtyard was completely rotten, mending and making do until now, the broken pieces had to be mended this year, and the next, I put up about 2000 yards of new wire fences, the old too rotten to turn any stock at all.

January 15th, there was a tremendous gale, it blew quite a few trees down and tin sections blown off the big Dutch barn slates off the house and buildings, the gale also blew down the Radar tower on Dun Fell—next to Cross Fell—gusts up to 134 m.p.h.—a record.

On 16.1.68, I took one of Lassie's pups to Craig Robinson, a specialist vet in Carlisle, the wee thing had a lump in its tummy, Craig was going to operate on it.

I phoned the next day, the operation was a success, the lump removed, all was well. It was a lovely pup, I was pleased, however, Craig phoned me on the 18th, the puppy had died that morning, I thought, what a pity, it had such a sweet, kind little face, in fact, Arthur Sowerby who had shot with me at Skirwith Hall a week earlier, had liked this puppy, over the other ones.

The day after all of this, I felt as if I had flu coming on, It always started with a sore throat, and this day, I had a catch and roughness in that region. Thursday, I took to my bed with a heavy dose of flu, two days later, I was worse, much worse, Monique phoned our doctor, now Donald Ain- scow from Temple Sowerby, Donald came and gave me a jab of penicillin, I told him this drug was no good for me after I had had massive doses of the stuff when I was about 17 or 18 years old with a severe sep- tic throat, I blamed this on Dad making me the clip and pull the wool of stinking carcasses of dead sheep, so that he could sell it, I with big doses of penicillin each day by the district nurse, got penicillin poisoning, now the drug had no effect on me, Donald did not believe what I told him, day after day I got worse and reached temperatures of 102.5, Donald was going to send me to hospital when I again told him not to give me penicillin—only then did the silly fool change the drug. He changed it, I think, for Terramycin or similar and within 24 hours, the fever had stopped, my temperature was dropping, I was, after ten days, on the mend. This had been the worst flu I had ever had, later on I was to have a similar bout in Germany, I was very shaky when I did get out of bed, I did not smoke a cigar for a full two months, I never felt like doing so.

Monique and I were invited to Kelso races by Sandy Taylor in this lovely Scots town of Kelso, in the hotel, Ednam House, a gathering place before the races of trainers and owners and punters. The racecourse lay only a mile away, a good days racing was had, I lost 2 pounds, then Sandy had a surprise for us, we were with him, invited to a cocktail party in the evening at the Campbell Walters large house, now a daughter of the house was Fiona who appeared regularly on the glossy magazines of the world as a model, and had then married Henri von Thyssen, the Swiss Steel magnate. Monique and I were introduced to the Campbell Walters—drinks and titbits were served nonstop by orderlies, from I took it, the local army regiment in their army evening orderlies dress, all was extremely laid on, Mr Campbell-Walters, I use Mr because I did not know his military title, was I thought by his facial features, a very kind man, Monique and I enjoyed the evening very much, we arrived home in the early hours, quite contented.

The next week, my little dachshund bitch, Juno came in season. I thought it might be a good idea to get her mated, so Monique and I took her to Dinwoodie Lodge Hotel, near Lockerbie, where the owner, Tom Mair, had a lovely dog called Fritz. This day, Juno would not stand for Fritz, no matter what, I held her, Tom helped Fritz until, nearly ill with laughter, Fritz was almost exhausted from trying, we had to give up, Juno just did not want Fritz for a husband.

Monique had an accident in the M.G.B. coming from Culgaith to Skirwirth. She had met a large lorry on this very narrow road, banked in at both sides, the lorry belonging to Frank Bird of Langwathby was driven by one of his men who had been collecting poultry from various poultry keepers in the area, these were for killing. Monique was completely on her own side, the high bank making it impossible to move further over. She had stopped, but the lorry came on, she had ducked down in the car to avoid the lorry deck side, hitting her head, but she struck the gear lever with her mouth, knocking one of her front teeth out. The lorry stopped when the M.G. was halfway along its side, the driver got out, but Monique was unable to get out of either side, but he came to the bank side window, Monique opened it and smelled and saw that he was drunk, then he went and drove off. Monique got part of the number and then she left the M.G.—mudguard was catching on the front offside wheel—and walked a mile to Mrs Metcalfe, who took her in, as she was bleeding and with facial bruises, Mrs Metcalfe then came running to Skirwith Hall to find me. I took the Land Rover and quickly drove Mrs Metcalfe Back to her house, there I found Monique in quite a state, shocked. She told me all that had happened, I asked if she could drive the Land Rover home and if I could get the M.G. going, she assured me she could, so off we set for the scene of the accident. I managed to get the mudguard off the wheel, there was quite a bit of damage, but the car would repair quickly enough, Monique then drove the Land Rover back home. I then took her straight away to her dentist in Carlisle, William Bousfield, William took her immediately, examined her tooth, and found it had snapped off at gum level, he gave her an injection, then with a needle-like thing, with a threader end, he inserted this needle up the hollow of the tooth, twisted it round and round, then pulled it out, and there twisted round the threaded end, was the nerve of the tooth. I had never seen this done and thought it quite clever. William cleaned the tooth stump in the gum and fitted Monique with a temporary crown until he had acquired a perfect porcelain one, now at least Monique could smile without embarrassment, it had been a hard day for her. When we returned home, I phoned my friend Harold Fell, the policeman at Langwathby, and told him about the accident and the part of the number plate Monique had Remembered, he said he would look into it and come and see Monique the next day. The next day, I decided to do some detective work on my own, I went to Melmerby to the pub there, the Shepherds Inn, run by my friend Wally Siddle, and asked Wally if any lorry drivers had been on the beer the day before, he told me yes, Frank Birds man had been pretty well oiled when he left the pub, I then went to the next village Ousby, the village leading to Skirwirth, I asked Mrs Curragh of the Fox Inn the same question I had asked Wally, she told me the same story, Frank Bird's man had had a fair load on board when he left, I asked the times, and they corresponded more or less to the time the lorry would travel to the scene of the accident. I told this to Harold Fell and in the meantime, Frank Bird had delayed by a night and half a day in declaring that one of his drivers had been involved in an accident. Harold came and told me not to worry, they would nail the driver—in time, sure enough, three weeks later, they and other police—Harold had passed the word—the driver was caught drunk in charge.

The end of April came, lamb tailing time and marking them with the farm mark in hot tar, at the same time as cutting their tails off. The lambs were castrated with the pincer type of castrators. We cut the tails off because, for one thing, it kept the lambs clean, and for another, Dad always reckoned when cut, the lambs would bleed, sometimes quite a lot—it did them good, saved them from getting pulpy kidney disease at this crucial stage, and after a good bleed, the lambs would thrive fast. At lambing time, the carrion crows, with eyes like eagles, would watch for these signs, which they knew well. They were clever, cunning devils, they would swoop down and quickly peck the newborn lamb's eyes out, quick work with their powerful hard beaks, then peck their way through the ewe's vagina, into her insides, then if she was unable to get up and peck her eye out for good measure, the eye facing upwards, as she would be lying with the other to the ground, these were diabolical birds, Dad and I used to every year, at their nesting and breeding time, shoot the adults from their nests, putting a few shots into the bottom of these isolated nests to break the eggs or kill the youngsters inside. Carrion crows build their nests in solitary trees at a great height, making it impossible to climb and destroy them by hand. This year, I decided to poison these crows, I had heard from Lord Lonsdale's keeper, Walter Drysdale, that phosdrin was a great thing to use; put one drop in a hen egg as bait, and that was it, well, I had plenty of eggs—still—I bought the phosdrin which was also good to do away with moles. I collected, for starters 2 dozen eggs, filled a small 5cc syringe and, injected one or two drops in each egg, then emptied the syringe back into the main bottle. Off I set in the Land Rover, placing the eggs here and there while making a note of the particular poison drops. The next day, I went along to see if any of the eggs had been eaten by the carrions, sure enough, I found 15 dead crows, some lying beside the remains of a poisoned egg, some 20 yards away. This phosdrin seemed to be very quick working, for the crows to die more or less on the spot and I also found two dead rats and a dead hedgehog. That same morning, one of the tractor drivers had reported to me of a crow flying in front of him, 20 yards up, when all of a sudden, it fell out of the air, stone dead. I estimated this last placement of poisoned eggs must have killed 25 to 30 crows because some must have died in very rough cover, where I was unable to spot them. I had another poisoning day or two later on, just before the young wild duck and pheasant were hatching. The carrion could play havoc with game birds.

The month of May saw the de-horning of many of the calves and the biggest to be castrated. Dad and I used to castrate the calves with hot irons and then run green salve into the empty ball sacks, but that was very hard work. First, it entailed putting 7 or 8 young bulls of 6 to 9 months old into a loose box, 4 or 5 men going in, catching one of them with a halter thrown around its head, dragging the bellowing and kicking animal outside, throwing it onto its side, tying its four feet and legs, each side to each side front to back. At this age, these youngsters were tough and very strong, if they had Angus or Galloway blood in them, they were demons, first trying to climb the loose box walls to get away, when they realised this was impossible, they would often bellow with rage and fright, then charge the catching men. One had to be sharp on one's feet, I have had, along with the men, my trouser legs ripped from top to bottom with flying and kicking hoofs. When the beast was on its side and its legs tied, the hot castrating irons would be taken out of the brazier, the testicle sack held tight, the hot iron would then be drawn across the skin on one testicle, the first pass, cutting the outer skin down to the testicle skin, then one more pass and the testicle would spring out, the same procedure for the second testicle. When both testicles were exposed, a quarter moon-shaped clamp would be put on the two testicle cords, making sure surplus membranes were not clamped down—another iron would then be used to burn through the testicle cords at the clamp, this done, green salve would be held on a widish flat stick, and run onto the severed testicle ends, hence the quarter moon dish shaped clamps, so that the salve would not run over the sides and be wasted, the clamps then gently, slowly, opened, if bleeding started then searing with the hot iron was needed, small amounts of salve being run into the open testicle sacks. I have castrated many by this method, but now we had a lot to do at once, so Dad had the vets in, by their method, two or three minutes to castrate one beast was quickly done. Now Kurt had built a cattle crush that fixed the beast by its neck, these were done standing, I watched the vet's method and thought, I can easily do this. I bought a pair of veterinary testicle clamps and, from 1968, castrated all myself and never lost a calf, one-eyed Willie used to ask me for all the young bulls' testicles, I used to castrate them at 6—8 months old, and the older calves had good sized testicles. One-eyed Willie swore by them as an aid to higher sex delights, he loved them. I had never tried eating them myself, but I thought they must be good if one-eyed Willie liked them so much, I asked him how he cooked them, he told me, so the next batch of calves I castrated, I kept 6 or 8 good sized testicles and gave Willie the rest, 50 or 60 of them, I prepared them myself in Willie's way on the Aga, sat down and slowly tried them, they were delicious, after that any castrating, Willie got a few, myself 80% of them. Monique refused to try them, but our two boys followed in their father's footsteps and came to love them.

July 3rd was the start of the three-day race meeting at Carlisle, these usually were three good and hectic days of betting, a vast amount of drinking and dining at night. Monique and I set off early, as we intended to dine at the race course, where some of the waiters were from the County Hotel, so it was very homely for us. This first day, a Wednesday, we entered the dining room, the same time as my favourite Newcastle bookie, Willie Whiteman, he asked if he could join us, I said, of course Willie, so the three of us took a table, wine was ordered, we all had soup, this was followed by large portions of cold salmon, here I saw how fas- tidious Willie was, he scaled off every single little piece of brown fila- ments and a small soft bone, until he had a small pile of the stuff on the side of his plate, I agreed with him to take the brown flesh off as this can spoil the taste of the pink flesh, Monique and I looked on in amuse- ments, then came the strawberries and cream, the waiters from the County knew I loved strawberries, a wink here and they served us all a double helping, Willie paid for the wine, thanked us for our company, and left to see his clerk, Monique and I dwelt a while, then we left to make way for other people wishing to dine, I knew 90% of the diners there, the dining room was on these days, a happy and busy place, a good atmosphere, I spoke to Leo the head waiter to make sure to keep a good lot of strawberries for Monique and

I for tomorrow and half way through today they had run out of them. The day passed well, but the weather was bad, very wet and very cold, the bars did a roaring trade, betting wise, I was about level when the last race was run. This was when the serious drinking started. Owners and trainers, friends etc. filled the owners and trainers' little bar, swapping their various horse and betting stories of the day, then I asked Robert Jackson and two other friends if they would join Monique and I for dinner at the County Hotel, they accepted. Into the County we went, Mr and Mrs Atkinson, manager and manageress, knew us well and joined us for drinks and more drinks before dinner. Monique and I went through to the great kitchens to see what our friend the chef Mr Cioli—I never knew his first name, it was always Chef—had on special for us that night, he himself was a great punter, studying form avidly in his little office in the corner of his kitchen, we had met at the races in the afternoon, he had some freshly caught salmon, from the Solway, but we had had salmon for lunch, however, the chef's salmon looked so good, we both decided to have it again, as did the others, but they had not dined midday at the racecourse as Monique and I had, at the end of the meal, surprises of surprises, Robert Jackson paid for the whole meal, a thing he never did before and never did since, we all thanked him kindly. The middle day of racing, Thursday, was the day of the one and a half miles Cumberland Plate, the big race of the three days meets, the weather was a little better. Monique and I dined by ourselves at the racecourse, Leo had done his job well, he had double strawberries put by for Monique and I, which I appreciated.

Friday, July 5th, the final day of the meeting, turned out weather-wise to be quite nice, this day was the running of the Carlisle Bell, supposed to be one of the oldest races in the racing calendar, worth 500 pounds. Willie Nevett, the champion Northern Jockey, rode a race finish this meeting, one of the best and fiercest, one of absolute artistry I had or have ever seen, it was good to see. He was a swarthy little chap as if he had some black blood in him. Also, Edgar Britt, the Australian, was there and an exceptional rider. One of our workers had been drinking in a pub near Carlisle and got into conversation with a man who claimed to be the man who put money on for Britt himself, telling our chap, Joe Wilson, the name of a horse that would win on the morrow Britts mount, Joe told me before I left for the races, it won.

The Bell was won by Red Swan, trained by Tommy Robson, and owned by Phil Hogg, a chiropractor from Newcastle I had a tenner on @ 3/1. Cyril Parker, Bridget's father, had not had a good" day. As usual, he had a pile on the least favourite, and again saved the day for him, calling this his getting out stakes. He always drove home after the races.

The various personalities at Carlisle during the three days were Phil Bull, the founder of Timeform, with his red beard and trilby, and always with a good-sized Havana. He and I were the only people to habitually smoke large cigars, I never spoke to Phil, but over the years, we met at many race meetings, and each would nod to the other in a silent greeting, a silent one each recognising in the other, a lover of good cigars. On race days, I would light up before I would set off and chain smoke cigars the day through, perhaps getting through 6 Havana's during the afternoon and evening, each lasting 1½ hours. Burma Cheroots the Scots No. 1, perhaps 4 to 5, they lasted rather longer, and I was not a fast smoker, as some would smoke a similar sized cigar inside 1 hour. Teddy Lampton and his wife were there. I have introduced to them five years ago. Teddy was a charming man and liked his drink and his wife, also I found most charming. They used to come up in their Rolls Royce, a nice car but an awful vulgar colour of violet.

Sam Hall the trainer, big bluff Sam, kindness itself, was a very clever trainer indeed, we became good friends, Jack Ormston, a trainer from near Scotch Comer, was a good friend of Monique's and I, Jack was an ex speedway driver, a gentleman, always dressed impeccably, an expert in getting a horse fit for a certain race. He once raced Monique and I for about 20 miles on the Ayr road. We were all going to the races, there I was driving the M.G.B. Jack had some high-powered car, we were really putting the foot down, but I found at high speed, the M.G.B. would not corner, but roll over the road, I had to give up and slow down at Ayr, Jack pulled my leg in front of Monique saying I could not drive a barrow, he asked what the matter was, I told him I could not corner, he asked what tyres were on the car, I told him Dunlop Cross-ply, he advised me to change to some Radial Pirrelli which I did that same week and what a difference, now the M.G.B. would corner on a sixpence at 80 or 90 m.p.h. I never had X-ply on any of my cars again.

August 21st, Richard Burton invited me to shoot grouse over on the Alston side of Cross Fell, his grouse moor adjoined Skirwirth Fell, the shooting rights of which I now had in perpetuity. Burton had Bracken- bank shooting lodge at Lazonby, he had acquired the sporting rights over a few moors. Ousby fell adjoining me being one. I had told him I would possibly shoot my own moor on the 12th, but I did not for some reason. Now, here I had my first invitation from him. I knew him well, a big bluff man. One had to watch him where the shooting was concerned, he would ask a farmer if he could shoot pigeons off either corn or turnips with a party of 4 or 5 guns, then proceed to shoot the whole farm and, when apprehended, apologise, saying he had misunderstood the particular field, a nice man though. On this shooting day, we mostly walked up, six other guns, the birds were scarce, we shot 14 braces, it was very windy too. Lassie worked very well, better than "the Brackenbank dogs, I noticed a large portion of my moor was being shot over and some new shooting buttes had been erected and realised that Mr Burton must have shot over Skirwirth fell or moor for many years before, myself I had not been shep- herding these fells since 1952, Burton must have shot this land free gratis all that time. Now it was time to stop all of that, Burton was not in the shooting party this day, we the guns were in the care of his keeper, I said nothing about a few new butts on my moor or that it had been shot over I would see to this at a later date, which I did I took Kurt with me and dismantled 6 new butts, putting a few large posts with a note nailed to them covered in plastic, saying 'No shooting beyond this point". Going by my map and what marker stones there were, I remember the ground from my young shepherding days. After a while, I had my friend Richard Burton on the phone uttering threatening noises about destroying his butts and declaring that I did not know the boundaries, I phoned Tony Holliday, who came up with his theodolite, just he and myself, and Tony declared I was, according to the maps, within my rights.

I told Burton this, but he would not agree to Tony's declaration and went to his solicitor, who was also mine, Quintin Little, he advised us to have another go at finding the exact boundary stones now some of this land was very peaty and some stones over the countless years, sunk out of sight, we could find odd ones, then draw a line, but it turned out, it was not as simple as that. The second effort to find the boundary's Burton himself was there with his surveyor, I with Tony Halliday, Burton pointed out to us an enormous boulder named the gray mere stone as one of the boundary points which was obliterated on my map by a sticker, once we had established this fact, Tony realised where we had gone wrong. Burton made growling noises, but I put my hand to him and apologized, he accepted with good grace for he at heart was a good man, but I had to point out he had 4 butts on my moor that had to remain demolished, this was agreed, and we both left the fells in a friendly mind. He invited Monique and I to dinner at Brackenbank later on and he was the perfect host, dining in the old and elegant style of yesteryear, together with 6 or 7 other guests staying at his lodge. The measures of whiskies being double-doubles, one glass was never left empty, he himself was captivated by Monique—the evening and food was a memorable one.

My little Dachsund Juno, had two months ago, jumped out of the Land Rover window when the vehicle was doing about 15 m.p.h. She rolled over and over, but she seemed to have hurt herself, then becoming all right, though she was quieter than normal, I kept an eye on her and within three days, she was very stiff walking on her hind legs. At the end of a week she could not use her back legs at all, dragging herself along by her front ones. I took her up to the Royal Dick Hospital for Animals in Glasgow, Robert Jackson also wanted to go there for something, so he said bring Juno, we will go in my car, which was good of him I wondered if they could operate on her, they said no, but would give her treatment. I left her for about 3 weeks, then brought her back home, she was not much better walking a yard or two, then her back end would collapse, I kept massaging her and moving her about. She herself would try hard to walk also. I would take her around the farm in the Land Rover, she liked this very much and looked forward to the ride.

This was in September, but she finally lost her heart and passed away on November 16th, she was only four years old, she had been grand company for me and I used to take her to Sedgefield races. She was quite popular there with the bar staff, and Juno loved being there because she was given parts of leftover pies and other goodies.

The September rains came and flooded the back for a week, so out came the fishing rod. The first day I got 40 but put 20 back again, as they were too small, it was a wonderful little beck, the Briggle, full of trout and full of wild duck and waterhens, of which I used to take quite a lot of eggs from their nests, in late spring, knowing that they would quickly lay another batch. These eggs were almost equal to plover eggs in texture and flavour.

I fished for another three days, as the water was just right, landing a total for these three days of 123 and putting 45 back in the back for another day.

Then, I thought it was a good idea to take a break, the year had been a very busy one indeed. I said to Monique on Tuesday, October 1st, pack the bags, we are off to see Heinz, and off we set on Thursday 3rd. The boys were back at school, we had now sent young Joey to Lime House School Dalston Carlisle for his first term, Adam would keep him company, he looked forward to this event Mrs Dickinson, the teacher at Skirwirth, said she would miss him a lot, everyone took to Joey right away.

Monique had a phone call from my cousin Barbara, telling us that her father, Uncle Bob, had died, he had been my favourite Uncle, he had introduced me to many racing personalities over the years, we had had a lot of fun together, hunted the fox with the Dumfriesshire hounds, and drunk a great deal of whisky together. He was only a young man in his 50s. He had, when a boy, a slight asthmatic problem that had eventually disappeared, but in the last two to three years, emphysema had developed until it took him from us. I would miss him at the race meetings, as would many more. Monique and I attended the funeral, where a little service was held in the little house he and Aunt Jean had retired to, Douglencleugh, above Langholm, then to the crematorium at Carlisle. He was the first of the 5 Tinning brothers to die, whereas the 3 Tinning girls, my mother, and her two sisters had all died youngish.

25

Now to our trip to Germany, we set off in the morning at 9 am for Dover in the M.G.B. We duly passed through the centre of Lon- don, it was quite easy and well signed, leaving the Northerly A1 and taking the A2 straight to Dover. We got to Dover and had time to kill as the next ferry boat to Ostende was not leaving until midnight, so we had a look around the town of Dover, which I thought was rather a miserable and sad place.

I took the autoroute to Brussels, which seemed pretty straightforward, but I missed the bypass to take me to the other side of Brussels and so had to pass through the middle of the capital. There was an enormous amount of road building going on through the city, making it hard going, I think the roadworks were for the construction of many over and under roads, for the future overload of vehicles.

I wished I had taken another route, the hold-ups we were having, I decided to take the first sign taking me out East, which turned out to be Leuven, what a relief it was once we were out of this construction jungle. Once at Leuven, I headed for Venlo, and, after that, took the road for Wesel. After this, it was straightforward for Munster.

At Munster—once there, I knew my way well, but during the last hour of driving, I noticed the water temperature gauge creeping up until it was almost touching the red danger mark, I pulled onto a wide verge and unscrewed the water filler cap, bit by bit for the radiator was beginning to steam, sure enough, the car was short of water, there were three or four houses nearby, so I drove to the first, knocked on the door, explaining my predicament to the woman who answered, she smiled and soon gave me a bucket with about 2 gallons of water, putting the bonnet up this time I noticed there was water on the engine side, I thought probably a cracked hose pipe somewhere telling myself the next day or so I would take the M.G. to a garage in Telgte, however, I filled the radiator, returned the bucket to the house, thanked the woman and drove on.

We arrived at Heinz's at 11 am, rather tired with little sleep in the night, we were greeted warmly, and immediately Heinz got a few bottles of beer on the table of Dortmunder Kronen. Monique and I loved the German beer, especially the beer made in the Rhur region, i.e. Dortmunder, then Maria started to prepare the Mittag Essen of her homemade soup, and then chicken, and to finish a sweet I always liked, the German name escapes me, but it was like thick creamy yogurt or like white custard, similar but much better with cinnamon sprinkled over it. Heinz's table at lunch never had wine on it, only if it was a birthday, wedding or communion etc, but always plenty of beer, the brewery lorry used to call at his house once a fortnight to drop off four crates needed at a very low cost I thought it was a great idea.

In the evening, we paid a visit to our good friend Emile, who's smile nearly split his face, he sat round the table with us, having a good old chinwag, insisting we had numerous Schnapps on the house as chasers with the beer, then as usual, off he went, sat down at the piano and played for me the tales of Hoffman.

In the morning, we, Maria also her sister looking after the children, motored down, not to the Moselle, but to the wine festival at Boppard. This was a great day and night of fun and dancing, and the wine was excellent, Heinz knowing the German wines ordered the best, with Father Rhine as Germans call their river, flowing by with numerous barges slowly heading for their destination, some with a little car on deck, the clothes washing on the line, the world seemed a nice place to be in.

We danced and drank until midnight, only then we left the other revelers, and Heinz driving his shooting brake Opel, we took the Hundsruck strasse over to the Moselle to see our friend and vineyard cum wine maker Herr and Frau Walter Pitch. He was a big friend of Heinz and Maria and had also become a good friend of mine. We arrived about an hour or hour and a half later. Both Walter and his wife were waiting up for us because Heinz had arranged we would all sleep there that night, which we did, all four of us in one bed, but a bed that would safely have slept 8 people, it was the biggest bed I had seen, Frau Pitch telling us her other bedroom at the very top of the house, I suppose the attic was not suitable, Monique was dead against such a thing, as sleeping all together in one bed, she was aghast at the idea, at the end, she condescended as the night was freezing, Heinz and I took the middle, with our wives on each side Monique sleeping with most of her clothes on. One thing about Heinz within one minute of hitting the pillow, he was fast asleep like a baby, I thought of the irony of it Maria would not sleep with him at home, now she had no choice.

Walter lived in a small village on the Moselle called Kloten, his vineyards were on steep, very steep slopes, there everything had to be carried up and down by hand, it must have been hard work for him, they had three sons, only boys at that time, but now when grown up none stayed to help Walter, the work was too hard. The wine Walter produced was of excellent quality, he gained the red seal year after year for quality. After breakfast this day, we were shown around his cellars of thousands of bottles and another cellar where the wine was in the making in great wooden barrels. We were then treated to some tasting of his wine, which lasted all morning, then Heinz bought 300 bottles, I bought 2 cases of 12 each Walter told us of another wine festival not far from Kloten, about 20 or 30 minutes away on the Moselle called Poltersdorf, a small village of which Walter was on the committee there.

e bade farewell to our host and hostess until evening time. We would meet up in the evening of Poltersdorf, we motored slowly on taking in the beautiful scenery; though it had been a very cold night, the day was sunny and warm, we had an excellent simple lunch of Pork Schnitzel at a lovely little restaurant looking over the Moselle river, it was so warm we decided to dine on the terrace, this went down well with a few bottles of this nice mild fruity wine, nicely chilled. One thing the Germans have is a good sized glass to drink wine in, not too large and definitely not too small, 4 glasses to one bottle, not as in England when one orders a glass of wine, it usually 8 glasses to a bottle and 4 or 5 times the price.

The day passed quietly, then came the festival of Poltersdorf, we made sure of good seating by arriving early, which was a wise thing because before we knew it, the great tent where the dancing and drinking was held filled up rapidly. Walter and Frau Pitch joined us, then we danced and sang popular old songs and drank wine until 2 am, Heinz joined the orchestra to play the trumpet, of which he was an expert, he was applauded loudly many times, with this we drank more than enough wine, people sending bottle after bottle to our table, he and I both went home well oiled, back to the 4 to a bed at the Pitch's, I kept two wine glasses from this festival at Poltersdorf and still have them 38 years later.

We all slept soundly, I was not bothered about breakfast the next morning, if I had looked at one egg, I would have been sick. I felt awful. Monique never a great breakfast eater, had a glass of water, the Pitch had no tea, Heinz and Maria were quite fit. I, so Heinz told me, looked awful. Walter said, "Take a glass of Schnapps quickly down in one go." I thought, well, I would try this remedy, though I did not feel like alcohol—just the opposite—Walter handed me a small glass of the fiery stuff. I looked at it and it looked at me. I could see myself holding that glass up even now, I said to the onlookers, "Down the hatch, Prost", and downed it in one gulp, it was hot stuff all right, then my stomach started to revolt against this shocking intrusion and heaved I started to run for the toilette, Frau Pitch shouted her father was sitting in there I was expressly directed to an outside loo, in the backyard. I ran, just reaching it as my stomach had had enough and thrust out the intruding liquid, together with a fair amount of old booze and bile from the night before. I now had a look around my loo, it was an old earth closet and still used by the look of it, the look of it down the hole nearly caused me to vomit again, so I got out in a hurry, thinking a bit backward these Germans down here, like in the house, there was no hot water taps upstairs, only cold to wash in. I suggested after this to Monique to take a walk along the river to see it if would improve me, I was feeling much better, though, by now. We set off and slowly walked hand in hand, Monique preferred this to arm-in-arm, after about a mile, we came to a very nice little pub with an outdoor terrace, we took a table in the sun, and ordered two Pilsner beers, drank half straight away, then lent back to see what medicinal purposes it may bring. The sun shone warmly, I ordered another, and now I was back to normal Heinz came slowly along the road in his Opel, looking for us. We waved him down and he then joined us for a few more beers—he had developed a thirst. By now the time was noon, none of us felt hungry, and Heinz wanted to be on the way, so we returned to the Pitch's and loaded up our wine, once we had the wine loaded, there was little room left, and the car was well down on its springs. We said goodbye to our friends and left. Monique and I have been friends with the pitch ever since, and if we were ever in that part of Germany again, we would always call on them. Walter would always get the bottles out, and we would drink wine and chat for 3-4 hours.

I called one day my cigar friend Sepple Poppenborg to top my supply up at home, bought two thousand at 40 pf each, Sepple gave me a discount of 7.5% and gave me a box of 25 of his best selection, had my hair cut at his brother's shop, where when the job was done, I was taken through to the living room, for Schnapps and beer, all over Telgte people had known me now for so long, had grown to like me, I was invited to their houses and treated like one of the family by many.

Heinz and I started to pack the cigars into the doors of the M.G. all had to come out of the boxes and put in soft cellophane bags, 30 or 35 at the door bottom, coming down to 20 or even 15 to a bag, keeping 175 in boxes for the customs at Dover, plus the wine, I took them out of the cases and laid the bottles behind the two front seats and a few in the boot, not a lot of room in the little car.

I had taken the M.G. to a garage just on the outskirts of Telgte, a friend of Albert Greveler who told us there was no burst pipe anywhere—but a thin trickle of water was coming from a point between the engine block and the head, they said it would perhaps be better for me to have it seen to back in England if I thought the car would travel okay, I thanked them and said I thought the car would travel home all right. There was no charge.

Monique and I noticed Maria was taking notice of a neighbour who lived only 100 yards away. His name was Charlie Tische, ten years older than she. Now, as I have said, Charlie was taking too much notice of Maria and she to him. We would see what would happen in the future.

We set off for home, leaving Dover at 2 am. I drove through the night, stopping 3-4 times for water and getting home at 9 am. The minute Monique was home, in the house, she told me someone had been here and moved various objects about, the office had been disturbed, I noticed Dad's desk drawers were slightly open, all had been emptied, Kurt came along, so I asked him if he had seen anyone about the house. Yes, he had, he told me Dad and Mrs Page had been in regularly, this made me angry. My father could have the run of the place, I did not mind—but that awful woman, who in her liaison with my father, had hastened Mother's death through her knowledge and worry over the affair, that woman, that slut who had the audacity to tell my mother to her face while attending her dead son's grave—"What's the matter with you, you look like death warmed up". Father had keys to one door in the house, the smoke room—cum office I straight away myself took the Yale lockout and replaced it with another. Three or four days later, Dad came to me saying he could not get his keys to turn the lock in the smoke room—I told him that I had changed the lock because he had brought that awful woman into my residence and that I did not like it, I asked why he had emptied his desk, he did not reply. There was on the desk a newspaper sheet of 1815 reporting Wellington's victory at Waterloo, together with fascinating adverts of a household requiring a wet nurse, "who must have a good breast of milk", otherwise I was ignorant of the contents as the desk was locked at all time, I also did not give Father a key to the new lock, and he never asked for one.

Since I had bought the farm a short few months ago, some of the men (workers) whom I had worked side by side with over the years were seemingly jealous of me now, not only the owner, but their boss also, here I had slight conflict with Dad I would give the men their orders for the day at 7 am, starting time, Dad would come along at 9 am or later and put the men into other jobs, the men, not knowing who to obey, usually went to Dad's side I told him either he comes at 7 am and gives orders for the day, for which I would respect or he had to stop giving orders after the men were at their work, under my orders, he obliged and gave me no more trouble.

Now one of the workers, Joe Frith, head tractor man I had known all my life, who had been at Skirwith Hall for 25 years, decided to leave. I was surprised and not surprised, suspecting this might happen, watching their moods since I became the great patron. The next day, I had a visit from one of Robert Jackson's men, George Western, he had heard—it must have been quick—that Frith was leaving, and could he take his place. I hired him on the spot because I had seen him working at Roberts and he seemed to do his work well.

On November 1st, I took Monique to Leeds to have her hair done and to do some shopping, she took her mother's fur coat in Canadian Squirrel that Cathy had given her, just because Josephine did not want it. Monique took it to Marshall and Snelgrove for re-fashioning, we called to see Mrs Morris, the head fashion buyer, she always had some good things put to one side and she did this day, she had an eye for fashion Mrs Morris, she did not ponder, she knew straight away if a thing was a hit or not, this day she had an outfit for Monique—a model—at 150 pounds, she let Monique have it for 35 pounds, this happened almost every time we called to see Mrs Morris, she had taken Monique under her wing so to speak.

November 8th was Joe Frith's last day at Skirwith Hall, any of my workers leaving, I always shook hands and wished them well, but with Frith, I could not bring myself to do this, solely through his attitude toward me, after my purchasing Skirwith Hall, people and many of them, could not understand why it was me the owner and not Dad, but then no one knew my story did they?

November 13th, Arthur Sowerby invited me to shoot at Newbiggin together with seven others. It was a nice day but cold, most of today's birds were driven, they were good high, strong birds. Arthur did quite a bit of walking with the beaters, and at one point, his dog (Labrador) took off too far in front was very reluctant to return to him, having a little hunt on its own, but when it did return to Arthur, I bet it wished it had stayed away, he gave it a beating then proceeded to try and twist the poor things ear off, Arthur was a terror at twisting his dog's ears, until they yelped like mad, I didn't care for this ear twisting, preferring two good hits when necessary with a thin stick, my own gun dogs after they were trained were seldom, if at all hit. However, the day's sport turned out to be quite good, bagging 46 pheasants and 25 ducks, the shooting dinner again held at the Kings Arms, Temple Sowerby, an excellent meal it was.

Monique and I took the children to Silloth for the day, it was where Ma had had her house, they liked Silloth; it was quite a nice place for children, the beach, paddling, and looking for shells, but on the return journey, the M.G. gave up the ghost, I had not had the water problem solved yet, so I phoned through to our local mechanic, Billy Marshall at Langwathby, he came out to see what the matter was and soon spotted the trouble, water from the leak had got worse and run into the distributor causing the car to cut out, Billy fixed it temporarily and we managed to get home. Billy later took the head off the engine and found the root of the matter, it was a thread-like length of metal that had been somehow stuck onto the head when it had been manufactured, placed on the block and gasket, now water had been found its way along this thread, getting slightly bigger over time and causing more water under pressure to leak out. This was what British cars were like in the '60s and '70s, always something wrong with them, Billy soon had it repaired.

I did quite a lot of flying duck during November, bagging 76 for the month. I took Monique with me for a little walk up of game down the farm one day and with Lassie. Monique, like the rest of her family, was allergic to feathers and could not touch birds at all, if she tried, goose pimples would rise, and she would feel sick. This day, she accompanied me, I got 8 pheasants and one hare. Monique did not care for the shooting, but she enjoyed watching Lassie work.

When I was in my teens, I used to say if ever I owned Skirwith Hall, the first thing I would do would be to take the big Middin stand down in the main courtyard. This I have now started on. Dad never said a word, but when I looked again, the space was indeed large, it needed something to cut the emptiness. I knew what, I would construct a fountain right in the middle, pity I had not thought about it before.

My next improvement was to widen and put a cattle grid in at the entrance to the farm from the main road, the present entrance was at such a bad angle for large cattle wagons to turn into coming from the Langwathby side, they had to go into the village and turn there and return. I put the men to work, Kurt with the McConnel digger I had bought for draining, there was a lot of draining to do—to dig the pit, I bought railway lines from the railway people at Carlisle and had them cut to the proper length, the cattle grid was going to be 12ft wide and 6 feet broad, the pit 3ft deep, the other workers took the stone walls down for a few yards. Then I had the sandstone from the Midden walls brought down, all lovely shaped stone and made a half-moon-shaped sweep in the entrance on each side. I took four yards of ground into the field, 4x12 yards approximately and put the original gate the low side of the new cattle grid for stock as usual, now at Skirwith Hall we had an entrance to grace any property, lorry's no matter how big could drive in at top speed, if they wished, every driver afterwards congratulated me on such a good job, the only comment from father was "you have taken up too much land". 12 yards long by 4 deep out of 1000 acres, I myself was most pleased with my men's work and told them so and treated them to a night at the pub.

We were busy sawing timber up for fencing posts, I was cutting quite a number of Scots pine out of Black Wood because I was thinking of selling the whole of this plantation next year. Many trees were dying each year, the acreage would be perhaps 10, the trees were mature, then when sold, I would replant. Now I wanted as many trees as would do most if not all of the fencing project. We had a good 60ft travelling saw bench to cut all our own timber, be it boards or posts, day after day the saw bench was busy, all the work I was now doing should have been done 20 years ago, fences were rotten from Kirkland Hall and most of Skirwith Hall.

Wednesday, I had an invite from Arthur Sowerby to shoot at Skirwith Abbey, Cyril Parker's land. Arthur had the shooting rented from him for the past few years. I started today with a bad cold and a sore throat, and to cap it all, the day was wet and wild, this was the day when Alex Beck, the owner of Edenhall Hotel, also shot with us, Bert Johnstone, now the tenant of the Abbey and farm, Robert Jackson and myself were sitting on our shooting sticks, about 50 yards apart, overlooking a valley watching for the driven birds to arrive, Alex Beck was in between Robert and I, he, as usual, had his hotel black striped trousers, dinner jacket and tie, we often thought he must sleep in his black striped trousers and jacket for no one ever saw him in anything else, he was 5 ft tall and sitting on his shooting stick, his legs barely touched the ground, we had a laugh together at his attire when all of a sudden a hen pheasant came down our line, then it was in front of Alex, we three shouted loud at Alex, "Go on Alex, down it". He blasted off and did something wrong, for both barrels went off at once, blowing him backwards right off his seat legs and gun in mid-air, it was a sight for sore eyes, we laughed our heads off loud and clear and the pheasant lived for another day, it was a hilarious few minutes, when told at dinner at night, more laughter, Alex took it in good part.

Only 40 pheasants were shot, usually at the Abbey, we would get 100 to 110, the rough cover and woods that had been felled in the war, now growing rough rubbishy brush, created good cover for pheasants.

The dinner at night was held at Alex's Hotel at Edenhall, it was an excellent dinner. Alex was a good hotelier, no doubt—as far as a meal went, but his kitchens were far from clean, the menu I jotted down and consisted of Smoked Salmon and Shrimps, Mushroom Soup, Grilled Trout, Kummel Dort, Roast Beef, Plum Pudding and a finisher like Welsh Rarebit, coffee, cigars and liqueurs, red and white wine were served, an excellent finish to the day. The trouble was the next day, my cold was worse and the day was again wild and wet. I stayed in-doors and on Friday, I went to pick the Christmas goose up from another village. It was a very good one weighing 18lbs with its feathers on @ 3/3per lb.

Saturday 21st, I took the gun and Lassie down the farm, had a look at a few fields of cattle, all was well, then started to walk rough ground up. In no time, I had bagged 12 pheasants and five pigeons, it was a fine, clear day, and had been very hard frost in the night. I had put three men to saw fire logs for Father, he was out of them, when finished, these were trucked up to Kirkland by tractor and stacked in his outhouse.

Boxing day, I took Lassie and lit a German cigar before I set off down the farm. I was shooting ducks today, it was an excellent day for them, being very hard frost indeed, down the beck I went slowly, after 200 yards or more, I got two, a right and a left, one winged, the other dead however Lassie soon had the winged one at my feet, on I went, now duck was getting up at regular intervals by the time I was within 200 yards of the Water Quarry I had 15.

They were too heavy to carry, I decided to leave them and collect them later with the Land Rover—I knew the Water Quarry would hold a good number, but I only had two barrels, so I expected to shoot no more than two, I approached quietly then stood up, the little place was filled with duck, easily 60 to 70, I should have flighted them in that morning really, all got up at once, I chose one, or thought I did, and 10 of them fell down. My second barrel got the one I aimed at: 11 ducks with two barrels. Lassie brought me the first—she looked at me with a very satisfied look on her face as if to say, well done, master. I piled these ones up to collect later on and debated whether to continue. I sat down and had another cigar, I thought if the frost stops and thaws, the duck will go, so I continued down towards Beck Mill, getting another 17 ducks. 43 ducks in all! I thought of the plucking of them but remembered there was a chap at Clifton, outside Penrith, Cocky Robinson, who plucked poultry and geese at Christmas time for a fee, I rang him up, he said bring them in, I think the charge was 1/- a duck, and he made a very good clean job, insides were left in. The deep freezer was starting to be very full, especially of game, we ate game about four times a week, and I gave some to friends, which reminds me, Monique had taken two fat ducks to the retired banker of the old Martins Bank, Mr Dick Ritchie. She took them to his house in Penrith, Dick was not in, but Mrs Ritchie was—now Mrs Ritchie was, as was her husband, extremely nice—but she was an alcoholic. Dick had to have a special lock made and fitted to his drinks cupboard. On this day of the ducks, Mrs Ritchie asked Monique into the house, took the ducks and put them in the kitchen, now she said to Monique, we will have drinkies, she only had gin, but couldn't find where she had hidden the bottle, so Dick would not find it. Monique said no, she did not drink gin, but her friend insisted, all the time hunting for the elusive bottle, which she did find, the only glasses were half-pint tumblers, which Mrs Ritchie filled to within half an inch from the top, she asked Monique if she would like anything in it, she said tonic, adding that there was no room for anything to put in, the whole tale was that Monique managed to put some tonic in the glass as she slowly emptied the tumbler, Monique came home very unsteady, the first time she had been so, how she drove home, I don't know, she did well. Dick Ritchie and his wife were among the clique, on Tuesday, market day and Friday's drinking days, these sessions were kept religiously, and lasted from 11 am until 5 pm, then whoever was left went on till midnight, Dick knew of the trouble I had had with father over the tenancy of the farm, etc., telling me that he knew father was difficult, and adding that he knew my grandfather very well, the one who had thrashed me when I was a child, telling me he had never liked him at all.

27th Friday, Monique and I, together with Archie and Pat, went to a Hunt Ball at Lockerbie, this time held at Castle Milk, the home of Sir John Buchanan-Jardine, the master of the Dumfriesshire Hounds, more of a small country mansion, than a castle, the place was a lovely one, and an excellent ball it was, Sir John's son, Rupert taking a shine to Monique, showing her round a few of the rooms, and art, and dancing perhaps too often with her, I think at about this time Rupert may have been separated from his wife. All in all a most pleasant evening, we got home at 5:30 am. The next day, there was extreme frost, so I went again to shoot down the farm, taking my good friend Lassie, bagging 7 ducks and 5 pheasants, 3 pigeons, then the snow started to fall, I instructed the shepherd to start and feed the in lamb ewes with hay from now onward. Sunday, about 4 inches of snow had fallen. Monday, the thaw started, I put the men to sawing fence posts while I took the gun and Lassie, on these outings with the gun, I would also inspect the breeding cows, now having their calves, and look around the breeding ewes, the men working down the fields at various jobs never knew when I was going to show up in their midst, so to speak, it kept them on their toes, two or three times I had caught them and watched for 10 to 15 minutes sitting down talking, doing nothing, they earlier had seen me set out early in the day with the gun, they thought, now he is out of the way, we'll take it easy, they soon found out I was not just playing. On Father's Day, when I had the hatchery, the men were supposed to be on the farm at 7 am, they got into the habit of arriving at 7.15 to 7.30. After lunch, the time to start was 1 pm, they got the habit of arriving at 1:15 pm, Joe Frith was the worst culprit, I had to put them right when I took the farm and stop two men doing one man's work, this probably rankled in their breasts.

The Ford Capri I had on order, I cancelled, because the garage could now not guarantee delivery for the months ahead. I called on Bobbie Dickson, my brother's friend at County Motors Carlisle, his father was the principal shareholder there. I asked Bobbie to get me a Triumph 2000, being a friend and Bobbie had good contacts, he said to leave it with me, and I did. Now, within days, he had a white 2000 for me at 1411 pounds on the road. He gave me 661 pounds for the M.G.B. Now, at last, I could get our two boys in the car in comfort, poor young devils, they were cramped up in the M.G. I took delivery of the new car on 26th April 1969.

On 1st May, Monique and I went to Hexham evening race meeting, where we had rather a good evening racing. I made 40 pounds, then we all went to my friend Jimmy Alexander at Sandhoe Hall, where the drinks flowed well. Jimmy was an excellent host, he liked a good cigar, but he could never get acclimatised to the Burma cheroots—he always refused them when I offered.

I decided in February to sell Black Wood timber of Scots Pine for a little extra cash, then replant it for shelter as at the moment it was too open for any use as shelter, one long side of the L-shaped plantation being 400 yards x 25 and the short L being 200 x 50 yards. I wrote to three timber merchants, Mr

Lowther, Mr Croasdale, and Mr Herd of Penrith, Lowther did not offer; Croasdale bid 1307 pounds and Mr Herd bid 1200 pounds, I then told herd, whom I knew slightly, he was the underbidder, he then upped his bid to 2000 pounds, I let him have it. For future timber for the farm gates and fencing, I still had 2 acres of Scots pine in Spring Field that was also mature but was quite a good shelter.

March and April found us at a lambing time again, the end of March was cold and snowy. Fortunately, while this was on, the ewes lambed slowly, the men were busy ploughing and sowing oats and barley, I was sowing more cereals than father had done, as I had to try to get the profits to increase from the 2000 pounds per annum that he had achieved of late. The tic beans, 5 acres of them, went in on 2nd April, later than usual, but the seed beans were a long time in coming after my order went in. They should have been sown a month ago.

On the beef herd, we had trouble with liver fluke, no doubt brought over from Ireland, where the butchers could not and did not use cattle livers for human consumption. Because of this problem, we had good healthy looking cows drop down dead in their tracks and young heifers of 2 years going down and unable to get up again, the vet told me it was a massive infestation of immature fluke, and immediately I set about to rectify and dose all and every one of the breeding stock, bulls included, after this the breeding herd was dosed for fluke twice a year, we had no more problems, but we had lost 12 female cattle, all good breeding stock.

The following Saturday, Monique and I went again to Hexham races after putting the men to work to sow the last of the turnips in the little 6-acre field that was my mother's. We did not dwell at Hexham after the races, we came back and drove to Appleby for dinner at the Royal Oak, now owned by two brothers, whom we named Happy and Grumpy. Happy real name! Lived up to his name, always a welcoming and sincere smile, saw to the dining room and the cocktail bar, Grumpy, real name George, never smiled, always had a scowl, looked after the public bar if he did not like anyone, he would be so nasty they would leave before being served, the food was always very good, they had a woman to do the actual cooking, as both brothers were not married. At the bar, I used to always ask Happy to have a drink, which he did, always of gin. At the odd time, Grumpy would look after the cocktail bar. If Happy was busy in the dining room, he would serve Monique and I, then I would ask him to have one with us. The first time I asked him, I think he nearly dropped to the floor in surprise, I think it must have been the first time ever someone had asked him to have a drink (from a customer). He hesitated, then thanked me and had a whisky—this was on one of our first visits to the Royal Oak. Monique and I would dine or call after perhaps Catterick races. By now, George was almost as happy as his brother when Monique and I walked in, he would leave his public bar to come and drink and talk with us both, swapping drink for drink, he was a very kind chap underneath that scowl. His pet thing was to look out of his bar window onto the hotel parking lot, and if anyone had not parked correctly, he was outside in a flash to tell them to park correctly, I have seen people come park—George breathing fire—and the potential customer(s) drive off, either disgusted or frightened, his other pet was his love of a vintage Bentley, with straps holding the bonnet on, he could talk for hours about this one. We all became good friends and both of the brothers would do anything for Monique and the odd time going to either Catterick or Wetherby races, I had forgotten to take money, George would ask how much I wanted, and never hesitate to hand the cash over—any cheques wanted by him—on trust.

My new car, the Triumph, was running well, but a few people kept telling me, from behind, the car seemed to be crab like the rear wheels quite offset, I took the car eventually back to County Motors and they told me the car was perfect, but again people still told me the car was like a crab from behind, I thought I best had a look at this for myself, I asked Monique to drive it on a straight stretch of the Skirwith-Langwathby road while I followed in the Land Rover and sure enough it was plain to see the car was far from right, I took it down to our faithful mechanic, Billy Marshall at Langwathby, Billy was a mechanic second to none, started work at 9 am and carried on till midnight and sent his bills in yearly, if he hadn't timed at two yearly intervals, Billy examined the car and quickly found the car wheel base's were offset causing the crab like effect from behind I left the car with him for a day while he rectified the problem—so much for County Motors, this problem seen to. Three weeks later, driving from Carlisle—by now, the car had done 4000 miles. I had taken it no more than 40mph for the first 2000 miles, so it had been run in very gently—I felt the car start to falter, I had been doing only 80mph just then, so I slowed right down to 25mph, the engine missing and coughing, I thought this is something serious. Monique and I were to meet three friends at the George Hotel on the way back from Carlisle, but such was the noise from the car, I took the shortcut over Lazonby Fell and went straight home. As it was dark when we arrived home, I did not bother to inspect the engine, leaving this until tomorrow, when I did so the next day, I had a surprise, a piece of metal the size of a side plate was cracked and bulging out of the side of the engine block, I notified County Motors, who picked the car up on a trailer and took it off to Carlisle where they had to put a new engine in, under the guarantee. I was told by many friends that it was unfortunate, but it seemed that I had bought a Friday night, Monday morning car. This was the era when the British car industry was at its lowest ebb, take over after take over until the industry was just one big mistake, bad management, and a worse workforce. On the continent, our car industry was a sick joke, they did not want our cars at any price. There were too many things going wrong with the cars like mine.

 I had no sooner had the new engine in the Triumph than at Newcastle races. A few days later, Monique and I drove up to the Gosforth Park Hotel after the last race. I parked beside the curb, only 5-6 yards from the hotel front door and as we went into the foyer, a young man of about 20 came staggering towards the front door, I said to Monique, "By Jove he's had a skinful" and went on to the bar to meet friends with whom we were dining with later at their house, we had only been in the bar 10 minutes when over the intercom system came a voice, asking for the owner of the white Triumph 2000 to come to reception I thought what is the matter now, I arrived at the reception, where I was told "We are very sorry sir, but your car has been involved in an accident", I thought this was rather silly my car is parked outside. I was invited to go outside and to my amazement, the Triumph had the driver's back passenger door shoved right in. The car had been pushed right over the six-inch curb and up a steep grassy bank, ripping the front tyre near the curb, right off the rim, the force had been so great, I asked who and what had been responsible for all of this. The hall porter told me a young man, driving a M.G. sports car had driven out of the hotel car park at full speed and just rammed my car full amidships, his friends had grabbed him, put him in their car, managed to get his car going and took off. The hall porter had notified the police who arrived shortly afterwards and took various statements, in the meantime the receptionist came looking for me, there was a phone call for me and I answered, it was the friends of the drunk who had rammed the Triumph, the same drunk man Monique and I had seen staggering past us on arrival at the hotel, I asked who they were, but they would not tell me, only if I did not get the police in would they talk, and admit liability. I told them too late, the police were already in the hotel—in the long run, I heard the police seemed to know who it was, I was informed by them he was named W. Muirhead of Rothbury—I had the car repaired under his insurance company. After this I had to get the spare wheel on, both drivers and rear passenger doors were completely jammed. I had to get in from the front passenger side and drive slowly, as I had to sit almost in the middle of the car, I did not let that spoil our evening, though, we went on to dine at Derek Strakers' and his wife Angela, just outside Newcastle, the latter being the sister of Phillip's new wife, the meal was like something the cat had sicked up I thought it was shocking, a tin of dog food would have been better, after dinner, if it could be called that, we went on to Needleshall—Col Cookson may have been the owner, but I'm not sure—to a grand ball held there. Derek Straker is a grand chap but is trying his best to get off with Monique.

Sunday, Monique, being a Roman Catholic, had been invited to John Cummings to be the mother of his new son Giles, Phillip Johnstone went with us to the christening, which turned out to be a very excellent affair. Phillip leaves Skirwith Hall at 5:30 am to return to his home near St Boswells and return to Hong Kong, Monique sets him off with 6 fried eggs and about a pound of bacon. The day after, I castrated 35 bull calves and dehorned 6.

26

On Tuesday 5th August, Monique and I decided to take a holiday with our two boys, we thought we would all go to Spain, the boys had never been to the seaside except Silloth, and we thought it would be a good thing for them to see and mix with a few foreigners. We set off at midnight on the 5th, driving for Spain, the ferry boat was an excitement for the boys; the sea was calm, and the weather was hot, we drove fairly quickly through France, having for our lunch a picnic from food bought at an epicerie and butchers for pate, fresh loaves of bread, big ones. The French call them Restaurant bread, wine and mineral water, coca-cola for the boys, although they liked to have wine with water, twice we stopped in some farmer's field of stubble, the corn just having been cut a few days before and stopping at small clean hotels at night, or a Logis de France. Those days, most Logis were excellent and served very good food at a realistic price, but in the 80's, I found a vast change in these places, and not for the best.

We duly sought out a place called Castelldefels just south of Barcelona, the car had run well, we were all pleased with it, very comfortable, at Castelldefels Monique asked at various hotels which we thought might be suitable for a family—not too excessive in price, but all were full, she tried the more plush ones, the same thing—full. Of course, being August, it seemed everyone was on holiday. The last hotel, the receptionist told Monique of a more or less bed and breakfast place, this it seemed was the last chance, so off I drove once again to a street, perhaps one might say on the outskirts of the small town, they were full, but they had an annex of which we had to climb an outside flight of stone steps, the annex had two other families staying, there were two rooms left, they were bare, only the beds and two upright chairs in the rooms, the price was peanuts, and as there was nowhere else, and it seemed every holiday place was full, we took it. One thing pleased Monique, the bed linen was spotless and our landlady seemed a kind, pleasant type. Anything we wanted, just ask, she said, the boys had their own room. In front of the outside staircase was a piece of ground with a thatched roof affair open on two sides for the family and friends barbecue, which it turned out they had on Friday and Saturday nights, a real jolly sing-song, dancing, eating affair, they often invited Monique and I but each time we declined, they were a rough and rowdy lot, we thought it better to use discretion.

For breakfast, we went to the local marketplace, like a small supermarket, where there was a food kiosk that served breakfast. I even got Adam to try his first Prairie oyster there and he liked it, the young chap who ran it was named Toni. I found this little supermarket to be really very good and also very clean, in fact, cleaner than the English or French, especially the dairy product counters. Toni used to look forward to our morning entrance, we used to linger on a bit as he liked to talk. For our dinners, we took in one of the best little restaurants in Spain—or so we thought—it was named Restaurant Fortuny.

Run by Senora Fortuny and her husband—Senora did the waiting at the table, and her husband the cooking, there were about 15 tables always full, we found the food so good, not exotic, but consistently good and here we dined every night the price was low. For lunch, the Fortuny's made us sandwiches which varied from ham, salami, chicken to omelet ones, the well-to-do of Caselldefels often came to eat here. The restaurant was only a couple of minutes from the beach—the days were spent sunbathing and swimming. The boys really enjoyed the sea and became very good swimmers. They were in the water most of the day—one day, the sea was just a trifle rough, I went in with the boys and found within 15 yards of the beach that we were swimming in a sea of fish, fish about a foot or more long, it was quite incredible if we had a net it would have been quite easy to just scoop them up, we could get hold of them in our hands, but they were too slippery to hold on to.

One day, we all went to a bullfight in Barcelona where one of the picadors horses got a severe goring in its belly, blood pouring onto the ground, the boys booed at this. Otherwise, I think they thought it interesting but not in love with this cruel sport. One of the most interesting part was a bullfighter fighting the bull from horseback, the horses were beautiful beasts when the bull charged, the horse knew in a split second which way the bull was going, side step with the speed and elegance of a ballet dancer. At one part, the bull's horns grazed the flank of the horse, a grey, slight streak of blood showed up brilliantly on the grey coat. The graze, very slight, was enough for the rider to take the horse out and re-enter the arena on a superb bay to continue. The finale was the killing of the bull from horseback, which I think took at least five passes before the bull was on the sand.

One day, we all went to see the monastery on the mountaintop of Monserrat, where they have a black virgin in the church I thought it very much commercialised. There was a restaurant where we dined, food so-so. The Sangria tasted good, though, I bought a little bottle of the monk's liqueur, named the liqueur of Montserrat, I still have it, quite an interesting trip. We sat in the church listening to one of the services and also said a little prayer. I believe a fortnight before we arrived in Castelldefells the actor and film star George Sanders committed suicide in one of the hotels there, one of the hotels Monique had asked for rooms, it seemed quite a good hotel. George Sanders was one of my favourite stars, had been for a long time, he could play the cad and be so suave, always immaculate, suicide—what a waste of such talent.

The days passed quietly and easily, after a month, we thought about returning to work. We all had a good rest, enjoyed ourselves, had good food and wine, we bade goodbye to our landlady. The only thing we had asked for was more loo paper. Mrs Fortuny, bless her, had tears in her eyes, she took us through to the kitchens to say our goodbyes to her husband. They had a little boy aged about ten who sometimes brought bread or wine to the table and was busy quite often catching butterflies in his little net—Mariposas, he called them—he had gone back to school. Mrs Fortuny had prepared sandwiches for our travel home, she would not accept money for them, they were a nice family indeed.

27

We set off on Friday, 5th September, heading for the black forest in Germany, where we would spend two or three days and where I would stock up with cigars. On the first night of the 5th, we stopped for the night in Nimes, an old city still had the Roman amphitheater, one can feel the oldness somehow. We ate at a brassiere, quite good, a little clean hotel cost 8 pounds for a family room, two twin beds and a double. The next day, I headed for Lyon, branching off for Geneva and skirting there. I made for Basel, having our picnic lunch in Switzerland, with food bought in France as I always found food bought in Switzerland too expensive, we got into Freiburg in the Black Forest, I asked at two hotels in the town for rooms, they had rooms but far too costly, I thought it best to drive outside the city to take a look for a country hotel. We stumbled on the village Sexau, where we had been before, Herr and Frau Gehri's Hotel Lerche, they gave us two rooms, very clean and comfortable. Sexau was near Emmerdingen and Waldkirk, it was here I was to stock up with cigars. Now was also the time of year for the neue zusse, the sort of first fermentation of the wine, the colours of grape juice, one could smell it on the streets, excellent to drink and quite strong too. Monique and I indulged in quite a few in the surrounding villages. Herr Gehri always stocked the best, so he told us. We motored to Titisee, I was not impressed by the place. We both liked the old city of Freiberg with its open market in the shadow of the great Cathedral. In Waldkirk, I knew of a good tobacconist there, run by a very old woman, who smoked what she sold, cigars, I selected 800 of them and had a good chat, I think she said she was 89 years old, I told her about my fathers age, she asked me if my mother was alive, I told her no—she immediately said, tell your father to come over here and I will marry him, we had a good laugh, she gave me 10 cigars on the house plus 5.5% discount, that I had to ask for, she without hesitation gave it to me.

The next day, with all of the cigars to pack into the car door panels, I drove to a secluded place, which seemed to have a lot of apple trees about. I posted Adam on the road to yell if any cars came along, as the car was about 25 yards inside this orchard looking place if any cars did come and slow down we would pretend to be picnicking, I took the panels off the doors and put what boxes I could in, then I had to resort to plastic bags, of which I had plenty in readiness for such an occasion. At the finish, I had a pile of empty boxes, so I piled them neatly under a tree and left. No cars had passed, Adam had become bored and gone far down the road to some plum trees, where he was busy filling his tummy with them.

Little Joey had wanted a real pipe to smoke at home and, Adam a sheaf knife, Monique a Cuckoo Clock, so on our final day, we went into Freiberg. Joey chose his pipe and tobacco, it was a very small pipe, Adam got his knife and Monique the cuckoo clock—Joey still has his pipe, Adam's knife has long since gone, Monique still has the clock and my cigars have gone up in smoke. We set off too late on 9th September— getting to Strasburg and feeling tired, we had not driven far either, thought it prudent to take a room for the night, we came upon what looked like a nice little place in the town itself, the price was right, and instead of looking at the rooms before declaring yes or no, we took them. There were two rooms, very tatty indeed, but for one night, we said we would give it a go. Downstairs, the little dining room looked quite pleasant, but the food was no good at all, when we went to bed, I went along to the loo; it was a stinking place, but most peculiar was that when one sat down, and what passed out, dropped down to the ground floor, it was an earth closet and a long drop one at that. Being so high to "our seat," there was created an upward draft, which filled one's nostrils with the stink from down below. Most unpleasant, a pity I did not take the name of the place, in the morning, we did not even think of having breakfast, the sooner we quit this hole, the better.

Leaving at 6 am, I drove in the direction of Metz, where we

stopped for breakfast. Here also, there was that taste and atmosphere of the Germanic side to things. The restaurants and people were not as refined as the French people inland, which I or we all did prefer, I was pleased before long to be out of the smoked meat and sauerkraut side of the French. I drove through Sedan and Charleville-Mezier, where the Maginot line, I believe, runs; one could see plenty of pill boxes from the 1st World War towards Arras. Little did I realise that in years to come, I would shoot over these areas six and seven days a week. We stopped for a good picnic lunch at Cambrai, passing a little village called Marquion, where the great Duke of Marlborough fought one of his battles. In fact, from here to the Channel, the English had fought the French time and again for a few hundred years, then on to Calais, onto the ferry boat. Late evening at Dover, we passed the Customs, no trouble with my cigars and drove on. I was determined to drive home in one swoop from Strasbourg, the car was running well—but I drove through the night, car still running well, until 200 miles from home, when all of a sudden I felt she was missing a bit on a hill or long decline. I had for the first time to take a lower gear. I knew or thought I knew what it was a valve stem broken because the old Bedford lorry used to break the odd valve stem, and now the Triumph had the same symptoms. In any case, I did not now push the car before I had been doing 80 mph, taking it easy in this way, I knew we would reach home, which we did in the daylight hours. I had a talk with Father, all seemed to be in order. I rested up and took the cigars out of the door panels the rest of the day.

25th September, old Major Parker, Cyril, had decided to sell his odds and ends of furniture in the market halt in Penrith, but reserving his best, together with drawings and oil paintings, for sale in London. I cannot remember if it was Christie's or Sotherby's, the sale of his bric-a-brac—with quite a few nice pieces, made him 6000 pounds, later I asked him what he thought of the sale, he told me he thought before the sale started, he would be lucky to get 500 pounds, Monique bought a copper bed warmer for 5 pounds and a beautiful gent's wardrobe for 35 pounds. I never heard what Cyril's pictures or furniture made in London, this was all kept hush, hush, the auctioneers the night before his London sale, dined and wined him at Madame Prunier's, he told me they dined him well. The old devil, when I was at my mother's knee and at the sales with her, Cyril would buy oil paintings by the score for I/-, 2/6 or 5/- never more. I can remember his struggle with them under his arms, taking them to his car, now he was reaping a harvest, no doubt the odd few he had had the correct signature. The old major was moving into a house in Penrith, he was getting on in years now and felt it better to be nearer help if needed, but perhaps more so—the bar of the George Hotel, his wife had died of cancer. Now, poor Bridget, my first love, had been stricken with multiple sclerosis and was unable to walk, having to have a wheelchair. It was indeed a tragedy, but Bridget never let it get her down, she was always cheerful and ready to laugh.

The same week I took my Bedford Lorry and the farm men to Keswick to help load a 30ft travelling saw bench, all in solid iron, from Mrs Sandy Allison of Sheep Close, Keswick, Sandy had died that year and Mrs Allison told me Sandy knew he was dying, and told her that when he did die—that same day—she was with him when he died—a big gust of wind would go through the house. A while later, in front of Mrs Allison's eyes, Sandy passed away and within a few minutes, 2 or 3, a huge gust of wind hurtled through the house, blowing windows off their latches, doors from their latches, straight through the middle of the house, "Sheep's Close" a large rambling place, and out the other side. She looked out at the orchard, there was not a branch stirring, except the path of wind where it had left the house, there, the trees as if in a corridor, were bent double—she said she was not afraid, she knew it was Sandy—myself, I knew the family well, Sandy and I sometimes got together in the Gloucester Arms Pub in Penrith and knocked a bottle of whisky on the head.

23rd was the main sale of the year for the beef suckling calves; 150 youngsters went to the sale and 11 small ones were left behind. The 150 head were not enough by far for the farm or to leave a big enough profit for the mortgage and the men's wages. This day, however, the top price bullock was 75 pounds and the top heifer made 70 pounds. Not too bad, but I was determined to raise the cow breeding herd up from 170 to 250 at least, then up to 500 eventually.

These were good days for shooting on Saturday, I thought to have a walk round with Lassie, it was a crisp morning, freezing hard, I got the game bag out, slung it over my shoulder, took my Westley Richards, and set off on foot leaving the Land Rover behind starting at the beck before 300 yards 8 or more duck got up, I downed two, both dead. Lassie had them back to me quickly. She was most pleased, I could see by the look she gave me. It is a fact Labradors and water go hand in hand, they just love the sport, another 100 yards more duck, I again dropped two, luck would have it, both were only winged. They were going to take some time to retrieve, I thought. Just then, I saw one move under some roots by the far bank 20 yards on, I got up with the gun and killed it right away. Now I thought, Lassie can get the other one if possible, she had quickly brought the first to foot, now I did not know where the other one was, I had seen no movement, it was up to Lassie's nose. She worked slowly but surely under one bank, nothing there, it seemed. Now she was trying the nearby side bank, there was an abundance of tree roots for ducks to hide, it was going to take some time this duck. All at once, Lassie lunged under the bank, she has it, I thought, good girl, out she came with a pleased look, and in her mouth was a live water hen, she brought it to me, I took it from her, the poor little water hen's heart was going 60 to the dozen, it seemed lively enough, I held Lassie and let the water hen go, throwing it in the air so that it would fly far enough away from the scene It did. Lassie watched, wondering what a stupid thing Master was doing, the water hen out of the way, I encouraged Lassie on to the last duck. Again, she hunted steadily, going further and further down, easily 30 yards from where the duck had dropped, there she was onto something, a flurry of yellow and water as she made her grab and she had the duck, this went into the bag after pulling its neck. On we went to the water quarry, a 22-carat piece of water for duck here 30 or more jumped up, two dropped with my first shot and a third with my second barrel, one was winged and had fallen in some rushes, so Lassie had it very quickly in my hand.

That was probably enough duck for today, I thought, *7 of them.* I thought now for some pheasant. There was some excellent rough ground from here, the water quarry, to the end of the farm at Beck Mill, also it was grand weather also for snipe. I expected a few to be in the soft, boggy bits, of which there were quite a few from now onwards. Lassie and I entered the rough only 20 yards past the water quarry, when up sprang a large cock pheasant, nearly frightening me, he got up so near me, with a loud cackle, I left him for a second, letting him travel further, rather than blow him to pulp being so near, before I fired, the gun on the way to my shoulder, 4 more pheasant got up, I downed the first one, then switched to one of the 4, fired and missed clean as a whistle. Lassie set off for the first, bringing the big bird back to hand. 30 yards further on, Lassie quartering nicely, 20 yards in front put three more up, two dropped quickly. While she was on her way to retrieve them, Lassie put five more up, I always reload immediately after I fire, which in this case, I already had done so, once again, two dropped, these in the bag, which was now far too heavy, I walked to the cart track and emptied the birds onto the ground putting some rough grass and reeds over them in case the buzzards or carrion crows would take a liking to them, swung the game bag once again over my shoulder, I went back into the rough, two woodpigeons flying by had a fright, or at least one did, the other I shot dead, it's one thing I like for a meal is woodpigeon, delicious birds they were.

Lassie was working nicely to one side of me, I was watching

her when again I was startled, a huge hare jumped out of his seat in a cluster of reeds only a yard from me. I let him run on till I thought right to shoot, but realized at the same time the rushes were too high just where he was running to. I fired quickly, just in time and he rolled head over heels, dead. Nice one for hare soup, especially in this cold weather, but I would hang the hare for five days with its insides in before skinning and preparing it for Monique to cook. I don't like carrying hares at all; they weigh a ton in no time, so I picked him up, walked back to where I had left the duck and pheasant, and put the hare with them. While Lassie and I walked, I never spoke to her when she was working, only using a whistle, which had a very thin tone and then only a very short blow of a split second, using hand signals for some directions, two short whistle blows for other instructions, because when all birds, game or otherwise and four legged game animals come to that, hear the human voice, they take off, and far too soon for the guns, so a lesson to townsmen who perhaps like the sport of shooting, do not speak in the shooting fields or grouse moors.

Anyway, after the hare was safely put by, my four-legged doggy friend continued, on we went, I shot six more pheasants but tried to concentrate on the very soft places for snipe. I knew exactly the location where they were in the rushes, now two snipe got up, with a chirp and the usual shite in mid-air, I managed to drop one, missing the other, then as Lassie was looking for the fallen one, another two got up, I dropped both, as the gun touched my shoulder, I had changed now to No 6 shot, from the 4's I always used for all other game or pigeon. I have shot snipe with No 4's, but I have also seen against a background the shot striking ground and snipe right in the middle of the pattern and carrying on unscathed. I finished up that day with 8 snipe, having the best sport with that little bird at the freshwater syke or spring in Black Wood—Beck Mill, which never froze over and at the same time getting another two ducks—at one stage, there Lassie came back to hand with two snipe in her mouth, she was indeed a good buy as a puppy.

The next day, the snow lay an easy 6 or 7 inches, a very heavy carpet all in one night, and that night of the 7th to 8th, the frost was the hardest for many years. The tractors and Land Rover would not start, the diesel had turned to jelly. At Culgaith there was 34% frost and Langwathby 40% frost. That day I cut the great fir tree down in the garden. She had succumbed to age, I suppose, year by year, branches dying until now the poor old girl's branches were all dead. I had climbed many times to the top of her 27 yards height when I was a boy, her branches almost like the rungs of a ladder, making it easy, and every morning in good weather, a thrush would perch on the topmost twig and sing her or his songs for the world to hear, this Sound was so beautiful, I could listen for ages to this bird. Now, writing this, I can still hear that thrush singing; nostalgia comes into my heart. When I lay in bed ill, I had all the illnesses a child could catch. Mother always left the bedroom window wide open on nice days, and I lay there listening to the beauty of the birds singing—the chatter of the sparrows in the ivy, but also in that great fir tree, there were a pair of wood pigeons who would give their coo-coocuk-cuk-coo, the softness of their gentle call I used to love too, and at no stage in my life did I ever shoot wood pigeons anywhere near the house—now my tree was felled, it was a sad day.

On the 21st, I took Monique up to the R.V.I. in Newcastle (the Royal Victoria Infirmary), for the operation on her bunion, saw her safely in and returned home. The next day I phoned her after the operation, she said it was very painful. The surgeon who did it, Mr Stanger, also shortened her big toe, he was a man I did not like the look of, really. I drove over to see Monique the day after this operation, she was hale and hearty, the pain she said, was much better, a few days later, I brought her home, the hospital lent her a pair of those long under-armpit crutches, which I thought were rather cumbersome, the type for the arms and elbows would have been much easier and handier, but they had none—so they said.

Monique, Major Parker and myself, one Tuesday market day night, called at Edenhall Hotel for drinks, this was 10 pm, we stayed until after midnight, there was a very large fireplace in his bar lounge, somewhere near midnight. Beck himself had one or two too many, there was a slight argument going on between us, Beck and his mistress, Mrs Grimes, a lady of 60-65, whom we knew well, Mrs Grimes disagreed with Beck over something trivial, then all of a sudden Beck lost his temper with her, he got hold of her, and pushed her right into the fire, fortunately, the fire, a very wide one, had begun to die down, I jumped to the rescue and pulled Mrs Grimes out of the fire with only a slight burn or two to her fingers, it was as well I pulled her out. Otherwise, she would have finished in hospital. I then turned on Beck and told him I had a good mind to put him out of his own hotel and gave him a good dressing down, he took the huff and went to bed. Mrs Grimes told Monique she often wanted to leave him, but when she tried. Beck knew the moves and took her car keys away.

On the 2nd of February, Monique and I drove down to Liverpool bound for Dublin, I had not asked Father to come, I wished to spend two days alone with Monique in Dublin. she, poor girl, was still on her crutches, making it hard going, such as going on board the ferry ship, and off again, the ferry was the "Munster," a comfortable and warm ship with good crew and good or fairly good food and bar. The crossing was rough and stormy. We docked at Dublin, and there, by bush telegraph, was our old friend, Cristy Collins, we took a taxi, dropping Monique off at the Gresham Hotel, where she could have breakfast and perhaps do some win-dow shopping in O'Connell Street. Cristy and I set off for the open air cattle market, nothing suitable there. The stock mostly being for the abattoir. We went on to Ganly's auction, there was none of the Angus and Shorthorn heifers at all. Nowadays I was told, the shorthorn cow was going out fast as farmers were going for Friesians, as the English farmers were doing, eventually I bought 14 good strong two-year-old heifers Hereford X Friesian with white faces at 68 pounds each, I wanted more but was unable to find what I wanted from Mr Jim Larnisy. I went across to the little pub near the auction, treating Cristy and myself to a few Guinness, the price of Guinness was climbing pretty high, I wondered how it was possible for the man in the street to drown his thirst at the day's prices. However, in the process, I ran into Hugh Walsh, of whom Dad had bought heifers from in other years. We sank a few Guinness, during which I asked Hugh if he had any of the Angus X Shorthorn heifers on hand, he had, he said, some very good, strong ones also, he knew of others he could get for me. We arranged a rendezvous for the following afternoon to give him time to get some of the cattle in for me to inspect, and in the meantime, would Monique and I have drinks at his house that evening? I thanked him and accepted. Cristy, looking after my new purchases for the night, giving them hay and water and holding them until I had maybe done a deal with Hugh.

Hugh drove me to the Gresham, where he dropped me off, coming later on to take Monique and I to his house in town (his farm was outside of Dublin). We showered and changed and went down to the large lounge for a few drinks, awaiting Hugh to pick us up, which he did at 5:30 pm. His wife was a charming, open-hearted woman—in my dealings with quite a few Irish people and visiting them in their houses, I found them to be the salt of the earth, great kindness and tremendous hospitality all around.

They would give their all and I should think if one was in trouble, they would never hesitate to help one. That is the impression I had over the years with the Irish, it made me think many times over what a tragedy the fighting in Northern Ireland, a few hotheads making tremendous misery for many.

I mentioned that in the morning. I would take Monique and myself around Guinness' brewery, as I had heard so much about it, Mrs Walsh, without prompting, immediately told us she would take us in her car and go around with us. We thanked her and accepted her offer, and then Hugh took us back to the Gresham, where we dined below in the grill room. It was good, fine food, as always, a pity I did not write down what we had that night, as I usually did. And as usual, the grill room had its quota of those black leeches of crows, the priests, feeding off the fat of the land while their parishioners went hungry.

Wednesday 4[th,] Mrs Walsh picked us up at 10 am after a very good large breakfast. The Gresham breakfasts were something to be remembered, and off to the brewery. It was a cold day, in fact bitterly cold, and Monique found it hard work on her crutches, but she battled on wonders of wonders, there was not another soul, tourist-wise, being shown around the brewery that morning. We were the only three to be escorted around by a gentleman of a guide, helping Monique up staircases and taking his time as if tomorrow was not coming. The place was immense, covering, I believe, 60 acres in all. Guinness had a rental agreement for a few hundred years at a peppercorn rent, which I believe was and is still running. On a most interesting tour, our guide explained the various procedures of brewing and at the finish of the tour, we were ushered into an office cum reception and offered a glass of Guinness. I had three in the course of time we spent there and, Monique two, Mrs. Walsh had one. We would be in the brewery for at least two and a half hours. Monique was tired out, being on her crutches all morning and on the move, I then invited Mrs Walsh for lunch at the Gresham. Then Mrs Walsh took me to her husband's farm, first leaving Monique at the hotel to recuperate and to take it easy.

Hugh had arranged a nice bunch of cattle for me to see and after haggling for an hour over the price, we struck a deal for 69 pounds each for 34 of them, 20 of which were for Archie up at Nethercassock, he had asked me to get him 20 for his farm there in Eskdalemuir, I had 28 for myself, Hugh arranged everything regarding shipping and TB papers, and trucked them off to the other 14 I had bought at Ganly's.

Hugh then took Monique and I to the airport, as for some reason, there was no ferry boat that night, we were flying to Speke Airport, Liverpool.

While we were sitting in the airport lounge, I started to talk to an Irish-man sitting beside us, he was a cattle dealer flying up to Glasgow. In the course of our conversation, I mentioned that I had never tasted the poteen, the illicit brew the Irish made, telling him I had heard a lot about it. He said, "You've never tasted poteen?"

"No never," I said. He looked around to see who was about and fished a bottle of Vodka out of his hand luggage, we had had coffee before, and the cups, empty, were still on the table in front of us, he poured me, not Monique, a large dose into my coffee cup. .

"Take that," he said, putting the bottle back in his bag.

I said, "Vodka?"

"No," he replied, "that's a blind for the customs, it's the real stuff." I put the cup to my lips and took a good measure, let the liquid rest on my taste buds for a second or two and swallowed – whoever had made this liquid should have been presented with a gold medal, it was superb, liquid velvet, I told our new friend this, he was so pleased he gave me another slurp, then said the remainder was for his landlady in Glasgow, then we were called to our plane. Shaking hands with the poteen chappie, we left and boarded the plane, arriving at Speke in the darkness of night, we waited for our luggage to arrive and waited finally I had to ask what had happened, it turned out our baggage had been sent on the wrong plane, it was on the way to Glasgow by mistake, we took a taxi to the garage near the docks, where I had left my car, getting home at midnight, both of us tired, especially poor Monique.

28

For some reason or other, I had kept a pig for the house, where I got it from, I cannot recollect, but one thing I can recollect quite clearly was the day we decided it was time it was butchered for the house. I had never butchered a pig, only lambs, and I had no intention of starting on pigs now, so I asked our local butcher to do the job for me, Bert from Langwathby had taken over Hubert Dyson's business after Hubert's death, two butcher's vans travelling round the villages.

This day, Sunday 22nd, was the only day Bert could come as weekdays he was doing the rounds in his van. He landed with his assistant butcher Duncan, who was possibly 20 years old, Kurt came to help as well, Bert and Duncan had a look at the pig first, saying it looked to be about 18 scores in weight, this was 10 am, I invited them into the main kitchen for a drink of whisky as it was a very cold morning, they accepted with obvious glee. We sat around a portable square table Monique had set up in the middle of the kitchen, as the large table 4 yards long was against a wall, so it was no good sitting all in a line on the long form. There we were, 2 butchers, Kurt and I. Monique brought the whisky bottle, I poured good measures and we sat and talked, I poured another round and we sat and talked, Bert was a home brew expert, so a good part of the conversation was about various recipes for winemaking. Eventually, I poured a third round of drinks, both butchers made no move to get down to work, and both of them, including Kurt, were in a mood for talking about anything. I went for another bottle of whisky, their eyes lit up at this, Kurt said he wanted no more, and now he himself was as red as a turkey jock. I filled the glasses again, and slowly, this bottle disappeared, so I got the 3rd bottle of Gloags Famous Grouse out, I was beginning to wonder if the pig was going to be killed that day or not. The time was now 2 pm and both Bert and his assistant Duncan were well oiled, I suggested we get the job done, then come back and finish this bottle off, that sounded great to both butchers. Kurt caught the pig with a noose around its snout, somehow we got the poor animal into the meal house nearby, but not before Bert fell over the pigs back, Duncan, going to help him up – he was more drunk than Bert – tripped himself up, falling flat on his face in the mud, I was beginning to wonder if it might be better to postpone the event, I mentioned to Bert that next week would do. He would have none of it. He brandished the Humane killer, and possibly with more luck than anything else, he put the gun to the pigs head and fired, I think he surprised himself as the poor pig collapsed, then the knife, the bloodletting and saving of this latter work, I did, stirring the big bowl on and on to stop, the blood-curdling. Then take the bowl into the warm kitchen, otherwise if curdled, the blood would be no goodto make black puddings.

The pig was eventually hung up all nice and clean, ready for the cutting up the next day. Then we all – except Kurt, who said he wanted no more drink – went back into the kitchen to finish the whisky off. Duncan seemed to go wild, jumped onto the little grey Ferguson tractor, thought he was Stirling Moss, went round and round the main courtyard at full speed – on and on, I let him. Bert and I slowly but surely got through the bottle of scotch, all of a sudden, Bert went quiet, I asked him if was all right, he did not reply, instead he vomited all over the table, I shouted at him to go outside and half dragged him to the door. Monique heard the commotion, came into the big kitchen, saw the mess, then we heard her very angry voice. Bert dared not go back into that kitchen, he realised Monique had her dander up, the silly fool, he should have felt ill and gone outside – Monique let me know – no more pigs had to be butchered at Skirwith Hall. We never did another pig killing, she'd had enough.

19th June, I bought 150-day-old pheasant chicks from Lord Lonsdale's keeper, Walter Drysdale, for thirty-six pounds, to rear for my own shoot, rearing them under gas heaters in a large portable hen house, the pheasant chicks were good strong, healthy ones, they did very well fed on chick crumbs and after a week inside, I opened the pop hole in the hen house, put a runway board outside so the chicks could run in and out of the house, outside I had constructed a pen of 10 yards long, 4 yards wide and 6 feet high, made of chicken wire. This was to be the home of the chicks until they were 6 weeks old, then I would halve them, putting half in a similar hen house with a similar wire pen, then at 10 or 12 weeks old, put the growing pheasants in poultry fold units of 25 birds to a unit, down the farm at various points, like turnip fields, corn fields and rough growth, etc. At this time, I had bought some partridge eggs, I had managed to get a few bantam broodies, and now these were hatching out. The fertility seemed very good, getting 53 chicks hatched from 60 eggs, these tiny chicks (grey partridge) were like little bumble bees, very lively, and the bantams were excellent mothers, looking after their babies very well, much better than the usual heavy farm fowl.

26th June was the Northumberland plate meeting at Newcastle, I had booked Monique and I in at the Park Hotel for this meeting, where some of our friends had also booked in. The day went well; me made seventy pounds for the day with my lucky bookie, Willy Whiteman. Sandy Taylor, who it seemed was not booked into the hotel, asked if he could borrow our room keys, as he wished to take a girl up to make love to her. "Of course," I said, handing him our key, "help yourself, the girl was named Sarah, whom a year or two later he married.

15th June, I took all of the men to the Royal Yorkshire show held at Harrogate for the day and young John Frith, son of Joe, who had left my employment. John was a young friend of our son Joey Jnr, they played together and had lots of fun together. John at the age of 12 or 13 was also an accomplished tractor driver, in fact better than many men and he helped out at hay time and harvest, or after school, he could drink beer as well as a man too. After the show, I treated the men to dinner at the A66 motel of Malcolm and Sonia fame, the one where the waitresses wore short skirts and used to bend over so that customers would see what they had further up, young John could not take his eyes off these delightful naughties, nor for that matter could my workmen, we dined very well, and had a hilarious evening there, our host and hostess being very good sports. Weatherwise, it was a hot, sunny day.

28th July, I left Dad in charge of everything, the hay was in and he had only the routine to see to plus some lambs. Monique and I set off on holiday with Adam and Joey to Spain, setting off at 9 am. I drove straight down to Dover, through the middle of London, arriving in Dover, we were in luck, there was a boat leaving within half an hour at 6:30 pm. We passed through customs at Calais and drove 150 miles into France, the weather was perfect. We were heading for a small town on the Spanish coast beyond Barcelona called Villanueva, one of Monique's uncles on the male side of her family had two apartments there, and we were renting one, I pushed on this time crossing France, stopping for breakfast en route to have those large cups of cafe-au-lait and croissant, the children loved this. Then for lunch, it would be a picnic one, liver pate and fresh charcuterie bought from the butcher shop in some small town, same with bread, and for the two boys a nice big cream cake for dessert, and of course wine, not too much as it would make me too tired to drive, then on driving I took a road over the hills to get to Villanueva, a mistake I found out too late, it was zig zag for miles, eventually we arrived at our destination at 9 pm on the 30th July. Went to Ernest, the uncle of Monique, first to get the key, and to my surprise and dismay, Monique's aunt Josephine, the one who had brought her up, was there waiting to stay with us at my rented apartment, she had been on holiday with her son Paul and decided to stay on and holiday with us, Monique and I were disappointed at this news, and to make matters worse, after driving all day, Ernest whom I had not met before, offered me lemonade to drink instead of what I wanted, a stiff whisky, I thought to myself, what a greedy sod. After small talk, we drove to the apartment – Aunt as well – It was only 2 or 3 minutes by car, the flat was big enough, with a balcony sideways onto the sea, but all there was in the place was a table and chairs for dining, no easy chairs, a bed in each bedroom (3), no pictures, only bare walls, the kitchen seemed to have what it takes to cook and that was it, knives, forks and spoons thrown in.

Being tired, we all hit the hay pretty quickly, I asked Monique if we were going to be saddled with her aunt for the duration of our stay, she did not know. The sea, this is what we had come for. Josephine, the aunt, stayed inside, she did not like the hot sun on her legs, with their varicose veins. We had the same routine day after day, but we could not go out on our own unless we had Auntie tagging along, she refused to "babysit" the boys. At one stage, the French family, Mr and Mrs Boison, downstairs were going to look after the boys, as Auntie had refused, while Monique and I went to a late dinner and cabaret together, when Auntie heard this, she threw a tantrum, so we did not get to the cabaret or our tete-a-tete dinner, Auntie would prepare lunch, not that we asked her to, she did it, and it got to the point where if we dallied on the beach before lunch, she would be in a black mood.

One day, Monique and I and the boys, plus Auntie, who gave us no chance to give her the slip, set off for Casteldelfels to present a pullover we had bought for our favourite bargirl, Elloisise, she had a kiosk bar beside the main road in Casteldelfels and she was such a kind soul, very poor, only about 20 years old and always cheerful, we had bought the pullover in Carlisle, just for Elloisise, when we parked and walked over to the kiosk, a year later, she recognised us right away, and when we gave her the present all wrapped up, she was like an excited child, and when she opened it up and saw the pullover – a good quality one – she squealed with delight, then she gave us big hugs, it was nice to see her so pleased, we knew her mother and her brother, and had been shown round her house, her brother had an automatic pistol under his pillow, that was one of our days out, we also called and dined at Madame Fortuny's, she was delighted to see us also.

After a fortnight into our holiday, Monique's Uncle had his granddaughter Dominique stay at his and his wife's apartment. Dominique was only 13 years old, she looked 20 and an absolute beauty, an Amazon of a girl, being 6 feet tall, long slender legs, a gazelle of perfect proportions, it was amazing how a 13-year-old could look like she did when she passed on the pavement, men's heads would turn, she was a statuesque beauty, everything was complete symmetry about her, she loved being in her bathing suit all day, she was not concerned about her beauty, she was just an innocent child – but some child.

There was 30 yards off the beach in the sea, a pretty big oval dip on the bottom, the dip or depression was 20 yards by 15 yards and at the bottom were mussels and a few sea urchins. Dominique and I used to dive down, possibly 20-25 feet and pick a few up one day doing this. Her elastic broke on her swimming pants, my word, what an eyeful I got, perfection. Dominique, in her innocence, did not care two hoots, shepulled the pants back on and continued diving, holding her pants up by one hand, twisting the front into a twirl. I thought I would see what happened if I tried to pull them down, so I got hold of her pants from behind and gave a good pull, but she had a good hard grip on them, they came halfway and that was that, she did not have another pair of swim pants to change into and the morning after, she turned up with the same ones, still holding them up with one hand.

One Sunday, Monique and I decided to dine at one of the best restaurants in town for a change. Of course, Auntie tagged on as well, she was like a Svengali. The Mare Nostrum, had in the middle of the street, covered in part, almost like a long bus shelter, except it was well equipped, cars, etc., would pass either side and to bring the food over, waiters had to be careful not to get knocked down, we had dined here before and the food was good. This particular Sunday, Dominique was being treated by her grandparents. As we walked in, there they were. We took a table nearby. They were having lobster and big ones at that. During this gastronomic delight, Dominique said she could eat no more lobster, she had had her fill. Ernest, her grandfather, told her, "This meal costs a lot of money, you eat it all up." Dominique told him she couldn't, he then ordered her out of the restaurant (not banished) but told her to run around the block twice to get the food down, this she did, came back and finished her lobster, we laughed over this for days, so did Dominique. Ernest had been when he lived in Oran – his family were also put out of Algeria by the Arabs – been in the tobacco and wine trade. One day he gave us an introduction to go and visit a friend of his, who was the owner of vineyards and made their own wine, at Villa Franca de Panades, off Monique and I went, this time on our own, leaving the boys in charge of the French couple, in the flat below, we did not tell Auntie a thing, the couple looking after the boys knew now, how difficult she was.

We spent an interesting two hours being shown around the winery. The friend of Ernest giving us a case of white wine by the label Vina Sol, or Sun wine, this was a rather good wine, I brought the full case back home to Skirwith with me.

On 29th August, we left Villanueva, heading for Marseille, I had to drop Auntie off there. Regarding the holiday, the boys really enjoyed it and it did them good. They were well-tanned and looked good with their blonde hair, and in the sea, they could both now swim like a fish, especially Adam, when they and I used to frolic in the waves, I began to realise they were now growing up, the strength they both had, or I myself was getting weaker.

For Monique and I, we had hardly been alone, Auntie had dogged our footsteps from the beginning and had had tempers thrown at us from time to time, if I had known she was going to stay a month with us, I would not have taken a holiday there. The flat itself had the barest of basics: a cooker, table and beds.

When I paid Ernest his rent money, he condescended to get his whisky bottle out.

I headed for the Black Forest once more to get stocked up with cigars. Going by way of Lyon, Chalon-Sur-Saonne, branching off there in the direction of Besancon and stopping the night at a little hotel near Belfort, not far from the German border, the hotel was small. Once inside, the bedrooms were quite good, but the bar and tables we thought for eating were not good, we sat and had a beer each, the children Coca-Cola, and then two or three Arabs came to drink, Monique said right away. "I'm not eating here tonight", well as it was dark and late, I was not going in search of a restaurant, because this hotel was on its own on the roadside, so we resigned not to eat because for one thing, the bar looked dirty and the Arabs being there, was enough for Monique. All of a sudden, on one side of the bar, two great double curtains were pulled aside and beyond lay an immaculately set dining room, very clean, in fact, spotless, I mentioned to Monique, "This looks okay, let's take a table," she replied. "No one is in it, it can't be good," within 15 minutes, people arrived and filled the tables. I told Monique there is one table left, and I am taking it, the boys were pleased, our table was in fact, the last one of, I think, 15. It was incredible how the place filled almost at the drop of a hat. It must have had a good reputation, and we were soon to find out, the boys and I had steak, I think we were all ready for this, Monique ordered with reserve, she was being careful, she ordered ham from the bone, the atmosphere in the dining room was like a beehive, everything had come to life, it was rather amazing. When our steaks came, they were huge and thick, not like the Cote d'Azur, small and paper thin, Monique's ham came, 3 enormous slices of ¼ of an inch thick, covering the whole plate, looking very succulent, I cut into my steak, it cut-like butter, so did the boys ones, the taste was excellent with a sauce to match. After the meal, I said to Monique that this was the best steak that I had ever had, and that included home, they were so good that as big as the steaks were, the boys finished theirs also, not a morsel left on the plate, Monique found her ham the same as the steaks, superb, but she could only manage 2 slices, as each slice would be the full round of a pigs thigh or (ham). We had two bottles of St Emilion to slowly wash everything down, the boys had theirs with a little water added, cheese to follow, about eight different sorts of cheese were put in front of us to help ourselves, wonderful cheeses the French have, then for dessert the boys had an enormous slice of chocolate cake, myself had crème caramel, I always have a softness for this dessert, Monique made it quite often for the boys and I, for dessert Monique did not take any. The meal had been so good, we had to go on to coffee and brandy, Monique had a whisky. She had been to so many parties and race meetings she now had graduated to scotch, or a glass of beer.

We dwelled at our table for quite a time and while I smoked a very good Havana, counting how lucky we were to stumble on such a hotel and restaurant, which from outside looked like nothing at all – but this is the secret of France, as I was to discover many times over. The price was not at all expensive, though I made no note of the total, if it had been outrageous, I would have done so.

In the morning, we left the Palace Hotel, for that was its name, crossing over Father Rhine as the Germans fondly called this big river and into Freiberg at 9 am, where we had breakfast. Had a look around, then at 12:30 pm we had an excellent lunch at a restaurant near the Dom Platz, accompanied by large glasses of Pilsner beer, the boys again Coca-Cola. Then we motored out to Waldkirch to my old 90-year-old cigar woman who had, the year before, wanted to marry Dad. There she was once more, large as life, still smoking her black cigars, she said she knew me from the year before and made a fuss of us, I was not sure though if she did or not, I bought 1000 cigars this time, black and blonde, the old lady, when I asked for the percentage gave me 7.5%, but for an extra present gave me only 5 very good cigars, I thanked her kindly, then we hunted another quiet place to put the cigars inside the car door's panelling, once again I had to take a few hundred from the boxes and put the cigars in cellophane bags Gabby had given me in Marseille for this purpose. We were not disturbed at all during the transformation, keeping 200 in boxes to declare at Dover, 75 each, which we were allowed, plus 50 as blind. I had bought a case of Keiserstuhl red wine to take home. Time was now getting on, it was 5:30 pm, I thought it was time we booked into a hotel for the night. Arriving in a village called Ezach, I saw a pretty little hotel, I went in and asked if they had two rooms. Yes, they had, I took them right away, as I did not feel like driving around anymore, the hotel was clean and warm, the beds as all German hotels, have had the lovely great thick goose down duvets. Monique and I liked these duvets very much, so did the boys, or I should say Adam did and Joey Jnr did not, even in later life he would not have a duvet, preferring a mountain of heavy blankets. The next day Joey Jnr wanted a cuckoo clock, so we bought him a little one, it worked well for years. Adam thought another knife would do for him. After that, we had an excellent lunch at Gegensbach, then set sail for France, where we stayed at a place called Soverne, not very good, nor was the food, and bedrooms so-so, after dining so well the last few days it came as a disappointment, as before we found the food with a German touch, as well as French, the marriage of the two, we didn't like and never have either.

On 4th September, we set off very early and drove through to Calais, having a good picnic lunch near Cambrai, getting into Calais at 5 pm, the car on the last 50 miles started to run badly, same trouble as last time, a valve stem gone, so I thought. With luck, there was a ferry boat sailing within the hour. I booked in, and we were soon on board, getting to Dover at 8 pm. When we had cleared customs no trouble, I decided to drive hard through the night. Going steadily, due to our engine trouble, getting home on 5th September at 4:30 am, tired but pleased to be home. The house was as cold as an iceberg, Monique had got to the stage when she could hardly stand the cold, her hands and feet going white as snow and cramps starting. I had bought her some fur-lined boots, but even then she got cramp in her feet if the weather was very frosty. Mrs Metcalfe had lit the Aga cooker and also the Agamatic that heated the water, which was something, otherwise, everything was cold.

Sunday, I took it easy, unpacked the cigars, and had a look around the farm in the Land Rover. I would have to wait until I saw Dad to see how things were, I never called or phoned him now Mother was gone, I had no wish to talk to that awful woman he had married.

Monday 7th Dad and I talked, all was well on the farm, he complained about me having a month's holiday and the cost of it I explained the cost of the whole holiday was 285 pounds including petrol and ferry boat, and 200 pounds had come from my horse money and bets. He never believed it.

With the hundreds of yards of new fencing I had done, plus cementing the big courtyard, plus extra breeding heifers I had bought from Ireland to get the numbers up, plus 50 breeding gimmers, also to help get numbers up, we were overdrawn at the bank by one thousand pounds. Now Dad, each morning come hail or rain, used to come into our breakfast room, sit down, take his wallet, about 2.5 inches thick, from his inside jacket pocket, unfasten the elastic band, and rail on about being over-drawn at the bank, how it was a bad way to do business, we would soon be bankrupt – I asked him one morning "What is the matter, are you frightened of the bank manager, because," I added. "It seems as if you are," He denied it but half-heartedly.

Then, sometime about now, a new bank manager was in the office at Barclays Stanley Farnsworth, he thought to start using his "new broom." One morning, I received a letter from this little man about the overdraft, I did not like the tone of his letter at all, I wrote by return that we at Skirwith Hall had never had such a letter from any bank manager before and that I did not like the tone of his letter to me, next day, a knock on the front door, I opened to find little Farnsworth on the doorstep, he startedapologising again and again, I told him, "I hope this sort of thing does not happen again," and it never did – I did not ask him in either, myself I have never been afraid to have a row, or to tell my bank managers where to get off, even when I was hard pressed in later years, they all backed off.

Dad continued this until it became a ritual every morning: sit down, give two or three coughs, hand into his jacket breast pocket, out comes the thick wallet, off with the elastic band, slowly opens the wallet, produces bank statement or similar, then starts to remonstrate, at the same time telling me he could have bought the farm for much less that I had given for it. With this, I always retaliated with the very words he had used at the time. "We would be far better off under a new landlord", he would give a cough and not reply, I would counter again with "Fleming-Smith (the valuer for A.M.C.) offered me twenty-five thousand pounds profit right away". It think it rankled even to the day he died that I had negotiated the deal on my own, behind his back, but I had to do so quickly before it became public knowledge that Skirwith Hall was for sale, he had had his chance once when I was in Algeria, and fluffed the whole thing. He and his brother-in-law, Alex Bayne, offering thirteen thousand pounds, I certainly was not going to let Father fluff it again, especially when I saw the road he was taking with that awful woman, Mrs Page.

If Mother had not died, I am not sure what my moves would have been, very possibly the same, but I would have told Mother of my moves.

But this daily or almost daily ritual of money complaints was getting on my nerves, he told me that Monique was spending too much and used too much lipstick. I thought of the year he emptied Skirwith Hall of every item, leaving things that was a fixture, the Aga cooker and Agamatic – his own desk in the smoke room, and a threadbare carpet in that room,

Monique was left with not even a bent fork to eat from, or plates to eat from, or even a table to put food on, except the old 20ft long servants table in the kitchen. Also, a house whose roof leaked like a sieve, the old maid's bedroom was shocking. The last of Mother's maids had to put half a dozen buckets to catch the rainwater. Monique's maids slept in one of the main rooms, the bathroom was the same, the large guest bedroom the same. We did not use this one for a long time, ceilings were falling down, really Skirwith Hall was on purchase day, in a bad way. Father would do nothing to the house, always saying it was the responsibility of the landlord, the result, nothing ever was done, the landlords had no money. Even Mother, when she sold her house at Silloth, every stick of furniture, knives, forks, spoons, plates, were sent off to Josephine in Paris, some exquisite furniture to boot, Josephine sold the lot right away for a pittance, I kept my cool, and said very little. Father also hadthe knack of always arriving to see what I was doing, just as we would be setting off for Penrith or the races. His looks said it all.

11th September, I took Bert Johnstone, Adam and Joey to shoot grouse over on my moor behind Cross Fell, Adam had one of my guns, but Joey was beating. When we arrived by Land Rover, walked down the fell for perhaps 100 yards, we stopped while I instructed Bert and the boys the direction to go, and in line, no talking etc, we were stood four square when all of a sudden, Bert's gun went off, blowing a hole a foot deep in the peaty soil, right in the middle of our square, one inch of elevation, either Adam's or my feet would have been blown right off, I asked "what the hell are you doing?" to Bert, he said "the gun just went off, I told him, "Well its a damned dangerous gun to bring out, get another one next time". He said he would, however, I noticed later in the day, when the shooters would be at ease, Bert's fingers would play about the trigger and trigger guard, there was no fault with his gun. I mentioned this episode to Dad and his advice was, do not to ask Bert again to any shoots, I wish I had taken notice of the advice.

I was most annoyed at Bert and told him so, we carried on, but I kept my two boys a good distance from him, Adam shot 3 birds, he was going to turn into a good shot, no doubt.

When our little group were close together, Bert had a habit of, without thinking, waving his gun muzzle in someone's direction, even standing still, his gun would be pointing at one of us. I came to the conclusion he was not to be trusted with safety in mind.

Thursday, 29th September my old friend and drinking partner and the father of my first love, Major Frederick Cyril Francis Parker, died aged 82 years, for the last 6 months, Cyril had been slipping away and had Alzheimer's disease creeping up on him.

My throat was still inflamed, and I was far from well, when Cyril's funeral was declared for the 2nd October, I decided not to go as I was not really fit to do so, however Bert Johnstone phoned to ask if I would go with him to the funeral as he wanted to be introduced to the two executors, Denholm Rowlands and Derek Pattinson, and the new boy owner, as he did not know any of them, he realised I knew them all and well.

When Bert phoned, I told him I had decided not to attend the funeral, but then he pleaded with me over the phone to go, and I relented to my regret. Cyril had left a sum of money to be spent at the George Hotel for his friends to celebrate after the funeral rites, at the George, which had been sold a year or so ago to Dutton's Breweries of Lanc's, they hadinstalled a new manager, Stuart Coulthard, it was he who opened the bar, a temporary bar in the dining room cum ballroom of the George. I duly introduced Bert to the various people he wished to know, whisky was flowing like water, it was Grant's Malt in the clear bottles, that was the only whisky on that day, and then I did not like malt whisky at all, but I drank it and rather too much in my "delicate" state of health. In bed for 10 or 11 days, getting up to go to a funeral, too much whisky, I must have been drowsy, for all at once, I had to sit down, or I would have fallen down and went into a deep slumber. Bert and Robert Jackson, who were also there, managed to get me home, Monique was not very pleased repeating that I was a fool to have gone to a funeral in my state of health, if I had been fit, I would have been there drinking old Cyril's voyage to the unknown till the day after.

On 3rd October, I awoke feeling rather low and weak, I suppose the antibiotic and whisky had not mixed too well, I got up late and then took it easy. The remainder of the week, I saw the men off to work and kept indoors as it was raining hard, and I did not wish another soaking as on the grouse moor.

Saturday, Monique and I had a day at Newcastle races, where we met up with all of our Friends. A few of us got together to dine at a new restaurant in a high-rise building, this was 6 or more floors up by lift. I never made a note of its name, but that night John Cummings and his bitchy wife Valerie were at the party when just about to take our table, something happened that made her very nasty to her husband John, who was always the gentleman, far too soft towards her, giving in to her every bitchy whim, I hated the way this night she started on John and I told her so in no uncertain terms, this made things much worse, she threw a real tantrum, John told me not to speak like that to his wife, so I told him "It's a pity you did not speak like that to her years ago, how many times has she spoiled your evenings for you, in front of friends," in the end she stormed out, John after her, the rest of the party decided now they did not want a meal, but before Monique and I got into our car; John who was on the pavement shouted to me "Don't forget I am shooting on Wednesday. I had invited John to my shoot on the 11th.

Wednesday, 11th November, I had arranged to have a shoot with a few friends at Skirwith Hall. The day started with an almost gale-force wind, not so good for a decent bag of game, the guests were Archie and Pat, who had learned to shoot and was shaping up quite well, she had a very nice gun, a Purdey, which speaks for itself, Robert Jackson and John Cummins, who had been the first to arrive, he had left his wife behind, thank goodness. We had morning drinks of whisky. Pat was also a drinker of whisky, Archie had his hip flask full of the Famous Grouse.

My farm men were doing the beating, the morning shoot was not too good owing to the wind, far too strong still – but I could see it dropping as we knocked off for lunch, we had shot 11 pheasants and two woodcock, 3 pigeons. Monique had arranged a very good lunch of Pistou soup. Lasagne and bread and butter pudding, Robert Jackson looked at the lasagne (he had never had it before) and asked Monique to give him only very little, when he tasted it, he finished his plate and asked for twice as much, saying it was one of the best dishes he had eaten – Monique's lasagne was indeed something special.

Lunch took quite a long time, in the end, I had almost to drag the shooters outside to finish the afternoon, the wind had dropped quite considerably, making the walking and shooting much more pleasant, 21 pheasant, 2 pigeons and 4 hares were shot in the afternoon, but the shooting was much poorer than in the morning. The wine, I think was the fault, Archie had been getting at his flask, too freely, pure whisky, he was feeling rather limp at the day's end. Pat had decided to stay with Monique for the rest of the day when lunch was finished. Lassie had worked so well. She was the apple of everyone's eye and deserved a gold medal. She was the only dog there, no one else seemed to have a gun dog. The total bag was 32 pheasant, 2 woodcock, 5 pigeon, 4 hares and Lassie had retrieved the lot, John Cummings had enjoyed himself so much, he gave Kurt, who had carried his cartridge and game bag, ten pounds for himself, the other men received five pounds each from the guests.

After more drinks, Monique laid on the dinner, once again the Pistou soup, then roast pheasant, half a bird for each guest, followed by crème caramel. Archie and Pat stayed the night in front of a roaring coal and log fire in the morning room, faces quite red from the elements and barleycorn and cigars. We chatted on till late, it had been a pleasant day.

Saturday 14th, John Cummings' horse was running at Catterick, he had told me to get there and have a bet that it would win. Monique and I decided to go, Catterick was only 1 hour and 10 minutes away, in any case, we both liked Catterick course, and the racing staff were a good and friendly lot. Catterick was also one of the fastest tracks in England, John's horse Quagmire was favourite @ 70/40 against, I was and never had been a heavy gambler, but I had my 40 pounds on and also 5 pounds forecast on the tote, the horse won nicely, that forecast paying just over 51 pounds. The day was a good one, though dry, it was a very icy wind. John and Valerie, who was there with him, were in an extra good mood with the win, knowing now she could ask John with certainty to buy her another diamond or some tremendously expensive outfit in London, celebrated with a few bottles of champagne, and after the races, in the Bridge Inn, just across the road from the track, an excellent watering place after racing, and later dinner at Scotch Corner Grill, again with Quagmires owner and wife, the manager also a good friend, Tom Jones, congratulated John and invited us for drinks after the meal, then home, once again late.

The following Saturday, the same procedures as last Saturday, except this time the venue was Wetherby Races. Monique and I drove down, once again, to back Quagmire, and once more, he obliged, this time 2/1, I had 50 pounds on him, another profitable day.

Tuesday, December 16th, was our wedding anniversary. Monique and I went to one of our favourite places, the simplicity of the A66 motel on the Scotch Corner road, there the food was guaranteed to be good, Sonia saw to that, not only the food, but the ambience was good, a most friendly place, the dinner was superb, as also the wine. The anniversary dinner went on with various people we knew and our hosts Malcolm and Sonia until we left at 5 am, getting home at 5:50 am. The trouble now was that I was shooting that same day with Arthur Sowerby on the Abbey Estate. Arthur had rented the shooting on the Abbey from old Parker for a few years now and still kept hard at it, in fact, he kept the shooting until he died, aged about 90 years, Bert taking it then, but now Arthur was expecting me at 9 am at the rendezvous, up the old Roman Road. The acreage to shoot was approximately 300, but quite a lot with excellent pheasant cover of scrub woodland having grown like this after the wartime felling of the trees. These areas had not been replanted and had now grown into useless scrub stuff, but the pheasants loved it Arthur reared about 200 birds to let off.

I slept until 8 am, then stripped to the waist, shaved, and splashed ice-cold water over myself (we had no shower). I had a quick plate of porridge, toast and tea while Monique made me sandwiches for lunch, let Lassie out for her ablutions, got into the car and went off. I had only 1 mile to go, thank goodness. I still felt a bit bleary from all the whisky and wine only a few hours ago; I shot well, though my first half dozen shots were bad. I shook myself up and then I was back to normal. I did not keep a tally of the birds I shot, but the bag at the end of the day was 79 pheasant, 10 hares, 4 partridges, 1 woodcock from 8 guns.

As usual from this shoot, Arthur had organised the shoot dinner at Edenhall Hotel, our dirty friend Alex Beck's place, but as I have said before, Alex, and especially for Arthur, could lay on an extremely good banquet, fit for the highest in the land, and this was one of the nights. There were, I remember, 5 courses, all of which were one better than the other, the wines also good, followed by liqueurs and Havana Corona cigars of Ramon Allones, then after this guests, guns and beaters had to buy their own, it's a pity I never made a note of the menu this night, we never left the dining table to drink at the bar, this was as usual, it seemed to keep us together, I remember I made a short speech that night, but what it was about I have forgotten. Again, it was late when I drove the 5 miles home at 2 am on the 17th. I took it rather easy. My system was tired from lack of sleep and clogged up with booze.

Saturday was a bonus day for the workforce, paying them their accumulated overtime for hay time, harvest time and holiday pay, lamb bonus for the shepherd and calf bonus for the cowman. They were well content, this payment would come in handy for them for Christmas. They had smiles on their faces as they left the smoke room cum office, but they had deserved it. They had their overtime and bonus paid tax-free, myself paying that tax for them, as when working overtime and paying tax on that, the workforce was not interested in overtime at all.

The two boys, Adam and little Joey were home for the Christmas holidays. They were as excited as we all were for Christmas to arrive. Monique and I took them shopping at Carlisle and treated them to a slap-up lunch at the County Hotel.

Christmas Eve day, little Joey came running into the house to tell me the Triumph 2000, standing in the garden car park, was full of smoke inside, I rushed out to see what the matter was, and there it was, the car inside so full of smoke I could not see through to the other side, I opened a door, put my head inside, and nearly chocked to death on the absolute acrid electric smoke, however, no flames were visible, so I opened all 4 doors, and put the bonnet up when the smoke had cleared, there were no burn marks on the inside at all, but then taking a good look under the dashboard, inside the boot and engine it turned out every wire in the car had burned out, from rear to front, a wonder the car had not gone up in flames, also I thought, a pity because from new, it had been a constant headache, I thought this is it then, the car goes, there seemed to be a hoodoo on it. I got it towed into Penrith to Armstrong and Flemings to rewire, where I hired a Hillman Minx until the Triumph was rewired. That night, Adam and I went to midnight mass. Monique, being Catholic non-practicing, stayed behind with little Joey.

Christmas Day, the boys, now of the age to wait and receive their presents from under the Christmas tree mid-morning, had an exciting time. Monique and I always opened our presents after lunch. This year, we had goose, and it was an excellent one, cooked to perfection with the trimmings of bread sauce, apple puree and mashed swede, the latter going well with goose and that stalwart, the potato, followed by plum pudding and rum sauce, but for the children thick jersey cream. Before the feast, I opened a bottle of champagne and while at one stage out of the room helping Monique to do something in the kitchen, Adam had taken advantage of my absence and helped himself to a great deal of champagne, with the result he missed lunch and had to go to bed until feeling better, he surfaced at 4:30 pm, his excuse being the champagne tasted like lemonade. We did not remonstrate with him.

On New Year's Eve, Monique and I went to a dinner dance at Ramsbeck Hotel on Lake Ullswater, owned and run by John Grundy and his wife, Beryl. Ramsbeck had possibly the best site of any on the lake, a beautiful Country mansion turned hotel. John Grundy, whom I knew well, could and did put a very good dinner dance on, good food also, but his breakfasts would probably be the best in England, he could drink 25 pints of Guinness on a market day in Penrith, no problem, latterly however, in the late 70's it seemed John had a touch of financial cramp, sold the hotel, bought a large country house from Lord Lonsdale, a house as it turned out, that needed a new roof, a very large roof, two years approximately after this, he died. He was great buddies with another of our hotelier friends, Malcolm Hunter of the Queen's Hotel Tirril, who also died a rather painful death from cancer, aged in his late 30s, I think, similar age to John.

Adam's birthday fell on the day he had to return to Dunrobin School, on January 11th, he is 15 years old, academically he was doing quite well, at the sport he was very good. He had taken his pet ferret to Dunrobin a year ago and used to go ferreting with the Countess of Sutherland's keeper and, in the holidays, left his ferret with the keeper when sometimes he had brought the ferret home on the train to give other passengers a fright, he would take the ferret out into the corridor, and put it up one of his sleeves, he would then return to his seat, then say to a passenger sitting opposite, "look at my hand" at the same time stretching out his arm, with the ferret in the sleeve, the person opposite would look carefully, then all at once the ferret would poke his head out, there would be loud screams, and sometimes a rush to the door, one oldish woman nearly fainted, that ferret could go up one arm and come down the other sleeve, Adam had it trained well, but I had to tell him not to try his trick on older women, scare the pants off others if he wished.

I had got the Triumph 2000 back, but in mid-January, it was running badly, so I took it to Langwathby to Billy Marshall, the complete mechanic was Billy. He found a badly bent valve stem and a missing piece of a valve insert, what a car; no wonder foreigners would not buy British.

I had by now planted two acres of young trees of Sitka spruce, just beyond the water quarry on each side of the beck, but keeping about 4 to 5 yards from the bank of the beck to give plenty of room for fishing, this small plantation was for the sporting aspect, i.e., cover for pheasant and duck as well as others, and also in the long term, timber for fencing on the farm. I also planted 2 acres on land halfway to Kirkland beside a 65-acre field that was open to the elements, this was primarily for shelter and, again, timber for the farm. Black Wood that had been felled, I was fencing this area and going to plant it next winter. The planting had been done by the three Margarets in the village, they were Kurt's wife, Margaret Wilkinson, whose husband used to work at Skirwith Hall, he now worked at Robert Jackson's, and Mrs Fawcett, whose husband had helped me out at hay time and harvest, in return I lent him machinery to work his small farm, these three women were all excellent workers, and would help out on the farm at any time, all first class sorts. Father was not too pleased with my planting of trees, considering them a waste of time, telling me I would have passed on before I saw them to maturity, but I considered trees a thing of beauty as well as of great use in many ways.

Saturday, Monique and I were up at 5:30 am to go to Eskdalemuir to shoot at Archie's farm, having to be there by 8:30 am Robert Jackson also went with us. The day was very cold and at times, quite misty, rather a poor day for birds to fly well, there were 8 guns, two of them were Lord Riverdale and his son Mark. At a stop for a "breather," Archie, shooting with Pat's gun, a beautiful Purdey, leaned it against the side of the Land Rover. In seconds the gun slid to the ground, hitting a sharp stone with the barrel, putting a fair-sized dent in it, not the sort of thing that should happen to a Purdey, it would be expensive to have it repaired. On hearing the news later, Pat was far from pleased.

Lunchtime came, with drinks beforehand, which was most welcome to kill the cold. Pat had both fires going in the dining room and living room, Archie filling the glasses as soon as they were empty. There was an enormous turkey to carve, I should think it would weigh at least 25 lbs. Archie attacked it with his new electric carving knife, as noisy as ever. We finished with plum pudding, with more rum than sauce. I don't think after all this good fare, none of us wanted to go out to shoot again; however, we did venture forth, shooting to start with a ten-acre field Archie had sown with oats and, due to continually bad weather, had been unable to harvest it, now it was a tangled mess of straw, with the head of corn either touching the ground or lying on it, first-class cover and food for pheasants, but there were not as many birds in this lovely piece of cover as there should have been. Robert Jackson and I were at the lower end of this field when 4 or 5 pheasants flew so high they were more like pigeons. Robert missed, and for some reason, so did I, clean as a whistle. However, at the end of the day, after some hard walking, we had bagged 16 pheasants, three woodcock and a duck, the day had been a most enjoyable one. At the end drinks were served, and then with Archie and Pat, we bid goodbye to the others as they left, Robert, Monique and I stayed for more drinks and dinner, finishing off the large turkey, getting home at 2 am.

On January 22nd, I had sent two men to mend a gap in a stone wall, the breeding ewes had been knocked down, the other side of the wall was Robert Jackson's farm, but the wall was mine, the gap was 3 yards long, and had been made in a place the ewes made a yearly habit of breaking through, I had rebuilt this same piece of wall a few times myself. This day I sent David Metcalfe, the son of Mrs. Metcalfe, Monique's daily help, and of the shepherd, Harold, the former poultry man, David was perhaps 18 years old and possibly missing 6d in the pound, he had worked here since leaving school a year or two earlier, the other was George Western, tractor man, quite a hard worker, and had to do quite a lot of the housework at his cottage, as his wife also had a problem, possibly missing 1/- in the pound, sometimes going round the village, with her very full breasts hanging right out of her blouse, no bra's or things like that, the village school lads, used to hide and watch her, although there was no need to hide. Kurt and I were sawing posts and rails all day at one stage, I wondered why it was taking Western and Metcalfe so long to return home. Eventually, late evening, they appeared and told me they had finished work on the gap, I remonstrated with them for taking most of the day - 5 hours - here were two men – young Metcalfe started to give me backchat and swearing, then told me to fuck off, I had no alternative but to sack him on the spot, which I did. Western took his ticking off as he should have done quietly.

I saw David's father, Harold, after work that night and told him what had happened, telling him I hoped it did not or would not alter our good working relationship – to my surprise, he said it did and would – I told him then not to be so narrow-minded and left him.

What happened next was that this particular week. Dad was out at Sil- loth in a house he and his wife had bought, David Metcalfe, the sacked man, Harold, his father and his mother drove down to Silloth that night to complain of my conduct towards their son, Dad phoned me up that same night telling me to take David back in work, I told Dad quite straight, that if I then took David back, it would undermine my position completely, telling him at the same time that I myself, the men must regard as the "boss', also, that in my position I was not going to have an overgrown schoolboy swear and tell me to fuck off, and that was that. I thought, let him come and apologise to me now, then will I take him back? David did not come to apologise.

On Monday, George Western, who had been with David mending the wall gaps, decided to start and tell me that I was not the boss at Skirwith Hall and that I had no right to sack David, I soon put him right on that matter, sacking him as well. Later on, he had a hard think because he came to me very apologetic, I took him back on the payroll. I hoped this would be a lesson that the men would think twice about before slagging me in the future. I had always bent over backwards to see their side of things, but familiarity does breed discontent.

Tuesday, I had a very sudden death of a healthy two-month-old calf, which had been in a large shed running with its mother and 25 other mothers and youngsters. The vet came, as one has to notify them for instant deaths, he thought it was virus pneumonia but was not sure. I took the calf myself to the government centre at Merrythought for a post-mortem on Carlisle Road. I phoned John Barr, the head vet, whose assistant had seen the calf that morning, I asked Barr to push the vets at Merrythought for a quick diagnosis as I was afraid whatever malady the calf had may prove contagious – I wanted to know quickly. To my surprise, Barr refused my request to treat this as urgent and started to become very officious and bombastic. I suggested that seeing the attitude he was taking, he should send his bill in right away and from hence I would no longer require his services, and put the phone down on him - this man had been one of my brother's big friends, but I had noticed since I had bought Skirwith Hall many people had become jealous of me somehow, probably because of my flamboyant way of life, but that was only one side of me they saw, they did not see the other side, the work side, I could work longer and harder and did so more than any of my own men. I played hard, too.

Little John Barr, the vet, he was like most little men of approximately 5' 2-3, bombastic and big-headed, endowed with his own importance, he phoned me the next morning to give me the results of the calf's post-mortem, apologetic, saying the post mortem was due to lead poisoning, I kept him on as my vet, but I never liked the man. However, his three assistants were gems of men. Barr, later on in life, dropped down dead in a London railway station enroute to the U.S.A. I did not shed any tears; his son, also in later life, became as big-headed as his father and as liked in the community as I liked his father.

Uncle David, we could see, missed his wife Kate, his childhood sweetheart and my mother's dearest sister and closest friend, he did not last many more years, dying quietly, I think, as he wanted to go and see his sweetheart.

A thing I hated to do, I had to shoot the boy's dog, Ben, he was Adam's really – he was a collie but a very strong dog, he loved the boys, but at the same time in his excitement playing with them, he would bite them, quite hard too. This day, Ben was caught worrying a large, strong ram, Ben going like fury in full rage, meaning to kill the ram, Ben was caught, put on a leash and I shot him. I told the boys a lie, saying Ben had got lost somehow, I could not bring myself to tell them he was dead.

Then, a phone call from my blood brother, dear old Heinz, reminding me that Karnival was going to start the following week, that was enough for me. I told Monique to pack one large suitcase ready for off on Wednesday, the 17th – I had to arrange the men's work while I was away, though Dad was there to see to things also.

Monique and I set off for Dover at 2:30 pm on Wednesday 17th. Looking back, it seemed to be a late start for me, this was in the Triumph 2000. We arrived in Dover with plenty of time to spare for the next ferry boat, which sailed at 12:30 am.

On we went in the direction of Koln, taking the Autobahn, skirting Cologne. I stopped at Remscheid Roadway restaurant for something to eat, where we had some goulash soup and roast beef and potatoes. The whole lot tasted very good, the drinks were coffee, now feeling much better, we pressed on and headed, as Heinz has always said, in the direction of Recklinghousen, passing Bochum, where the red light girls would stand in their doorways or windows beckoning one in to sample their feminine delights. These places at Bochum were government licensed and fully doctored to see that the girls were healthy. Soon, we were rolling through Munster, the streets I knew so well, and drove straight to Ienenerstrasse, Telgte, arriving in time for lunch and fun. The welcome was a warm one; out came half a dozen bottles of champagne (Matteus Muller) and into Heinz's cellar bar, "The Shepherd's Inn," warm as toast, music from the Karnival songs, and Strauss, this I knew was my second home, we had a close bond my blood brother and I.

After a long and liquid lunch, Heinz, myself and Monique drove the 250 yards to Emil's pub here once again, the welcome was a warm one from Emil and Mitze, especially the former; he just enjoyed seeing Monique and I turn up, once more, the drinks flowed and flowed, we took them as they came, I myself was in top drinking form, on we went, this time on foot, the ½ mile to town. We knew the police at Karnival time could and often did block all roads into and round towns breathalysing all drivers except taxis and buses, I've seen that happen many times, by now, our other good friends had joined us, Willie Hesselman, the big farmer whose brother had a factory where he made 250,000 bottles of cocoa a day, half a million small packs of butter for restaurants a day etc, and Alfons and Nane Lutkehous, we were set for a night out, we did not return to Heinz's house till 3 am the next day, meeting Maria at 7 pm in the Wildman pub, we danced, sang and drank and smoked the hours away. These Karnival days and nights I chain smoked cigars from breakfast time until bedtime, usually this was about 3 am, only putting a cigar down to have some food, this was quite often taken in pubs, where at least in Telgte and Munster, the pub food was very good indeed and most substantial. We had lunch quite a few times at the Althaus hotel, run by our friends Erica and Helmut Schrade, they themselves had invited Monique and I, Heinz and Maria to their private Karnival party on Saturday night, together with approximately 50 other guests, no outsider being allowed in, the doors being locked. We accepted and looked forward to this, as it was also going to be a fancy dress do. Alfons and his wife and Willie Hessleman had not been invited for some reason. Heinz wanted to go to this dressed in the Scottish kilt and insisted that I do the same, but at this, I refused point blank because I had knobbly knees and very slim legs, whereas Heinz had good, strong, thick legs that would do justice to a kilt. I know this: if I did happen to have good thick legs, I would have made the kilt my habitual dress, and in full evening dress of the kilt, there is no finer dress in the world. However, nature had not endowed me with such limbs, and on this occasion, I was not exposing anything that would embarrass me. I was determined to dress as a gypsy prince. Monique was dressing herself in her own dresses, arranged in exaggeration.

    Friday was the same, except that we visited almost all of the 35 or 40 pubs in Telgte, meeting people I had known as children in the '50s and '60s, now young adults starting on their great adventure of life of girlfriends and boyfriends, and early marriage for a few, I was greeted by these young men and women most warmly, all still insisting on calling me Oncle

Joey, it made me wonder sometimes, why the hell we were ever at war with these people, who were more like the English than most – but of course they had been led onto the path of such a terrible war by thugs who had come to power.

Now here, in their Karnival time of 1971, all of these bad times seemed rather far behind, we were among warm-hearted people, welcomed open-heartedly into their houses day after day, and told, "do not forget to come back."

Saturday night arrived and at 7 pm, we went to the Althouse, Heinz and I in our costumes. The hotel, always nice and warm in winter, was well decorated, just like Christmas time. We were introduced to the other guests, some I knew, quite a few I did not. Titbits to eat were on the tables. Helmut gave us the first round of drinks, then we had to buy our own. Karnival music was played on tape and discs. Willie, the head waiter and a waitress were there to see that everyone's glasses were kept full and they were. Willy was only about 22 years old but perfect in everything in the restaurant and hotel world. We danced and danced, then at one time I danced with a blonde woman of about 35, perhaps more, who spoke very good English, a little later, I asked Helmut more about this woman, as I was piecing bits together, what I had gleaned from her and now what Helmut told me, she was the woman who had been married to an Indian living in England, he and his brother, where they reared pigs. One day, the two Indians disappeared, thought by the police to be murdered, it was headlines for a week or so in the News of the World Sunday paper in England. The culprit, they thought, was the wife of one of the brothers, this woman whom I had been dancing with. The police dug up some of the small holdings, even some of the pigs were slaughtered to see if any human flesh or bones were in the pigs' intestines and the dung heap was inspected and analysed for human remains – because the police believed this woman had fed the bodies of the two Indians to the pigs, but not a thing could they find, they could not pin the murders on her, she sold the small holding and stock and left England, quite a rich woman. Now here I was dancing with her in Telgte, she was dressed to kill (some pun – not intended) and had not a care in the world, she was there with a slim, well-dressed businessman – whether he knew of her past I don't know - but I did not dance with her again. Round about 4 am, we thought as a few others, to call it a night. Helmut had, so he said, kept an account of our drinks, now brought the bill to Heinz and me, we both thought it was rather a steep bill, but paid up, next day we reckoned up and realised that the money we had paid was the equivalent of over 250 beers, which we certainly had not drunk. We had known from events before concerning Helmut he would stick quite a lot of extra on drink bills if he could, both Heinz and I had tripped him up before and had become wary of him, we did not say anything, seeing it was Karnival and we had spent a most enjoyable night at his and Erica's invitation.

Sunday evening we passed at Emil's, danced and drank, while he played the piano, this was the night Monique lost the big diamond from the ring I had bought her for our 1st wedding anniversary, it was a platinum one with one big diamond and two lines of rubies.

At the stroke of midnight on a Tuesday, all music stopped every – whereas one. All decorations were dismantled instantly, no more drinks were served, for on the last stroke of the clock, it was now Ash Wednesday, and Lent had started, we took the taxi home and to bed – for today, Ash Wednesday, Monique and I were heading back home, I had already bought a thousand cigars from Sepple Poppenborg and put them all ex- cept for 200 behind the car door panels. Heinz had to start work also. We were up at 6 am, had breakfast, drank a couple of beers in the kitchen, said our goodbyes, Willie Hesselman had come over to see us on our way and had breakfast with us. We left the house at 7:30 am and drove down Elnenerstrasse, there was Emile sweeping dead leaves up outside his pub, he gave us a big wave, and then we were on the road to Munster.

We took a later boat but arrived in Dover in the dark and

took rooms just out of town, not a bad little place run by an Indian. We were up early next morning and on our way, albeit slowly, stopping at Canterbury to have a look and buy some bread baked in the oldest ovens in the world, I had read about this place in Canterbury in one of the Sunday papers, this bakery was run by a woman and her son, she was round about 98 years old and her son 80 years old, she served the bread and her son baked it, in according to the papers, 900-year-old ovens, Monique and I went into this quaint little shop, more or less in the shadow of the Cathedral, there was this very aged, but active, physically and mentally fit woman, I told her I had read about her and had quite a chat, she told me she could not cope with the new coinage (the decimal one) and was going to close down. She showed us the ovens, in full work, her son busy baking and indeed they were ancient, built of very small bricks, the roof of them inside, oval-shaped, Monique bought three loaves, then we bade goodbye to some of England's history. I hoped that these ovens would be preserved for posterity, they were the only ones of their kind left in the country.

That week the man from the M.A.F. came regarding the cow subsidy, he was Mr McHattie, a very fair and good-natured Scot, he used to, on these days, get into the smoke room, a bottle of whisky between us and a box of cigars, and chat until the bottle was finished, this day was the same, except my number of cows eligible for the subsidy did not tally with his, for Skirwith Hall I had 146 and he had 143, I had 3 too many–Kirkland cows had a separate hill cow subsidy – I checked my diary, as I had the numbers of what cows were in each field, and each time they were moved, this movement was entered into the diary, as it turned out, Mr McHattie was correct, my fault had been not to have deducted three deaths a few months ago, he realised how I had gone wrong, so we drank to it. Most of the M.A.F. men who visited me were jolly good chaps and had no bother from them, maybe the whisky and cigars had something to do with it because all who came, including the police, had the same treatment.

The George had been sold by Frank Street a few years before, Frank had had a slight stroke, his brother-in-law, Leslie Walker and wife had left to open their own place at Middlesbrough, the running of the George put in the hands of Christine, Frank's adopted daughter, later to marry Robert Sangster of pool fame. Christine, a lovely girl, had no idea how to run a hotel, and it went slowly down, Frank selling to Duttons Breweries of Blackburn. Now, Duttons had a young manager in Stuart, he seemed the man for the job.

Friday, Robin Rowley from Glastonbury, who had a tree nursery, brought me 7000 Scots pine, young trees to plant, these were for Black Wood. Adam and Joey came from school for the Easter holidays, they both set to work loading turnips out from the big heaps by tractor to the various fields of ewes and lambs and on Monday 28th, I set my three women, Misses Witteck, Fawcett and Wilkinson to plant the little trees in Black Wood. Young Joey relished the tractor work and he harrowed a 25-acre field for me prior to sowing the barley, Adam would work a bit then leave off, fed up. After the barley was drilled in, little Joey harrowed behind the drill.

In Black Wood about 500 young trees had the top buds nipped off and I got the womenfolk to replant 500 more. On inspection next day, more trees had been nipped off at the top bud, I started to suspect hares, and put gin traps where there were holes in the stone walls, there was two of these, and put rabbit wire on the gate bottoms, there were two of the these also into the tree's section, I also put rabbit netting beside the sheep fence, the entire length of the plantation. This seemed to do the trick, though 3 or 4 trees a night seemed to be nipped off. I decided to go down at daybreak each day with the gun. One week, as dawn was breaking, I went stealthily behind the stone wall with the gun, making no noise, peeping over, very slowly at times, I saw one rabbit and shot it, the only other animal was a large tom cat in one of the gin traps. These, of course, were illegal. I recruited little Joey at night to drive the

Land Rover over Black Wood field of barley, this was only an inch or two high, around about 10 pm, also for a week. Joey would drive the Land Rover, headlights on full, round the growing corn, feet barely touching the pedals, he was 13 years old, I think, while I sat on the bonnet with my 12 bore. Sometimes I had a hard job keeping myself from being thrown off, as one night we saw a rabbit in the headlights 100 yards away, with its eyes glinting, Joey spotted it and put his foot down hard on the accelerator, I fell back onto the windscreen, nearly going over the side, but Joey had the bit in his teeth because I had told him if he saw a rabbit to go after it, he was following instructions all right, maybe too much, however, I recovered my posture of sitting up, feet on the front bumper, Joey got within 30 yards of the rabbit when it decided to run. However, after a couple of jinks, I shot it with one shot, that was the only rabbit in a week of nightly runs with the Land Rover, little Joey enjoyed this work and wanted to continue night after night, but I did not, the trees were now more or less free of 4 legged pests.

On April 11th, Easter Sunday, the boys and I went to church. Harold Metcalfe, whose son David I had sacked, told me on April 30th that he was leaving my service. I accepted without saying a word, he had not been content since his son's dismissal, I had been more than fair towards him, also his wife had been Monique's daily help for years, now she came to see Monique and asked what she should do, as things were not the same, Monique told her what I had told her husband, that the affair was between David and myself, but Harold had disagreed saying it was now between him and myself, I then told him not to be so narrow-minded - Monique then went on to say that as far as she was concerned everything between herself and Mrs Metcalfe was as before. Tears were flowing down Mrs Metcalfe's face, she said she did not want to leave, Monique told her, "I hope you do not, you have been a good friend and help." That clinched it - Mrs Metcalfe did not leave and continued until we left England, a few years ahead yet.

Harold had cut his nose off to spite his face, he had to move house, and the only one vacant in the near vicinity was one at Ousby, 3 miles away.

At first, when I dismissed David, he found work (without my reference) at the local paper mills at Little Salkeld, here he met a girl of about 18, like David, missing a 1/-. She and David got together, she sex mad, David dying for sex - he had in earlier days offered a school girl, Janet Sped- ding, half a crown for sex, she had gone home and told her Mum and David had a good telling off by his parents. However, at that moment, this girl – I forget her name - and David would have sex anywhere, they were so keen on it, I myself have seen them on the roadside hard at it, and so did many others, one day, these two vanished, the police were notified, people were alerted to keep an eye out for them, reports came in they had been seen in London, then somewhere in Scotland. This went on for about three weeks, possibly more, not one reliable sighting of them. About three weeks later, the two surfaced, they had been camping in a tent in a small wood beside the Drove road, the old Roman Road, running between the Langwathby Road over to Culgaith, only a mile as the crow flies from Skirwirth, they had come up for food, during those almost three weeks they had not set foot out of that wood, living on sex no doubt, because they could not keep off each other, inside a few more weeks they got themselves married and lived with David's parents. The girl, Mrs Metcalfe said, would never change her panties for months on end until Mrs Metcalfe almost had to forcibly take them off her, she would not take a bath either, so one day in front of David, Mrs Metcalfe ordered her to take a bath, she cried, with tears, even David insisted she takes one, eventually the girl locked herself in the bathroom, ran the bath- water, on and on, the taps then stopped, splashing noises were heard, David looked through the keyhole, saw his wife sitting fully clothed on the bath side, splashing with her hands - she never took that bath yet, according to Mrs Metcalfe.

The next day, Sunday, May 9th, Monique and I had a surprise, Josephine my niece, now married with two children and living in Paris, turned up, she said she had left her husband, Henri Gabriel. Would we put her and the children up, as her mother Cathie, living at Dumfries with Robert McGeorge would not? McGeorge did not want any children about. Josephine also told us if her husband phoned to tell him she was not with us, she had a little girl Helen, a prim little girl of about five years and a little boy, Antony, of 2 years, who promptly got stuck in the garden cattle grid the next day and promptly messed his pants, this grid was only a foot deep, the wee fellow did not fall through the bars, he was kind of spread-eagled over them, all he could say day after day was "me cowboy."

We were also looking for a new school for little Joey, he was now 13 years old, both Monique and I did not wish to send him to the same school as Adam, thinking it better if they were separate, for one thing, Adam was prone to bully him, Joey would not retaliate at all. In our search, Silcoates School near Wakefield was recommended by two masters at Lime House, his present school, we also wanted him away from the pervert headmaster Peter Inghams. Monique and I took little Joey down to Silcoates on June 15th, it seemed a very good place, the headmaster and his wife were just what we wished for, a kind family couple. We had tea with them and were shown round the school by the head, they seemed to have everything needed for a boy's first-class school, the dormitories etc. first class. We decided this was the place for Joey. He would go in September.

After seeing round the school, we drove on to Leeds, I had my farm books to give to my new accountant Ken Cope, on the return home I de- cided we should dine out, so we called at the Black Bull, Moulton, just below Scotch Corner for dinner, after drinks in the bar, we ate - the meal was all right but nothing to write home about. Quite a few of my friends had dined there and raved about the place, but some people would rave about beans on toast, I have come to the conclusion over the years that en-masse, the English had not much of a palate, and as for wine, their taste buds were zero.

29

971 would be the last sunny hay time for a few years, each following year proving more difficult to make good hay due to week after week of rain. It got to be a headache.

My personal little sheepdog Maid had been off-colour for about a week, she would drink water and more water as if she had a permanent thirst, I took her along to the vet, he told me she would have to have her womb removed and they could not operate just that day. Our M.A.F. friend Mr McHattie came the next day to look over the cows for the subsidy, I took him around in the Land Rover, then that done, back to the smoke room for a bottle of Grouse Whisky and cigars, the ministry men liked coming to Skirwith Hall for they usually made a whole day of it.

Thursday, I took Maid in for her operation, when I was leaving her there, she looked up at me with appealing eyes as if to say, why are you not taking me home? She was a grand little worker at all times, and for shedding sheep i.e. taking one or two sheep out from a flock, she always kept her eye on the ones to come out or to shed neighbours sheep out from my own flock, behind hedges or stone walls. She seemed to know these strange sheep should not be in my fields, almost as if she could read the tar marks of the farm on the wool. The vet told me she would be ready to take home the next afternoon, and the next afternoon, I took the Land Rover to pick her up, as soon as she saw me, one could see joy on her face, I took her out to Post Office Square and opened the Land Rover passenger door for her, she leapt in nearly finishing up over the gear stick, she flew in so fast, this was her favourite place, she always leant her head over the middle arch where the gear stick was. One would not think she had just had some of her main organs removed, never a whimper at all. I did not work with her for two weeks, but she travelled each and every day, as a habit, in front of her favourite vehicle, the Land Rover.

I had more or less got the grouse moor boundary sorted

out with Mr Burton of Brackenbank. Seeing there was a dog leg in his and my moor, I asked if I could shoot his dog leg, and when he shot, he could shoot my area of the dogleg, to this he agreed, so far, for the 12th all was in order.

I had asked my guests to arrive on the 11th for a pre-shoot dinner that evening, which was going to be held at Leeming House on Lake Ullswater. Some of the guests were staying at the Kings Arms, Temple Sowerby and others with us. The guns were John Cummings, Derek Straker, Jack and Phillip Johnstone, Sandy Taylor, Robert Jackson and myself. Seven guns, no wives had been invited. The guests duly arrived at Skirwith Hall for cocktails, then on to Leeming House, on arrival there, things seemed to get off on the wrong footing, shown the menu by the owner, Carlson, Jack Johnstone asked how he roasted his salmon, immediately the owner took umbrage, telling Jack more or less not to be impudent, saying he did not roast salmon, I wondered why Jack had asked this question, but he had the ace answer, Jack showed Carlson his menu at the same time pointing to the fish selection, saying "what is this then?", Carlson went as red as a turkey jock with rage, snapping at Jack, "this is a misprint", snatched the menu and stalked off, the rest of my guests, laughed loud and clear, making Carlson, I should think worse tempered.

The meal, which was very good (a pity I did not make a note of it), progressed quite well except for Carlson, who made a point of continually passing some caustic remark at my guests. Not wishing to put him in his place and have a row with him, as this would spoil the evening, I kept quiet, at the end of the meal, I asked my guests what drinks i.e. liqueurs they would like, to my surprise Carlson refused to serve them to us, I pointed out that I had spent a good deal of money eating this night, his reply was he did not care about that at all. My guests were equally amazed. They could not believe the arrogance of this hotelier, I told them, we would go now, I went to the desk to pay, Carlson prepared the bill, I paid him, telling him that his food was very good, but his manners and attitude towards my guests was abominable and left him, it was quite a while before I went back there - then I had the laugh on him.

After this, I took my guests on to our old friend John Grundy at Ramsbeck Hotel, just a little further on, also sitting on the side of Lake Ull- swater. Here, if known, one could drink until dawn, this is where my guests started to let their hair down, we left Grundy's at 1:30 am, then set off on the return home, but calling at another old friend, Malcolm Hunter at the Queens Head Hotel, Tirril. John Grundy came along with us, here we were made more than welcome, this was the second hotel I had taken Monique to when I first met her that night in 1954. The Queen's was a very old English coaching house with low ceilings, oak beams, a big fireplace and very good hosts in Malcolm and Audrey, his wife. Finally, we all got to bed at 5 am after a hilarious night out. Monique did not go to bed on our return, she was going to prepare the picnic for all the guns to eat on the moors.

The glorious 12th opened to a clear day, thank goodness, for if Crossfell would have been covered in fog or mist, this mountain over which I shot – both sides also - was in full view from my garden, checking it to see at 8 am, all was clear, I had bought a case of champagne to clear the various heads in the morning, my farm men were ready for beating. As they were waiting, I sent a bottle out for them, they were looking forward to all the fun. The guns were to arrive at 8:30 am sharp, but it was 9 am before they arrived from Temple Sowerby. John Cummings, who had stayed with us, came down bleary-eyed. Robert Jackson, who lived ¼ mile away, came on time, then the others drifted in: Derek Straker, large as life, a very strongly made man this one, Jack and Phillip Johnstone, eyes like tomatoes, Sandy, rather tottery on his feet but after an hour of champagne, everyone perked up and were full of beans, off we set, my beaters had gone off half an hour ahead in the Land Rover with Lassie, to meet us at the George and Dragon Inn at Garygill, a small village at the bottom of the fells. The other side of the fell, not far from the highest market town in England, Alston, the guns and picnic in two cars, John Cummings D.B. 8 cylinder, and my Volvo.

Off we set at 10 am, getting to Garygill at approximately 10:30 am, where we got the landlord to open up, he was a young man, and seemed reluctant to oblige but was eventually persuaded to do so, in we all piled, beaters as well, the first round was on me, the bar – stone flags on the floor, an enormous open fire going great guns and good easy chairs for half of us made a good atmosphere, the drinks were now coming like confetti, I thought to myself I bet the landlord is now very pleased he did open up. At one stage, I went to the men's toilet for a leak, this was situated semi outside when I entered, I was just in time to see Sandy being sick, through an open window and his false front tooth flying through the air into the yard beyond – poor Sandy, I did not know he had a false tooth – it was his only one - he did not look too good, I then decided to get going, we had 4 miles at least of fell track to go through, very rough indeed, we left the two cars outside the pub on the village green, and somehow all piled into the Land Rover. Two or three beaters sitting on the bonnet and roof, the picnic basket, a large one, took a lot of room, plus Lassie, it was a veritable squeeze. On arrival at our starting point Cash Wells, an old lead mine marked on the map, and before us lay a few thousand acres of grouse moor, it looked flat and easy until one got started, we would walk approximately three miles and three back shooting both ways, as the moor was amply wide enough for this, as time was now 11:30 am we had a chat about the time for lunch, and thought that by the time we returned after 6 miles of gruelling walking over peat hags, bogs etc., it would then be too late for lunch, because I had a dinner laid on for tonight at the Kings Arms, Temple Sowerby, and if we ate too late we would not have much of an appetite, unanimously we all agreed to have Monique's picnic on arrival at Cash Wells old mine. The road up the fells was, at times, very bumpy, going through potholes 6-7 inches deep, over rock, avoiding soft, boggy places. This old mining road was now being used widely by hikers on the Pennine Way walk from Derbyshire to the borders, we encountered two or three of them, fortunately, they stuck to the old mine road and were not much of a nuisance. We unloaded the picnic baskets, beer, wine and three bottles of champagne, the latter to drink at the end of the shoot, which we put in a small stream there, well anchored, to keep cool. Now, we unpacked Monique's delight. She had done a good job, only going to bed when we had left the house. She had been up 24 hours. Monique had prepared for us before going to bed our gastronomic picnic of three roast pheasant, one leg of suckling lamb, one good sized "Beef en Croute", one whole cold salmon from the Solway, and salads, some champagne, one dozen bottles of red wine, three dozen tins of beer, one box of German cigars (50), also some lemonade to make shandies with.

After eating, and there was quite a lot of food left, we set off to shoot. I think Lassie was wondering when we were going to start. We spread out, I took the high side of the stretch, which was not the best, wanting my guests to have plenty of birds, the beaters in between guns, which were 60 yards apart. We had not gone far, I had to walk around a hillock, out of sight of the rest, for 5 minutes – when 8 grouse got up unexpectedly, I downed two right away... the other side of the hillock, I heard 4 or 5 shots, but was unable to see if any birds dropped. Lassie quickly brought my two birds back to me, my beater, George Western, was also out of sight from me, but a couple of minutes and we were all within sight of each other again, George took my two birds, he told me 2 birds had fallen from guns below. The dead birds had been collected and while the birds were being picked up, the line, of course, had been halted, Lassie was the only gun dog, or dog there that day, none of the other guns had gun dogs if so they were kept as pets, it was not long before I had to stop the line and stop Kurt talking loudly to Derek Straker, whom Kurt called "Mr Streicker." Kurt was beating for him and carrying his cartridge bag and any birds

Derek shot, the grouse were a bit thin on the ground and shooting could have been better, but due to the amount of alcohol consumed the night before, plus this morning, the guns did pretty well, we tramped on and on, when we reached the source of the (South?) Tyne, we had 15 minutes of rest, everyone was ready for this.

We then moved higher up here. It was good grouse land. Spreading out, we set off on the return journey, four birds went down at once, one bird was picked up straight away, the three others, no one could find them, the line waited on, after 10 minutes, I descended from higher up with Lassie and within a few minutes she had the other 3 in the bag – it made me proud to watch her, she was never in a hurry, dashing here and there, but took her time, quartering to pick up the scent, she was admired by all for her feats there.

Now, I had to climb up the fell to my position, but I was used to fell climbing, keeping in trim with shepherding. The same thing happened three times with lost birds, but three single ones. Lassie had to go to the rescue, unfortunately, one of these birds, she just could not find it, she tried and tried, but it was no good, after 20 minutes we had to give up and start again. At the end of the moor, finishing at Cash Wells, we had 35 birds, which was, considering, quite good, we had had a good day's sport, everyone had enjoyed themselves. The guns and beaters were now ravenous, the remaining food of Monique's picnic disappearing quickly, together with the beer, wine and champagne. Here, we lingered for an hour, taking a well-earned rest. The beaters were tired also with the weight of the birds.

We all piled into and on top of the Land Rover and off we went to the George and Dragon for some more lubricant. The place was closed, but I persuaded the young landlord to open it up. He must have been thinking of his profits with this morning's binge, he quickly obliged. As we all piled, he had the fire going full blast, which alone created a good atmosphere, this time the guns had a thirst unquenchable, drink was going down as fast as the owner could pour them. The beaters thought they had landed in a heavenly brewery, young John Frith, only 14 years old, drank with the rest of us, but in pints of beer, he could sink these better than many a man, he was a grand young chap, he could drink, but never smoked. John always helped out on the farm and shoots, he was almost indispensable and a kind and good nature to boot.

I had almost to drag the guns out of the pub, for I was giving another dinner that night, this time at the Kings Arms, Temple Sowerby, when we arrived home, the beaters got their monetary reward from the guns, I believe Derek Straker gave Kurt 10 pounds, of which he was over the moon. What the other guns gave, I'm not sure, and I did not ask. From myself, they received 5 pounds each and had a good day outing, John Cummings was always a tremendous tipper, my men liked over the years to carry his cartridge bag and birds, he always had, a gentle and kind manner towards everyone.

At Temple Sowerby, the guests were J. Cummings, D. Straker, Jack and Phillip Johnstone, Sandy Taylor and Robert Jackson, also joining us were Ken Straughan and his mistress Nancy, a very tall long, legged beauty, and Stuart Coulthard, the new manager of the George Hotel in Penrith, and Monique and myself, the meal was extremely good and very well presented by Peter and his wife Brenda.

After the meal, we adjourned to the public bar, where there was room to dance to the record player, where we danced and drank until 4 am, at which time Peter wanted to go to bed, Stuart chirped up, "All come along to the George," this was in Penrith, 8 miles away, we did not need asking twice, off we went and in 15 minutes we were in the comfort of George's cocktail bar, where we gave the bottles another good hiding and danced until we left at 8 am, once again for the Kings Arms, Temple Sowerby, where 15 minutes later we had breakfast of vegetable soup, bacon and 2 eggs each, after a few drinks with Peter, we left to return to the George Hotel, collected Stuart, then on to the Queen's Hotel, Tirril, to our friends Malcolm and Audrey, Malcolm always liked a fun day like this. After more bottle hitting, we all left, including Malcolm, to John Grundy's, at Ramsbeck Hotel on the lakeside, where John's chef made us a sumptuous lunch, John also liked a fun day like this, it was just up his street. Here, we again gave the bottles a beating up, the amazing part was no one was drunk, all were, of course, seasoned drinkers in their own sphere, we left Ramsbeck at 5 pm and returned to the George Hotel until 8 pm, when we bade goodnight to our friends.

My cousin Betty, the daughter of Dad's sister Hilda and Uncle Alex, came with her husband Harry, an Australian. They brought with them their young daughter Judy, a redhead about the same age as Joey Jnr. It turned out on the spur of the moment Judy was going to spend a fortnight with us, she was indeed a lovely girl. Harry and Betty were staying at the George Hotel for a day or two, the next day, the Triggs, Harry's family name, came out from the George to see us, I had an idea Monique and Betty did not care for each other, for Betty, I think jealously, because Monique was mistress of Skirwith Hall and on Monique's side, she did not like snobs of which Betty was one, looking down her nose to speak at Monique, also she had a habit of contradicting Monique in sort of undertones, possibly how her mother, Hilda, had treated my mother on her marriage to Dad.

Also, Aunt Josephine and Marie-Jose, daughter of Paul Pineda, came to stay.

Monique went shopping for groceries on Thursday 19th. Monique took Judy, little Joey and her Aunt with her and locked up the house, on her return, there was Betty sitting in the garden, most displeased at not being able to get into the house, Monique by now, was getting tired of Betty's attitude, however on 20th they left to return to their home in the South.

On Friday, it was the usual Penrith binge at the George Hotel, the children wanted to go, to have a look round the shops, I asked Judy if she had plenty of money, in case she wanted anything she liked, she told us her parents had not given her a penny, Monique and I could not believe it, a young girl of 13 years – on holiday and her parents not giving her even a pound for a bar of chocolate or similar, I immediately gave her 3 pounds – in case of – by now Judy and Marie Jose were competing for Joey's favours, they were both in love with him, one evening they had been playing round the farm buildings, with the dogs, coming in to the house at dusk, Monique's Aunt Josephine, she was again staying with us, was becoming most agitated, she had the Spanish mentality thinking, a boy outside with a girl (Joey had two girls) they must be thinking to have sex, when the children did come in, through the back door into the big kitchen, Josephine yelled something to them, then before I could say anything – she slapped Marie Jose so hard twice – I could almost feel it myself, this in front of me, Monique and the other children, poor Marie Jose her face marked by the hard slaps, was sent to bed by her grandmother Josephine, this attack on Marie Jose was what Monique endured her whole young life. I felt very sad for Marie Jose, it was not just the slapping, it was done in front of her young friends, that I certainly did not like. I said nothing, perhaps I should have told this nasty old woman, "These things were not done in my house." I still regret not putting Josephine in her place.

On 21st August, Monique and I went to Stockton races. However, this day, Phillip had a horse running, he had told me to get there and have a good bet on it, the horse was trained at Newmarket by, I think, Jarvis, which Jarvis, I forget, there were two at Newmarket. The horse named Samfoo got up, especially for this race, Phillip asked me to put a few hundred on for him, which I did. Samfoo won nicely at 8/1. That is what I got for my money, I won 400 pounds. After the win, champagne flowed freely, it turned into a most pleasant day.

Aunt Josephine and Marie Jose left us to go back to Marseille on 25th August. We were pleased to see Aunty go, Marie Jose had been no problem, I pitied the poor girl.

This was a day we could not harvest the corn, rain had started and as we were unable to work, Monique and I went to the Newcastle races, where I won 70 pounds from Dan Flyn, the Scottish bookie with whom I had a credit account at the same time as Willy Whiteman, Willy Whiteman died sometime about now, I have not marked the year of his death down – poor Willy passed away very quickly.

Monday, Monique and I decided to return to Newcastle races, we took little Joey, Adam and Judy, my cousin's daughter, who was still with us, I lost 20 pounds. John Cummings asked us for drinks at his house. Sands Hall at Sedgefield. The children had enjoyed their day out. Judy now that she had Joey Jnr to herself, she was in her element, I gave her another 3 pounds to play about with that day, she was such a nice natural girl and good looking, it passed my mind for an instant that she would probably make an excellent match for Joey later on in life, they hit it off so well, alas it was not to be.

Thursday, 2nd September, was the village show of Brough near Appleby. The boys wanted to go and show Lassie and Sandy, a pup of Lassie now 2 years old, plus Titch, Joey's Jack Russell and Adam's rabbits. I myself was never too interested in showing stock of any kind, however I put the boy's dogs and rabbits in the Land Rover and set off for Brough, dropping the boys and pets at the entrance, leaving them to see to their own thing, promising to pick them up later, giving them enough money for entry fees, food and drink, when I returned later in the day, the boys were as excited as if it were Christmas, Titch had got 3rd prize in his class and I think 5/-, Adams rabbits had won 1st prize and 10/-. The two gundogs had won nothing, I knew Sandy would not get a prize for he was a lean dog, no matter how much he ate, he never put any fat on, but he was a good gundog. The boys really had enjoyed their day at the show. I wished I had stayed with them to enjoy their fun, but I had told the shepherd to bring a few hundred lambs in for dosing for worms and treat them for footrot.

The next day, Saturday, I castrated 34 bull calves in the

morning, keeping ¾ of the testicles for myself and the rest for One-Eyed Willie. In the afternoon, Kurt and I started the combine harvester up and set off to cut the corn in Black Wood, starting at 3 pm and cutting till 8 pm. This was oats and a good crop, too. The day, weather-wise, had been quite sunny. On Sunday we could not start cutting until 1 pm due to a very heavy morning dew. Kurt and I cut until 9 pm. The day being very hot, cutting corn was a pleasure on days like this. During this period, the corn was being bagged on the combine, myself on the bagging end, Kurt driving, George Western, whose weekend off it had been, turning up today without being asked to do so, and Ernie, the shepherd loading the oats onto trailers and taking it home to pile up and store in one of the large ex-poultry houses. Monday was the same workload, finishing Black Wood at 9:30 pm. Kurt baling straw in the next field, another good hot day.

On Tuesday 7th Sept, I took the combine myself and, with little Joey on the bagging end, started to cut barley while the other men were leading sacks of corn from the day before and baling straw. Little Joey liked his work and did very well, he and I knocked off at 9:30 pm. Wednesday was the same pattern: little Joey and I cut, the others leading the corn in. Kurt Baling and my three faithful women workers I roped in to put the straw bales into heaps of 8, ready for the bale lifting machine to lead into the barn later, another lovely hot day. We were progressing well with the harvest, field after field was being finished quite quickly. So far, so good, no breakdowns. Little Joey and I stuck to the cutting, he was at the dusty end of the machine, at night, when we finished for the day, he was like a little blackamoor, each night, it was 9 or 9:30 pm when we finished, each day nice and hot. The bales of straw being led in, my three ladies now helping to load the sacks of corn onto the trailers, we were getting through the work at express speed, these three women were a tremendous help and they thoroughly enjoyed the work. It got them from out of the kitchen sink, so to speak. Many times in other years, I could not have finished the work before the rains came without them.

My good little helper, Joey Jnr, had to go to his new school, Silcoates, at Wakefield on Friday 10th September. Monique and I took him down as we also had to buy him some school clothes at the same time. We left him with 3 or 4 of his newfound friends, he seemed quite happy, but I knew he preferred life at home. After seeing and paying for these sorts of schools, and having the same choice again. I would never send my children away from home to boarding schools, they are not cracked up to be what they are. I, having my life again, would have as many children as possible into the teens and employ private teachers.

Saturday, 25th September, I decided to go myself to shoot grouse, Monique came with me, she had never seen my moor, or fells as we called them, where the grouse were. She packed a picnic, I put Lassie in the Land Rover, and we set off, the day was nice and quite warm. Monique could not stand the cold, her hands and feet would be the colour of snow, deathly white, at times, she could not move her fingers. However, this day suited her. On arrival at Cash Wells, we had a cup of tea and a couple of sandwiches, then set off, in the first 100 yards, I shot 4 birds, after another 200 yards, the going was too rough for Monique, she said she would sit in the heather as it was warm, in fact she could see me for the next 1000 yards, she made herself comfortable and off I went, there were quite a few birds. Before I got halfway, I had shot ten birds, by the time I had reached the source of the South Tyne, I had 13. I debated whether to descend to the river, which lay in a steepish valley and climb the other side, the other side was borderline with Richard Burton of Brackenbank, as he shot my moor, had done so for years, I told myself he owes me a few, so down I went, crossed the river, or rather a source of, it would be only 20 feet across here if that. I remember Dad telling me when he was a boy, he caught a lot of trout here. Up the other side I climbed, fairly steep, then gently leveling out, a pack of grouse got up on the high side of me on my left, they would be 50 yards higher up, they flew away from me, but one broke away from the others passing in front of me 60 yards away and 60 yards high flying downhill like a rocket, I gave it an enormous lead with the gun, the most I have ever

done, the bird only faltered and flew on, as I watched it about 500 yards away by now, all of a sudden it rose vertically, then on its tail shot up 30 or more feet, then fell to earth, stone dead, when birds shot at do this, it is called towering, this was always said to be a heart shot. I was not going to go that far down the fells to pick it up, I had plenty of climbing to do on the return trip, and Lassie would probably never go 500 yards or more, I glanced down at her and by the look on her face I knew she had watched that grouse fall to earth, I gave her the command "fetch it Lassie," off she set at full speed, on and on she went never faltering, until she was only a speck, still at speed, then suddenly she swerved, stooped, picked something up, which I presumed to be the grouse, for at that distance I could not distinguish what she had in her mouth, but straight back she came at speed, though not as fast as she had left me for the grouse. Soon, she put the grouse into my hand, my heart went out to her, this retrieval deserved a gold medal, it was the finest retrieve I have ever witnessed by a dog, absolutely superb, for her to have watched that bird all that distance was a feat in itself, I made a fuss over her, she, I think was also proud of herself. For myself I was most pleased that I had hit the bird, for without doubt, it was the fastest flying bird – ever through my life – that I had knocked down at such speed, I can see that grouse today in my mind's eye as clear as a mirror, watch it towering and fall to earth and the tremendous superb retrieve of my lovely Lassie, Lassie and I then made the return over the fells back to Monique, but higher up so that I covered new ground, my game bag was getting heavier. I did not let Lassie work ahead, as the grouse being shot before were getting up at 35 to 40 yards ahead. By the time I got back to Monique, I had 22 grouse in my game bag, three or four grouse had been winged, but Lassie had found them all, one had taken 15 minutes to find. This bird had fallen on a very wet and rather boggy piece of land. The scent being poor kept Lassie sniffing, eventually, she found this bird up a hole, made by melting snows or rainstorms, 20 yards from where it fell. Monique was tired of being in one place for so long, it must have been 3 to 3 ½ hours, but was frightened to walk on or go back, the Land Rover was out of sight under the rising ground for fear of being lost, but at last she saw me a long way off on my return. I was pleased to get the game bag off my shoulders and have a well-earned rest, I told Monique of Lassie's great feat, so Lassie got more fuss made of her, then to the Land Rover, and a bottle of beer and some sandwiches, which we shared with Lassie.

Stuart Coulthard, the manager of the George Hotel, asked if I could supply him with some grouse or other game, as he had a dinner for some committee or other coming up. I told him I never sold the game I shot but kept it for myself, but if he was stuck I would see what I could do for him, the end of that week, I took him 17 brace of pheasant, 4 brace of wild duck, 4 teal ducks, 6 pigeons and 4 guinea fowl, 8 brace of grouse, and two large salmon. I did not like the idea of selling my game, but Stuart was pushed to have a variety, so I helped him out.

30

On Tuesday, the 19th, I collected the men up and we all went up to the high wood fields. There were 5 fields, all of them big, to take down 450 yards of rotten fencing and posts to renew, this took most of the day.

Friday, October 22nd, my throat got worse, however I was planning a holiday and drove to Carlisle to withdraw money from my bank there, the Clydesdale, this was where I kept my betting money – separate from the farm, then father could not throw this holiday, or any other for that matter, in my face, then I called on Stuart at the George Hotel for the money he owed me for game, £130.

Monique and I were planning to go to that island in the Canary Group, Lanzarote, near the Sahara of Africa, we would motor to Spain first, we also decided to have a cholera injection, which Donald Ainscow gave us on the 22nd, this was our 2nd injection.

October 29th, we set off to Penrith for the last-minute bits of things, looked in at the George Hotel, at 10:30 am there were two or three friends having their morning lubrication, I had 4 or 5 large whisky's – we were now on holiday. My workforce had the usual routine on the farm, ploughing and fencing. The shepherd knew his job; Dad was always there if anything went wrong. Monique and I left Penrith at 11:30 am, down the A1, we went straight through London onto the A2, getting to Dover at 7:30 pm. We had two hours to wait for the next ferry to Calais.

We docked at Calais at 11:20 pm and, after passing through Customs, drove into town to find a bed for the night, we stumbled on the Hotel Belle View, Monique enquired within, yes they had a room, when she asked the price, the receptionist told her 23 francs, we took it, shown to our room, we discovered it to be very nice and also warm, we were too tired to make love, we both fell asleep quickly.

Saturday 30th Oct, we were up at 8 am motoring on to

Boulogne, where we had breakfast at a Brasserie – cum Chacuterie, which was excellent and also warm. After eating, we were fit for the road. I had had a large rum in my cafe au lait; it had a grand, mellow taste. We bought two different sorts of pate and some chacuterie and cheese, gruyere and a bottle of wine for a picnic later on, we had dwelt quite a while over breakfast, one thing, because the place was well heated, secondly we were in no hurry. We were taking at least a month's holiday, maybe more, and we were in love. We treated this as another honeymoon, I lit a grand punch and we motored, stopping at a village for bread at 11:30 am and at 1:30 pm we pulled into a quiet side road and had our picnic, we ate in the car because the day was at times rather foggy, and not too warm, however, the pate's were very good, also the chacuterie. Monique had packed in the car forks, knives, spoons and glasses, corkscrew and bottle opener, as usual, all went down well, the bread newly made was just right, the gruyere with plenty of holes in it, soft and mellow, went well with the wine, we always ate gruyere with mustard and a pinch of salt, Monique had not forgotten this either.

We then drove on, stopping for the night at Chateau Renalt, booking into the Golden Lion, which was a Logis, this was at 8 pm, having driven 310 miles, the car on topping her up, doing 28mpq approx.

As the dining room was full, we had to wait, we went up the street to a cafe, where for a change, we both had a few Pernods and then switched to beer, Monique went back twice to see if we could have a table in our Logis, at last after one and a half hours they had one free, down we sat – for a start, the soup was cold, then we had frog's legs, these were good, then chicken, so-so, the wine was a house wine, also so-so. On the whole, I did not like the place, but Monique did so.

Sunday, we set off at 8 am, it was quite foggy, I drove slowly and seeing it was the Sabbath, we made sure to buy our paté and bread early, this was paté champagne. It looked lush and fresh and some more gruyere, another bottle of wine with a label I did not know, stopping for our café au lait in those massive cups and bread and croissante for breakfast. Stopping for our picnic lunch at 1 pm. By now, the fog had disappeared (this was at 11 am). The sun was getting out well, the day was now nice and hot, we dined in some farmer's meadow on a blanket. My sheep and cows seemed a long way behind. We had already stopped at about three nice little cafés en route for a glass or two of beer. By 1 pm, when we stopped, we had motored 200 miles.

We then carried on, stopping twice for a beer in small villages heading for Lourdes. We were making for another Logis there the Auberge & Logis, Maurice Prat. This proved to be excellent and well run by Madame. All was scrupulously clean, the staff impeccable, the meal super, though our bedroom was very much on the cold side. We had frog's legs each, veal escalope, and plentiful yoghurt, homemade and a variety of superb cheeses. Here we dispensed with wine and had four beers each with the meal and to bed. The car had done 400 miles exactly that day.

The trouble that night was I had chronic diarrhoea. I was up all night to the toilette, it must have been the frog's legs, I thought, but I was not sure – In the morning, we went downstairs to the breakfast room, the waiter asked what we would like, I told him a very large brandy and port, he brought the two beverages in separate glasses, he watched in surprise as I mixed them, and downed them both in one. I then told him that is an Englishman's breakfast, I thought it would give him something to talk about for a while. Then we left the hotel at 8:10 am, put our bags in the Volvo and drove into the middle of town, I now had to look for a cafe, my tummy trouble was at it again, this call was urgent, there was a brasserie in front of us, I pulled in the pavement side, quickly locked up, dashed into the toilette, the barman looking puzzled, no doubt thinking, crazy English. I came out of the gents, Monique had taken a table, we had decided to get out of the car to have breakfast here, the only other customer was a gendarme, Monique ordered cafe au lait, bread and croissant. For myself, I was determined to cure my fox's trot, I ordered another very large brandy and port. This, again, was served in separate glasses – and only dry bread for myself. Croissants are not the thing to take when one has a tummy upset. The gendarme started eyeing my two glasses, watching carefully as I poured one into the other, this time I drank the mixture more slowly, I could have done with another of the same, but I thought our gendarme friend might cause trouble if I did so, thinking me to be an alcoholic, he had watched me drive up, discretion is the better part of valour. Monique finished her breakfast and off we went outside. The gendarme, coming to the brasserie doorway watching us get in the car – then we were off.

This was now November 1st and a lovely bright sunny day, we had been driving for only 10 minutes when I had another call of nature, and in a hurry, another cafe was in sight, into the toilette at a gallop, Monique ordered me a large brandy and port, served as before, this time Monique had a beer, I downed the mixture and ordered another, our gendarme friend was now well out of sight. One thing about brandy and port mix is that it is a most pleasant drink. Feeling better we drove on, 5 or 6 miles along the road, now not too far from the Spanish border, I spotted another cafe, and pulled in just to take more of my medicine, then at 9:30 am, we were at the border and into Spain. We headed for Huesca, in the direction also of Zaragoza. Here, en route, as there were for many miles no cafes, I had the call of nature a few times, it was getting on my nerves, this diarrhoea. I parked the car on the roadside and went behind trees or bushes, I thought to myself, at least I'm leaving old Franco a few visiting cards. I stopped at Huesca for more of my tummy mixture, made now with their Fundador brandy, more fiery than the French, but still with the port, quite palatable.

On we went, driving over difficult roads, poor surfaces and very twisting mountain terrain. I stopped when I could for more of my medicine, the diarrhoea had more or less stopped by now. Also by noon I had had plenty of my medicine. Otherwise, I might endanger my driving. We drove for 250 miles that day, 1st November. The scenery had been one of superb wild beauty. Through and over the mountains, one could see quite a few Falcons or Eagles gliding on air currents in the bright sun, quite majestic are the mountains, I love them.

We stopped at Albacete for the night, it was a huge place, a Government Parador, newly built only a year or so ago, the furnishings were splendid, the bedroom sumptuous. We both thought the food would also be five-star stuff, the cost for the night was 400pts, roughly about £3 – for such a palace, I thought it dirt cheap, our bags were carried in by the immaculately dressed porters. Once in our palatial bedroom, we approached a long corridor with many beautiful chandeliers hanging from the ceiling. Beautiful, what looked like antique chairs, dotted about, old paintings on the walls, we both thought to prepare for a gourmet meal, we would take a good hot bath, and linger in it for a while, in fact, have a good soak – ever since we married Monique and I always bathed together, and still do, at 70 years old, at least that's my age now. Monique turned the hot tap on, let it run while we undressed, in a minute or two, she felt the water to see if it was too hot, but it was stone cold. I told her to try the cold tap, saying, knowing the Spaniards, they might have got the pipes reversed, but alas, no, the cold tap also ran cold, as this was winter time, and neither of us felt like having an icy bath. To compromise, we made love and went downstairs. I had three large whiskies, Monique three sherries of Tio Pepe, these were pretty large too, then into the dining room, this room was most tastefully decorated, it would have done justice to any great English house. We ordered our meal, which turned out to be very poor indeed myself. I could not believe it and told the waiter so he understood and spoke English. No apologies were given, however, the wine was very good. Afterward, we dwelt in the bar while I smoked a cigar and had our digestives of the brandy Soberano. I found their brandys just a bit fiery, and so to bed, we had Madrid to cross in the morning.

On the 2nd, we set off in the Volvo at 8 am prompt and drove straight for Madrid. I thought it couldn't be worse than London, but Madrid was full of traffic. Halfway through, Monique spotted a good-looking brasserie, I quickly pulled in; we wanted breakfast and indeed, this brasserie was as good as it looked, the bread and croissants were beautifully fresh, the coffee excellent. However, we had to press on. Eventually, we were out of Madrid, not counting our breakfast, it had taken hours of driving to get through.

I took the road in the direction of Ocona, down to Valdepenas, it was wildish countryside, quite picturesque, as we were in no hurry we stopped in quite a few villages for a beer, usually if I remember right it was a San Miguel, this beer was quite good, seemed to be all over Spain. In each bar we stopped at, all eyes would be glued on us, conversation would stop while the customers sized us up, we would bid all a hearty Buenos Dias, I would try my one or two words of Spanish on purpose to get them to talk, asking for a cigar, which at most places the barman did not understand, Monique would interpret for me and then customers would crowd round us, everyone vying to get their word in first. In no time, Monique was in full swing, answering questions as fast as she could. You see many of these villages were isolated, even on what could be called main roads, the inhabitants had no cars, only the family donkey or a bicycle to travel perhaps to the next village only. They were keen to know what the outside world was like. These were still the days of Dictator Francesco Franco, only the very rich Spaniard would or could travel – but at the same time, Spain was waking up just.

For us this travel across quite a large part of Spain was an adventure in itself, we came across, once again, whole villages dug out of hillsides or mountainsides only chimneys visible – then on this rout we saw an advert on a huge boarding on the land beside the road, of a red partridge, advertising a restaurant of that name, mile after mile of this same advert, we thought this place must be something special, so we decided when we eventually reached the Perdri restaurant, to have lunch there. These adverts went on for at least 100 miles. I thought it could not really exist, but the last two or three boardings showed us we were almost there, the time approx 2pm, in we pulled and parked. This elusive restaurant at last, first we walked into the bar and had a beer each, which I thought at 3/- each was the most expensive, but the whole place gave off that expensive feeling, everything was of the best. The waiters, of which there were plenty, were immaculate. We were shown a table, chose our food, I did not make a note of what we ate, but the meal was quite good, we drank two more beers with our food, a good luxurious restaurant, very well run, but not to be compared with one on the same lines in mid-France. After our meal, we decided to motor on to Seville via Cordoba, the car was running well, this time we did not stop, getting into Seville at 8:30 pm, into a lot of traffic. I tried to visualise where exactly we were from our last visit, thinking after a while we were more or less near the dockside of the Guadalquivir River, but in town we spotted a hotel that would suit our purpose, the Ducal Residencia, in Monique went to see if they had a room, they had, but no restaurant, that did not bother us, as we mostly ate outside our various hotels if possible.

The hotel on inspection was so-so, the bedroom not bad and we had our own bathroom, this Monique liked, she hated going down hotel corridors to the bathrooms or toilets. The hotel reception clerk was a most pleasant young man who spoke good English. As I had almost no pesetas left, we did not have dinner but went to a bar round the corer where we had a few beers, leaving the car parked by the pavement side outside the hotel. We had motored 470 miles that day and it had been nice and hot, considering our numerous beer stops, I thought we had done very well. We slept well that night but were awakened at 7 am by a loud knocking on the bedroom door. It was our nice reception chappie, he said the police wanted my car removed from outside the hotel, it seemed there was going to be some fruit market stalls put up for the weekly sale of fruit and veg, I went down, got into the car and parked round the corner 50- 60 yards away, then we dressed, had coffee, bread and croissants, and drove to the shipping office on the riverside, our receptionist had given us good directions how to get there. I was right last night it. The shipping office was very near.

Monique asked the shipping clerk the times of ships to Las Palmas, then from there to Lanzarote, where we intended to spend our holiday, this was November 3rd there was not a ship from Seville until 11th and from Cadiz on 12th too long for us to spend here in Seville. We decided to take a plane to Lanzarote, now we had to have more pesetas, off we went to a bank to replenish our pockets, this done we had a look at the shops. Seville has a good selection of these, and of quality also. Passing a furniture shop, we spotted some chairs, which would just do for our breakfast room at Skirwith Hall, made from wood but with a thick leather seat and back. In we went and bought four of them @ £3 each. I paid there and then for them. Monique asked if the chairs could be kept for a few weeks, explaining that we were off to the Canary Isles, the shopkeeper was only too willing and obliged. Off we went again, seeing a shop selling lanterns in the old-fashioned style made from iron and tin, Monique liked one priced at 1800pts, it was a beauty, so we bought it. It would hang nicely in the hallway back home. Again, Monique asked the shopkeeper to hang on to it for a few weeks, explaining why he also was pleased to do so.

We went to an airline ticket office for tickets to Lanzarote and got fixed up without any bother. On On 4th November, I garaged the Volvo at the same garage as I had put the little MG 1100 in, The Torres del Oro, taking a taxi to the airport, we flew out at 11:40 am en route for the first stop at El Aiun, but the plane was unable to land there due to a terrific sand storm, this was easy to see quite plainly out of the plane's windows, the plane was quite a long way above this terrific storm, it was a fascinating spectacle, rather like Dante's Inferno, of enormous billowing, swirling, yellow clouds of devilment.

The plane was diverted to Las Palmas, where we landed safely. Now we had to get to Lanzarote. I enquired at the Airline office about a plane out to this island where we were heading, to my delight, there was a plane flying to Lanzarote within 30 minutes, and seats were available, I booked two immediately. Tickets in hand, luggage on the way to the plane, we went on, within a few minutes, every seat was taken, the plane not a big one, looked rather like the French Caravelle's, it may have been, but did not ask if it was a Caravelle, they were super planes indeed.

The plane took off climbing very steep, just as the Caravelles used to, and in no time, we had landed at the airport of Lanzarote. Monique grabbed a taxi while I saw to our baggage and off we went to the principal town there. On the way in the taxi we were both surprised and disappointed with the complete drabness of the scene, in fact instantly we both did not like what we saw, however into town, we went. I thought we best had taken a first-class hotel, as we thought a 2nd class place, perhaps would be just too dirty.

From the taxi, we saw a big hotel sign saying Lancelot Hotel and had either 4 or 5 stars. Monique told the taxi to drive to this place, she went to find out if they had a room, they had. The taxi driver put our bags out, a hotel porter came smartly dressed and took charge of them, in we went, the hotel was plush, I thought this would do fine. We had a bath together to freshen up, taking plenty of time.

Dinner time came along, down we went. The dining room tables were well set, the waiters very smart. We ordered 1st and 2nd courses, the first was soup, which looked and tasted like dishwater, we both left it, the meat course came and was so terrible I told the waiter – he spoke English – as I was by now most annoyed, that I would not give my dogs muck like this, he tried to tell me that a party of 15 English had been in that weekend, they had the same food, and had liked it very much, I told him straight, the English people did not know what good food was, at the same time telling him on no account was this food to be put on my hotel bill, also telling him to send the Manager to my table immediately—he left us very sheepishly, returning within a couple of minutes to say the Manager was not available, Monique and I got up and left the table. I went straight to the reception office and told the girl there exactly what I had told the waiter. About an hour later, a waiter approached us while we were in the bar, telling us we could only stay one more night, I took no notice of him but thought the Manager must have a small brain.

When Monique and I left the dining room, we went straight to the bar, a pleasant little place with comfortable chairs, we took one not far from the entrance doorway, I ordered 2 large whisky. I needed my nerves calmed down, I was most annoyed that a 5 star place like this could put on such rotten food and smile at the same time, I had a good mind to take the matter further and get the Manager sacked, but Monique talked me out of this.

I lit a large Punch Corona. I had taken a box with me, Monique and I settled down in our comfy chairs, chatting about things when both at the same time looked up and just coming through the doorway was our old friend Isidor from Fuerteventura, he recognised us in an instant, we invited him to join us, which he did. Monique told him of our experience in the dining room. He had had the same food as had been placed in front of us earlier on, he had also left his table, the food, he said, was too horrible to eat, this pleased me, it showed that, indeed, this place was no good. Isidor's plane had been diverted from landing at Fuerteventura by the sand storm. He thought, was leaving for that place in the morning, Isidor stayed with us for two hours, in which time we had given the whisky bottles a good thrashing, he must have thought these alcoholic friends are back again, for he left the bar cross-eyed and wobbly, so to bed.

The next day, 5th November, was very hot, we had a well-earned lie-in, we both bathed and felt fresher we decided to have a look and see what the town was like, on the way down, I called at the reception desk, again asking to see the Manager, the girl went into another room coming out again too soon, saying the Manager was out. I knew he was hiding and was too scared to face things out with me, I laughed at the girl and went on our way.

We had a good look around the little town and were not impressed at all, it was a dirty place, even the local inhabitants seemed dirty. Compared with the local people on Fuerteventura, they were poor, but extremely clean and very pleasant to converse with. We had the odd beer here and there. By now the time was 3 pm. Monique was hungry. We sat ourselves at a small restaurant and dined on the fish Rougie, these were quite good, in fact, rougie were Monique's favourite fish, after this we walked a while, stopping for a beer at an open fronted bar, where Monique spotted a fruit tart the size of a large dinner plate, she asked if she could have a slice, the barman said of course, I had seen a few flies on the tart, also the barman looked rather sickly, I cautioned Monique, but she was determined and had her tart, I stuck to my beer, in the course of conversation the sickly looking barman said his stomach had been giving him trouble for a few days now, and the poor devil he did look ill, I thought of the tart but kept my thoughts to myself.

By now, Monique and I had decided to leave Lanzarote, we were disenchanted by the place, the dirt and the look of the people, I bought tickets there and then for a flight to Fuerteventura in the morning, I was not going to spend a holiday on an island I did not like. Monique was agreeable at once.

That night, Monique spent the whole of it on the loo, she had chronic diarrhoea, in fact I would say a good dose of food poisoning, brought on by that fruit tart, she now realised she should not have eaten it, agreeing with me on the flies and the looks of the poor barman. By morning Monique was tired out and had little sleep, we booked out of the hotel late. I again asked for the Manager, once again the same reply, I studied my account, found only the bedroom was charged for, paid and left, leaving our suitcases to be picked up later by taxi. Monique had not to be far away from a bar that she could dash into. This was very frequent, she was lamenting the eating of that tart, so was I, for her.

We collared a taxi, collected the cases and headed for the airport, getting there by the skin of our teeth, almost missing the plane, it turned out that Monique's watch was not correct, we took off at 3:30 pm, Monique kept the loo busy or was it vice-versa.

Getting into Fuerteventura we took a taxi to our old friend Andre's hotel – immediately when in the taxi we realised we had made the right decision to leave dirty Lanzarote, strangely we both had that homely feeling here, the taxi man told us Andre had built a new hotel further back from the previous one which he rented, to this new one we were driven, Andre' and his wife recognised us right away, greeted us with great delight, of course, there was a room for us, the best one he said.

The hotel had been finished, I think only the year before and was very good, most pleasant our room was, with our own bathroom and toilet, tastefully decorated also. We took it easy because of Monique's predicament, she was still with her tummy trouble, telling Andre of this and that she would eat only something very simple. He was concerned and asked if he should have the doctor called. Monique said no, she would see what the morning would bring.

We descended to the bar, I wanted Monique to try two or three brandy and ports to see if this would help, she had two but did not like them. We went to dine, where we found Andre's new dining room most pleasant, he himself was very proud of it also. Monique had a light veg soup and a small helping of fish, very light and very fresh. Andre's wife is still seeing to the cooking, I had the same as Monique but double helpings. For drinks, Monique had bottled mineral water I had three beers. It was a relief to eat good clean, fresh food in very clean surroundings. Andre's waiter, a young chappie, was a most pleasant youngster, always obliging, we did not venture out after dinner, Monique was not up to it.

The next day, the 7th, we did not bother to have breakfast, we were going to walk the two miles over to Playa Blanca, Monique asked Andre's wife if she could make us sandwiches, she was overjoyed to do so, these were of fresh chicken. Monique's tummy was getting better, but she was still troubled by the call of nature, I asked if she would not rather take it easy. She said no, she felt like a swim, as the day was hot. Off we set to walk and in no time, like our last visit here a few years ago, a car, a very old one, stopped to give us a lift, we accepted and were duly dropped at Playa Blanca, where we sunbathed and swam until 7 pm. Monique's tummy seemed to have settled down now, we packed up took the road to town, this time, we were picked up after half a mile of walking. We showered and dressed, when all of a sudden Monique's tummy trouble started again and again, once more, she only had a light soup and a little chicken breast, she herself was fed up with this bug. It had been a most virulent bug alright, and an elderly person might have been hospitalised with a bug as she had had.

By the next day 8th Monique was fine. She was looking forward to a day of no troubled tummy, the day was windy, a good day to get bronzed.

Afterwards, we went to see our old barkeeper friend, Rosie. Rosie, of course, was not old, being in her late 20's, she was delighted to see us, and when she poured our whisky's she made sure of make them extra large, we spent an hour there chatting away with her. Isidor I thought was rather self-conscious in Rosie's presence, Monique suspected there may be more than meets the eye here. Afterwards, we bought some tablets for Monique's tummy upset, it bothered her slightly still.

We went to the hotel had a rest, Isidor told us about a newly opened little nightclub that had dancing etc, we arranged to meet him there. Monique and I had dinner at Andreas (our hotel) and left for the nightclub at 11 pm. We were greeted warmly in the entrance of the club by a youngish waiter, no more than 20 years old, as we were being ushered in he spotted that I was wearing sandals, he apologised saying that sandals were forbidden by the management, my sandals were almost shoes, being well latticed and firm, but no sorry I was not permitted entry – I realised now I had made a mistake, I had left my shoes inadvertently in the Volvo in Spain, I must have forgotten completely to pack them, it was rather too far to go to Seville, Monique explained the situation, the young waiter left us to, I suppose ask the Manager, whom we got to know later and referred to him as "greasy bug," why, because he had very lanky greasy hair, with a face to match, the waiter came back, saying no, I had a quick thought and asked him if I could borrow his own shoes for the night for 25 pts. The nice young chap agreed right away, saying he had an old pair, which he himself would wear, in his cloakroom, there and then I gave him the 25 pts, he handed me his shoes and we were admitted, with a big smile from our new friend. The young fellow was onto a good thing because Monique and I were at this club most nights, each time, our friend handed over his shoes and he got 25 pts. No doubt it augmented his low wage – I was pleased and he was pleased, also I appreciated his gesture and bought him a few beers now and then.

The club Las Garvies was small, very cosy, a small dance piste in the middle of the room, comfortable seats, nice tables, good music from records, drinks were cheap, no gambling – I don't like gambling clubs really, a good atmosphere all around. It was never crowded, more or less the same faces most nights. We danced till 2:30 am, in our newfound place, the trouble was, though, no single girls were there on their own, this I suppose, frowned upon by the Spanish community. Girls there did not gad about like ours in Europe. Monique had, that first night, two of us to dance with, Isidor and myself, however, we were pleased with our newfound little club.

Monique and I went along to Las Garvies after having a few drinks with or rather at Rosie's bar, she still had about 7 cats in the place, sleeping on the shelves among the glasses, the place smelt of them, why we drank at Rosie's was, she was a most pleasant young woman, her bar nicely placed in town, where bars were a scarce item, also we drank large whisky's, these Fuerteventura measures would be equal to 5 singles in England. For the price of 2/- to 2/6, and I thought whisky is a good disinfectant, if the cats leave any bugs on the glasses, the whisky will soon kill them. My friend, the club waiter, immediately gave me his shoes, I parted with 25 pts and we went. There were 10 or 12 people sitting around drinking. Monique and I took a table on the far side of the dance floor, ordering our drinks there. The whiskies were not quite as big as at Andre's or Rosie's, but they were big enough. At this time, most bars seemed to have that scotch whisky 100 Pipers in stock. I found it most agreeable.

We danced on to some rather lovely melodies, one always stuck in my mind, it was Maripossa, I even bought the record, there were many more, and when we danced, and the others there also, danced in each other's arms, not this stupid jig a jig modern junk, where one's partner is 3 yards away, both partners wriggling like maggots, this little club was just great. This night a man in a corner kept looking continuously at us – I began to think here's another nutter, eventually this man came over to our table, saying he had heard us speaking English, he himself was a teacher of English on the island, in English he said his name was Prof Rienna, but please call me Mr Queen, (the English of Rienna). I got up, shook hands with him, introduced him to Monique, and invited him to sit and take a drink with us, he saw we were drinking whisky and ordered the same, we talked for three hours with our new friend, then we left to return to our hotel at 2 am.

The next day, we both swam for three or four hours, the wind was still strong. In the late afternoon, I thought it a good idea to visit the Military Camp to see if our army friends were still there, off we set at 5 pm, and we marched to the bar in the officer's mess, knowing the layout well, nothing had changed in this respect, at the bar Monique had just started to ask for the Colonel – the one we had known before – when two orderly's surrounded us, ordering us out. Monique explained to these two chappies the reason for our visit, we were treated very coldly, told the present Colonel was not the one we had known, told to leave and more or less not to come back. This was a disappointment, as we had had a lot of fun here on our last visit, but more surprises were to come, more than ever we thought.

We backtracked to the town and had a few drinks in the Casino, as I have said before, Casino was only the name of the place, there was no gambling, it was the village hall, so to speak, of the little town of Fuerteventura. Here we came up with Christobal, Isidor's brother. A large, kind man, one look at this man and you liked him, large honest face, kind eyes. He was in Real Estate. I think Christobal would finish in later years very rich because by now, the Germans were buying up land to build on, right and left. Christobal, later on, took us to see the largish tracks of land just outside the town that was all marked and lined up for the Germans, who were going to build their holiday houses or villas.

From there, we went and saw Rosie, then as an after thought at midnight, instead of returning to our hotel, we thought to have a few dances at Las Garvies, "my" shoes were duly taken off and put on, 25 pts handed over, in we went, there was Mr Queen, the Prof, he was delighted to see us, his face beaming with pleasure. What I forgot to mention earlier, in our conversation with him, was that Mr Queen was pro-English from the hair on his head to his toenails, almost fanatically so, he adored the Royal Family, and Ted Heath, I believe, was Prime Minister, he thought him the tops too, he had told us he had written two or three times to the Queen and Mr Heath, he loved all things English, I invited him to join us, he was overjoyed. All the time he was with us during our stay, he never spoke one word of Spanish to Monique, insisting on the English language.

During our drinking and conversation, I mentioned to him our experience at the Officer's mess that afternoon, telling him of our friendship with the Colonel on our last visit, he was shocked and immediately said, you both go to the Officer's mess at 11 am tomorrow morning, I shall be there. By now, a lot of whisky had been drunk and I thought poor little Mr Queen had had one too many, eventually Mr Queen left and we followed, we shook hands on a junction of three roads – built up area – tracking off from these was a "footpath," if it could be called that, over some ruined buildings, Mr Queen took this rough track, we both just happened to glance back, as he entered this dark, one could almost say hole, he glanced backwards and sideways, most furtively, like someone about to commit a crime, to see if anyone was coming or watching, then he was gone. Monique and I began to examine our Mr Queen in our minds. We had known him twice in 24 hours. We noticed no one spoke to him ever at the nightclub – he kept himself very much to himself, except he delighted in our company. Mr Queen, we thought, was a mystery man.

The next day we debated whether to go to the Military Camp or not, neither of us wished to be given the order of the boot again, then something in our minds told us to go, Mr Queen was, as we thought, a mystery man. The walk was only about 400 yards, we arrived at 11 am sharp, there was indeed Mr Queen, he had seen us arrive, he came out of the foyer, took us both inside the Officer's mess, there before we stood the two orderlies and 6 or 7 highish up officers – he had arranged this I knew by the officers more or less standing to attention – he addressed them as one, telling them in Spanish, which Monique well understood – that Mr & Mrs Swinbank-Slack had to be given access to all the club's facilities, here and the beach club and treated with respect at all times, during our stay on the island, Mr Queen then addressed us and repeated to us what he had told these officers. I could hardly believe my ears, with all of this and my amazement, the Lieutenant Colonel Jose Martin Villoria was present, if he was not, then his adjutant certainly was with a few Majors and Captains thrown in. Mr Queen then invited all present to the bar for drinks and all present did so, one thing I noticed Mr Queen did not pay.

We then, on exit from our military friends, invited Mr Queen for lunch at Los Angeles, outside town, we had been a few times before, it was run by Alberto, another super character. We, of course, thanked Mr Queen for his kindness. I never did pry into how he had so much swing here, he then told us if ever we had trouble in any way, contact him. This is when the jigsaw began – so I thought – and I don't think I was wrong, he was one of Franco's political spies, or commissar's his cover was as a teacher, he actually did teach children because we saw him at work. We mentioned him to Isidor, he hated him but would not say why in fact. During our stay, we knew almost everyone hated or was frightened of Mr Queen, strengthening my guess 100% that he was one of Franco's men.

Day by day, we saw people avoid Mr Queen, even crossing the street to be away from him. However, Monique and I basked in his protective net and enjoyed our days and evenings at the Officer's mess, the officers, on their part, became most friendly once they knew we were just plain English tourists, and when Monique told them of our fun and games with the Colonel on our previous visit, we were accepted as good friends and invited on our visits to join various groups for drinks and two or three times for dinner.

On 12th November, we had breakfast in our room, then took a taxi to Castello beach, this was in the region of about 6km, we had a quick swim, because all of a sudden the sky darkened and rain threatened, from nice sunshine to within minutes to this, and in no time at all the rain started, great big drops becoming heavier until it was torrential. We kept our clothes in a plastic carrier bag, nicely rolled up and set off to walk the 3km to Los Angeles Bar & Restaurant, where Alberto, the owner knew us well. Once there, we dried ourselves, dressed, had a couple of whisky's each, then asked Alberto what he had on the menu for lunch fresh fish he said, landed this morning, that was enough, we both liked fish, especially freshly caught, he showed us the fish, what sort I don't remember, but they looked sparkling fresh, we asked Alberto for two each. They were served with baked potatoes, they turned out to be absolutely super. We were ready for this, after swimming, getting drenched (in our swimsuits), and 3 km walk, we drank three bottles of wine over our meal and stayed chatting to Alberto, the meal and drinks were 146pts. Alberto giving us one of the bottles of wine, very cheap.

We left Los Angeles on foot, walking only about half a mile or thereabouts before we were given a lift. The rain had long since stopped. Later, we had dinner at Andrea's and went out on the town with Isidor, finishing up at Las Garvies, once again changing shoes with my waiter friend, I still had not asked his name. Mr Queen was there, alone at his table. Isidor did not want him to join us, saying no one here liked him, meaning Mr Queen – however, I liked Mr Queen, for one thing, he loved the English, he also had a good and intelligent crack in him. I took no notice of Isidor and invited Mr Queen to join us. Monique introduced Isidor to him, but the two never conversed at all. Mr Queen did not seem to like his fellow countryman.

The next day, 13th, we again took a taxi to Castello Beach rather early, getting there at 10:30 am. On a nice sunny day, swam for two hours, then the sky darkened once again. This time, we thought, for some reason or other, we dressed. Of course, this was simply dressed, me light trousers and a shirt, Monique the same, blouse etc, we had walked 1km when the heavens opened, within seconds we were soaked, on we walked almost to Alberto's, when we were given a lift, the one and only vehicle, a very ancient Austin truck, a real old rattletrap driven by a very kind-faced old farmer, he and Monique had a good old chinwag, I think he was sorry to say farewell when we got to town. That night Monique and I had drinks in the old Fuerteventura Hotel in the little bar opening onto the pavement, as usual, Isidor was sitting up at the bar, this was all he ever did, also this was his favourite bar, after perhaps an hour Monique told him we were on our way to dine with some of the army officers, we asked if he would like to come for a drink, he stated emphatically not any Spanish civilians admitted there, we did not insist, sensing trouble if we did, however, Isidor offered to drive us the 400 yards to our destination, to please him we accepted. We had a very pleasant evening and had an excellent dinner with our officer friends.

My cigars on the island were, as on our last visit, huge 7-inch long black cigars, I was told they were made from Canary Isle leaf, 3p each, a perfect smoke. Indeed, this was a pleasant isle to holiday on, with drinks, cigars, and food so cheap it was unbelievable, immaculate and beautiful girls, extremely kind people, much better mentally than the Spanish mainlanders, in fact, most of the inhabitants had never been to Spain, some preferring to visit Argentina, rather than Spain. I could see, to be correct, we both could see, that not many years ahead, possibly 4 or 5, this lovely, more or less barren island would be forever spoilt by the tourists, especially the arrogant Germans, whom were busy buying up every piece of land they could. When that happened the mentality of the people would change, the school children indoctrinated into the ways of vulgar tourism or tourists, but just now, in 1971, it was a lovely place to be, and nice people to be with, our honeymoon was idyllic.

That night of 16th November, there was a tremendous storm of thunder, lightning and torrential rain all night. In the morning, gale force winds, heavy rain and sea's far too high and rough to even think about swimming. Isidor was downstairs in the bar, the watchdog, ever watchful, he drove us out to the airport, where we had lunch, a long one. After 5 or 6 hours there we all went to see Alberto, here we arrived at 7 pm, there was a countryside dance going on, so we joined in, this time I had no trouble with girl partners, I suppose we had become quite well known now in the locality, the music by records, were good old melodies, music that made us want to dance. There we stayed until 5 am.

In Isidor's car, we got three abreast on the front bench seat, we sang some of the songs we had danced to, but I could not follow them in Spanish, Monique and Isidor singing in full swing, then things gradually quietened, we were driving along a road that was elevated above the land on either side by possibly 10ft when the next thing I knew, I was looking at the stars and all was quiet, then something moved underneath me, all of a sudden I realised we had run off the road, the car completely on its side and all three of us lying in a heap, we had all gone to sleep more or less simultaneously, fortunately, as I said before, Isidor never drove fast, we had rolled off the road at about 20m.p.h, we were in the middle of nowhere, Isidor said he would walk 3km to some friends who had a tractor, and pull the car over and up the embankment, off he set, he was not too long arriving with what I took to be a Forson Major Tractor and 3 friends laughing their heads off, they quickly had the car righted and pulled out, then we were off again. The car seemed none the worse, and to the hotel, where Andreas and his wife were starting work.

9:30 pm Friday, November 19th Isidor picked us up and had driven only 2km outside of town when there in the middle of the road, waving us down with his torch, was a Spanish Policeman, the ones with a flat side to their hats, these Police were sent out from mainland Spain to the islands at various intervals – with no warning – to see that law and order was maintained, now here was one of them, first he saluted the driver Isidor then invited him to get out of the car, then asked to see his driving license. Monique quietly interpreted to me as things went on, Isidor had not either got it or never had one, then flat hat asked for his, either car or insurance papers, poor Isidor had none. I then started to explain – trying to help Isidor – and spoke in English – that we were tourists blah blah. I was told sternly to mind my own business – Monique's interpretation – so I did. The Policeman then took his time and wrote some form out from a booklet he produced. Then he let us go. Also, now, Isidor told us one side and one main front light was not working and both backlights did not work, I had never noticed before, this was an offence put on his Police form also. Poor chap, it spoiled his evening because when he had added the fines up, these monetary penalties must have been on the ticket he'd collected, they totalled roughly £75, a large sum of money then, especially for these islanders. We stayed chatting and drinking until 3 am.

On 20th, Monique and I were up and swimming by 10:30 am, then after an hour, she started to feel not well. So much so that we immediately returned to the hotel where she went straight to bed, I told Andreas, he told me she must have the Dr and insisted on phoning him there and then, the Dr came and a very kind man he was, he took Monique's temperature, then her blood pressure, finding the latter very low, saying Monique's system was completely low also, he gave her an injection and gave her some pills to take, telling me she had to take it easy for a few days, I will say we had been living it up far too much, and too fast.

That evening, I ate alone and then went to keep Monique company, Isidor sent word to our room to come down, as there was a function in the hotel—a wedding party, I think – of a friend of his, Monique told the waitress we were staying put tonight, which we did.

In the morning, the district nurse or chemist came to give Monique another injection at noon, she was feeling like her old self, but I insisted she stay inside and in bed, only getting up for lunch, which was fish, nice and light for her and dinner at night of vegetable soup and pork. Andreas' meals were straightforward and simple but always tasted very good, and a bottle of wine, which we took slowly. Monique was ready to go out for a few hours, but I thought another early night would be best and this is what we had. Also, today, the 21st, was little Joey's birthday. He is now 14.

Monday 22nd was rather overcast in the morning. We strolled along the streets on the way to say hello to Rosie, passing a building with shutters and windows wide open and from inside, children's voices, chanting, sing-song, counting in English from 1 to 10, one and two and three and four and so on, we poked our heads over the window sill, this on ground level, there was Mr Queen teaching a roomful of children aged 5 to 7 years old. He saw us, his face beaming he came over to the window, we chatted for a minute, then I asked if we could meet later in the evening, he said of course, at the Las Garvies 6 pm, because I had a plan to get Isidor off the hook regarding the Police with his car fines, we would test the power of our friend Mr Queen. While Rosie and she talked as women do, after an hour, we walked to our rocks and took the sun, which had decided to come out smiling.

At 6:00 pm, we strolled along to Las Garvies, there was Mr Queen, I ordered large whisky's, and for Monique, she decided on a small Tio Pepe, I lit a large local black cigar priced 3p. then started to explain to our spy friend the problems and troubles, Isidor had with the police over his car, we gave full particulars of the incident, Mr Queen did not hesitate, he said, tell your friend to come to see me at 10:30 am tomorrow morning at my classroom bring his police paper, and I will see that the police do not bother him again, now I was sure beyond doubt, that our friend Mr Queen, was a top political spy of Franco, later within 24 hours I was more sure, Monique also had no more doubts, I thanked Mr Queen, we had two more rounds then he left, saying to meet him midday in the officer's mess tomorrow 23rd.

We asked around for Isidor but could not find him, to give

him the news of Mr Queen, at the old hotel bar, a friend of his told us he would see him before long. Monique told the friend to tell Isidor to meet us at 10:30 pm that night at Las Garvies, in the meantime Monique and I had dinner at our hotel. At 10:30 pm we went to Las Garvies where my friend, the waiter, duly took off his shoes, and was 25pts richer, now I had his name, it was Pedro, he was always happy to oblige, there was a greasy bug, with his records, Isidor had not arrived, we took our usual table, Monique stuck to her small Tio Pepe, me whisky and the black local cigar, we had a dance or two, nice slowish ones, I did not want Monique to get into anything fast – it might upset her, though she was full of beans and looked it – absolutely lovely.

At 11 pm or thereabouts, Isidor came in and sat down, Monique told him we had something important to tell him, I listened carefully, trying to understand the language. I was picking bits of Spanish up by now, but the talk was too rapid for me. Monique explained fully when she had finished explaining, he thought for a while, and then to my astonishment, in fact, us both, he refused to see or speak to Mr Queen, he made some silly excuse for not doing so, I tried to impress on Isidor the cost to him, I knew even though his family had a lot of land, they had little or no cash, but he was adamant not to see Mr Queen. Monique and I put it down to "losing face." Isidor was a very proud and suave man-about-town sort of thing, he wasn't going to ask a little insignificant Spaniard a favour. It was beneath his dignity and so it remained, neither of us could budge him. We left and went home to bed.

In the morning, we took it easy, had breakfast in our room, showered and dressed we had a rendezvous with our friend Mr Queen in the officer's mess at 11:30 am. Dressed, we slowly made our way to the military end of town, we entered this holy of holy's, there was our friend Mr Queen at the bar, straight away he said, "Your friend has not been to see me." Monique told him that Isidor refused to discuss his case and left it at that, Mr Queen then said, "Stupid man."

We sat up at the bar, ordering whisky's, Monique had a beer, we drank steadily, Mr Queen and I, for two hours, Monique had two beers in this time, then we adjourned for lunch, taken in the Officer's Mess, a good one it was too, after lunch Mr Queen, by now well on the way to Mandalay, we again adjourned to the bar. Now, there were six or seven Officers drinking; what ranks they held I don't know, but Mr Queen by now was singing English and Spanish songs, the Officers, Monique and I joining in, then Mr Queen would recite poems from Tennyson and Byron, our group listening to him with interest, for he was good. Then to Monique's and my surprise, he had the six Officers lined up, he, Monique and I faced them and instructed them to sing God Save the Queen, not once but twice and they did – very lustily too, it amazed me this made me again realise I had not been wrong in my first assumption of what our friend Mr Queen really was, undoubtedly he was Franco's man. I thought then that if Franco could see him at this moment, Mr Queen would have been in deep trouble, however the afternoon wore on, the drinks were coming steadily in, the only one holding back was Monique, she was taking it easily, the Officers were still with us and going strong, Mr Queen now was drinking his whisky with a large quantity of milk, thinking it would help him survive I suppose.

8:30 pm arrived. One of the Officers asked Monique if she and I would stay for dinner with them, she asked me, I thanked the Officer and accepted, Mr Queen then said he would also stay – inviting himself. We had a superb evening, good food, excellent wine and Cuban cigars, Mr Queen was in his element, quoting poetry, singing and plenty of jokes. We parted from there at 1 am, very happy.

We were up the next morning and went straight to swim. We had done the right thing because in the afternoon it rained quite heavily, we had lunch at our hotel. In the evening, we had a few drinks at Las Garvies, returning early to the hotel for dinner and bed. There had been no sign of Prof. Reina, he must have had a solid hangover. However, he surfaced on Friday 26th.

This day was cold and overcast, we did not swim, we ran into Mr Queen in town, he greeted us with great enthusiasm, wanting us to take drinks with him at the Casino, which we did, then to the hotel of Andreas for lunch, by the time lunch was over at 3:30 pm Monique had to leave us, she had an appointment at the Hairdresser, Mr Queen and I drank on and on, when Monique returned we were in quite a happy state, Mr Queen himself did not smoke, but he was quite fascinated how I managed to chain smoke the double Corona sized black cigars continuously, these, though, were a very mild smoke. We then all went for dinner to Los Angelos, Alberto's place, where he and I had rabbit and Monique fish. Here it was another hilarious night, quite a few locals, whom we had got to know, joined in singing and joking. Alberto himself threw a few free rounds of drinks in for us, we left at 3 am.

We continued our swims and sunbathing, dining and drinking. On 29th, Monique had her period, so swimming was out for her, these periods laid her low for two or three days, as they were very heavy, lasting a full week, sometimes longer. However, our holiday on Fuerteventura was drawing to a close, for this day, I bought the return air tickets for Seville. We planned to leave on Wednesday, however today, Monday, we slowly did the rounds of all our haunts, myself drinking my fill and the health of the friends we had made. Monique sticking to a small sherry now and then, the friends we had made all over were, I think, genuinely sad to see that we would be leaving them in two days' time, we were also sad, for these were kind-hearted people living a simple way of life, we had enjoyed their company immensely.

I bought 200 of the enormous black cigars, these were too good to leave on the shopping list. We spent the last evening saying our goodbyes to Rosie, the Officers at the military camp, the casino, then met Mr Queen at Las Garvies, he was sad to see us go, my friend Pedro, the waiter, looked rather sad also, when I told him we were leaving the next day, no doubt thinking of his 25pts four to five times a week, he had been a grand little chappie during our stay, always a big happy smile and always willing to help. Then we had a run out to Alberto's to again sample his bottles with Isidor, Alberto had, so he said, enjoyed our visits to his pub restaurant and, as if to prove it kept our glasses well charged, most of it on the house, he presented me with 10 of the big black cigars, which I thought was a very kind gesture. Then back to town at midnight, calling again at the Casino for the last few for the road, with various members of the town, including Christobal, Isidor's brother.

Wednesday, December 1st 1971. Isidor, this time, arrived to take us to the airport. The latter was now quite a fashionable and smart little place, much different from the first holiday we had here, the plane took off at 11 am, landing at Las Palmas, where we had time to go into town, but once again, I did not like the place, neither did Monique, it seemed sleazy, we boarded the plane and were off again at 3 pm touching down at El Aiun in the Sahara. Flying low over the black tents of the nomads, sand dunes as far as one could see, here we bought and posted a few postcards from the Sahara, had a couple of beers, then on the plane again with a few new passengers from the military – probably going on leave. About 10 soldiers had been dropped off in El Aiun.

31

The plane touched down at Seville Airport at approximately 8 pm, we took a taxi straight to the garage, Torres del Oro, to pick up the Volvo, paid the bill, about £15 and took off for our hotel, the Ducal, we booked in, still the kind-faced receptionist, leaving the car as before beside the pavement outside the front door of the hotel, then, feeling hungry, walked 100 yards round the corner to a restaurant for something to eat and a good bottle of red wine, as we were still in our summer clothes, we suddenly realised it was quite cold. We left the restaurant to get our winter clothes from the car, as we drew nearer to the car, I saw the small window on the driver's side smashed and my winter clothes gone from the back seat, one thing gone was my alpaca jacket. I blew the car horn to attract attention – I thought someone might come and tell us they had seen the thief, but all I got was a volley of apples thrown from an upstairs window of a house beside the hotel, I shouted at them in Spanish "thank you very much," which probably made them more mad.

Into the hotel we went, told the receptionist what had happened and asked him to phone the Police, he said, "It's no good, sir, they will not come."

I said, "Right, we will go to them." He rang for a taxi, in we got, Monique instructing the driver to go to the nearest Police Station, this building was not too far away. In we went, there was a plain-clothed chap behind the desk, Monique told him what had happened, he just shrugged his shoulders and said he could do nothing at this I called him Uste Tonto, which means "you are stupid," about the only Spanish I knew outside of "thank you", that little statement by me put the tin hat on properly, Monique told me, "you should not have said that." He asked me to repeat what I had said – Monique told me, "Say nothing." He did not understand English, he asked again to repeat my words, I remained silent, he then told Monique, "Your husband does not leave here tonight." She tried to pacify the man, but he ignored her, except to say that she could go, I had to stay, I was under arrest.

Monique told me what he had said, I thought then, in my anger, I had done the wrong thing in telling the chap he was stupid. The thief also had gone with a set of car keys, which were in my stolen jacket, this was told to our civil-suited Gestapo chap behind the Police counter, he took no notice, now I realised that this was Franco's Country, I might be put in jail for six months, English boys and girls in this period, holidaying in Spain were sent to jail for a kiss on the cheek if seen by the Police, in towns or on the beaches, Monique had told me to be careful of the Spanish mentality.

I said to Monique, "Come on, let's get out of here," and made for the door to open out into a small courtyard, but in the courtyard we were stopped by an armed Policeman and ordered to stay where we were, we were not allowed back into the room, after an hour we were still in the courtyard, it was also freezing cold, Monique banged on the door, which was opened by another armed chappie, demanding to know what was going on, she was told, "Soon you will see." At 11:30 am, we were shivering. It was so cold, we still had our summer clothes on, though I now had shoes instead of sandals.

Two Police came to me, one on each side and marched me outside to a waiting car. Monique followed behind demanding where they were taking me, I was hustled into the car, Monique insisting to go with me, they allowed her into the car, once inside the car, I gave Monique all the cash I had and my cigar case, in case they were stolen from me. Our companions watched this move but said nothing. After passing 15-20 minutes in the car it pulls up at the main Police Station in Seville, I was to be put in the cells. They pacified Monique by telling her she could collect me at 9am that morning. She insisted on coming with me, but once through the main big doors they roughly got hold of her and pushed her outside, I thought to myself, "Now, my boy, your temper has let you in the soup this time" – but then thinking about it, I reckoned I was justified, my clothes had been stolen, my car window broken, and the thief, for all I knew, had taken off with my car, he had the keys and the damned stupid Police had shrugged their shoulders.

Now I was marched down flights of steps to the underground cells, I was put into one of them, one to myself, the iron door clanged shut and the key turned noisily just as one sees on the films of prisons and prisoners, I took stock of my surroundings, the cell was about 12ft x 8ft, solid walls except the front which was iron bars from floor to ceiling, in this was the door, at the far end was a cement platform about 3ft 6in wide to lie on with a bump at one end to serve as a pillow, no blankets or anything else, I lay down on my cement "bed", but it was so cold my feet started to cramp, I rubbed and twisted them and lay back again, as soon as I relaxed the cramp started again, my cement pillow was too hard for my head, so I took my shoes off and had them for a pillow, it was no good, my feet got worse – just then I heard a noise like a cannon going off from the next door cell, I could not see my neighbour but I could hear the snoring, then the "shot" – my neighbour had let a fart off that could have blown the wall down, he carried on farting, it seemed every 5 minutes, like gunshots, sleep was impossible.

I shouted for a guard, who, after 5 minutes, condescended to come, I gesticulated to him that I was cold and would like a blanket, he understood and brought me one, I wrapped the end around my feet and pulled the rest up to my chest, my shoes still as pillows, meanwhile my friend next door continued to snore loudly and fart even louder, but within minutes I started to scratch, then more and more, the blanket seemed to be alive with bugs, I threw it away from me in disgust, put my shoes back on my feet and just sat on my cement bed with my back to the wall as a backrest. I thought, hell, what a mess I had got myself into. I sat the night through, listening to my neighbour, I have never heard anyone fart like a shotgun and snore like a pig grunting all through the night, this was the worst night of my life.

At about 6 am I wanted to go to the toilette for a No.2. I shouted for the guard, he came, I gesticulated what I wanted, he let me out, showed me the toilette, a dirty hole, but no paper, I went in search of him again, gesticulating, he handed me a sheet of newspaper and off I went to the filthy dirty toilette hole when I had finished I was locked up again, the door clanging loudly, I think the guards like this bit of clanging the iron-barred door shut as hard as they could.

At 7 am I was taken from my cell and marched along the corridor, the end of which widened out into a reception area, hallway etc. Here, I was put into a large cage-like cell with a kind of semi-circular front of iron bars. I had some cellmates, all youngsters in their teens, two of them for smoking or having pot on them, the other, whom became a friend, had been locked up for not paying his phone bill – he had telephoned his girlfriend in America from the local Post Office, been connected and spoken to his girlfriend for half an hour when he had finished the call he had walked out of the Post Office without paying – only 3 or 4 yards then the hand of the Law on his shoulder and locked up. He had been there three days, his name was Jose Lopez Garcia of Feria 140, Seville, he spoke very good English, so we had no problem conversing, he told me his mother was a gypsy, of which he was intensely proud, she was a beauty he said and a Flamenco dancer, he was a good and kind youngster of about 19, he had a packet of cigarettes on him, he insisted I have one, in the end I smoked most of them for him. At 8 am a woman came around selling cakes and coffee, as I had no money, Jose bought me my breakfast of one insipid cake and the coffee was not much better, but it was a great kindness on his part.

We made a pact, whoever got out of jail first would do a favour for the other, for example, if I was first, I had to get in touch with one of his relations and his Lawyer, he gave me the telephone numbers and addresses, but I seem to have lost these – If he got out first, to contact Monique at Hotel Ducan, we shook hands on it. The other two youngsters inside were also very kind, nice young men, clean and very tidy, they had just been larking about, as all youngsters do, but then, in the Franco era, the iron fist of El Caudillo was everywhere.

Then, surprise, there arrived Monique, my was I glad to see her, she was accompanied by the British Consular agent Peter Bolton (or Baldwin) – I think I have his name correct. Monique had contacted him, he, I thought looking at him, was a smoothie, it transpired that he was married to a Spanish woman, I think he was more pro-Spanish than wanting to help a fellow countryman, he was, or had been, a Northerner, educated at St Bees, Cumberland. I told him to get cracking and bribe whoever was necessary to get me out, he said he couldn't as my case was already on the books, he said he would be at the tribunal later in the day to help, but somehow, I had no faith in this smoothie individual, then they had to leave but before they left I asked Baldwin to telex my bank at Penrith, explain and to send me £100 immediately, he said he would do so that morning, I needed a little reserve of money just in case!

At 11:30 am, a guard came for me to go with him to be photographed and fingerprinted, my friend Jose interpreted this to me, then Jose asked the guard if he could accompany me, as my interpreter, the guard agreed. Upstairs to the second floor we went, where I was photographed and fingerprints taken, when I gave them my full name, Lancaster came up the fingerprint chap said, "Ah, Lancaster, the Royal House." this Jose interpreted, I said yes. The Spaniard then said a few words to his colleagues, who then gathered around, looking at me quite with respect, I thought I'd scored one here.

Back in the cell, Jose and I continued to smoke his cigarettes, I had, in my linen jacket breast pocket, a large red silk handkerchief, about as big as a flag, Jose admired it so much I took it from my pocket and gave it to him, he was delighted and gave me a big bear hug.

I had asked Monique to bring me some money and a box of cigars so that I could share them with my new friends, my cellmates, but it seemed she did not have the time – she had reminded the Police of their promise to her, that I would be released that morning at 9 am, they just shrugged her off.

Thirty minutes after noon, my three companions and myself were taken out of our cage and assembled in the hallway together with a few others – I cannot remember how many, but I should guess at about 8 to 10, I was then handcuffed to an enormous dirty bloke who stank like a ferret and carrying a great big lorry jack easily weighing 3 or more stones, he carried it as if it were as light as a paper, Jose told me he was a lorry driver and had been in the next cell to me that night, now here I was not only face to face, but handcuffed to my farting neighbour, he must have been 18 stone and 6ft 6in tall, but missing it in the £.

Then we were escorted outside, I thought, just like a chain gang, the sunlight was quite dazzling in contrast to the gloomy cells below, once outside we were ushered into the Black Maria, and off we went to, I presumed, the Courthouse. About 10 to 15 minutes driving our transport stopped, the rear doors opened, as my farting friend and I were on last we were first off and lo and behold, there were 5 or 6 photographers on the pavement, flashbulbs going full blast, friends and relatives of the prisoners shouting goodwill to them, then into the Courthouse we went, we were assembled in a long large wide hallway-cum-room, in line but it seemed we were not the only prisoners by now in line with "my gang" there would be 10 or 12 more making 20 or more to face the "Beak."

As we stood in line at one side of this large hallway, still handcuffed together, the doors at one end opened and a crowd of people came in and stood opposite us; there would be 40 or 50 of them. 4 yards approx would separate us from them, they were wives, sweethearts, fathers, mothers, sons, daughters, friends of the prisoners, they shouted greetings and joked, laughed, and flung cigarettes over to their friends and relatives – it was like something out of a circus, quite hilarious, all of this quite lifted my spirits, a few took pity on me – kind souls – and threw me cigarettes as well, the time was 30 minutes after noon.

Prisoners were called for at various very slow intervals, a Policeman would then unlock his handcuffs and he would be off to see the "beak", with a volley of cheers from the other side, in looking back, it was really quite good entertainment, but just then it looked black, I had read plenty of Franco's "medicine" in the papers.

Monique turned up at about 1 pm, she saw where I was in the lineup and came right over, a guard tried to stop her, she faced him and gave him such a dressing down that he turned away and went back to his place. Once Monique has her dander up, people should beware. I suppose the guard would be too used to his regular "visitors" to court, the poor and uneducated of this band of prisoners. I would put my friend Jose as the most educated. He was well-read and knew his history, the guard had not come across a sophisticated, well-dressed woman with a tongue, like a whiplash, as Monique.

Monique told me the Consul agent Baldwin had returned to his Consulate and was not coming back. I told her to get back onto the little so and so and get himself back here to the Courthouse to act on my behalf, or I would see that he got the sack when I returned home. An idle threat perhaps, but in my eye, these fellows are there to look after their fellow countrymen in cases like this, Monique went off to get hold of Baldwin and bring him here to back me up.

Time passed slowly, the handcuffed line was going even more slowly. The crowd opposite were still shouting jokes, throwing cigarettes by the dozen over to us. They still inclued me, which I still consider most kind, but I find that the poorer people are much kinder than the rich. The former will share his crust, the latter very seldom will share anything. It was now 2 pm, we prisoners were still standing, but my good friend Jose had been in front of the judge and was free to go, his Lawyer had somehow been contacted and freed him, probably on bail, he saw Monique was now here, he wished me luck shook hands and left. There were no seats for us, or anyone else for that matter.

The crowd opposite now had 20 or 30 more people there; they were enjoying their day out, or so it seemed. 2:30 pm Monique arrived with Baldwin, he told me everything was going to be alright, he had spoken, so he said, with the judge on the phone, I did not know whether to believe him or not, I had not much confidence in him somehow, he said he could not stop to see me through, he had his work. Also, he said it could be a long time before I went before the bench, I then excused him, thanked him and he left. Monique continued to stand beside me, the guards were eyeing her angrily, the crowd also was eyeing her, I could see that they were thinking, why should she be over there and not us, I told her this and she should join the crowd opposite, which she did, I could feel the crowd relax somehow, now she was one of them.

At 2:30 pm the line was now thinning out, also my giant farting friend had gone and I no longer had the handcuffs on, but we were still standing in the same place. At 3:30 pm I was the very last prisoner, all prisoners had gone, no one was opposite. Monique came to my side, then I was called for into a small room of about 12ft sq. I could not believe it, I expected a Courtroom as such, no, there was an old desk at one side of the room with a rather kind looking grey-haired man, probably 60 years old, he beckoned to me to sit on a small upright kitchen like a chair, the first sit since I was in the Black Maria.

This then was my judge, he smiled and asked me in English, "Did you tell that particular Policeman yesterday evening "Uste Tonto", I said straight out yes, he then laughed his head off, then still laughing, he told me I was free to go, as I went through the door he was still laughing.

Monique and I took a taxi to our hotel, the receptionist told me he was so sorry what had happened to me, he was a kind chap and genuinely so, then I took a hot bath, I needed it. I felt very dirty, especially after my bed blanket was filled with bugs, the bath was an old one, good and big, I filled it half full and soaked and soaked, Monique sat beside me, telling me of her experiences, the night the Police pushed her out of the main Police Station and shut the door in her face.

She had sat on the steps of the police station, determined to be there in the morning for my release, even at that time of the night/day, lorry drivers and the odd car would stop and ask her how much she charged, thinking she was a prostitute. She was enraged she said, she was in a thin summer dress and the night was freezing. During this, with all the stress, her periods had started, she had nothing on her person, with regards to pads or tampax, she continued to wait for me, at 5 am the Police came out and threatened her with arrest if she did not leave, she then started the long walk back to the hotel Ducal, she asked the way from various persons now coming to work, to find the Hotel was not too far away. She told me she was a "bloody mess", she ran the bath to more than half full, jumped in and, like me now, had a good long soak, then a short sleep until 9 am. When she returned to the main Police Station where I was held, went in and asked if I had been released and was told no, your husband goes to Court at midday, she then thought about what should she do next, then took a taxi to the British Consulate, where she got hold of Baldwin, then came to see me in my cell, poor Monique she was pos- sibly much more distraught than I was.

After my long soak and a good scrub, we both dressed went round the corner to the bar we had been in when the car was broken into, I myself ordered four large whisky's and filled the half-pint glass to the top with milk, then another and another. Monique herself had good single mea- sure whiskies, then we took it slowly. Later, we had a fairly decent meal and bed, we both were dog-tired.

I had asked Peter Baldwin yesterday to ask my bank, Barclays, to fax me £100 to a bank near the hotel just in case it was needed, now Friday Monique and I called this bank at 11 am to see if the money had arrived, nothing had, - so far, Monique told the cashier we would call at noon, which we did – still nothing, I was not going to hang about any longer, I wanted to get on the way, I paid the hotel, collected the suitcases, put some plastic as best I could over the ¼ window shut it in with the door, because it was still winter and cold, the hotel receptionist shook hands warmly and wished us bon route. We went and collected our leather seated kitchen chairs, then we were off, in our hurry, we forgot to pick up the chandelier, as far as we know, it is still there, and regarding the £100, I had asked Baldwin to ask Barclays to send, Barclays of Penrith had never been requested to send any money at all, so much for our Consulate.

On our way out of Seville, a most charming city, I must have missed the way because on our first visit, we found ourselves driving through terrible slums, filthy dirty children with hardly any clothes on, slums, I should think as bad as anywhere else, the part of Seville no tourist ever saw or probably ever heard of.

We motored on, taking the road to Cordoba, crossing the Rio Guadilquivir, the same river from which our ship had sailed to Fuerteventura, the weather was very sunny but cold, there was no heat in the sun. Passing a little town named La Carolina, where we stopped for a sandwich and a beer or two, then motoring on, we stopped at Valde- penas, thinking of staying the night, but decided to have a beer and pass on through, we somehow did not care for the look of this town. We drove through, stopping only a few miles further on near Manzanares at an Alberque, which proved to be a very good one indeed. This was at a village named Alberque. The waiters insisted we take our chairs out of the car in case they were stolen in the night, and carried them into the hotel, where their dining chairs were exactly the same, we had an excellent meal in warm and happy surroundings, all of the staff seemed at all times to have a big smile, and quite genuine too, we had driven 230 miles this day.

In fact, we were so comfortable we overslept, had a bun for breakfast and left at 9:30 am. The same waiters put the chairs back in the Volvo and waved goodbye to us. We drove on straight for Madrid, passing through Madridejos, Ocana and Villaverde and headed for the centre of Madrid. I thought from there I would soon find a way out, for the direction of Zaragoza. However, I seemed to hit a multitude of traffic all of a sudden, three or four cars abreast, many times at a standstill, cars almost touching the sides of each other, it was quite easy to shake hands with other drivers, we were so near, which I did quite a few times as we asked directions from other drivers, Monique would shout over to the driver by our side, directions given, I would shake hands, then crawl for 50 yards, stop again and so on, however the drivers were most helpful and one of the last ones we asked told us to follow him, which we did for perhaps two miles, he then stopped and got out, as he was turning off, and told us the way to go looking at our map and telling Monique to take the road to Alcala de Henores, which lay on the Zaragoza road. Eventually, we were out of Madrid and once again on full sail. We were heading up the road we had been on before.

We stopped at a little place named Medinacell, where Monique bought Charcuterie, cheese, bread and a bottle of wine, which we had for a picnic lunch, which we had in the car as it was very cold outside, though sunny. After this, we did not loiter, wanting to be on the French border by night-fall, I was heading for Pau, passing Zaragoza, Huesca, very wild and beautiful countryside, savage in itself.

We made it to Jaca, not far from the frontier. The last 100 miles had been rather twisty. We had driven 425 miles, the Volvo running well, she was petrol injection and quite economic. At Jaca, we stayed at the Hotel Mur, getting there at 6:30 pm, the hotel was nice and warm, but our bed-room window let the wind in – it was quite blowy outside – so I slept with my cap on, we put our chairs in the hotel, the clerk helping us, he was a kind young man, this done we bathed together to freshen up then had a look in the town. Finding it quite a nice little place, there were quite a few very good bars where we had quite a few beers, the night was cold and there was snow over all. Back to the hotel, where we had an excellent meal, with more beer to wash it down, this was December 4th, a Saturday. Sunday, we were up at 8:15 am having breakfast myself. For some reason, we had milk to drink, which was rare; I still don't know why, but it was very good.

Outside, the frost had been iron-hard, but the morning was nice and dry, very clean-tasting air, I suppose, from the mountains. It was a plea- sure to breath air like this, worth its weight in gold if one could weigh it. Monique and I bought our lunch to eat on the way, which consisted of a large slice of pate, bread, goat's cheese, yoghurt and a bottle of red wine. On we drove, the route being hilly and very twisty, the snow ploughs had been through but had left some hilly stretches with just a covering of ¼ to ½ an inch of hard snow, making getting up some places very skiddy. I kept the Volvo in as high gear and as slow as possible on hills, steep and semi-steep. At one point, rounding a corner and facing a long low climb, I found the road in front covered with a multitude of snow hikers and skiers going somewhere. They covered the road from side to side, which was a good wide one, but a sheet of an inch of snow, some hardened. I dare not change gear or slow down; that would have made the wheels spin, and I would never have got up without retracing back for two miles. These people just would not move out of the way, my head lights full on, horn blowing, I motored towards them, I thought damned fools, I still did not slow down, and had no intention of doing so, if they want to be hurt, so be it. When I was 10 yards from this medley, the horn still blasting, they started to jump out of the way, I was not sure if I had clipped anyone or not, I did not stop to ask. Their shouts were pretty loud. The Volvo was through and the crest of the incline was in near sight, then, we were going downhill. We made it to the border at Condanchu, where formalities were soon over and we were on the way again. Once through into France, we pulled into a wide area for our lunch, which, once again, we had in the car, too cold to dine outside, even though we had our own chairs.

Through Pau, I headed for Angouleme, where we aimed to spend the night, passing through Marmande, Bergerac, and Perigueux. At each place, we stopped at a Brassiere or good-looking bar for a few refreshers. After all, we were still on holiday. The day was pleasant and sunny, a bit warmer than in the mountains. Not a lot of traffic on the road. We got into Angouleme at 6:30 pm, Monique went into the Hotel Coq D'or to ask for a room and the price. She came out and told me yes, they had a room and the price was 24F. She said the hotel did no meals but seemed very comfortable, this was enough for me, Monique had a good nose for a good hotel and or restaurant. Sometimes, I had insisted on staying and eating at some hotel or restaurant, which Monique had told me she did not like, for me to be proved wrong quite often. The hotel was indeed very comfortable. We unpacked our chairs, much to the amusement of the hotel clerk and our suitcases, had a bath together, then out on the town, where we had a few beers before deciding on eating at what looked like a good and busy restaurant. This was the L'Union Hotel restaurant and it was as busy as a beehive. In we went, and were shown to a table for two. They had menus from cheap to middle to expensive, we took the middle one as, by now, I was getting rather short of cash. It was a 4-course meal with the wine thrown in, at 14F each. We had soup, I had two helpings, quail, cassoulet and cheese, all of which were excellent, I somehow was still hungry even with a big helping of cassoulet, which is a meal in itself. I was going to order a whole wild duck for myself, but Monique stopped me, saying something must be wrong for me to eat so much. That night, I had, for some reason, an insatiable appetite, our bottle of wine was now empty, the waiter spotted it and immediately replaced it with a full one, the atmosphere in this grand little restaurant was humming. From what we could see, most of the customers were local. The meal was such that it demanded good digestion. I took 3 or 4 brandies and Monique made do with 2 whiskys. I had a good Havana to round things off, I remember that meal to this day, it was so good, so did Monique, we have had some extra special meals over the years, but somehow, this one stood out, I kept the bill and have it still.

December 6th I wrote in my diary, "out of bed at 8:15 am tired from our big meal last night". We had breakfast where we were staying, the Hotel Coq D'or. This was the only meal they produced and was very good, we each had a big cup of Cafe au Lait, freshly baked bread and jam, and freshly baked croissant, two each, then we were once more on our way. Took the road to Poitiers, then on to Tours, where Monique bought pate, pate campagne, Gruyere cheese and bread and a bottle of wine for our picnic lunch. It was a lovely sunny day. I parked the car on someone's field and sat outside on the sunny side of the car, we had a good thick rug, then we had an excellent picnic lunch. Monique always had her own supply of salt, pepper and mustard, plus cutlery brought from home.

On we went up the Loire Valley to Orleans. This is one of the most lovely and picturesque drives through Orleans, where Joan of Arc came from. Approaching Paris, the weather changed to rain. The other side was drizzling and foggy, making driving difficult. Skirting Paris, we made for Beauvais, we had in our mind to book in for the night at a Logis, Monique had the book on the Logis of France. These Logis were mostly very good and value for money, we were looking for the Logis, Golden Cross in Beauvais. We arrived there at 7 pm. Monique went to ask for a room only to find they were full, I thought, hard luck. We motored on, but 100 yards down the road was another hotel. Monique booked a room, we took our chairs in, leaving them in the foyer and went up to our room to find it rather crummy, in fact, the whole place when we took stock was crummy. Anyway, we were in now, but we did not bother asking about food, we went straight back to the

Logis, which was very active, it had a good atmosphere, smelt good and was spotlessly clean, obviously a well-run place. We were ushered to a table where we had a leisurely aperitif of Ricard, then the meal, which was excellent, a great tureen of vegetable soup, I had two big helpings; one thing I like is a good soup, not many restaurants or hotels put soup on these days, and when they do, it is usually tinned. Then we had an escalope of veal, I have remarked in my diary - a tremendous helping, myself unable to take the cheese, but Monique is a great cheese eater, so she helped herself to a tremendous selection of these French delights. France, for me, is the only country to produce cheese; as such, the English at one time were good, but with few varieties. Now they produce plastic instead of cheese. I finished with crème caramel, another of those things I rather like. We had two bottles of house wine, very cheap and very good. We went to bed at 9:30 pm, tired but content.

On Tuesday, 7th December we were up at 7:30 am and drove to Abbeville, where we had breakfast in the town square. Monique bought herself some perfume and, for home consumption, black pudding and andouette sausage. From Abbeville, we drove past Rue, little did I know it, but I would be shooting duck and woodcock here in later years. Here was the region of the Somme battlefields of the 1st World War, thousands of acres of marchland, covered with 7ft high bog grass or reeds, strong stuff. Also, here lies great sadness of the many military cemeteries we passed, holding many thousands of our dead young soldiers, the cream of the British youth, hurled to their deaths by unrelenting and brainless leaders, who themselves should have been shot. The graves and grounds were immaculately kept – we drove slowly on, it is a great pity that our army's could not have been led in this first world war by such as the great Duke of Marlborough, who did his best to keep casualties low, his strategy was impeccable, no wonder Napoleon read all he could of this greatest of soldiers, but also kept a bust of him in Malmaison.

We drove into Calais at noon, there was a boat at 2:15 pm, but we wanted to shop for a while. Also, I needed some money for this, we walked into Barclays' Bank there, asked for the manager and told him I wanted 50 pounds right away in 30 pounds and 20 pounds in francs. Within minutes I had it, he had phoned Penrith and was told, "Give Mr Slack what he wants, as much as he wants." Now we had a stroll round the town, where Monique bought some jam, various pots, various cheese and Framboise liqueur, and two bottles of Ricard in the port itself. We had quite a decent meal on board in the restaurant, plus a bottle of so-so wine, getting into Dover at 7:45 pm. We stayed the night at the Red House Hotel. On the morning of the 8th, we had breakfast in bed at 9am, getting up at 10am to a nice dry morning, and setting off at 11 am. We had a good run to London and no trouble crossing, in fact, straight through, without a hitch over London Bridge, I drove up the A1 to the A66 motel near Scotch Corner, arriving there at 5 pm, by now a dense fog had set in, so we stayed the night. Sonia, our hostess, laid a marvellous dinner for us of scampi followed by trout, followed by fillet steak for myself, Monique had a mixed grill in place of the fillet and two bottles of their best red wine, which I think was a Volnay, an excellent meal and beautifully prepared by Sonia herself. We had two digestives with Malcolm and Sonia's whisky, then went to bed.

32

I only went outside to see the men to see how things had been going. All had gone smoothly on the farm; thank goodness, there were no catastrophes. Saturday 11th, I took both Labradors, Lassie and Sandy, her son, for an outing down the farm, following the beck to the water quarry, getting 6 ducks, then flighted pigeons in the turnips, shooting 15, which pleased the dogs and myself, I loved pigeon to eat, a great tasty bird I reckon.

Christmas Eve, the boys and I went to midnight mass held in our own village church, many people were there, some from other villages, including Eden Hall, for our church of St John was the Cathedral of the fells, the midnight mass was a lovely and touching one.

Christmas day, the boys had their presents opened, excited about it all, as usual, their grandfather – my father – gave them nothing, not even a small present and my two boys were the only grandchildren bearing the Slack name. Father gave me a round tin of 25 panatelas, the ones sold in pubs of very poor quality, he handed them to me, I thanked him and handed him a box of 25 Havana's, I think they were Ramon Allones. Later in the day, I opened Dad's present to me to find only 12 panatelas in the tin tube, I thought, my word, the shop had diddled him. Boxing Day, I told him he had been short-changed on these panatelas, telling him there were only 12, his reply astounded me. "I know," he said. "I took the others out for myself – I could not believe my ears, cheap jock stuff and he had to keep some for himself. As for Monique, she got nothing from him."

We had a roaring fire in both the morning room and dining room, everywhere was cosy. A Christmas tree reaching to the ceiling in the morning room, with all the lights on - still here was Christmas, yet something was missing in this family festival season, it was not hard to know what was missing, it was the family split. Mother gone, my sister gone, my father only 1

½ miles away, gone also, the whole family split by a tramp of a woman and my father's stupidity. If one's mind wandered backwards a few years, one's thoughts could be terribly sad.

However, I now had my wife and two sons and their lives to look forward to, the show must go on, little was I to know the trouble our eldest would bring on our shoulders later on.

For Christmas lunch, there was a large 18lb goose I had bought from a local farmer, Monique was busy basting it, delicious smells were drifting around the large kitchen, to start with there was hare soup, the queen of soups, Monique using mother's recipe and now adding some of her own ideas, herbs, sauces, etc. The aroma of the hare soup with its port and brandy additives together with mother goose, the kitchen was now full of cooking gastronomic perfumes, wafting through the half-open window onto the courtyard, Kurt shouted in, "my word missus, something smells good in there". Then there was Christmas pudding, Monique's own made by the chef Mr Cioli, from the County Hotel Carlisle had made us a Christmas pudding one year, but it was so heavy you could have played cricket with it - served with rum sauce and lashings of rum creating a heady aroma. For the boys, they had either thick cream or custard with the pudding, for the wine, I had bought two cases of Chateau Beychevelle, a Bordeaux, I had opened the two bottles to breathe at 9 am, leaving them in the warm atmosphere of the morning room. The boys had got and opened their presents quite early, leaving Monique's and mine under the tree until after lunch, the men had been given theirs that morning, for Ernie the shepherd – a great smoker – a few packets of cigarettes, for the tractor drivers, 3 pairs of good thick socks, same for Kurt plus a manual on mechanics that he wanted badly. The stock fed in the morning, the men had the rest of the day off.

Tuesday 11th, Kurt's turn now to go down with the flu. Friday 14th, I gave a shoot. The weather had eased off, thank goodness, but it was threatening most of the day. Sport was quite good, though the turnip fields were very wet to walk through, waterproof overalls were needed. Monique put on a splendid lunch of steak and kidney pie, which went down well. For starters, we went through 4 bottles of champagne and 3 bottles of red and 2 of white wine. My farm men were beaters. The guns were Derek Straker, Archie and Pat, George Fabi, an Italian P.O.W left over from the war married to an Englishwoman - Bert Johnstone- and Ken Stamper - an eventual Brutus. This was a walk-up shoot, and the latter person, Stamper, was shooting on the left side of Straker, myself on the right-hand-side, when pheasant got up, even at 25 yards range, instead of waiting, as the others did, for a few seconds for the birds to fly a few more yards to 35 or 40 yards, Stamper would shoot them down, at the short range even if some had been sitting so tight and got up at 10 yards, he would shoot, making such a mess of the killed birds, they were not fit to eat, I asked him to let his birds fly on before he shot, he took no notice, then I noticed he was shooting his neighbour Derek's birds, birds that got up in front of Derek were his. It is the unwritten law of gentlemen shooters not to take your neighbours birds, this Stamper was doing until I noticed Derek put his gun over his shoulder to show his disgust and did no more shooting for that drive, I put Stamper in another position after this. The bag was 35 pheasant, 4 hares, 6 pigeons, which was quite good considering the weather the days preceding the shoot.

On Saturday, 22nd January, we had a surprise telegram from Willie Hesselman in Germany, saying he was coming to Newcastle airport on Monday 24th, at noon. Sunday, it rained all day.

On Monday the 24th, I had a caterpillar digger with an extra long arm arrive to start excavating a fish and flight pond for me in a boggy bottom 200 yards from the water quarry. Simon Ballantyne was the digger owner, I got him started explaining the length and breadth, then I had to leave to pick up Willie Hesselman at Newcastle, I arrived with half an hour to spare, the plane, as far as I can remember, was leaving

Amsterdam, Willie had gone there, as it was not too far from Telgte. I watched the plane touch down, then went to arrivals to await him, I waited and waited until I asked if any more passengers were coming off, "No more, sir, that's it," I was told. I asked when the next plane was due in from Amsterdam, I think it was about 3 hours later, I thought Willie must have somehow missed the first plane and would no doubt be on the next one. I phoned Monique to give her the news, also as we had two dinner guests dining with us this night to introduce Willie to.

With that done, as I had three hours to kill, I went into Newcastle town to see Derek Straker at his office in the town centre. He was pleased to see me. He, so he said, had just made love to his secretary on the floor of his office, I did not disbelieve him because it was Derek's style. His secretary was, I saw, very good-looking, about 19 years old, and very sexy in a feminine, not a vulgar way. She was quite refined, a splendid figure and very good legs. Derek invited me to go for lunch with him, but first, he said, "I'll ring the gang". By this, he meant John Cummings and Ken Stroughan, the doctor who peed on the dining room carpet of John Cunningham's father. We all met up at a restaurant not far from the law courts, where businessmen dined and drank, this particular lunch was very good, then turned into a very liquid affair, which continued until half and hour before Willie Hesselman's second flight came in, then we all set off for the airport and waited for Willie. Of course, Willie never came, he was not on that flight either, I went up to the information desk and explained what had happened, they very kindly phoned through to Amsterdam airport and asked if Herr Hesselmanm was booked into any flights or any information on him. I could hear them over the phone paging Herr Hesselman over and over. They tried hard to find him, to no avail. There was another flight at 8:15 pm, Amsterdam, London, Newcastle. I would wait for it. I phoned Monique to tell her the news and to delay the dinner. After this, the 4 men had a few more drinks at the airport, then Derek would have us go to his home in Ponteland, which was very near. There, the bottles came out and a session in serious drinking started, Derek was most kind and phoned the airport every now and then for news of Willie, by now, everyone at the airport was on the lookout for Willie, I did not return for the 8:15 pm flight. Derek phoned through, no Willie. That I thought was that for the day.

I set off for home, the journey over the Pennines, rather too full of whisky and terribly late for dinner. A ruined dinner for Monique, who had gone to a lot of trouble and effort to make a pleasant first visit for Willie. Our guests, Bert and Christine Johnstone, Monique and I dined together at 10 pm on my return. I apologised to them for having drunk too much, explained how I had drunk so much, all the episodes of the day for everyone. The hunger had gone, the meal of roast pheasant eaten half-heartedly.

The next day 25th, Tuesday, before Monique and I got out of bed, the phone rang, it was Derek Straker, he said Willie had arrived, the airport people had most kindly kept Willie in mind and on his arrival triumphantly phoned Derek with the news, I asked Derek if he could run him up to the Gosforth Park Hotel, and leave him there. Monique and I would pick him up there. This Derek did - now another trip over the Pennines, off we set. I saw to the workforce and the progress of my new fish and flight pond. I was not going to hurry today, Willie had put me to a lot of bother yesterday. We set off at 1 pm, and just before the drive entrance to the hotel, Willie was taking a walk in his German hunter's suit, sticking out like a sore thumb. Of course, he was stuck to ask his way or anything, for he did not speak one word of English.

We stopped and picked him up, he was glad to see us, he thought we were not coming for him, I asked what had happened the day before, it turned out he had been night clubbing in Amsterdam and got himself bedded down with a young girl, she taking precedence over his plane.

Friday in Penrith was, of course, the boozy day. We took

Willie into the George, the Woolpack, the Monkey House to let him have a look at the pubs, he was introduced to our hard-drinking friends in the George, where even he found the going hard, we stayed till 9 pm then set off for home but calling round at Edenhall on the way, a slight detour of ½ a mile, calling in at the Edenhall Hotel, run by Alex Beck, (the one who fell off his shooting stick when he let the two barrels off at once) to find the place a hive of activity, it was the police dinner dance. By now, all were either dancing or drinking, I had forgotten about it. Our local police, Sid Hetherington and Harold Fell, had asked me if I would give a prize towards Tombola or something similar, I had given 2 brace of pheasant. Now, we had landed in the middle of their fun. As I knew quite a few of these chaps, we were soon asked to join in the fun and soon we were all dancing away merrily, Willie enjoyed himself to the hilt. We got home at 4 am.

Stuart, the manager at the George Hotel, invited a few friends to a dinner at his hotel in honour of Willie, Stuart had taken a liking to Willie, hence the dinner. Monique and I were of course invited, and Bert and Christine and Stuart himself at the table. The meal was excellent indeed, I have entered in my diary the courses: shrimp cocktail, lamb roast, mint Bavoriose, 6 different kinds of cheese, coffee, etc. Four different wines were drunk to go with their respective dishes. The whole meal was prepared by Stuart himself – we knew from experience he was an excellent cook and knew the preparation of such. Also, in my diary, it was one of the best meals in years.

February 3rd, I had to take Willie to Newcastle airport, once more, I had to go round by Carlisle as Hartside over the Pennines via Alston was still blocked by snow. His plane left at 11:15 am for Amsterdam, we waved goodbye to our friend, somehow both Monique and I, with tears in our eyes. We both liked Willie very much, since his big love, his wife, had died after only six months of marriage – she died of cancer – Willie had been an unhappy and sad man trying to drown his sadness with booze and night-clubs, he was a great hulk of a man with a rugged face, tremendously kind, little did we know, he had not much time left on this earth, he was 50 years old in 1972.

Saturday 18th Monique wanted to see the Ideal Home exhibition in London, we set off early, and ran into the intense fog from Scotch Corner onwards, as we approached Doncaster, it became so bad, I was going to turn round and go home, when all of a sudden we were passing the rail- way station, whether I'd taken a wrong road in the fog, I don't know, however, here was an alternative. I went in to ask if there were any trains to London shortly, there was one in 15 minutes. I parked the Volvo and bought tickets, and we were on the way, getting into London at 11:30 am. At least now I could relax in the train, the first I had been in for years – and smoke a Burma cheroot, a Scott's No1. I hated driving in fog. The Ideal Home exhibition was absolutely crowded out, but neither Monique or I were enchanted with the show, considering it very poor indeed, we would definitely not go to another. We had dinner at the Connaught Hotel, this was our second visit to the Connaught, and we both thought it was the best place we had eaten when we were in London. Also, the staff was very kind.

We left London to return to Doncaster, arriving there at 3:45 am, and to my great disappointment, found I had left the car side lights on, of course, the battery was flat, but in any case, the fog was once again a pea souper, I could not have driven out of Doncaster. I could never have found the correct road, I asked the station staff for the nearest hotel and was directed to the Danum, where we got a room, we were not impressed with the Danum and never stayed there again, even when the yearling sales were on, staying at Punch's just outside or going on to Bawtry to the Crown. In the morning, I got the A.A. to jump lead the battery for me, and we were off, the fog had lifted.

March 27th, we had a snowstorm, everywhere was covered by about 2" and very cold, there the storm carried on all day, with a lot of hailstones thrown in. On inspection of the lambing ewes, I found only 3 newborn lambs dead, 29 ewes had lambed, all having gone behind the straw bales or the lee side of stone walls to give birth, I had expected 20 or more dead lambs. The stone walls enclosing most fields at Skirwith Hall were a godsend in times like this, creating shelter whichever way a storm blew. There was one field next to the lambing field where the ewes and lambs had to be moved, these lambs were 3 or 4 days old but were in the teeth of the storm. They were difficult to get going, but eventually, the 45 ewes with their 90 lambs were moved 150 yards into complete shelter behind a good solid wall, it took 2 hours for this short stretch to be covered; all newborn lambs were as usual if the weather was cold, put into lambing huts dotted round the four walls of Spring Field, each ewe and lamb to her own hut, bedded with 2 or 3 inches of clean sawdust. These huts had roofs and sides and front covered in 3 huts combined like semi-detached houses. In the wood, there were 6 semi-detached huts in line, 3 of them making 18 in the wood alone, once inside the warmth of these, the lambs were safe from the severest of tempests. The ewes would be given 3 or 4 turnips, already placed by the hut, for moisture and food, then at 4 pm, a feed of 3lb of oats.

Easter Sunday, the boys and myself went to church, the vicar now was Father Burdon, the previous vicar, JC Wilson, the one with his boyfriend Jim Peel, had died of lung cancer. Father Burdon never seemed to go down well with his flock, for one thing, he did not visit, even when someone was ill. To talk to, he was quite a nice man, I asked him one day if, supposing my father's wife died, I did not wish her to be buried in the family plot, he agreed, telling me to leave it to him to see she was not.

Easter Monday was cold with showers, not many ewes left now to lamb. I left the lambing field now in charge of the shepherd while I went around all the fields with ewes and lambs in to feed them with oats and see all was well, keeping an eye out for mastitis in the ewes, not many ewes got mastitis, only one or two each season. The signs were if a ewe happened to be walking very stiffly on one of her hind legs, then I would catch her with the aid of Maid. If it was only a slight attack, then penicillin would do the trick over a 3-5 day period, if the case was severe and blood poisoning had started, then I would disinfect the affected side of the udder and lance deeply with a good razor-sharp knife, if the poison had started to travel up the ewe's body, turning the flesh purple, then this would also be lanced, but not too deep. This would allow the poison to seep out and then be injected with penicillin, but before penicillin, there was only the knife and carbolic and it worked well. Dad had always taught me with "a sharp knife and a cold heart" whenever something like this had to be done and I have had to install this into my shepherds, but all, when it came to lancing, were frightened to cut deep, leaving possibly, a ewe to die a slow, painful death, myself, I can boast I never lost a ewe through deep lancing.

Saturday night, the 15th, Monique and I went to the Jockeys Ball, held at the George Hotel, Penrith. This was a very good evening. Stuart put on an excellent buffet but rather a poor band. John Cummings and their wife Valerie are staying with us tonight at Skirwith Hall. That night, there was a very strong story going that Valerie had been caught with Gordon Richards in a delicate situation, I believed it, so did Monique, as Valerie was mad keen over Gordon. Di Thompson-Jones, a beautiful girl, was there with her current boyfriend, Barry Brogan, Brogan had ridden for me a few times, he was a good, strong jockey, I liked him very much, he was there that night, with a mouthful of metal teeth, poor Barry, he later on seemed to get in with the wrong crowd, eventually going to prison.

Ken Oliver himself and his wife Rhona were in attendance, Rhona's horse having been placed in the Grand National a few times. Ken, himself a great toper, was dressed up while asleep in his chair at 3 am, like a Bishop, and by Jove, he looked exactly like one and was named the Benign Bishop. Alan McTaggart, a Scottish farmer and amateur jockey and his wife

Marty was there. One time I met her and hubby in the George cock-tail bar, she was sitting up on one of the bar's high stools, I was sitting on a low-down stool to one side, they had just come back from Spain and were well-bronzed, Marty sat all the time in front of me with her legs wide open. Fortunately, she had on the tiniest of panties, almost a G-string.

On 21st April, I had my three women workers planting trees again in Black Wood, on an area that had not yet been covered, and plant in blanks, caused by either rabbits or deer, plants were Scotch Fir and Norway Spruce. Robin Rowley, from whom I bought the plants, threw in 1700 free gratis, i.e., 1000 Norways and 700 Scotch.

On Sunday morning, I was going to have a lie-in, but I was knocked up by the shepherd, there was a ewe trying to give birth and he could not manage. Would I come to lamb her, I did, to find the ewe having triplets, when I entered my hand and arm into her, there was a tangled mass of legs and two immediate heads all trying to come at once. I soon had them sorted out and within minutes the mother had her 3 little ones in front of her. She herself gave little bleats of delight, it surely was a wonderful thing watching and listening to a mother's delight at her new offspring, be it cow, mare, or ewe.

My womenfolk were still planting trees for shelter and pheasant cover in various parts of the farm, on 28th, I drove over to Robin Rowley's and got 4000 more plants, comprising 3000 Norway Spruce and 1000 Sitka. Father thought I was stupid to plant, complaining all the time of the waste of money and time, also of the land, but what I was planting and underplanting were odd corners here and there, soft places, where grazing was well nigh impossible, but also I was creating a good shelter for stock, to him, what I was doing was a waste. He still, almost every morning would descend on me at breakfast or 10 o'clock for a cup of tea, out came his thick wallet with the elastic band on, then it was the same old record of the bank manager on and on, he never stopped to think I had lifted the profits from 2,000 pounds per annum to almost

16,000 pounds per annum, the overdraft never above 1,500 pounds if that, this continual harassment was slowly reaching through to me, I was considering selling the place up. Here, I was the owner, not the tenant, my father would not give this up. I remembered the advice of Uncle Bob, the racing one. Mother's brother. His advice was to have a complete farm sale of everything and get your father out of the way and start from scratch – good advice, but I did not wish for a complete family split. Dad had been a very good father, giving almost complete leeway when we were growing up. But of course, now, he had another wife, and a bad one at that, Uncle Bob, I believe, was not too fond of Dad, now, with Dad marrying such a woman as he did, there was no more contact between them up to Uncle Bob's death.

On May 4th, I drove in the Land Rover to the farm, with another 1000 tree plants, to find Dad in a bad mood, we had a major row, then he stalked off, a pity, nothing had gone well with the family since Ma had died – the same day the womenfolk finished their tree planting, they had worked very well indeed and I told them so.

On Sunday, 14th May, Monique and I went to little Joey's confirmation at Alverthorpe, near Wakefield, Yorks, he was confirmed by the Bishop of Wakefield, Bishop Tracey, with whom afterwards we had a chat, he seemed a kind and good man, if I remember rightly, his great hobby was training the old steam locomotives.

On Monday, 22nd May, I took a few empty ewes to the auction. The sale finished quite early, so I thought I would go and have a drink at the George Hotel with Stuart. I went to the cocktail bar to find George Fabi, the Italian prisoner of war, who had married and stayed behind, he had been drinking by the sound of him, for some time, for some reason or other, he started talking about coloured people, while Stuart and I listened, then he came out with a bombshell, saying to my face, that Monique was a half-caste, instantly as I was facing him sitting on a bar stool, I slapped him so hard across his face, I knocked him off his stool, where he hit the floor, I was enraged, he got up and left the hotel, Stuart, who had witnessed the whole thing said "He deserved that one" and poured a large Grouse whisky, Monique had the Latin skin colour, but her blood lines were French and Spanish. Fabi afterwards apologised, but after that, I kept my distance from him.

On 28th July, I took the boys' ponies to the Kelso horse sale, as the boys were now too tall for them. It was rather sad, really, Adam's Bronco making 100gns and Joey's Struan Gold bid to 60gns, I did not sell him.

The next day, Monique and I took the boys to the game fair at Raby Castle, the day was lovely, hot and sunny, an excellent fair, but the food was awful. Little Joey had his eye on a Darne shotgun, my father had had two Darne's made to measure for himself and little Joey had taken a liking to them and had saved up hard for one, now at the game fair he saw the Darne guns, and instead of a .410 he wanted a 12 bore, that would last him his life, "all right" I said, "if you're sure", the gun he chose was 131 pounds 10/-. He was disappointed, saying he only had 90 pounds, which he had on him in preparation for the purchase, I saw the disappointment on his face and told him I would pay the rest for him, his face lit up to a glow, so the gun was bought and treasured by him to this day, having a good tight pattern of shot. We met many we knew at the fair and, in the process, had a large quantity of champagne, culminating in a lengthy and excellent meal at the A66 motel, which lay only 5-6 miles from the game fair.

1st August, I phoned Willie Hesselman, inviting him to my grouse shoot on 12 - the glorious 12th – and he said he would come.

On 2nd August, Derek Straker and his wife Angela asked us to dinner at a place they had rented at Penton near Carlisle, off we went, a good dinner was eaten and rather for me, too much of the digestive afterwards, Monique drove the Volvo, taking the relatively new motorway to Penrith, just as she left the motorway on the slip road for Penrith and actually on the slip road, a police car stopped her, myself I was sound asleep, I opened my eyes and saw Monique outside of the car and two policemen, starting to get rather nasty with her, I jumped out, threatening to put them on the ground, but Monique stopped me, so I quietened down. She refused to be breathalysed. The police then told her to get in their patrol car and must go to the police station, whereas I told the police I was not driving my car, as I myself had been drinking, my wife had not, which of course was a big fib, one of the police then drove the Volvo with me in it, behind the patrol car and Monique. The police station was only a mile away, Monique went through to one of the, I suppose, questioning rooms, and lo and behold, there was our old friend Harold Fell, acting inspector that night, and behind the reception desk, another good friend Sid Hetherington, now I knew we would be all right. It turned out they were expecting us as the patrol car had phoned in the car number. Harold and Sid thought it was me, not Monique, who was being brought in, to cut a long story short, Harold ordered the patrol policeman out of his room, told Monique to blow into the breathalyser. Monique told him it was no good, she had been drinking, he said, "never mind - blow" - Monique put the tube to her lips, Harold said stop - Monique said, "I haven't blown into it yet," "Never mind," said Harold, "that will do," he called the patrol chappie back in telling him Mrs Slack is clear, she can go now. I said nothing then, not to show our friendship to any of the other police. Two days later, I thanked him most kindly and Sid – at the same time Sid – who had been our village Bobby was now based in town due to his wife's ill health – told me to keep out of the way of patrol cars, he said, "these fellows are so bad they would run their own mothers in, they are rotten" – Sid went on. This is from a policeman. Monique then finished off driving me home, but from that day, the police patrols were determined to catch us, they followed us at every turn, even following us halfway home, many times only 20 yards behind until I had had enough of this harassment, I called on Harold and told him, he was angry, and told me he would see that this harassment would stop at once – and it did, he was a good friend Harold – he would have made a very good superintendent or higher but the exams were just that tiny bit far for him, for more junior police with A or O levels, but absolutely no police experience, were promoted above him, which to my mind an experienced policeman of many years would be my preference instead of a bookworm, he retired from the police later on, fed up with this system, the chief constable lost a first-class man.

Take the case of Sid's daughter, I knew her well as I did her mother, father and brother. She in 3 or 4 years, she reached the rank of, I believe, Inspector due to her academic prowess, perhaps today, she is a chief constable – who knows – Sid and her mother were proud of her–justly so.

On Monday the 7th, I butchered and dressed a very good Dorset Cross lamb, giving a back leg each to Harold Fell and Sid.

On Friday the 11th of August, the lead-up to the grouse shoot, I gave a small dinner party at the Kings Arms, Temple Sowerby. Present were George Bate, a major in the Black Watch, now working for Rubery Owen, I had met George a few times in the Corporation Hotel Middlesbrough, where I used to stay for the horse sales at Stockton, he was quite a card. Jack Johnstone from St Boswells, my two boys and Stuart from the George Hotel, John Cummings phoned to say he could not come, he had a horse running, Willie Hesselman phoned to say he was in bed with a dickie heart, so there were few guns, the dinner was excellent as usual, cooked by Brenda, the evening went so well, we did not get back home till 5 am. The 12th opened as yesterday, sunny and hot. Out came the usual case of champagne, my neighbour Robert Jackson was shooting as were George Bate, Jack Johnstone and myself – Derek Straker also had given backword, he had quickly to go to Majorca to sell some villas he had a hand in, and Ian Duncan, a major in the Northumberland Fusiliers had a car crash, that put him out of the shoot.

We started later than usual, setting sail at 10:30 am, lunched with a superb picnic prepared by Monique, fit for a Maharaja, with 2 cases of wine, 4 bottles of champagne, 2 bottles of Crofts Port. We, as usual, first paid a visit to our habitual first watering hole, the George and Dragon Garrigill where we quenched our thirst for a good half hour. Then up the moor, starting at Cash Wells, little Joey had asked me if I would shoot with his new Darne gun, I told him no, I preferred to shoot with my old Westly Ritchards with its 30-in-Damascus barrels, he was so downcast I took pity and told him I would, this pleased him, as later it did me, I had George Weston carrying my cartridge and game bag, the other's beaters were John Frith, Kurt and my two boys, Adam and Joey. Before we started, we attacked the picnic, the guests praised the quantity and quality of Monique's handiwork. After the dinner at Temple Sowerby, she had not gone to bed but started cooking. Examples: one big leg of homebred lamb, 3 chickens, a large beef enroute – genuine fillet, salmon etc, with crème caramel and two other desserts.

During this meal, George Bate, whom it turned out, had come prepared for the shoot in city low shoes and a lounge suit - dark, I had to lend him a pair of my boots and also a gun - had got going on the wine, too much so, I had noticed in the pub at Garrygill he was kicking off on doubles not waiting for a round to end and start, getting drinks for himself alone. Well, now he, I could see, had enough already, enough perhaps too much for a shoot. All at once, he attacked the port wine, emptying a ¼ bottle into his glass - I thought it now better to start at once, otherwise, for George, it would soon be too late. I lined the guns and beaters up, Adam was next to George, I told him to keep an eye on him regarding his shooting, at a signal, the line of guns advanced, within five or six minutes 3, grouse had been dispatched by Johnson and Robert, the line halted until the birds were retrieved, then once again, more birds were downed and retrieved by the same shooters, I began to think the Dame gun might not be too lucky today when just then a covey of 8 got up, I downed two, nice shots, in fact, that day 51 birds were shot, myself shooting and downing 36 birds, I never missed a bird and twice I downed 2 birds with one shot, George Weston, my beater, became most enthusiastic, when I downed 3 birds twice with two shots, could not help himself, shouting to Jack Johnston "that's the way to shoot", as for myself, I was mighty pleased for little Joey's sake, he was thrilled at his gun's performance, and so was I, it had a very good pattern.

But to get back to George Bate, the line of guns had gone no more than 200 yards when he gave his gun to Adam, he was in a state of collapse, a sorry state indeed to be in, he had to be helped up small hillocks etc., then we left him behind, as he had become a hindrance, a great pity, for without drink, he was a most interesting man, Monique did not take to him at all, even before this day, he was so far gone he was not fit to have his dinner that night, having to be put to bed, an excellent dinner it was too, which again we had at Temple Sowerby.

On Sunday the 13th, we had drinks at Skirwith Hall, Peter and Brenda Brown, our hosts at the Kings Arms, came to partake with us, then we drove over to Temple Sowerby to the Kings Arms and had lunch, George Bate left very early without saying goodbye, no doubt ashamed of himself, I had a brace of grouse for him, so posted them on to him to his home near Bakewell, and so ended the glorious 12th for 1972.

The following Saturday, I took my two young sons over the fall to shoot grouse. This was, I thought, a good time of their life to initiate them to the grand art of shooting this very sporting and noble bird, just the three of us, and the two Labradors, Lassie and her son Sandy, the boys did very well indeed, Adam not quite as good a shot as little brother Joey, shot 7 and the latter downed 9, I shot 9, all good big strong birds, the boys were overjoyed with themselves and I was proud and pleased they had shot well, the dogs had I think enjoyed working with the boys, 25 birds in total, was a good bag. On the Sunday, I put the young reared pheasants out into the turnip and rape fields, they would like the cover these crops gave them, and at the same time, I scattered good quantities of wheat at various points.

Monday, August 28th, we took Adam to Newcastle races with us. Little Joey stayed to look after some sheep. Adam had good luck, backing all six winners and making himself 5 pounds 10/-, I myself, have not made a note of profit or loss.

On Thursday, September 21st, Monique and I set off for Germany to see our friends there. Harvest was all finished, we motored over to Hull to catch the overnight ferry to Rotterdam instead of the long haul to Dover, it was only about 100 miles to Hull, easy driving too. We arrived in nice time, having to wait about an hour in the car park, then eventually we drove on to the large ferry, this one was run by Dutch personnel, a most friendly lot indeed. We were shown to our cabin for two; it was very cosy. This done, I doused my face to feel fresh. Monique repaired her makeup, then we went up to sample the bar, at I think round about the 10 pm mark, dinner was ready, a smorgasbord affair, which was rather a novelty for us, but well arranged and well put, there was food for an army, and very good, and well cooked, and of a good taste, we were surprised and pleased, I don't think we ever took the Dover ferry again when going to Germany.

After dinner, we retired to the bar, getting into conversation with two or three officers of the ship. They made us feel quite at home, themselves standing round after round of drinks. Eventually, we retired to bed at 2 am, well pleased with our choice of Hull instead of Dover.

We docked early in Europoort Rotterdam. We were wakened up by a steward with two large cups of hot tea first, then to breakfast, as much food for this meal as for dinner last night.

We disembarked drove out of this huge complex of docks and shipping, there were a number of roads to Munster, which seemed equal to take, I took the higher road on the map rather than go too low down, this route took to Arnhem, but first, I missed the road, so stopped and asked in German for the road I wanted, the Dutchman understood my German, but I could not understand him at all, I showed him the map, he soon pointed out where I had to go, thanking him, off we went, across that bridge in Arnhem that had been the centre of a great battle - a bridge too far - a badly organised affair and going against the advice of the Polish general and against aerial photo's showing tank formations in or near the woods. Also dropping the parachutists far too far from their targets Montgomery's first defeat. The buildings still showed their scars of bullets and shells. Having seen the film and read the book of "Bridge Too Far", I could visualise the great effort our soldiers had put in there, and passing the heath found further on where a great number of our parachutists landed, too far from their target. From Arnhem, I took the road for Zutphen, Hengelo, Enschede, running right down to Munster, in the latter, I knew the streets well and were soon out onto the Warren- dorf road leading to Telgte and to my second home. It had been only a short drive from Rotterdam compared with the drive from Calais, we both arrived full of beans and not tired like the journey from Penrith to Dover, that was a long leg.

That first night, we spent in the Shepherd's Inn dancing and drinking with neighbours Alfons and Nane Ludkehaus and Charlie Tische, the man Maria was having an affair with, it was 3 am when he hit the hay.

We holidayed for three full weeks, in which we had only sunshine, not a drop of rain. One weekend, Heinz and Maria, Monique and I drove down to Berncastel on the Mossell for the wine festival, which we had been to before, always a good festival there, where we drank and danced until the early hours. This time all hotels and B & B's were full, so we all slept in Heinz's shooting break, this did not suit Monique at all, she liked something more refined, next day, Heinz drove us over the Hun- sruck Strasse to Rudesheim, where once again we danced and drank the night away in the Drosselgasse, on arrival though, that morning, we were lucky booking into one of the biggest hotels there, this place had a very large courtyard, with bedrooms and balconies overlooking it and rather a nice fountain, the name of which I omitted to write down, the bedrooms were most comfortable and well appointed. Monique was satisfied, not only her but Maria as well, she did not like sleeping in the car either, as for Heinz and myself, we did not mind at all, here we danced the night away.

From Rudesheim, after 3 days, we retraced our route back over the Hunsruck Strasse to visit our wine-making friend, Walter Pitch and wife at Klotten on the Mossel, here we lingered another 3 days this time Monique and I had a room for ourselves for Frau Pitch now took B&B guests and also there was a village wine festival of which Walter was on the committee. At Poltersdorf on the Mossel, this was an exceptional night, because of Walter, we were treated like V.I.P.'s and given top seats in the big marquee where we danced to a very good band, returning to Walters full of the best wine, round about 4 am. We were not in a hurry to get up that morning but had to, of course.

One night in the "Shepherd's Inn" we danced and drank until 2 am. Alfons, Nane and Charlie had been there. Heinz had retired to bed at midnight, Alfons and his wife left at 1:30 am, Monique and I went upstairs to bed at 2 am, leaving Maria and Charlie, we had been in bed only 10 minutes when we heard Heinz leave his little room next to ours, 2 or 3 minutes later we heard an almighty row from the cellars where the Shepherd Inn was. Heinz was shouting at the top of his voice, and we also heard Maria's voice. Neither Monique nor I ventured out. In the morning, I asked Heinz what it was all about. He told me he had gone down quietly to the Shepherds Inn, tried the door handle very quietly and found it locked, hearing noises from the other side, he took one mighty kick at the door, breaking the lock, and there was Charlie on top of Maria, he threw Charlie out, and only because of Charlie's age – he was about 70 – did not give him a good hiding. Maria shouted her innocence as hard as she could, blaming the locking of the door on Monique, which was in itself pathetic.

I had bought 2000 cigars from my friend Sepple Poppenborg and had them safely tucked away behind the door panels, Sepple giving me the usual 7 ½ % and a good box of 25.

Our holiday finally came to a close, and we set off for home on the 11th of October, getting home on the 12th by sailing from Rotterdam and arriving in Hull, a good crossing and, once again, pretty good food, arriving in Hull, we both thought at the same time what a dreary dismal and dirty place it was, in fact, depressing indeed.

The Monday before we came home, Dad had decided to sell some fat lambs and sent 146 to Penrith, but had made rather a poor selection, as 43 of them did not pass for the subsidy and had to be brought home.

On Saturday 4th November, Monique and I went to Newcastle races, little Joey stayed at home. After the races, we drove back to Penrith to dine at the George Hotel, as we entered Penrith, a police car heading towards us turned round and followed us on our tail to the entrance to the George Hotel garage. Monique was driving and she had not had any alcohol that day, we left the George at 1 am, within one minute, a police car was on our tail and followed us for 5 miles, the harassment started again on Wednesday, 8th the police again followed Monique at 5:10 pm from 2 miles north of Penrith to 6 miles southeast of Penrith, where she turned off for Skirwith.

On Sunday 19th, Monique and I dined at Sharrow Bay Hotel on the lake side of Ullswater. This place had a very good name, and people came from London to stay and eat there, run by two partners, one was named Sacks and the other, I forget, the main course we ordered was one of Monique's specialities. Beef en croute. We were served, but this dish was not a patch on Monique's, I told Sacks this because he came over to our table, I told him the farce plus the crust was not of the best, at the same time telling him it was a speciality of my wife, he made a stupid remark for a restaurateur – "What can you expect with 20 or 30 to cook for" - this was his job though to see that all should have been perfect, I also told him his soup was not too good, of course, the reputation of the place was pretty high, and as Sacks went round the other tables asking the same question "everything all right?", all and everyone chimed up "oh yes, beautiful - thank you". The trouble with the English when dining out they dare not open their mouths to complain about the food, preferring to keep quiet in case they made fools of themselves in front of others, and under their breath, vowing never to come back to this place again, Mr Sacks moved on, we dined two or three times there, over time, it could be good, but for us, the reputation it carried, it was not good enough.

In later years, Egon Ronay raved about Sharrow Bay, it was a lovely place, no doubt about that, but many places Egon Ronay raved about were found quite useless in my view, he was just a raver.

On 28th of November, was I note the exact day in which Dad had bought 20 Irish breeding heifers from a man named Towey, they had landed at Sil- loth docks. Dad now lived weekends at Silloth. These heifers were dropped off by lorry in the spring field - the lambing field – I went to see them and could not believe what I saw, these cattle were rubbish, I just could not think Dad, knowing his cattle, could have purchased such miserable articles, I asked him the next day when he turned up at the farm, how much he had paid for them, he replied 132 pounds each, I told him then and there he had been swindled. I even marked in my diary—"It is bloody robbery", I asked about the papers for health clearance – all in order, Dad said, I told him, "As far as breeding from them, you can't get rats out of mice" – and let the matter drop.

I am sure Dad bought these cattle because I had not asked

him to accompany Monique and I to Dublin on our previous trip there to buy cattle, he was jealous, no doubt encouraged by his wife, to buy what he wanted.

It turned out the papers for these heifers were completely false, issued by Towey to Dad, I enquired as to the character of Towey from two or three reputable cattle dealers, each story was the same – keep off – he's a rogue.

Within a few months, three of these poor small heifers slipped calf, they should not have been in calf, they were meant to be virgin heifers, the embryo's we found were small, I isolated them on instinct, these three in a small byre, tied up and fed well, to fatten up to sell. I did not want them around, a month or two further on four more aborted of Dad's consignment, he really had bought a pig in a poke. Little did I realise it just then, but dear Father, through his jealousy, had bought and brought contagious abortion into Skirwith Hall and introduced this awful malady into a perfectly fit and healthy herd of fine beef cows, never had we been troubled before with cows aborting. In my grandfather's – that nasty man – day, his herd had a contagious abortion, but that was way back in 1936. The next calving season in 1973 started to show the results of our own healthy herd starting to abort, at first slowly.

Monique and I went to Sedgefield races on Saturday, 2nd December, we had a good day. I made 50 pounds – we dined at Hardwick Hall Hotel with John Cummings and wife, and Sandy Taylor. We left at 10 pm, heading for home via Scotch Corner, there was roadwork's on the motorway, they were erecting a centre crash barrier at least in the day time, just now at 10:15 pm all was quiet, no traffic, I was doing 80 m.p.h. When all of a sudden I saw at the last second, a large lump of metal lying in the road, right in our path, then the Volvo was spinning round like a top, the road-way was covered in a cloud of sparks, from something metal, there had been a bang like a 12 bore let off in one's ear, next second we were over a steep bank facing the opposite direction, I had managed to stop the car, now we were sideways on this bank and we were leaning over at a rather dangerous angle, in fact so bad, it would have been easy to have tipped the car over by hand from the top side, we both got out gingerly, by the lights I could see the near side front tyre had been badly ripped open and a cut in the mudguard from underneath, this was all from some piece of iron bar or rail left or placed in the road by some irresponsible idiot, I switched the lights off, collected my binoculars, and made our way up the bank onto the road, only 20 yards away was a roadside phone, I thought right I will phone for a taxi to take us home, though it was 65 miles and leave the car for tomorrow, I picked the phone up, told the person who answered what had happened and that I wanted to get to Scotch Corner, the voice said that it would be seen to, I replaced the receiver, then we waited a few minutes, I then thought, if a police car comes along we will be breathalysed and that would be no good, within seconds a small truck came along, so I waved him down, the driver stopped, I explained the situation, told him I had phoned for help, he then told me something I did not know, that the roadside phones went straight to the police station, this was a surprise for me, if I had known that, I would never have used the phone.

The truck driver dropped us off at Scotch Corner Hotel, we thanked him and into the cocktail bar we went. Tom Jones, the manager, a very kind and gentle man, a true Welshman, treated us to a couple of large whiskys, the place was very busy, bars were open, some function or other was taking place, in the meantime I phoned John Cummings at his home, Sands Hall at Sedgefield, told him our trouble, he told me not to worry, he would send a breakdown wagon straight away, from his local garage at Bowburn, which he did, we chatted to various people we knew at the hotel when all of a sudden in walks a policeman, he comes straight up to me and says "Mr Slack", I had given my name on the roadside phone - I told him "I'm not Mr Slack" he then said "Yes you are, you have been pointed out to me, by one of the staff, he added, "don't worry I'm not going to breathalyse you", I then told him I was Mr Slack. We then sat at a small table in the bar, while I gave him what he wanted, particulars of the accident, he sneered at my telling him that it was some large metal object lying in the direction of my path that was the cause of my accident, telling me that I had been drinking, I told him he could be- lieve what he wanted to, signed the statement and he left.

I then asked Tom Jones to get me a taxi, which he did, then home we went. For some reason, I, forgot to mark down the cost in my diary.

The same day, I got Kurt to run me over to Bowburn for the Volvo, where the mechanic verified the car had run over some large metal object for the damage done to the car and tyre.

33

A Sad Affair

On 8th December, I gave a small shoot, it was a day I look back on with regret and great sadness, for during that day, Bert John- stone, one of my guests – he was from Cyril Parkers farm, Home Farm, Skirwith – was following directly behind me, Lassie my Labrador on my heels, when all of a sudden a gun goes off almost in my ear, then Lassie screaming in awful pain, jumped in front of me, there was a gaping hole in her side with her entrails hanging out, she was in terrible pain, I had no option but to put her out of her pain, I put my gun to my shoulder and shot her. There were now no screams of agony, there was complete silence. I turned on Bert Johnstone in silent anger and asked what the hell he thought he was doing. He replied that his gun had gone off on its own, I did not accept this as once before, on the grouse moor, he had nearly blown me and my two sons' feet off while talking in a square, the trouble with him, he would fiddle with his guns triggers, I realised if Lassie had not have been there behind me, I could very possibly have had my legs blown off, I said, "you bloody fool", I never asked that man to another shoot.

When I told Monique the sad news, she broke down crying, I went down in the Land Rover to pick her body up, my heart was broken, I shed tears over my great little friend, she was, without doubt, the best Labrador I have ever had, she and I had had some great moments together. I wrapped her now still and cold form in one of my riding macks, stroked her little lifeless head, and with a heavy heart, lowered her gently into her grave in the garden of Skirwith Hall beside where my great dog Spot was buried. They are two of the great doggiest friends in my life. She was 8 years old.

I had little contact with that fool of a man Johnstone, after this, my father also was most amazed at the irresponsibility of Johnstone.

When I first got Lassie, I told my eldest son, Adam, that he could claim Lassie as his own dog, he loved dogs, I thought it would be a nice gesture towards him and he loved her immensely and she him. When he came home ten days later, Monique and I told him the sad news when we returned from Carlisle after picking him up from his train. At the news, he became so silent did not say a word. Monique found him crying in his room, he never forgave Bert Johnstone, even many years later.

Monique and I went to Carlisle to shop for Christmas for the boys, we got them, amongst other things, a cassette recorder and a small record player each that would also run off a battery as well as electric, the reproduction of sound was crystal clear, and after the boys had left for school in January, I used to polish up my German on small records on the little players while on my own, at the breakfast table before Monique got up. The boys still have them.

I was, according to my diary, though I cannot remember, having trouble with my eyes, it seems I was getting cysts on and under my eyelids, I paid a visit to Dr Ross Weir, my left eye cysts were cut out top and bottom of the eye, where my diary reads, it hurt quite a lot.

Christmas Eve, Sunday 24th, the boys and I went to midnight mass at St. Johns Church in Skirwith, it gladdened the heart to sing the Christmas hymns, there is always something extremely soothing to one's heart to be in the Lord's house on Christmas eve, the service, the Christmas hymns and carols, one goes home with a sense of humility, but at the same time of good feeling, heart-lifting.

We had a quiet Christmas. The boys were growing up now, they were excited at their various presents, but for Adam, his excitement soon evaporated when he thought of his dog Lassie, who would not be there to go down the fields ferreting with him or for her to be just there with him, as his friend. But there were no presents for them from my father, their grandfather, Monique was quiet, I think Lassie's death touched her more than I thought, especially when she noted

Adam's quiet attitude.

She had made, as usual, a marvellous meal and, as usual, started with hare soup, the boys loved this, then came the goose, an excellent one too, and the finale, Christmas pudding and cigars. Monique had now taken to smoking cigars, graduating from the little Manikin for which I bought her a special holder of amber with an 18ct gold rimmed end (cigar end). Now, she was smoking my Corona with great expertise, too. There, we rested in the morning room, at each side of a great blazing fire, while the boys went outside to do their thing.

The week passed quickly, I had no heart to take the boys shooting, it would have been too painful for Adam, so I never mentioned it. The first week in the New Year was quite good weather, on the 3rd, I had a 5-pound double on the horses, winning 200 pounds, this was quite a good start, I thought.

I had Kenneth Oliver looking over the farm to give me an idea of the day's value, at the back of my mind, I had the idea that one day, I might sell the place. With Labour governments becoming more and more communistic, in fact, more red than the reds, heaven knows what the future held, death duties were enormous. I thought if I was killed in some accident, the estate would have to go to pay them. At the moment, this was only a thought.

Heinz had arrived for a short holiday, Monique and I dined at the George Hotel, Penrith, a very good meal but a very hard night, there was the opera singer, once again keeping us rapt in the beauty of her voice, then a company of hard drinkers kept the bar open until 8 am Sunday morning, we left for home, where Heinz and I had a quick look round the cow herds seeing if anything was calving, worse luck, there was one cow quite handy to the farm trying to give birth, only one leg visible. Heinz gave me a hand to bring her into one of the byres, I took off my jacket and pullover and rolled my shirt sleeves as far up as possible, Heinz rolled his sleeves up to help, I discovered one leg was completely facing backwards, this meant me, shoving the calf head and another leg back into the womb so that there would be plenty of room to manoeuvre the other leg into a proper position, it was quite hard to do, as the cow would have contractions so hard, one's hand felt like breaking at times, however eventually I had both legs in line, and the head nicely placed, I attached two leg ropes, one on each, gave one to Heinz and took the other myself, then we pulled, waited a few seconds for each contraction when the cow had these, we pulled hard, within a few minutes we landed a nice sized Hereford bull calf, Heinz took one end of the calf, I the other and carried it into a clean loose box, untied the cow and put her in with her baby. We watched the mother, licking her new-born with great love in her eyes, and gentle, low mooing to her son, it was somehow, even with the hundreds of calves I have seen born and calved, a new birth was always a joy to witness and watch the love of a mother for her new-born, sheep, cows, mares, dogs, the love shown was most touching to see. Little did we know what repercussions of this morning's birth would have for both Heinz and myself. I will explain later on. We went to bed at 11 a.m. on Sunday, January 21st, 1973.

The next day, Thursday, Heinz and I walked around the whole estate or almost, inspecting the various cow herds, taking the guns with us, doing so, we shot 5 pheasants, 7 ducks, 2 hares. This is a gourmet meal in Germany. He, like myself, also went mad over hare soup and in due course, Monique had them prepared for him, he was in his element. Always after breakfast, he and I would light up our cigars and continue smoking until bedtime and invariably, during his visits, great quantities of whisky and wine would be consumed from midday on.

The next day, Wednesday, 27th January, Monique and I took him to Newcastle airport, we were up at 6:30 am and at the airport by 9:30 am. Heinz's plane was due to leave at 11:05 am with sad hearts, we bade each other farewell.

I was now preparing the top courtyard for cementing, this was where most of the stock was sorted, and in a wet time, was always in a state of 2 or 3 inches of mud. I was determined to clean the place up, Kurt and myself did all the measuring, sloping, and levelling, the base needed very little added metal as the base was good, I was putting 5 inches of concrete where the heavy lorries passed through with loads of 20 tons, the rest only 3 to 4 inches, I ordered the ready mix from Edenhall concrete products this time. The courtyard was approximately 35 yards long by 25 wide, at the moment the weather was mild, Kurt and I laid and levelled 4 loads of concrete on Wednesday, 7th February, this was hard work for the two of us, it kept us going from 9:30 am until 5 pm, but looked very well, when down, only the building sides were to finish off, in a day or two when we took the levelling boards up. I allowed no traffic on it for one week.

Saturday, I phoned Hugh Walsh in Ireland for the price of a dozen bulling heifers, 2 years Aberdeen A x Shorthorn, he quoted me 140 pounds each. I told him to ship me 14, he agreed.

Monday, 19th February. I had a new tractor man start work, he came from working for a woman farmer at Culgaith, he was Bill Allan, he seemed all right but was rather slow.

Wednesday 21st the 14 breeding heifers from Hugh Walsh arrived at Birkenhead at 140 pounds each, twice tested for T.B., also for brucellosis, all was okay and all in order, I phoned the lorry driver, Peter Farrel to go and pick them up, he returned with them all safe and sound at 9 pm that day. On inspection, they were excellent stock, strong and healthy looking.

On Monday the 26th, Monique and I set off to drive to Hull, it was Karnival time in Germany, where we took the ferry boat to Rotterdam, we arrived in plenty of time, booked in and waited until we were called, we sat in the car for about an hour then we were called to drive onto the ship, now our short holiday had started. We always looked forward to setting foot on the ferry boats, even the short trip over from Dover, the feeling was always – now we're on holiday. So it was now we were shown to our cabin, which was quite cosy. The personnel were all Dutch and most pleasant, we wandered off to the bar, which was already serving drinks, even though we were still in port. I ordered two large whiskys, and we both sat at a small table for two, quite handy to the bar, got out my cigar case, pulled out a large Simon Bolivar and lit up, time passed gently, then we cast off. Then dinner was ready, smorgasbord, help yourself. As I have said before, the food on this crossing to Rotterdam was always good and plentiful. We tucked in, had two bottles of red wine, and eventually finished, returned to our table - no one had taken it and enjoyed our digestifs of large whiskies. In due course, a couple of the Dutch officers invited us to join them for drinks at a nearby table, which we did, we swapped yarns for three hours or more, drinks were coming in fairly fast. The two Dutchmen were Peter van Stoveren and Jaap Hagendijk, both lived in Rotterdam, and both were very nice chaps and invited both of us to stay for a day or two with them and their families at any time, and if stuck in Rotterdam to ring their houses directly for help, we still have the visiting cards from these two kind chaps. But at about 2am the sea was getting very choppy indeed, a few travellers still up, were starting to be seasick, this made me uneasy, and eventually feel decidedly queasy, I bade goodnight to our two new friends, Monique stayed to have final nightcap, but I definitely had to get to our cabin, if I did not, I could feel myself getting worse, then a bad headache started.

    I found our cabin, undressed quickly and, lay down with the blankets over me, and felt the nausea pass, within 10-15 minutes, Monique came in, deciding it was time to hit the sack. We both slept solidly, being woken by the steward with a cup of tea each at 6 am. For the first time in ages I felt very groggy, however we took our time to dress, went upstairs to the breakfast room, I could not face eating at all. Monique was quite all right, fresh and breezy, Jaap and Peter came to see us, took one look at me and smiled, making the odd joke, however, I rallied to bid them both farewell for the time being.

    Off we drove, I found the way out without much bother,

but starting to feel very sickly, I started to look for a lay-by in which I thought to make myself sick, the sooner, the better, in no time, there appeared to be a good sized lay by ahead, I pulled in, by now I was almost vomiting, I saw only a lorry or two, and two or three cars, by now, I had to stop, rea- son or non, I opened my door, leant over and a jet of stale booze, wine and whisky gushed forth, not onto the ground, through my watery eyes, I saw a pair of black shoes, covered in what I had jettisoned, I looked up and there was a strongly built chap, quite unconcerned I had made a nasty mess on his shoes, all he was interested in was trying his best to flog me some watches, he was a spiv, he took off his jacket, rolled his shirt sleeve up on his right arm, and displayed a multitude of gold wrist watches, all strapped round his arm from wrist to elbow. However, he soon realised I was in no state and no mood to buy or be bothered with such stuff. He went off with his smelly shoes to another car that had pulled up.

Now that I had got rid of the sour fluid resting in my stomach, I started to feel much better and, after resting for ¼ hour, drove on in the direction of Arnhem – Zutphen – Enschede – Burgsteinfurt, where we stopped at a little pub and had a couple of cool beers, which put me 100% fit again, and on to Munster, up the Osnabruck road and into Telgte, where we stopped for another couple of beers at Albert Grevelers. Alberto, as we called him, was delighted to see us and would not take payment either for the beers or cigars and onto Inenestrasse to see my blood brother. Heinz was most pleased we were back over to see him, out came the beers, we drank long into the afternoon, reminiscing over old times. It was good to be reunited with my best friend – once a Nazi, now more English than the English, we just got on well together, many times out shooting or whatever, we did not speak, there was no need to, we seemed to have telepathy.

That week, we were hardly in bed, dancing the nights away in Munster with our many friends, Willy, Alfons, Heinz, etc. Alfons always gave a big evening, eating and dancing at his house in Kettlerweg, only 100 yards from Heinz, and as always, drinks were in abundance, this was grand because we could walk home in two or three minutes, Alfons was one of the top men in the Armstrong factory in Munster, his job took him quite often to Milano in Italy where a new factory had just been opened up.

I paid my usual visit to my good friend Sepple Poppenborg, my cigar man, once again, I chose a selection of Black Brazilian and blonde cigars, buying a total of 1000. Sepple gave me a 7 ½ % discount and a box of 25 very good blonde German cigars. On Sunday, I packed them all carefully behind the Volvo door panels.

The affair with Maria and Charley was still going on, but behind Heinz's back, Charlie was forbidden to enter Heinz's house, Maria did not care, as she saw plenty of Charlie when Heinz was out all day at his work, Heinz was still not accepted into the marital bedroom.

Ash Wednesday, we took it relatively easy, visiting as many friends as possible for tomorrow. Thursday the 8th, we were setting off for home, I had to get back for lambing time. Also, I wanted to buy some wine and beer to take home. I bought two cases from Heinz made by Walter Pitch on the Moselle, Auslese, and Beerenauslese, extra good and two cases of Warsteiner beer, usually called Wappie in the pubs, this is an excellent beer fit for a connoisseur. Heinz had a cousin as one of the directors.

Thursday 8th Monique and I were up at 8 am, had a good breakfast, a few beers in the kitchen with my old friend and brother, then left at 10 am for Rotterdam, where we arrived at 3 pm.

On arrival at Hull customs, I was approached by an official, not the usual customs chaps, he asked me to please get out of the car, which puzzled me, I did so, then he asked me to open the boot, I told him you will have a surprise when this is opened, he smiled and said "I don't think so", however, I opened the boot lid, and there in all the glory in front of us lay the crates of beer and wine, their necks did up in gold and silver wrappings. Our man then turned to me and said, "yes a pleasant surprise", he then told me to close the boot and carry on to the customs proper, I asked what he had been looking for. He told me there had been some Pakistani people being smuggled into the U.K. recently in lorries, car boots, anything they could hide, that's what he had been looking for. At customs proper, I was through in no time, paying only for the wine and one box of cigars.

I had a contractor, Mr Allen from Pooley Bridge, arrive to make my fish lake bigger, he's charging 3 pounds per hour. I was extending the little lake on the higher end, knocking a wall down in the process. The extension would be another 40 yards long by 30 wide and make it easier to trench fresh water into the lake, as the fall was just right. It took Mr Allen, who worked off and on, more often off, a few weeks with his J.C.B., which I think had seen better days. However, eventually, the little lake was fully made. I would have liked the extension to have been bigger, but Allen, who worked one day on and 7 off, was being bogged down with water filling the lake bottom to a depth of about 2 feet, making it impossible to continue, all I wanted now were some trout to put in it, wild duck were already busy inspecting the lake for nesting sites.

Adam came home for his holidays on 29th March. Still, the mornings were cold and frosty, with very cool breezes during the day.

Adam and Joey were good helpers just now; they fed turnips with tractor and trailer to the various fields of ewes and lambs. The boys, Adam and Joey, did well on this awful blizzard of a day.

On the 8th, Sunday, some friends from Carlisle whom we had met in Tossa del Mar, on our first visit there a few years ago came to visit us, they were Tom and Sandra Preston and their daughter Angela. The latter, whom when we first meet in Tossa was about 5 years old, she was the most beautiful child one could ever have seen, her parents spoilt her enormously, justly so, now she was growing up, she was becoming a beautiful young girl, well mannered and poised.

My new man Bill Allan was off with a sore throat and was off work for a whole week, a thing I was not impressed with as he was seen walking the streets of Penrith.

On Friday 4th, I was shepherding the sheep at Kirkland and discovered over 70 stray sheep in the allotment, they had come in over the fell stone wall, creating a gap 5 yards long, with my dog Maid. I soon had then sorted out from my own sheep and back onto the open fell, then the hard bit came, the repairing and walling up of the 5-yard gap, I set to work, I had been walling for half an hour when the rain started in a steady stream, I had no waterproof coat and before long I was wet to the skin, it took me 2 hours to finish the job, I was pleased when the last stone was in place, this work was done by my bare hands. I see nowadays, industrial gloves are worn for the slightest of work, soft workers these days.

On Sunday, I had a visit from Stan Payne from Cockermouth, he had a fish hatchery there, he came to see what my little lake was like, Stan had only one arm, he had been a Sergeant in the Korean war, had his hand shot off, he'd tied it with a tourniquet, but the latter had been rather high and been left on too long before he was got to a field hospital, gangrene had set in with the result the arm had to be amputated well above the elbow, but Stan could handle anything he could put his hand to quite easily, he came this day with his wife, his opinion of my lake was in his own words, first class.

On the 18th, Friday, I had a busy day castrating 75 bull calves on a nice breezy day, I took one-eyed Willie Chapelhow 25 testicles and kept the rest my-self, having an excellent dinner that night of them, with a couple of bottles of Walter Pitch's wine from the Moselle, in fact, also finishing the testicles off in the pan, with Walter's wine, this put the finishing touch to these delicate gastronomic delights. Monique always refused to eat them, this evening, I also cooked them myself.

On 22nd May, Joey's ferret had a nice litter of 7 young ones, and on 24th May, I went to Carlisle to see about getting a new Volvo, but the price offered for mine was, I thought, an insult at 1200 pounds, myself having to pay almost 3000 pounds in for another the same model.

The same day, 4 N.H. racehorses arrived from Gordon Ritchard's stable at Greystroke. I was going to summer them for him, for cash.

Monday being a bank holiday, Hexham races were on, so off Monique and I went, the day was warm and sunny, I made no money, in fact, I lost 30 pounds. We did not dally too long afterwards in Hexham, having a few rounds with friends, then motoring back to Temple Sowerby, where we had dinner, this time no good, I was beginning to wonder what was going on with our catering friends.

On Tuesday, I went to Aspatria in West Cumberland on the advice of Lord Lonsdale's keeper, Walter Drysedale, to purchase a yellow Labrador puppy from a Mr Reid, the puppy was 10 weeks old and was to replace my beloved Lassie. I liked the puppy very much, and Mr Reid seemed to be an honest and kind man, we did a deal, but strange to say, I have made no entry in my diary of the price I paid for this second Lassie, for that is the name I gave her, she was to prove an excellent gun dog.

Also to arrive this day was Stan Payne, from Cockermouth, with 1000 rainbow trout fry, two months old, these were put in the water quarry, at the same time, I took delivery of 150-day-old pheasant from Jim Peat, son-in-law of Arthur Monkhouse. Also, 2 more horses landed from Gor- don Ritchards, these were put in a 65-acre field named High Close, halfway between Skirwirth and Kirkland. All in all, it had been rather a busy day, from fish, pheasant and horses.

On Friday, 1st June, I went to see my accountant in Leeds, Kenneth Cope, with a view to turning the Skirwith Hall estate into a family trust, his advice was too costly and too late. Myself, knowing nothing in this sphere, took note of his advice and did nothing. Casting my mind back, I am sure this was false advice given with some ulterior motive in Cope's mind. I had voiced to him that I may one day sell Skirwith Hall, but that was all, perhaps he saw a bigger financial fish to land later on.

On June 2nd, my birthday, Monique gave me a box of 25 Romeo and Juliette Corona cigars. They were perfect, also Cathie, Robert MacGeorge and a friend of theirs, Freddie Brain, came for lunch, only phoning up that morning to tell us, Freddie was a charming man, who I think was in charge of Simpson's of Picadilly, we had home killed leg of milk-fed lamb with mint or onion sauce. This lamb was superb, there is no lamb in the whole of Europe to compare with lamb from the British Isles. Finishing off with some lovely bought strawberries, Freddie also helped to lower the level of the whisky bottle.

On Wednesday, 6th June, Morston won the Derby, I had 10 pounds on him @ 33/1 after reading the write-up on him by Audax in Horse and Hound, my week's winnings were very good, I was rather pleased and had one of my birthday cigars and a few whiskys after listening to him win on the radio, the rest of the day I gave to "The Queen". Cova Dura ran 2nd with Lester up. Eddie Hide rode the winner, he was a very canny jockey. Hide, with his longish angular face, the jockeys then were a great breed of sportsmen, much different from today's spivs. The day was boiling hot, in the end, I had decided to buy a new Volvo, so on 7th June, Monique collected a new petrol injection 144 Volvo from Patons garage in Carlisle, while I had my hands in sheep muck all day.

The next day, 8th we decided to give the new car a good run-in and set off for Adam's school at Golspie Sutherland. The day was hot and sunny. The county hotel had been sold, the inside torn out of it downstairs and made into a sort of night club dining effect with cubicles, trade had dropped off to nil, the food was rubbish, there was no lounge, they had even done away with one of the best money spinners, the off licence, turning this into a tea room, trade poor, service and food poorer, now Monique and I never entered the doors at the county.

We drove on to Perth, where we stayed at the George Hotel. We found it good, but for what it was, it was far too expensive. The car was running well, though we were never over 50m.p.h, she did on this first run 23 ¾ m.p.g.

On a Saturday, 9th we arrived at Golspie and took Adam out, we dined at the Palace Hotel, a 4 star place not far away, the exact location I have omitted to put down, but seeing it was a 4 star place, we thought a good place to treat Adam to a good meal, the meal turned out to be no good at all, a great pity, the weather also turned cold, very cold. That night, we all slept at Abernethy at the Breadalbone Arms, once again, another useless place for food and the rest. These hotels and their food were a great disappointment to us.

On Sunday, we had lunch at Pitlochry in Fishers Hotel, and thank goodness, this was good. The school kitchens were a showpiece and scrupulously clean. The boys I talked to, as well as Adam, told me the food was very good, they all liked it, I couldn't believe this, so could Monique.

Now it was time for us to head for home, we dropped Adam off at the school at 6:30 pm, kissed him goodbye and left for Edinburgh to stay the night with Colin Strange-Steel and his wife April; both of the Strange-Steels were extremely charming and kind people to meet. They had not been married too long. April said she has something in common with me, our initials A.S.S. April gave us a beautiful dinner and Colin some excellent wine. They were very good hosts indeed.

13th cold, wet and high winds. This day, Stan Payne from Cocker- mouth, brought me 95 rainbow trout for my new lake, some of them were 2lbs in weight, on the whole, they were a beautiful sight, these glistening gems of the water with that lovely rainbow stripe on their sides - now my little venture for sport was complete, I took Stan into the house and thanked him for such a grand lot, then we settled down and knocked 1 ½ bottles of Grouse Whisky off and a couple of Bolivar

Corona's each, Monique had a grand fire going in the morning room, even though it was mid-June, she knew I liked a good fire, a very friendly thing is a good open fire, even if one is alone – with such a fire one is never alone.

Stan eventually made tracks for his home, for he was coming back with 100 more trout tomorrow, these ones were going to be smaller at approximately 1lb each, which to me was still a nice-sized trout.

Thursday, Stan duly arrived with 102 lovely rainbows, fascinating things live fish - now I was well and truly set up. Dad was quite excited also after giving me plenty of criticism for digging up so much land, which he said should have been reseeded down to grass instead. Land that had been a bog for the last 400 years of the Slackline. Once again, Stan had done me a good favour, nearly 200 grand trout, out came the Grouse Whisky and cigars, this was early afternoon, and today was very hot, no fire till nighttime, we talked on and on till the second bottle was nigh but gone 2 cigars, Bolivar had been gently smoked and enjoyed, Stan stayed and enjoyed a dinner of roast pheasant with 2 bottles of Volnay to wash it down, he was a happy man when he left for Cockermouth later that night.

Thursday night, Monique and I were invited by John and June Lowthian to dine with friends at Wetherall Carlisle. John's Uncle Alan Peck was or had been the master of the fell pack of Hounds, the Ullswater Foxhounds, he had branched out on his own and had become a very successful accountant indeed. His office was in Lonsdale St, Carlisle, he was a follower of racing and had roped quite a few jockeys into his net, seeing to their accounts. John himself was a grand chap to meet, he and his wife June were excellent hosts, she also was an excellent cook but also a determined social climber.

The same day, we received a phone call from the Reverend Jon Mc- Clintock, the vicar who had christened Adam, he was coming to Skirwith or in the vicinity of, and wondered if he could stay the night, Monique explained that we had a dinner engagement, but he could stay with plea- sure, she would prepare a cold meal for him, his reply was one of joy, he knew even a cold meal of Monique's was something not to be missed, so before we left, Monique prepared for him, one of the trout I had caught specially for him from my lake, it was fortunately only 1lb in weight, I had only wanted the one, this she cooked and left it cold for the entree, she had a whole roast pheasant with the trimmings, a bottle of Dupy Lagarde, Bordeaux and a bottle from Walter Pitch to go with the trout, with about 3 or 4lbs of strawberries for dessert with a jug of thick jersey cream from Penelope the house cow, together with another jug of jersey milk, holding 3 pints, Jon always when here, liked to take a pint of milk to bed with him, to round off, I left him an almost full box of Punch Coronas and a bottle of brandy, plus various liqueurs, all this was set and beautifully presented for him on his arrival on the dining room table, all covered, of course, he had to hunt for nothing.

When Monique and I returned at 2 am, for curiosity, we looked in to see how much he had consumed, for Jon was not only a gourmet but a gourmand. The trout had been finished, for it had been a plump beauty, most of the pheasant, half the strawberries, half the wine of Walter, all the Dupy Lagarde, half the bottle of brandy, which had been full, the cream jug of a good half pint empty, and ¾ of the milk gone, I did not look to see how many cigars he had smoked. My word, we thought, he'll be sick in the night with all of this mixture, but no, he was as, or so it seemed, full of beans in the morning, he said he had enjoyed his meal and thanked Monique, he had an enormous breakfast, and after this, seeing he seemed not to be in a hurry, and the day was sunny and warm, we moved into the garden, whereupon I opened a bottle of champagne, lit two of the Punch Corona's, sat back and chatted away, Monique could see that Jon was here for a few hours more, and put a leg of home killed lamb on for lunch. She had taken it out of the deep freeze before we left for the Lowthians dinner party. Suckled lamb from the grey ewes was for me and everyone who had eaten it, the finest in the world, absolutely succulent, with mint sauce from the kitchen garden, in the meantime, Jon and I had finished the first bottle of Champers and had opened a second, the lawns at Skirwith Hall were completely natural, with apple trees and one pear tree growing there, planted very many years ago, and against the sandstone wall of the house at one side, climbed a magnificent rose of great beauty and great perfume, the rose was a "Fleur de Dion", the ivy was full of chattering sparrows, blackbirds nested all over and quite a few song thrushes, the beck ran 30 yards away from the lower garden wall, and over the beck was a small woodland of oak trees and from these at this moment, wood pigeons are giving their soft and seductive coo-coo-coo-coo, then giving a display of wing, slapping and gliding. We had plenty of water hens below, these would call out frequently, we watched the trout jump for flys making a good splash; cigar smoke drifted lazily up into the air as the vicar and I sat back, enjoying nature at its best, we had lunch which lasted till 4 pm, and three bottles of wine, then Jon left us, he had enjoyed himself enormously, and we enjoyed having him.

After Jon left, I had the shepherd, Ernie, bring some lambs in for me to inspect for fatness. I drew 56 of them for Monday's fat market. Monique and I took it easy that night.

Monday, fatstock day, my 56 lambs weighed from 35Ibs to 40Ibs, made 6/- per Ib.

John Cummings and his wife, Valerie, an out-and-out snob, came over this side of the Pennines to stay at Sharrow Bay Hotel on Lake Ullswater. This was on Friday 13th myself, now clear of flu, they invited Monique and I to dinner there. Now, this place is supposed to be the place in the North of England, Monique and I had dined there two or three times over the last year or two and found it to be wanting, I had told Mr Sacks this and had been frowned on - this night dining with John Cummings was no exception, Monique and I found it bordering on poor, so did John, as a guest I said nothing to Brian Sacks.

Monique and I then invited John and Valerie to Skirwith Hall for dinner on Saturday evening 14th, we waited and waited. Eventually, the phone rang, it was John, he had had an accident in his car hitting another car on these very sharp bends on very narrow roads, leading to and from Sharrow Bay, would I go and pick them up, at once, Monique and I left to see what we could do to help, when we got to the scene of the accident, no-one was badly hurt, John was unhurt, Valerie was cut about the face and had small superficial cuts and needed a few stitches behind one ear. The car was not too badly damaged and could be driven slowly, a bit of mudguard to pull out here and there, and the police were there, two of whom I knew. They told me they would have to breathalyse John – I told the constable to go easy with this – John was clear, he told me later he could not understand why because he had been drinking all day with friends – I smiled and left it at that.

Eventually, we sat down to dine at 11 pm, poor Valerie, I felt sorry for the first time for her; her head had taken a fair knock, but she put on a brave front, she became very tired, I suppose due to shock, they went to bed by 12 midnight, none of us really had a great appetite that night, least of all Valerie.

Little Joey and I fed the pheasants and in the afternoon, I thought it was about time we fished my new lake, I asked Dad to see if he would like to have a go, he said he would. In the event, Dad got 2 trout, fishing for 2 hours, one 2 ½ pounder which put up a lively display of jumping out of the water before being landed. His 2nd trout was a lively 1 pounder, this made his day, and he relished later on with me digging into and leaving a hefty mark on a bottle of Grouse, I thought then, what a pity Mother wasn't here to sit with us, not to drink, because Ma did not drink, only a little tot for medicine sake, if she felt ill, and I thought of the road Dad had chosen by marrying such a slut of a woman, and in the course of, breaking the family up, a great pity, however, what was done, was done. Little Joey also caught one, Adam, who had arrived for his holidays, caught two trout of approximately 2 ½ lbs each, I landed two of about 1lb each. All in all, we had all enjoyed ourselves.

August 12th came round again. The opening of the Grouse shooting season being Sunday, it was illegal to shoot, so we had to wait till the morrow, in the meantime, some of my guests arrived on Sunday: Sandy Taylor, John Cummings, Derek Straker, Phillip Johnstone, on his leave from Hong Kong, with his wife Liz, we had many drinks on the lawn, because it was a red hot day, Robert Jackson, my neighbour was with us. We dined at Temple Sowerby at the Kings Arms, with our usual hosts Peter and Brenda, the meal was excellent, we danced in the public bar until 3 am, then went home, only John Cummings stayed with us, the others went to the George Hotel, Penrith.

The 13th opened with blue skies and a very hot sun indeed. As usual, a case of champagne was opened up and drunk before we set off, this was taken in the garden, Kurt and my other beaters, my workmen, had a crate of beer to themselves, then a bottle of champers for them. They liked these days out, for they knew there would be plenty of fun, also my guns were lavish tippers, especially John Cummings and Derek Straker, off we set for the little pub at Garrygill, the George and Dragon, where the young landlord was once again to knock up out of bed, he soon opened up however, as he knew my crew could empty a few bottles in short time, which we did, Adam and little Joey were beating, I should have let them shoot as well, but they would shoot plenty, just the three of us later on in the weeks to follow, present was Sandy, the son of Lassie, my new Lassie was too young to bring onto the grouse moor. Sandy was a character, any commercial traveller – or in fact, any male who came to Skirwith Hall - quietly Sandy would circle them, then approach from the rear, cock his leg up and with great accuracy pee into the chappies shoes, also if a tea flask top was open, and on the ground, he again with nonchalance, as if to walk past, pause, cock his leg and a direct hit was scored, right inside, it was uncanny how accurate he was. The men had to watch their bait tins he would do the same trick. Going through the village of Skirwith one day, Bert the butcher's van was there. As I passed with some sheep and Sandy, the van door was open. Sandy saw all this lovely meat, had one look and grabbed a fair big roast and took off, I don't know if Bert missed it or not. Young John Frith was beating also, he had been an enormous help at hay time, he was enjoying a pint of beer, his age about 15 years, my two boys - Joey was having a half shandy and Adam a pint like John.

We left the pub after an hour and a half, all of us well revived. John Cummings had driven just too fast around some of the S-bends on Hartside for the comfort of some of our drinking glasses. A few had been broken, he was driving a big Jensen Interceptor. He had taken, in fact, most corners too fast myself being a passenger in the back began to feel rather queasy, and had to change to the front, Sandy gave me his front seat, I was better right away. Also some of the food had a rough ride, Monique had not gone to bed the night before, after Temple Sowerby making her usual Royal picnic. Avocado mouse, cheese straw fingers, ratatouille, crown of lamb, 4 roast chickens, potato and onion omelette, crème caramel, selection of 5 cheeses, biscuits etc. A case of 1966 Chateau Beausejour, 2 bottles of Grouse Whisky, 2 gin, 2 port, 3 cases of beer, lemonade tonic etc. We were well supplied. We all piled into the one Land Rover, and set off for the moor, following the small miners road to the direction of Cross Fell. The weather was just too hot, the sun blazing down. On the way, we met quite a few grouses on the little road or track. Once we were at our rendezvous, we as usual, decided to sample Monique's picnic food, all was perfect, and of course a beautiful day on the fells to have a picnic. The odd raven passed overhead cronking, then after an hour and a half of food and more drink, I spaced the guns. Each gun had a beater and a game carrier, and at a signal from me, I was on the high side, where I could keep an eye 70% of the time on everyone below me, I gave Kurt explicit orders not to talk to his gun, Derek Straker.

Kurt called him Mr Striker. Phillip's wife walked with him.

The day sport proved good, though the birds sat tight, we walked past quite a few, these getting up behind, perhaps my line was rather long and at the far end of the shoot there was a stiff hill to climb out of the valley where the South Tyne starts its voyage. Most guns were too hot and sweaty, and did not wish to go further, but after a rest, we proceeded on and up, it was a long trip back to base, poor Sandy's tongue was hanging out a mile, he was jiggered, but he had worked exceptionally well, so far we had lost only one bird, he could scent and find, he was worthy of his mother all right. Adam was working with him because even in Adam's absence for weeks and weeks at school, Sandy just adored him.

Finally arriving at the base, the beer was attacked with ferocity by everyone. On counting the grouse, I was pleased with the result of 57 heads.

We sat and rested our legs, quenched our thirst, I told all, guns and beaters, to help themselves to the rest of Monique's food, there was not a crumb to take back home. Then, after 1 ½ hours, we descended to the George and Dragon, whereupon closed as usual, I had to persuade the landlord to open up, which he did, realising there would be a jump in his profits. He made a roaring trade, and as usual, I got the first round, for guns and beaters, my guns, bless them, never let a beater be without a drink. All glasses had to be charged at all times. Now Sandy in the bar of the pub of the George and Dragon blotted his copybook, nobody saw him until the last minute or second, he had just done an enormous No 2 in the middle of the bar floor, like a small mountain, with the crowd of drinkers, the pub owner did not see the mess, Adam came and told me, so I told him to get some paper from the Land Rover and clean it up, which he did, I don't think the landlord knew about it to this day.

Home at Skirwith Hall after everyone had cleaned and freshened themselves up, we retired to the bar at the end of the house, french doors opened up, chairs inside and outside, cigars were lit, strange to say no one else smoked cigars, except Kurt, he loved to smoke one.

Stuart had a special menu for us, consisting, for starters, game soup, well laced with port, followed by a good big trout each, this was then followed by half a duck each and for sweet his own - made by Stuart – Crème de Menthe bavois, ripe Stilton and 40-year old port from his cellars, the wine was Chateau Haut Brion, a very superior wine.

All guns departed with a brace of grouse each, Stuart had 5 brace, the rest were in my cellar, then 2 braces would be prepared for myself, Adam and Joey, a bird each. Monique did not care for them, the rest were in the freezer, except for a brace for Dad.

The weather had now turned to light rain, we could not cut the corn. Tuesday 28th, I fished in my lake, passing a tranquil 3 to 4 hours, catching 4 nice fresh rainbows, I walked further on - only 100 yards to see the rainbow fry, to see a kingfisher streak off from catching them, his colours extremely brilliant. Now, after all the time I had been at Skirwith Hall, this was only the second time that I had seen a kingfisher, and of course, the fry was just his size for taking. After this, I netted a good part of the pond over.

The next weekend I took time off for fishing in my lake, spending Saturday afternoon in quietness with Sandy and my new young Lassie, the latter watching me fish intently and when a fish was hooked, I could see she wanted in to see what it exactly was, each one I brought to land, I let her have a good sniff and inspection of them, then she could know what they were, because seeing she was so interested, I knew one day, I would ask her to retrieve the caught trout, instead of using the nets, this day I got 6, 2 @ 2 lbs each and 4 1 pounders, we had them that night, in Papaillot, myself finishing off with 2 large calf testicles, done in a smattering of olive oil and garlic and finished in white wine, excellent, with some of Walter Pitch's Moselle.

I had Stan Payne bring me 70 more trout of approximately

1 pound each, of these I wanted 12 of 1 ½ lbs each, I thought to put a dozen in my fountain in the courtyard, my idea was that I liked a trout for Sunday breakfast, Monique was not a breakfast eater, only coffee or tea and toast, except when on holiday then she liked and ate the full English breakfast, at home – no. I would cast a fly into the fountain and have a nice fresh trout for myself, Stan thought I was a bit loopy, however, the 12 larger trout were put in, I left them for a week before attempting to catch them, I fed them on fish pellets so they did not go thin, though there were plenty of flys and insects landing about the water, the rest we took down to the new lake.

A week later, on Sunday morning, I thought now, I would like a good breakfast of trout, I got the rod and fly tackle ready and cast into the fountain from 10 yards away, no sooner had the fly landed than it was grabbed like a piranha after a piece of meat, I tightened the rod and had one hooked, I could not play him too much because of the centre piece and electric submersible motor, I kept the reel tight and netted him – rather easy, but I had what many people had not, freshly caught trout for breakfast, any time I wanted.

34

Now the harvest was all in and finished, the big Dutch barn full from end to end with large corn stacks built outside, I had the most winter fodder ever at Skirwith Hall, I was pleased and pleased with my men's work, the boys, John Frith and Heinz.

Monique, Adam and I set off to France for a holiday, we motored down to Dover took the ferry boat, this was 17th September, the ferry was not too full, once on board, that feeling of being relaxed came over us, we were now on holiday, customs was passed with no bother. We motored on to stay at a little hotel near Arras had a very good meal and wine. We were heading for Cannes for some of the late summer sunshine. The next day I took the Meaux to Melun road by-passing Paris, motoring along, we had our picnic lunch of 2 baguettes, wine, chachuterie and cheese in a field near Beaune.

The weather was sunny and warm, there was not a lot of traffic. I took the road for Grenoble, I was going to take the route, Napoleon. I loved the mountains and in summer, they looked and felt good. From Grenoble, I took the road to Gap, where we stayed in a very good hotel and ate at a restaurant that also had a balcony overlooking the main dining room, where we chose to eat. The place was full, a good sign, in fact, Gap itself was pretty full of tourists – we had an excellent meal, then after a few beers, we returned to our hotel to sleep. I was tired, Adam was enjoying his holiday so far.

The next day, the 19th, we were up and about for breakfast of those massive cups of cafe au lait, fresh croissants, etc., by 8 am and hit the road, then of all things to happen, I started with tooth ache, I thought perhaps it would go away, stopped the car and bought some aspirin and took a couple, however on the way to Sisteron it got worse, my gum was swollen and had a swelling on a back bottom tooth. At Sisteron, I thought to hold some neat whisky on the swollen gum, now more swollen, this did no good. I realised I would have to see a dentist.

Monique enquired for me. Yes, there were three dentists in town, so off we set for the first one on foot, only 50 yards or so, to find he was on holiday. We went to the second mentioned, to find he was on holiday. The 3rd we were told was a woman. *Good grief*, I thought, just my luck, I am frightened of dentists at the best of times, having as a boy rough treatment by Ronnie Morton in Penrith, he always managed to break my teeth, (two) when extracting them leaving the roots in, he - Ronnie - used to tell mother, "You know, I have to use colossal leverage," my third visit to him with mother when I was perhaps 12 before he could start on me, I jumped out of his chair, ran downstairs and took off, I never went back to him. One tooth I had saved, taken out when I was 14 with gas, by Sidney Barren, whose daughter Netta I was to court for a while, the tooth had tremendous roots on it, no wonder Ronnie broke them. Now here I was with a woman dentist, I told Monique I would not go and adjourned to a bar for a few large whisky to think it over, Adam was drinking shandy's, after half a dozen down the hatch, my tooth was raging mad, I thought that woman would not have the strength to pull my molars. Then I thought, perhaps she is a very strong woman, conjuring up thoughts of a woman dentist with wrists like saplings. Then I decided and remembered Robbie Burns' poem on toothache - the hell of all diseases, and off we set across the square to my doom, on entering the dentist's premises - she herself proved an extremely nice person with an open personality and she seemed strong enough for the job, I duly sat in that chair, I opened my mouth on command, "Ah," she said. "You have an abscess, I'll soon deal with that." She then got her tools ready, I watched and saw her holding a thing with a small, thin, red hot needle on the end, "Open up," she said. I did as I was told, then she stuck this long handle and red hot tip in my mouth, I heard or felt – I don't know which – a slight sizzle and that was that, she massaged my gum, telling me, now all the puss has come out, now rinse your mouth out, I felt better right away, the nice dentist gave me some antiseptic in a bottle to rinse my gum at the rate of 3 times a day, my, was I pleased not to have the tooth pulled out, I thanked the dentist, paid her, it was very reasonable and drove on down to Cannes. En route over Napoleon Road, we took our time, the scenery was magnificent and the weather was getting hotter. There were numerous cafes, which we stopped at for liquid refreshment, signs galore advertising Napoleon's brandy, each one saying theirs was his favourite, it was 7 pm when we descended on Grasse and stayed the night at a hotel by the roadside, quite a good cheapish one and very clean, we ate in Grasse at a brasserie, but it was not too good. We had heard tales of how beautiful Grasse was, famous, of course, for its perfume, little did we know then that in the future, we would be living and looking down on Grasse and when we came to know it, neither of us would give it even half a star, I thought it a hideous place. We also got to know personally and dine and boated, with the president of the perfume trade of Grasse. A very greedy, selfish man indeed – of that later.

In the evenings we used to take two or three beers only at a small bar just down from the main prefecture on the opposite side of the road. This place was run by 2 brothers, where their mother cooked their meals for them in a kitchen at the far end of the bar, we christened the mother P.G. Tips because she was the exact twin of the female monkey in the T.V. advert for P.G. tea. At this bar each night, there was what seemed to be a rich German woman with her gigolo each night they occupied an adjoining table to us on the pavement; she seemed drunk each night and each night from her wicker cane chair, all at once, came forth into the gutter across the pavement for all and sundry to step over, a stream of urine, she never once attempted to go to the loo. The two brothers shrugged their shoulders, because she drank a lot of brandy, good money for them. One day, I had a telegram from Colin Strange-Steel. He had a client that was interested in Skirwith Hall, Mr Roberts, he was bidding 800,000 pounds for the estate as a whole, I sent a telegram back asking if he could squeeze any more out of Roberts. Land was going up and up fast, in the meantime, Strange-Steel approached Dad to ask him to give up the tenancy. I was the owner, but Dad had kept the tenancy to himself, Colin Strange-Steel was most disappointed when Father refused, and Roberts withdrew from more ado.

One night, October 14th, a Sunday, Monique, Adam and I were having our evening beer, for we were leaving on the morrow for the Black Forest, all three of us were at a table on the pavement, quietly watching passersby, sipping our beer when an argument started on the pavement across the road, a lot of shoving and pushing was going on between 4 or 5 men. One of them, obviously the leader, taking it out on another chap, whom I heard speaking English, eventually, the leader of the French gang began slapping the Englishman hard and pushing him about like a rag doll, I commented on this bad treatment to Monique, she told me not to look at them, she then went to the toilet. Just as she left, the Englishman fell to the ground and the leader of the group started to put the boot in, kicking the victim on the ground for all he was worth, this was too much for me, so I left my chair, strode across the road, got the leader by his shoulder and asked what he thought he was doing, he looked me right in the eye and what I saw I did not like, I didn't hesitate, I slammed my right fist into his jaw with full force, the man went down like a log, I then helped the Englishman to his feet, what he said surprised me – he blurted out - that I shouldn't have done that - I thought, crikey, what gratitude, then I was surrounded by members of the group who had been slapping the Englishman, telling me to get out quickly, otherwise I would be killed, not by them, it turned out, but by the man on the ground when he recovered, he was "Johnny the Greek" the top gangster in Cannes, I retreated back to my table, just then Monique appeared, she had fortunately missed all the fracas. Some people ran up to her and told her to "get your husband out of here quickly, this man (meaning Johnnie the Greek) is a killer", now I was becoming a bit worried myself, with that, Monique, Adam and I left and started to walk quickly away, we had only gone 25 yards when Johnnie, recovering from his knockdown crossed or started to cross the road straight for me, his shirt was out of his trousers and open to the waist, he had a very wild look about him, I thought, *You bastard, I'll meet you head on,* and started to cross the road to meet him, we met in the middle, I got my blow in first and felled him again, I thought, he's not tough, this guy, he's soft, but Johnnie grabbed my legs and pulled me down onto the road and there we set to again, but in no time I had his neck in an arm stranglehold, this is when his henchmen dragged him clear, at that same moment a large car drew up, a passenger shouted for us, Monique, Adam and I, to get in quickly, he was, he said, from the American embassy, we got in and drove away at high speed, he told us he and his friend the driver had been watching "Johnnie the Greek" for some time, and that he was a really bad egg, Monique told them where to drop us near our apartment, we thanked them and they drove off. On thinking about what we had been told of this "Greek" fellow, I should think he had and was under surveillance by the C.I.D. of perhaps America and England because all came off to pat, even on thinking back, the Englishman on the ground being kicked and what he said to me, he was probably infiltrating into Johnnie's gang. The American "diplomats" or whatever, just on hand at the correct moment – I got hold of my little finger of my right hand and twisted it, that's where the swelling started – now it hurt with the twist. I realised then I had broken the bone leading to the joint of my little finger and when I pressed, I could feel it was broken in two.

As we had packed our bags in the early evening, due to leave the next day, we thought it not a bad decision. However next morning, I decided not to run away and before we left, we all went to the P.G. Tips bar for a farewell drink, one of the brothers smiled broadly when we arrived, we had told him the night before we would be leaving today. He placed the beers in front of us, we drank them up, he placed three more in front of us, he said nothing when we went inside to say our goodbyes and pay. Then said, "The drinks are on me," giving a big smile at the same time. We shook hands, said goodbye to P.G. Tips and left, he wished us bon voyage, outside all was quiet, no sign of my Greek friend. He was, no doubt, nursing some massive bruises and probably a broken jaw, I think our friend the bar owner and others were very pleased to see their 'mad dog' get a good hiding. Then we were driving away out of Cannes heading for the Forest Noir, I took the route Napoleon again, we reached Chambery in the mountains. There, here we booked into a nice-looking small hotel and had a super meal. I myself was tired from driving the mountain roads, though good, were nothing but bends and corners, and my right hand was becoming very sore with holding the steering wheel.

On 18th October, my hand was rather sore, so I thought it time I had it seen to, I drove to the hospital in Lahr and was attended by Prof Mourath, who put my hand in plaster, with my little finger encased along with the finger next to it, but along with the finger plaster was a long piece of metal inside to stop movement of these two fingers, the charge was approximately 75 Deutschmarks.

I afterwards motored into Waldkirch to the same old woman who, a few years ago, said she would marry Dad - for some cigars, the old girl was still there, I asked if she remembered me, and she said she did, but I had my doubts. In any case, she had a pretty young girl of about 19 years helping her, I bought a thousand cigars from blonde to black, I again asked for a 7 ½ % discount, which I got.

I motored to a quiet country road, parked in a field, took the door panels off the Volvo and bit by bit put the cigars inside the doors. Some, as usual, had to be put in plastic bags as the last lot of boxes were too square and bulky.

At the Hotel Lerche Sexau that evening, at dinner Adam and I had venison, Monique had chicken, one main dish was all we ordered for the helpings were massive, huge servings of spaetle, a type of house-made pasta, we had this with red wine from Kaiser Stuhl, this wine is pretty good, and has hefty alcohol content. I bought 2 cases of Kaiser Stulh and 3 cases of beer to take back home with me. The waitress was the usual one, her name I can not remember, she was not only a marvel at waiting on tables, she looked after the dining room, always fully booked, plus a few tables in the bar, she was a beauty to boot, blonde hair in plaits, peaches and cream complexion, in her Bavarian costume. Her breasts were plump and full, her costume with its low cleavage showed her breasts to perfection, perfect figure, and perfect legs, and always with a merry smile on her face, she was indeed a very good catch for any red-blooded young man.

19th Friday, Monique, Adam and I set off for home, we arrived in Dover at 6 pm. As usual, the customs asked if I had anything to declare, I told him yes, wine and said I had, I thought, too many cigars. I paid for the 50 cigars I had declared extra and for some wine.

Going round the farm in the morning, the main courtyard was a terrible mucky mess, but the top yard and entrance into the farm yards were 4 inches or more in mud, everything was in an awful mess. Dad had been having cattle in to these yards, off and on, what for, I don't know. No cleaning up had been done, but when I went to inspect some cattle at the end of the farm Black Woods, near Becks Mill, my heart sank to my boots, all Black Wood, the timber stretch of approximately 14 acres that my 3 Margaret's had so diligently planted with spruce and scots pine, the little trees now 18 inches high, Dad had deliberately told the cowman to put 40 cows and their calves in amongst this young plantation, the cattle either ate or trampled everything there, this I could not understand of him when I asked why he had done this, his answer was "They had to go somewhere, it is just wasteland," I just walked away. Most of the heifers Dad had bought, aborted, and no doubt this contagious abortion was now passed on to the main healthy herd.

On Monday 22nd I started to sort the calves with Dad for the October suckler sale. In the evening I noticed my throat was starting to be sore. The usual sign before flu. Sure enough, I had to stay in bed the next day, I felt rotten. Maria had phoned us on our first night home, saying she had tried to get hold of us for the last 10 days, Heinz had been in hospital for that period, she told me the doctors were treating him for malaria, but he was not responding, in fact getting worse and she was worried. I thought it's rather late for her to be getting worried now when she would not have the poor chap in her bed. Each evening after this, I phoned Maria to see how things were with Heinz, he, she said, is getting weaker, he was getting big doses, she said of penicillin, I thought to myself, good heavens, my dear old friend cannot die, but what his wife was telling me over the phone, led me to believe time was running out for him. However, I myself was in the middle of a bad bout of flu and feeling very poorly.

The suckler sale on Thursday 25th I was unable to go. Dad had to sell and see everything. He was far from pleased with this, thinking I was swinging the lead.

Monique went to Penrith to get some pills the doctor had prescribed for me, I phoned Heinz that night from my bedside phone; he was still very ill and weak. On Saturday, Heinz himself phoned me from his hospital bed with the very sad news that our good friend Willie Hesselman had died, I was shocked, so was Monique, Willie was larger than life. Heinz then gave us the news Willie had been killed in a car accident on the 25th two days ago and Heinz had just heard the news. Willie had been on a binge and because he was disqualified from driving, he had a student girl driving him, the girl had had too much to drink, driving at too fast a speed, came to an L bend, went straight on and instead of turning – I knew the bend well - had driven at full speed head-on into an oak tree, Willie died instantly, his neck broken and the girl was taken to hospital she was now in intensive care, in a bad way.

Willie had been a good friend for 14 or 15 years, he was 51

years old, poor chap, he had never got over his wife's death, being married only 6 months before she died of cancer. He had loved her deeply – now they were united, his property and farm, he left to his nephew Ludwig, whom I knew well. For myself, I had my doctor in as I was still feeling fluish and feverish, I told him on this visit to take a blood test, as I suspected brucellosis, he did so, the result came through after two or three days, yes I had brucellosis, no wonder I was feverish and it would not go away. I immediately phoned Maria to tell her to contact the hospital where Heinz was and tell his doctors he had contracted brucellosis from my cattle, she did so, the doctors stopped treating him for malaria and he gradually got better and was able to go home after only a few more days.

Heinz had helped me to calve some cows on his last stay in September, I knew some of the cattle had brucellosis thanks to Dad buying heifers with false papers at Silloth docks.

Willie had been killed on our suckler sale day on 25th October, Heinz phoned me on 29th October from his home to say Willie's funeral was going to be held on Wednesday 31st October at 2 pm in Telgte, I told him I would not be able to go, as I was too ill, but would he purchase the best wreath he could for me, which he did - Albert Greveler, Willie's good friend, from Gasthof Greveler, told me he put a bottle of schnapps in the open coffin at Willie's feet – he knew and I knew, Willie would have liked that.

Then, when I inspected the tic beans that Dad had cut when I was on holiday (this is a late-cutting crop), he had the men put them in plastic sacks, I did not like plastic at all as they sweat. This is what was happening now. The sacks were sweating, and the beans were covered in mold. There were a few tons to sort through. Eventually, these beans had to be put through the combine harvester and then into clean hessian sacks. These were then put on the grain drier until dry, then another batch to dry and so on. This worked my men and I should not have had to do if Dad had put them in hessian sacks to start with. This work took, in between other jobs, 9 days.

On 10th November, I took delivery of a new Land Rover, white, with according to the garage County Motors, all extras, what they were I don't know. The cost was 1607 pounds total on the road, I got 75 pounds for the old one, she was 13 years old and had done 105,500 miles, 80% of this in the fields.

On 24th November, Monique and I went to Newcastle races. The day was windy, but by the time we crossed over the Pennines and reached Newcastle, I started to feel very ill and returned home, When I went to bed Sunday, I was feverish. This is what brucellosis is like – a fever all at once. I started a streaming head cold on 18th December. The next day, it was worse, but on Friday, I was much better and decided to take Lassie 2nd on a little training spell with the gun. I took her, as I had with my great Lassie the first, round a few selected coverts where I knew there to be the odd pheasant or two, sure enough, the first covert, a good big strong cock bird got up far too near, he made a tremendous racket as he rose and off. I gave him a few seconds till he was 40 yards range and downed him stone dead, I glanced quickly at Lassie as the bird was falling, she also was very intent at watching the great lovely bird fall amidst tall, rough grass and reeds. I told her to fetch, but she hesitated, I told her again, "fetch, good girl", this time she set off with vigour, I noticed she went straight to where the pheasant had fallen, no doubt she had "marked" where it fell in her mind, with this I was pleased. I added no other words to her, remaining mute, she had been told to fetch, that was enough, I have seen many good shots with their dogs at shoots, shouting their heads off for the dog to fetch.

Lassie, I could not see her where the pheasant had fallen due to high vegetation until she was halfway back to me, the dead pheasant held proudly in her mouth, her eyes shining with quiet satisfaction as if to say, "Does that please my master", she knew it would. I shot 3 pheasant down and Lassie never put a foot wrong, everything was perfect, little did Lassie and I know that in the near future, she and I would be shooting partridge in the beet fields of the Pas de Calais and pheasant in Provence.

Boxing Day, I took the boys shooting down the farm with Lassie and Sandy, they enjoyed themselves and shot well. The bag was not big, as it was just a walk here and there, but we shot 11 pheasant, 5 hares, 3 duck and one partridge. Little Lassie now thought she was an expert, which she now was, so quickly had she learnt. The hares had her baffled by their sheer weight, but she struggled through it all bravely.

Thursday 27th, Dad came telling me he was going to shoot, would I go with him, I said I would, so off we set. I insisted that he leave Shot his pointer behind, otherwise we would get nothing, he was reluctant but did so. Shot was a beautiful dog and would have won beauty prizes at any show, but once let off in the shooting field, that was the day ruined from the start. Shot did not know the meaning of the words "come back", until 4 or 5 hours later when he was exhausted. In the event, Dad and I shot 10 pheasants, all cock birds and 7 pigeons, he enjoyed his day and was very taken with the puppy Lassie, secretly thinking, I should say, that he wished he had one like her.

Then all of a sudden it was 1974, we celebrated by ourselves, the two boys, Monique and I at home, like Xmas Day, we had hare soup, turkey this day, and plum pudding, for New Years Day, it was nice and quiet, with just my own family, the New Year what surprises was it going to bring.

1st January 1974, the weather now was nothing but rain and hard too. One week later, still the rain just sheeted down, now the rain is still falling in torrents.

Adam, by now and for the last few months, even in Cannes, had been becoming difficult to control, I would set him off with the shepherd to go around the various fields to see all was well, mend the wall gaps, light work in all, but as soon, of late, my back was turned he would leave his work and hitch or walk to Penrith, into the pubs, the lower end of pubs, and with the layabouts and hobos, spend the day drinking with them.

When I came home from moving cows onto dry ground, Monique told me Adam had been swearing at her, he had for some time been against his mother, I phoned my friend Ken Hogg, who had Glendowling Country Club and also was building Chalet's there, just out of Penrith on the Tirril Road, he knew Adam was becoming difficult and had told me to send Adam to him, as he had three or four sons of Adam's age group, and Ken said he himself had a way with young lads in their teens.

Adam's birthday was on 11th January, he was 18 years old, he spent it, so I heard, at Rounthorn Club on Penrith's beacon edge, run by Nora Wilson, a good club, run by a very capable Nora, she kept her eye on Adam, by this I mean a motherly eye, Nora and her husband were long time friends of mine. It was my weekend for work, so I was kept busy, gales were in force.

Monday 14th, still the rains fell, the beck was a raging torrent. Tuesday 15th January, the gales got stronger, so strong half of the saw bench roof was torn off, flying over other roofs into the main courtyard, this had never happened before.

Adam had not settled at Ken Hoggs, in fact, Ken said he could not get through to him at all and asked me to take him home, which I did, for a while, he settled.

My new Land Rover had been consuming petrol at the rate of 8 miles per gall, I had taken it back to County Motors Carlisle to be seen to, and got it back on 13th February, only to discover it was not a bit better, I sent it back again, I took it back a few days later, still it was no better, I had my own petrol pump, but at 8 miles or less to the gall, it was no joke.

On Tuesday, 19th February, Monique and I set off for Germany and the Karnival, leaving Mrs Metcalfe in charge of the house and Adam staying with Kurt and his wife, Joey Junior was at school. We were sailing from Hull. I had already booked a passage by phone, we were somehow late in starting off from home, getting to Hull just in time for the ferry boat, another 20 minutes would have been too late, all cabins had been booked up except some 1st class ones, well we did not fancy sleeping in armchairs, so we took one of the 1st class cabins, very nice they were too. Our little holiday had started, the ambience on the big ferry boat was good, everyone seemed to be in a good mood. We, as usual, took a table near the bar and sampled a few Johnnie Walker Black Labels before it was time for dinner, which again was always good, plus two bottles of red wine, the personnel were English this trip and a good set of chaps they were.

Thursday, 21st, Heinz took us to see Willie's grave in the morning, Monique and I put a dozen roses and laid them on the grave and said a little prayer for poor Willie when we had called on Albert yesterday, Al- bert looked upward to the ceiling and said Willie would be watching us from Heaven, and maybe having a schnapps up there.

Saturday night, we went along to the Kolpinhaus, from what I can gather, it is a working man's centre – in many German towns, there is a Kolpinhaus, we had been here numerous Karnivals and enjoyed our- selves enormously, Heinz had reserved a table for us, I knew many of the people there, and this time I was introduced by the Master of Ceremonies, from the rostrum, as our good friend Joey, is once more with us, and his wife, we welcome them both, many cheers to this. I was then asked to the rostrum to make a short speech, which I did, in German, I was listened to in polite silence and then to hefty cheers when I had finished, we had a tremendous night, Monique getting slightly jealous when, for one game dance, I had a young girl of 16 on my shoulders, quite a good looker too, galloping round the dance floor the girl enjoying herself, too much for Monique's idea, but all was good fun, at 2 am we adjourned to the Shepherds Inn for drinks.

Monday, I had a breather that morning and let rip again in the after- noon, the weather was beautiful, that evening, we all went to a country pub well outside Telgte, run by Bernard Geismann and his wife Hanna or Emma, this place was as if one was stepping back 150 years in time, the Geismann's were aged 60 plus, very kind, never in a hurry either of them, time stood still here, the place was spotlessly clean, the toilette outside about 30 yards away in the corner of an orchard, the speciality of the house was home killed and cured ham, we used to have plenty of this, and found it always delicious, Bernard cutting it very thick, served with homemade wheat bread baked by Hanna, one could make a meal out of what was supposed to be a snack. Both the Geismanns were very tall, well over 6 feet and all muscle, male and female. When shaking hands with Bernard, one's hand was lost in his great mit, but one soon knew it, because he had a grip like a gorilla, almost breaking one's knuckles, he did not realise I think, how strong he was, but he was kindness itself.

Bernard was a big cigar smoker, he liked to sit by my side and talk of everything, from cigars to politics. To light his enormous fire, about 4 feet long x 4 foot deep, Bernard would put a dozen cigar boxes in, a fat depth of twigs, these always caught well, then came his great 5 feet long logs, very dry, in no time at all there was heat. There and in the company of host and hostess, time never mattered.

The days passed quickly, I bought 2,000 cigars from my friend Sepple Poppenborg.

On Sunday, 3rd March we packed our cases and put them in the car. Then, on the garden terrace of Heinz's house, we steadily drank a few bottles of beer, setting off at 11:30 am, we waved goodbye.

Getting to Rotterdam at 5 pm I found the ferry boat full, but I had phoned 2 days ago reserving cabin and car, a good thing I had done so. The crossing to Hull was calm, but it was raining and on the hills was snow, it was very cold and Hull, as usual, was dull and depressing, how anyone could live in such a dismal place was beyond me. The young women on the streets were wearing the thinnest of frocks, cheap I suppose from Marks & Sparks, one could see the cheapness of everything, I felt sad and sorry for these young English women.

We had arrived in Hull at 6:30 am, had breakfast and went off. The snow at Scotch Corner was about 2 inches deep, Monique was driving, a vehicle in front was idly doing 15 miles per hour when Monique decided to pass, she did so at 25 to 30 miles per hour, all of a sudden a Police car stops her, she asked what was the matter, the Policeman told her, "you have passed on a solid white line", I laughed and told him, "a white line in all of this snow, no one can see it", his reply was, "ok but we know where it is", I thought, here we are once again in stupidity land, he handed her a paper, she having to produce her driving licence etc.

35

On our return home, we had a nasty surprise: Adam had broken into Skirwith Hall, punching the front door off its lock and bolt, breaking some wood. He had had 7 or 8 of his yobbo friends in, they or Adam had pulled the claws from the feet of a tiger skin, drunk my best booze, smoked umpteen cigars, splashed the breakfast room walls with tomato sauce out of sardine tins, slept in all the beds except Joey's – (he was home on half term the night before, Mrs Metcalfe had let him in, then when Adam and his friends arrived, locked himself in his room) – not only slept in the beds with dirty boots on but urinated into every bed, including my own, it was a stinking mess. Monique's dresses had all been worn as there had been girls there also, not only that, Monique's hats, some very lovely hats, had been in the bottom of a wardrobe and all had been trampled underfoot, spoiling them all, the whole house was in an awful mess.

Adam did not turn up for three days, and when he did, I gave him a severe dressing down, told him not to do such a thing again and left it at that.

I asked Adam this day, 13th to help Ernie the shepherd, he went a few hundred yards and then came home, I asked him to help Kurt crush corn, he refused, this made me angry, but now he was too big and strong for me to take him in hand, up to now he had only been impudent to his Mother and been quite a good lad at his work, I gave him £5 a week pocket money, he had seemed content, now it was open rudeness and a refusal to do any work.

Saturday 16th, was Bill the tractor man's weekend off; his lots of cattle to feed, I put him in charge of Adam, the tractor-trailer was loaded up with hay – straw – and cereals the night before, ready for Adam on Saturday morning, that morning I had a lie in till 8 am. Kurt came to the house to tell me no one seemed to be taking Adam's tractor and trailer, he said Adam was nowhere to be found, I went outside to find him, but he had just taken off, leaving his tractor and hay, etc., I immediately took the tractor and fodder, to go round and feed certain lots of cattle myself, he, Adam was now testing my patience.

Adam did not want to work on the farm, so Monique and I took him to the Labour Exchange in Penrith. I explained to the manager there, but all he had to offer was forestry, cutting down trees, Adam did not fancy this.

This day Thursday 21st March, Stuart asked if I could lend him 5G to help with the purchase of the old Crown Hotel, now named the Hussar, his father had died and left him £20 odd thousand and he would borrow the rest, I have forgotten exactly how much, Stuart said he would pay 16% interest, as he was a good hotelier I thought alright, I lent him the 5G, he wanted a Hotel on his own, as the Hotel in question had never been really, in the last few years anyway, a popular place, rather run-down, large, it had 60 rooms. I asked him if he felt he was doing the right thing and he assured me he did know and that was that.

March 27th, Adam was not content to live at home. His refusal to help with any of the work, he could not and had no desire to get on with his Mother, only impudence, moved us to get him lodgings at Penrith, in a place called Mill House, Mill Street, Penrith, it was not a posh place by any standards, a poor place, but as Adam insisted on taking up with the riff-raff and baddies of Penrith, this was good enough for him. I paid his lodgings and he took some sort of work in Edenhall Brick Works.

This was Stuart's opening of his own Hotel, the Hussar, originally the Crown Hotel, all of his old customers from the George Hotel were there, including a great number of business people, the evening was a great success, Monique and I had back home at 5 am.

Stan Payne arrived with another 100 Rainbow Trout for my lake, I had not had a lot of time for fishing during the last few months and promised myself a few spare moments for this good sport in the future.

I had a good cow die from what looked like milk fever or

staggers, one of the troubles with the stock had been the atrocious winter of incessant rain day and night, undermining the cattle's health to such a degree that when ill, they lose the desire to live and will themselves to die.

Saturday, 13th, was a nice sunny day, the ewes had almost finished lambing except for a few stragglers, so I put my fishing rods in the Land Rover, Lassie and Sandy, and went down to my little lake, the setting was a paradise, only the pee wits, curlews, the larks singing their heads off, the wood pigeons cooing, moor hens giving their funny cry, I sat down beside the lake for a while, pondering over the past few years, the good and the bad, and thought what a bad lot the Brit Government were, becoming more and more bolshi, redder than the Russians, a bad lot all round, my eldest son a great disappointment, death duties meant that if I was run over by a No.10 bus so to speak, all my estate would go to this bolshi Government. I decided to sell Skirwith Hall and become a tax exile, getting my money out of the country eventually. It would mean pulling my roots up after almost 400 years of my family being in Skirwith Hall, but, after all, I was the only one to have purchased the place.

I remembered fathers very words when he had told me, "We would be far better under a new Landlord", I could not believe why he said a thing like that, that is when I got to work and bought the place - now it was mine to sell, also Dad had or tried continuously to put a spike in my wheels, cementing the courtyard and yards to put a cattle grid in the main entrance and made a good sweep in for the cattle and feed wagons, my planting of trees, all had been ridiculed no end, putting cattle, no doubt on purpose, into my young plantations, so that all were eaten off, refusal to give up the tenancy, even when Quintin Little, my Solicitor (and Lord Lonsdale's Solicitor), had asked him to do so, I remember Quintin telling me, "I cannot get through to him" (Father) "I can make nothing of him".

I caught 7 nice trout, which Monique cooked, two each for

us and one for little Joey, they went well with Walter Pitch's wine, halfway through fishing, I noticed when I had a trout on the line and jumping and fighting on top of the water, Lassie was extremely interested, wanting to be in on the act, when I had my 4th trout. Lassie was again excited and interested in this new game, I told her to fetch, she needed no more than that, with a bound like a kangaroo, she jumped easily 10 yards, swam to where she had seen the trout, looked around to see where it was, just then the trout jumped high out of the water beside her, it landed, flopped about for a second or two and in that time Lassie had the trout in her mouth, she swam to the side, climbed out, came over and laid it at my feet. The trout, of course, started jumping. Lassie thought it probably was going to fly away and grabbed it in a flash. I took it from her, telling her she was a good girl, she shook herself, most of her shower coming on me, then that satisfied look of hers, there was not a tooth mark on the 1 ½ lb fish. After this, I did not bother with the landing net, Lassie took that part on herself, she would thereafter when I was fishing, sit motionless by my side, only her eyes moving, she was a marvel, I think Lassie No.1 looking down from doggy heaven would have approved of her, whom had taken her place.

I went through the remaining ewes to inspect them for empties and found to my dismay 67 empty, in fact, most since Dad had insisted on keeping on ewes that had slipped or aborted lambs, I had got rid of these, and after this we had had no more than in the tens, one year only 9 empties.

Monday, 15th April being Easter time, Monique and I went over to Newcastle races, it was a nice hot day with us, but at Newcastle, it was very cold. I had a good day betting, I had been watching a horse belonging to a farmer near Appleby, Confluence, owned then by John Carrick, I looked the horse over, he looked very fit indeed. Had my bet on him and won £250, we then stayed behind and dined at the Park Hotel with a few friends, getting home reasonably early by 1 am.

Heinz had phoned me several times for Monique and I to

go to his Silver Wedding, I had at first declined as there was too much work to be done, but poor Heinz was so aghast that at my suggestion of the workload, he was almost crawling down the phone, I promised to go, because Adam had been causing trouble in getting into the house, when or if we were racing (he had left his brickworks job) he was continually on the prowl with his riff-raff friends, even Mrs Metcalfe refused to stay and look after the house, saying she was afraid of him. He, Adam, had had a fight with Ernie, and the latter was afraid of him, that is why Monique stayed behind, my heart was not in going, but Heinz was an exceptional friend.

I flew from Manchester airport on Thursday, 16th May for Düsseldorf, my blood brother met me there at 11:30 am, getting to Telgte by 2 pm, Heinz was overjoyed I was with him, we celebrated by drinking in his Shepherds Inn. Alfons Ludkehaus, and wife Nanne were there, as was Charlie (Karl Tische) who once again was on friendly terms with Heinz. Heinz and I finished off an enormous bottle of Asbach Brandy and when we went to bed at 1 am he insisted his blood brother and he sleep in the same bed, which we did, both of us slept the sleep of the dead, we were full to the gills.

The next day opened up to bright sunshine, a veritable marvellous day - myself I felt very groggy indeed, under the weather.

We were together with many guests invited to the ceremony in Church for the religious ceremony and take communion, there for me and a few others standing room only in Church and during the service, I felt myself starting to perspire, sweat started to run into my shoes, I felt as if at any minute I would keel over in a faint. I immediately went outside to the fresh air, with movement and fresh air, I soon recovered, then sat on the Church steps for a few minutes. A late comer, a woman I knew, came along and wished me, Gutten Morgen, she went in and I followed to take communion, then back at the house, I told Heinz I was going to bed for a while, I felt rotten and feeling sick, he was so disappointed, his face showed it, he said, "You can't do that on my Silver Wedding day, but if so, have a glass of champagne with me," I shuddered at the mention of drink. However, I was handed a glass of bubbly, preparing if necessary to make a rush for the toilette, I raised my glass to my brother and toasted him, I took a good swig and down the bubbles and liquid went, and hey presto, within 10 seconds, I had completely recovered, I felt as fit as ever I could be, it was indeed a miracle, it astonished me and delighted Heinz, so now he and I set to with a will. At noon Heinz had invited a select party of friends to lunch at the Althaus, where Erica herself had prepared everything, this lunch and drinks lasted till 3 pm, then back to the house for more champagne, cases and cases of the stuff. At about 4pm Heinz had organised a tea at Brandhof, with all the cream cakes and pasties one could imagine, then at 7:30 pm, a massive dinner was given there for over 100 guests, the Brandhof was on the outskirts of Telgte, a very large place on the crossroads of Telgte and Osnabruk, Heinz and I often had drinks there each year, it was run, most capably by a woman whose husband had run off with a young waitress, the food she had prepared was a six-course meal, superbly prepared and served, drinks came in an endless stream, we danced and danced till 3:30 am.

    The next day, again sunny and hot, Heinz had not finished yet, we were up early and had drinks on his terrace at the rear of the house overlooking his small orchard and fields beyond, then Heinz surprised us by telling us there was lunch ordered at Brandhof, this was for a dozen of us, the lunch was excellent, then someone laughed at me and said, "Joey you've still got your slippers on," I looked down and so I had, I did not care, neither did anyone else. John & Claire Cronin, who came from Chorley Lancs, were with us.

    The next day we adjourned to the Althaus, where we got tanked up rather too much. Heinz and I had now drunk our fill and smoked cigars non-stop for 3 days and 4 nights, it was pleasant going.

John and Claire left for Manchester airport, Heinz and I drove them to Düsseldorf, and surprise, surprise Monique had landed as a surprise, saying she did not like us to be parted, this was nice, so she and I stayed on another week, we drove back and had further celebrations at the Althaus, where Helmut and Erica greeted Monique with great affection, Karl Tische, whom I had nicknamed Charlie Van Gough, gave a buffet dinner party on Thursday 23rd Charlie I will say was an accomplished chappie, he prepared everything himself.

Friday 24th, Monique and I called to say hello to Emile and Mitze, they were overjoyed to see us and hated to see us leave.

On Saturday, another party at Maria's brother Helmut's, I think he was called, for a 1st communion, eats and drinks in their garden, in the hot sunshine was very relaxing with a nice big black cigar between our teeth Heinz and I, we settled with beers under an apple tree, rather than face any more cream cakes the size of footballs, we had enough of them to last us a long time.

Monday 27th May, Heinz took us to Dusseldorf airport, saw us safely in, we said our farewells, always sad between three friends, then Monique and I adjourned to a little bar in departure, we looked at the wall clock, it seemed so late and no take-off announcement, this went on, we had another drink, then a woman in a uniform dashed up to us – we were the only ones in the bar - asking if we were Mr & Mrs Slack, I said we were, she told us the plane had been waiting for us for 15 minutes and told us to run after her, so at a gallop she escorted us on to the tarmac to the plane, we were indeed the very last, as inside a couple of minutes we were taxing along then off, it had been a narrow squeak. We arrived home at 9:30 pm to find the house in an awful mess, Adam had broken in, together with about 10 or 12 others, they had had a wild party. Monique phoned the Police, they came and had a look around, the next day, the Police picked Adam up at Stuart's Hussar Hotel, it seemed the Mill House landlady had put Adam out for sleeping in his bed with his work boots on and taking his riff-raff friends to his room and them spending the night there, also late at night he would go into the kitchen, open a new packet of bread, make some toast, this was alright the landlady told Monique, but he would split the packet and leave it on the table open and in the morning the bread would be bone dry. Monique would not press charges against Adam, the Police gave him a verbal telling off, Monique gave him £10 - told him to find new lodgings and not to come home until he straightened himself up.

My brucellosis fever started again on the 26th until the 28th. Wednesday 3rd Monique and I went to Carlisle races, where I won £70 and lost the lot the day after. On the evening of the 3rd, I invited them to dine at the Hussar Sam Hall, the trainer, I had known Sam for years, he was a very kind bluff Yorkshireman, always jovial, Sam just now had not been too well, he was half the weight he used to be, but he enjoyed this dinner, cracking a lot of jokes, among my guests were also Guy Reed, whom years ago I saved from bankruptcy, in the chicken world, now he owned Nidd Hall Stud near Harrowgate, and Sam trained his horses. Guy, with his R-R Chaffeur-driven car, was also a charming, likable chap. The other chap I invited was Tug Wilson, also a most charming man, we dined very well, good food presented by Stuart, and good wine, the main dish was sea trout.

Monique and I, two weeks ago, had gone to see my horse Eastern Dove gallop at Ken Payne's Middleham stables. He, Ken, had told us to be there at or before 6 am a couple of weeks ago to watch her gallop, we set off and arrived at his house by 5:30 am. I knocked at the front door, no reply, I looked around, all was very untidy, I looked or tried to look through the window facing the lawn, they were so dirty it was impossible to see through, I rubbed them with my hand to make a clear patch to see through, but the dirt was on the inside, I thought we were at the wrong house, it seemed so abandoned. I went back to Monique in the car and told her I could not raise anyone, I could see some stables nearby, so I walked over to them, there was a young chap working there, but no one else, I asked him where Ken Payne lived, he pointed to the house I had come from, "There" he said, I told him I had knocked a few times and had no answer, "Oh" he said, "They will not be up yet." I told him I had come to see my filly do a gallop, he asked what its name was, I told him, he then showed me to her box. In I went and stood in amazement, the filly's nose, both nostrils, were smothered in thick yellow mucus, there was no doubt, she had the father and mother of a severe cold or flu and had been like this for either a few days or a few weeks. I told the stable lad this filly is not capable of work and has not been capable for a while, but he did not seem to know anything about anything.

I returned to the house, got round to the back door and knocked hard, I heard noises on the other side, the door opened, there stood a chap in his underpants and as I told him I wanted Ken Payne, my glance took in the scene, this was the kitchen, and lying on the floor were 4 or 5 sleeping men on mattresses, later Ken Payne himself came into the kitchen, half asleep, he had forgotten we were coming, and apologized, I told him I had been to see my filly and that she was not fit to work, he feigned surprise, that she had a cold, - my impression was that he had not seen my filly or for the matter any of the others for days, he said he had been in London, it came out later that he spent more time in London than with his horses.

At 3 pm, we left for home, I told Ken that it looked to me as if my filly would not be at work for quite a time, I would take her home, I told him it was a good idea, she was dropped off later on, it was then I was told by one of the lads, this one, meaning mine, had been like this, (flu or cold) for two months.

On the 18th, I had John Frith and Joey Junior digging me a small duck pond in a soggy piece of ground near the beck and below spring field wood, duck used to frequent this place, I thought it would make a good flight pond, 400 yards distant from my lake, cage wheels were fitted and the McConnell digger mounted on the 135 Ferguson tractor, and the two youngsters set to work, I wanted the pond no more than 2 feet deep, and sloping sides, 20 yards across in a circular form, dug round an elder tree as an island feature, it would fill by natural seeping in from the bottom and sides. Two days later, they had it finished, the boys had indeed made a good job of it.

Adam, he had kept breaking into Skirwith Hall for food by the look of things, for the bread used to disappear, also quite a few tins of sardines, and to eat the latter with, take the table forks each time he entered, then when he would finish eating throw the tin down and the fork with it, we lost quite a few forks this way.

I put locks on all the downstairs windows, but Adam was so strong he could bend these with lifting and forcing the window's frame outside, also he could enter by the cellar, there was a window, one of the iron bars was broken, Adam had found this loophole, I put a bolt on the cellar door leading up the cellar stairs to the top, I opened this door one night and there he was sitting on the steps, nowhere to go, I took him in, telling him if he had mended his ways he could stay, he stayed for a week, needled his Mother constantly, would not work one bit. Monique bought him a leather shirt, the kind of jacket style he had always wanted, it cost about £18 – he would stay away for days and nights, he kept company with the lowest type of lads in Penrith until once again I told him not to return to Skirwith Hall.

Adam then turns up once more, this time with a black eye, he had been in a fight but would not elaborate.

On 10th August, we had an unwelcome visitor in the person of Rene Agulo, Monique's cousin, the one who was a she-devil. I had asked Gabby, Rene's husband only, to come to the grouse shoot, but he had brought his wife. Unfortunately, now she was here, I suppose we had to put up with a bad job.

Guests invited to the shoot were Sandy Taylor and wife Liz (2), John Cummins (1), Robert Jackson (1), Gabby (1), Seamus O'Connell (1), Derek Straker (1), and myself (1), 8 in total on the moor, but only 7 shooters, Liz was going to be a beater,

Rene, dining with the shooters at night.

When all arrived, some stayed with us at Skirwith Hall, the others were in the Kings Arms Temple Sowerby. I had arranged a dinner at Stuart's Hussar Hotel, the entree was melon with port, followed by a 1 ½ to 2lb sea trout for each person, but in the cooking of the trout, Stuart had made a mess of these beautiful fish, on removing the skin, the flesh was found to be so dry one could hardly masticate them, I believe Stuart had cooked them by immersing them in boiling oil beforehand then re-cooking them later when needed, of this I'm not sure, but that is what I believe, once again the dinner plates were so small the trout heads as were their tails lying on the tablecloth at either side of the plate, absolutely beautiful fish ruined, after a few chewy forkfuls, I left mine as did the rest of the party, I was most disappointed and told Stuart so, he gave some lame excuse, he also had taken Adam in to help as a waiter, otherwise I might have said more.

The 12th was anything but a good shoot, bagging only 18 birds (9 braces). A very strong wind had gotten up, a terrific downpour of rain early into the shoot; though this passed, also there were a great many cheaper, very young, late hatched birds, just learning to fly, of course, were not shot. That night, we, the shooters, etc, dined at the Kings Arms Temple Sowerby and by contrast to Stuart's, a superb meal was had.

By now, I had sold the little farmhouse and a few buildings, the little house where I first saw the light of day on 2nd June 1927. Dad one day said, "I have found you a buyer for Kirkland", (the little house).

I said, "Oh yes!" He was over the moon, I asked how much for, he said £1,000, I looked at him in amazement and could not stop myself from saying, "I could spend that amount in a weekend," he, Dad, looked at me and walked away, now six months later, through Colin Strang-Steele of Knight, Frank & Rutley, it was sold for £15,000, when I told Dad, he just walked away.

Now, on August 23rd, a firm of landscape gardeners from

Ambleside Hayes Bros started to landscape the lawns at Skirwith Hall and incorporate the beck, this made into bays and islands, with post bridges over to them, making the old kitchen garden into lawn and car park, rose beds, etc., the price quoted was in the region of £12,000, but Hayes did not stick to this always quibbling, about one thing or another, the bridges over to the islands, instead of being nicely arched as in the quote turned out to be flat, in any case, the sale of the house at Kirkland paid for these works and also central heating. I had nothing left over, but if Father had his say, the house would have gone for £1,000, like the sale of Mother's two houses, one for £500, the other at £1,000, to his tarty woman friend be- hind Mother's back. I was content at the sale and content at the garden works.

Saturday 24th August, we went to Newcastle races, taking Gabby and Rene with us, the day was quite enjoyable, at night we dined at the Park Hotel, in our company at our table there was Robin Terry of the chocolate firm Terry's of York, a long time friend and a charming man, we both enjoyed his company always, poor Robin he had not much longer to be with us, a few months later he was knocked down by a car as he was coming out of Terry's shop in York and died, others at the table were John Cummings and wife and Sandy Taylor and wife. After dinner, we danced on and on, as Monique danced with Robin, Rene was getting very jealous, as when she heard the family history of Robin and the chocolate firm, she thought as usual of money – she wanted to dance with him, - in passing our table Monique and Robin dancing made a remark in French, at Rene's expense, of how bad-tempered she looked, this put the cat among the pigeons, Rene heard this, and immediately her temper, as usual, got the better of her, ordered Gabby from the table, she, she said was staying here not a minute more. Rene had always been jeal- ous of Monique, from Monique's childhood, then Monique, until she left on that bus trip overseas, when she and I met, she had one pair of shoes and one dress, Rene always telling her mother,

Mr Pineda; not to buy her, Monique, anything – now she saw Monique's lifestyle - beautiful, the belle of the ball so to speak, wearing far superior clothes than herself and whatever Monique dressed in, she wore it well, tall, elegant, with a walk like a model - now Rene's jealousy was coming out in force, she could not contain herself and burst forth like the spoilt brat she was, this said in real fury, as everyone else including Gabby was enjoying the evening, I told her to sit down and be quiet, no one was going anywhere until I said so, I had the car I told her, I also told her, that whenever peo- ple are enjoying themselves, you have to spoil it for them, with that she stormed out into the hotel lounge. Gabby, henpecked, after her – I let them go. Monique and I carried on for another hour until Gabby pleaded with me to go home, and him frightened to death of his wife, I relented.

In the morning, I saw the men in to work at 7 am and was back in the house by 7:30 am, Monique called me to one side and told me Rene was packed and was leaving there and then unless I apologized to her for the previous evening, insulting her, as I had not insulted her, but told her the truth about her behaviour, I felt I had no apology to make, I told Monique this, well she said they are leaving – I said, let them. Gabby came down and explained and tried getting around me to apologise, poor soft man or should it be a mouse? I told Gabby what I had told Monique, Gabby was most unhappy; however, within 10 minutes, Rene, the she-devil, came down the stairs Gabby behind with their suitcases into their car and left, I told Monique good riddance to her, that's the last time I ask Gabby.

In the meantime, little Joey had bought himself a car, a Hillman, an old one at that, for £12, he was going to learn to drive on the farm, he said.

On 18th September, Monique had to appear in court at Barnard Castle. This was for crossing a white line, which was covered in snow at the time – while passing another vehicle. She was fined 15 pounds and costs 3 pounds. John Marsham defended her, then we went off to celebrate at the A66 motel, which was only a few short miles away.

That same late afternoon, I discovered some cheques missing from my cheque book, torn out together with the counterfoil piece, I set off to hunt Adam up in Penrith and confront him. I eventually found him in the Grey Goat pub, I asked what he thought he was doing, stealing my cheques, he had no excuse; he just hung his head. I noticed his shoes were worn out, but rather than give him money for some, I told him to meet me the next day at a certain time by the guest shoe shop. He was there waiting. I took him in and bought him a strong pair of good brogues. He did not want to come home, so I left him.

I went down to the bank to see about the cheques Adam had stolen and cashed – he had stolen and cashed six cheques to the value of 117 pounds. I thought what a rotten thing for him to have done to his father. I had given him a good upbringing and spent a fortune on schooling, all for nothing. A most ungrateful boy, our first son and heir.

On Thursday, 3rd October, I took Adam to the Labour Exchange to get him fixed up with a job. Unfortunately, a suitable job for him had just been filled, they had nothing else. The next day, the Labour Exchange phoned Barrets the house builders needed someone. Adam said he'll take it, he goes to work for Barrets on Monday the 7th, yet he won't work for his father, much easier work, too.

For new lodgings for Adam, Monique and I hunted for something better than his last place, Mill House. Adam seemed incapable of looking for somewhere to lodge. He only looked for pubs; however, Monique and I found very nice digs for him in Portland Place, run by Mrs Rickerby, a very nice elderly lady and spotlessly clean. I paid a few week's rent for him, then he would have to pay himself out of his wages. On Monday 7th, Adam started to work as a builder's labourer.

On Thursday 24th October, was the annual suckler sale at Penrith. We were 5000 pounds down on last year for the same amount of cattle, more or less. There was a panic slump for no reason, I wanted to take the lot home again. Father said no, he wished differently because, within 4 months, prices were soaring. On Saturday 26th October, the police paid me a visit. They were hunting Adam and another friend of his called Watson, it seems they had broken into Dad's house at Kirkland and stolen 29 pounds from Dad's wife and she was pressing charges, the police caught up with them both in Penrith, where they spent the night in the cells. He now had no work; his landlady had put him out for misbehaving, so Monique and I took him back under our wing again.

Monday night of 4th November, in the middle of the night, Adam stole the Land Rover, and it had a full tank of petrol. The Land Rover was returned sometime the next day, empty of petrol, by Adam, he had parked it and run away. Fortunately, no damage had been done. The next night, Adam stole the Volvo when we were in bed, he was getting the keys from my trousers, which I took off before bedtime in the bathroom, where I hung them in the cylinder cupboard to keep warm, I gave him a good talking to and thereafter kept the keys on my person, or on my bedside table.

To cap it all, he had not listened to me one iota. On Saturday, 9th November, he stole Joey's old Hillman car together with his friend Wat- son, also three more of my cheques, of which he cashed two, Sunday 10th the police came for him at 9:30 am and took him away. 'What a silly boy' I marked in my diary. I went down to the police station in Hunter Lane and asked for news of Adam. He was still locked up, they were sending him to a detention centre in Durham until he had to appear in court next week on Tuesday. At this court held in Penrith, Adam was charged with 15 offences of breaking and entering, including Father's wife's charge of 29 pounds, and stealing Joey's car, though neither we or Joey pressed charges, poor Adam was sentenced to 3 months in a detention centre at Durham, Monique and I were very sad at this turn of events, but at the same time thought and hoped Adam would have learnt his lesson, unfortunately, future events proved us wrong. Adam did not learn but got worse.

The next day, 20th November, a Wednesday, Monique and I motored down to Hull and took the ferry boat to Rotterdam – enroute to Telgte. Getting to Heinz's at 5 pm, once there, we adjourned to the Shepherd's Inn with Heinz and Maria. Music was played, cigars lit, Heinz had 6 crates of beer in stock. We were nicely settled.

Monique and I went to the Bahnhof pub in mid-afternoon to take a drink with Theo, our host. On opening the pub door, we were unable to see for a while, the room was one big smoke screen of cigar and cigarette smoke, the place was so full, about 40 men and women, of whom I knew a few, they had all been to a funeral of one of their buddies, now they were drinking the dead man's health. By now, our eyes had become accustomed to the smoke screen and we were able to take stock of the people. There were about 35, almost all smoking. I have never seen a room so thick with tobacco smoke one could almost cut it. We were made most welcome, and after perhaps half an hour, Theo got his accordion out and started playing. Within minutes, everyone was dancing, we stayed there until 6 pm, at which time Heinz would be home, then off we went. We had an agreeable 3 hours of fun.

Another thing stuck at the back of my memory was the occasion one night, a knock on the door, a customer had come to pay his bill. Maria answered and took the man into Heinz's house office, the bill was settled in cash for DM 2000, of which Maria next day seemingly put this sum into her own account in her maiden name of Gehr. Heinz, on hearing this, went berserk, telling her in most strong terms the money should have gone direct into the firm's account, later on, I was to learn the meaning of this.

We docked early morning on Friday, 6th December. By now, I was all right and had a hearty breakfast, then set off home, passing customs quickly, we arrived at Temple Sowerby and had lunch there at the Kings Arms.

On talking to the cowman, he told me that 4 cows had

aborted, one of them being from this season's first crop of heifers, this I realised was the beginning of more bad news of this type.

The 10th of December remained very cold, with hail showers all day. This was a good day to duck shoot, so with Lassie II, I set off down the beck, Lassie did not seem to mind the hail as long as she saw I had the gun, she was satisfied she would enjoy herself. Before long, beyond the first quarry, this quarry rock had been used to build Skirwith Hall and outbuildings, 4 Mallard got up at a corner dub, I fired twice and two dropped, one on land, the other in the beck. Fortunately, both stone dead. Lassie had them at my feet in no time, wagging her tail and that proud look as if to say, 'aren't I a good retriever'.

However, on we went down the beck getting two more before reaching the water quarry, where 95% of the time, I was guaranteed duck. Lassie and I approached silently, myself bent double to avoid being seen too soon by any duck that might be there, now I was near enough, I straightened up, all at once the air was full of duck and beating wings. There were or must have been 50 ducks in an area 8 yards by 10 yards, I quickly tried to focus on one fired. The duck dropped, so did 5 others, they were so tightly packed when rising, I fired again, dropping two more, only 3 ducks were dead, and fortunately, the wounded had fallen back into the water quarry.

Lassie had her work cut out to retrieve the 5 wounded ducks, which she did after half an hour of hard work. I could have helped her and shot them dead, but I thought this experience would do her a world of good, in any case, it was a pleasure watching her work, if these ducks had fallen in the back, she may have found two, the other three escape in the midst of tree roots and holes etc. I now had eleven ducks, too heavy to carry on my back and continue, so I hid them from the carrion crows behind a fallen tree trunk, covered them over with reeds, then Lassie and

I went on our way, by the time I got to the boundary of

Beck Mill, I had another 5. I then walked over Beck Mill field to the little fresh water syke, which had an abundance of excellent water cress – Alf Britton used to sell this from his stall in Penrith market - approached the syke, which lay in a hollow, again bent double. Lassie at my heels, full of expectations, I straightened up, there were about 10 or 12 ducks, just in range, they launched up and I fired twice, downing only one.

I now had 17 ducks, a very good days sport. By now, I thought to fly the wood pigeon in, by Spring Field Wood. I had a little while to wait before the flight began, perhaps ¾ of an hour, the weather was still bad and very cold, though with walking and carrying the game bag, I had kept warmish. Lassie must have felt cold, though she never showed it, however, in Spring Field Wood to while away the time, we took shelter in a lambing hut which was dry and sheltered from the tempest - a great flighting evening, I thought – I lit a black German cigar, sat down on an old bucket and enjoyed my smoke, time passed quickly, I stationed my- self behind the stone wall of saw steps, facing the beck, the tempest at our backs. The pigeon flew into the teeth of the almost now blizzard. Now, we both felt the cold. Lassie's teeth began to chatter, she also shivering. I put her in front of me, covering her a bit, however, when the 1st pigeons started to arrive, she soon forgot how cold she was. The pigeon were kept low by the storm, and there were plenty of them. Lassie retrieving on both sides of the wall kept her warm, there was no need to hide from the pigeon, they kept coming regardless. I shot 15 with 16 shots, then had no more cartridges left. I could not get the birds in my Game bag so I left the lot in the lambing hut until morning, when I would come with the Land Rover for these birds and the duck at the water quarry.

On reaching home, by now dark, I rubbed Lassie as dry as possible, put her to bed with a good supper and went into the nice big log and coal fire Monique had built up. Got my boots off, a clean pair of trousers, sat down beside this great comforter of cold feet and tired bodies, with a large whisky and water and a good Cuban cigar before dinner while outside the tempest continued. What a pleasure to come into a warm welcome and a beautiful wife after tramping in a blizzard most of the day.

Monday 16th December was our 20th wedding anniversary. We both dined by ourselves at the Kings Arms, Temple Sowerby and as usual, Brenda's food was excellent, we were still in love as on our 1st wedding day and Monique was more beautiful than ever, turning heads wherever she went. On this day, I had all cows inoculated with the vaccine 45/20 to halt or try to halt the abortion in the herd.

36

Thursday 19th the central heater boiler was all sooted up, I asked the chappie who installed it all what was wrong, he told me the fault, he thought lay in the height of the chimney. The two young builders of this chimney had not gone quite high enough, thus, instead of a sucking, there was a downdraft. I had one good long drainpipe of 3 feet long and about 9 inches width of the interior hole, I put Kurt and Bill the tractor man, to build this into and on top of the heating chimney, they had it done in no time, and ever after that, the boiler ran perfectly. The heating system had taken ages to install, roughly six months, due to various industrial strikes. The heaters were from Sweden, but once the system was going, the whole of Skirwith Hall was warm within 30 minutes, possibly due to the very thick, warm sandstone walls. It was indeed a pleasure to come into in the cold winter day. Monique no longer had her hands as white as snow, wearing gloves and a warm overcoat to do her housework.

While this was going on, I decided to shoot a nice hare, ready for hare soup for Christmas day lunch. I took Lassie and went to one of the outlying fields near Ousby called Hungary, where I was almost guaranteed one.

All at once, a lovely big hare bounced out of his seat in a tuft of reeds, he was a beauty, as the gun was coming to my shoulder, I admired him, I fired and he somersaulted, stone dead. Lassie brought him back gently, she always seemed to carry these big hares very gently indeed, as if to salute a noble animal, which I think hares are.

We walked on, I had now changed my cartridges from No 4 to No 6 shot, I did not want another hare; I knew there would be snipe here, and there was, I shot 5, two being left and right. Lassie must have thought it a big change from a heavy big hare to something that she could easily swallow with one bite. Two more hares got up, I watched them lope away with great elegance. Lassie's eyes not believing this was happening, I laughed at her, which seemed to settle her mind that I had not gone bonkers.

Christmas Day came, the day itself was a pleasant day, not cold nor rain. Monique made an excellent lunch, starting, of course, with hare soup and goose.

On February 5th, Monique and I drove down to Hull and took the ferry boat to Rotterdam. We were en route for Telgte and the Karnival. Once on board, we relaxed after our month of rain, arriving at Milterweg 5 Heinz's house at 4 pm. My blood brother was there to greet us, it was good to see him again. Once our baggage was installed into the Shepherd's Inn, we went to celebrate. Later on, off we went to the 'Wild Man' to greet Joseph, the owner, whom resembled a high priest in manner, then on 40 yards to see our good friend Albert Greveler.

Alfons Ludkehouse had a bad attack of flu and was confined to bed, so we ended our first day in Telgte, the weather was kind, mild but dry, thank goodness.

The 8th Saturday was the day of the cavalcade of lorries and trailers with their entourage on top in various costumes, throwing handfuls of sweets over the crowd, the Karnival Prince in all his splendour, attended by beautiful girls showing plenty of bosom and legs.

Off we went to Munster by train for a tour of our favourite pubs and hotels, returning by taxi to Telgte, Heinz had arranged for a table at the Kolping House for Saturday night dancing and drinking, here we had a great time. Alfons turned up for this, from his sick bed, and danced with gusto, until I spotted that his suit, shirt and himself – face and head were soaking wet, he was absolutely drenched in sweat, I felt him and discovered he was almost on fire. He was so hot, I persuaded him to go home before he had an attack of something, he realised what I was saying and reluctantly he left, I've never seen before or after anyone so drenched in sweat and hot in all my life, however Alfons was in good health and spirits next day and thereafter accompanied us on our

Karnival pub crawls each day.

On Monday, Alfons and wife Nanne gave a dinner of chicken, one each and done on the spit. Alfons always did a great job of these chickens, we spent an enjoyable night with them, 8 of us all told, dancing, talking, drinking – calling it a day at 4 am.

Friday dawned, we were up at 6 am for breakfast. Heinz was a lot better and was also up. In fact, he was so fit he called Maria a drunken pig, when Heinz was like this, Maria dared not utter a word. After breakfast, Monique and I left with Heinz, he wanted to inspect a building his men had just finished installing electricity to in Munster.

On Saturday, 15th we packed our bags, took them downstairs, had breakfast, then Alfons, Nanne and Charlie came to say goodbye. Heinz took us all into the Shepherd's Inn, where we partied on Pilsner beer and Sekt until 12:30 pm, then we set off for Rotterdam via Arnem, passing over the bridge where a fierce battle was fought in the war, getting to Rotterdam ferry boat at 5 pm. Then, on board, straight to the bar for a refresher, then a good meal, a couple of drinks – then bed for a well-earned rest.

We were home at 12 noon Sunday, having enjoyed our Karnival holiday and ferry boat immensely. Now, back to work on the farm. Then we had three heavy nights of rain, making everywhere soft again, making it impossible to sow the cereals.

37

This week another cow aborted, I cursed the foolishness of father who had introduced this current disease by stupidly bringing, in a peak of temper, the bulling heifers from Silloth docks, just because I had not asked him to go to Dublin with me – now the whole herd of beautiful cows was slowly, so far, reaping the dreadful results.

Thursday, Monique and I went to town, myself, to see what the price of beef cattle were in the market. On our arrival back home, we found the front door had been kicked in, smashing the lock and the bolt inside. Quite a force must have been used, we were told by the staff, it was the work of Adam, he was again causing trouble all around.

Later, I discovered Adam had stolen some cheques from one of my chequebooks and stolen a cheque valued at 120 pounds, which was the price I had got for my mare, Eastern Honey, from a farmer, a racegoer near Penrith, Bobby Elliot. Adam had found this cheque and picked it up - I was very fed up with the behaviour of our eldest; he did nothing but create trouble for everyone, I phoned the C.I.D. in Penrith. They soon had him under lock and key. Now I discovered he had also stolen my Barclay card. The detective on the case was Neil Bruce and a colleague named Keith, they came to see me on the evening of 22nd March and stayed until 1:30 am sampling my whisky and cigars, which they seemed to enjoy.

This was a sad weekend to once again see our first born deliberately getting himself into trouble. He spent his time with others of his age, some who had been to Borstal and others who would no doubt end up there. He would not listen to me or his mother and had become most un- trustworthy. We did not want him in the house.

On Sunday 30th, March, almost 2 inches of snow fell and 18 ewes lambed, all twins, except little Joey's own ewe, Girty Gimmer, she had a very big single lamb.

This was Easter weekend, and as I was in the lambing field

or at Kirkland. I left word with Kurt for the tractor man, Bill Allen, to put two trailer loads of turnips into 3 fields for the ewes and lambs there. This was not done, he seemed to have refused. As it was Easter Monday, though, this would mean him getting double pay or more.

On April 1st, Monique and I took Joey Junior to Hull to catch the ferry boat for Rotterdam, he was going to visit Heinz.

After two weeks, I was up at 4:30 am and set off at 5 am to drive to Hull to pick Joey Junior up from the ferry boat. He had enjoyed himself staying with Heinz. He had made good friends with the children there, especially with Ulli, Heinz's third child, more or less the same age as Joey.

The next day, I was moving lambs to various fields but found myself get- ting very tired. This was Friday 18th. On Saturday, I seemed to be aching all over, my back was so bad I was hardly able to sleep that night. I stayed inside all day on a Sunday – now the symptoms seemed like Brucellosis. On Monday 21st, my back was so bad I stayed in bed for the day, Kurt came to tell me later that 3 more cows had aborted and the day was heavy rain. Wednesday, I was still in bed, the symptoms were now very fluish.

On Saturday 26th, I was feeling better after being in bed for 7 days. It had been a bad flu or Brucellosis for me, and feeling rather waffy, went downstairs. The day was warm and sunny. I found I had lost 7lbs in weight.

On 30th April, Adam was sentenced to one year in Borstal at Carlisle Crown Court, neither Monique nor myself attended, we were both very unhappy. Monique was shedding tears but Adam had been asking for this for a long time, he seemed bent on self-destruction, he was sent to a place near Wetherby.

On 6th May, Tuesday, Monique and I went to Powfoot, the other side of Annan, to buy some salmon and sea trout from the netting men. I got 3 nice salmon at 1 pound 4/- per lb and 6 beautiful sea trout at 1 pound 2/- per lb, total I paid was 55 pounds 4/-. The taste of these freshly caught fish was absolutely superb, especially the sea trout, so delicate. The wine from the Moselle of Walter Pitch went well with them, we had one of the sea trout for dinner that same night and froze the rest immediately, first painting water on them (both sides), wrapping them in grease-proof paper, then in cellophane bags, leaving the insides in them, as I also did with all my game birds.

My 3 lady tree planters were busy planting Douglas fir seedlings in the Beck Mill bottom and underplanting big Mill wood. This one was 400 yards long and 40 yards wide.

38

On May 15th, Monique and I were up at 4 am and drove down to Hull to pick Maria, Alfons and Charlie up, they were coming for a holiday, they disembarked at 8 am. The day was sunny and hot, we had coffee at the A66 Motel on the way home. Monique had prepared a cold lunch of pheasant and home-killed lamb, which we sat down to eat at 2 pm. They had brought with them a quantity of bottles and pre- sents including a painting Charlie had done of a woman and signed by all my friends in Telgte, not the best of paintings, but an extremely kind thought of all concerned. Heinz had to stay behind to attend to his work.

At this moment in time, the weather decided to be at its best behaviour. Each day, the sun shone, the skies were blue, and the full blast of summer descended upon us.

The next day, Friday 16th after showing my two male guests some of the farm, we dined at night at Stuart's. He excelled himself this time for me. The first course was Dover Sole, then lamb to follow, one of my own lambs, then the choice of two of Stuart's desserts, wine was Volnay. I paid the bill, which was 40 pounds. I thought it rather a lot.

I had prepared my bar in what used to be Mother's drawing room with plenty of whisky, gin and brandy, together with a keg of beer that pushed the beer out with a foot pump, Charlie enjoyed himself with this as he took a liking for our beer, in the afternoon of the 15th. I took them down to my lake to fish, the weather was hot and sunny, we fished for a while, and we managed to catch a trout each, which excited my guests because the trout size were very big, at 3 ½ lbs each, we had them for dinner, Monique preparing them style papyot, with some of Walter Pitch's wine, strange, neither of my guests smoked, so my cigars were left to me.

We did not bother to have big lunches, just some good sandwiches, but at night, we had excellent dinners. The Germans liked game, and I had plenty of that in the freezer, the French windows were open all day, from the bar onto the garden, the weather was so perfect we spent a lot of time in the garden, having drinks there or on one of the islands below the house in the beck.

Alfons persuaded us not to visit Stuart, as he - Alfons - had taken a dislike to him, and to boot, Alfons did not care for the Hussar, as it was, he said, filthy. In this, of course, he was dead right.

Thursday 22nd, we all repaired to the Royal Oak at Appleby for lunch, this time, Charlie paid. It was an excellent lunch served to us by Happy, his brother Grumpy George, who was not a keen man on Germans, but all went well. We were there for 5 hours and as we left. Grumpy wrung the hands of my guests as if they had been lifelong friends.

On the 23rd, it was very hot, we all had just 2 hours of sleep, then up for breakfast, then champagne in the garden until noon, an early lunch, then all into the Volvo and off to Hull to catch the ferry boat to Rotterdam, my guests were leaving to return to Telgte. On the way over the Yorkshire moors to Scotch Corner, my eyes would hardly keep open, I was rather tired, it must have been the champagne, so Alfons kindly offered to drive from Scotch Corner. We saw them off onto the boat at 6 pm, then home, calling nowhere.

On May 29th, Monique and I got ourselves dressed and set off for Sands Hall, Sedgefield, the home of John Cummings and his wife, the renowned Valerie, John was giving a party. When we arrived at 7 pm, quite a few cars were already in the parking ground in front of Sands Hall, we were warmly greeted by John and I will say, also by Valerie. The drinks on entry were Buck Fizz or straight champagne, this was drunk the whole night, before long, the place was crowded. Approximately 120 guests arrived, we knew almost all of them, at one stage in the early hours, Ken Straughan and Sandy Taylor were on the point of throwing their empty glasses at the very expensive paper on the walls of the living room, John had gone to a lot of expense decorating his house throughout, however, Valerie's entry soon made them think otherwise.

We finished the party at noon on the 30th. We thanked our host and hostess and made our way home. Cathie, my sister, phoned to say she and Robert MacGeorge had got married that day, 3rd June, it was about time, I thought, now at least she had security.

Saturday 7th, Stuart paid me 500 pounds off the loan and 336 pounds interest @ 15% on the money I had loaned him on his hotel, this was encouraging.

Now the weather had turned to real summer, in the afternoon, Monique made a nice picnic and we went down to the little lake where we sunbathed, away from the hustle and bustle of the last weekend. We listened to only the birds singing, the pigeons coo-cuck-cooing, the curlews and their special tunes, my word, it was perfect bliss to be quiet.

On Sunday the 15th, I took delivery of a 200-day-old pheasant from Jim Peet @33 pounds per 100. I put these under gas heaters in the old hatchery, the same day I took delivery of a handmade split cane fishing rod, the second I had bought from the maker Cecil Beaty from Blackpool or Morecombe, the first I had given to Adam, two years ago, these fly rods were beautifully made by Cecil as a hobby, and very cheap at 13 pounds each, I am afraid Adam sold his for two or three pounds for beer money if I had known, I would have bought it from him.

The next day, I cut the lawns, we now had quite an expanse of lawns, reaching down to the beck and the little islands, in the evening, it was a grand sight to see my reared wild ducks flighting in at 40 or 50 at a time into the pools at the garden bottom, as if they knew where they had been reared. Of course, they had been reared in one of the lofts at the farm, but somehow, I believe they knew their rearing place, it was a lovely sight to sit out on the lawn on a warm summer evening.

On Thursday 26th, I sold my oldest Hereford Bull in the store market at Penrith. He had almost lost interest in the opposite sex, he had had so much sex over the years he had

had enough. Almost like having too much strawberries and cream, one would gradually get fed up with them, he had been a grand fellow over the years and was very quiet, so much so that when moving cattle – cows and him – to Kirkland, Kurt would ride on his back for most of the way. He was bid for 190 pounds sold to Frank Jackson.

That week, I started with a sore throat, the prelude of worse things to come.

On the 15th, Tuesday, Joey Jnr came home for his summer holidays, bringing back his 8 wild young stoats, he had found these 8 baby stoats with their eyes shut under an old poultry fold unit, collected them up, put them in a box with plenty of cotton wool, they were practically bare of hair, and let them suck bread soaked in milk and to suck soft bloody minced meat he reared the lot, they grew very fast, he eventually kept them in a good solid hen house 8x6 with a bale of hay and a sack or two hanging over the bale, where they could hide and make a nest. They knew Joey very well, they would play with him, their agility was amazing. They would take his fingers or hand in their wide open mouths, full of sharp needle teeth, but never biting Joey at all. I went into the stoat 'house' with him one day to see them perform their tricks with me however they scarpered like little rockets into their nest behind the hay bale, before long, curiosity got the better of them, little heads would suddenly peer round the edge of the bale, Joey moved over the other side of the hen house, the sharp little beggars would run all over him, frolicking, jumping, pretending to bite him, but of course only mouthing his hands, I kept absolutely still not moving a finger - all eight of the youngsters would be round Joey or on his knees, and when I did move one of my feet, as one and like lightening, almost quicker than the eye, the stoats would vanish behind the bale of hay into their nests, it was quite incredible to watch them and their understanding of Joey. No doubt they thought Joey was their mother.

I had a young man come to do some work, I put him to hand weeding the growing turnips, he came from Blencarn and was about 6ft 4inches, a poorly dressed and clad young chap but of a very kind nature, he was the grandson of Dad's old foreman, Arthur Durham, who had died while working for Dad. As readers will have read, Arthur was a gem of a man, this newcomer was David Thompson, Arthur's daughter Hazel was his mother. His father, I believe, was a merchant seaman and never at home.

David was a good worker, I had him for about a week or ten days, at 4 pounds per day, the weather was wet, but David worked quietly, he received 32 pounds in all. One of his friends, Les Wilkinson, whose father had also worked at Skirwith Hall, got 26 pounds for 6 ½ days, poor Les was run over and killed while walking home one night, only 50 yards from his house, by one of Bert Johnstone's workers.

My throat was still not so good, and I felt like flu. I had Dr Aniscow call on 1st August. He gave me some tablets and took a blood sample – this day, the weather seemed to take up because it was a lovely hot day.

On August 12th was the opening of the grouse shoot, my party, this time, included Joey Junior, Sandy Taylor, Seamus O'Connel, John Cummings, Ken Stamper (later my Brutus) and myself, plus Sandy's wife Sarah, who was beating.

The day was incredibly hot and very sultry indeed. On arrival at starting point Cash Wells, we started on Monique's food, once more, she had made Beef en Crout, a leg of home-killed suckled lamb, and six chickens, with all the spices etc. There was a case of Volnay, 4 bottles of champagne, and a bottle of Crofts port, 2 dozen tins of beer, after this satisfying repast, I lined the guns and beaters up and off we set, I took notice of Sarah, she had brought a very bright yellow plastic jacket as some black clouds had appeared, I thought to myself, this jacket is going to scare the grouse, I was right. Many birds got up much too far away, in the meantime, the weather did change, it came down quite violently, sleet slashed down with a wind that came with it, it lasted only 5 minutes, then came savage rain for another 10 minutes, then hey presto, back to sunshine again. In the end, the bag was only 11 brace, the shooting was not brilliant, together with Sarah's coat. The bag was not a big one, Joey Junior shot very well with his own Darne gun.

The usual dinner in the evening was held at Stuart's Hussar Hotel (the old Crown). This time the food was very, very good, consisting of smoked salmon, game soup, with sherry, saddle of suckling lamb from Skirwith Hall, crepe suzette, the wine I forgot to mark it down, the bill came to 70 pounds, plus 11 pounds in tips, the chef's 5 pounds inc. I now had my blood test result back from Donald Anscow, I had a good dose of Brucellosis, he told me, no wonder I had been off colour. This ailment was to plague me almost monthly for years, then in the 1980's and 1990's, about three or four times a year.

On Sunday 17th Monique, her Aunt and I went down to Wetherby to see Adam in Borstal, it was not a pleasant thing to see him there, but he was as large as life, we saw what type of youngsters were there, a very ill-bred looking lot indeed, this was not the place for Adam. We hoped he would learn his lesson, but unfortunately he did not. When we were seated around a small table, Aunt Josephine slipped him a 1 pound note, folded up like a small stamp, later he told us he had told his 'best friend' there that he had 1 pound – his friend immediately shopped him, that's the type that he was in with, ones that would shop their own mothers.

Also, I started my 3 new youths on weeding turnips at High Wood, two days later, I noticed they had not covered much ground, on the third day, I kept a discreet eye on them from a nearby vantage point, unseen by them, I watched for quite a long time during which nothing was done, except sitting down and talking, I approached them and of course when they saw me, all were suddenly very busy, I told them I had been watching them and that little ground had been covered during the two previous days, they said not a word, so I sacked them on the spot, I had no time for such, they were getting good money, I was sorry for Arthur's grand- son, I think he was led on by the others.

On 21st I gelded 33 bull calves, I also gelded 16 bull calves on 22nd keeping ¾ of the testicles for myself, Joey Junior also liked them and gave one-eyed Willie the rest, he was over the moon when I took them to him, he invited me into his house in Carelton Drive, Penrith, for he was now retired, and we settled down to finish a bottle of whisky off, reminiscing over the good days just after the war, we had had some fun, his one eye used to sparkle, thinking of these times when he would pull a fast one on the bookies at the flapping meetings.

Little Joey went back to school at Wakefield from Appleby railway station with his 8 stoats and a dead and half-eaten rabbit in their cage, he told us later that people would not stay in his carriage because for one thing, the smell, and secondly, people were frightened of them.

I had Bill Allen sow some winter rye for stock feed grazing in winter, 16 acres of it for a first-time try, when I went to see how he was doing, the silly chap had sown the first few acres at double the rate, much too thick, I had to set his drill correct for him, he had not even checked that he was sowing the stuff correctly.

The pigeons had gone mad on the bean stubble, so I thought to have a shot at them, with Lassie, I built a sort of hide behind a fence and had good sport shooting 30 of them and one wild duck, earlier on that day 20th I castrated 20 bull calves, these were the smaller end of the calves, the testicles were also rather small, but quite delicate to eat, though I preferred the almost full-sized ones.

Monday was cold and wet, so I put the men to saw logs for the house, also I had them put a big trailer load for my old friend Sid Hetherington, who used to be our village policeman and who was now on duty in Pen- rith, Sid was always a genuine man, but his health had not been too good, also his wife. He had asked for a transfer to town for her sake, Kurt took the load in for Sid the next day. Sid still liked to have a shot at duck at my Black Wood stream, which I liked him to do with his big black Labrador dog, so fat it waddled.

On the 24th Wednesday, I had missed dehorning some of the calves earlier in the year, so this day, I had these calves with horns, big and small, brought in, I set to work on them, the small horns, quite a few with just large 'buds' were burned out with electricity, but a dozen older calves with quite long and strong horns, I took off with a thin wire saw. This was hard work, I had to say, as quickly as possible, as it was quite a painful process for the animal(s) and exhausting for the operator, smoke would come out of the horn as sawing was in the process because of the speed, Kurt and I took turns at each animal, one horn each. By the end of the day, I had done 35 of them. I was pleased at the finish of the day.

On September 30th, Monique and I set off for a short holiday to be spent with my blood brother in Telgte. We docked early as usual, our steward knocking loudly with his key on the cabin door. With two cups of strong tea, we took our time, eventually surfacing in the restaurant for breakfast to find most of the passengers had finished theirs. However, we were not worried, we had all the time in the world, we had no timetable to keep.

We drove off the ferry, winding our way through the great port of Europoort Rotterdam. To my disappointment, the traffic was very heavy all the way to Munster.

At luncheon, we in time noticed there was something in the air, it eventually came out Maria wanted to build a house in their rear garden and incorporate the new building into the original house of No 5, with a swimming pool and sauna and showers, built down where the cellars would be, she was copy booking Charlie's house, Maria had already had the plans drawn up for all of this, by an architect costing according to Heinz DM 5000. This same architect had a sauna at his own home – in Telgte – and only 4 weeks earlier, his wife had gone into her sauna, shut herself in, of course, eventually fell asleep and, with the sauna going full blast, did not wake up, she died.

Later in the day, I questioned Heinz about this new affair,

he admitted he did not want to build another house, I said, 'well stop her (Maria) from going further on with it'. He shrugged his shoulders, I realised he was frightened of his wife, I asked how much the thing was going to cost, he thought in Sterling 45,000 pounds - this was in 1970 - he added that the money was in the bank, so I said no more, it was none of my business, but it was easy to see he was most unhappy about the whole thing.

One morning, Maria got the plans of the new project out for us to see, Heinz was out at work. She adding that she was going to put Heinz outside in a shed with his canaries. Monique and I could not believe we were hearing right. Heinz the breadwinner and an exceptionally good husband and father, being treated like a leper, this woman now sunk very low in our esteem, also it turned out she and Charlie were thicker than ever, I could not understand why Heinz did not kick him out of the house and forbid Maria to see him. Things in the family were not happy.

I slowly began to think or realise that Heinz was resting on his laurels with his British army contracts instead of concentrating more and more on the German civil side of things. I mentioned to Monique if he lost his army contracts, he is in big trouble. His workforce had shrunk to 3 men. But my mind went back to the evening a year or two back, when a customer came to pay his bill in cash, DM 2000 and Maria took it and put it into her own account. Heinz had blown a gasket.

As usual, we called on our old pub friends out in the countryside, Bernard and Enna Geismann, they were overjoyed to see us, a huge fire was in full swing, Bernard got the cigars out and a session was in full swing, Bernard getting the round in when it was his turn, always including a schnapps as well as beer for me. After a couple of hours, Enna disappeared into the kitchen and returned with enormous plates with enormous portions of their home-cured ham with two fried eggs in each – this was her present to us.

The next day, I paid a visit to my good friend Sepple

Poppenborg, my cigar friend, buying 2000 of the best brands @ 40pf each. As usual, Sepple gave me a 7½ % discount and a box of his choicest ones @ 70pf each and spent the late afternoon putting them in the car doors.

On Thursday, 16th October, we said our goodbyes and left for Rotterdam at 11 am, getting into the dockside by 4 pm. The ship was pretty full, but I had reserved a cabin for us from Telgte, the crossing was calm.

On Wednesday I was asked to shoot at Ken Stampers of Culgaith, only 2 miles away. I have no note of the quantity of game shot but a note stating that I shot ¾ of the bag myself. This day, I took Sandy, Lassie's son. Sandy was starting that eye problems in many breeds of dogs, particularly in Labs and Alsatians, eye retina problems, his eyesight getting shorter each year, this particular day, Sandy worked like a champion. For one retrieve, I wish that I had my camera with me, for I shot a hare 60 yards away. Sandy made the retrieve by jumping over a full stretch of sheep netting with two strands of barbed wire on top, clearing it with grace and ease, and on the return with a big fully grown hare of perhaps 10lbs in his mouth, cleared the same fence with a foot to spare, this performance was watched by 2 or 3 guns and beaters, Stamper himself saying he would never have believed it, if he had not have seen it. Sandy brought the hare to my feet, I do believe he understood, by the voices of praise, that he had done very well.

However, on Wednesday, I decided to shoot grouse, I took both Lassie II and Sandy, put them in the Land Rover, and set off, I took nothing to eat. This time, I drove to the top of Ousby allotment, and walked away over to the west side and below Cross Fell.

The dogs were excited and looking forward to some sport, I walked around by the top side of Bulman Hills, almost to Cash Wells mine, our usual rendezvous, it was a long walk and a long way back, the grouse were very wild indeed, getting up much too far in front, however I shot and killed 7 birds, all full grown, big and fat, I hit 2 harder, but they carried on, over the horizon. Into the Land Rover – and home, to a big roaring fire, Monique had going in the morning room, a large whisky and a black German cigar. In no time, I had dozed off, Monique taking the lit cigar from my fingers, she often did this, though I very seldom dropped a cigar whenever I dozed off.

On the 30th, Monique and I went over the Pennines to Newcastle, firstly, to have my spinal discs put right, I could barely lift my left arm up high. Mr Wedderburn was the osteopath who put the discs back again. He said, I had two out just below my neck, also I had a capsule on my shoulder point out and one of my fingers was out of joint. These were all put right in no time. When I came out of the surgery, I could put my arms as high as before I had disc trouble. This was a relief, my finger was also back to normal.

Saturday, I had my shoot at Skirwith Hall. Guests were Hamish Alexander, Seamus O'Connel, John Lancaster, Ken Stamper, Joey Junior and myself. Beaters were Kurt, Bill Allen, Tractor Man and John Frith. The dogs were Lassie and Sandy.

John Lancaster was the son of an old friend, Frank, who had now passed away. Frank was a great racing man, a farmer, and a complete gentleman, known and liked by a great many.

We all enjoyed the day shoot, the only trouble was, as usual, Ken Stam- per, he shot his game far too near, if a pheasant got up only 10 yards from him, it was downed at 12 yards. He ruined quite a few birds, always.

This day we shot 29 pheasants, 53 ducks, 7 hares, 2 pigeons – 91 heads. The dogs worked extremely well, especially flighting the duck into my new little lake. Lassie needed no bidding even when we could hardly see in the shadows, she piled the duck up at my feet. Many, of course, were shot by my guests. Monique put on a very good dinner for us, unfortunately Hamish and John Lancaster could not stay for it.

We had to start onion tart, smoked salmon, main dish, Cogau-vin, with either homemade apple tart and thick cream, or creme caramel, cheese and biscuits before the desserts as in France, fresh ground coffee, various liquers – brandy – whisky, cigars. The wine was Volnay. We had a pleasant evening. The beaters were well tipped with 5-pound notes from the guests, each would get 15 pounds.

On Friday, November 7th, Dad and I set off for days walking up of pheasant, I asked him to leave his pointer, Shot, at home because it was a headache to go out with that dog, we went with only Lassie, we bagged 15 pheasant, 2 hares and 5 ducks. Father was most pleased, one of the cleanest of shots I had seen ever - walking some turnip ground, a black hen pheasant got up and flew crossways past Dad at 40 yards range, he fired once, and the pheasant fell a dead shot, we stopped walking and watched Lassie retrieve it, when she brought the bird to hand I was amazed, the pheasant was minus its head and half its neck. Dad had made a complete clean kill alright, he was using his made to measure 28 bore Darne gun. Then, Dad was about 77 or 78 years old, I was most pleased for him – one thing, Dad never shot in a hurry at birds, but in one instance, his gun would be at his shoulder, then he would let the bird get to a reasonable distance away.

On Monday I had all the breeding cows from the far ends of the farm and Kirkland nearby, for tomorrow was the TT and brucellosis test.

On Tuesday, Tom Barr, the vet and his assistant vet, Mike, tested the cows on 243 of them, it took until 3:30 pm and it was very cold and frosty but thankfully dry. At lunchtime, Monique made an excellent meal of hare soup, followed by roast pheasant, then apple tart, two bottles of Volnay, both vets refused brandy and whisky after as a digestive, having had two good snorts each for the aperitif.

Friday 14th, the 2nd run-through for the cows, all were clear for the T.T. test, but the ministry phoned from Carlisle to say of the brucellosis test, 128 were positive, it was as I suspected.

I buttonholed Dad not to let him forget that it was through his jealousy of Monique and I am going to Dublin without him and without a word to me, buying female breeders, straight from the docks at Silloth, false papers, a very devious Irish dealer, that now my beef herd was ruined, he of course denied all, but the facts were there.

On Tuesday, the vet came to swab cow no. 188. Bred on the farm, I thought she seemed to have aborted. The vet took blood, what little 'milk' was in her teats, and vaginal swabs, she was to prove aborted and brucellosis positive, one Friday the Ministry vet came to ear tag the cows for compulsory slaughter, and Norman Little, the auctioneer, for valuation of them.

It was indeed an extremely sad day to see these beautiful home-bred cows ear-tagged, carted off to be killed. 141 were reactors and a good many were doubtful. I could have wept, I again thought of the stupidity of father, not wanting me to even farm on my own account, then not wanting me to even buy cattle on my own. All gone for the sake of jealousy and a spiteful woman, whom no doubt egged Dad on against me.

The men trucked 90 odd young calves, which, under Ministry orders, went to British Beef. However, many cows were still waiting to be trucked to their death, many of whom Kurt and I had pet names for. By 3 pm, on Monday 24th all cattle had gone from the farm, the atmosphere was eerie, almost like the period when we had foot and mouth disease.

On Tuesday 25th, I had Ministry orders to clean, muck out and disinfect all loose boxes, byres, stalls, etc.

On Friday 5th December, Dad wanted to shoot a few pheasants, he had invited one friend just for a knock around, this friend was Willie Relph, his brother was famous for his film star sheepdogs. Willie was a character in his own right, he was built like a Toby Jug, in fact, quite a few people knew him as Toby Jug, he was perhaps 5'5" tall and as round as tall. He had been a hill sheep farmer in the hills around Ullswater. Now he had a few years ago, started a little business selling farm implements, boots, feeding troughs, gumboots, minerals, medicines and lately, antibiotics, etc. He was so good at this job because he had an excellent rapport with him, even if one did not buy anything from him, he would treat you as if you had just bought his whole van load of materials, all of this with his shining and brilliant smile, almost always in knickerbockers, I used to ask him in for a wee dram, which he loved. Somewhere in the conversation, he would think, females - and come out with 'Joy' – meaning me – 'what is it Willie?' I would say, 'ahh, think aal have a clim on to neet'. 'A good idea, Willie, why not', I would say. He would almost always come out with this, his possibly secret desire, I'm not sure he ever got his climb on, his tummy was so round and large that he would have rolled off any woman he got on top of – his wife was a gentle, very well spoken woman, with a cultured accent, a school teacher I think, I spoke to her on the phone a few times and met her once or twice.

Regarding the antibiotic side of Willie's business, he would sell penicillin or streptomycin bottles at 2 pounds 10/-. Our vets would charge 5 pounds, a big difference. Willie got his antibiotics from his brother or brother-in-law, which I forget.

Willie arrived at Skirwith Hall just after Dad, he had a beautiful one-triggered Boss 12 bore.

I took them both into the breakfast room for a few wee drams of Grouse, then off we set with Lassie and Sandy and we 3 men.

Willie shot quite well and enjoyed his outing enormously. Dad, as usual, was on target, the dogs worked very well, I told Dad he should have had a Labrador instead of a pointer. In fact I was going to give him a puppy out of Lassie's litter, the one Sandy was born into, I was keeping it as a surprise, but two weeks before I was going to give him the puppy, he sprung his own surprise, he got Shot the pointer.

This day we shot 14 pheasant, 2 hares, and 2 rabbits. This was a good bag for just taking it easy.

Back home in the smoke room, we sampled some more

Grouse whisky and cigars, we were all ready for a few drams, then the pair of them left, I knew Willie would not be going to Kirkland, as Dad's wife hated visitors.

The next day Monique and I set off to Hamish Alexander's party, set up by his father Jimmy, at Sandoe Hall, near Hexham, Jimmy had rented Sandoe Hall, a large country mansion. When we arrived, there were al- ready quite a lot of people there. I have marked in my diary 350 attended, it was an excellent party, people started to leave at about 4 am. There was a bedroom put by for Monique and I, but Monique was adamant she wanted to go home, at the same time, a young chap by the name of Stordy, whose family were biggish farmers, wanted a ride over to Penrith to see his father's horses at Gordon Ritchard's place at Greystroke, Monique was equally adamant he was not going to have a lift in my car, she was getting now in a temper. I don't know why, for myself, I then told her I was staying, she could like it or not, and off she went home on her own in the Volvo, by then, most or all had left the party, so young Stordy and I bedded down in one of the lounges, myself on a very large and long sofa with bags of soft cushions, young Stordy in a large armchair, I had a very good sleep indeed. I awoke at about 9am, Stordy was sound asleep, but eventually, hearing people move about, he surfaced, a few minutes later Hamish's sister came downstairs, surprised Monique was not there, telling me about the bedroom, she made us tea and toast, then I tried to phone Monique, but got no reply. By now, 3 or 4 more of the party's guests were surfacing, one was Johnny Harrington and his future wife Jessie, an extremely nice couple. They were going on to Lanchester, where Jimmy and Robin Alexander had their small stud. Partridge Close, would I go with them? I said, "Of course I would." I wanted to see Jimmy, I tried to phone Monique again, no reply. She was in a huff, I phoned my neighbour Robert Jackson to ask him to go down and knock Monique up and tell her to bring the Volvo over to Lanchester, to the stud, giving Robert directions on how to get there, at the same time I told Robert to tell Monique, take Kurt to drive her, which she did.

In the meantime, I set off with young Johnny Harrington, Jessie and young Mr Stordy for Lanchester. Jimmy was putting a big lunch on for us, but before setting off, we had 3 or 4 large gins for revivers. It was the first time I had met Johnny, he was one of the heads of Curragh Bloodstock, and later when in Ireland, he kindly invited me to a marvellous dinner. By then, he was married to Jessie, an extremely kind woman.

Arriving at Partridge Close, we were made heartedly welcome by Robin and Jimmy, extra large drinks were served all around. One thing, we had the best ever host and hostess. Just before lunch, Monique arrived with chauffeur Kurt. Jimmy knew Kurt from racing days, looking after my horses, and made him most welcome and put him at ease, for poor old Kurt had never dined in such company before, but Kurt had an easy way with him and was quickly at home, Derek Straker and Hamish had long chats with him, they knew him from shooting days.

We were called to the dining table, a magnificent lunch was served, Kurt put between Jimmy's daughter and Straker and held his own conversation. After a two-hour lunch, Brandy's, whisky's etc and cigars were thrust on one, we spent the next few hours chatting and emptying the bottles. Kurt drank only 2 or 3 beers, he was never a 'drinker' in that sense. I made our farewells at 6:30 pm, but before I left, Jimmy, who told me he had enjoyed our company so much, insisted on giving me a Christmas present, which to my surprise, was a case of whisky and a box of 25 large Corona Cuban cigars, which I accepted with great delight, he, Jimmy was always the most kindest of men, when in later years he had cancer, I was the only person he ever came downstairs in two years to speak with. It really was an honour. Kurt drove us home.

Christmas Day, Joey Junior and I went to mass at 9:30 am. The day, weather-wise, was very pleasant. Boxing Day, I took it quietly, as I was far from well, no doubt the bru- cellosis was taking its toll.

New Year's Eve, I had the men ditching near Beck Mill, the rain was pouring down. I went to see them and told them to knock off and go home. This is at 4 pm. It was snowing hard, so it ended in 1975. The next year was to be our last in England.

On Thursday, 1st January 1976. The workforce with no cattle to feed had the whole day off, and paid as if they had worked their morning shift. Since the cattle had gone from the farm I could legally have cut the wage of each man by a couple of hours per day and done away with weekend work completely, saving me quite a few hundred pounds a year, which of course, would lead to my men seeking work elsewhere, so I kept paying them the full wage as before. To refresh the memory of readers, my men were in first-rate cottages, rent and rates free, as much free firewood as they wanted, free potatoes, free milk for the cowman from the house cow (this before the herds exodus), free eggs for the two poultrymen, their income tax paid for them, no income tax on their overtime, my workers were very well off. If they were off sick for any length of time, I paid their wages in full, as I did not want any stress on their families, the shepherd Ernie lived with his mother.

On Friday the 9th, Joey Junior and I had a walk around 3 of my outlying fields with the guns, Sandy and Lassie to see if we would get a hare for Monique to make into hare soup, for my blood brother was coming next week and he loved hare soup and hare meat. We started at High Close, a 60-acre field ½ way to Kirkland, this and the field named Hungary was always a certainty for hares. Sure enough, we had only walked some rough in a small gully for a couple of minutes, then a monster hare got up, ears pricked only 25 yards away. Joey Junior shot and missed, I gave the hare another second or two, fired, he rolled over and over, stone dead. Little Joey had been too quick to fire. I told him, first take a good look at the target, with the gun already on the shoulder, judge the distance and never be too near, then all this fire, of course, all of this happens in split seconds.

Sandy brought the hare to hand, very proud of himself carrying such a weight. The hare, indeed was a beauty, and popped him into the game bag, on we walked, then the unexpected happened. A couple of pheasant got up. It was seldom pheasant were in High Close, Joey shot and dropped one, a very nice shot at the correct distance; he had his own 12-bore Darne, I fired and glory be, missed the bird. Again Sandy brought the bird to hand, on we walked. A single pheasant got up, I left it for Joey, he dropped it nicely, then as he fired, another hare got up, now it was my turn, as Joey's gun was still in the air, I downed hare no 2, also a beauty, I did not want any more hares from High Close - I told Joey if hares got up to leave them and we'll go for more pheasant, before long we had two more, also another 2 hares got up, but we let them go, I think the dogs thought we were quite mad, they watched intensely the hares, then a quick glance at us not understanding almost asking why, it is a wonderful sight to stand back and watch a hare loping away quite nonchalantly.

After High Close, we piled all into the Land Rover, I was glad to empty the game bag, one hare is heavy, 2 of them is like lead, this done we drove over to Hungary. I only wanted one hare out of this field, and sure enough, after only a couple of minutes, a beauty got up. Joey fired in- stantly and again was much too quick, he missed, I had my sights on the hare, in case Joey missed, when he did so, I took the hare and rolled him over, a nice full grown one, again I told Joey, take your time with these chappies, by now Sandy had brought him to hand, again those Labrador eyes said it all – he was as proud as punch. I told Joey, no more hares, we will hunt for some snipe, always good here in Hungary, we changed cartridges from No 4 to No 6, and sure enough, we dropped 6 snipe in quick succession, these were the small Jack snipe, Joey got 2 of them, which was pretty good going, then off we set for home, most pleased with ourselves, 3 hares, 4 pheasants and 6 snipes.

These would be a good start for the menu for Heinz.

On Saturday, 10th January, Heinz landed at Manchester airport, but for the first two days, he stayed with a 2nd cousin of his at Chorley, Klair Cronin and her husband John. Klair had been a field telephonist in Hitler's war, had married an English army captain, who had, after a few short years, died, then later, as a widow, married John Cronin.

On Sunday, 11th January, Adam spent this day, his birthday, in Borstal, very sad.

Thursday, January 15, 1976 was Heinz's birthday, he was 51 years old. He insisted on treating us to a diner, which was held at Stuart's place, the Hussar in Penrith. Heinz loved to eat lamb, so he asked Stuart to put on a leg of lamb, which he did. We started with a prawn cocktail, thick with prawns, then trout, followed by a leg of lamb, then crepe suzette, finishing with cheese and biscuits, 3 bottles of Chateau neuf du pape, the cost 24 pounds for 3, Joey Junior having gone back to school the day before. The meal was very good indeed, as was the wine. We left for Skir- with Hall at 6 am. We had an excellent birthday night.

Friday 23rd January, I had the grey breeding ewes started on their turnip break, as the frost had started.

Saturday was very hard frost. Heinz and I drove to Penrith for him to say goodbye to Stuart, as Heinz was leaving the next day. We were home by 2:30 pm and flighted duck in on the little lake, Heinz wanted to take some home with him, the ducks were not plentiful, only getting 4, which Heinz stuck into his suitcase together with 5 pheasants and one very large hare, his suitcase now weighed very heavy indeed. The same day, J and J Grahams sent their lorry for the 10 ½ tons of oats, as I had no cows to eat the cereals, the crop was to sell.

The next day, Sunday the 25th, I drove Heinz to Manchester airport, Monique stayed at home, not liking goodbyes. Both Heinz and she had tears in their eyes, Heinz of course was a part of my family; we did not stand on ceremony, and Heinz was the same. We set off at 7 am, getting there at 9 am. Heinz's plane took off at 10:25 am.

On arriving home, we both realised there was a large emptiness in the house. Heinz was never in the way, like many guests, many of whom 'we wished would leave', never did we feel like this with Heinz, I was sad.

Now, there was no cattle on the place, I had both cereals and hay to sell, I had an articulated lorry call on the 31st, a Saturday, to load up with hay, ready for the sale on Monday, at Harrisons auction mart Carlisle of fodder. The weight of hay was 5 tons 8 cwt, it went for 45 pounds per ton, which was quite good. I think it was possibly the first time in history that Skirwith Hall had sold hay.

I sent two trailer loads into Penrith on Tuesday to be sold before the livestock, one of hay, and one of straw, which weighed out at 2 ½ tons of hay and two tons of oat straw. The hay made the same at Carlisle, 45 pounds per ton, the straw at 24 pounds per ton.

Adam, on leave from Borstal, came to Penrith with me, but on looking later on for him to go home, he refused to do so, no matter how I tried to persuade him, he still refused, I went home without him.

That same day, I sold Jos Bowness of Cliburn some hay, the chap I sold a foal to years ago when he was drunk, for 35 pounds, and it turned out to be one of his best. Jos wanted 30 tons, we bargained for quite a while over a few whiskys. Eventually, I sold him the hay for 42 pounds per ton, as there was no commission to pay, the produce to go to him in 3-4 weeks' time. Jos lived only 6 miles away, a nice easy distance for my tractors and lorry. All of this time, the weather was very frosty.

Joe Clark, the butcher from Penrith, wanted ten tons of hay. My men delivered, Joe was a canny man, a good buyer of fat lambs, but as soon as he knew Stuart the hotelier, 1st from the George Hotel, then the Hus- sar bought one or two lambs per week from me, a few years ago, he never bid for any of my lambs, a very petted mind I thought, Monique still bought her beef from him - I charged him top price.

On Monday, I had to go and see Jos Bowness, he had phoned to say the quality of hay delivered to him was not the best, I knew Jos, he always complained if he bought something so that he might get things at a lower price, Jos could be nice but he could be sometimes rather nasty. I went to see him, vowing to keep my temper because for myself, I had not seen the hay my men had taken him, on arrival at Jos' he and I inspected the hay from Skirwith Hall, to me it was good hay. I told Jos this in nice terms, he disputed this, then invited me in for a drink, I knew Jos' ca- pacity was very good, but when oiled up, could be very argumentative. However, we sat down, a bottle of whisky between us, a good fire going, Jos' pipe came out was lit up, I always had, when dressed, my cigar pouch. I lit up a Burma cheroot and we talked horses, racing, people for 4 hours, the 1st bottle, now finished long ago and another in its place, now well down. The room was thick with smoke.

Time was getting on when the subject turned to the thing in question – hay. Jos said finally, 'oh reet, a'll pay the price, but aah still say't hay could be better.' We shook hands and that was it. I think a year later, Jos fell ill with cancer and died. He was a character all right, he left a son and his wife, a charming and kind woman.

On 17th, a load of hay was delivered to an old friend, George Bowman, of carriage horse driving fame. George and his family were an extremely nice bunch of people and most honest. George had a constitution like iron, his work entailed demolition of machinery and buildings, one day was dismantling an aircraft hanger when one of the huge doors fell on top of George crushing him into the ground and almost to death. His workers managed to lift the doors up an inch or two so that poor George could breathe and eventually jacked the great metal door up and drag George out, he was in the hospital and out of commission for months. Also, he, George, was an expert horseman as a rider and a driver.

Bill Allen was doing quite a lot of ploughing at the moment

and he was making quite a mess of the whole lot, I remonstrated with him to do a better job, but he did not seem to care, I was not pleased.

On Wednesday, 25th February, Monique and I set off in the Volvo to Hull, we were off to the Karnival in Germany at Telgte, staying with Heinz, we had an enjoyable trip over on the ferry, crewed by Dutchmen.

Ash Wednesday, people who had been to early mass would have a cross on their foreheads of ash this day I went down with flu or was it brucellosis, there was a flu epidemic around Munster and Telgte at the time, however within two days, I was fit again.

Heinz told me about Maria insisting on building the new house, but he seemed to do nothing about stopping it from going ahead, she herself also seemed occupied with Charley. About now Heinz lost his contract of work with the British Army, also the American contract. He now had only 3 workforces, doing a lot of electricity installations himself, I could see the future not too rosy for him. Maria's carrying on with Charley and her not letting Heinz into the marital bedroom. She treated him almost with contempt, he only came to his old self when he and I were together, I realised he did not confide these things to me, because underneath, I think he was ashamed to mention them. Monique had the same views as I did.

I paid a visit to my old friend Sepple Poppenborg, my cigar man, topped myself up with 2000 @ 40 pf each, and as usual Sepple gave me 7 ½ % and a box of de Luxe cigars @ 80 pf. Heinz helped me stash them away in the doors of the Volvo and, as usual, keeping 200 to declare.

Monday 8th March there was a snowstorm in Telgte. Monique and I went around our friends saying goodbye as we were leaving the next morning for home. That night, quite a few people came to the house to have a goodbye drink with us.

Tuesday 9th we were up at 9 am, had breakfast, then a few beers with Heinz, wished everyone well and left at 11:30 am, getting into Rotterdam at 4:30 pm.

Wednesday, once customs was cleared we were off and home by 11:30 am, to the start of lambing time, already 6 ewes had given birth.

On 6th, I had Bill Allen sow 25 acres of barley next to the farm steading, Mazurka barley @ l0st per acre. The shepherd and I went to inspect the allotment above Ousby to find over 200 stray sheep.

On finishing on Friday night, coming down from the allotment rather late, I called on Kurt to see how the work had gone, I was surprised and not surprised to hear him say that Bill Allen had a lot of barley sacks left over from sowing the 25 acres, I went to see how many sacks he had not sown, as I had weighted it all out for him in the morning, exactly the correct quantity. He had almost half the number of sacks left over, sowing it at the rate of 6st per acre instead Of l0st, I was very angry at this crass stupidity as also the drill had the settings on it to also make it easy for the sower, also, I had stepped an acre out for him, to be sure of the first sack of l0st, he had ignored everything, all this work to do again, and it was his, Allen's, weekend off, his work, ploughing recently, had been poor, his attitude seemed to be, couldn't care less, I had had enough of him so there and then, I put his pay plus holiday pay into an envelope, put a note in, telling him he was sacked and why, and took it up to his house, handed it to him and left, without speaking, he knew what was coming.

The next day, without me knowing he went to Silloth to see Father, who was down there at weekends. He told Dad what had happened and asked if he could rent his farm cottage from him, Father, for 1 pound a week. Father, without consulting me, told him yes, so without more ado, Father had done me out of a house for another man to take the place of Allen, I did not have another farm cottage empty, and now I was unable to hire a replacement, this stupidity on father's part all for 1 pound per week, put more work on my shoulders.

Allen also had made another faux pas, he had mixed some

pedigree barley seeds @ 190 pounds per ton with other ordinary barley of a different brand, I had Kurt sow the field over again and Joey Junior did the harrowing.

Saturday 17th, Monique and I went to Carlisle races, where Gordon Ritchards had his 100th win of the season, he invited Monique and I to dinner, which was held at Stuarts Hussar Hotel, 20 other people were at the dinner, which was very good, drink flowed freely. We got home at 5 am after having a look around the fell ewes on lambing, all was well, I took it easy.

39

Friday 14th May, I set off for Ireland with Hamish Alexander. Monique could not go, as she did not want to leave the house with Adam alone in it.

I had been invited to stay with an old friend for the Irish 1000gns and 2000gns, run at the Curragh, Willie McCauley, Willie had shot my grouse a few times, Willie's place was close by where the Tetrarch was foaled.

On arrival, Willie met us with one of those little French cars that, going round bends, leans right over on their sides, not a deux chevaux, but similar. From here it was straight into a bath of booze from daybreak till bedtime, it was one mad whirl of drink parties. On Saturday 15th it was lunch at Willie Robinson's, the famous jockey and one of natures gentlemen, I made a faux pas, though only to Hamish and Willie MacCauley, on arrival in his yard of horses as I mentioned to Hamish as we came to a little tin hut, surrounded by boxes, "what a nice tack room Willie's got", Hamish said "shut up, it's Willie's house", and so it was. Willie welcomed us in and once inside I found the place very pleasant indeed and of course the Irish hospitality as always, was fantastic, they, the Irish, will give one the clothes they stand in, lunch was buffet, and very good, it was there I met Julliette de Chair and her husband Somerset de Chair, Julliette I remembered clearly was the daughter of Earl Fitzwilliam who owned the largest house in the British Isles, Wentworth Woodhouse in Yorks. Her father was killed in an air crash when Julliette was about 14 years old, the only child, I believe – now here she was. I had a long chat with Somerset about I think, some books Winston Churchill had written, drinks kept pace with events, I told Julliette I was going that afternoon to the races, could she provide me with a pass or members badge for the day, she told me to be at a certain point near the entrance to the stands, so I did as I was requested to and Juliette duly got me my pass, after lunch and a torrent of more drink, John Harrington shouted, "Come on

Joey, we're off to see – so and so." John, I had met at Hamish's father's party a few weeks ago at Sandhoe Hall with his wife Jessie, I had an enormous crystal glass almost full of whisky and was busy talking to Somerset. I shouted, "Hold on a while, I'll finish my drink," John H said, "No time, bring it with you." Into the front seat of John's car I jumped with my glass, and off we sped to see a friend of Harringtons, I forget exactly whom, I eventually finished my drink then placed the expensive glass close in by the front of my seat. I don't know if Willie Robinson ever got it back.

I met another Irishman there at the races, whom I was told was the biggest whisky drinker in the whole of Ireland, his name was 'Bruiser' nickname, I met him again at each drinks party we were at, these went on nonstop I had quite a few talks with Bruiser, I realised eventually that Bruiser was not as tough a drinker as his reputation suggested, quite often I would say to him, "Come on Bruiser, have another one," he often declined. Without boasting, I had no trouble in out drinking him at all, also when he had had a fair fill, he would become rather loud-mouthed. In later visits to Ireland, Bruiser, who again appeared at each and every drinks party, avoided me and when more or less came face to face, he would quickly move on – so would his wife, I mentioned this to Hamish, as he also was there most times, he told me Bruiser's reputation had been shattered by me, and that his pride was such, he was insanely jealous of me, after hearing this, I never bothered talking to either he or his wife.

Saturday at the races, I did not know any of the bookies, so Willie Mc- Cauley introduced me to one of them, he informed me it would be a pleasure to do business with me, which I did, and thought it most decent of him to take me at face value, however, I had no luck and lost 30 pounds. It was a tremendous day all around and met more and more of these delightful Irish horsy people that night I was invited to dine at John and Jessie Harringtons, they were marvellous hosts, Hamish warned me not to tell any of my joke stories, as they may offend some of the ladies at table, there were possibly 15 people dining, conversation was good, jokes started to flow, so I thought I can't let my jokes go amiss, no matter what, so let forth. They were quite risqué, in fact, one was very sexy, an oldish lady only two seats away from me, was so pleased with the jokes she congratulated me and asked for more, John Harrington, our host, told me, "Joey, you will have to come and visit us more often," then he took me into his study, and hunted round for something, which turned out to be a box of Cuban punch cigars, double coronas and handed me one and had one himself, we lit up and laughed. The evening was excellent, later on, we left for home, which was Willie McCauley's and bed. The day had been a hectic one but a super one.

On Sunday, we got out of bed at 9 am to more cocktails. After breakfast had a look round Willie's stables, he had the vet in, and as one of his horses had something wrong with it, we set off to a country pub where Willie was well known. Bruiser was there with his wife, not wanting to speak to me. I wondered why, but later, I was told why. Drinks came in on an endless belt and they went down my throat like Jersey cow cream, then back to Willie's for a large and good lunch with a few of Willie's friends, Hubie de Brugh, Simon Sherwood, Oliver Sherwood, who were now well up in the racing world.

Then, to the airport where we flew to Liverpool, Monique was there in the Volvo and as I had told her to bring Kurt as chauffeur, Hamish, before I could turn around, had vanished.

On Monday, 17th May, Monique and I took Adam down to Lytham St Annes for an interview with the manager of the Hotel Dalmeny, he thought he would like to start learning hotel work. We told the manager, a very nice young man indeed, the full history of Adam. He understood, and he liked the look of Adam, so he said he would take him on, he could start in a weeks time, the manger showed us all around the hotel, and the staff quarters, which were excellent, he told us, "I am the oldest person in the hotel, I am 44 years old." He said, "The staff are from 17 years to 25 years old, and so Adam should get on well with them, all youngsters," Adam was told when off duty, he could use all facilities, such as the swimming pool and ballroom, as there were dances once or twice a week.

Sunday 23rd Monique and I took Adam down to St Anne's to the Dalmeny Hotel, to start his new career, Monique gave him her own large canvas and leather suitcase lined, also packed it well for him and saw him into the hotel, we stayed a while, chatted to some of his new young colleagues, said goodbye and thanks to the manager, who said he would watch over him for us and left.

I had three professional shearers to shear 500 ewes, Dad helping to wrap the fleeces, 500 grey-faced ewes were finished that day. We started at 9 am sharp and finished at 6:45 pm. I had a 9 gallon barrel of beer in for those thirsty enough, this went down well. Next day, I drew 80 fat lambs for auction on Monday and on Friday, I went to Carlisle to see a man interested in buying Skirwith Hall, he was Willie McCrone, a big cattle dealer and a dairy farmer. I knew Willie well, he was a very clever man, self-made, he had bought land all over the place, though he was interested in Skirwith Hall for someone else. I was fed up with the continued hassle with Father, the weather always soaking wet, the government Labour, more communist than the Russians, the capital gains tax. All, I thought, looked bleak for the future, my eldest son an ogre on our back, a continual headache, we hardly dare leave the house for a weekend.

On 18th June, Friday, we set off for France at noon, getting to London ap- proximately 6 pm. The traffic was at a standstill there, however at length, we arrived in Dover at 8 pm. We waited a while and for a change and the first time and the last time, we took the hovercraft and were in Calais by 10 pm.

We had breakfast in Beaune in a small square there, at a cafe we had been to many times before, we were heading for a place in the South called Bandol, not far from Marseille, arriving at a place named La Cio- tat, where we stayed the night. A very good bedroom indeed at F40, but it had no restaurant, its name was Hotel Rotund. We ate out nearby and it was quite good.

In the morning, we entered Bandol and were surprised to see how many people were knocking about, the place seemed full, we parked and had breakfast of croissant, bread and those enormous heavy cups of coffee au lait, this done, we set about asking at hotels for rooms. Alas, all were full, from end to end. There was nothing to be done but to move on, I did not wish to be to near Marseille and Monique's family, who lived there, so we motored in the opposite direction, getting to Sanary, all hotels there were full, so Monique asked at the info place, there we struck luck, if it can be called that, a Mr Santor had a ½ a villa to rent for a week, ½ of the villa was quite a good one, but inside the bare essentials. However, we took it for the week and a further 3 weeks in an apartment owned by a Madame Coulete, which was not the best. However realising everywhere seemed chock-a-block, we took this also.

Mr Santos right away took a distinct liking to Monique and became a nuisance. His wife had, he said with seeming glee, been killed by a motor car on the side of the road while walking, only a few weeks before, he asked one day if Monique would like to go and see the fish market in Toulon, she said yes, on the day, he arrived in his car – he lived nearby, and when he saw me going also, he more or less told Monique to tell me to stay behind, but Monique told him where I go my husband goes also, he did not like this at all, and on the trip to Toulon was in a huff.

At the end of our week at the Santos villa, we were rather pleased to get away from him.

Sanary was quite a pleasant place, there were excellent beaches for children or any adult learning to swim, as the sea was only 2 feet deep for 50 yards in, then only 3 to 4 feet.

Freshly caught fish were to be had every morning, the local butcher had the best andouettes I have ever tasted, good local wine and quite good restaurants, we enjoyed our stay there taking it easy sunbathing and swimming, there was an excellent beach bar 'snacks' called Drakar, very nice people had it and we became friends with them.

We set off slowly for home on 14th July, arriving home on Sunday 18th to hear bad news regarding Adam: he had been sacked from his hotel job, firstly the manager told us, Adam would not get up in the mornings, Adam's excuse was that he had not an alarm clock, the manager gave him one, then Adam got in with the bad boys from Blackpool's South shore fun fairs and not turning in for his work, the result, the sack.

He had taken one of my two Land Rovers, an old one, ran it so hard and so little oil in, in no time, the crankshaft broke. He was in trouble with the police for other things, he had broken into someone's house, the police caught up with him at Carlisle - such was our homecoming. Monique enquired through the police where was her suitcase, she had lent to Adam while he was at St Annes, they later told her Adam had said he had left it on the beach at St Anne's, a few weeks later, the local police came over to Skirwith Hall with a suitcase and asked if it was Monique's, yes it was hers, but completely ruined by salt water, the weather, etc. It was thrown onto the rubbish dump, what a waste, I thought, and Adam had grown no better.

On calling Stuart's in Penrith, he told me he had lent Adam 10 pounds, I immediately refunded it and told Stuart to lend Adam no more money at all in the future.

Monday, that day, I paid Dad back out of the farm money he had lent me when I had sprung on him that I was the new owner, £30,000.

7th August, I had Lassie mated with one of Ritchard Burtons dogs from Lazonby, the dog was a black lab named Brackenbank Mike.

The next day, Sunday 8th, I drove down to Manchester airport to collect my blood brother, Heinz and another good friend Alfons Ludkehaus. I collected them at 5:50 pm. They had come for the grouse shoot, both of them had brought lots of bottles with them, tucked away in the suitcases and not declared, 150 cigars for me, perfume for Monique.

11th August, the weather was fine and hot, Heinz and Alfons helping with the harvest, Heinz baling straw behind the combine with his shirt off, enjoyed himself to the hilt, the only thing I did not like he had grown a goatee beard, which was grey as grey, making him look as old as Methusela, as normally he had a pink and smooth face and looked much younger than his years. Now, this beard, I told him to get it off, he just laughed, however a few months later, he cut it off. Alfons helped on the combine and in the lofts and barns, where the corn was stored, he also enjoyed himself, his wife Nane was from farming stock.

Now the evening of the 11th, I had some guests arrive, Hamish Alexander, Willie McCauley from Ireland and John Cummings stayed with us.

That night we had dinner at home, later we adjourned to the party room, while Monique started work at 11 pm, preparing one of her super picnics for the morrow. We retired to bed at 2:30 am, Monique was still working.

I was up at 6:30 am, there was no work on the farm that day, my men were acting as beaters along with John Frith, who had got the day off from Monkhouse's Mills and Allan Kiching, the village joiner's son.

Off the set for our first port of call, at the village of Garrygill, the George and Dragon and as usual, we had to knock the landlord out of his slumber, however, he did open up with a protest, but he knew there was profit in my grouse shooting parties for him. We spent a lot in a short time and there was the return trip for him to think about, 12 of us, all told, the beaters, were treated royally on these shoots.

Eventually, we arrived at the rendezvous on the moor, Cash Wells, we adjoined Ritchard Burtons of Brackenbank and with his permission we started at Cash Wells on a dog leg bend of his, while to reciprocate I let him shoot a dog-leg bend in my moor. Once at the rendezvous, the time was midday or almost, so we started on Monique's picnic, which was avocado mousse, cheese twists, savoury omelette, beuf en croute, suckling racks of lamb home killed, all with their sauces, chicken whole, to carve on the spot, vegetables of various, potato salad etc, creme caramel, champagne, St Emilion and Walter Pitch wines, and beers. The white wine, champagne and beers were cooled and left to cool after the meal in the little cold stream right on the spot, which came right out of the fell side, a little further up.

Lassie and Sandy, whom I have not mentioned, were I could see, eager to kick off. Sandy was under Joey's direction, Lassie under me, and off we went, the birds somehow were not too plentiful and at the end of the day, we had 29 birds, all had enjoyed the sport, as for Alfons, he was as excited as a boy at Christmas time.

Monique had an excellent meal for us, after first settling everyone in our party room and bar, everyone was now completely refreshed, I had seen that the beaters had had plenty of refreshment at Garrygill.

The meal consisted of smoked salmon, followed by a large gammon steak, sprinkled with brown sugar, two fried eggs on top with creamed mashed potatoes, the gammon was delicious and well received, especially by my two German guests. The wine Gevery Chambertin I had bought through Stuart a while ago, this was an excellent wine, all right. We finished with strawberries and thick cream, possibly a simple meal but a good and satisfying one, French coffee followed with port, brandy, and various liqueurs, cigars were lit and more serious drinking was taken in hand, Hamish and Willie stayed the night and John Cummings left for home after dinner, he had an early engagement the next morning. We re- tired to bed at 3 am and slept well.

The next day, 14th Willie still with us, I decided to shoot my moor again for the sake of Alfons, who was returning to Germany the next day. On Sunday, 15th, I thought I would take the tractor with a carry tray up the front of the fell past

Kirkland and start shooting from the Ousby side of the moor, as the Land Rover was running badly, Adam having smashed my other one up, I got the tractor quite a long way up the fell front but eventually felt obliged to be prudent and leave it, as there was a definite risk of the thing turning over, this I did, walking rather farther than I wished. However we soon arrived on my moor and started off in line, Heinz, Alfons, Willie and I. We walked steadily on, bagging birds quite well, in the end, we had 25 birds, losing none, I had taken the two dogs. Lassie and Sandy worked in complete harmony, they were worth watching. Now came the long slog back from Cash Wells, which we had reached with 14 birds. The way back over peat bogs, then down into the valley, where the South Tyne starts and up the other side. We rested beside the quite wide stream, crystal clear, for a while, taking a breather, before climbing up and out.

Then on and up we went, by now we had 20 birds and the weight was beginning to tell, poor Willie, not the most robust of people, was now lagging 200 yards behind, I could see he was fatigued, so I took his gun from him to make it easier, Alfons took his cartridge bag, but still Willie could hardly make it. Then I thought it best to take rest periods so that he, Willie, would not be too fatigued or demoralized, this seemed to help him, in the end there lay the tractor, about 1000 yards away or more, but downhill, we reached it with much pleasure, all of us, the weather was extremely hot. This is what I think lay heavily on Willie's head.

Monique made an excellent home meal of Sole Veronique, then a whole grouse each, which were very good, but I like them hung for 4 or 5 days, though the weather was almost too hot to do that, and an iced pudding.

On Sunday, 15th Alfons had to return to Germany, for he was on the management ladder of Armstrong in Munster, so we packed 3 races of grouse into his suitcase and drove him down to Manchester airport in the morning, leaving Willie McCauley behind, he being collected later on by Derek

Straker.

In August, I had decided now was the time to order myself a Rolls Royce, I wanted one now when I was young enough to enjoy such a car, and not when I was old and tired. Dad always wanted one and never got around to own one. They were 25,000 pounds and to help pay for it I planned to sell the field lying on its own near Ousby, named Birch Lands of 7 or 8 acres, this field would never be missed, Monique and I motored down to Harrogate ordered a Shadow II through Applyards garage. There was a two-year waiting list.

Also, on the 19th, Heinz and I returned to the grouse moor, this time with the Land Rover, and had an excellent walk-up shoot, with only Lassie bringing 18 birds, all good sporting shots and losing none, thanks to good old Lassie, what a pleasure it is to have a good dog to shoot with, such a dog makes ones day at any shoot, and is the envy of many.

The next day 20th, John Cronin came to collect Heinz as he was leaving for Germany on Sunday 22nd Heinz did not want to go at all, we had had a full night drinking in my party room, now with more whisky after breakfast the old booze was starting to work, he was adamant he did not want to go, I told Cronin, let him stay, but Cronin told him he had to get back to this business in Telgte, in the end, Heinz realised he must go, he left my parking place, with tears rolling down his face, I and Monique were most upset and were unable to speak.

That evening, late, John Cronin phoned to say he had had a hard job getting Heinz to Chorley, Heinz insisting on calling in at Vera's at the X Keys inn, Carleton, Penrith, then at Stuart's, drinking like a fish and on the way back over Sharp Fells, Heinz threw his passport out of the car window when John was doing 80 mph, taking quite a while to find it.

However, on Sunday, Heinz, I was told, was back to his old self and flew to Düsseldorf, where Alfons collected him, he phoned the same night and we talked for half an hour. We were very close. Heinz and I. Later, there was a tragic end to our brotherhood.

On casting my mind back to Heinz's stay, during the last few days, when he was in a drink mellowed mood, he would ask me to lend him various sums of money, which sums were small, to help him build this new house Maria was keen to build, yet he himself was not, I said, "you told me you had the money in the bank, what has happened?" His reply was, "It has gone." I left it at that, not wishing to ask interfering questions of a private affair.

I told him to forget about building another house, and to put his foot down regarding Maria, and that I had no cash, especially after paying Father back.

Monique and I thought Heinz was in mental turmoil over this house – money – his loss of the contract for the British Forces, plus the U.S.A. base and his wife's never-ending spending, we were unhappy for him, I said put your foot down.

On 3rd September, Dad came over with Tom Lancaster, a neighbour of Dad's at Silloth, Tom was a retired farmer and a nice chap, and a straight one, who, he told me, couldn't stand the sight of Dad's wife, so we had something in common there. Tom had driven Dad over and was to do so for quite a few weeks, we settled in our little breakfast room, a bottle of Grouse on the table, which slowly disappeared except for a couple of inches in the bottom, Tom liked his whisky and spoke the broad Cumberland dialect, we chatted for about 3 hours before they decided to go.

The 11th opened up to a mild day but turned to gales and torrential rain, I went fishing but got only one, the beck had not recovered from the thick carapase of silage sludge, washed down the drains from the silage pit of Ronnie Wilson in the middle of the village 2 years before, there had been dead fish by the hundred for almost ¾ of a mile. This sludge was traced directly back to his farm by the M.F.F, then Bert John- stone's man did not put the plug back into his huge milk vat, one morning I awoke to find the beck white for half a mile or more, Kurt and I traced this directly to Bert's farm, at the same time

Bert had refused an offer from me to dig him a soakaway hole, via Kurt and my McConnel digger, free of charge. He was very vehement not to do so, which I could not understand as I had offered all free – now, with all this milk coming down my beck, the trout or what was left of them vanished. All of the slug life etc, on the beck bottom was dead.

Monday 13th Adam once more in trouble, he had stolen 3 money boxes for spastics from the Bee Hive Inn at Eamont Bridge, also he had broken into the Crown Hotel, Stuart's place and stolen cigarettes, the police came out to tell us that Adam was now in custody.

Monique, on her own, was frightened of him, so was Mrs Metcalfe, so was Ernie the shepherd.

Then, when on remand 4 weeks later, he broke into a chocolate machine and the offices of Roper Street Garage, owned by friends of mine, at Crown Court at Carlisle in December, I pleaded for him, and he got sentenced to two years probation, home he came.

In the meantime, I had made movements to finally sell Skirwith Hall, the weather, my family, and father, both Monique and I were quite fed up with the hassle, also with the Labour Government getting redder than the Russian communists, I felt, one day would come when the communists, under the banner of the Labour Party, would take over the country, I had decided to leave my country.

On Wednesday, 15th September, I took Joey junior to Flight Duck to my little lake, the evening flight, it was a cold night, made colder by a very cold breeze; however, these were good nights to Flight Duck, I took only Lassie, the sport was good, duck came in steadily, and were shot down steadily. Lassie brought all of them to my feet, in between retrieves she, soaking wet with continual swimming, sat beside me, her teeth chattering, like castanettes.

After 1½ hours, we both had shot very steadily, now Lassie had a large pile of duck beside my seat, I looked down at them, quite amazed at the quantity, when I saw a movement amongst them, and one of the shot duck started to run to the beck, which was only 10 yards away, however Lassie forever vigilant spotted the duck and brought it to hand, where- upon I pulled its neck, - by now the flight was more or less over. I called to Joey to come over to me, he saw Lassie's pile of ducks, he could not believe what he saw, as Lassie had brought his shot ducks to me during the whole of the flight, we started counting, we had 33 ducks all told, I don't think Lassie had missed one, we loaded the duck into the Land Rover, gave Lassie a good rubbing down with a dry Hessian sack and put another over her for the drive home, we had an enjoyable shoot, now Monique had a big log fire on in the morning room, where I had a large whisky or two, and a good Havana double Corona, Joey junior had beer, Lassie a warm deep bed of straw and a good supper, she was a marvellous dog.

On Monday 20th, my solicitor Andrew Thornely and I went to meet my accountant, Ken Cope from Leeds, to discuss the tax problems, which may arise if I sold Skirwith Hall, all went well, but it seemed as if to escape capital gains, I would have to be a tax exile.

That night, Joey and I flighted my little lake again, Lassie also with us, the duck once again came in steadily, and Lassie was as busy as the time before, we shot 21 ducks, all good heavy plump mallard, rather strange, I never shot teal on this small lake.

Lassie gave birth to 6 puppies; alas one was dead, but there seemed 5 good, healthy ones remaining. 3 yellow, 2 black, as Mike the father, was black.

Wednesday, we went to Carlisle – Patons garage. They had a 6-year-old Volvo saloon in. I thought it might suit Joey. On inspection, it looked quite good. I told Patons, I would buy the car, the price was 825 pounds. Joey put his savings towards it, which was 100 pounds. He was most pleased with his first car, a mustard coloured 144.

Thursday, 7th, October, Monique and I went to Leeds to converse with Ken Cope and Nathan Apfel, a solicitor from

London, who was supposed to be an expert on tax evasion and whose father was a Rabbi in Leeds, this meeting was with regard to a future sale of Skirwith Hall. If I wished to sell and be free of capital gains, I had to be out of the country and have put and call option on the property.

Also, on this day, I had an invitation from Rolls Royce to go to Crewe to see around the factory and choose the colour inside and out for my future Rolls Royce, we duly went down to Crewe and took Joey Junior with us, I thought he would learn something here, the visit was indeed a marvellous experience, to see the finest car in the world is made. We were allowed and even encouraged to talk to any of the personnel, which we did. There was no endless belt system. Each car shell was on a low trolley and pushed from one worker to the next worker and when he finished his part of the work, he would push the trolley onto the next worker and so on. Monique chose the colours, exterior paint was Silver Sand, the interior roof and sides beige, floor chocolate, I wanted a bar in the car but was told I would have to wait 3 to 4 years for one, as with a bar, the chassis had to be longer, as it was I had to wait 2 years, they had just made a Rolls for Ronny Corbett, but with his legs so short, they had to build the pedals up quite a lot. Lunchtime came, we were invited to a local hotel, not far away, where we were entertained to a very good lunch, with a glass of excellent wine, I was asked after the meal if I would have a cigar, this was music to my ears, a box of Punch Coronas were produced and I chose one, now I was quite content. The time was 3 pm, we decided to head home, I thanked the Rolls people for their hospitality and off we went.

Anyhow, this day, I set off with the dogs, the day itself was covered and later, rain set in, but not too heavy. The dogs enjoyed being together, quartering the ground when asked, the command only by hand or whistle, the bag was a mixed one, consisting of 6 pheasants, 1 partridge, 3 pigeons, 2 ducks and three hares, I was not out to shoot a large bag, but what I had shot I had enjoyed. The duck and pigeon and two hares had been good, difficult shots, which I was most pleased about. The dogs had worked very well, as always. I left the whole bag of game, as it was too heavy, in one of the Spring Field lambing huts and collected them later with the Land Rover.

The day after, Joey's Volvo had a puncture in the rear wheel, he had the car jacked up, but as he was taking the wheel off, the car slipped off the jack and jammed his hand between the mudding top and the half-off wheel, luckily I was with him and saw his hand jammed, I grabbed the mudwing with both hands with my back to the car, heaved with all my might, I got the car an inch or two up, and Joey managed to get his hand out, thankfully I dropped the car, it was heavier than I bargained for, his hand now swelled to double its size, I then put the cold water hose pipe on to stop any more swelling and to take the heat out of it, he said it was very painful, it looked it. The next morning, however, the swelling was reducing well due to quickly using the cold hose pipe.

Friday, Monique and I did a little shopping in Carlisle, I went to Hous- tons a grand class shop for men, I bought 3 jackets, a long suede overcoat with an extra large fur collar, which, when turned up, protected one neck and cheeks beautifully and a pair of trousers, the quality was such that 45 years later I still wear them for best.

Saturday, Joey Jnr and I decided to have a walk round with the guns and dogs, on the exterior border of much of the land, not into the best coverts. We shot 6 pheasants and 5 pigeons, we both enjoyed shooting together, he, Joey, was getting to be a good shot.

Saturday 4th it was cold snow right to the fell bottoms and very hard frost. I took Lassie and we went to shoot a few ducks, this was good weather for ducks and pigeons.

I shot on this little promenade 11 ducks and 25 pigeons, flighting the pigeons in late afternoon and evening standing behind saw steps high stone wall, this was always a good pigeon flight path, the other was Spring Field, small wood of Scot's pine.

40

Lassie was most pleased at having plenty to take home. by now in mid-December, I had made a deal with Willie McCrone, who was buying on behalf of Bibby's farm foods pension fund, to sell Skirwith Hall and Kirkland, I had wanted to keep Kirkland and two farm cottages, but on Nathan Apfel's advice I had to sell everything to escape capital gains when I became a tax exile, as I proposed doing, which as later this advice was false like the man giving it.

Sunday 19th, Monique wanted to go and visit Adam over in Durham, where he was on remand. Young Joey went with her, driving over Hartside. The weather was bad with snow falling, and at Nenthead had to turn back due to heavy snow and a gale-force wind, they were lucky to get back because these roads are small and fill up quickly in a snowstorm.

Monday 20th, was Adam's Crown Court case, held at Carlisle, I pleaded on his behalf, he was lucky, the sentence was probation for 2 years. The weather was bitterly cold. Adam came home with Monique and I.

On Tuesday 21st, Monique put the Christmas tree and decorations up around the rooms, with the tree in the morning room.

Christmas was a happy one, we had goose, hare soup, and plum pudding, a bottle of champagne in the morning, the boys and I had been to midnight mass, Dad had given the boys 1 pound each and for myself a bottle opener from Woolworth's, with the price still on, as far as I can remember about 12/-.

Boxing Day, I took the boys shooting with both Sandy and Lassie, Adam long ago, had claimed Sandy as his own strangely Sandy seemed to sense this because when Adam was about, Sandy would never leave his side. Another thing regarding my little lake, I had had roughly 15 call ducks on it, now they had all gone, Adam earlier in the year had shot the lot and sold them to the local poultry merchant, Frank Bird of Langwathby. And so the old year went out and a new one in -

1977 - I wonder what it would bring.

Details were being worked out to finalise the sale of the estate. Dad was not pleased, so I reminded him of his words a few years ago when the estate was to sell from the Le Flemings. His words were, "I think it would be far better to be under a new landlord rather than buy." That is when I decided to get in myself, with or without his help. Also, he did not like if Quintin Little, my solicitor at the time I bought the estate, said, "You will want to be on your own." He tried hard to convince Father of this, to no avail, I remember Quintin telling me, 'I cannot talk to him, he just will not listen to common sense." Now, with all the hassle I had had, coming back from a holiday to find thousands of my newly planted woodlands eaten off by cattle, deliberately put in - together with the red Labour government, I was quitting.

My old friend and blood brother Heinz decided to come over for my last month at Skirwith Hall, pleading with me not to sell. We shot almost every day and in between getting farm machinery and the ewe flock ready for sale and visiting old friends roundabout, we drank and smoked the nights away, shooting duck on the frosty mornings, sitting on a tree trunk to take a breather and have a good cigar each.

Adam was also quite a good help at this time, on 11th January, it was his 21st birthday. This was the day I sold my ewes and hoggets at a special sale in the auction mart at Penrith – just over 2000 head – trucking started at 5:30 am. But on the count in the morning, I realised the shepherd must have missed some ewes, I sent him looking for them the next day, he found 38 of them, stupid fellow, I was not pleased with his poor shepherding, however these ewes were sold at the machinery sale day on the premises.

The sheep sale went very nicely, the auction mart was crammed full from all the Northern Counties, the bar was free to all purchasers, but when I received the bill later on, there had been more than purchasers drinking.

In the evening, Monique and I treated Adam to a very

good dinner at Stuart's, which he enjoyed, I also gave him 20 pounds, which probably was not a good thing, I also gave the staff of the auction mart, the drovers 5 pounds each, the foreman, I think 20 pounds. He was an extra special good man, Norman Watt, he would help anyone in distress, poor Norman had not long to live, his heart was giving up, a big loss to many people. I marked it in my diary re the sale, I put, 'a very sad day' and indeed it was.

On 13th we put all of my implements and machinery in lines in the first field, The Croft.

The weather was very frosty and snow forecast.

The Finale

During the first week of January 1977, Border TV called to see if I would speak to them for a while on TV in Skirwith Hall, I said I would and did, the camera's zoomed in on my entrance to the house, then gardens, then myself in my armchair in the morning room, showing my wall shelves stocked with over 2000 cigars and myself with a large tumbler of whisky on my cigar stand ashtray, the great TV lights were switched on, Heinz and Monique and the boys watching from be- hind the lights, I was told to say what I wished, why was such an old established family like mine after almost 400 years at Skirwith Hall going to leave the property and the country, the TV chaps told me to say what I wished, so I tore into the government, how communist and redder than the Russians were the Labour Government. I still hold the same views today, even with Blair's government – a leopard never changes its spots. I spoke to the camera for perhaps 10 minutes or more, this programme was shown after the Border TV news the same night, I say it myself, it came out very well, the next day Father came to see me and told me "After that speech last night, they won't let you out of the country," I just laughed.

On machinery sale day, Saturday 15th, it could have been a disaster, 2 or 3 inches of snow had fallen in the night covering all of the bits and pieces of machinery in the field with snow. I had 3000 fencing posts covered completely. I phoned the auction company, asking them if it would not be better to cancel the sale, and put this over the radio and TV, I was told it would be no good at this hour, 8 am, as the sale was due to start at 10 am and many people were coming from Yorkshire, Scotland, Northumberland and many would have set off. I resigned myself to a failure of a day.

However, at 9:30 am, cars rolled in and in half an hour there were hundreds. In midday, there were reckoned to be 3000 people there. The Croft was full to overflowing with cars, and luckily the snow began to disappear.

All went well, two or three people were caught taking riding saddles and bridles that were not for sale.

I had prepared a bar inside my old hatchery, in fact, it was situated in the sexing room, I had rolls of cinema seat tickets to hand out to farmers I knew, friends and genuine purchasers, bar staff was Joyce, the daughter of the people who had the pub in Skirwith, she was a great help and Jack Waring, from Langwathby, a retired forester, always willing to help at any time. Non buyers had to pay for their drinks at half price.

Late afternoon, some people from Penrith came, by this time, the sale was over, I had invited quite a few friends into the house for drinks, some of whom wandered to parts of the house they should not have, later we found ornaments had been stolen and 25 pounds of Joey Junior's taken from the breakfast room mantelpiece, I suspected by whom the money had been taken, but could not prove it.

By now, 9 pm, the snow had started to fall again, this time heavily. The partying went on till 5 am Sunday morning, odd people were left sleeping on the floor in the party room: one local farmer from Kirkland, a young married chap, Robert Ridley and his brother-in-law Chris, whose father had at one time been cowman for father at Skirwith Hall, left at 3 am to return to his farm at Kirkland, only 1½ miles to 2 miles away, his farm, Ranbeck, lay through three or four fields from the road, they did not reach Ranbeck until 7 am Sunday morning, they were rather drunk. The snow was so deep at Kirkland and big snowdrifts the car got stuck, they started to walk and got lost only ½ a mile from home, when they eventually turned up, they, I was told, were completely exhausted.

On Tuesday, 18th January, Skirwith Hall house was sold, this was in the plan devised by Apfel; the buyers, of course, Bibby's were also buying the land in the "put and buy" sale programme, now things here and there were to tie up, furniture to store, etc.

Just after this, John Cronin called to pick Heinz up to take him the day after to Manchester airport, poor Heinz, he did not want to leave, we had had a good few rounds of drinks that morning, solid drinking, even our local policemen from

Melmerby, Mr McMonnies, came in his panda car to wish us bon voyage, he was a nice young man, it was quite a party we had. So good, I had to ask Kurt, who was with us, to take P.C McMonnies back to his police station and home to his wife in the panda car, while I organised a vehicle to bring Kurt back, our P.C. was legless. So it went on, my time at Skirwith Hall was drawing to an end.

We were asked to a few dinners out, in our last week, I was becoming rather sad at leaving all behind, all I had kept was the shooting rights over Skirwith and Kirkland fells, the grouse moor, nothing material.

I had given Heinz 2000 pounds in cash, I had made from cash sales, for him to keep for me when next I was in Telgte, as I was only allowed a small amount of cash, no capital at all, so Apfel informed me.

Monday 24th, I was informed for tax exile purposes, I had to pay for the Rolls Royce in advance, which I did, 23,000 pounds, plus the deposit, it turned out later on Apfel had not advised me properly this, as far as Appelyards greed went, I ordered a dust sheet to come with the Rolls, they even charged me 12 pounds for it, this for a straight sale of a car, no trade-in with another vehicle.

Binnings, the removal people came, lan Kellet in charge, a capable and likeable chap, to lift out all the furnishings, Monique left some carpets, curtains and blinds and other household goods, telling Mrs Metcalfe, her daily help for years, and also Kurt, to help themselves. At the same time, I gave Kurt a few hundred pounds so that he could buy himself a good car, he threw his arms around my neck, thanking me over and over again, it was getting harder for me to leave, Kurt promised to look after Lassie and her 2 pups I had kept by Brackenbank Mike, until I sent for them. Sandy, I gave to my cousin Arthur Slack of Appleby, but I learnt later that Sandy would not settle and ran away from Arthur's farm on the other side (South) of Appleby, Sandy was seen and caught only 2 miles from Skirwith Hall trying to cross the River Eden, he had either crossed or bypassed Appleby and numerous villages, travelling 10 miles with very short eyesight, to almost back home, poor Sandy, I also heard that Arthur had shot him, the excuse, a poor one I thought and not true, Sandy had worried sheep.

Dad came to see me during this period, I hugged him, said goodbye outside the smoke room, then he left without a word, perhaps this may never have happened if (always an if) he had not married such an awful woman and if Mother had been alive, I know I would never had sold and perhaps if I had been left on my own from the beginning of my purchase of Skirwith Hall.

Joey Junior was billeted with Mrs Ridley in Skirwith, mother of Robert, lost in the snowdrifts after the sale party and Adam had good lodgings in Penrith, paid for and also a weekly allowance paid to him by Andrew Thorneley, my solicitor.

Monique and I had our last night in Skirwith Hall, almost all the furnishings had gone. This night there remained the beds otherwise all rooms were more or less empty. Joey's little Jack Russell terrier, Titch, came up the stairs and sat on the bathroom floor watching us with a very sad look on his face, a thing he had never done before, he was never allowed upstairs, I wonder what was going through his little head, Joey was looking after him until we were ready for them in France.

Rather odd, the week we left, the George Hotel was sold to a German and Roundthorn Country Club to a Dutchman in January 1977, things were changing and the sad news on the day of departure was our good friend Malcolm, the owner of the Queens Head Hotel, Tirril, died of cancer of the spine, I believe he was only about 40 years old, and his best friend and also our friend, John Grundy of Rampsbeck Hotel was to follow Malcolm within a few short years, the same age as Malcolm.

Saturday, I got a set of new tyres on the Volvo in the morning, then this done, I set off for Calais, reaching

Canterbury, where we slept, and on the 30th, my time limit had come. Monique and I took the ferry boat into France and exile, just getting the ferry in 5 minutes.

Now, a new chapter was being turned in my life. My next chapter was to be in France.

About the Author

Joey Swinbank-Slack, a retired farmer and landowner from Cumberland, North England, lived his life with a love of sports, travel, shooting, fishing, racing, and cigars. At the age of 96, he is writing the story of his life full of adventures and his great love story of seventy years.

www.ingramcontent.com/pod-product-compliance
Lightning Source LLC
Chambersburg PA
CBHW070451120526
44590CB00013B/638